SO-AYI-905

THIS BOOK WITHDRAWN FROM
THE RECORDS OF THE
MID-CONTINENT PUBLIC LIBRARY

JUN 2 8 2007

DICTIONARY OF ORNAMENT

It would be far beyond the limits of the powers of any individual to attempt to gather together illustrations of the innumerable and ever-varying phases of Ornamental Art. It would be barely possible if undertaken by a Government, and even then it would be too voluminous to be formally useful.

Owen Jones *Grammar of Ornament* (1856)

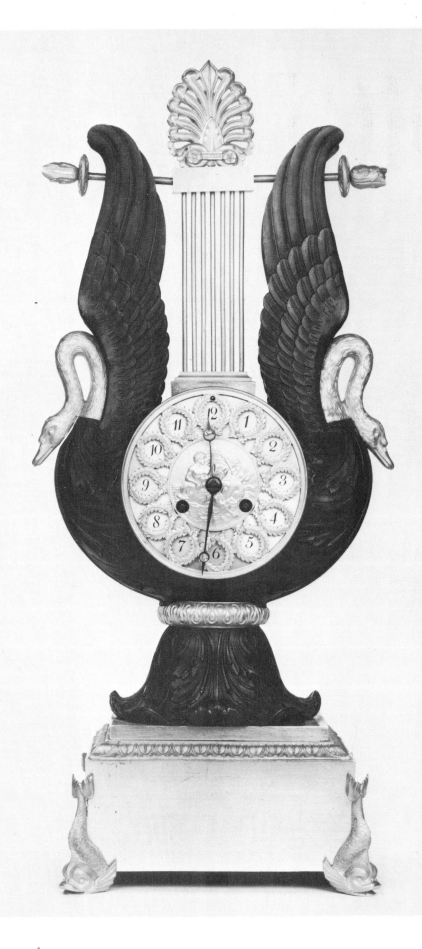

DICTIONARY

of

ORNAMENT

Philippa Lewis & Gillian Darley

PANTHEON BOOKS
New York

First American edition

Copyright © 1986 by Cameron Books

All rights reserved under International and Pan-American Copyright Conventions. Published in the United States by Pantheon Books, a division of Random House, Inc., New York, and simultaneously in Canada by Random House of Canada Limited, Toronto.

Library of Congress Cataloging in Publication Data

Lewis Philippa
  Dictionary of Ornament

  Bibliography: p.
  1. Decoration and ornament—Dictionaries.
I. Darley, Gillian. II. Title.
NK1165.L48 1986   745.4′03′21   84-26579
ISBN 0-394-50931-5

Edited by Jill Hollis
Designed by Ian Cameron
Produced by Cameron Books, 2a Roman Way,
London N7 8XG

Manufactured in Great Britain

9008674

Ref.
745.403
L588

745.403 L588   RF
DICTIONARY OF ORNAMENT
PANTHEON   WE MCPL

3 0000 01443786 1..

Frontispiece:
French ormolu, bronze and steel mantel clock, early 19th century.

The authors received help, advice and encouragement from many people, in particular Miles Thistlethwaite, Dan Cruikshank, Jill Lever, Ben Weinreb and staff, Deborah Nevins, Andrew Saint, Eileen Harris, Margaret Richardson, Elisabeth Cameron, Michael Snodin, Alain Gaucher, Dillwyn Knox, Harry Teggin, Randal Keynes, Briony Llewellyn, Peter Flagg Maxson and Donna Thynne; also the staff of the London Library, the British Library, the Department of Prints and Drawings at the Victoria & Albert Museum and the Library of the Goldsmiths' Hall.

  It would be difficult to quantify the thought, effort, energy and patience that our editor, Jill Hollis, has contributed to the preparation of this book, and we owe her very many thanks.

About this Book

This book is a survey of ornament, pattern and motifs in the applied arts and architecture. The coverage is mainly of European and North American buildings and objects from the Renaissance to the present day, with reference, where relevant, to ancient and oriental sources and precedents. The text is arranged alphabetically with cross references indicated by asterisks. In addition to entries on specific styles, patterns and motifs, there is coverage of the pattern books through which successive vocabularies of ornament were disseminated, and of recurrent themes and their various decorative expressions. Although, for example, architectural and technical terms are covered where they have an ornamental significance, this book is not intended as a comprehensive glossary of architecture or the decorative arts.

The selection of pictures is designed to demonstrate the wide variety of ways in which a motif, pattern or theme may be interpreted in various media. Numbering within blocks of illustrations works clockwise, starting at the top left-hand picture. Limitations of space have dictated that the captions be kept as brief as possible, and styles are excluded from cross referencing within them.

The visual key on pages 6 to 16 is intended to lead the reader to the appropriate entry where the specialist name or term would otherwise be the only route. 'See also' in a visual key caption indicates a related entry or entries that might usefully be consulted. The visual key is not an exhaustive guide to the contents of the book; the wider issues of styles and themes have not been included here, and easily recognisable motifs have also been omitted. The arrangement of pictures in the key is evocative rather than formal; its ambitions are not to classify but to suggest cues to be followed up.

VISUAL KEY – Motifs from antiquity

△ **caduceus**

△ **rod of Aesculapius**

△ **torch**

△ **thunder and lightning**

△ **eye of Horus**

△ **tripod**

△ **fasces** (and **spear**)

△ **vase** (see also **urn, sarcophagus, cinerarium lid**)
▽ **columna rostrata**

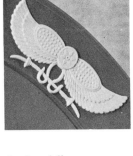

△ **winged disc**
▽ **obelisk**

△ **pelta**

△ **cornucopia**
▽ **canopic jar**

△ **wreath**

△ **trophy** (see also **panoply**)

See also: **labarum, menorah, Phrygian bonnet.**

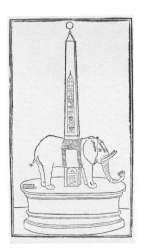

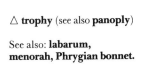

Plant forms

△ **acanthus** (and **caulicoli**)

△ **scrolling foliage**

△ **husk**

△ **fleuron**
▽ **crabstock**

△ **stiff leaf**

△ **waterleaf**

△ **palmette**

△ **anthemion**

△ **peapod ornament**
▽ **kikumon**

△ **crocket**

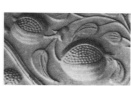

△ **poppyhead**

△ **pomegranate**

△ **lotus**
▽ **pine**

△ **ballflower**

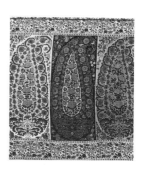

△ **fleur-de-lis**

△ **papyrus**

△ **pinecone** (see also
pineapple)

△ **paisley**

Animal forms

△ **aegricanes**

△ **bucranium**

▽ **kylin**

△ **dracontine**

▽ **dog of Fo**

△ **salamander**

△ **claw** (see also **paw**)

△ **monopodium**

▽ **unicorn**

△ **hippocamp**

△ **hoof foot** (see also **duck foot**) ▽ **beakhead**

△ **pelican**

▽ **phoenix**

△ **griffin**

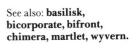

△ **scarab**

See also: **basilisk, bicorporate, bifront, chimera, martlet, wyvern.**

Human or part-human

△ **atlantes** (see also **persian**)

△ **herm**

△ **half figure**

△ **gargoyle**

△ **gorgon**

△ **grotesque mask**
▽ **foliate mask**

△ **caryatid**

△ **portrait head** (see also **cameo, medallion, romayne work**)

△ **femme-fleur**

△ **wild man**

△ **mermaid** (see also **triton, nereids, siren**)
▽ **sphinx** (see also **harpy**)

△ **canephora**

△ **putto**

△ **cherub**

△ **pagod**

△ **satyr**

See also: **boxers, nymph, personifications.**

△ **espagnolette**
▽ **mask**

Linear and surface decoration

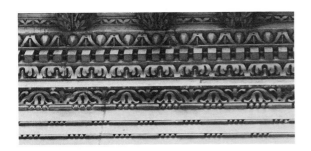

△ **mouldings** (others illustrated on this page)

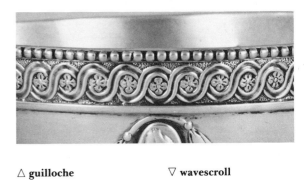

△ **coin moulding** ▽ **key pattern**

△ **beading**

△ **banding**

△ **bead and reel**
▽ **bead and spindle**

△ **guilloche** ▽ **wavescroll**

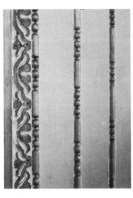

△ **vertebrate band**
▽ **undulate band**

△ **scoop pattern**
▷ **fluting**

▽ **ribbon moulding**

Linear and surface decoration

△ piecrust   ▽ feather-edged

▽ strigillation   ▽ linenfold

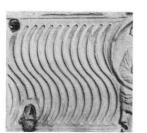

▽ gadrooning

▽ chevron

▽ **scale pattern** (see also **diaper**)

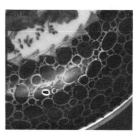

△ blue dash border

△ caillouté

△ rustication
▽ **gyronny pattern** (see also **counterchange, chequer**)

△ dogtooth

△ billet moulding

△ **treillage** (see also **trellis, fret**)
▽ **coffering**

Surface decoration   # Architectural and

△ **grotesques**

▽ **pulvinated frieze**

△ **balustrade** and **baluster**

△ **arabesque**

▽ **candelabra form**

△ **cartouche**
▽ **margent**

△ **bandwork**

△ **interlacing**

▽ **flushwork**

△ **strapwork**
▽ **chintz pattern**

△ **Laub und Bandelwerk**
▽ **rocaille**

▽ **festoon**

decorative features

△ **patera**

△ **rosette**

△ **label stop**

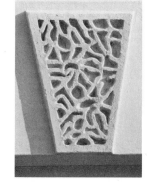

△ **keystone** (with **vermiculation**)

△ **corbel**
▽ **console** (see also **bracket**)

△ **label**   ▽ **volute**

△ **crossette**   ▽ **pendant**

△ **triglyph** with **metope** and **guttae**   ▽ **dentils**

△ **modillions**
◁ **lesene**
▽ **bolection moulding**

Architectural and decorative features

△ **quoin**

△ **spiral column**

△ **banded column**

△ **knotted column**

△ **long and short work**

△ **colonnette**
▽ **arcading**

△ **annulet**
▽ **tracery**

△ **vesica piscis**

△ **pilaster**

▽ **star vault**

▽ **fan vault**

△ **foil** (and **cusp**)

Architectural and decorative features

△ lunette

▽ batswing

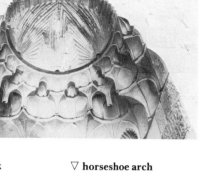

△ stalactite work

▽ horseshoe arch

▽ fanlight

▽ oeil de boeuf

△ spandrel

▽ ogee

▽ triumphal arch

▽ Palladian window

▽ aedicule

△ relieving arch

▽ niche

▽ baldacchino

Architectural and decorative features

△ antefix   ▽ cresting

△ **brattishing**   ▽ **Gothic cornice**

△ **pediment** with **acroteria**

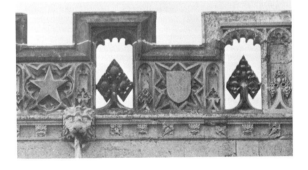

△ **tabernacle work**
▽ **town canopy**

△ **floriated merlon**   ▽ **battlement**

△ **swallowtail merlon**
▽ **Dutch gable**

REFERENCES

The Acanthus Motif in Decoration, Metropolitan Museum of Art, New York, 1934.

The Aesthetic Movement and the Cult of Japan, exhibition catalogue, Fine Arts Society, 1972.

Age of Neo-classicism, Council of Europe Exhibition, Arts Council, 1973.

Allwood, John, *The Great Exhibitions*, Studio Vista, 1977.

The Arts & Crafts Movement, artists, craftsmen and designers, 1890-1930, exhibition catalogue, Fine Arts Society, 1973.

Aslin, Elizabeth, *The Aesthetic Movement*, Paul Elek, 1969.

Aslin, Elizabeth, *Nineteenth Century English Furniture*, Faber & Faber, 1962.

Atterbury, David, and Irvine, Louise, *The Doulton Story*, exhibition catalogue, Victoria & Albert Museum and Royal Doulton Tableware, 1979.

Banham, Mary, and Hillier, Bevis (eds) *A Tonic to the Nation: The Festival of Britain*, Thames and Hudson, 1951.

Banham, Reyner, 'Ornament and Crime: the decisive contribution of Adolf Loos', *Architectural Review*, Vol. 121, February 1957.

Basford, Kathleen, *The Green Man*, Brewer, 1978.

Battersby, Martin, *The Decorative Twenties*, Studio Vista, 1969.

Battersby, Martin, *The Decorative Thirties*, Studio Vista, 1971.

Battersby, Martin, *Trompe L'Oeil*, Academy Editions, 1974.

Becker, Vivienne, *Antique and Twentieth Century Jewellery*, NAG Press, 1980.

Berlin: Katalog der Ornamentstichsammlung der staatlichen Kunstbibliothek, Berlin and Leipzig, 1939.

Berliner, Rudolph, *Ornamentale Vorlage-Blätter des 15 bis 18 Jahrhunderts*, 1925.

Brønsted, J., *Early English Ornament*, London, 1924.

Brooke-Little, J.P., *An Heraldic Alphabet*, Macdonald, 1973.

Byrne, Janet S., *Renaissance Ornament Prints & Drawings*, Metropolitan Museum of Art, New York, 1981.

Chafer, Denise (ed.) *The Arts Applied, a catalogue of books* B. Weinreb Architectural Books, 1975.

A Choice of Design 1850-1980; fabrics by Warner & Sons Ltd, travelling exhibition in Britain, 1981-82.

Christopher Dresser 1834-1904, exhibition catalogue, Arkwright Arts Trust, 1979.

Clark, Kenneth, 'Ornament in Modern Architecture', *Journal of the Royal Institute of British Architects*, 3rd December 1934.

Clayton, Michael, *The Collector's Dictionary of Silver and Gold*, Country Life, 1971.

Coleridge, Anthony, *Chippendale Furniture*, Faber & Faber, 1968.

Colvin, Howard, *A Biographical Dictionary of British Architects 1600-1840*, John Murray, 1978.

Comstock, Helen, *American Furniture*, Schiffler Publishing, 1981.

Comstock, Helen (ed.), *The Concise Encyclopedia of American Antiques*, Connoisseur, 1958.

Conner, Patrick (ed.), *The Inspiration of Egypt*, exhibition catalogue, Brighton Museum, 1983.

Conner, Patrick, *Oriental Architecture in the West*, Thames and Hudson, 1979.

Cooper, J.C., *An Illustrated Encyclopedia of Traditional Symbols*, Thames and Hudson, 1978.

Crane, Walter, *The English Revival of Decorative Art*, 1892.

Crook, J. Mordaunt, 'William Burges and the Dilemma of Style', *Architectural Review*, July 1981.

Cruickshank, Dan, 'The Georgian House', *Architects' Journal*, No. 13, Vol. 175, 31st March 1982.

Cruickshank, Dan, and Wyld, Peter, *London, the Art of Georgian Building*, Architectural Press, 1975.

Darby, Michael, *The Islamic Perspective*, World of Islam Festival Trust, 1983.

Davis, Terence, *The Gothick Taste*, David & Charles, 1974.

Decoration and Art Trades Review, London, 1888-89.

Decoration in Painting, Sculpture, Architecture and Art Manufactures London, 1880-89.

Dolmetsch, N., *The Historic Styles of Ornament*, Batsford, 1898.

Dresser, Christopher, *Principles of Decorative Design*, 1873.

Durant, Stuart, 'Ornament in an Industrial Civilisation, *Architectural Review*, September 1976.

English Romanesque Art 1066-1200, exhibition catalogue, Arts Council and Weidenfeld & Nicolson, London, 1984.

Evans, Joan, *Pattern. A Study of Ornament in Western Europe from 1180 to 1900*, Clarendon Press, 1931.

Evans, Joan, *Style in Ornament*, Oxford University Press, 1950.

Evans, Joan, *A History of Jewellery, 1100-1870*, Faber & Faber, 1953.

Fastnedge, Ralph, *English Furniture Styles*, Herbert Jenkins, 1962.

Fastnedge, Ralph, *Hepplewhite Furniture Designs*, Tiranti, 1947.

Fastnedge, Ralph, *Shearer Furniture Designs*, Tiranti, 1962.

Fisher, Stanley W., *The Decoration of English Porcelain 1750-1850*, Derek Verschoyle, 1954.

Fleming, John and Honour, Hugh, *The Penguin Dictionary of Decorative Arts*, Allen Lane, 1977.

Focillon, Henri, *The Art of the West in the Middle Ages*, edited and introduced by Jean Bony, 2 vols, Phaidon, 1963.

Freeman, Margaret, *The Unicorn Tapestries*, Metropolitan Museum of Art, New York, 1976.

Freeman, Rosemary, *English Emblem Books*, Chatto, 1948.

Gask, Norman, *Old Silver Spoons of England*, 1926; reprinted Spring Books, 1973.

Gerson, Martha Blythe, 'A Glossary of Robert Adam's Neo-Classical Ornament', *Architectural History*, Vol. 24, 1981.

Girouard, Mark, *Sweetness and Light – The 'Queen Anne' Movement, 1860-1900*, Oxford University Press, 1977.

Glazier, Richard, *A Manual of Historic Ornament*, London, 1899.

Gloag, John, *A Short Dictionary of Furniture*, Allen and Unwin, 1969.

Gombrich, E.H., *The Sense of Order: a study in the psychology of decorative art*, Phaidon, 1979.

Gombrich, E.H., 'The Priority of Pattern', *The Listener*, 1st March 1979.

Grandjean, Serge, *Empire Furniture 1800-1825*, Faber & Faber, 1974.

Guinness, Desmond, *Georgian Dublin*, Batsford, 1979.

Hall, James, *Dictionary of Subjects and Symbols in Art*, John Murray, 1974.

Hall, James, *A History of Ideas and Images in Italian Art*, John Murray, 1983.

Hamlin, A.D.F., *A History of Ornament Ancient and Medieval*, Batsford, 1917.

Hamlin, A.D.F., *A History of Ornament Renaissance and Modern*, Batsford, 1923.

Hamlin, Talbot, *Greek Revival Architecture in America*, Oxford University Press, 1944.

Harris, John, and Lever, Jill, *Illustrated Glossary of Architecture*, Faber & Faber, 1966.

Hartland Thomas, Mark, 'The Festival Pattern Group', *Design*, May/June 1951.

Hayward, Helena, *Thomas Johnson and English Rococo*, Tiranti, 1964.

Hayward, J.F., *Virtuoso Goldsmiths and the Triumph of Mannerism 1540-1620*, Sotheby Parke Bernet, 1976.

Heaton, J.A., *Furniture and Decoration in England During the 18th Century*, 1892.

Hillier, Bevis, *Austerity Binge: the decorative arts of the forties and fifties*, Studio Vista, 1975.

Hillier, Bevis (introductory text) *The World of Art Deco*, exhibition catalogue, Minneapolis Institute of Arts, 1971.

Himmelheber, Georg, *Biedermeier Furniture*, Faber & Faber, 1974.

Hind, Arthur M., *A History of Engraving and Etching*, Dover, 1963.

REFERENCES

Hind, S., *Early Engraving and Engravers in England, 1545-1695*, third edition, 1905.

Hitchcock, Henry Russell, *American Architectural Books*, Oxford University Press, 1946.

Hoever, O., *A Handbook of Wrought Iron from the Middle Ages to the end of the Eighteenth Century*, 1962.

Honey, W.B., *French Porcelain*, translated by Ann C. Wearer Faber & Faber, 1950.

Honey, W.B., *European Ceramic Art*, Faber & Faber, 2 vols, 1949 and 1952.

Honour, Hugh, *Cabinet Makers and Furniture Designers*, Weidenfeld & Nicolson, 1969.

Honour, Hugh, *Goldsmiths and Silversmiths*, Weidenfeld & Nicolson, 1971.

Hope, Henry R., 'Louis Sullivan's Architectural Ornament', *Architectural Review*, Vol. 102, October 1947.

Howarth, Thomas, *Charles Rennie Mackintosh and the Modern Movement*, Routledge & Kegan Paul, 1952.

Hussey, Christopher, *Early Georgian English Country Houses*, Country Life, 1955.

Hussey, Christopher, *English Country Houses: Caroline 1625-1685*, by O. Hill and J. Cornforth, Country Life, 1966.

Impey, Oliver R., *Chinoiserie: the Impact of Oriental Styles on Western Art and Decoration*, Oxford University Press, 1977.

Jervis, Simon, *The Penguin Dictionary of Design and Designers*, Penguin, 1984.

Jervis, Simon, *Printed Furniture Designs before 1650*, Furniture History Society, 1974.

Jervis, Simon, *High Victorian Design*, The Boydell Press, 1983.

Jessen, Peter, *Meister des Ornamentstichs*, in four volumes: *Gotik und Renaissance, Das Barock, Das Rokoko, Der Klassizmus*, Berlin, 1923-24.

Jourdain, Margaret, *English Decorative Plasterwork of the Renaissance*, Batsford, 1927.

Kedourie, Elie (ed.), *The Jewish World*, Thames and Hudson, 1979.

Kimball, Sidney Fiske, *The Creation of Rococo*, 1943.

Kimball, Sidney Fiske, *Domestic Architecture of the American Colonies and The Early Republic*, Dover, 1966.

Lambert, Susan (ed.) *Pattern and Design: designs for the Decorative Arts 1480-1980*, Victoria & Albert Museum, 1983.

Lynn, Catherine, *Wallpaper in America, from the 17th century to World War I*, Norton, 1980.

Madsen, S.T., *Sources of Art Nouveau*, translated by Ragnar Christophersen, H. Aschehoug & Co., Oslo, 1956.

Montgomery, F.M., *Printed Textiles. English and American Cotton and Linen 1700-1850*, Thames and Hudson, 1970.

Moyr Smith, John, *Ornamental Interiors*, 1887.

Musgrave, Clifford, *Adam and Hepplewhite and Other Neo-classical Furniture*, Faber & Faber, 1966.

Musgrave, Clifford, *Regency Furniture*, Faber & Faber, 1974.

R. Neve, *The City and Country Purchasers' and Builders' Dictionary*, 1703.

Nicholson, Peter, *Architectural Dictionary*, 2 vols, 1812 and 1819.

19th century America, Metropolitan Museum of Art, New York, 1970.

Oman, Charles, *Caroline Silver*, Faber & Faber, 1970.

Oman, Charles, *English Engraved Silver 1150-1900*, Faber & Faber, 1978.

Park, Helen, *Architectural Books Available before the Revolution*, Hennessy & Ingalls, Los Angeles, 1973.

Parker, J.N., *Glossary of Terms*, Oxford, 1845.

Parsons, Ian, *Silver Flatware, English, Irish and Scottish 1660-1980* Antique Collectors' Club, 1983.

Percival, MacIver, *The Chintz Book*, Heinemann, 1923.

Petsopoulos, Yanni (ed.), *Tulips, Arabesques and Turbans – Decorative Arts from the Ottoman Empire*, Alexandria Press, 1984.

Pevsner, Nikolaus, *Studies in Art, Architecture and Design*, 2 vols, Thames and Hudson, 1968.

Pevsner, Nikolaus, Fleming, John, and Honour, Hugh, *A Dictionary of Architecture*, Allen Lane, 1975 edition.

Pevsner, Nikolaus, *Pioneers of Modern Design*, Penguin revised edition, 1960.

Pevsner, Nikolaus (ed.), *Buildings of England* volumes, county by county.

Phillpotts, Beatrice, *Mermaids*, Russell Ash/Windward, 1980.

Physick, John, and Darby, Michael, *Marble Halls*, Victoria & Albert Museum, 1973.

Radice, Betty, *Who's Who in the Ancient World*, Anthony Blond, 1971.

Rawson, Jessica, *Chinese Ornament, the Lotus and the Dragon*, British Museum, 1983.

Robertson, E. Craeme and J.R., *Cast Iron Decoration: a world survey*, Thames and Hudson, 1977.

Rococo, Art and Design in Hogarth's England, Victoria & Albert Museum, 1984.

Savage, George, and Newman, Harold, *An Illustrated Dictionary of Ceramics*, revised edition, Thames and Hudson, 1976.

Schéle, Sune, *Cornelis Bos: A Study of the Origins of the Netherlands Grotesque*, Almquist & Wiksell, Stockholm, 1965.

Saxl, Fritz, *A Heritage of Images: a selection of lectures*, edited by Hugh Honour and J. Fleming, Penguin, 1970.

Scott, W.B., *The Ornamentist or Artisan's Manual*, London, 1845.

Scully, Vincent, *The Shingle Style and the Stick Style*, Yale University Press, 1971.

Sheehy, Jeanne, *The Rediscovery of Ireland's Past: the Celtic Revival 1830-1930*, Thames and Hudson, 1980.

Spencer, Charles (ed.), *The Aesthetic Movement 1869-1890*, exhibition catalogue, Academy Editions, 1973.

Spittle, S.D.T., 'Cufic in Western Art,' *Archaeological Journal*, Vol. XI, 1955.

Sullivan, D.M., *Meeting of Eastern and Western Art from the 16th Century to the Present Day*, Thames and Hudson, 1973.

Sternberg, S.H., *Five Hundred Years of Printing*, Penguin, 1955.

Stillman, Damie, and others, *Architecture & Ornament in Late 19th century America*, University of Delaware, 1981.

Summerson, John, *The Classical Language of Architecture*, Thames and Hudson, 1980 edition.

Tait, Hugh, 'Commedia dell'Arte in Glass and Porcelain', *Apollo*, October 1963.

Talbert, B.J., *Gothic Forms Applied to Furniture*, 1867.

Thornton, Peter, *Baroque and Rococo Silks*, Faber & Faber, 1965.

Thornton, Peter, *Seventeenth Century Interior Decoration in England, France and Holland*, Yale University Press, 1978.

Thornton, Peter, *Authentic Decor*, Weidenfeld & Nicolson, 1984.

The Universal Decorator, London, 1861-63.

Valentine, Lucia N., *Ornament in Medieval Manuscripts*, Faber & Faber, 1965.

van Marle, Raymond, *Iconographie de l'art profane au moyen-âge et à la renaissance, et la décoration des demeures*, 1931.

Victorian and Edwardian Decorative Art, The Handley Read Collection, Royal Academy, 1972.

Wagner, Anthony, *Heraldry in England*, Penguin, 1946.

Ward, James, *Historic Ornament*, 1897.

Ward-Jackson, Peter, 'Some mainstream and tributaries in European ornament from 1500 to 1750', *Bulletin of the Victoria and Albert Museum*, Vol. III, 1969.

Ward-Jackson, Peter, *English Furniture Design of the Eighteenth Century*, H.M.S.O., 1958.

Watkin, David, *Thomas Hope and the Neo-Classical Ideal*, John Murray, 1968.

Watson, F.J.B., *Wallace Collection Catalogue; Furniture*, H.M.S.O., 1956.

White, Norval, and Willensky, Elliot, *AIA Guide to New York City*, revised edition, Collier Books, New York, 1978.

Williams-Wood, Cyril, *English Transfer-printed Pottery and Porcelain*, Faber & Faber, 1981.

Wornum, Ralph N., *Analysis of Ornament*, London, 1879.

THE
DICTIONARY

Aaron's rod. 18th and early 19th century plasterers' term for a staff twined with leaves. Alternatively, a rod with a serpent coiled round it, known more usually as the *caduceus.

abacus. Flat upper element of a *capital supporting the *entablature. It sometimes bears simple ornamentation such as indentations or chamfered edges, which may vary according to the *Order or style.

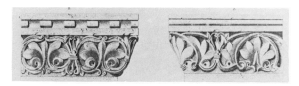

*abacus. Abacuses on Romanesque Revival *capitals from* Romanesque Architecture in the South of France *by A. Revoil, New York, c.1880.*

Abbotsford. Style of furniture named after the home of Sir Walter Scott, whose immensely popular historical novels were an important element in kindling a general enthusiasm for *Gothic, *Jacobean and *Tudor Revivals in the 1820s and 1830s. Predominant motifs in the furniture are *cusps, twisted columns, bulbous carving. High-backed chairs are typical.

A so-called 'Scott' chair is illustrated in L. Gruner's *The Decorations of the Garden Pavilion in the Grounds of Buckingham Palace* (1846). This pavilion (now demolished) had one room decorated with frescoes showing scenes from Scott's novels.

acanthus. The most widely used type of foliage ornament. Based on the leaves of plants of the Mediterranean species *Acanthus spinosus*, it may also resemble thistle, parsley or poppy leaves. The full leaf was employed in *classical architecture (sometimes with its *caulicoli exposed) both in its own right and as a decorative masking device. It was an essential component of the Corinthian and Composite *Orders. T.*Hope, an 18th century patron of the arts, presented the Vitruvian explanation of it as 'a wild acanthus, accidentally lodged on the top of an ancient sepulchral cippus and with its foliage embracing a basket placed on the pillar and compelled to curl down by a tile that covered the basket.'

The Roman acanthus was more elaborate than the relatively sparse Greek form and was used as the basis

*acanthus. 1) Windblown acanthus *capitals, Kelat Seman (St Simeon), North Syria, 6th century. 2) Silver tankard, Norwegian, 1709. 3) Table made by Tobey & Co, Chicago, Illinois, 1880s. 4) From* A Collection of Ornaments in the Antique Style *by G.*Richardson, 1816. 5) South porch, Bayeux Cathedral (Calvados), France, 13th century. 6) Italian Baroque giltwood chair, 17th century. 7) South doorway, Church of San Polo, Venice, Italy, 14th century.*

of *scrolling foliage with the leaves generally appearing heavy and drooping. The *Byzantine treatment was harsher and spikier; though modified in *Romanesque and *Gothic styles, it led to increasingly naturalistic representation. Widely adopted in the early *Renaissance, the acanthus has rarely been out of favour for long, appearing in many materials and many forms. The Marsuppini tomb, designed by Desiderio da Settignano in 1456 (Santa Croce, Florence), possibly marked the Renaissance reintroduction of the acanthus and showed its new adaptability: it formed the base and feet of the tomb. A structurally convenient motif, it could be used as a scroll forming a bracket, as a *cornice frieze, as carved or ormolu furniture feet (particularly during the 18th century) and to mask or reinforce a join in metalwork (e.g. between cup and stem, or *knop and cover).

The Greek Revivalists in the 19th century used the acanthus sparingly. However, *A Guide for Drawing the Acanthus* by J. Page (London, 1839-40, 1886) presented itself as 'a valuable instructor to all inlayers, modellers, cabinet makers, ornamental workers and carvers, and also to students in every department of the fine arts ... at this period when the florid ornamental style is so predominant.' This provoked a complaint from O.*Jones in *Grammar of Ornament* (1856) that 'the fatal facilities which the Roman system of decoration gives for manufacturing ornament, by applying acanthus leaves to any form and in any direction, is the chief cause of the invasion of this ornament into most modern works. It requires so little thought, and is so completely a manufacture, that it has encouraged architects in an indolent neglect of one of their especial provinces, and the interior decorations of buildings have fallen into hands most unfitted to supply their place.'

C.L.*Eastlake echoed this in *Hints on Household Taste* (London, 1868) referring to 'the inevitable acanthus leaf as if in the whole range of vegetable life this was the only kind of foliage worth imitating.' Although the acanthus was not used in most late 19th century styles, it did not disappear entirely and even occurs in some 20th century designs.

achievement of arms. Representation of all the armorial devices to which the bearer is entitled. It evolved into its present, full form during the 16th century and was systematically presented by John Guillim in *Display of Heraldry* (1610, 1632, 1638, 1660, 1664, 1666; republished as *The Banner Display'd*, 1726-28).

Knights first began to carry personal devices on their banners (*see* banderole) and subsequently on *shields in the 12th century. These devices were added to the old hereditary seals and thus became incorporated into heraldry. Crests, which became general during the 14th century, consisted of a metal, wooden or leather device fixed to the top of the knight's helmet so that, when it was closed, the wearer could be identified. Around the base of the crest, depending on the owner's status, was a *coronet or a wreath of twisted scarves (a relic of the custom of ladies giving 'favours' to knights before tournaments) often represented as a diagonally striped bar. On full armorial bearings, the *helmet is shown as the proper vehicle for the crest. From the early 17th century, different types of helmet were assigned to different ranks, e.g. a peer's

helmet is silver with gold bars and faces right; knights' and baronets' helmets face frontally with the visor raised; esquires, gentlemen and, latterly, corporations have steel helmets with closed visors facing right. From the helmet streams the *mantling – scallop-edged drapery which was worn over the helmet to prevent the metal from overheating in the sun. The supporters (pairs of humans, animals or mythical beasts, placed on either side of the shield) were originally a 15th century device, but by the next century they had been formalised and could be used only by royalty, peers, and Knights of the Garter, Thistle and St Patrick. War-like objects were omitted from women's armorial bearings, which appear on a lozenge rather than a shield and bear no crest or helm. Ecclesiastical arms are surmounted by either a mitre or an *ecclesiastical hat. *See also* heraldic decoration.

Ackermann, Rudolph (1764-1834). Bookseller and publisher who is thought to have been responsible for the introduction into Britain of lithography for book illustration. His most influential publication, *The Repository of Arts, Literature, Commerce, Manufacture, Fashions and Politics*, which appeared monthly from 1809 to 1828, was not strictly a *pattern book, but among its law reports, commodity prices and listings of bankrupts were coloured plates of 'Fashionable Furniture', which provided the consumer with an important guide to prevailing tastes in architecture and decoration. Included were designs by George Bullock, A.C.*Pugin and G.*Smith as well as the products of commercial firms. Fashions noted include the Grecian style (from 1809), Gothic (from 1810), military ornamentation (from 1813), drapery (from 1812), and French Empire decoration. The early furniture plates were reissued c.1815 in a volume entitled *The Upholsterer's and Cabinetmaker's Repository: consisting of seventy-six designs of modern and fashionable furniture*. In 1816, Ackermann began to produce patterns, in general dreary, called *Ornaments for Painting on Wood and Fancy Work* for the 'recreation of the fair sex'. Between November 1817 and January 1819, *A Selection of Ornaments in forty pages, for the use of sculptors, painters, carvers, modellers, chasers, embossers* was produced in three lithographed volumes. This workman-like pattern book included a full range of *classical motifs and demonstrated the influence in Britain of contemporary French design, with such motifs as ribboned *wreaths, double *cornucopias and

Rudolph Ackermann. 'A Gothic Side Table' by J. Taylor from The Repository of Arts, *July 1821.*

*swans, as well as a variety of *friezes composed of naturalistic flowers, e.g. roses, buttercups and poppies.

acorn. Motif in Roman art. More widely used in Celtic and Scandinavian art as a seed form to symbolise life, fecundity and immortality. It could also embody the important symbolism of the *oak tree itself. Easily produced on a lathe, it is a popular form in woodwork, particularly as a *pendant or terminal (e.g. on chairs), and an obvious embellishment for pieces made out of oak. Similarly, the shape works well as a finial — English spoons (from the early 14th to the 16th century) often had acorn *knops. Brass drop handles on late 17th century furniture could also be acorn-shaped. Later, acorns were a common ornament on *American Colonial case furniture, and appeared in *Gothic Revival metalwork, e.g. the door hinges at Arundel Castle, Sussex. Like *fir cones and *pineapples, acorns often appeared on gate piers or on posts or turrets: Sir Christopher Wren (1632-1723) used them in his restoration schemes for Westminster Abbey. In the 18th, 19th and 20th centuries, turned wood acorn shapes were used to end curtain cords and sashes (important features when drapery and upholstery were becoming increasingly heavy and needed elaborate arrangement) and for roller blind cords.

The sentiment expressed in the proverb 'Great Oaks from Little Acorns Grow' is sometimes reflected in ornament, with the acorn appearing, for example, on savings banks and commercial premises.

acroterion (Greek, extremity). *Pedestal or *plinth with or without an ornament or figure, applied to the three angles of the *pediment in *classical architecture; may also refer to the figure or motif and the base together. Acroteria are often statues or forms with

*acroterion. *Pediment on 19th century commercial building, Bristol.*

interesting profiles, chosen for the striking effect of their silhouettes against the skyline. In the *Baroque period exuberant forms like flaming *torches or symbolic beasts and birds were used. Globes, *vases and *urns were popular in the late 18th century, when they were sometimes referred to as parapet ornament. Occasionally, pedestals in English or American 18th century furniture may be called acroteria, e.g. the ornament placed at the centre of an *open pediment on a tallboy, bureau or bookcase.

Adam style. Buildings, interiors and objects in the style of the Scottish architect Robert Adam (1728-92) and his less influential brothers James (1732-94) and John (1721-92). In 1755-57, Robert Adam studied in Rome, where he met Sir W.*Chambers and G.B. *Piranesi, who dedicated his book on the Campus Martius to Adam. On an expedition in 1757 with the Rome-based French classical architect and teacher Charles-Louis Clérisseau (1722-80) to what is now Split in Yugoslavia, Adam gathered material for his first publication, the folio *Ruins of the Palace of the Emperor Diocletian at Spalatro, in Dalmatia* (1764). His style as a designer was based on close study of the architecture and artefacts of classical antiquity and the Italian Renaissance and on other published sources, e.g. Piranesi and R.*Wood. He made use of Roman, especially *Pompeian motifs (he had visited Città, later known as Pompeii, in 1755), later broadening his vocabulary with Greek and Etruscan examples and even extending his repertoire to the *Gothick castle. The *Works in Architecture of Robert and James Adam* (published in instalments, 1773-79, with a posthumous volume in 1822) records the elevations and plans of the principal buildings by the two brothers and, more influentially, the interiors, furniture and fittings.

The reputation of the brothers Adam came from their integration of architecture with the design of interiors and objects, and from their use of distinctive motifs: *swags and *festoons, *guilloche friezes, *griffins and *chimeras, *vases and *urns, *husks, *paterae, *anthemions and *palmettes. Nevertheless, the Adams were attacked as lightweight by critics such as Horace Walpole, who referred to their work as 'gingerbread and snippets of embroidery', and Chambers, who called the *Works* 'a presumptuous book' and saw the interiors as 'filigrane toy work' which 'excite no

*acorn. 1) *Knop on Dutch porcelain sugar bowl, Amstel, c.1800. 2) Late 18th century iron railing, Ockbrook, Derbyshire. 3) Plaster ceiling, Chastleton House, Oxfordshire, 1606.*

other ideas than that of a desert [sic]: upon the plates of which are dished out bad copies of indifferent antiquities.'

The Adams criticised the Palladians for failing to distinguish between the interior and exterior architecture of the Romans, and used *grotesques 'as a small-scale alternative to the more massive ornament which they felt was fit only for exteriors. The Adam style brought new life to many areas of the decorative arts in Britain, notably silver and furniture – both G.*Hepplewhite and Robert Adam himself designed silver for Matthew Boulton's Soho Manufactory. In silverware, archaeological finds of bronze and marble artefacts provided the forms that were then converted to domestic objects, e.g. vases, coffee urns and soup tureens, ornamented with simple, slender ornament such as *bead moulding and fine swags. This type of design was widely adopted for Sheffield plate, which began to be mass-produced c.1770. The earliest American silver in this style appeared in 1774 in Philadelphia. Many pattern books in the 1770s and 1780s were influenced by the Adam style, among them the work of G.*Edwards and M.*Darly, Emmanuel Eichel of Augsburg (1718-70) and the French Louis XVI *ornemanistes*. G.*Richardson and the Italians M.A.*Pergolesi and P.*Columbani all worked for a time with Adam.

Two other painters trained in Italy and working in England, Giovanni Battista Cipriani (1727-85) and Angelica Kauffmann (1741-1807) were responsible for classical, allegorical paintings that were used for many of the ceilings and panels in Adam style interiors. Their work was widely disseminated, particularly in the stipple engravings of Francesco Bartolozzi (1728-1815), Richard Earlom and others. These small engravings, many of them mythological scenes in the style of classical cameos and engraved gems, were

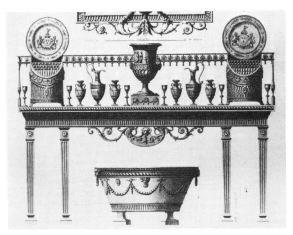

Adam style. 1) Ceiling, Belvedere House (now College), Dublin, designed by Michael Stapleton, 1786. 2) Furniture from the Dining Room, Kenwood House, London, from Robert Adam's Works in Architecture, *1773-79. 3) English painted giltwood side table made for Carlton House, London, c.1795.*

adapted for enamels and painted decoration on furniture and ceramics.

The Adam style spread to Russia with the architectural work of Charles Cameron (c.1740-1812) for Catherine the Great, and to America where, for example, architect and furniture-maker Samuel McIntyre (1757-1811) used Adam-style door-cases, chimneypieces, etc. Adam ornamentation formed a basis for the early *Federal style, and ornaments made of stucco and plaster composition were shipped to America until the embargo of 1807.

There were frequent revivals of the style from the 1880s. J.A. Heaton wrote in *Furniture and Decoration* (1892) of the Adam brothers that 'a large proportion of their ornament is capable of being executed cheaply in carton-pierre and plaster, and often forms the chaste and delicate ornamental touch of many a burgher's house of somewhat later date. If only our speculating builders would take their plaster cornices . . . architects and decorators of public buildings might here find a quarry from which they might dig nearly all their material, greatly to the advantage of the whole nation.' An article in the magazine *Decoration* (May 1881) indicates how the interest in the style was purely for interiors: 'the whirligig of time has brought the Brothers Adam to the front again'. While the architecture was described as 'monotonous', the ornaments were 'inspiration' for interiors and furniture.

aedicule. 1) Heavily eroded aedicule, Temple of Baal, Palmyra, Syria.
*2) 'The Great Temple' from R. *Wood's The Ruins of Baalbec, 1757.*
3) West Front of Church of St Rémy, 1522-1640, Dieppe (Seine-Maritime), France.

In the 1930s a still more refined version of the style appeared and selected motifs such as fluted paterae for chair-backs (with oval inlays) were used by Oliver Hill and others, according well with *Neo-Georgian domestic architecture.

aedicule (Latin, *aedicula*, small dwelling, shrine). From its original meaning – a shrine in a Roman temple – the term widened to describe any framing device consisting of columns or vertical supports bearing a *pediment, gable or other terminal, used as a surround for windows, doors or *niches. The Romans themselves used it widely as an ornamental architectural motif, and it was used consistently in classical work from the *Renaissance onwards. It was also used in furniture and metalwork. R.*Wood's mid 18th century publication of the great Roman ruins of Palmyra and Baalbec gave the aedicule added currency, as it had been used with particular effect on the temples and public buildings of both Middle Eastern cities.

aegis (Latin, shield). 18th century term for *shield or breastplate motif, particularly when used as an attribute of *Minerva or Jupiter; form often adopted for *cartouches.

aegricanes. Head of ram or goat, a motif in Greek and Roman art that appeared in temple decoration, especially on altars, reflecting its connection with ritual sacrifice. *Festoons or *swags might be attached to the horns, which sometimes curled into *volutes; some commentators saw this as an explanation of the Ionic capital (*see* Orders). In *Renaissance decoration, it

aeroplane. 1) Smoker's compendium: cigar cutter propeller, cigar box body, cigarette case wings, probably German, early 1920s. 2) Cotton print made in Ivanovo, Russia, early 1930s.

aegricanes. 1) Handle to English silver vase, c.1775. 2) English black jasper ware vase with *festoons and *ribbons, made by Wedgwood, c.1800. 3) 18th century English pier table, Wimpole Hall, Cambridgeshire. 4) Dutch porcelain vase, Amstel, c.1800.

was preferred to the *bucranium, which was often considered rather morbid, particularly for domestic settings.

A common motif during the 18th century, notably in the *Adam style, where it was often combined with festoons in a repeating frieze decoration, but also appeared singly on furniture where it might be combined with cloven hoof *monopodia (especially on tripods or side-tables). In ceramics and metalwork aegricanes sometimes appear as handles.

aeroplane. Like the *railway train and the *motor car, the aeroplane has been a popular symbol of modernity, speed and invention. Used as a repeating motif in fabric and wallpaper – Enid Marx's 1930s design was aptly used to line suitcases, although it had to be adapted as aeroplanes changed shape. In the 1920s, objects such as electric fires and cocktail shakers were made in this form. Aircraft also appear on souvenir ware to commemorate important technological advances and aeronautical events.

Aesop. *See* fables.

Aesthetic movement. A decorative style that arose in Britain in the 1860s as a reaction against the over-elaborate productions of industrial mid-Victorian

Britain. The ideal of Art for Art's Sake was expressed through styles and ornament from a variety of sources: objects from Japan (which were first shown in any quantity at the 1862 International Exhibition in London), 17th and early 18th century design (*see* *Queen Anne Revival), blue and white Chinese porcelain, certain kinds of flowers and birds, and craftsman-made metalwork.

During the late 1860s and 1870s, furniture, metalwork and ceramics were produced which satisfied the criteria of the movement, but these well-made, simple objects with carefully confined ornament were an exclusive taste, adopted only by a culturally aware section of the middle class, and despised by many for being self-consciously artistic. For the Aesthetic movement, according to Walter Crane (1845-1915) in 1889, 'plain materials and surfaces are infinitely preferable to inorganic or inappropriate ornament.'

Walter Hamilton's *The Aesthetic Movement in England* appeared in 1882, but the movement also gained notoriety through attacks on its attitudes in *Punch*, and the satirical comments on it in Gilbert and Sullivan's *Patience* (first performed 1881). Oscar Wilde (1854-1900) did much to publicise the movement in America with his lectures there in 1882.

The legacy of the style was an enduring taste for its ornament: *sunflowers, *lilies, *peacock feathers, *fan shapes, *bamboo, *cranes, sparrows, apple and cherry *blossom, marigolds, plants in vases and pots, figures in 'rational' dress (so-called because it allowed freedom of movement) and medieval drapery. Another popular manifestation of the Aesthetic movement was the book illustration of Walter Crane and Kate Greenaway (1846-1901), re-used to decorate tiles. Published sources of Aesthetic design included C.L.*Eastlake's *Hints on Household Taste* (London, 1868; New York, 1872), J. Moyr Smith's *Ornamental Interiors* (1887), some of the textbooks of ornament by L.F. *Day and W. Watt's *Art Furniture from Designs by E.W. Godwin . . . and others* (1877), which illustrated Godwin's much copied *Anglo-Japanese furniture in ebonised wood as well as including other suggestions for domestic decoration such as wallpaper with dados and

Aesthetic movement. English earthenware teapot, c.1880.

Aesthetic movement. 1) Rubbed brick panel with *sunflower, 6 Chelsea Embankment, London, by E.W. Godwin, 1876-78. 2) 'Jacobean Furniture' from E.W. Godwin's Art Furniture, *1877.*

'Jacobean' furniture. *See also japonaiserie.*

African. The discovery of black African art in the late 19th and early 20th centuries was influential in European fine arts – a display of artefacts from the Belgian Congo at the Exposition International in Brussels (1897) provoked serious consideration of African art. In the decorative arts, however, the negro figure and head appeared on ephemeral and fashionable objects more as a reflection of contemporary interest in American black jazz, e.g. Cartier dress clips in the form of black heads made of onyx, gold and enamel. *See also* blackamoor; Continents.

Ages of Man. Theme in Renaissance painting where the Ages of Man are usually divided into three, seven or twelve periods. It is used in decoration as a device to represent the *Seasons: childhood, youth, maturity and old age standing for Spring, Summer, Autumn and Winter; the twelve *Months are sometimes similarly personified. Figures may be accompanied by attributes of *time. The Ages of Man (and, more rarely, of woman), divided into ten scenes representing each decade from 10 to 100, were used to decorate German 16th and 17th century enamelled glass *Humpen* (tankards).

agriculture. *See* husbandry.

aigrette. *See* feathers.

air. *See* Elements; wind.

Alberti, Leone Battista (1404-72). Italian polymath whose *De Re Aedificatoria* (manuscript form, 1452; published in Latin, Florence, 1485) was the first architectural treatise of the *Renaissance. His own works of architecture, though few in number, were to be enormously influential as they became known in later publications. Since *Vitruvius no such attempt to theorise upon architecture had been made and although Alberti followed Vitruvius he introduced a far more profound analysis of Roman buildings. He also noted a fifth *Order, the Composite. Ornament was a matter of no great importance to Alberti, in

fact he considered it to be 'auxiliary Brightness and Improvement to Beauty . . . somewhat added and fastened on, rather than proper and innate.' In 1550, Alberti's treatise was published in an illustrated edition and in 1553 a French translation appeared. It was not until 1726 that G.*Leoni published an English translation, *The Ten Books of Architecture* (3 vols; second edition 1739), which became an important source-book for early 18th century *classicism.

Albertolli, Giocondo (1742-1839). Italian architect who was instrumental in introducing the heavy style of French *Neo-classicism to Italy. He was the director of the School of Ornament at the Accademia dei Belle Arti in Milan from 1775. From there he published designs, principally for room interiors, ceilings and wall panels in the Neo-classic style: *Ornamenti Diversi* (Milan, 1782); *Alcune Decorazioni di Nobili Sale ed Altri Ornamenti* (Milan, 1787). His favourite motifs included *eagles with flower *festoons suspended from their beaks, flaming *lamps, *wreaths of *laurel and *oak, *medallions enclosing classical portraits and the *thunder and lightning symbols. He also published two guides to ornament: *Miscellanea per Giovani Studiosi del Disegno* (Milan, 1796) and *Corso Elementare di Ornamenti Architettonici Ideato e Disegnato da G.A.* (Milan, 1805).

Alciati, Andrea, called Alciatus (1492-1550). Scholar and commentator on Roman law and history. His collection of *emblems, although known in Milan from 1522 (possibly from very small editions), was first published in Augsburg in 1531. During the next 80 years

G. Albertolli. Stucco vault, Gabinetto Nobile delle Llaarr, Milan, from his Ornamenti Diversi, *1782.*

there were over 130 editions and translations published across Europe. Alciati's work appeared less frequently in England. Geoffrey Whitney's *A Choice of Emblemes, and other Devices* (Leyden, 1586) contains 86 of his designs.

Aldegrever, Heinrich (1502-c.1558). Prolific German engraver of designs for ornament. Member of a group of artists and craftsmen called Die Kleinmeister. Among his designs are panels, vase mounts, *keystones, plinths, jewellery and arms and armour — particularly dagger sheaths. Although the foliage in his designs for *arabesques has a *Gothic feel, most of his motifs are typically *Renaissance: *dolphins, *satyrs, *putti, classical portrait *medallions, swags of *drapery and *sphinxes. Aldegrever also produced series of classically inspired engravings, e.g. the Labours of Hercules (*see* Herculean decoration), the *Virtues and Vices, which provided ornament for painted enamel dishes, plates and wall-plaques from Limoges, relief work on Rhenish stoneware from Cologne and engraved English silver until the end of the 16th century.

Alhambresque. 19th century term for the *Moorish style of architecture based on the Alhambra (Granada, Spain) that was championed by O.*Jones in the second half of the 19th century.

alphabet. Decorated initial letters first appeared in early medieval illuminated manuscripts, and were later a popular embellishment for the printed book. An alphabet was included in one of the first Italian printed *pattern books, a collection of embroidery and weaving designs by G.A.*Tagliente. From the 16th century engraved or woodcut alphabets were produced, some of which were highly imaginative, e.g. Ludovico Vicentino's ribbon alphabet (Venice, 1533), T. and J.I.*de Bry's human alphabet (1576) and J.B. Silvestre's *tree alphabet (Paris, 1843). Most alphabets were intended for the printing industry, but some were designed for other media such as carved wood or engraved silver.

*alphabet. 1) *Rustic alphabet engraved by Joseph Balthazar Silvestri, Paris, 1843. 2) South Islington Public Library, Bridgeman Road, London, 1906.*

In the mid 19th century, a large number of alphabet books were published, covering every conceivable style, e.g. William S. Ford's *Ancient and Ornamental Alphabets* (1850, 1858) and Freeman Delamotte's *Examples of Modern Alphabets* (1858, 18th edition 1935). Gothic examples, such as H.*Shaw's *Alphabets, Numerals and Devices of the Middle Ages* (1845) and *The Handbook of Medieval Alphabets and Devices* (1853), were the most popular. E.G. Stagoll's *Alphabets, Medieval and Modern* (1873) offers a geometric alphabet. *See also* cypher; inscription.

American motifs in ornament reflected a new consciousness of nationality within the early Republic, which was expressed, for example, in the adoption of the bald *eagle (an indigenous North American subspecies) as the national bird of the United States and the invention by Benjamin Latrobe (1764-1820) of 'native Orders' for the Capitol in Washington, utilising native vegetation, the *corncob, tobacco and cotton boll. A vocabulary of alternatives to European *classical motifs was being developed in line with Mrs Trollope's remark: 'if America . . . would be less imitative, she would be infinitely more picturesque and interesting.' The thought was echoed by others such as Robert Mills (1781-1855), a *Greek Revival architect, who suggested: 'study your country's tastes and requirements, and make classic ground here for your art. Go not to the old world for your examples.' Thus,

American. 1) Late 18th century wallpaper with allegorical scene of Britannia weeping for the loss of her colonies. 2) 19th century printed cotton commemorating the political campaign of William Henry Harrison (1773-1841).

American. *Trophy, Museum of the American Indian, West 115th Street, New York, architect Charles Pratt Huntington, 1916.

American. 1) Parian ware jug with Niagara Falls motif, made by the US Pottery Co., Bennington, Vermont, 1852-58. 2) Wallpaper 'curtain' or windowshade commemorating New York's Crystal Palace Exhibition, 1853. 3) Bison head *cornice, New York Central Building, 230 Park Avenue, architects Warren & Wetmore, 1929. 4) Early 20th century ceramic panel ornament on office building, Newark, New Jersey. 5) Indian head on Woolworth Building, 233 Broadway, New York, architect Cass Gilbert, 1913.

cast-iron railings in Louisiana combine corncob *finials with the *anthemions and *palmettes of classical Greece, while furniture made for the mansions of the Southern States was carved with rice plants. As each new state joined the Union, it was represented by an additional star on the Union flag, and the star became an increasingly important motif (see Texan Order).

*International exhibitions like the Philadelphia Centennial (1876) and the World Columbian Exposition in Chicago (1893) fostered national spirit in the arts and widened the range of motifs, which now included American Indian elements. Commemorative ceramics were produced using many of these themes. By the 1890s, American flora and fauna were used widely, for example in the ornamentation of *Gothic Revival *capitals, as at the Chicago Exposition where they were adorned with tobacco, moose, turkey and bison (which was also used as a substitute for the

*aegricanes in classical styles). The Woolworth Building (1913) in New York, was decorated with carved Indian heads.

Frank Lloyd Wright used Mayan elements on Hollyhock House, Los Angeles (1920) and Midway Gardens, Chicago (demolished 1929). An exotic vocabulary, whether of primitive jungle or Babylonian grandeur, was transferred from the silent screen to domestic and commercial interiors in prosperous areas of the country. The geometrical decoration of *Art Deco was enriched by patterns from Central American pre-Columbian art (especially weaving and temple architecture) and by American Indian motifs, such as the feathered arrow shaft or bison horns. Many of these motifs were later taken up in Europe. See also Spanish Colonial Revival.

American Colonial. Style of architecture and furniture developed by settlers in the thirteen British colonies in America between 1620 and 1775, deriving broadly from English styles.

The first permanent dwellings in 17th century America were solid timber buildings loosely based on provincial Elizabethan town houses: built round a main hall, with overhanging upper storeys. However, the buildings usually known as 'Colonial style' or 'Old Colonial' architecture are the clapboard (weatherboarded) timber frame houses with posts and beams and, sometimes, a verandah. These are a modest version of the *Georgian styles in Britain, their character determined by the relatively unsophisticated skills of early craftsmen and the exclusive use of wood (the most easily available natural material). During the 18th century a wealthy merchant/landowner class appeared and the *Palladian style gradually became further refined, though it was still fairly simply interpreted. A wide range of publications was available from 1700 and although practical manuals were the most commonly used source, e.g. W.*Salmon's *Palladio Londinensis* (1734), ubiquitous works such as those by B.*Langley, or, at a more scholarly level, J.*Gibbs, were highly influential in architectural design and detail.

Gradually, different architects and craftsmen produced quite distinct regional interpretations of the classical style: cabinetmakers from Albany, Boston, Philadelphia and Salem all earned special reputations. Early furniture followed Elizabethan and *Jacobean styles with an emphasis on turned wood decoration:

American Colonial. 1) Doorcase, The Hunter House, Newport, Rhode Island, c.1760. 2) Oak bible box from Massachusetts, late 17th century.

split *balusters, knobs, spindles, *spiral turning, balls. Painted decoration sometimes replaced more expensive and elaborate ornament.

The lacquering, carving and *cabriole legs so typical of the *William and Mary and *Queen Anne periods were enthusiastically adopted in America until the mid century when the plainer forms of T.*Chippendale became fashionable.

The first *pattern books to be published in America appeared around the time of the Revolution, beginning with a reprint in Philadelphia of A.*Swan's *The British Architect* in 1775. A.*Benjamin's *The Country Builder's Assistant* (1797) was the first American pattern book. English and French pattern books remained influential after the Revolution, but a more distinctive national style gradually developed (*see* Federal style).

ammonite capital. *Capital decorated with ammonite forms, which is found almost exclusively in Sussex towns. It was probably first used in the early 19th

ammonite capital. Oriental Place, Brighton, Sussex.

century by the architect Amon Wilds (c.1762-1833), who established a practice with his son Amon Henry Wilds in Brighton and built 2-3 Castle Place for the geologist Dr Gideon Mantell, decorating the capitals of the porch with actual fossils picked up locally. It travelled further afield as a decorative variation on the Ionic *Order.

amoeboid shapes. *See* Organic Modernism.

amorino plural *amorini* (Italian, cupid). Alternative term for *cupid usually used with reference to Italian *Renaissance ornament.

anchor. Often indicates a *marine and, by extension, commercial function, appearing, for instance, on port authority, marine insurance or shipping agency buildings. An anchor fouled with rope is a symbol of death – an obvious ornament for mariners' tombstones. The anchor was also an early Christian symbol of hope and steadfastness, found in the catacombs of ancient Rome as a disguised form of the cross. An anchor combined with a *dolphin has been a favourite typographical ornament since the *Renaissance.

anchor. 1) Stone panel, Palais Royale, Paris, 1780s. 2) Early 20th century ironwork, Naval Ministry, Avenue Octave, Paris.

anchor. Dart or arrowhead repeating motif usually used in *ovolo or *astragal moulding enrichment. For egg and anchor *see* egg and tongue.

ancones or **elbows.** *Consoles projecting from the corners of a doorframe to support the *cornice. Term also applied to the arms of a chair.

angel. Winged figures were symbols of divine communication long before the Christian era, e.g. the guardians of the dead on Etruscan sarcophagi, *Mercury and personifications of *Victory. Angels became important in *Christian iconography from the 4th century AD and were divided into nine orders, each with its own characteristics and emblems: the seraph is red and sometimes holds a candle, the *cherub is blue (occasionally gold or yellow) and may have a book – both cherubim and seraphim are represented as a head with one, two or three pairs of wings. The lower orders of angels are represented full figure and are usually winged.

In the sparse decorative vocabulary of *Anglo-Saxon architecture, angels were one of the few representational elements (e.g. flying angels on the rood

angel. 1) Ornamenting 15th century hammerbeam, Church of St Mary, Bury St Edmunds, Suffolk. 2) Façade of St Carolus Borromeüskerk, Antwerp, Belgium, by Pieter Huyssens, 1615-25. 3) Guardian angels on christening mug designed by Richard Redgrave, 1865. 4) West front, Bath Abbey, Avon, begun 1500.

screen at the Church of St Lawrence, Bradford-on-Avon, c.900). Angels are often portrayed as winged musicians in the choir of a church, and the nine orders may appear as nine choirs. Angel roofs appeared during the *Decorated period of English *Gothic, particularly in East Anglia – the angels were carved on *bosses or were finely sculpted and sprang from the beam ends, reinforcing the symbolic identification of the roof with heaven. Angelic heads with outstretched wings made a particularly convenient shape for decorating *spandrels. Angels also became commonplace on *cornices and on canopies (especially for musicians' galleries).

From the mid 14th century, angels began to feature in *heraldic decoration, usually where it was introduced into churches, e.g. on tombs, most often those of women and ecclesiastics, who, according to heraldic practice, were not entitled to proper supporters (*lions, *unicorns, etc.). The angels appear as supporters of *shields or hold mantles of the livery colours.

In the *Baroque period, angels became hyperactive, leaning over balustrades, adhering to ceilings or holding back heavy curtains. Angels have sometimes appeared in secular decoration; the stretchers of late 17th century chairs were occasionally decorated with reclining angels playing trumpets amid elaborately carved *scrolling foliage. Guardian angels appeared on children's cots and christening mugs and became popular in the 19th century as a motif associated with repose, e.g. on beds and armchairs.

Funerary art depicts the Recording Angel, who is shown writing on a tablet while other angels hold pillows or, a specifically English convention, are portrayed as weepers (usually representing the family of the deceased).

Anglo-Japanese. Style of furniture developed around 1867 during the fashion for *japonaiserie by the English designer and architect, Edward W. Godwin (1833-86). Where commercial producers of Japanese-style furniture tended to apply Japanese decoration to recognisable European forms, Godwin produced original and elegant Japanese-inspired designs for both the form and decoration of the pieces, which were usually in ebonised wood with simply shaped silver mounts and were decorated with Japanese motifs such as the *kikumon. Some of his designs were published in the catalogue of the furniture manufacturer William Watt, *Art Furniture from designs by E.W. Godwin with Hints and Suggestions of Domestic Furniture* (1877), and were then copied in England and America. *See also* Aesthetic movement.

Anglo-Japanese. Two pieces of drawing room furniture from E.W. Godwin's Art Furniture, *1877.*

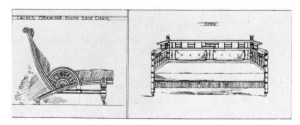

Anglo-Saxon. Earls Barton Church, Northamptonshire, late 10th century.

Anglo-Saxon (5th-11th centuries). Only a small number of buildings in England survive from this date; they are sparsely decorated and motifs tend to be simple, bearing no resemblance to the classical tradition apparent in contemporary Mediterranean architecture. Applied strips of decoration – *lesene and *long and short work which form intricate meshes of geometric shapes – are characteristic and hark back to primitive timber-framed buildings. The *animal art of Nordic and Iron Age cultures was also important source material. Jewellery and manuscripts, which were easily portable, were often responsible for the dissemination and exchange of motifs.

Angoulême sprig, barbeau, cornflower or **Paris cornflower.** In ceramics, painted decoration of small sprigs of cornflowers in blue, green and pink that was popular in the 18th and 19th centuries. It was first used on French porcelain made at Chantilly in the mid 18th century, and then adopted by a Paris porcelain factory belonging to the Duc d'Angoulême. Thomas Turner of the Caughley factory (Shropshire) brought the design to England after a visit to Paris in 1780 and it subsequently appeared on Worcester, Derby, Bristol, Lowestoft and Pinxton wares until well into the 19th century.

Angoulême sprig. Early 19th century English porcelain teapot lid.

animal motifs appeared in the art of the earliest prehistoric societies, which lived by hunting. The animal art of the early nomadic cultures of Central Asia provided the basis for the *zoomorphic forms of *Celtic and *Viking art. Sacrificial and ritual practices in both oriental and occidental cultures assured such animals as *bulls, oxes and rams a place in the decoration of temples and altars; the *aegricanes of Graeco-Roman ornament, a staple motif during all periods of *classical revival, is the most widely used example. From its early days, the Christian church incorporated a wide range of animals in its decoration, depicting such scenes as the 'peaceful Kingdom' described in the Book of Isaiah or symbolising aspects of Christ and his church.

Medieval rulers made a practice of collecting exotic animals and presenting them as gifts to one another. Thus, in 1235, Henry III of England was given three leopards by the Holy Roman Emperor, Frederick III, which were exhibited at the menagerie in the Tower of London and aroused great public interest. In addition, myths, *fables and the *bestiaries, as well as travellers' tales such as the mid 14th century *Marvels of the East* by the fictitious Sir John Mandeville ensured

animal. 1) Late 16th century bronze doors, Duomo, Pisa, Italy.
*2) Woodcut from J. *Le Moyne de Morgues's La Clef des champs, 1586.*
3) 15th century bench end, Church of St Andrew, Norton, Suffolk.
*4) *Keystone over entrance to Inverness Market, Scotland, 1890.*
5) English silver wine label, c.1840-50.

Latinè CAMELVS. Gallicè CHAMEAV.
Ger. KAMELTHIER, Anglicè CAMELL.

*animal. 1) Town Hall, Liverpool, architect John Wood the Elder of Bath, 1749-54. 2) *Moulding on late 19th century commercial building in Eastcheap, City of London.*

that a wide vocabulary of animal forms was established. This included both mythical or fabulous beasts and real creatures, particularly those thought to possess magical qualities. The ornament of *Romanesque and *Gothic churches included exotic animals such as *tigers, leopards and *elephants, often inaccurately depicted, alongside fabulous beasts such as *dragons, *griffins and *unicorns, and familiar European species, both wild and domestic. In Britain alone, over 60 different types of creature have been recorded in medieval sculpted church decoration. Animals were no less widely depicted in the secular arts, and in the later medieval period, *heraldic beasts became common decorative motifs.

The *Renaissance brought a new desire to observe and record the animal kingdom, although the early zoological writers retained their credulity towards the inventions of mythology and folklore: *grotesque ornament is often scattered with bizarre creatures. The first large-scale illustrated work on zoology was Conrad Gesner's *Historia Animalium* (Zurich, 1551-58) which was a source for artists and for many subsequent books, including Edward Topsell's highly fanciful *Historie of Foure-Footed Beastes* (1607), itself widely used as a basis for needlework designs. During the 17th century, the level of accuracy in zoological illustration improved; by the end of the century, the carefully observed animals based on zoological illustrations formed an entirely distinct decorative theme from the fanciful creatures of grotesque decoration. In the 18th century, animal illustrations became increasingly elegant in their engraving and were often richly coloured; they were copied on ceramics, textiles, etc. Among the most influential were the engravings (principally after Jacques de Sève, 1742-88) in the *Histoire Naturelle* (1749-1804) of Georges-Louis Leclerc, Comte de *Buffon.

Favourite decorative themes for domestic interiors in late Renaissance and *Rococo styles included animals associated with *hunting, fables and an odd development, *singeries. Under the *classicism of the

late 18th century, a stricter approach to ornament prevailed, and the naturalistic depiction of animals (whether real or imaginary) in ornament lapsed.

In the 18th and 19th centuries, the *Picturesque theory of the desirability of ornament reflecting the function of a building led to the use of, for example, horses' heads over stable block entrances or *capitals for livestock markets decorated with the animals sold within. Later in the century, Alfred Waterhouse's Natural History Museum in London (1881) was decorated with zoological and palaeontological motifs. Interest in oriental arts introduced, for example, the Persian gazelle into the work of the *Arts and Crafts ceramic tiles of William De Morgan in the 1880s. In the 1920s and 1930s, slender, leaping animals, antelopes, gazelles, deer and greyhound-like dogs, were a recurring theme of ornament in almost every medium, but especially in textile design.

annulet, shaft-ring or **corbel ring.** Thin, flat ring encircling the shaft of a column; used beneath *mouldings, often several at a time in the Doric *Order. It appears singly on *Romanesque columns, and around clustered columns in *Gothic architecture.

annulet. 1) Nave, Rouen Cathedral (Seine-Maritime), France, built by Jean d'Andely, 1201-20. 2) 18th century doorcase, Hadleigh, Suffolk.

anta. *See* pilaster.

antefix (Latin, *antefigere*, to fix in front). Ornamental tile or block used in series to mask the exposed tiles where a roof meets the eaves in Greek and Roman architecture, and usually based on the *anthemion. Appears on Etruscan sarcophagi. Whenever a strict *classicism was in fashion the antefix would appear, thus it was an important element in early 19th century *Greek Revival buildings. *Neo-classical, *Regency and *Empire-style furniture also made use of the device as a corner stop to hold a cushion in place on stools, chairs or windowseats.

anthemion (Greek, *anthos*, flower). One of the principal motifs of *classical ornament, thought by some commentators to be based on the flower of the *acanthus, but loosely resembling the honeysuckle flower and leaf. Possibly a development from similar forms

antefix. 1) Church of St Pancras, Euston Road, London, architects H.W. & W. Inwood, 1819-22. 2) Die Grosse Neugierde, Glienicke, Berlin, architect K.F.*Schinkel, 1835-37. 3) Strand Palace Hotel, London, F.J Wills, 1925-30.

occurring in ancient oriental cultures. 19th century writers on ornament spent much paper and ink on the baffling (and apparently insoluble) question of its origins, citing either the Assyrian hom (sacred plant of the Parsees and ancient Persians) or Egyptian *lotus as the precedent. Its similarity to the *palmette has led to the two terms often being used interchangeably. Used in classical architecture as a horizontal repeating ornament in banding for *friezes, *architraves, *cornices or the necking of Ionic *capitals, it also appears in its own right, e.g. as an *antefix or *acroterion. It survived into French and German *Romanesque architecture, copied from fragments of classical sculpture

anthemion. 1) Wedgwood jasper ware vase, c.1790. 2) *Frieze, Royal Scottish Academy, Edinburgh, William Henry Playfair, 1822 onwards. 3) Early 19th century ironwork balcony, Chequer Square, Bury St Edmunds, Suffolk. 4) Ironwork verandah, Menger Hotel, San Antonio, Texas, 1859. 5) 'Running Anthemion' border on Wedgwood black basalt jug, c.1770.

in southern France and around other Roman outposts. During the *Renaissance, the anthemion became as popular a motif as it had been in Greek and Roman art, often appearing with one bloom facing up and one down. The 18th century marked an enthusiastic readoption of the motif: J.*Stuart and N. Revett did much to re-establish it, taking as their model examples from the Erechtheion, and *Adam style work used it extensively. There were many combinations of the anthemion with other motifs, most notably, single anthemions enclosed between or sprung from two palmettes and scrolls – a favourite *Empire motif similar to the *lyre and *heart shapes so popular in France and America – or as a running ornament (both horizontal and vertical) where flowers alternated with buds. The motif appeared in the decorative arts wherever the *Neo-classical style was taken up. A specifically American use was the crowned version on splat-back chairs made in Massachusetts, c.1790.

antick. 18th century term for *grotesque ornament. It was used by John Neve in *The City and Country Purchaser and Builder's Dictionary* (1703); he described it as 'confused Composure of figures of different Natures... Comical, Pleasant, apt to make one laugh: also ridiculous.'

antique. Term used from the *Renaissance to denote works of Greek and Roman art, which until the middle of the 18th century were not differentiated. In *The City and Country Purchaser and Builder's Dictionary* (1703), John Neve referred to 'a time when the Arts were in their greatest Purity and Perfection among the Ancient Greeks and Romans. We likewise say the Antique Manner to signify anything done according to the strict Rules and the good Taste of the Ancients.'

'After the antique' referred to work deriving from classical originals.

antlers. Motif in 19th century *Scottish ornament and in schemes of decoration using the *stag. Antlers

were used as the material for furniture, candelabra, etc., in some of the most bizarre products of the *Gothic Revival in Scotland and Germany.

Apolline decoration first appeared in Greek and Roman art; the theme was widely adopted and elaborated during the *Renaissance, usually reflecting Apollo's chief significance as god of the *sun and patron of *music and poetry. A popular form of ornament during the reign of Louis XIV in France: a medal decorated with Apollo was struck to commemorate his birth in 1638 and from the early 1650s the king cultivated the identification assiduously; he even appeared in several ballets in the character of Apollo. C.*Le Brun created the Galérie d'Apollon at the Louvre (c.1663), and the Grands Appartements at Versailles (1671-81) where a series of rooms were each named after a planet, culminating in a throne room called the Salon d'Apollon. The most common motif in these decorative schemes was the head of Apollo surrounded by sunrays.

The sun moving across the sky was a popular image signifying the passage of *time, and Apollo's rayed head or Apollo driving his chariot across the sky were frequent ornaments for clocks, particularly in 18th century France. The *lyre motif (another Apolline attribute), though generally reserved for objects and places with an obvious musical association, such as music rooms and music stands, was also used for

Apostles. 1) External decoration on Westminster Cathedral, London, architect John Francis Bentley, 1895-1903. 2) Early 17th century English silver spoon. 3) Early 17th century stoneware tankard made at Kreussen, Bavaria.

*Apolline decoration. 1) Engraving after work by W.*Kent from I.*Ware's* Plans, Elevations and Sections of Houghton, *1735. 2) 18th century marble chimneypiece, drawing room, Belton House, Lincolnshire. 3) Dutch porcelain vase, Amstel, c.1800. 4) Plate by J.*Berain, early 18th century.*

clocks, neatly combining the Apolline associations with time and music.

Because of the importance of Versailles, these motifs achieved wide popularity and continued to be used well into the 19th century; Apolline ornament was advocated as classically correct by R.*Brown. In pre-19th century interiors, where the hearth was often an important source of light after dark, the theme was an obvious choice for the embellishment of chimneys and mantelpieces.

Apostles. Popular decoration for spoon ends in England from the late 15th to the 17th century; similar sets were also made in Germany. Occasionally a thirteenth spoon representing Christ was included. In Holland very large spoons were produced ornamented with figures of saints, but as individual pieces. The Victorians revived the decoration for coffee spoons.

Like other biblical subjects, the Apostles appear in ceramic decoration, e.g. relief decoration on Rhenish stoneware, painted decoration on Swiss faïence drug jars made at Winterthur, enamelling on German and Bohemian 17th century glass and stoneware. Charles Meigh of Hanley, Staffordshire, registered a design for an Apostle jug in 1842; later he used the theme on a teaset in the fashionable *Gothic Revival style.

Apostles often appear with their emblems: St Andrew – X-shaped cross; St Bartholomew – knife, flayed skin; St James the Greater – scroll, pilgrim's staff, scallop; St James the Less – fuller's staff; St John – eagle, book or palm; St Matthew – money bag, or book and pen; St Paul – sword, book or scroll; St Peter – keys, fish; St Philip – Latin cross attached to top of staff; St Simon Zelotes – saw, cross; St Thomas – builder's rule or square. *See also* Christian motifs.

apple. *See* fruit.

apronwork. Panel below a window sill or oriel or bow window, often ornamented with a *fan or scroll form. Feature of late 17th century and late 19th century architectural revivals. A similar semi-circular shape was used in furniture below the seat-rail of chairs, sofas, and at the bottom of chests of drawers, highboys, cabinet stands, etc. *See also* lambrequin.

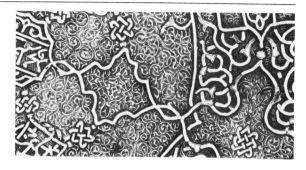

apronwork. 1) Late 19th century office building, Eastcheap, City of London. 2) English card table, c.1700. 3) Early 18th century plaster apronwork, Prague.

arabesque. 1) Early 16th century Venetian Saracenic metal bowl cover. 2) Woodcut by F.*Pellegrino from La Fleur de la science de pourtraicture, 1530. 3) Mid 16th century inlaid stone monument, Church of St Mary Magdalene, Cobham, Kent. 4) Design for goldsmiths by Marcus Grundler, 1617. 5) Tin-glazed earthenware dish, Venice, 1543.

arabesque. Term generally used to describe the stylised interlaced foliage patterns which became a major element in European ornament from the mid 16th century to the early 17th century. Moresque was the contemporary term, still used to describe the earliest foliate patterns that do not include *strapwork. Both 'arabesque' and 'moresque' indicate the origins of the patterns in Near Eastern design: they derive particularly from damascened and engraved metalwork produced in Mesopotamia, Persia and Syria. Moslem craftsmen settled in Venice at the end of the 15th century and produced engraved and inlaid metalwork (known as Venetian Saracenic) densely decorated with such ornament; it was mainly via this route that arabesques became absorbed into the mainstream of European design. Indeed in the 16th century the patterns were sometimes referred to as *damascins*.

G.A.*Tagliente's *Opera Nuova* (Venice, 1527) and N. *Zoppino's *Esemplario di Lavori* (first edition 1529, sixth edition 1539), which were intended primarily for needlework, both included moresques. An unknown artist called Master F. who worked in Venice during

the 1520s and 1530s was responsible for an early collection of moresques described as suitable for painters, rug weavers, needleworkers, goldsmiths, stonecutters and glass engravers. He described the patterns as laurel leaves in the manner of the Persians, Assyrians, Arabs, Egyptians, Indians, Turks and Greeks, thus taking no chances in mistaking their true origins. Some of this set were subsequently copied by Augustin Hirschvogel (1503-53) in Germany and then by Hieronymus Cock in Amsterdam in an influential edition entitled *Variarum protractionum forme, quas vulgo Maurusias vocant*. P.*Flötner also copied some of these. Once established in the ornamental canon, the abstract curving foliage from the East was combined with Western formal and symmetrical *bandwork or *strapwork, and arabesque designs of this kind were included in *La Fleur de la science de pourtraicture et patrons de broderie façon arabicque et italique* (Paris, 1530) by the Florentine F. *Pellegrino; these were the first such patterns to be published in France. Balthasar Sylvius published some influential patterns in Antwerp in the 1550s. The first to appear in England were T.*Geminus's *Morysse and Damashin renewed and increased Very profitable for Goldsmythes and Embroderars* (1548).

Gradually the use of the arabesque spread from metalwork to a wide variety of other media: e.g. pottery produced at Gubbio, Venice and St Porchaire, Italian and Spanish brocade, bookbinding and printed ornament, marquetry and lace. In the early 17th century there was a fashion for jewellery and enamel decorated with arabesque designs carried out in white on a black ground. Many engravers published work in this style, among them Daniel Mignot (1590), Hans Hensel (1599), M.*Le Blon, Jacques Hurtu (1615-19), Marcus Grundler (1617), Jean Toutin (1618-19) and Esias van Hulsen (1617). This lasted until c.1650 when a more floral style incorporating *peapod ornament was developed.

The *Renaissance Revival in the mid 19th century saw the reappearance of much arabesque patterning, particularly in the fashionable inlaid and elaborately decorated metalwork. Original 16th and 17th century designs were republished, notably by O. Reynard in London.

18th century French designers applied the term *arabesques* to what were essentially panels of *grotesque designs that incorporated figures, bandwork and *scrolling foliage.

Arabian style. Just as the 18th century antiquary went to classical Greece, so his 19th century counterpart often travelled to the Middle East, and painters such as John Frederick Lewis (1805-76), David Roberts (1796-1864) and, later, Lord Leighton (1830-96) helped to spread the enthusiasm for what were called the Arab countries – Islamic North Africa and the Middle East. This was not a specific or historicist interest, and motifs were adopted from a wide range of oriental cultures, from the *Byzantine to the Ottoman. Some travellers went to record the places mentioned in the Bible, and theoretical investigation of the relationship between Arab and Christian art ironically resulted in oriental decoration becoming absorbed into that most Christian of movements, the *Gothic Revival. The Great Exhibition of 1851 was much concerned with the Orient, and O.*Jones wrote that 'the mosques of Cairo are among the most beautiful buildings in the world.' Importantly, he distinguished between Arabian and *Moorish styles: 'the constructive features of the Arabs possess more grandeur and those of the Moors more refinement and elegance.' The French (who invaded and took Algiers in 1830) published works on the Arab countries: E.-V.*Collinot and Adalbert de Beaumont included Arabian work in their *Recueil de dessins pour l'art et l'industrie* (1859, much extended in the 1880s), and A.C.T.E.*Prisse d'Avennes began publishing accounts of Arab monuments as early as 1847; his *L'Art Arabe d'après les monuments du Cair depuis le VIIe siècle jusqu'à la fin du XVIIIe* (1869-77) covered the buildings in detail, down to interior design and furnishings. The Germans were interested too: F.M. Hessemer's *Arabische und Alt-Italienische Bau-Verzierungen* (1842) had examples of geometric designs from Cairo.

*Arabian style. 1) 14th century interior windows from Queycoun Mosque in A.C.T.E.*Prisse d'Avennes's* L'Art Arabe, *1869-77. 2) In O.*Jones's* Grammar of Ornament, *1868 edition.*

In 1880 George Aitchison (1825-1910) designed the Arab Hall for Leighton House, London, an example of the literal approach to the Arabian style. Liberty's imported Arabian cabinets, *mushrebîyeh* screens – Egyptian bobbin-turned screens like those in the popular paintings of J.F. Lewis – mosque lamps and stained glass windows with Islamic *tracery were all listed in J. Moyr Smith's *Ornamental Interiors* (1887), and using them together was said to produce an oriental effect 'further emphasised with Eastern-patterned ceiling papers and Arabic forms used in the constructional lines.' *See also* eclectic.

arcading consists of linked arches, round-headed or pointed and sometimes interlaced, supported by piers, columns or *colonnettes. It may be freestanding (as in covered walks, cloisters) and serve both a structural and a decorative function, or *blind (against a wall) and purely decorative. It is common in *Anglo-Saxon,

arcading, Duomo, Siena, Italy, 12th to 14th centuries.

*Romanesque, *Gothic and *Renaissance buildings as a useful device for lending interest to large, blank walls and for defining changes of level. In *Lombardic architecture, arcading became an overall decorative device often rising in series to the full height of a façade. It was much used for courtyards and *logge* in the early Italian Renaissance, and when it was applied on successive levels, the *Orders were observed (based on a classical prototype, the Colosseum in Rome.) Arcading has been much used in an ecclesiastical context, e.g. Saxon fonts, where it may be incised or applied as relief patterning, on sedilia or triforia, on reliquaries and censers. It was used on secular furniture and woodwork during the 17th century, and reappeared in the architectural ornament of the 19th century *Romanesque and *Renaissance Revivals. *See also* pillar and arch.

Archaeological style. Mosaic pendant by Ernesto Pierret, c.1860.

Archaeological style. 19th century jewellery designs based on a variety of ancient styles, notably *Etruscan, *Greek, *Celtic, often using or imitating original metalwork techniques, e.g. filigree, *granulation, mosaic and *cloisonné enamel. The style was particularly popular in Italy and reflected the growing interest across Europe in archaeological excavation and trade in ancient jewellery.

architectural elements have been used as motifs in ornament since Greek and Roman times (e.g. *columns framing motifs on sarcophagi). They appear frequently in the *Romanesque and *Gothic styles, particularly in an ecclesiastical context: choir stalls and funerary monuments make use of canopies, *arcading, pillars, turrets as well as the more common *finials, *cusps, *crockets and *cresting. Miniaturised architectural features also decorate church treasures such as reliquaries and illuminated manuscripts. In *classical styles, features like *aedicules, temple fronts and *triumphal arches are used in ornament – a very early example of this is the city-gate motif used on Early Christian sarcophagi. 16th century panelled interiors and *cassone* (15th and 16th century chests) decorated with *perspectival inlay sometimes depicted whole streets. Occasionally a group of buildings has been

*architectural elements. 1) 123-127 Cannon Street, City of London, architect H. Huntly Gordon, 1895. 2) Late 16th century English Nonsuch chest. 3) Design for pendant, Hans Collaert, Antwerp, c. 1573. 4) Marquetry table with view of Venice by Gio Ponti, c.1957. 5) Doric bookcase from B.*Langley's The City and Country Builder's and Workman's Treasury of Designs, 1740.*

used symbolically, e.g. to represent the holy city of Jerusalem. Particular towns were commonly personified as female figures, the head encircled by a *crown composed of a city rampart, often called a mural crown.

18th century classicism made extensive use of *broken pediments, *columns, decorated *cornices and *friezes; any object with a frame was well-suited to an architectural treatment, e.g. wall mirrors designed by W.*Kent (1730-40). 18th century cabinet-makers were expected to have a working knowledge of architectural composition, and most of the *pattern books they used contained summaries of the *Orders.

architrave. The lowest of the three sections of the *entablature, the other two being the *frieze and the *cornice. Term also generally applied to the *moulding, often enriched, around a door or window frame.

archivolt. A *moulding around an arch which may be plain or decorated. Alternatively, the undersurface of an arch.

armorial bearings. *See* achievement of arms; heraldic decoration.

arms and armour. *See* military decoration.

arrow. Used by *Cupid to pierce people with love, it appears, sometimes in a quiver, on *trophies representing love, along with a flaming *torch for setting hearts on fire. The arrow piercing a *heart appears as a motif in 16th century jewellery, but this symbolism was particularly favoured in 18th century French ornament, e.g. quivers of arrows forming bed posts. The quiver of arrows and torch also appear in *au carquois* [quiver] decoration on mid 18th century Rouen ceramics.

The jagged arrow is a symbol of lightning, an attribute of Jupiter, often used with motifs representing *thunder in heavy *classical decorative schemes.

Arrows appeared in schemes of *military decoration long after they had been superseded as weapons. Arrow-heads ornamented railings and gates well into the 19th century, giving a suggestion of fortification. In the early 19th century arrows supported fashionable drapery, appearing as curtain poles and holding bed curtains; examples are illustrated in the work of P.*La Mésangère and R.*Ackermann. Windsor chairs with arrow-shaped spindles appeared in America at the same period. *See also* American motifs.

arrow slit. Narrow vertical slit, first used in medieval walltowers for defence. A horizontal slit was soon added to form a cross shape, improving visibility and making it easier to fire a crossbow. Like other signs of fortification, it remained as a decorative feature long after it had become redundant, giving an appearance of strength to manor houses and sometimes even appearing next to a mullioned Tudor window. Commonly used around gates and entrances, arrow slits reappeared, mainly in the more decorative cross form, during the 18th century *Gothick vogue for fake fortifications in the *Castle style. 19th century *Gothic Revival architecture used the motif unstintingly.

Art Deco loosely describes the decorative styles that superseded *eclecticism and *Art Nouveau in the years before and after World War I. It derived from elements in the work of the Deutscher Werkbund and the Wiener Werkstätte, from the early 20th century art movements of Cubism, Expressionism, Futurism and Fauvism, from the designs (particularly those of Léon Bakst) for the Ballets Russes, which had their first season in Paris in 1909, and from a growing awareness of African art (via the French colonies) and Indian art from Central America.

An exhibition was planned in Paris by the Société des Artistes Décorateurs in 1916 to display ceramics, glass, graphics, furniture, interior design, bookbinding,

metalwork and lacquer, all produced in the new styles. Postponed until 1925, the Exposition Internationale des Arts Décoratifs et Industriels Modernes gave rise to the term Art Deco, acting as a catalyst in a post-war burst of creativity, but also revealing a split within the movement between the 'decorators' and the modernists. The official publication for the exhibition, the *Encyclopédie des arts décoratifs et industriels modernes au XXième siècle* consisted of 12 volumes and contained over 1,000 illustrations. The works on show in 1925 were decorated with rounded and romantic motifs: closely packed flowers in garlands and baskets, the ubiquitous stylised *rosebuds, *doves, prancing fauns, oval shapes, *fountains, *tassels, tightly whorled spirals and ropes of pearls. In the late 1920s and early 1930s, the designs became more abstract and geometrical. Art Deco also spread from France to the rest of Europe and to America, absorbing different national influences. Current archaeological discoveries contributed: in Britain, *Egyptian motifs were assimilated after Howard Carter's excavation of the tomb of Tutankhamen in 1922; in America, discoveries of Aztec temples suggested stepped shapes, particularly in architecture, and *sun motifs. Late Art Deco included motifs suggesting speed, dynamism and *streamlining which were particularly suited to objects, buildings and materials of the machine age. The change of emphasis was noted by the French designer, Paul Iribe, who wrote in 1930: 'for thousands, the flower is as necessary as the machine – shall we sacrifice the flower on the altar of cubism and the machine?' Essentially a matter of decoration, Art Deco could be applied equally to the façade of a building or the surface of a plastic powder

Art Deco. 1) French scent bottle with black enamelling, 1920s. 2) Silver tea service, made in Birmingham, England, 1930s.

Art Deco. 1) Railway Station, Cincinnati, Ohio, Fellheimer & Wagner, 1929-33. 2) Hoover Building, Greenford, Middlesex, architects Wallis Gilbert & Partners, 1931. 3) Lexington Avenue entrance, Chrysler Building, New York, architect William Van Alen, 1930.

compact, and many of its main designers worked in several media. An exhibition in Paris in 1966 commemorated the 1925 one; it aroused interest in Art Deco, aspects of which were subsequently revived.

Art Nouveau. Decorative style, equally important in architecture and the decorative arts, that first appeared in the 1880s. Influences that fed into it included the linear ornament of some *Arts and Crafts designers, e.g. A.H. Mackmurdo and Walter Crane, the sinuous interlacings of the *Celtic Revival, the serpentine line of *Rococo, the asymmetry of Japanese design and, above all, the strong return to *naturalism prompted by the *Gothic Revival coupled with the Symbolist fascination with the forms of nature. Apart from the consistent asymmetry, the vocabulary varied: stems, roots, elongated blooms and foliage, dream-like figures of women with half-closed eyes and drifting hair, set among undulating lines and *whiplash curves or surrounded by entwining plant forms (*see femme-fleur*). The Art Nouveau woman was embodied by the American dancer Loie Fuller (1865-1928). Her 'serpentine dance' (first seen in Paris in 1892) combined movements with flowing swathes of silk and special lighting effects. So entranced were artists by her that she became an ornamental motif of the period, notably forming electric lamp bases.

*Art Nouveau. 1) Porcelain chocolate pot designed by Georges de Feure, Limoges, France, c.1900. 2) Brooch designed by E.*Grasset for Henri Vever, Paris, c.1900. 3) English silver mirror back ornamented with lily-of-the-valley, early 1900s. 4) Casa Batlló, Barcelona, Spain, architect Antonio Gaudi, 1905-07. 5) Corner cupboard designed by Hector Guimard, c.1900.*

Apart from Victor Horta (1861-1947) and another Belgian, Henry van de Velde (1863-1957), who was strongly influenced by the Arts and Crafts movement, the most innovative Art Nouveau designers were French: Hector Guimard (1867-1942), Emile Gallé (1846-1906), designer of glass, pottery and furniture and a leading member of the group known as the Ecole de Nancy, and René Lalique (1860-1945), who designed glass and jewellery.

The style took its name and focus from Samuel Bing's shop 'La Maison de l'Art Nouveau', opened in Paris in 1895 and designed by a group of artists including van de Velde and the American designer and manufacturer Louis Comfort Tiffany (1848-1933). The shop displayed and sold pieces by most of the artists and craftsmen working in the idiom. In graphic design, Art Nouveau was widely promoted by artists such as A.*Mucha and E.*Grasset. The style was well suited to commercial use, catching a popular mood of reaction to *Historicism, and spread across Europe. In Italy it was called the Stile Liberty; a closely related style termed *Jugendstil appeared in Germany and Austro-Hungary; Spanish Art Nouveau was termed *Modernismo. In Britain, although some parallel may be found in the work of the *Glasgow School, there was little response to the style. The movement reached its peak at the 1900 Exposition Universelle in Paris, and its commercial spread began in earnest. Within a few years, however, the movement was fading rapidly, although echoes of it (sometimes referred to as Quaint Style) lingered on in mass-produced goods of many types.

A revival of Art Nouveau in the 1960s, particularly in textiles, wallpaper and graphic design, was triggered partly by a large Art Nouveau exhibition in 1960 at the Museum of Modern Art in New York and by later retrospectives of Mucha (1963) and Aubrey Beardsley (1966) at the Victoria & Albert Museum, London.

Arts and Crafts. 1) Tile, William De Morgan, made at Merton Abbey, 1880s. 2) English silver and enamel buckle, made in Birmingham, 1910. 3) Late 19th century English silver candlestick made by James Dixon. 4) Art pottery vase, Marblehead Pottery, Massachusetts, 1910-20.

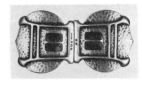

Arts. *See* Liberal Arts; Muses.

Arts and Crafts. A movement that originated in England but subsequently had a much wider influence in the development of the Modern Movement (*see* Modernist decoration) and of industrial design. Its central figure was the socialist writer and designer William Morris (1834-96), and its essential aims were to revive medieval standards of craftsmanship and to make the idea of truth to materials the basis of design. The firm of Morris, Marshall, Faulkner & Co., founded 1861, offered to undertake 'any species of decoration, from pictures properly so-called, down to consideration of the smallest work susceptible of art beauty.' Apart from Morris, its founders were three painters, Ford Madox Brown (1821-93), Dante Gabriel Rossetti (1828-82), and Edward Burne-Jones (1833-98), an architect, Philip Webb (1831-1915), an engineer and surveyor, P.P. Marshall, and an Oxford don, Charles Faulkner. The combination indicates ambitions remote from those of mass-manufacture, which was then characterised by over-ornamentation, *eclecticism and novelty for its own sake. Taking the creative craftsmanship of the Middle Ages as an ideal, Morris and the others replaced the ecclesiastical emphasis of the *Gothic Revival with political and social consideration, and addressed themselves to a secular world. Many of the company's early works (stained glass, painted furniture and embroideries) are decorated with medieval subjects.

The textile and wallpaper designs by Morris were very successful and encouraged simple, unpretentious patterns incorporating English motifs (daisies, wild *roses, rabbits), a vein continued in the work of C.F.A. Voysey (1857-1941). In the 1880s and 1890s, much of the ornament and decoration in Arts and Crafts products was closely allied to structure and to the qualities of the materials: hammered metal in simple shapes, *waggon chamfering on wood, stencilled ornament in linear patterns on architecture, plus a variety of traditional or vernacular touches.

Craftworkers associated with the movement banded themselves together into groups: the Century Guild, formed in 1882 by the architect A.H. Mackmurdo (1851-1942), the Art Workers' Guild (1884) with Walter Crane (1845-1915) as a founder member, and the Guild of Handicraft, started in 1888 by C.R. Ashbee (1863-1942). Exponents of the Arts and Crafts movement were also powerful in the art schools that were being established, notably Walter Crane at Manchester School of Art and then as first principal of the Royal College of Art, London, and William Lethaby (1857-1931), Professor of Design at the Royal College and first principal of the Central School of Arts and Crafts; others produced textbooks for the students, among them L.F.*Day, a founder member of the Art Workers' Guild, who was responsible for a series of textbooks on ornamental design published in the 1890s. Much Arts and Crafts work was quickly published in the illustrated art magazines that were then flourishing both in Britain and in Germany. The German writer Hermann Muthesius (1861-1927), who was in London from 1896 to 1903, praised the utility and simplicity of much of the architectural work,

Arts and Crafts. 1) Office building, Cannon Street, City of London, 1899. 2) English oak wardrobe, Ernest Barnsley, c.1902. 3) English ironwork hinge designed by Ernest Gimson, early 20th century.

Assyrian motifs. English gold brooch, c.1850.

publishing it, for example, in *Das Englische Haus* (1905). The Arts and Crafts Exhibition Society was set up in 1886, followed by similar organisations in Birmingham and Liverpool. The Guild of Handicraft exhibited in Vienna, Munich, Düsseldorf and Paris, exercising a strong influence over designers and manufacturers – in fact, commercial manufacturers plagiarised their designs to the extent that the Guild could not compete with its imitators and went into liquidation in 1908.

The two most influential adherents of the Arts and Crafts movement in America were Elbert Hubbard (1856-1915) and Gustav Stickley (1857-1942). Hubbard visited William Morris in the early 1890s and set up a craft community, the Roycrofters, in Aurora, New York, marketing the products through the Roycroft Shops. Typical work (in 1905 called Aurora Colonial Furniture) was plain, unornamented oak furniture, metalwork with hammered finish and leatherwork, sometimes decorated with simple *Art Nouveau motifs. Stickley abandoned historical style furniture after meeting Voysey on a trip to Europe in 1898 and began to produce well-made pieces with emphasis on construction: dove-tail and mortice and tenon joints. His books explained how people could produce their own versions of his furniture. The style was successful and was rapidly copied by manufacturers. It was an important strand in the *Mission style. *See also* Old English.

Assyrian motifs. The *lotus, *rosette, geometrical *diaper patterns, hom (*see* Tree of Life) and winged

bull are all motifs of Assyrian origin that played an important part in *classical Greek ornament.

Apart from an indirect influence on *Neo-classical styles via Greek prototypes, Assyrian forms were not taken up again until the mid 19th century when they were one of the latest discoveries of the *Archaeological style. Sir Austen H. Layard discovered evidence of the Assyrian civilisation and published his findings in *Nineveh and its Remains* (1849) and later, *Nineveh and Babylon* (1853). These publications encouraged interest in Assyrian art and provided examples for ornament; around 1850 jewellery was made from miniature gold plaques imitating the huge stone tablets found in the Throne Room of Assurbanipal at Nineveh, and electroplate wine coolers engraved with human-headed bulls and an Assyrian king were produced in 1855 by Henry Wilkinson & Co., London. In his *Grammar of Ornament*, O.*Jones expressed scant regard for the Assyrian, describing it as 'a development of the Egyptian, but, instead of being carried forward, descending in the scale of perfection, bearing the same relation to the Egyptian as the Roman does to the Greek . . . A borrowed style and one in a state of decline.' The winged lion or bull used as a *bracket was fairly common in late 19th century architecture both in England and in France.

The exoticism of Assyrian motifs brought about the occasional revival of the style in the 20th century, e.g. in New York, the SJM building of 1927 by Cass Gilbert has lions guarding the entrances and Mesopotamian *friezes arranged up the height of the building.

astragal or **baguette.** Thin, semicircular *moulding in *classical architecture, often enriched with *bead and reel ornament (referred to in 18th century glossaries as 'paternoster') and associated with the Ionic *Order. A larger version of the astragal used on the base of a column is known as the *torus.

In cabinet-making, an astragal is a glazing bar. *Pattern books, such as that of T.*Shearer, provided alternative designs in *classical or *Gothic styles. A related form is *cock beading.

astronomy. *See* Liberal Arts.

atlantes, gigantes or **telamones.** Male figures or half-length figures acting as supports for an *entablature.

*atlantes. 1) Baroque doorway, Palais Caprara-Geymuller, Vienna, 1698.
2) 17th century house, Via San Cosimo, Verona, Italy.*

They were originally used in *classical Greek architecture, and may be nude or lightly draped; the arms are usually raised with the weight supported on the hands and forearms. Atlantes derive from Atlas, the god whose role in Greek mythology was to hold up the heavens. A variant, the telamon, sometimes had a loincloth and headdress in an *Egyptian style. Examples modelled on ancient Egyptian statues in the collection of Pius II (1405-64) at Tivoli in Central Italy were well known to Renaissance artists; for example, Raphael and Giulio Romano incorporated them into the picture surrounds in the Stanza dell'Incendio in the Vatican (1514-17). Atlantes flank a doorway in the Palais de Fontainebleau (c.1540); they were widely illustrated in 16th century engraved sources for ornament such as those by J.A.*Ducerceau, where they appear as supports for furniture and notably for chimneypieces. Well-muscled and contorted to show the effort of support, they were much used by *Baroque designers of the late 17th and early 18th centuries. Early 19th century French and Italian *Neo-classical designers followed their earlier use as supports for tables and chimneypieces. In Second Empire France, atlantes served as ornamental columns for balconies and entrances. Like other elements of Baroque ornament, atlantes were adopted in a flamboyant form in the late 19th and early 20th centuries. *See also* caryatid; herm; persian.

Attick Order. An additional Order relegated to the topmost storey in which the supports are small *pilasters or *columns or sometimes sculpted figures. Often in *Renaissance *palazzi* this storey is an open *loggia*.

Audsley family. William James Audsley (b 1833), George Ashdown Audsley (1838-1925), Berthold Audsley and Maurice Ashdown Audsley were all writers of books on ornament and *eclectic decoration at the end of the 19th and beginning of the 20th century. George Audsley was the most prolific; an expert on Japanese art, he wrote several books which were influential sources of motifs for *japonaiserie: *Descriptive Catalogue of Art Works in Japanese Lacquer in the Possession of James L. Bowes Esq* (Liverpool, 1875), *Keramic Art of Japan* (Liverpool, 1875; London, 1881) and *The Ornamental Arts of Japan* (London, 1882-84; New York, 1883-85). In 1878, George and William Audsley published a joint work, *Outlines of Ornament in the Leading Styles* (London, 1881; New York, 1882), which was both a historical survey and a practical guide. In 1882 they also published *Polychromatic Decoration as Applied to Buildings in the Mediaeval Styles*, which examined 13th century geometric ornament. The most elaborate production was George and Maurice Audsley's *The Practical Decorator*, published simultaneously in Britain and France in 1892, and then in Stuttgart in 1893. An expanded version of the earlier *Outlines of Ornament in the Leading Styles*, it contained large chromolithographed plates, and although much of the polychromatic formalised ornament illustrated was no longer very fashionable by the time the book was published, the authors emphasised its practical application, describing it as 'a series of designs capable of being executed by the simplest means . . . namely, stencilling . . . suitable for the decoration of all ordinary classes of buildings and for the ornamentation of articles of furniture and other objects of utility and beauty.' In the early years of the 20th century, George and Berthold Audsley produced several guides to the application of ornament, notably on illuminating, turning and stencilling.

auger flame. *See* flame.

aureole. *See* vesica piscis.

Auricular style, Dutch Grotesque style, Lobate style, Cartilaginous style or **Oleaginous style.** (In Dutch, *kwabornament*, from *kwab*, earlobe; in German, *Knorpelornament*, from *Knorpel*, cartilage.) Style of ornament modelled with a smooth undulating surface of flowing

Attick Order. Grecian Chambers, 336-356 Sauchiehall Street, Glasgow, architect Alexander 'Greek' Thomson, 1865.

Audsley family. *Diaper patterns developed from 13th century examples, from W.& G. Audsley's Polychromatic Decoration as Applied to Buildings in the Medieval Style, *1882.*

lines, creases and ripples, that was developed by Dutch silversmiths in the late 16th and early 17th centuries using forms resembling earlobes, sinews, intestines (perhaps because there was great interest in anatomical dissection at the time), also parts of animals and fish used together with the *grotesque masks typical of the period.

The most dramatic examples of the style were produced by the van Vianen family of Utrecht: Paulus (c.1558-1613), his brother Adam (c.1565-1627) and Adam's son Christiaen (1587-1669). Johannes Lutma (1587-1669) and Thomas Bogaert also worked extensively in the style. Lutma published two series of engraved auricular designs: *Veelderhande Nieuwe Compartmente* (1653) and *Verscheide Snakeryen* (1654). Christiaen

Auricular style. 1) Dutch silver candle sconce, Adam van Vianen, 1622. 2) Dutch *cartouche design, c.1655, probably by Gerbrand van den Eeckhout.

van Vianen published the designs his father had developed from the work of Paulus, *Modelles Artificiels de divers Vaisseaux d'Argent et autres Oeuvres Capricieuzes et Dessignees du renomme Sr. Adame de Viane* (1650). By the time the book appeared the fashion for Auricular ornament had to some extent subsided, but this record of the work may well have been the reason why lobed decoration in silver survived throughout the 1650s and 1660s. The van Vianens travelled from Holland to work in England and Germany, and watered-down versions of Auricular shapes spread to carved furniture and plasterwork as their work became more widely known. An early application of Auricular ornament to woodwork is illustrated in Nikolaus Rosman's *Erster Theill: Nieuw Zierat Büchlein invent Grad.* (1627); other designs were published by Georg Caspar Erasmus of Nuremberg in *Seülen Buch*, (Nuremberg, 1666, 1667, 1672), by Friedrich Unteutsch, a cabinetmaker, in *Neues Zieratenbuch den Schreinern Tischlern oder Künstlern und Bildhauern* (Nuremberg, c.1650) and by Daniel Rabel in *Cartouches de différentes inventions* (c.1620-30).

Ayres, Philip (1638-1712). English author, translator and poet whose emblem book on the subject of love contained many engravings depicting *Cupid.

Bacchic ornament. 'The Triumph of Bacchus', design by E.*Delaune, mid 16th century.

Bacchic ornament. Decoration related to Bacchus, Roman god of wine and fertility (and his Greek equivalent Dionysus), and generally alluding to the myth concerning Bacchus's discovery of wine (and honey). His attributes include the *grapevine, *ivy, *laurel, *dolphin, *serpent, panther, *tiger, ass and ram, and he is often depicted as a youth with a sweet, if drunken, smile. Bacchus and the panther appear in bas relief on the Choragic Monument of Lysicrates (Athens). In the *Renaissance, Bacchus and his attributes were widely used in decoration, sometimes as a symbol of living by the senses to contrast with Apollo who personified reason; there are many examples in *emblem books. Bacchus's companions in the Bacchanalia are the Maenades (or Bacchants), the Thyiades (wildly dancing females crowned with vines, clothed in animal skins and carrying the *thyrsus, cymbals, swords or serpents), and the fat figure of old Silenius clutching his wine-skin, too drunk to stand and often astride an ass. The figures decorated *friezes on Roman sarcophagi. Engravings of the subject such as those by A.*Desgodetz in *Les Edifices Antiques de Rome* (1682) and by J.*Stuart and N. Revett were eagerly copied. The *Adam style decorators Diana Beauclerk and William Hackwood produced many variations for the ornamentation of Wedgwood jasper ware, stone-glazed

ballflower. 1) St Andrew's Cathedral, Inverness, architect Alexander Ross, 1866-69. 2) South front of Gloucester Cathedral, mid 14th century.

Bacchic ornament. 1) Marble chimneypiece carved by Sefferin Alken in the dining room of Wimpole Hall, Cambridgeshire, 1740s. 2) Relief of the Drunkenness of Silenius on a silver tankard by Rundell, Bridge & Rundell, London, 1815. 3) English electroplate fruit stand with two Bacchic boys and a panther under a vine, 1840-46.

jugs and painted furniture. Bacchic decoration was considered eminently suitable for dining-room furniture and tableware. Later, commercial architecture, hotels and pubs endlessly exploited the theme, either as detail or in overall decorative schemes, particularly where the *Rococo Revival and *Art Nouveau styles were used. In the 19th century the subject was sentimentalised with the characters often transformed into *putti. These 'bacchanalian boys' were popular throughout the Victorian age, pulling silver wine chariots and trailing vine garlands on engraved glass, e.g. H.J. Townsend's design for champagne glasses, 'Bubbles Bursting', in which boys cavort in fountains exploding from vine tendrils.

baguette. *See* astragal.

baldacchino. Originally a damask canopy over an altar, throne or doorway; it later appeared in carved stone and wood as well as fabric, either suspended from a ceiling or supported on columns (often *spiral) usually over an altar, a characteristic *Baroque feature. It was used two-dimensionally as a motif in *grotesque panels by J.*Berain and subsequently by French *orne-manistes* of the early 18th century. Also occasionally used as a framing device.

balistraria. Cruciform apertures cut in the *battlements of medieval fortified buildings, through which a crossbow could be used. Later applied to castellated buildings as an ornamental motif. *See also* arrowslit.

ball and bar. Row of spaced beads linking the uprights of a chair-back – a typical feature of 18th century chairs produced in eastern England.

Also, a style of thumbpiece with a bar stretching from the centre of the lid to a ball at the top of the handle in 19th century Scottish lidded tankards and wine measures, usually of pewter.

ball and claw. *See* claw.

ballflower. Small stylised flower form used to enrich both interior and exterior mouldings in English Gothic architecture of the *Decorated style; it replaced the earlier *dogtooth motif. Found widely in the west of England. It was popular in *Gothic Revival enrichment. *See also* tablet flower.

ballon. 18th century term for stone or metal ball most commonly placed on a gate or newel post.

baluster. A form that developed in the *Renaissance, and was used either singly or in a *balustrade. The classical shape which corresponds most closely to the baluster and from which it probably developed is the *vase (or krater) shape, usually with a flat top, found on antique bronze candelabra. The 'double vase' baluster, consisting of two opposed *candelabra forms connected by a *scotia, *torus or *bead moulding, appeared frequently from the late 15th century. The 'single vase' baluster appeared later, possibly first used by G.B. da *Vignola in his design for the central fountain and courtyard of the Villa Farnese (1547),

baldacchino. St Carolus Borromeüskerk, Antwerp, Belgium, by Pieter Huyssens, 1615-25.

bamboo. 1) Design for a teapot in the Chinese style by W.*Chambers, c.1750. 2) Caneware bulb pot, Wedgwood, 1788.

baluster. 1) Design from J.*Gibbs's A Book of Architecture *1739 edition. 2) English glasses with baluster stems, c.1715-45. 3) Chest tomb, All Saints' Church, Newland, Gloucestershire, 1792. 4) Oak table by A.W.N.*Pugin, c.1830.*

Rome. Because of their columnar form, balusters lent themselves to treatments according to the conventions of the *Orders; Vignola produced designs in the Tuscan and Doric manner. Balusters used with *pilasters may be square in section. By the 16th century, the form had been applied to furniture legs, chair-backs, candlesticks, the stems of chalices and drinking glasses, and used as supports for pulpits, water stoops and lamps. In some cases the baluster was elaborated with additional *knops and curves or enriched with foliage, *fluting or other details. The development of the lathe in the 16th century made the form easier to produce and thus more widespread. The *split baluster was common in 16th and 17th century furniture in England and subsequently in America.

balustrade. Usually, a series of linked *balusters joined by a rail or coping, although the term sometimes describes supports in shapes other than balusters. It has been widely used at parapet level, on balconies and on bridges. Sometimes it is used blind, purely as ornament. Balustrades were much used in formal gardens, both *Baroque and 19th century, as a device to mark changes of level. They were an obvious form for interior stairs and communion rails, and furniture echoed architectural usage, e.g. balustrades along the top of bureaux. The form appeared in Baroque *trompe l'oeil* painted ceiling decoration. At Petworth House, Sussex (1688-96), the outer balustrading on the principal stair is echoed by a perspectival rendering on the wall side. Sir Christopher Wren did not want to use a balustrade in St Paul's Cathedral (built from 1675) but the Commission insisted; he commented: 'Ladies think nothing well without an edging.'

bamboo. Both the foliage and the stems of bamboo are used as motifs. The stems are also used as a decorative material in China and Japan, a practice copied in Europe from the mid to late 18th century. The bamboo plant appears in Chinese art (with plum *blossom and *pine) as one of the elements of winter. Bamboo and a sparrow together denote friendship, bamboo with a crane represents long life and happiness. Simple Chinese domestic furniture was made from bamboo, as illustrated by Sir W.*Chambers in *Designs for Chinese Buildings* (1757). With the fashion for *chinoiserie during the latter half of the 18th century, simulated bamboo

balustrade. 1) Pierced giltwood balustrade (or gallery) on a German rosewood cabinet, 17th century. 2) Loreto Pilgrimage Church, Prague, 17th century with façade rebuilt by K. Dientzenhofer, 1721. 3) Nave of Church of La Trinité, Falaise (Calvados), France, 15th century. 4) French wallpaper frieze designed to be hung below a landscape paper, c.1820-30. 5) Window of apartment, Champs Elysées, Paris, 1930s.

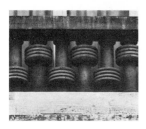

bamboo. 1) Examples of bamboo foliage from O.*Jones's Grammar of Ornament London, 1868 edition. 2) 18th century bed at Belton House, Lincolnshire.

chair legs, *cock beading and picture and mirror frames became popular. In the 1780s, Josiah Wedgwood even produced ceramics that appeared to be made from bamboo. The *Regency decoration of Brighton Pavilion, Sussex, included a bamboo cast-iron staircase, as well as bamboo-style furniture. During the late 19th century craze for *japonaiserie bamboo again became fashionable, particularly in ceramics and metalware, e.g. Wedgwood's Sparrow and Bamboo service (1873). E.W. Godwin produced a wallpaper with bamboo designs in 1872.

George Hunzinger, a New York furniture maker, used simulated bamboo from the 1860s to the 1880s, but in general the extremely low price of imported Japanese bamboo furniture, such as hat stands, magazine racks and small tables, rendered its imitation pointless.

banded column. A column whose shaft is broken up by the addition of (often *rusticated) bands or blocks of stonework. A common feature of *Mannerist and *Baroque architecture.

banded column. 1) *Flemish Mannerist doorway in Korte Nieuwstraat, Antwerp, Belgium. 2) Palazzo Madama, Rome, remodelled 17th century.

bandel column. 18th century term for *banded or *rusticated column used by P. Nicholson (1819).

banderole, bannerol or **banner.** Narrow streamer or flag with a cleft end. It played an important part in medieval English and French pageantry, and usually bore *coats of arms, *heraldic badges, mottoes or diagonal stripes representing livery colours. Its use continued as a field for a motto, sometimes below a coat of arms, and reappeared during the *Gothic Revival in its original form as a type of *frieze ornament or as an ornamental drip mould (*see* label).

banding. In woodwork, a decorative effect achieved with different coloured veneers cut at varying angles to the grain: straight-banding along the length of the grain, cross-banding across it and feather-banding or herring-bone banding diagonally. It is generally used to finish edges and rims of furniture.

bandwork. A development from the linear elements of *arabesque ornament, decorative bandwork is used to contain and frame elements of decoration within an overall scheme. It originated in late 17th century French decoration. The *C scrolls and foliate scrolls combined with flat bands are similar to the forms that appeared in embroidery designs and *parterre* garden designs, such as those published in Claude Mollet's *Théâtre des plans et jardinages* (1652). Bandwork subsequently became an important element in the work

banding and cross-banding. 1) Mid 18th century English mahogany tallboy. bandwork. 2) Stone staircase, Oberes Belvedere, Vienna, 1722. 3) Early 18th century English sidetable, carved and gilt.

J. Barbet. Plate from Livre des cheminées *(c.1630).*

of such leading Louis XIV *ornemanistes* as C.*Le Brun, and J.*Berain (who incorporated it into his *grotesque designs). The use of bandwork marked the beginning of a tendency in decoration for the framing element to assume greater importance, culminating in the *Rococo when the ornament within was often secondary to the borders. It appeared through the 18th century, often combined with scrolls and interlacings, on room panelling, furniture and then silver and ceramics. German *Laub und Bandelwerk* used bandwork for its basic structure and added other elements.

Barbet, Jean (1591-c.1650). French architect whose *Livre d'architecture* (Paris, 1632; second edition 1641) – a set of *Baroque altarpieces and chimneypieces dedicated to Cardinal Richelieu – was influential in England and Scandinavia as well as in France. I.*Jones adapted some of Barbet's designs, for example at Wilton House, Wiltshire (1630s). Barbet's designs were redrawn and reissued by Cornelis Danckerts in Amsterdam (1641) and also in Paris. Some of the plates were published in England in 1670 by R.*Pricke in *A book of archetecture containing seeling peeces, chimney peeces and several sorts usefull for carpenters, joyners, carvers, painters, etc.* and a selection in *The Architect's Storehouse* (1674).

bargeboard. Wooden cladding at eaves level for gable ends, sometimes called vergeboard in America, which is found in *Carpenter Gothic and *Gothic Revival architecture. *See also* Picturesque.

Barleycorn, John. Personification of malt liquor deriving from a figure in Robert Burns's poem 'Tam o'Shanter' (c.1789): 'Inspiring bold John Barleycorn,/ What dangers thou canst make us scorn!'. John Barleycorn is usually presented as a beery child or man lying among the sheaves and appears in the ornamentation of English drinking vessels, e.g. on the lid of a beer jug designed by H.J. Townsend for Summerley Art Manufactures in 1846.

Barlow, Francis (c.1626-1702). English engraver whose two sets of illustrations to Aesop's *fables, published in 1665 and 1668, were influential during the *Rococo fashion for fables as decorative subjects. W.*Ince adopted some of Barlow's illustrations for his designs in the Rococo style.

Baroque. A development of elements of *Mannerist design rather than a historically fixed period. From the 1620s, Italian architects produced this lively variant of *classicism, characterised by the use of elaborate effects, including sculptural forms, painted decoration and *architectural elements applied purely ornamentally. They regarded the architectural design of the building as inseparable from its ornamentation. Curving lines were used both in overall plan and in detail, and the effects of light and shade, texture and form, were maximised. In Italy, designer/architects Pietro da Cortona (1596-1669), Gian Lorenzo Bernini (1598-1680) and Francesco Borromini (1599-1667), all working in Rome, were the first to produce High Baroque work. They were followed in northern Italy both by G.*Guarini and by Filippo Juvarra (1676-1736), an architect who was also skilled in stage design, a field in which Baroque forms were to be widely adopted and which, itself, reinvigorated the late Baroque via the work of the Galli da Bibiena family – a veritable dynasty of early 18th century painters and designers, who were masters of the art of *trompe l'oeil* schemes of

Baroque. 1) Oratory of S. Filippo Neri (1637-50) by Francesco Borromini from Studie d'Architettura Civile *by Domenico de Rossi. 2) Monstrance by G.*Giardini from his* Disegni Diversi, *1714.*

Baroque. Doorway of school, Prinsstraat, Antwerp, Belgium, 17th century.

Baroque. Audience Chamber from Fürstlicher Baumeister oder Architectura Civilis, 1716 editon by P.*Decker (1677-1713).

ornament. There were also architects in the family, so their decorative schemes for interiors of theatres and churches were perfectly co-ordinated with the buildings' structures. In Italy, the growing wealth of the Jesuit Order (constituted 1543) was to prove an important source of patronage for these designers. Counter-Reformation churches were used to demonstrate the richness of the Catholic church triumphant and, ironically, the effects of splendour could be achieved relatively cheaply by the use of stucco – techniques of application rapidly became more sophisticated. Ecclesiastical silver was produced in the new Baroque forms to replace that lost in the religious wars (especially in Holland).

In architectural decoration, ornament based on human figures, *angels and *cupids spilled on to the previously sacrosanct areas of *archivolts, *pediments and *cornices. Architectural elements, especially the roofline, gables, entrance points and *broken pediments, were elaborated with vast scrolls and *volutes, *urns or flaming *torches, *spiral columns (emulating the *baldacchino motif introduced by Bernini in St Peter's, Rome) and various forms of *rustication.

The principal works of the Italian Baroque were known from a number of influential printed sources: among them were G. Guarini's *Architettura Civile*, A. *Pozzo's *Perspectiva* and *Studio di architettura civile* (3 vols, 1702, 1711 and 1721) published by G. Domenico de Rossi and edited by Alessandro Specchi; the first two volumes were published in a simplified German edition

in 1712 and concentrated largely on the works of Borromini. The publisher Sebastiano Giannini also produced detailed illustrated accounts of Borromini's S. Ivo (in 1720) and the Oratory of Filippo Neri (in 1725). These volumes were known throughout Europe and as far afield as the Spanish and Portuguese colonies in Central and South America.

Baroque furniture was often highly sculptural in character. The motifs derived from architecture, the basic shapes formed by great leafy scrolls, *swags, *putti, figures. The dominant techniques used were illusionistic inlay (using marbles, semi-precious stones and *scagliola*), gilded carving, elaborate mirrorwork, japanning and lacquerwork. Silver, ceramics and glass tended towards bulbous shapes, elaborate moulding and modelling.

The influence of the Italian Baroque was to leave few European countries untouched: in England the work of Thomas Archer (1668-1736), Nicholas Hawksmoor (1661-1736) and Sir John Vanbrugh (1664-1726) displayed Baroque tendencies, with deep-cut rustication, *Orders used full height, *broken pediments and a variety of idiosyncratic detail. The *Palladians found the style distasteful. C.*Campbell's introduction to *Vitruvius Britannicus* typified the reaction: ' . . . the *Italians* can no more now relish the Antique Simplicity, but are entirely employed in capricious Ornaments, which must at least end in the Gothick . . . How affected and licentious are the books of *Bernini*, and *Fontana*? How wildly extravagant are the Designs of Borromini, who had endeavour'd to debauch mankind with his odd and chimerical Beauties where the Parts are without Proportion, Solids without their true Bearing, Heaps of Materials without Strength, excessive Ornament without Grace, and the

Baroque Revival. Passmore Edwards Museum, Stratford, East London, by J.Gibson and S.B. Russell, 1895-98.

Baroque. Early 18th century carved and giltwood *console table after a design by W.*Kent.

whole without Symmetry?' In mainly Catholic southern Germany, Bavaria, Bohemia and Franconia, the style was largely promoted by families of architect/decorators, the Asam brothers, Cosmas Damian Asam (1686-1739) and Egid Quirin Asam (1692-1750) in Bavaria, and the Dientzenhofers. Balthasar Neumann (1687-1753), the most important German late Baroque architect, was much influenced by the Dientzenhofers' work. Germany and Austria, rebuilding after the destruction wrought by the Thirty Years' War (1618-48), and Spain and Portugal all adopted particularly exuberant versions of the Baroque. In France, the style of *Louis XIV was grandiose and well ornamented, but a more heavily classical version of the Baroque. One regional variation was the revival of northern European *Flamboyant Gothic architecture into a kind of Baroque, with particular reference to vaulting patterns, by practitioners such as J.B.S. Aichel (1677-1723) in Bohemia and Moravia. In the early years of the 18th century, the style encompassed the new wave of the bizarre and the exotic, the *Auricular and *chinoiserie.

The *Rococo style, which followed the Baroque, was lighter but shared many of the same approaches to overall ornament.

Baroque Revival. As the *Renaissance was followed by the *Baroque, so the *Renaissance Revival was followed throughout Europe and America by the Baroque Revival. The style differed from true Baroque in that materials were less lavish, though motifs survived and if anything the original forms were exaggerated with increased density of ornament. The style developed in France during the period of the Second Empire, 1852-70 (*see* French Second Empire), with buildings such as the Paris Opéra (1861-75), but the popularity of the style was at its peak during the 1880s and 1900s. In Britain, it remained dominant for large-scale commercial and civic structures until the First World War. The growth of interest in art history in the 1880s, especially in Germany, led to a clearer appreciation of the qualities of the style, and the scale and high degree of ornamentation that characterised the Baroque were deemed appropriate for buildings of importance. Examples include the Law Courts in Rome (1888), Frankfurt railway station (by Herman Eggert, 1879-88) and the work of English architects such as John Belcher (1841-1913) and Reginald Blomfield (1856-1942) who blended the Baroque of Vanbrugh and Hawksmoor with the more restrained tones of the *'Wrenaissance' (sometimes known as Free Classicism). In America, the Baroque Revival was treated with a more classical approach, based on a *Beaux-Arts education and a more thoroughgoing attitude to historicism than was current in Europe, to produce a style also known as Romantic Classicism, e.g. the New York Customs House by Cass Gilbert (1870). Although the terms Baroque Revival or Neo-Baroque are usually applied to architecture, furniture, ceramics and metalwork were also manufactured in the style in Europe and America c.1850-c.1880; many of the items of furniture shown at the Great Exhibition in 1851 were Neo-Baroque in style. Characteristic features are heavy architectural elements, elaborate figure sculpture and richly *scrolling foliage. In the decorative arts the style was sometimes called Louis Quatorze or Louis style.

During the 1930s some fashionable interior decoration contained a so-called Baroque element, manifested in elaborate inlay and the profuse application of quilted satin.

Bartoli, Pietro Santi (c.1635-1700). A prolific engraver (with his son Francesco, fl.1706-1730) of Roman antiquities from large relief carvings to small domestic pieces such as lamps. Collections of engravings by the Bartolis, such as *Admiranda Romanorum Antiquitatum, Vestigia Pitture Antiche delle Grotte di Roma* (1706) and *Le Antiche Lucerne Sepolcrali* (1729), provided an extensive fund of classical detail on which 18th century *Neoclassical designers could draw. Their work was included in books by the Comte *de Caylus, B.*de Montfaucon and R.Adam (*see* Adam style) among others.

basilisk or **cockatrice.** Mythical animal with the body of a snake, referred to by classical authors as King of the Serpents and believed to be exceptionally venomous. During the Middle Ages, the creature (which was thought to be an aspect of the devil) developed the crested head and claws of a cock and many legends about it grew up, notably that it could kill with a single glance. It appears in medieval ecclesiastical decoration.

basket capital. *Capital imitating woven straw, adopted in the *Byzantine and early *Romanesque styles in place of more naturalistic forms. It may reflect the legend of the origins of the Corinthian capital (*see* acanthus). *See also* canephora.

basket of fruit and flowers or **corbeil.** Flowers and plant forms were an important part of 17th century European ornament. Baskets of flowers (or fruit) combined well with the luxuriant *festoons of the period as an applied ornament, e.g. on wall panels, or as a free-standing form, e.g. carved in stone on gate piers. Newel posts carved in the form of fruit and flower baskets appear in Carolean houses such as Thorpe Hall, Northamptonshire, and Tyttenhanger, Hertfordshire – a feature typical of the work of virtuoso carvers of the period such as Grinling Gibbons (1648-1721) and his contemporary Edward Pearce. Schemes

basket of fruit and flowers. 1) Carved wood newel, Ham House, Surrey, 1637. 2) Silver bed, Chirk Castle, North Wales, 1693. 3) 18th century panelling at Polesden Lacey, Surrey, remodelled 1906-08. 4) Ironwork balcony, Paris, 1930s.

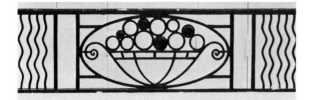

representing the *Seasons often include a basket of fruit and flowers for Spring or Summer. Botanical illustrators of the period, e.g. J.B. Monnoyer (1635-99), who provided important source material for carvers and craftsmen, often presented their subjects arranged in baskets.

Lighter, more floral baskets were a frequent motif in French *Louis XVI *pastoral decoration, combining well with *trophies and *arabesques. Hepplewhite style chair-backs, particularly those produced in America by furniture makers such as Samuel McIntire of Salem, were often decorated with fruit and flower baskets frequently including *wheat sprays. Chinese-inspired flower baskets were sometimes used on 18th century porcelain (in Chinese art, they are a symbol of plenty and fruitfulness and denote longevity and a fruitful old age). Free-standing ornamental baskets of flowers were also produced.

In the mid 19th century the motif appeared stencilled on the crest rails of American chairs mass-produced by Lambert Hitchcock (1795-1852). Luxuriantly filled baskets of flowers were a common motif in the Victorian period, particularly on textiles and wallpapers, reflecting the great popularity of *naturalistic decoration. A stylised realisation of the form was part of the vocabulary of *Art Deco ornament, particularly in furniture and metalwork where the influence of the late 18th century is evident.

basketweave patterns. Patterns imitating interwoven rushes, cane, willow, or straw applied mainly to ceramics and metalwork. They were popular in the early to mid 18th century fashion for *pastoral decoration. Relief basket patterns on the borders of porcelain plates were introduced at Meissen in a variety of forms: *ordinair-ozier, alt-ozier, neu-ozier.* These were copied soon after at the Tournai porcelain factory. Frederick the Great, in an excess of enthusiasm for *fêtes champêtres,* commissioned from the Berlin porcelain factory a service imitating the wicker platters used by peasants. From about 1730, improved technology in the rolling mills led to easier production of silver and metal wire, and silver baskets became a fashionable form. By the mid to late 18th century, ceramic baskets containing flowers, technically difficult to produce, were achieved. There are many examples of basket patterning in ceramics, metal and pressed glass during the Victorian period, although C.*Dresser, in line with late 19th century theories concerning authenticity of design to materials used, specifically mentioned basket pattern as an unsuitable decoration for ceramics.

Blind basket ware is moulded ceramic basket ware that is unpierced.

batik. Method indigenous to Java and Mandura of patterning fabric by using wax resist in the dyeing process. In the wake of general enthusiasm for Japanese and oriental art c.1860-c.1880, interest in the art of the colony grew in Holland, and Dutch artists adapted the batik effects of soft delineation and abstract patterning to other media. Theodore Colenbrander (1841-1930) recreated them on porcelain and textiles, Jan Thorn Prikker (1868-1932) produced carpets and Carel Adolph Lion Cachet (1864-1945) used them in bookbinding.

batswing. Suffolk Place, Haymarket, London, architect John Nash, 1820-30.

J.J. Baumgartner. From Neues Teil Buchel von Laub und Bandelwerk, *c.1725.*

batswing. 18th and 19th century term for a motif composed of radiating flutes. An elaborate version appears in French *Rococo ornament, and it is a typical feature of *Adam, Sheraton and Hepplewhite style furniture. Also known as fluted *patera.

battlement. Parapet with regular indentations, sometimes coped. It existed on Roman fortifications to protect often flimsy roofing hidden behind stone walls, also providing convenient cover from which defenders of the castle could see and attack assailants. It was reintroduced from the 11th century in European castle building. Battlements were later used purely decoratively although in some cases (e.g. the city of Cracow, Poland) medieval laws ordained high parapets (often ornamented with battlements) to protect roofs from fire. In England during the reign of Henry II (1154-89) it was necessary to obtain a license to crenellate or fortify as a result of legislation designed to curb the power of the nobles. Although in Britain the form remained relatively plain, the *merlons were sometimes elaborated, particularly in eastern Europe, in keeping with intricate gables. An Italian variant was the *swallowtail merlon.

Battlements appeared as *cresting on church furnishings of the *Gothic period. The device reappeared on secular furniture in the 18th century *Gothick style and in such unsuitable positions as the tops of chimneypots. The motif remained popular in the *Gothic Revival (sometimes with *floriated merlons), e.g. on furniture by William Burges (1827-81).

Baumgartner, Johann Jakob (fl early 18th century). Ornamental engraver based in Augsburg. Some of his output included designs for *Laub und Bandelwerk, such as *Neues Teil Buchel von Laub und Bandelwerck* (c.1725) and *Gantz Neu Inventiertes Laub und Bandwerck* (1727). He also published designs for metalwork, borders and *cartouches.

Baumgartner, Johann Wolfgang (1712-61). Painter and engraver who worked in Augsburg and produced a series of *rocaille ornamental borders enclosing mythological and allegorical subjects: the *Continents, the *Ages of Man, the *Elements, the *Liberal Arts.

bay. *See* laurel.

bead and leaf. *See* mitre leaf.

bead and reel. *Moulding in which bead shapes alternate with small, elliptical forms resembling reels. The combination of the two shapes, which often decorate

*battlement. 1) Palazzo Pubblico, Siena, Italy, 1297-1342. 2) Church of St Ethelbert, Hessett, Suffolk, late 15th century. 3) Battlemented *cresting from W.& G. *Audsley's* Polychromatic Decoration as Applied to Buildings in the Mediaeval Styles, *1882.*

basketweave pattern. 1) 'Ozier' border on Meissen porcelain saucer dish, c.1735. 2) English silver gilt hot water jug by Paul Storr, 1806.

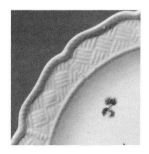

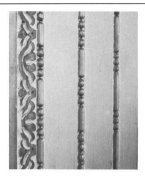

bead and reel. 1) Engraved ornament on Scottish silver flask, c.1715.
bead and spindle. 2) *Moulding on doorcase at Chiswick House, London,
built 1725-29.

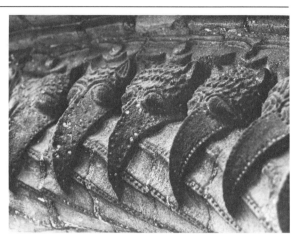

beakhead. Caldbeck Church, Cumbria, English Romanesque.

the *astragal, varies widely in *classical usage. In 18th century *Neo-classical decoration, it provides a contrast with the more exuberant mouldings such as *egg and dart. It is associated with the Ionic *Order and in 18th century glossaries was known as beads and berries, pearls and olives or paternoster.

bead and spindle. Circular bead and long spindle forms used in various combinations in woodwork and *mouldings. It was popular in 17th century turned decoration, and was revived in the 19th century. Mainly used on furniture, particularly chair-backs.

beading or **pearling.** Enrichment consisting of a line of tiny beads. Originally an element in *Romanesque decoration, it became popular in 18th century silver and furniture. From the 1780s beading on silver could be machine-made and it became even more common. It was subsequently applied to ceramics, particularly creamware and queensware.

bead moulding. A small half-round *moulding, equivalent in scale to the *astragal but not projecting. Series of bead moulds used together produces *reeding.

beakhead. Stylised head of bird, beast or monster with its beak or tongue wrapped over the *roll moulding from which it projects. Sometimes rows of beakheads are used. This Scandinavian motif appeared frequently in 12th century English *Romanesque architecture, and subsequently in France. Rarely found on grander buildings, it appears to have been regarded

as suitable for decorating arches and doorways in small, relatively unimportant churches. *See also* Celtic.

Beauvallet, Pierre-Nicholas (1750-1818). French sculptor and painter who published a *pattern book in the *Empire style: *Fragmens d'architecture, sculpture et peinture dans le style antique* (Paris, 1804, 1820). Beauvallet acknowledges help and some plates from C.P.J. *Normand, another propagator of the style, and describes his work as *'une sorte d'encyclopédie artielle et mobiliaire'* for painters, sculptors, architects, *ornemanistes*, marble-workers, coach painters, jewellers and metal casters, tapestry makers, carvers, snuff-box makers, carpenters, manufacturers of chintz, mousseline and printed calico, wallpaper, porcelain, faïence, japanned ware, enamel and glass. The book, which was relatively cheap and therefore accessible, contained an assortment of ornamental motifs, designs for *friezes, furniture and metalwork, etc., and essays on the origins and principles of ornamentation.

Beaux-Arts style. A vein of late 19th century *classicism based on the teaching at the influential Ecole des Beaux Arts in Paris, which had replaced the former royal schools of painting and sculpture (founded in 1646 by Cardinal Mazarin) and of architecture (founded by Jean-Baptiste Colbert in 1671). The school, which was transformed 1793-1815, adopted a new, rigidly classicist attitude to architecture which was to remain unchanged from 1819 to 1968. In 1864 the school was placed under state control by Napoleon III. Outstanding students, the winners of the Prix de Rome, were sent for a five-year period to Italy, where their studies included measuring, drawing and reconstruction (on paper) of noted monuments from Roman antiquity. The Pantheon was the most popular of all subjects but many students also studied Pompeii and Herculaneum. Because a large number of American students followed the Beaux-Arts course from 1846, the school had a fundamental influence upon the course of American architecture during the second half of the 19th century via the work of such architects as Richard Morris Hunt (1827-95) and was

beading. 1) Church of St Mary, Iffley, Oxford, c.1170-80. 2) English silver hot water jug, c.1810.

much used on substantial public buildings. The Society of Beaux-Arts Architects was founded in New York in 1895 and became the Beaux-Arts Institute of Design in 1911. There was no equivalent system of training in England, where the approach was less academic and therefore closer to an apprenticeship.

bee. Symbol of industry and order, and less commonly, of rebirth and immortality in ancient Greek, Chinese and sometimes Christian art. It was adopted as a device by the powerful and wealthy Barberini family of Rome, one of whom, Pope Urban VIII (1623-44), had the buildings he commissioned ornamented with bees. Napoleon Bonaparte took the bee as his personal emblem – metal bees had been found at the excavation of the tomb of Chilperic I, a 6th century Frankish king, and Napoleon valued this allusion to a link with the early rulers of France. The Imperial household had bees woven into textiles for hangings, upholstery

bee. 1) Design for sucrier *with Napoleonic bees by H.*Salembier, 1807-09. 2) Beehive on Cooperative Society headquarters, Halstead, Essex, late 19th century. 3) *Keystone over arch leading to Honey Lane, Cheapside, City of London, late 20th century.*

Beaux-Arts style. Grand Palais, Paris, 1897-1900. The details are probably by A.F.T. Thomas and L.A. Louvet.

and robes, and applied in ormolu to furniture, most of which were designed to order by C.*Percier and P.F.L. Fontaine. Napoleon III retained the emblem, and bees ornament the chimneypieces of the Château de Pierrefonds (Oise), which he had restored as a royal palace (though he never lived there). Bees (as a symbol of industry) appear in the mosaic floor of Alfred Waterhouse's Manchester Town Hall (1868-77), a monument to the Industrial Revolution at its height. The worker bee became an emblem of 19th century self-help groups and was taken up, notably, by the cooperative movement.

In the mid 18th century, when insects were a popular decoration on ceramics, goat and bee jugs were produced at Chelsea c.1745 and the exotic *Bienenmuster* design was devised at Meissen. Bees are an obvious ornament for honey pots (sometimes made in the form of hives). Increasingly elaborate tableware produced from the early 19th century resulted in a range of silver, Sheffield plate and ceramic pieces specifically for serving honey and honeycomb; these were usually in the form of dome-shaped straw hives (skeps) with bee *finials. Art Deco-influenced ceramic honeycomb containers with bee finials were produced in England by Poole Pottery in the 1920s.

Occasionally bees (sometimes around a bee hive) allude to eloquence, e.g. on a memorial to a speaker, echoing the expression 'honeyed words'.

Hans Beham. Woodcut dated 1546.

Beham, Hans Sebald (1500-50). Designer and engraver who was a member of a group of craftsmen called Die Kleinmeister (so-called because they made very small-scale pieces) and worked in Nuremberg and Frankfurt. Besides woodcuts of historical and biblical illustrations, he produced ornamental engravings, which included some of the first German examples of *Renaissance subjects, e.g. the Labours of Hercules (*see* Herculean decoration), the *Liberal Arts, and incorporated typical *Renaissance motifs, e.g. *grotesques, *hippocamps, *sirens, *laurel wreaths, triumphal chariots, and the *Orders. Late 16th century Rhenish stoneware jugs and tankards were impressed with versions of Beham's mythological and biblical scenes.

His brother, Barthel (1502-40), also a member of Die Kleinmeister, visited Rome and Bologna in the early 1520s but produced less engraved ornament than Hans.

bell. *Chinoiserie* ornament deriving from illustrations of pagodas with bells hanging from their many eaves, as shown in one of the earliest published accounts of China, J.*Nieuhof's *Atlas Chinensis* (1673). Bells occur both on *pagoda form furniture and as part of the general vocabulary of *chinoiserie* decoration.

Sir Edwin Lutyens (1869-1944) used a bell form to ornament the angles of *capitals in his work in New Delhi, a feature reminiscent of the drop ornaments of Moghul architecture. *See also* guttae.

bell and baluster. Turned bell-shape surmounting a slender baluster, commonly used on late 17th and 18th century English and Dutch furniture legs.

bellflower. American term for *husk.

bells. 18th and 19th century term for *guttae.

Benjamin, Asher (c.1773-1845). Author of *The Country Builder's Assistant* (Greenfield, Massachusetts, 1797), the first architectural *pattern book to be produced in America by a native American. It was regularly reprinted and updated over the following decades. It included standard *Georgian details, by then considered old-fashioned in England, such as the *Palladian motif and traceried *fanlights. Benjamin was also co-author with Daniel Raynerd of the *American Builder's Companion* (Boston, 1806). He produced another five volumes including *Rudiments of Architecture*

(1814) and *Practical House Carpenter* (1830), the latter with at least 17 subsequent editions in which the *Orders (following W.*Chambers's account in his treatise), *moulding details and information for carpenters were further explored. Benjamin's publications helped to spread the *Federal style and then the *Greek Revival style across America at a time of great building activity along the eastern seaboard. *See also* commerce.

bent ribbon. Flat, ribbon-like looping patterns in late 18th and early 19th century cast iron.

Berain, Jean (1639-1711). French *ornemaniste* of immense influence, who was responsible for the creation of the light, linear designs of the late *Louis XIV style. Berain's family were gunsmiths and his earliest published designs (1659) were for small arms, *Diverses Pièces très utiles pour les Arquebuzières*, followed in 1662 and 1663 by designs for locks, *Diverses pièces de serruriers*. In 1674 the King made him Dessinateur de la Chambre et du Cabinet du Roi, and in this capacity he published both existing schemes of interior decoration by other architects and artists and his own costume and set designs for masques and festivities. From the mid 1680s a succession of Berain's designs were published covering architectural details, panels, furniture, clocks, *vases, *trophies, etc., and were subsequently republished in foreign editions across Europe. The year Berain died a large collection was gathered together and published under the title *Oeuvre de Jean Berain*,

Asher Benjamin. Design for meeting house from the 1827 edition of the American Builder's Companion.

Jean Berain. 1) French style Berain faïence dish made at Moustiers, c.1710. 2) *Pilaster capitals and *cornice from his Ornemans, 1711 edition.

recueillies par les soins du sieur Thuret (1711). The most innovative elements of his style, which were to influence ornament until the 1730s, were his light *grotesques. These appeared not only on wall panels, but also in tapestries, goldsmiths' work, faïence (e.g. Moustiers) and *boulle inlay. The framework of the grotesques (at that time referred to as *arabesques* in France) is usually fantastic architecture and *bandwork interlaced with foliage, inhabited by classically derived satyrs, *sphinxes, *putti, gods and goddesses and terminal *caryatids, combined with newer elements such as *singeries, *chinoiserie and *Moorish figures. Other motifs are the *baldacchino, the tasselled *lambrequin and the characteristic looping *festoons, some forming swings for figures and birds. Some sets of panels were based on themes: mythology, the *Seasons, etc. Berain's influence quickly spread over Europe. Claude Berain (d c.1730), his brother, was also an *ornemaniste* who concentrated on small pieces of metalwork and

produced designs for *cyphers. Jean Berain's son, also Jean (1674-1726), worked in the style of his father, causing much confusion in the identification of their work.

bestiaries. A crucial source of *animal ornament (both ecclesiastical and secular) in the Middle Ages. The *Liber Physiologus* was the best known medieval bestiary and many subsequent manuscripts derived from it and from other early sources such as the *Moralia* of St Gregory, the *Etymologiae* of Isidore of Seville, Rabanus's *De Universo* and Aesop's *fables, as well as the natural history writings of Pliny and Aristotle. In the 6th century, the *Physiologus* was stated to be heretical but its popularity seems not to have abated. The 12th century English vernacular version on which *Gothic masons and woodcarvers drew was a mixture of fact and fantasy (e.g. the *unicorn was given the attributes of a rhinoceros), further confused by the fact that many of the animals, such as *elephants and *crocodiles, had rarely been seen in Europe. Bestiaries, often illustrated with woodcuts, classified animals as birds, beasts or fishes, and each chapter began with biblical references to the creature, its habits and its spiritual significance. Alongside fairly accurate information were garbled descriptions of real creatures (the *pelican was more like a dove, the ostrich was said to have feet like a camel which were often depicted as cloven hoofs) and accounts of mythical monsters – there were 25 species of *dragon. Other versions of the bestiary stories spread across the world and are found in the languages of Ethiopia and Iceland as well as in innumerable Latin and French editions. The bestiaries were most influential in establishing the symbolism used in ecclesiastical decoration in psalters, sculpted ornament, misericords, etc.

Beunat, Joseph. 19th century French manufacturer of composition ornament whose trade catalogue of decorative details from *rosettes to complete interior schemes was an important influence in spreading the *Empire style both inside and outside France. The *Recueil des dessins d'ornements d'architecture de la manufacture de Joseph Beunat* (Strasbourg and Paris, 1813; reissued in a lithographic edition, 1823) contained 700 illustrations by various designers, many of whom subsequently became known in their own right. It is not known what medium the ornaments were to be carried out in, perhaps a kind of *papier-mâché* or in stone-mastic. The catalogue continued in print until at least 1848.

bicorporate. Mythical animal with two bodies and one head that originally appeared on cylinder seals describing the myths of Sumeria, Babylon and Assyria, c.3000 BC. Classical and oriental art both used bicorporate forms, and they appeared, usually resembling a *lion, *sphinx, *stag, *bull, *bird, lizard or goat, in Europe during the 11th century, and increasingly during the 12th century. The motif was used on Italian woven textiles from the 12th century in designs introduced by weavers from the East.

Biedermeier. Style of furniture and interior decoration associated with the German middle classes, particularly in Vienna and Munich, which spread through

Biedermeier. Early 19th century German commode with swan handles.

Austria and Germany from c.1818 to c.1860, and was sometimes adopted in the rest of Europe as a reaction against ornate 18th century styles. The emphasis was on the economical production of comfortable, relatively informal pieces. The two influences on it were the French *Empire and English *Regency styles. However, the cabinetmakers' skill at producing expanses of fine veneered wood tended to dominate the designs, with the decorative motifs (usually of flat, stamped brass) appearing almost incidental. The dependence of cabinetmakers on such Empire *pattern books as those by C.*Percier and P.F.L. Fontaine is evident from the *palmettes, *caryatids with Egyptian heads, *swan-neck sofas and chair arms, *monopodia legs, *swags of drapery and *lyres. T. *Sheraton's work was also influential. The overall shapes of the furniture derive from the earlier and stricter *Neo-classicism: architectural forms, scimitar legs, curves and *volutes, but in Biedermeier furniture comfort and ease takes precedence over adherence to classical precepts. For reasons of cost, the style had only a small amount of marquetry decorations mainly with simple patterns such as stylised *shells and flowers and *geometric shapes – circles, stars, ovals. Some decoration, such as *egg and dart moulding, *festoons and *cameos, was painted, often in black. Ceramics and glass picked up elements of the style: shapes were plainer, often slightly concave, and lion's *paw feet and swan-neck handles appeared on, for example, Berlin porcelain. By the end of the period the style was lusher, the curves and ornament moving towards the richness typical of the mid 19th century.

bifront. Figure with two heads or with two faces on the same head looking in opposite directions. Certain classical gods were depicted in this form, for example Janus, the Roman god identified with the month of January and all beginnings, was a guardian deity and therefore looked both forwards and backwards on doors and gateways. A bifront might also signify past and future, e.g. in personifications of Prudence. Like the *bicorporate, it was an image originally taken from Middle Eastern mythology. Bifront figures were sometimes adopted in *heraldic decoration and also in 13th to 15th century woven Italian textiles with a heraldic flavour.

billet moulding. Ornament of small rounded or squared blocks placed regularly along a *moulding in *Romanesque architecture. When it is used in quantity, it is sometimes known as a billet frieze.

billet moulding. The Norman Gate, Bury St Edmunds Abbey, Suffolk, built by Abbot Anselm, 1120-48.

birds. Only the most grandiose and splendid of birds, the *eagle, had a major place in Roman ornamentation, but in medieval *naturalistic ornament, birds frequently appear. Falconry and hawking were popular activities and the French are known to have kept birds in cages from at least 1200. Birds decorated stonecarving, embroidery, enamels, woodcarving, etc. The *bestiaries contributed mythical birds such as the *phoenix, or exotic birds such as the *pelican, many of which were endowed with *Christian symbolism. The motif of birds in a tree became a medieval emblem for the Holy Ghost and the Virgin Mary.

In the late 17th and 18th centuries, game birds (both dead and alive) were among the motifs used in the ornamental theme of *hunting, sometimes combined with guns, powder-flasks, knives, etc., in *trophies. This theme was particularly popular in England: on the plasterwork at Melton Constable, Norfolk (1687), there are pheasant, duck and snipe, and at Denham Place, Buckinghamshire (c.1693), there are partridge, pheasant, woodcock and pigeon. Illustrated natural history books were an important source of bird designs, some produced specifically for the purpose, e.g. the 1666 catalogue of the London printseller Robert Walton which was entitled 'Divers Maps, Pictures, Coppy-books, Books of Beasts, Birds, Flowers, Fish, Fruites, Flies, neatly cut in Copper, and worth buying; and also extraordinary useful for Goldsmiths, Jewellers, Chasers, Gravers, Painters, Carvers, Embroiderers, Drawers, Needlewomen, and all Handicrafts.' Gottlieb Friedrich Riedel (1724-84), who worked at the German porcelain factories of Meissen, Höchst, Frankenthal and Ludwigsburg, published a guide to birds especially for porcelain modellers: *Sammlung von Feder-Vieh besonders Haus-Geflügel nützlich Fabriquen* (Augsburg, 1776). During the 18th century, more exotic birds were chosen for ornament. The influence of *chinoiserie introduced adaptations of phoenix-like mythical birds, such as the fêng-huang or *ho ho, in ceramic decoration a kind of quail or partridge was adapted from *kakiemon patterns. Parrots, cockatoos, macaws and other non-European birds were copied from *chintz designs. R.*Hancock's engravings showing parrots and macaws pecking at assorted fruit were illustrated in the *Ladies Amusement* (see drawing books) and used at Worcester and Caughley porcelain factories. The Meissen *Fantasievögel* pattern, based on birds collected at the Moritzburg aviaries but with a dash of *chinoiserie* influence, demonstrates the new use of a wide range of coloured enamels on 18th century porcelain. The designs were copied on Sèvres and Worcester porcelain and the 'bird of paradise' became a favourite motif of the porcelain decorator and gilder James Giles who worked in London in the 1770s. Coloured plates in natural history books were used by porcelain painters: the Comte de *Buffon's *Histoire Naturelle* was used by Sèvres, Meissen and Tournai in the 1770s and 1780s and George Edwards's *Natural History of Uncommon Birds* (1743-47) was used by Chelsea in the 1750s for the production of bird models. Textiles, particularly the woven silks produced in Lyons by Philippe de La Salle (1723-1805), exploited the same rich and colourful quality. Consistent with the use of lush, overblown flowers of the sort grown in hothouses, brightly coloured tropical birds (observed in aviaries) were popular in the mid 19th century. The vogue for *japonaiserie made the long-legged *crane and the sparrow popular motifs. William Morris, C.A. Voysey and the *Arts and Crafts designers used common garden birds in their designs.

biriga. *See* quadriga.

birds. 1) Carved wood panel in Ely Cathedral, Cambridgeshire, 12th century. 2) Exotic birds on French porcelain plate, Sèvres, 1792. 3) Parakeet on French Louis XV ormolu firedog.

Bishop Sumner pattern. An adaptation of a Chinese design consisting of a *kylin and a *ho ho bird in an oriental landscape, first produced at Worcester in the third quarter of the 18th century and imitated by European factories.

bison. *See* American.

bizarre patterns. Style of silk design popular in the first two decades of the 18th century. These jagged and abstract patterns combined with exotic plumes and foliage often have a very long repeat. It is likely that they were produced to compete with the exotic appearance of the highly popular *chintz designs. The forms seem to be adaptations of oriental textile and ceramic designs – Indian, Chinese, Turkish and Persian originals were imported in quantity at this point. At one time it was thought that bizarre-patterned silks were woven in India, but they were in fact produced principally at Spitalfields in London and at Lyons in France. Fashion in silk design changed rapidly and the bizarre phase was short-lived.

blackamoor. Negro heads were a fairly frequent decoration for *classical and *Renaissance *cameos – the subject was well suited to the composition of the black

blackamoor. 1) 18th century French candelabrum base. 2) Anti-slavery symbol on early 19th century English cast-iron plaque. 3) *Keystone from Liverpool Town Hall, England, by John Wood the Elder, 1749-54. 4) American cast-iron clock made in Connecticut, c.1875.

blind arcading. 1) Tower, Church of All Saints, Earls Barton,
Northamptonshire, late 10th century. 2) Lincoln Cathedral, 13th century.

and white gem-stone, sardonyx. In the mid 16th century, J.A.*Ducerceau produced engraved designs for *Termes Nègres*, one of many variations on the columnar figures produced at the time, and in 1682 he published designs for a black figure as a candlestand. A black woman wearing a coral necklace was traditionally used to personify Africa in decorative schemes depicting the *Continents. Although the blackamoor first appeared in Europe in ornament as an exotic curiosity, an increasingly flourishing slave trade led to the arrival of black figures in ornament. By the end of the 17th century the Venetian carver and furniture maker Andrea Brustolon (1662-1732) had produced *guéridons* (named after a black vaudeville actor popular in Paris in the mid 17th century) in the form of ebony negroes with chains around their necks. Throughout the 18th century they appeared crouching to form footstools, or as bent figures supporting brackets. Black figures often appeared in servants' livery, perhaps with a jewelled turban, rather than in rudimentary native costume, reflecting the fashion for exquisitely dressed black pages. With the growth

of the anti-slavery movement, this form of decoration declined, although it was revived in the late 19th century and again in the 1930s for *Baroque Revival interiors. In 19th century America the emancipated but still picturesque figure of the black minstrel appeared cast in metal and brightly painted on clock-cases, money boxes, etc.

Blaublümchenmuster. *See immortelle.*

blind arcading. Linked or interlaced arches used 'blind' on a flat surface as decoration. Patterns of arches, often interlaced, were widely used in *Romanesque architecture to break up expanses of blank wall and to articulate space between principal features.

blind basket ware. *See* basketweave pattern.

Blind Earl pattern or **Earl of Coventry pattern.** In ceramics, modelled decoration of very large rose leaves and buds interspersed with insects and small flower sprays, typical of the mid 18th century enthusiasm for botanic subjects. It derived from a Meissen design and was used as an all-over decoration for plates at Worcester, Bow and Chelsea. It was named, over twenty years after it was first produced, after a blind Earl of Coventry who was said to enjoy the relief patterning.

blind tracery. Gothic *tracery applied to a blank wall but using the motifs and forms associated with window tracery. While *blind arcading tends to be used on exteriors, blind tracery was popular as an internal wall decoration in situations such as cloisters where a sophisticated architectural design involved a play between solid and void. Increasingly complex schemes of blind tracery added to the elaboration of vaulting in late Gothic *Perpendicular or *Flamboyant architecture. This form of decoration was much used in ecclesiastical Gothic woodcarving, e.g. pew ends.

blind trumpet. *See* trumpet pattern.

blind window. *Gothic blind windows composed of *blind tracery were used purely decoratively, to break up large expanses of wall. In 17th century domestic buildings, blind windows sometimes balanced real windows to produce a symmetrical fenestration pattern.

blind tracery. 1) Choir of Rouen Cathedral (Seine-Maritime), France,
13th century.
blind window. 2) Ely Cathedral, Cambridgeshire, 12th century.

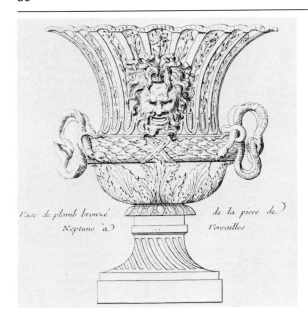

*J.-F. Blondel. Engraved design for cast *vase for the grounds at Versailles from his* Cours d'architecture, *1771-77.*

Blondel, Jacques-François (1705-74). An important figure in mid 18th century French architectural theory as a teacher and then professor at the Académie Royale de l'Achitecture. One of his main beliefs was that if architectural proportioning was correct there was no need for ornament. However, the second volume of *De la Distribution des maisons de plaisance et de la décoration des édifices en général* (2 vols, 1737-38) was devoted to ornamental detail such as *sphinxes, *trophies, *vases, classical gods and various allegorical themes in a restrained *Rococo style; he included formal garden designs with items such as a '*parterre de broderie à compartiment'*. Blondel gave precise instructions for the application of ornament: chimney decoration, for example, should become increasingly rich as the principal rooms of the house are approached. In France, plain *classical exteriors often disguised riotous and flamboyant interiors. Although he did refer to 'a certain licence which novelty in these times has authorised', Blondel believed that the exterior of the building should determine the decoration of the interior, that allegories used on exteriors should announce the purposes of buildings. He advised that if economy was required, the *Orders should not be used; where they were used, they should be rendered in marble or stone, never in woodwork. He stressed the importance of lighting, to be achieved by strategic positioning of candles, the placing of mirrors (to make a pleasant repetition) and the use of gilding. He felt that cheaper ornament should be well painted or gilded and that furniture should be designed to fit the overall scheme of the room. Above all ornament should not be too 'busy' for 'relaxation [in the rooms] is indispensable.' Other publications of J.-F. Blondel include his *Livre nouveau ou règles des cinq ordres d'architecture* (1767) based on the work of G.B. da*Vignola, and the *Cours d'architecture* (12 vols, 1771-77), a vast project based on his teachings which was completed by his assistant Pierre

Putte. Throughout his writings he maintained his early view that 'simplicity of form, economy of ornament' were essential. It was an unusual view, important amidst the excesses of the Rococo, and anticipated French *Neo-classicism.

blossom. Prunus blossom, particularly, is a common motif on Chinese ceramics; it is considered a flower of Winter as it flowers very early in Spring, and symbolises strength and endurance. The motif was taken up by 18th century European porcelain factories, e.g. St Cloud, Chantilly, Meissen, Mennecy, Chelsea, Bow, either painted or applied in relief in imitation of Chinese *blanc de chine* pieces made at Tê-hua.

A similar type of blossom spray is found in *japonaiserie* decoration. William Morris (*see* Arts and Crafts) and the designers of his circle made frequent use of apple blossom on textiles, wallpaper and stained glass.

blue dash border. Decoration of slanting blue dashes giving an impression of a *cable moulded or *gadrooned edge (probably in imitation of contemporary silver) on the rims of Dutch and English 17th century lead and tin-glazed earthenware plates and dishes. Blue dash chargers (large ornamental English delftware dishes) were made from c.1640 until the early 18th century, mainly in London (at Lambeth) and in Bristol.

Blum or **Bloem,** Hans (fl 1550). German author of an influential treatise on the *Orders, *Quinque Columnarum exacta descriptio atque delineatione* (Zurich, 1550; four editions by 1668), which was known in England by 1570 (English edition, 1608). Blum based his work on that of S.*Serlio and his designs were included in some later editions of Serlio's *Architettura*.

boar. This much hunted animal has appeared in the art of most European cultures. It was sacred to the Celts, used by the Romans as a symbol of *Mars (denoting destruction and strife) and in *Christian decoration signifies evil and brutality or, occasionally,

blossom. 1) French porcelain coffee-pot with applied chinoiserie *blossom, St Cloud, c.1740.*
blue dash. 2) Dutch tinglaze dish, early 17th century.

Cornelis Bos. Design for a panel of ornament in the Netherlands Grotesque style, c.1550.

Boler, James (d 1635). English compiler of a highly popular volume, *The Needle's Excellency*, first published in 1632 and into its twelfth edition by 1640. Patterns were prefaced by a poem in praise of needlework by a John Taylor. Some of the designs were taken from J.*Sibmacher, others were lace patterns from *Nouveaux Pourtraicts de point coupé* (1598) by Jacques Foillet (1554-1619). They included a variety of flowers and designs influenced by *emblem books and heraldry.

bonnet top. *See* scrolled pediment.

Bos, Cornelis (c.1510-c.1560). Netherlandish engraver and silver designer, born in 's Hertogenbosch (also known as Bois le Duc). Like C.*Floris, Bos was one of the creators of the *Netherlands Grotesque style of ornament which emerged during the 1540s. He travelled to Antwerp in 1540 and in 1548 visited Rome, where he engraved *grotesques by Raphael and Giovanni in the Vatican *logge* before returning to the Netherlands. He then published a series of Northern Grotesque designs which consist of grotesque figures framed with elaborate *strapwork and frequently incorporating *swags of vegetables. Bos also designed trophies, *caryatids, *herms, and *friezes of armour. *Moresken* (Antwerp, 1544; Paris, 1546), his book of *arabesque designs, was mainly derived from the work of F.*Pellegrino.

boss (French, *bosse*, knob). A carved and often also painted ornamental form, usually roughly circular, which covers the join or intersection between the various ribs of *vaulting. Bosses are often carved with human or animal heads, *heraldic motifs, flowers,

the cruelty of princes and rulers. In decorative schemes depicting the *Seasons, the boar sometimes represents Winter. Also a frequent *heraldic beast and a common device in *emblem books. The boar occasionally appears in *Herculean decoration – a reference to one of the Labours of Hercules.

bobbin turning. Decorative wood turning with sections cut to look like bobbins, more elongated than the elements of *spool turning. Most common on pre-17th century chair-backs and arms and cottage furniture.

bocage (French, copse). In ceramics, closely packed leaves and flowers used to provide background and support to figure groups. *Bocage* was much used from the mid 18th century, first at German factories such as Frankenthal and Nymphenburg and later in England at Chelsea and Derby.

bolection moulding. Convex *moulding consisting of *cavetto and *torus mouldings with *fillets devised to disguise and elaborate the join between two surfaces on unequal levels. Used both as interior panelling and as external decoration from the late 17th century, it rarely appeared after 1710. Bolection moulding also appears in furniture where it performs a similar function, covering the joint between panel and frame.

bolection moulding. 1) Façade at Stamford, Lincolnshire, late 17th or early 18th century.
boulle work. 2) Cupboard in the manner of A.C. Boulle, c.1870.

foliage, and even scenes from *bestiary stories and *fables. They appear in *Gothic wooden or stone ceilings, and late 16th century and early 17th century plasterwork. *Gothic Revival examples are often very elaborate. Also used on woodwork to disguise the intersection of mouldings.

Also a decorative knob or stud on metal or wooden object, e.g. at the centre of a shield.

boteh. The leaf motif of the *paisley pattern, most extensively used on oriental carpets.

Boucher, François (1703-70). French Rococo painter who also designed directly for the Beauvais and Gobelins tapestry works (which he supervised from 1734 and 1755 respectively) and the Vincennes and Sèvres porcelain factories. In 1731 he published *Diverses Figures Chinoises* (after Watteau), and further *Rococo ornament such as *Nouveaux Morceaux pour des paravents* (1737), *Recueil de fontaines* (1736), *Livre de cartouches* and *Livre de vases*. His pastoral paintings, *fêtes galantes*, his groups of *putti, and scenes showing *children pursuing activities such as dancing, gardening and painting were influential in providing a basis for the design of printed textiles, marquetry, and porcelain groups. Engravers such as C.-N.*Cochin the Younger and P.A. Aveline produced prints after Boucher's paintings and drawings. In 1752 Vincennes produced thirty-eight 'Enfants d'après Boucher' as well as repeatedly producing the 'Leçon de flute' from 1753. Mennecy and Chelsea also produced groups modelled after Boucher engravings. These subjects reappeared on painted porcelain both in the 18th century, on Frankenthal and Lowestoft pieces, and during the mid 19th century *Rococo Revival, e.g. at Coalport. One of the most successful contributors to 18th century *drawing books, R.*Hancock, produced designs clearly based on the work of Boucher and others in *The Ladies' Amusement, or the Whole Art of Japanning Made Easy* (1762). During the 19th century G. Aubert reprinted groups of Boucher *putti for a collection called *Le Compilateur Artistique* (Paris, n.d.).

Boucher, Juste-François (1736-81). Son of F.*Boucher, he produced some 65 suites of designs in *Neo-classical style which were published c.1775. These designs are mainly for furniture of almost every type, but there are some for architectural and interior details.

boulle or **buhl work.** Marquetry decoration using brass and tortoiseshell was introduced to France by Dutch craftsmen in the first half of the 17th century. The great master of this technique was André-Charles Boulle (1642-1732), furniture maker to Louis XIV. His innovation was the use of *première partie* (brass on shell) and *contre partie* (shell on brass) in which one layer of brass and one of tortoiseshell are cut in the same pattern, separated, then reassembled to combine the two materials. In the early 18th century he collaborated with J.*Berain to publish marquetry designs in *Nouveaux Desseins des meubles et ouvrages*. Boulle also collected Renaissance drawings, from which he drew ideas for classical subjects to ornament the ormolu mounts for his furniture.

Furniture with marquetry in this style was made throughout the 18th and into the 19th century by Boulle's sons, apprentices and imitators reproducing similar designs with mounts that invariably repeated the same stock themes. The Prince Regent bought new *boulle* furniture in 1810, but its popularity reached its height during the mid 19th century revivals of French styles when much existing furniture was heavily restored and many reproductions made. *Boulle* (or *buhl* as it became known from the 1820s) was originally produced by continental cabinetmakers, but it later became a popular technique in England. In *The Practical Cabinet Maker, Upholsterer and Complete Decorator* (1826), P. and M.A.*Nicholson describe it as 'lately revived in England, where it has risen to superior elegance.' Henry Lawford included a series of designs in his *The Cabinet of Practical, Useful and Decorative Furniture Designs* (1856) and expanded the theme in *The Cabinet of Marquetry, Buhl and Inlaid Woods* (c.1870).

bowtell or **edge roll.** A *roll moulding, three quarters of a circle in section. The name supposedly derives from *bouteille* (French for bottle).

boxers. English embroidery motif of unknown origin which appeared in 17th century samplers. It consists of small naked men (usually shown in rows) with upraised arms, often holding a trophy or leafy plant. Boxers sometimes have wings on their shoulders, which may well indicate that they were originally a variation on *cupids. Towards the end of the 17th century, they were dressed in clothes and wigs. By the mid 18th century the motif had dropped from use.

boys and crown. Motif of *crown supported by two flying *cherubs. It was used in *Restoration woodwork on chairs, daybeds, etc., as a *cresting detail for chair-backs or stretchers, and survived into the 18th century.

Boyvin, René (1530-after 1576). French engraver from Angers, who worked in Paris and at *Fontainebleau. His work derives from that of the leading Florentine

*René Boyvin. Engraved design for ewer with *marine decoration, c.1560.*

and Mannerist painter at Fontainebleau, Rosso Fiorentino. Boyvin published designs for metalwork, nefs, salts, jewellery, etc., decorated with *strapwork, *monkeys, *tortoises and frogs as well as more standard *Renaissance ornament such as *trophies of ancient Roman armour. He also published a series of *grotesque masks, and scenes set in elaborate strapwork frames.

bracket. Used either as a structural feature with or without ornament, or purely decoratively. Brackets are applied below sills, ledges, balconies, parapets, in fact any projecting element, and may be further decorated with *pendants or terminals. Brackets composed of *scrolls and *volutes are known as *consoles, and in the *Mannerist style are highly exaggerated. *See also* ancones; corbel; modillion; mutule.

brattishing. Type of *cresting associated with English late *Gothic openwork which has a repeating motif of foliage, *battlements or floral devices. It is used especially in ecclesiastical interiors, as the ornament for edges of shrines, canopies, screens, panelling, etc.

*bracket. 1) Interior, Chiswick House, London, 1725-29. 2) Bracket ornamented with *lion masks, Stadhuis, Zutphen, Holland, 1729, rebuilt 1956. 3) Brackets for marble slabs from T.*Chippendale's Director, 1754. 4) Densely bracketed *cornice, Albert Buildings, Queen Victoria Street, City of London, by F.J. Ward, 1871. 5) Porch of Edwardian block of flats, Knightsbridge, London.*

brattishing. 16th century wooden screen, Stokenham Church, South Devon.

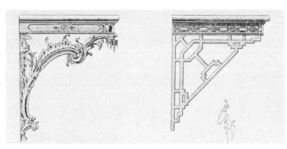

Examples often have a *Tudor flower motif. Widely used in the *Gothic Revival.

bridge fluting. Mid to late 18th century term for faceting that extended from the stem of a glass to bridge the junction with the bowl. By the late 18th century bridge fluting also ornamented the lower part of the bowl.

Bridgens, Richard. English architect, furniture designer and author of *Furniture with Candelabra and Interior Decoration* (1838), a collection of designs for furniture, principally chairs and sofas, *cornices, panelling, window drapery and doorways, which provided straightforward designs in three styles: *Greek, *Elizabethan and *Gothic Revival; it included some of the Elizabethan Revival pieces Bridgens had designed for Aston Hall, Birmingham, in the early 1820s. The intention was to suggest the style by choice of ornament rather than to reproduce it with any great historical accuracy. The relative simplicity of the ornament is indicative of the advent of machine carving. A few authentic examples of Elizabethan and *Gothic work were included, some contributed by H.*Shaw. *See also* eclecticism.

bright cut. Shallow, bright, faceted engraving that was popular on late 18th century silver, producing ornament in fashionable thin *festoons with *husks and light flowers. Bright cutting was less popular after the 1790s, but continued in use throughout the early 19th century.

briqueté (French, bricked). In 18th century ceramics, a ground decoration simulating brickwork that was first used at Sèvres and later copied by other porcelain factories such as Worcester. Early examples have gold lines over dark blue.

Britannia. Female personification of the British Isles that first appeared on Roman coins in the 2nd century AD and reappeared as a medallic figure in 1665. Britannia wears a helmet which is clearly based on that of *Minerva, and holds a shield on which there is usually a representation of the Union Jack and a trident to symbolise Britain's naval prowess. In the heyday of the British Empire, Britannia appeared on commercial buildings, railway stations, docks, etc.

Britannic Order. Order incorporating *lion, *unicorn and *crown motifs, invented by Robert Adam

Britannic Order. From R. Adam's Works in Architecture, *1773-79.*

*brocade patterns. From W. & G. *Audsley's* Polychromatic Decoration as Applied to Buildings in the Mediaeval Styles, 1882.*

(*see* Adam style) for the gateway to Carlton House, London (1767). It was occasionally called the 'German Order'. Another variant appears in the *Works in Architecture*, with Prince of Wales *feathers replacing the foliage on the *capital.

brocade or **brocaded patterns.** Designs supposedly derived from Japanese textiles and used on ceramics. Usually red, blue and gold, they consist of circular or fan-shaped panels of differing *diapers and *frets. They were used on early 17th century Ming porcelain for the Japanese market and subsequently by the Japanese themselves, who exported the wares to Europe. Patterns were then freely adapted by Western ceramic manufactures: at Ansbach in the 1730s and 1740s, Meissen, Chelsea, Derby and Worcester in the late 18th and early 19th centuries. These patterns were revived, though in more correct form, during the craze for *japonaiserie in the 1870s.

At the end of the 19th and beginning of the 20th centuries, 'brocade patterns' referred to the ogival shapes of *pines and flowers typical of Italian woven silk brocades or damasks.

broccoli decoration. Term occasionally used for foliage or *scrolling foliage of the *acanthus type; the term *parsley is used in a similar way.

broderie. French 18th century term for *lambrequin. *See also rayonnant.*

broken column. *See* death and mourning.

broken pediment. In architecture, a form of *pediment broken at the base, whereas an *open pediment is broken at the apex. One of many variations and elaborations of the classical pediment, it was introduced in the *Mannerist style and thereafter widely adopted. Also used on furniture, especially Chippendale-style pieces.

Broseley Blue Dragon pattern. *See* dragon.

Brown, Richard. 19th century painter and architectural draughtsman who produced *The Rudiments of Drawing Cabinet and Upholstery Furniture* (1822, 1835) with twenty-five plates of designs for furniture in *Greek Revival style. In 1822 he also published *An Elucidation of the Principles of Drawing Ornaments*, which is clearly influenced by T.*Hope and demands purity of ornament and symbolically appropriate motifs: e.g. sofas carved with heartsease and couch flower, the Three *Graces and their attributes for a dressing table, the figure of Narcissus – and the flower of the same name – for the decoration of a dressing-glass. These suggestions were to be 'varied according to the taste and judgement of the designer.' For example, the design for a library and withdrawing room chair included two *putti striving for *wreaths (back), two horned *owls sacred to *Minerva and emblematic of wisdom (front legs), and the *lyre of Apollo, god of poetry and the *Muses (sides).

Richard Brown's *Domestic Architecture* (1842) fielded the longest list of *Picturesque styles, providing a rich picking for the *eclectic designer. He covered no fewer than fourteen, including such oddities as 'Protestant Baroque', 'Soaneian' and 'Anglo-Italian'.

Brunetti, Gaetano (d 1758). Italian-born designer who worked in England from c.1730. He produced

broken pediment. Doorway of mid-Georgian house, Long Melford, Suffolk.

Gaetano Brunetti. Engraved design, 1736.

the earliest *pattern book to include *rocaille* published in England, *Sixty Different Sorts of Ornaments* (1736), which described itself as being 'very useful to Painters, Sculptors, Stone-Carvers, Wood-Carvers, Silversmiths &c.' It included designs for asymmetrical *cartouches with *rocaille* decoration, as well as *trophies, mirror frames, *niches and *grotto ornament with a tendency toward Italian *Baroque. It was reissued in Paris in 1857.

buckle. *See* love.

bucranium. The skull of a ram, ox, bull or goat in *Graeco-Roman classical ornament. Bucrania appeared on altars, reflecting the animals' significance both as sacrificial offerings and as fertility symbols, and on sarcophagi and other funerary items. The bucranium was used in *friezes, often combined with garlands or *festoons, and on the *metope of the classical temple. In the *Renaissance and to a greater degree in the 18th century, it became a favourite decoration for any projecting element in an interior, e.g. the corner of a *tripod, on the corner or centre of mantelpieces, on *cornice friezes, even as a handle. In a particularly literal use of the motif, ceramic tiles decorated with bucrania were sold for butchers' shops.

Buffon, Georges-Louis Leclerc, Comte de (1707-88). Highly influential 18th century zoologist. The engravings from his massive encyclopedia, *Histoire Naturelle,*

Générale et Particulière avec la Description du Cabinet du Roi (1749), were widely copied and used on textiles and ceramics, notably at Sèvres, Meissen and Tournai, from the 1760s to the 1780s.

buhl. *See boulle* work.

bulb. Bulbous decoration on late 16th and early 17th century turned and carved wooden furniture uprights, e.g. table legs, bedposts and supports on court and press cupboards. The bulb is either roughly circular (melon bulb) or shaped like a cup and cover and may be carved with foliage or *gadrooning. Bulbs reached their grossest shapes in the very early 17th century. Motif frequently used in the *Jacobean and *Elizabethan Revivals of the late 19th century.

bull. Symbol of strength and fertility in many ancient cultures, and often sacred to solar deities. The Assyrians depicted a winged bull, sometimes with a human head. Bulls figure in various classical myths, and these themes appear on Mycenaean and pre-Hellenic artefacts, e.g. Europa and the Bull, Minos and the Minotaur, the chariot of Zeus pulled by a bull. In the Roman Imperial period, the bull was viewed as a sacrificial beast and was worshipped in Mithraic temples. Bulls are represented at the sanctuary at Delos and appear on a capital at Salamis, Cyprus.

The winged bull appears among *grotesque ornament and *scrolling foliage in the Renaissance and, subsequently, in *Neo-classical decorative schemes. The Brahmin bull, a sacred beast for Hindus, makes an unexpected appearance in England, in Coade stone at Sezincote, Gloucestershire, an early 19th century *Indian style country house. *See also* bucranium.

bucranium. 1) Fragment of ancient altar in the Forum, Rome. 2) From early 20th century catalogue, Plastic Decoration Company's Enrichments. 3) Base of statue to Giovanni dalle Bande Nere by Baccio Bandinelli, 1540, in the Piazza San Lorenzo, Florence, Italy.

Byzantine. Three sculptural fragments at the Cathedral of St Mark, Venice, Italy.

butterfly. A frequent motif in oriental art which was adopted in *chinoiserie* and *japonaiserie* decoration. For the Chinese the butterfly symbolised immortality, abundant leisure and joy; combined with a *chrysanthemum, it signified beauty in old age, and with a plum, longevity. For the Japanese it signified a vain woman or a fickle lover, although two symbolised conjugal happiness. Disproportionately large butterflies appear in the earliest *chinoiserie* designs, e.g. in the patterns of J.*Stalker and G. Parker (1688), and were commonly engraved on silver and painted on tin-glazed blue and white earthenware. One curiosity in engraved ornament is the *Essay de papilloneries humaines* (1748) by Charles Germain de Saint-Aubin (1721-86) in which butterflies perform human activities. J.M. Whistler was one of the first European admirers of Japanese art and adopted the butterfly as his symbol. In Western Europe and America, butterflies were minutely observed at first hand and included in *naturalistic ornamentation. The *Art Deco designer E.A.*Séguy produced a series of ornamental patterns called *Papillons* in 1927, primarily intended for textiles. Like all winged insects, the butterfly was a popular motif in *Art Nouveau jewellery, a natural subject for virtuoso enamelling techniques. *See also* insect.

Byzantine. The Byzantine Empire, partitioned from the Roman Empire in 395 AD, reached its artistic apogee in the 6th century with the great works of Justinian in Constantinople. It borrowed the forms of *Graeco-Roman classicism which had survived in early Christian architecture and artefacts, and merged them with oriental motifs from the Arab countries that were part of the Empire until the 7th century AD. Decoration was abundant and the medium of sharply cut, low relief marble altered classical forms such as the *acanthus into a spikier, more defined type of ornament (compared to the loose, abundant forms of late Roman ornament). *Vines, *peacocks, *palmettes, geometrically patterned brickwork and highly gilded and coloured mosaics (both representational and geometric) were part of the vocabulary of Byzantine ornament. Hagia Sophia, Istanbul (which

was dedicated in 537) was a storehouse of these forms, with carved *capitals, e.g. *basket capitals, in which the ornament obscures the structural definition between capital and *abacus. Many of the craftsmen working in Constantinople came from the Aegean region where skills originating in classical Greece were still in evidence. Across the Empire which, at its height, included North Africa, Italy, part of Spain and the Balkan countries, the architecture and artefacts exchanged and transmitted native and imported styles. In the 8th and 9th centuries the Iconoclasm intervened, causing a break in the development of Byzantine art, but the 10th and 11th centuries saw a resurgence of ornament in works at St Mark's, Venice, in Ravenna, and in the areas of orthodox Christianity in Eastern Europe and Russia. Southern Italy and areas of Spain and France (Languedoc) were all affected by the Crusades and thus were influenced by Byzantium. *Christian motifs became mingled with those of classical antiquity; oriental motifs, such as the *Tree of Life became absorbed within Greek or Roman forms such as the palmette or *acanthus.

The Byzantine style was the basis for *Romanesque decoration and underlies regional modifications such as the *Lombardic style. Motifs from jewellery (e.g. a bracelet of 600 AD in which pairs of *swans and *peacocks are enclosed by a vinescroll), were taken up by French metalworkers of the *Romanesque period (in *cloisonné enamel, for example). In Venice, where fragments from Byzantium were to be seen everywhere, early printed books (illustrated from 1476) used Byzantine knotwork or *interlacing for page borders (e.g. Alessandro Paganino's *Apocalipsis Iesu Christi*, Venice, 1515).

Byzantine Revival. As with *Neo-classicism, it was the scholarly publications on *Byzantine buildings and artefacts that spurred 19th century designers to re-examine the style. Sulzenberg's *Alt Christliche von Constantinopel* was cited by O.*Jones as an influential publication. Earlier only the 6th century church of

Byzantine Revival. Three details from the exterior of Westminster Cathedral, London, by John Francis Bentley, 1895-1903.

Byzantine Revival. 1) 103 Cannon Street, City of London, by Fred Jameson, 1886. 2) Administration Building, Rice Institute, Houston, Texas, by Cram, Goodhue and Ferguson, 1910-12.

San Vitale in Ravenna, St Mark's in Venice and the cathedral of Monreale in Sicily had been regularly published and usually for their famed geometric mosaic pavements. The Byzantine Revival was not a widely adopted branch of *Historicism, except in Germany, but isolated examples (usually ecclesiastical) reintroduced the barrel vaults, round arches, dense, prickly foliage carving and brilliantly coloured mosaics associated with Byzantine art. J.F. Bentley (1839-1902) seems to have chosen the style for Westminster Cathedral (1894-1903) partly in order to differentiate the Roman Catholic Cathedral of London from the nearby Anglican Westminster Abbey. In America the style blended with the *Romanesque Revival and in work by architects such as H.H. Richardson (1838-86) it became highly influential. Publications such as Charles

cabled fluting. 1) English silver candlestick, made in Exeter, 1718.
*cable moulding. 2) *Pilaster base, Mosteiro dos Jerónimos, Belém, Portugal, early 16th century. 3) Silver ewer made in London, 1700-01.*
4) House doorway, Ardross Street, Inverness, Scotland, c.1900.

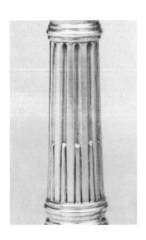
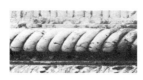

Vogue's *Byzantine Architecture and Ornament* (Boston, 1890) were aids to designers in search of authentic detail. The motifs shared by Byzantium and the pre-Christian Middle Eastern cultures were considered appropriate ornament for some synagogues and other Jewish institutions. More directly, the Greek Orthodox communities scattered outside their home countries adopted Byzantine forms for their churches. *See also* Rundbogenstil.

cabled fluting. A variation of *fluting, where the lower section of the flutes have convex infillings. *See also* reeding.

cable moulding or **ropework.** Enrichment carved to resemble twisted *rope. In architecture, a characteristically *Romanesque form used on arches and *arcading. An adaptable edging decoration in metalwork, sometimes in plaited form, cable moulding appeared widely on early 18th century silver and occasionally on ceramics. Well-suited to the casting process, it became popular in 19th century ironwork. In some instances cable moulding indicates an earlier use of actual rope, e.g. on fonts, recalling Early Christian wooden fonts that were sometimes 'bound' in this manner.

T.*Sheraton, in his *The Cabinet-maker, Upholsterer and General Artist's Encyclopedia* (1804-06), included furniture with *marine emblems, alluding to Nelson's naval victories: the simplest and most commonly used motif was cable moulding to decorate chair-backs (sometimes referred to as Trafalgar chairs). *See also* interlacing.

cabochon (French, smooth domed gem). Raised oval or circular ornament in carving, stonework, etc. It appears in both *Gothic and *Gothic Revival ornament. It occurs in *jewelled strapwork on Elizabethan and *Jacobean woodwork and metalwork, sometimes alternating with a *lozenge. A cabochon may be used at the centre of a repeating ornament, e.g. in *guilloches on late 18th century *classical furniture.

Cabochon may also refer to a small convex *cartouche form with a carved surround on the knee of a *cabriole leg in *Rococo furniture.

cabriole leg. Ornamental curving leg based on the animal *monopodia used for Roman *tripods, etc. It came into fashion on European furniture from the late 17th century and remained popular until the late 18th century. Cabriole legs often have feet in the shape of *claws, *paws or *hoofs. The 'knee' of a cabriole leg is also sometimes ornamented, occasionally with carved fur or feathers, but more often with a fashionable motif such as a *scallop shell or *cartouche.

caduceus. A winged staff entwined with two serpents, which are thought to have evolved from the traditional ribbons of a herald's staff. In classical mythology, the caduceus is an attribute of the Roman deity *Mercury (and his Greek counterpart Hermes), messenger of the gods, who was also credited with the invention of the *alphabet. It is therefore a favourite motif in the decoration of objects and places associated with the written word, e.g. printing presses, and, notably, post offices. R.*Brown considered it an appropriate ornament for writing tables.

caduceus. 1) English library table, c.1810. 2) Post Office, Lisieux (Calvados), France, late 19th century.

Mercury was also the protector of merchants and traders, thus the caduceus became a part of the decoration associated with *commerce, e.g. it appears on the bronze doors of the Bank of England in London, and on many office buildings.

caillouté (French, pebbled). In ceramics, a form of decoration devised at Sèvres during the 1750s and 1760s in which a ground colour, usually rose pink, apple green or *bleu du roi*, is overpainted with a network of pebble-shaped outlines in another colour, often gold. *Caillouté* patterning, which appeared on cups, saucers, plates, *jardinières*, etc., had the effect of softening brilliantly coloured enamel grounds. It was copied at Derby, Swansea and Worcester from c.1800.

Callot, Jacques (1592-1635). French ornamental designer who trained as a goldsmith. Although Callot never became an ornamental artist in his own right, he was one of the earliest exponents of etching, and his work was therefore relatively widely known. His most popular designs were a series of twenty-one grotesque dwarfs (Callot had sketched a troupe of performing hunchbacks in Florence), published as *Varie Figure Gobbi* in 1616. Some of these designs were reworked and republished in Amsterdam in 1716 by the engraver and printseller Wilhelm Kooning under the title *Il Calotto Resuscitato oder Neu-ein-gerichtes Zwenchen Cabinett*, which became a well-used source for porcelain figures of dwarfs made at Meissen, Vienna, Chelsea, Mennecy, Venice, Capodimonte and Derby (the Mansion House Dwarfs). 'Callot Dwarfs' also appeared on glass: e.g. enamelled c.1665 by the German Johann Schaper (1621-70) and stipple-engraved by the Dutchman Franz Greenwood (1680-1761). Callot's etchings of *commedia dell'arte* figures, *Balli di Sfessania*, were also used by Schaper. Some of the beggar figures from his *Misères de Guerre* (two series, 1632 and 1633) were adapted by R.*Hancock and printed on Bow porcelain.

calyx ornament. Classical ornament resembling the botanical form. Calyx ornament appears, often combined with other motifs, in *Adam style decoration.

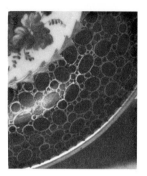

Jacques Callot. 1) Engraving of dwarf from Varie Figure Gobbi, *1616.*
*camel. 2) From S.*della Bella's* Ornamenti o grottesche, *c.1640.*
caillouté. 3) French porcelain saucer, Sèvres, mid 18th century.

camel. In medieval *bestiaries any creature with a hump that kneeled to receive its load was taken to be a camel, and a very confused picture of the animal resulted. It appeared in representations of the Magi, but was also used as a symbol of Christ's humility, e.g. on misericords at Boston, Lincolnshire. Camels' heads appeared with *grotesques in S.*della Bella's *Ornamenti o grottesche* (c.1640). As a beast of burden, the camel makes a suitable support: on the Thames Embankment, London, pairs of kneeling camels support Victorian cast-iron benches. A camel occasionally appears as an attribute of Asia in decorative schemes incorporating the *Continents, and sometimes in connection with trade with the Orient: it is an emblem of the medieval London guild, The Pepperers, later called the Grocers' Company, and appears on buildings endowed by it.

cameo. Unlike engraved gems which may be used as seals and can be traced back to about 5000 BC, cameos are a purely decorative device. They first appeared in Greek jewellery c.300 BC, and were subsequently popular in Roman jewellery and furniture. Stones with stratified layers of dark and light colours, such as onyx and sardonyx were usually used, with the top layer of stone being cut away to leave the design in relief. Although cameos were still cut in the Middle Ages, they were relatively rare.

However, interest in them was revived during the Renaissance, and 15th century artistic patrons with collections of antique cameos commissioned new ones. In the mid 18th century cameos became a general decorative motif, suiting the fashion for *Neo-classical

cameo. 1) English silver slop basin made by Boulton & Fothergill, c.1780. 2) Late 18th century silk waistcoat. 3) English jasper ware vase with cameo relief of Apollo and his *lyre, made by Josiah Wedgwood, c.1795.

and in ceramics (with the *pâte-sur-pâte* technique developed at Sèvres).

candelabra form. A decorative form much used in the *Renaissance and based on the classical candelabrum. Like the *Tree of Life, it is used in vertical panels of decoration (e.g. on *pilasters), is symmetrical, and incorporates curving forms that provide a focus or framing device for surrounding patterns and motifs. Antique examples were found in the Domus Aurea of Nero in Rome and provided the source for many of the earliest Renaissance *grotesque patterns. The candelabrum foot (usually a *tripod with animal feet), the candelabrum shaft of *baluster and *vase shapes and the branching lamp holders provided the basic skeleton around which *scrolling foliage, mythical animals, *putti and *festoons were entwined. Engravings of the form, sometimes referred to as *a candeliere* designs, were produced by A.*Veneziano, Nicoletto Rosex da Modena (fl 1500-12), Zoan Andrea (fl 1475-1505) and Giovanni Pietro da Birago. The candelabra form was originally used in painted decoration, but it

candelabra form. 1) Design by Robert Adam, published 1821. 2) *Pilaster panel, Mosteiro dos Jerónimos, Belém, Portugal, early 16th century. 3) Carved wooden timbers on house near the cathedral in Le Mans (Sarthe), France, late 16th or early 17th century. 4) Lamp standard, New York Public Library by Carrère & Hastings, 1911.

and specifically for *Pompeian decoration. Examples of antique cameos were illustrated in such influential books as A.F.*Gori's *Museum Florentinium* (1731-66), and the Comte *de Caylus's *Recueil d'antiquités* (1752-67). During the 1760s both Sèvres and Meissen produced wares bearing painted cameos, at first depicting a profile and later more complex mythological scenes. Cameos were also painted on satinwood furniture, echoing the fashionable *medallion form. Wedgwood's development of jasper ware in the mid 1770s (which was the culmination of a search for a ceramic body that looked like stone and was hard enough to be given a lapidary polish after firing in order to imitate the Greek and Roman examples) exploited and extended the fashion for cameo decoration. The finest examples of jasper ware were modelled by John Flaxman (1755-1826) in impeccable Neo-classical style using such subjects as the Apotheosis of Homer. Jasper ware plaques were used in many ways: set into jewellery, into steel grates, into furniture and fireplaces (they were subsequently copied by Sèvres). Cameos were copied by the silversmith Andrew Fogelberg (fl 1770-93), who ornamented his work with applied silver examples, as did Paul Storr (1771-1844). Cameos also appeared in textiles, on *toiles de Jouy* (printed cottons), and were even, occasionally, painted on waistcoats.

In the 19th century, cameos again became popular in jewellery, and coral, shell and jet were all used in their manufacture. In the second half of the 19th century, cameo effects were achieved in glass (by overlaying several colours and then cutting through them)

canephora. 1) Early 19th century French Empire cabinet with ormolu mounts.
canopic jar. 2) English caneware inkwell, Wedgwood, c.1800.

was soon carved in marble and stone, particularly for mullions. Engravings by Veneziano and Rosex were used by decorators of ceramics in Italy at Castel Durante and Cafaggiolo. Although the form was initially most popular in Renaissance Lombardy and Tuscany, it spread northwards and appeared in France as early as 1526, carved on the door jambs of the choir screen at Chartres Cathedral. It was adopted as one of the most popular ornaments for printed books, particularly on title pages, as in Johannes Monteregio's *Calendarium* (Venice, 1476), designed and printed by Erhard Ratdolt, and in Coverdale's Bible (1535).

The candelabra grotesque was revived in the 19th century, frequently in terracotta or majolica, for internal and external architectural decoration.

canephora (Greek, basket carrier). A female figure (sometimes a *half figure) bearing a basket on her head. The full figure canephora performs the same supporting function in *classical, or *Neo-classical architecture as the *caryatid. The canephora was extremely popular in *Louis XVI and late 18th century furniture and interior plasterwork, the basket sometimes replaced by a cushion, and appeared in many media both on small-scale objects and in architecture. Gwilt's *Encyclopaedia* (1867) commented that they were 'frequently confounded with caryatids from their resemblance in point of attitude and the modern abuse of their application.'

cannon. A component of schemes of *military decoration. When used in *trophies and *panoplies, cannons often have a ramrod and powder keg next to them. The Porta dei Bombardieri in Verona (1687) is supported by stone cannon barrels standing on plinths of drums. Blenheim Palace, Oxfordshire, built for the Duke of Marlborough in the early years of the 18th century in recognition of his military prowess, has a gateway with columns that have cannon balls as bases. Later the cannon was not confined to exterior use: at the Bagatelle, Bois de Boulogne, Paris, built for Philippe Comte d'Artois (Louis XVI's brother and Grand Master of the King's Artillery), the boudoir

(designed by F.J. Bélanger in 1777) was ornamented with *colonnettes formed from groups of cannon barrels; Napoleon had the same device used as bed-posts. After the defeat of the French, R.*Ackermann's *Repository* reported a planned colossal column, decorated with French cannon in the manner of a *columna rostrata. Crossed cannons, symbolic of victory, were used in American *Federal style commemorative ware, textiles and wallpaper.

canopic jar or **canopic vase** (Canope: a town in ancient Egypt). Ancient Egyptian jars, ovoid in shape, usually of stone and in sets of four, were used to hold the mummified viscera of the dead. Those of the New Kingdom period (1552-1069 BC) often had stoppers carved to represent the demi-god sons of Horus: ape-headed Hapy, jackal-headed Duamutef, hawk-headed Quebhsenuef, and the human-headed Imset. The latter was adopted in late 18th and early 19th century *Egyptian style ornament: T.*Hope used a canopic jar as a *finial on furniture; Wedgwood reproduced them in his *rosso antico* ware, and a black basalt ware inkpot was also made in this shape.

capital. 1) Nave of Rouen Cathedral (Seine-Maritime), France, built by
Jean d'Andely, 1201-20. 2) Capital from the Temple of Bacchus from
*A.*Desgodetz's Les Edifices Antiques. 3) Incised capital, Peck House,*
Eastcheap, City of London, architect A. Peebles, 1884-85. 4) House,
*Houtmarkt, Zutphen, Holland, 1615. 5) Egyptian capitals from O.*Jones's*
Grammar of Ornament, 1868 edition.

capital. 1) Design for a cast-iron capital engraved by Thomas Langley from B.*Langley's The City and Country Builder's Treasury, *1740. 2) Detail on a Paris shop, 1930s.*

Carpenter Gothic. Porch of house, Galveston, Texas.

capital. The head of a *column or *pilaster that supports the *entablature. The capital is subject to endless variations in its ornament, although these are most frequently based on foliage and flowers. Basic capital forms include block capital, cushion capital and scalloped capital. In classical architecture, the form and decoration of the capital denotes the *Order. *See also* ammonite capital; basket capital.

caprice. Term sometimes used to denote the decorative *vignettes devised by *Rococo *ornemanistes. Caprices* frequently depicted fantastic architectural ruins inhabited by emblematic figures (e.g. the *Seasons, *Ages of Man) and surrounded by a border of scrollwork and **rocaille.* They were produced in quantity, particularly by German artists, and were transfer-printed on ceramics, enamelled on glass and carved on overmantels or panelling.

Caramanian pattern. *See* topographical decoration.

card cut. In wood, a type of *fret ornament that is carved in low relief, and not pierced. It was used, principally from the mid to late 18th century, in horizontal sections on furniture, for example along the top of a tallboy, and was particularly favoured in the *chinoiserie and *Gothick tastes.

Carpenter Gothic. In America, a popular mid 19th century expression in wood of *Gothic Revival forms. Fenestration, verandahs and porches, and, above all, *bargeboards and *finials, were carved in elaborate

card cut decoration on English side-table, c.1740.

forms using conventional Gothic motifs such as *cusping, *Tudor flower *cresting, or foliate forms, with the addition of some classical motifs such as the *wave-scroll. The effect of the decoration was maximised by the play of light through pierced or fretted woodwork. The origins of the style lay in the English *Picturesque movement interpreted by American designers, notably A.J.*Downing and Alexander Jackson Davis (1803-92). Later influential English publications such as C.R.*Eastlake's *Hints on Household Taste* (published in America in 1872) contributed other motifs, in particular the machine-turned finials, *balustrading and knobs that were to become important components of the *Shingle style, which followed Carpenter Gothic by the end of the 19th century.

carquois, au. *See* arrow.

cartouche (French, escutcheon or scroll). A framed panel, often elaborately decorated, and thought to be based on the shape of the *scroll; it may be concave or convex, with a plain, decorated or inscribed centre. In its later forms, the distinction between border and central motif became increasingly blurred. Cartouches were widely used in *Renaissance decoration, particularly in northern Europe, where they often came to be used as heraldic *shields. Albrecht Dürer (1471-1528) placed inscriptions on animal skins to create a cartouche effect, as in the lion pelt in his woodcut of the Triumph of Maximilian. *Pattern-book engravers promoted the device: Melchior Tavernier, in his *Cartouches de diferentes inventions* (1632), depicted Arcadian landscapes with rustic figures enclosed in the draped skins of imaginary creatures. During the 16th and 17th centuries, *strapwork was most commonly used in the borders. *Baroque cartouches typically had swelling, curving forms, which were often markedly convex or concave. Examples designed to resemble scrolled paper were much used in 17th and 18th century printed books as an obvious ornament for title pages and book plates. Winged cartouches were sometimes applied as a corner detail on picture frames. Numerous pattern-book authors addressed themselves to the form, and its period of greatest popularity was undoubtedly the *Rococo, the characteristic asymmetrical versions first appearing in examples engraved

by A.*Mitelli. Almost every *ornemaniste* of the period contributed examples, often with pastoral *vignettes or themes such as the *Seasons, *Months, etc. Despite their popularity, many of the more extravagant engravings were too difficult actually to apply in decoration; nevertheless, Rococo cartouches appeared on carved *boiseries*, on interior plasterwork, enamelled or transfer-printed on ceramics and engraved on silver (usually to serve *heraldic purposes). Occasional attempts were made to use the cartouche as a three-dimensional form: the silversmith Paul de Lamerie (1688-1751) tried to create cartouche feet for a cream jug. For wall monuments in churches or datestones on houses the cartouche was used to frame inscriptions, a practical as well as an infinitely variable decorative motif, and an alternative to the more classical *label or tablet. The form was little used in *Neoclassical styles but returned to favour during the 19th century fashion for *eclectic ornament.

In 18th century parlance, cartouche, cartooze, cartouze, etc., also referred to an interior equivalent of the *modillion.

caryatid. A draped female figure that acts as a column supporting the *entablature. *Vitruvius related the legend of the caryatid's origin (and Fra Giocondo

*caryatid. 1) From *Vitruvius's* De Architectura, *Fra Giocondo edition, Venice, 1511. 2) High Point 2, Highgate, London, architects Berthold Lubetkin and Tecton, 1938. 3) Late 19th century lamp standard, Prague. 4) Doorway to the Palais Palavicini, Vienna, 1783-84.*

*cartouche. 1) Cooper's House, Grote Markt, Antwerp, 1579 (rebuilt). 2) *Auricular design from D. Rabel's* Cartouches de différentes inventions utiles, *c.1620-30. 3) Letter box, Florence, Italy.*

illustrated it in his 1511 edition of Vitruvius's work): during a period of hostilities between the Greeks and the Persians, the Caryae, a people living in the Peloponnese, became allies of the Persians. After a Greek victory, the Caryae womenfolk were punished for their treachery by enslavement and forced to carry burdens on their heads. This, Vitruvius considered, was the kind of explanation 'which architects ought to know . . . A wide knowledge of history is requisite because, among the ornamental parts of an architect's design for a work, there are many the underlying idea of whose employment he should be able to explain to inquirers.' The earliest known examples of the caryatid were on the Erechtheion in Athens (1409-06 BC), and at Delphi. In Rome, they were adapted for Hadrian's Villa at Tivoli, and as a result of Vitruvius's account became central motifs in the vocabulary of classical Roman architecture.

Caryatids were popular in the *Renaissance, although generally applied to small-scale objects. In the School of *Fontainebleau, the caryatid became a less rigid form; *drapery was often depicted as though in movement, legs might be crossed or in a relaxed pose, bodies were sometimes contorted. As a result, the function of the caryatid as a supporting column was often abandoned and it was frequently used as a purely decorative form though still usually in a supporting position, e.g. on chimneypieces, screens or small-scale artefacts. Caryatids are included in works by H.*Vredeman de Vries, J.*Shute, J.A.*Ducerceau and H.*Sambin; soon no pattern book was complete without them, together with *atlantes, *canephoras, *herms and *persians. In the *Mannerist and *Baroque periods, sheathed caryatids, heavily swathed in robes, appeared in current taste. With the adoption of *Neo-classicism, however, more orthodox versions reappeared. One of the caryatids from the Erechtheion porch was brought to London in the early years of the 19th century to form part of the Hamilton Collection at the British Museum. Soon after, William and Charles Inwood built the church of St Pancras (1819-22), with a porch copied from the Erechtheion complete with a full complement of caryatids. Sir J. Soane used the form to dramatic effect on his Bank of England offices (1790s). The Coade manufactory of artificial stone mass produced replicas in the late 18th and early 19th centuries. One of the most recent and most surprising architectural uses of caryatids is at Highpoint, North London, where they support the entrance to a block of flats built by Berthold Lubetkin and Tecton, 1936-38, and supply the only decorative feature in an otherwise unadorned International style building.

Small-scale caryatids appeared in furniture, woodwork and metalwork mainly from the 16th to the 18th centuries. Their use often reflected 'architectural' considerations: they appeared as miniature supports replacing *balusters in the 16th century, as furniture legs (e.g. in designs by J.A. Ducerceau), as bronze furniture mounts and handles and as stems in silver. *Half-figure handles on metalwork and ceramics are sometimes known as caryatid handles. In the early 17th century, caryatids occasionally framed the title pages of printed books.

castellated or **crenellated**. Decorated with *battlements.

Castle style. A light-hearted adaptation of forms and motifs originally associated with fortified structures. John Vanbrugh built a mock fortified gateway at Castle Howard as early as 1699. The style was originally confined to *Gothick follies, gateways, fake ruins and false-fronted farmhouses or cottages, but by the late 18th century it was adapted for larger houses. The vocabulary consisted of battlemented rooflines, *arrowslits and brackets, and even, on occasion, drawbridge and portcullis. Though it had its origins in the *Picturesque, the style was taken up by *Neo-classical architects such as Robert Adam, and subsequently led to the *Neo-Norman and *Romanesque Revival styles of the early 19th century. Medieval revivalists were attracted to the secular associations of the style (in contrast to the predominantly ecclesiastical sources of the *Gothic Revival). As a highly ornamental genre, the Castle style could cloak buildings of regular classical form or of Picturesque asymmetry with equal ease. John Nash (1752-1835) was particularly fond of the

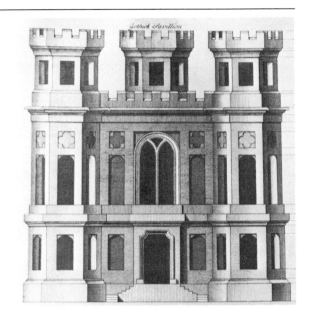

*Castle style. 'Gothick Pavillion' engraved by Thomas Langley from B.*Langley's* Gothic Architecture, *1747.*

style and used it in many of his country villas. In Scotland a distinctive version, the *Scottish Baronial style, found considerable favour in the mid 19th century.

In the 19th century many new industrial buildings were given the outline of a Norman castle, sometimes echoing an original structure nearby; for example, Lancaster railway station below the castle, or the bridges across the Menai straits near Conway Castle, Gwynedd. In both Britain and America, the Castle style was popular for 19th century prison buildings.

catenary. *Festoon composed of *chain links, usually used as carved architectural detail in the 18th and early 19th centuries. Catenaries were sometimes applied as an alternative to the more common fruit and flower festoons but they also appear more specifically as an appropriate decoration for prisons and lock-ups, occasionally with manacles on the ends of the chains.

Cathedral style. Term sometimes applied to the English and French moves towards *Gothic forms and motifs, c.1810-40, that predated the fully-fledged *Gothic Revival led by A.W.N.*Pugin and others later in the century. In France it was called the *style cathédrale*. It implies the use of *architectural motifs, especially window *tracery, *lancets and *rose windows. The Cathedral style was popular in jewellery and bookbinding and is also found in woodwork, e.g. chairbacks and chests with panels of *blind tracery.

caulicoli. Fluted *acanthus stalks that support each of the eight *volutes on a Corinthian capital (*see* Orders).

Cauvet, Gilles-Paul (1731-88). French architect, sculptor, designer and engraver who produced ornament in the *Louis XVI style. His *Recueil d'ornements à l'usage des jeunes artistes qui se destinent à la décoration des batimens* (1777) included designs for panels, *scrolling foliage, *friezes, *vases and *grotesques, many incorporating large nymph figures.

cavetto moulding or **hollow chamfering** (Latin, *cavare*, to hollow). One of the principal forms of *moulding, a concave version of *ovolo moulding, usually a quarter of a circle in section.

Celtic. From about the 5th century BC, Celtic ornamental art spread from the Rhineland eastwards to the area of present-day Czechoslovakia, Romania and Hungary, southwards to Austria, Yugoslavia and Italy, then to Ireland and France, and finally, in about 250 BC, to Britain. As they spread, via Celtic invasion, these art forms combined Greek and Etruscan motifs with the abstract and *zoomorphic forms which probably originated, respectively, in the Orient and Central Asia. They also absorbed the influence of work by early Christians in Syrian and Coptic churches, and the oriental motifs of *Byzantine art. Typical motifs are spirals, *knots and *interlacing forms, stylised animals, birds and reptiles as well as abstract designs such as *triquetrac, *triskele and *trumpet pattern. Many of these motifs and patterns were disseminated through Christian illuminated manuscripts. Borders and initials were often highly decorated with geometric designs and what O.*Jones described in his *Grammar of Ornament* as 'strange, monstrous animals and birds with long top-knots, tongues and tails, intertwining in almost endless knots.' The early 9th century *Book of Kells* contains representations of the *Elements; wheels composed of figures and animals also appear, as does the Christian cross superimposed on a circle to form the characteristic Celtic *wheel cross. Metalwork

catenary. 1) 18th century house at Nag's Head, Gloucestershire.
Cathedral style. 2) French necklace and pendant, c.1851.
caulicoli. 3) King Charles's Block, Royal Naval Hospital, Greenwich, London, by John Webb, 1662-69.

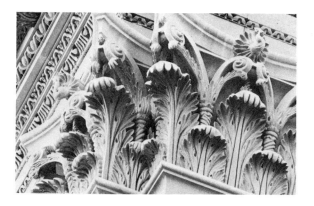

Celtic. Stem of Celtic cross, Ruthwell, Dumfriesshire, probably 7th century.

patterning, often achieved with a high degree of technical skill, as in *cloisonné* work, was similar to the designs that appeared in manuscripts; typically, the whole surface area of an object was covered with curvilinear designs – this effect was achieved on some metal objects with the application of spirals of gold wire. In Brittany, Ireland and Scotland, Celtic forms remained predominant in architectural ornament until the 11th century, although by then they were often incorporated into subsequent styles, notably the *Anglo-Saxon, *Romanesque and *Hiberno-Romanesque.

Celtic Revival. The 19th century revival of Celtic motifs and forms dating from between c.650 and 1150 was largely confined to Britain and Ireland, and those countries to which the Irish and Scots had emigrated. It paralleled a revival of the *Viking style in Scandinavia. Reports of archaeological discoveries and accurate topographical accounts such as those by George Petrie and Henry O'Neill in Ireland made available illustrations of Celtic artefacts: the stone crosses of

Celtic Revival. 1) Watts Chapel, Compton, near Guildford, Surrey, built by Mary Watts, 1896 onwards. 2) 'Cymric' vase designed by Archibald Knox for Liberty & Co., Birmingham, 1902.

Ireland and Northumberland, metalwork and jewellery with intricate patterning and the great illuminated manuscripts. The Tara Brooch, discovered in Ireland in 1850, was exhibited the following year in Dublin, at a time when there was a nationalistic literary and political revival in Ireland, and sparked off the production of jewellery in the Celtic style. The Dublin Exhibition of 1853 included many *Irish style exhibits. *A Descriptive Catalogue of the Fine Arts of Ancient Ireland*, published in 1855, points out that recent archaeological finds served 'to show that a truly national and beautiful style of Art existed in Ireland from a remote period till some time after the Anglo-Norman invasion.'

William Morris, who had studied Nordic culture and read translations of the sagas, took an early interest in Celtic art; in 1861 he produced a cabinet decorated with inlaid *interlacing. Illuminated manuscripts were recognised sources of fine abstract ornament, as shown by Edward Sullivan's *Facsimiles of National Manuscripts of Ireland* (1874-84) and Thomas K. Abbot's *Celtic Ornaments from the Book of Kells* (1892-95). These publications undoubtedly influenced *Arts and Crafts designers such as Arthur Heygate Mackmurdo (1851-1942) and Walter Crane (1845-1915) and subsequently the *Art Nouveau designers at the turn of the century. Members of the *Glasgow School drew on Celtic motifs to varying degrees. O.*Jones and C.*Dresser wrote on Celtic ornament and late 19th century manuals such as the magazine *Decoration* (1881-89) devoted considerable space to variously named 'Scotic', 'Scandinavian', 'Saxon' or Celtic ornament. Liberty launched a range of silver and jewellery called Cymric (1899-early 1930s) and a pewter range called Tudric (c.1903-c.1938) much of which was designed by Archibald Knox (1814-1933), a student of C.*Dresser. He was a native of the Isle of Man, an important repository of Celtic art. The Irish exodus to America, Canada and elsewhere spread the Celtic Revival beyond Britain; wheel crosses, often decorated with interlacing and other abstract designs, stand in cemeteries worldwide, dating from the mid 19th century onwards. The entrance to the 1893 World's Columbian Exposition in Chicago was a full-scale replica of Cormac's Chapel, Rock of Cashel (1127-34), which represents a high point in *Hiberno-Romanesque architectural decoration (1127-34). The Arts and Crafts movement in

Ireland continued to look to Celtic forms well into the 20th century, and jewellery is still produced in Celtic style in Ireland and Scotland.

centaur. A creature from Greek mythology with the head, trunk and arms of a man and the legs and body of a horse. As in the *zodiac sign of Sagittarius, the centaur often has a bow and arrow. The most famous legend is that of the battle between the centaurs and Lapithae; this appeared on the Parthenon and was a popular theme for *Renaissance engravers and painters. The centaur was also mentioned in medieval *bestiaries where it was sometimes described as a Christian symbol, representing the contrast between man's lower animal nature and his higher spiritual nature, or man torn between good and evil. Sometimes the centaur symbolises his lower nature alone: sensuality, adulterous passions or even the devil with the arrows carried by the centaur representing the fiery darts of evil. The centaur appears in medieval ecclesiastical carvings, tiles, misericords, etc., and also in schemes of *Bacchic ornament.

Ceres. Goddess of agriculture and the fruits of the earth, the Roman equivalent of the Greek Demeter, whose attributes, a crown of *wheat, corn sheaf, *poppy, *cornucopia and sometimes a *scythe, appear in schemes of ornament depicting *Plenty and *husbandry. Ceres often appears in conjunction with *Bacchic decoration, in the ornamentation of places and objects associated with eating, as a symbol of food and wine. She sometimes holds a *torch, a reference to the legend in which she searched for her daughter Proserpine in the underworld. Occasionally she appears in medieval ecclesiastical decoration, symbolising the Church itself, holding two torches which represent the Old and New Testaments. Where the *Seasons are depicted, Ceres may stand for Summer.

cerquate. The arrangement of *oak leaves and *acorns on Italian *Renaissance *maiolica*.

chaînes. Vertical strips of (often *rusticated) masonry consisting of blocks of alternating width that echo the placing of *quoins, used to mark bays or surround doors, windows etc. *Chaînes* were a popular form of ornamentation in 17th century French architecture that was occasionally copied in Britain.

chains. In *Renaissance allegory, chains symbolise man enslaved by his natural desires; thus personifications

centaur. 1) 13th century English earthenware tile.
*Ceres. 2) Ornament for a rich *frieze from G. *Richardson's A Collection of Ornaments in the Antique Style, 1816.*

chains. 1) Tympanum ornament, Kilmainham Gaol, Dublin, by Sir John Traile, 1796. 2) Naval Ministry, Ave. Octave, Paris, early 20th century.

of the Vices (*see* *Virtues and Vices) are fettered. However, chains appear most often in schemes of *marine and naval decoration, e.g. looped around *anchors, as *catenaries, and in the decoration of prisons: Newgate Gaol, London (built from 1770, demolished) had chain-festooned doorways; the Georgian gaol in Dublin is ornamented with chained *serpents signifying captive evil.

chain trailing. *See* trailed decoration.

Chambers, Sir William (1723-96). English architect who made several visits to China in the 1740s and then studied in Paris and Rome under J.-F.*Blondel and later C.*Clérisseau. On his return to London, he published the results of his observations in China, *Designs for Chinese buildings, furniture, dresses, machines and utensils* (1757). This was a milestone in the establishment of *chinoiserie* as an architectural style rather than a purely decorative vogue. A French edition of the book was published in the same year, a Russian translation in 1771, and plates were pirated for another French publication by G.L. Le Rouge. Catherine II of Russia ordered Charles Cameron to build a Chinese village at Tsarskoe Selo, based on Chambers's illustrations. His own buildings at Kew (1757 onwards) included influential works such as the Pagoda, as well as a *Moorish-style mosque and an Alhambra. However, the main influence on his work was the *classical French mode, tempered by a familiarity with Roman and Italian *Renaissance work and a background of the early 18th century English *Palladian style. Chambers campaigned energetically against the *gusto greco* (the *Greek Revival), and was an early champion of the *Gothic Revival as a national style that had been overlooked for too long. Chambers disliked the Greek style because he felt it lacked magnificence and variety. His varied interests and wide knowledge formed the background to his work on the *Orders, *A Treatise of Civil Architecture* (1759, 1768; revised as *A Treatise on the Decorative Part of Civil Architecture*, 1791). In the *Treatise*, he discussed at length the decorative accompaniments to the Orders but counselled against over-zealous ornamentation such as that exemplified by the Adam brothers' 'bad copies of indifferent antiques'. Further editions, revised and amended, appeared in the 19th century and formed the basis for even later summaries of the subject.

chamfering. Finish on stone, wood or metal in which right-angled edges are flattened, sometimes as a purely decorative device, sometimes to protect a corner from damage. *See also* waggon chamfering.

chandelle (French, candle). Decoration of the lower section of fluted columns, *pilasters or furniture legs with infilling, for example, compact foliate forms and *beading. *Chandelles* appear most commonly in 18th century French architecture and interior decoration, and are especially associated with P.*de l'Orme's *French Order in which *banding and sections of foliate infilling are alternated on columns. When *chandelles* appear on French furniture they are generally in ormolu.

Chantilly spray or **Chantilly sprig.** In ceramics, a painted motif of a stylised spray of flowers (often blue) and what appear to be grasses, wheat ears and twigs. It was first used on French porcelain made at Chantilly in the mid-18th century and taken up across Europe by factories at Mennecy, Tournai, Caughley and Derby.

chaplet. Narrow, ring-like *moulding often decorated with small beads.

Château style. *See* François I; Renaissance Revival.

Chenavard, Claude Aimé (1798-1838). French designer, decorative painter and draughtsman who was a pioneer in 19th century industrial design. Through

Sir William Chambers. Plate by Chambers used in G.L. Le Rouge's Jardins Anglo-Chinois, *1774-89.*

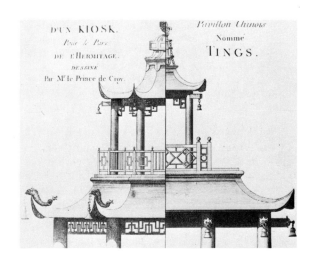

*cherub. 1) Bureau des Finances, Rouen (Seine-Maritime), France, built by Roulland le Roux, 1509-10. 2) *Spandrel on English clock face by Thomas Tompion, late 17th century. 3) *Keystone on St Mary Abchurch, City of London, by Sir Christopher Wren, 1681-86. 4) 17th century church near Volterra, Italy. 5) Cherubs with *scale-patterned fishtails supporting a roundel with Aikman's portrait of Lady Burlington, Chiswick House, London, by Lord Burlington, built 1725-29.*

the family firm run by his brother Henri, and his own official positions as a consultant designer at the Manufacture Royale de Sèvres and director of the Beauvais tapestry works (1829), Chenavard was well-placed to promote his own particular brand of *eclecticism. This he did in a series of publications, first published in parts and then as a single volume. His *Recueil de dessins* (Paris, 1828) was the first, followed by *Album de l'Ornemaniste* (12 parts, 1832 onwards; in book form, 1836); and the *Nouveau recueil de décorations intérieurs* (1833-35; in book form, 1837). Styles included the *Gothic, *Louis XV, *Assyrian, Chinese, *Egyptian, *Greek, *Renaissance, *Persian and Arabic (*see* Arabian style), and the plates showed original pieces as well as a wide selection of decorative objects designed in these styles.

chequer. The chequer produces the simplest form of *counterchange pattern, consisting of regularly placed squares of alternating colour. Its bold, geometric form made it popular in heraldry where it is also referred to as chequy, checky or chacquy. Chequer patterns appear where it is easy to mix contrasting colours in the same material, e.g. in Roman and medieval tiled floors, in *Tudor and 19th century brickwork, in inlaid *banding on 16th and 17th century furniture, and in textiles,

as the chequer is one of the simplest woven designs to achieve. The introduction of *engine-turned decoration in the late 18th century allowed chequer patterns to be easily incised on metal and ceramics.

cherub. In *Christian iconography, cherubim belong in the first hierarchy of *angels and represent Divine Wisdom. In medieval art they were often coloured gold or blue, had two or four wings and sometimes held a book. Later, cherub came to designate simply a beautiful winged child, or even a winged child's head; both of these forms were popular in ecclesiastical *Baroque ornamentation and often indistinguishable from *cupids in secular schemes. From the 16th century they appeared on monuments, pulpits and ecclesiastical embroideries. The winged child's head, with wings either outstretched or crossed downwards became an immensely popular motif in the late 17th century and was particularly favoured by Christopher Wren (1632-1723) among others. Whereas its use had been ecclesiastical, it now spread into secular decoration. It frequently decorated the eye of a *capital, supported *consoles or ornamented *spandrels. In the 17th century cherub spoons were produced in Britain and Europe with a cherub's head and neck as the *knop; clock-faces were decorated with cherubs' faces on their four corners. A cherub with puffed-out

chevron. 1) Roman mosaic pavement, Kourion, Cyprus. 2) South porch, Le Mans Cathedral (Sarthe), France, 12th century. 3) English oak and mahogany sideboard in Gothic Revival style, c.1870. 4) Woven fabric designed by Enid Marx, 1946.

cheeks was sometimes used to represent the *wind. The cross-winged cherub remained popular in funerary and memorial decoration; in the Baroque period it was sometimes echoed by a *skull flanked with bat's wings. Victorian sentimentality ensured the survival of the child angel both in ecclesiastical and in secular decoration, but particularly in funerary contexts.

chevron. One of the simplest *geometric forms composed of Vs used either singly in a vertical series or in a string to form a zigzag, the chevron appears in the earliest woven materials and as an incised ornament on ceramics. It was an early symbol of both water and lightning. The chevron was one of the first architectural ornaments within the *Anglo-Saxon style and, in a zigzag form known as the dancette, it appears as an incised *moulding enrichment in *Romanesque work. Later, the tooth-like protrusions of the pattern were decorated with *fluting or *reeding. In 17th and 18th century brickwork, it appeared as a form of coursing and it was sometimes used in relief at *cornice level to replace the rectangular *dentil. The chevron was a key motif in the 19th century *Neo-Norman style. Chip-carved ornament on furniture is often in chevron form and *Gothic Revival pieces frequently include bands of chevron inlay. In heraldry, the shape (in the form of a single, inverted, wide V) was to be found on shields from which it was adopted for the flashes on the sleeves of military uniform. The Italian Renaissance embroidery pattern known as *bargello* consists of a fluid chevron form. Chevrons were among the most favoured geometric patterns used in 1930s *Art Deco ornament.

children. In the early 17th century, the painter and engraver Jacques Stella (1596-1657) produced a series of decorative engravings, *Les Jeux et plaisirs de l'enfance*, which were later used for the decoration of both Vienna porcelain and Moustiers faïence. But it was not until the 18th century that the *putto was portrayed as a realistic, clothed child in ornamentation. F.*Boucher and other mid 18th century designers used children in decorative schemes pursuing such adult occupations as painting, gardening, building and dancing, or personifying the *Elements, *Seasons or *Months. J.B.*Huet laid down rules for the drawing of children: they should be five heads high, the thickness of the thigh should be two thirds that of the head, the knee should have the thickness of the distance between eyes and chin, the bottom of the legs and the arms should be half the thickness of the neck. Series of engravings were published of children playing games such as marbles, blind man's buff, battledore and shuttlecock, etc., and were adapted for use on delftware tiles. *Le Jeu Volant* and *Le Jeu de la gobille* by H.F. Gravelot (1699-1773) were reproduced by the engraver R.*Hancock and transfer-printed on Worcester and Bow porcelain. A growing concern with education during the 19th century produced designs showing children in the schoolroom. Scenes portraying children were often realised with great sentimentality by the Victorians. Typical of the period is the enamelled decoration on Mary Gregory glass with figures of children in opaque white on jugs and decanters made

*children. 1) School doorway, Prinsstraat, Antwerp, Belgium. 2) Sèvres biscuit porcelain figure, La Petite Fille au Tablier, from a design by F.*Boucher. 3) English wallpaper with a Kate Greenaway design showing the months of the year, 1893.*

in America by the Boston and Sandwich Glass Co. and subsequently copied in Bohemia. The wallpaper manufacturers Jeffrey & Co. of London first produced a Walter Crane children's paper in 1875 called 'The Queen of Hearts'. In the new belief that childhood might be made fun, nursery furniture, wallpapers and china with decorative designs incorporating children were produced, often (as now) derived from the work of children's book illustrators, e.g. those by Walter Crane and the Evans Toy Books of the 1870s, Kate Greenaway in the 1890s through to Mabel Lucie Attwell in the 20th century.

ch'i-lin. *See* kylin.

chimera. Creature from classical mythology that breathes fire and has the head, mane and legs of a lion, the tail of a dragon, the body of a goat, and often the wings of an eagle. It did not appear in the *bestiaries, but was adopted in the *Renaissance from such classical sources as *Pompeian wall paintings and used in *grotesque ornament. It was a popular motif in 18th century *Neo-classicism and subsequently an important *Empire and *Regency motif. T.*Hope used chimeras on the sides of arm-chairs and G.*Smith used them as supports for *console tables and *chiffoniers*. They reappeared in late 19th century buildings, on *brackets, *apronwork (beneath oriel windows) and on terracotta and rubbed brick panels.

Chinese paling or **Chinese railing.** Chinese *lattice or *fret applied to railings, gates, bridges, staircases

and balustrades; it became popular when *chinoiserie* was fashionable during the 18th century. J. Shebbeare commented in 1756 that 'at present fox hunters would be sorry to break a leg in pursuing their sport in leaping any gate that was not made in the eastern taste of little bits of wood standing in all directions.' Chinese paling was also used on furniture, e.g. to form the glazing bars on china cabinets, for bedheads, parapets, around tea-tables and trays, bookcases, chair-backs. It was copied on wallpaper, especially for the dado paper, often with a complementary design above it.

chinoiserie. Marco Polo first brought back tales of China to the West after he had travelled there overland c.1271. The land or silk route between China and Europe allowed for a limited, slow trade of easily portable textiles, and the influence of Chinese brocades and embroideries was gradually absorbed into the work of mid 14th century Italian silk weavers, sometimes incorporating Chinese motifs such as firebreathing *dragons and the phoenix-like fêng huang (*see* ho-ho bird). After 1498, when Vasco da Gama discovered the new sea route to China, imports of Chinese artefacts into Europe vastly increased, particularly the highly prized porcelain which had previously been very difficult to transport. During the 16th century, links between China and the West strengthened. Portugal and Holland set up trading stations in China and the Jesuits established missions there in 1542. By the next century the Chinese were producing large amounts of blue-and-white ware specifically for the European export market. Imports of lacquerwork also proved extremely popular. Demand soon far outstripped supply and by the early 17th century European imitations were produced: Western craftsmen wanting to decorate in the Chinese style took their patterns from authentic porcelain or lacquer pieces. A few orientally inspired designs were engraved, notably those by Valentin Sezenius in 1623 for enamelled jewellery; these include long-tailed Chinese birds and rickety buildings on stilts. Early *chinoiserie* decorations were applied to the interiors of the Rosenberg Castle, Copenhagen, between 1655 and 1668. Towards the end of the 17th century *chinoiserie* became still more fashionable: tin-glazed earthenware manufacturers at Delft, Nevers, Rouen, Marseilles, Southwark, Lambeth and Bristol all began to produce blue-and-white wares painted with *chinoiserie* motifs. There were more sources for designers to consult in the form of reliable travel books such as J.*Nieuhof's *Atlas Chinensis*, which ran into at least six editions in five years in Dutch, English, French, German and Latin and contained descriptions and engravings of the people, buildings and landscapes of China. Nieuhof included the towering pagodas hung with bells, mandarins, dragons, the archetypal chinaman with moustaches and a coolie hat, carrying an umbrella,

*Chinese paling. 1) Late 18th century English mahogany dining chair. chinoiserie. 2) Combined with Rococo ornament in A New Book of Chinese Designs by M.*Darly and G. Edwards, 1754. 3) English silver tea caddy by Paul de Lamerie, 1747. 4) English satinwood and lacquer chair, 1920s. 5) English wallpaper, c.1770. 6) English mid 19th century transfer-printed earthenware plate. 7) Le Pagode (now a cinema), rue de Babylone, Paris, early 20th century.*

and the hilly landscape about which Nieuhof commented 'there is not anything where the Chinese shew their ingenuity more than in these rocks or Artificial Hills'. A similar book, *Monumenta Illustrata* (Amsterdam, 1667), was published by A.*Kircher. The craze for japanned furniture, particularly in England and Holland, was served by manuals such as the *Treatise of Japanning and Varnishing* (1688) by J.*Stalker and G. Parker, which included a selection of suitable Chinese designs. Although the earliest *chinoiserie* designs on silver were probably those decorating the European mounts that protected the precious pieces of porcelain, Chinese motifs were soon engraved on small decorative silver pieces such as toilet sets. At the court of Louis XIV in France there was a growing taste for Chinese artefacts, mainly imported through the Compagnie des Indes. Chinese wallpapers were fashionable and provided a range of motifs. *Chinoiserie*, with its haphazard and asymmetrical decoration, offered an alternative to the principles of symmetry and proportion that had dominated the Renaissance, and it was these characteristics that fitted in with the growing movement towards the *Rococo.

However, it was a passing fashion for a distinct taste and few people would risk decorating more than one room in their houses in the style. J.*Berain included monkeys (*see singeries*), mandarins, *pagods and umbrellas in his *grotesque designs of the late 17th century, and *chinoiserie* became a frequent element in Rococo schemes. The fashion had become fully established by the 1720s and spread to all media, whereas it had previously been mainly the province of ceramics and lacquer decoration. Nearly every ornamentalist of the period produced *chinoiserie* designs; those of J.*Pillement were widely available and influential. Architects and furniture designers, for example B. *Langley and T.*Chippendale, produced complete ranges of *chinoiserie* designs as well as the ubiquitous general ornament for *cartouches, grotesque panels and *vignettes that could be easily translated on to silver, porcelain, wallpaper, marquetry, printed textiles or even used in the ornamentation of garden pavilions. Lady Mary Wortley Montagu wrote in 1740: 'sick of Grecian eloquence and symmetry or Gothic grandeur, we must all seek the barbarous gaudy gout of the Chinese.' Robert Morris in the *Architectural Remembrancer* (1751) described a cavalier attitude to the style: 'the principles are a good choice of chains and bells, and different colours of paint. As to the serpents, dragons and monkeys etc. they, like the rest of the beauties may be cut out in paper, and pasted on anywhere, or in any manner. A few laths, nailed across each other, and made black, red, blue, yellow or any other colour, or mixed with any sort of chequer work, or impropriety of ornament, completes the whole.' An additional encouragement to the use of *chinoiserie* was the growth and success of European porcelain manufacture. Decorators imitated Chinese designs such as the *chrysanthemums and peonies of the *famille rose* and *famille verte* wares, to produce, for example, Meissen *indianische Blumen* designs. *Blossom sprigs were applied to white Chantilly porcelain and *pagods were a popular form for pastille burners. The development of blue cobalt glazes, used so frequently

by Worcester, Lowestoft and Caughley, also suggested *chinoiserie* subjects, often imitating original Chinese blue-and-white designs, which were then given English names such as *Lady and Squirrel pattern, or *Long Eliza.

Despite attempts by Sir W.*Chambers to provide accurate topographical descriptions and illustration of large-scale Chinese buildings, *chinoiserie* was never adopted as a serious architectural style. Its frivolous aspect appealed to certain European monarchs and princes, who had the resources to indulge in fantastic schemes: at Drottningholm the Swedish King Adolph Friedrich built a Chinese house for his Queen with interiors painted after F.*Boucher and J.*Pillement; at Dresden, Augustus the Strong built a 'Japanese' palace (to house his porcelain collection) complete with mandarin *caryatids; Frederick the Great built a Chinese-style tea house in the grounds of his Potsdam palace, Sans Souci (1754-57); the Landgrave of Cassel attempted the creation of a *willow pattern village and Catherine the Great also commissioned a whole 'Chinese' village. The last *chinoiserie* whim on a grand scale was probably the interior of Brighton Pavilion created for the Prince Regent between 1802 and 1820. As the taste for the Rococo faded and was replaced by the clean lines of *Neo-classicism, the fashion for *chinoiserie* largely disappeared, although it lingered on throughout the 19th century for the ornamentation of fairgrounds, garden teahouses, cafés, and buildings with Chinese associations, such as the tea warehouse built by George Wightwick in Plymouth in 1848. There are many examples of *chinoiserie* garden buildings such as the pagoda and Chinese bridge designed by John Nash (1752-1835) for St James's Park, London (1814) and, in America, John Haviland's Pagoda and Labyrinthine Garden (1828) in Philadelphia.

Elements of *chinoiserie* design were revived for interior decoration in the 1920s: black and red were fashionable colours, admirably complemented by lacquered furniture. Reproduction red lacquer pieces were produced, using motifs from 18th century *drawing books, such as *The Ladies Amusement* published by Robert Sayer. Chintz and damasks with oriental themes were also popular.

chintz. From the 17th century hand-painted calicoes from India were greatly admired in Europe and imported in quantity. The East India Company was licensed to import chintz into Britain in 1631. The Dutch and French also imported chintz. Large hangings, often with a *Tree of Life design, were vastly popular in Europe: their designs consisted of a tree form sprouting rambling foliage with lush blooms, exotic fruits and, often, birds. The vivid colours and intricate patterns of Indian chintzes produced results far beyond the capability of British fabric printers and by 1700 the importation of printed fabric from India, Persia and China was forbidden, in an attempt to protect the livelihoods of English wool and silk weavers. As a result, chintz became irresistibly fashionable and there were attempts to copy Indian designs. Even stricter legislation was introduced in 1722 when no printed, painted, stained or dyed calico was allowed to be worn or used for furnishing, nor 'any stuff made of cotton or mixt therewith, which shall be printed or painted with any colour or colours or any calico stitched or flowered in foreign parts with any colour or colours or with coloured flowers.' There were similarly restrictive laws in France. As chintz motifs could not be printed or painted they were used in embroidery, particularly wool crewel work, as they had been before the new legislation. The prohibitions were lifted in France in 1759 and in England in 1774, and Indian chintz designs were once again pillaged by European textile printers who tended to use details such as sprigs, flowers and birds, rather than the whole tree designs, which were difficult to use in dress designs and complicated to print either by the woodblock method or the new plate printing (introduced c.1770). By the early 19th century the influence of Indian chintzes had waned. In the late 19th and early 20th centuries fabrics printed to accompany the *Jacobean Revival turned once again to chintz motifs, though tending to reproduce them in the more sombre colours of English crewel embroidery rather than those of the bright Indian originals. Chintz patterns have remained enduringly popular for furnishing fabrics. *See also* pines.

chip carving. One of the simplest methods of ornamenting woodwork, chip carving is achieved with a

chintz pattern on late 17th century English embroidery, wool on linen.

Thomas Chippendale. Shelves for china from The Gentleman and Cabinet Maker's Director, *1762 edition.*

chisel or gouge and consists of chipped out indentations that usually form geometric patterns, often based on a circle. It was used from the late Middle Ages until the 19th century. Chip carving is particularly suitable for softwoods which cannot be carved with more intricate patterns, and was common in northern Europe.

Chippendale, Thomas (1718-79). English furniture maker and author of one of the most famous and enduring *pattern books for British and American furniture ever produced. *The Gentleman and Cabinet Maker's Director* (1754, 1755, 1762) was intended as an advertisement for the range of household furniture produced by his firm; its 161 plates make it the first comprehensive book of furniture design, with only a few pieces that were impracticable for manufacture. The English furniture trade was at that time concentrated in one area of London (between Leicester Square and Tottenham Court Road), so the exchange of ideas, designs, carvers, apprentices was rapid and continuous. The *Director* included schemes from other English and French pattern books and possibly the work of designers other than Chippendale. Of the 310 subscribers to the first edition, 130 were cabinetmakers, carvers and joiners and among the rest were architects, plasterers, founders, painters, engravers and upholsterers. The first and second editions were identical, offering designs in the *Gothick, Chinese and 'modern' taste – an anglicised version of French *Rococo which was properly established by the publication of the *Director* although M.*Lock had presented and interpreted the complexity of Rococo design some ten years earlier. The Gothic element was provided by *tracery, *cusps, *crockets, pointed *arcading and other late medieval motifs often combined with *chinoiserie and Rococo elements. Apart from M.*Darly's chair designs of 1750-51, these were the first published designs for Gothick furniture. Chippendale's designs in the Chinese taste used angular forms and square sections with *lattice and *fretwork; cabinets and standing shelves were often surmounted with *pagodas and *bells, the whole frequently japanned black and gold.

The third edition of the *Director* appeared in weekly sets of engravings from 1759 to 1762, with the Chinese and Gothic designs dropped in favour of further Rococo designs – the 'most fashionable taste'. A French edition was published in 1762. Chippendale's designs were in competition with those of T.*Johnson and W.*Ince and J. Mayhew, who had also recently published work in the Rococo style. But a move towards *classicism is clear in this edition: *trophies of arms, *masks, *putti, *dolphins, strings of *husks, *herms, pedestals and tapering and fluted legs appear. Chippendale did not, however, publish any of the *Neoclassical furniture which he made for Robert Adam (*see* Adam style).

By the third quarter of the 18th century a large number of cabinetmakers were working in the style of the *Director*. American cabinetmakers, such as the Goddard and Townsend families, were working to Chippendale patterns, sometimes adapting the forms by adding typical American characteristics such as the block-front shape. Generally they did not make pieces in the extreme Chinese, Gothic or French styles. In Philadelphia, the centre of Colonial wealth, cabinetmakers such as Randolph Benjamin (c.1750-90) and William Savery (1721-87) evolved (particularly for

Chippendale-style English mahogany display cabinet, c.1890.

highboys and lowboys), a version of Chippendale's style sometimes known as Philadelphia Chippendale with characteristic details: bonnet or *scrolled pediments, auger *flame finials, *cabriole legs and rich carving.

To profit from the revival of interest in French Rococo during the late 1820s and 1830s, John Weale republished some Chippendale designs as *Old English and French Ornament*, first in 1833 and again in 1858. The facsimile reproductions in J.A. Heaton's *Furniture and Decoration in England during the Eighteenth Century* (1892) included the 'choicest examples' of Chippendale, Adam, Richardson, Hepplewhite, Sheraton, Pergolesi, etc., and their purpose as stated by Heaton was to 'restore and copy' the furniture that 'our great-grandfathers bought and valued'. The endurance of the Chippendale style was noted by the magazine *Decoration* in December 1886: 'Chippendale, the cabinet-maker, is more potent than Garrick, the actor. The vivacity of the latter no longer charms (save in Boswell); the chairs of the former still render rest impossible in a hundred homes.' A similar line was pursued in the introduction by Charles M. Stow to a reprint of Chippendale, Hepplewhite and Sheraton designs published in America in 1938: 'Furniture that is made and sold today follows one of two sorts of designs: either it is modern, with no touch of the past in its ornamentation, or it is traditional, and traditional means, in the majority of cases, Chippendale, Hepplewhite or Sheraton.' He was of the opinion that a modern reprint of the relevant pattern books would help bring elegance into the American home.

Christian motifs were, in the Early Church, based upon a repertoire of pagan and mythological themes, varying according to the cultures from which early converts came. Until Constantine proclaimed the Peace of the Church in 313 AD, overtly Christian symbols and representations of Christ were avoided because of the risk of persecution and instead the *peacock, *dove, *fish and *palm frond were taken from *classical sources and used as Christian motifs. The fish was particularly favoured because it was a symbol of baptism (as it cannot live without water). Pre-Christian cults lent other iconographic features and provided useful disguises: classical winged *Victories reappeared as *angels; the image of Helios from solar pantheism could be reinterpreted as Christ upon a chariot; the *Bacchic cult was echoed in the metaphor of Christ as the vine, 'I am the vine, ye are the branches' (St John 15:1). In addition, the Old and New Testaments themselves provided a wealth of themes and symbols.

Early Christian art was largely confined to funerary work, especially sarcophagi, upon which *friezes or framed episodes or scenes were carved. The first considerable body of Christian ornament developed during the 4th and 5th centuries in the *Byzantine Church, appearing in architectural decoration, church furnishings and artefacts, mosaics, metalwork and illuminated manuscripts. Gradually, different strands of Christian art mixed, for example, the Eastern styles of the Coptic Church combined with the imagery of the *Celtic Church. In *Romanesque and *Gothic church ornament, everyday life and activities began to be depicted alongside animals from the *bestiaries and *plant and abstract ornament. Early illustrated texts helped to establish the Christian ornamental vocabulary, and the advent of printing in the mid 15th century and the development of woodcut techniques further disseminated it. Bibles and illustrated compendia of bible stories such as the *Biblia Pauperum* formed a large part of the output of early printers and engravers. By the *Renaissance the ornamental vocabulary of Christianity was well established and much of the symbolism was elaborated and extended.

Many plants have specific Christian meanings, often adopted from earlier pagan cultures: the *oak, an important element in Druidic worship, became a symbol for Christ and the Virgin Mary; the Roman palm, symbol of victory, became the martyr's palm, signifying triumph over death. The Bible provided a large number of symbolic plants, often with complex significance, for example the almond, as a symbol of the Virgin Mary and the unfertilised producing of fruit, from '. . . the rod of Aaron for the house of Levi was budded, and brought forth buds and bloomed blossoms, and yielded almonds' (Numbers 17:1-11). The tripartite clover leaf signifies the Trinity; the columbine flower's similarity to a dove resulted in its use as a symbol of the Holy Ghost; the red spot on a cyclamen flower signifies the bleeding sorrow in the Virgin Mary's heart, the *lily symbolises her purity; the *pomegranate, having many seeds within one skin, suggests the Church (or sometimes chastity); evergreen plants represent everlasting life.

Animals, birds and insects are imbued with similar symbolism: the goldfinch, fond of eating thistles, is an accepted allusion to the Crown of Thorns and thus the Passion of Christ; the cock alludes to Peter's Denial of Christ; the *pelican piercing her breast to feed her young appears as a symbol of the sacrifice of Christ on the cross; the frequently used *lamb usually symbolises Christ himself, as in references such as 'Behold, the lamb of God, which taketh away the sins of the world' (St John 1:29). The *bestiaries also provided a wealth of both real and imaginary animals.

Numerical configurations with Christian significance include three for the Trinity, the four *Evangelists, the seven Deadly Sins, the twelve *Apostles. Geometrical forms were also used: the circle of Eternity, a triangle for the Trinity, the oval of the *vesica piscis.

Christian *inscriptions and *cyphers include the Greek letters Alpha and Omega, from the biblical reference, 'I am Alpha and Omega, the beginning and the end, saith the Lord' (Revelation 22:13); Chi and Rho, the first two letters of the word Christ in Greek; INRI, *Iesus Nazaremus Rex Iudecorum*, meaning Jesus of Nazareth King of the Jews (St John 19:19-20). IHS was originally a monogram for the name Jesus formed by abbreviating the corresponding Greek word; later, explanations of the three letters as the initials of separate words became very common, among them the Greek 'Iesous Hemeteros Sotor' [Jesus Our Saviour], the Latin *Iesus Hominum Salvator* [Jesus Saviour of Men], a medieval motto *In Hoc Signo*, alluding to the saying 'In this sign ye shall conquer', and the Jesuit interpretation, *Iesum Habemus Socium* [We Have Jesus as our Companion].

Heraldic usage of Christian motifs includes the bleeding *heart and the *Instruments of the Passion within *escutcheons. The *ecclesiastical hat (established in the late 15th century as a sign of rights within a papal cavalcade) and the mitre, given to papal legates, were more worldly signs of hierarchical privileges within the Church. *Personifications such as the *Virtues and Vices sometimes appear, as do, occasionally, representations of the *Seasons in which the renewal of life (the Resurrection) is equated with Spring following Winter.

The Victorians used Christian stories as ornament in secular contexts in much the same way as classical legend had been used in the 18th century, e.g. the Coalbrookdale ironworks produced wall drinking fountains with reliefs of Moses and the Bulrushes (Exodus 2:3) or Christ and the Woman of Samaria (John 4:5-30), etc. The Great Exhibition catalogue (London, 1851) illustrates a sideboard decorated with a carving of the Return of the Prodigal Son (Luke 15:1). *See also* mermaid; water.

chrysanthemum. Flower imported into Europe from the East. It was a popular motif in Chinese and subseqently in Japanese art, particularly on ceramics, and a symbol of longevity to Taoists. It also represented Autumn for the Chinese. It was adopted from those sources for use on Western ceramics. Johann Friedrich Böttger (1682-1719) decorated his early white porcelain with applied chrysanthemums in imitation of Fukien *blanc de chine*. Formalised into a *rosette, the Japanese chrysanthemum became the *kikumon, sometimes called the Japanese pie ornament when imitated in *japonaiserie*.

Churrigueresque style. A manic late *Baroque decorative style concocted in the first half of the 18th century by the three Churriguera brothers from Barcelona and their followers Pedro de Ribera and Narciso Tomé. Architectural details and motifs were contorted and elaborated beyond recognition. Churrigueresque decoration, widely popular in Spain, later spread to the Spanish-speaking parts of South and Central America, largely via buildings endowed by the Roman Catholic Church. In Latin America it mingled with the Amerindian liking for pattern, texture and colour to produce some extraordinary results. The style also reached the Spanish-influenced states of America: Florida, New Mexico, Arizona and California. It even saw a revival in the California Building, which was designed by B.G. Goodhue (1869-1924) for the Panama-California Exposition of 1915 in *Spanish Colonial Revival style.

cilery. 18th and 19th century term for carved decoration of flowers or foliage applied to stone or wooden *capitals.

cinerarium lid. A variant on the *Neo-classical *urn or the more bulky *sarcophagus which was popular in the *Greek Revival and used as a *finial for gateposts, as *acroteria and as an ornament on parapets.

cinquecento. Term applied by late 19th century art historians to works of the Italian High *Renaissance dating from the 16th century. More popularly the phrase came to denote the *Renaissance Revival style in late 19th century interiors.

cinquefoil. Five-lobed *tracery (*see* foil). In heraldry the cinquefoil is called a fraise, frase, fraisier, quint or quintfoil.

cippus (Latin, post or stake). Small low column, square or round, sometimes without base or *capital, but usually bearing an inscription. It was used by the Romans as a landmark or sepulchral monument. In the mid 18th and early 19th centuries the cippus was a popular decorative form, mainly used in funerary decoration (*see* death and mourning), e.g. for tombs, mourning jewellery, but also for clock-cases.

claustra. Term used at the beginning of the 20th century to denote geometrical designs in early reinforced-concrete work usually on ornamental walls, e.g. as a parapet or screen.

classicism. The forms and ornamentation of *Graeco-Roman classicism have been revived constantly and since the Italian *Renaissance have provided the theoretical basis of architectural form. The approach to classicism was determined by what was known of Greek and Roman antiquity at any particular period: for example, the *Byzantine and *Romanesque styles adopted a range of motifs based upon the revealed fragments and monuments of the eastern and southern Mediterranean. With the dissemination in the

*classicism. 1) From the Comte *de Caylus's* Recueil d'antiquités, *1752-67. 2, 3) State Capitol, Austin, Texas, architect Elijah E. Myers, 1882-88. 4) Palazzo Chiericati, Vicenza, Italy, designed by A.*Palladio, 1550, completed late 17th century (pinnacles and statues not part of original design). 5) From A.*Quellin's Afbeelding van 't stadt huys van Amsterdam, 1665-69. 6) *Architrave moulding at the Villa Adriana, Tivoli, Italy, from Oeuvres de Philibert de l'Orme, 1648.*

Renaissance of printed illustrated treatises and *pattern books, the monuments of Rome and the Roman Empire became more accessible. Engravings of classical ruins were popular in the 16th century, as in the work of E.*Vico. Soon, the rapid dissemination of the classical vocabulary led to distortion or reinterpretation, notably in the *Mannerist style and its northern variants (*see* Flemish Mannerism). Classicism in the 16th century was still challenged by, and sometimes combined with, the *Gothic but by the early part of the 17th century designers were returning to the originals and there was a new regard for authenticity. I.*Jones visited Italy in 1613-14 and this experience, combined with his knowledge of works such as A.*Palladio's *Quattro Libri* produced a profound classicising effect on English architecture. In France, the influence of the Italian artists working for Francois I at *Fontainebleau was considerable, and classicism held sway from the mid 16th century onwards. The style was retained for exteriors well into the 18th century, long after the *Rococo had invaded interiors. In the Netherlands Jacob van Campen (1595-1657) adopted the style in works of pure classical character. In America classicism took the form of a colonial version of English *Palladianism. During the 18th century the classical vocabulary was enriched by increasing knowledge about its

sources. Towards the mid century, Greek classical forms, in particular, were sought out, leading to the *Greek Revival. The later phases of classicism are known as *Neo-classicism since they reflect the full gamut of the originals, often accurately reproducing ancient structures or artefacts.

By the middle of the 19th century, however, the veracity of classical sources was again obscured. Walter Crane observed, 'the elegant lines and limbs of quasi-classical couches and chairs . . . had grown gouty and clumsy in the hands of Victorian upholsterers.' Late 19th and early 20th century classicism followed two directions. The *Queen Anne Revival was a reinterpretation of earlier domestic architecture in which the classical elements were used asymmetrically. Alternatively, the so-called Free Classicism was a much wilder version, developing at the extreme into the *Baroque Revival. At the St Louis International Exhibition of 1904 the British Pavilion was a recreated version of the Orangery at Kensington Palace and the French Pavilion was based on the Grand Trianon, originally built in 1687 (by Jules Hardouin-Mansart) at Versailles.

Much *Modernist decoration in the inter-war years was loosely based upon classical forms; some ostensibly unornamented buildings incorporated a panel or two with classical motifs, commemorating rather than fully adopting the style. Large-scale commercial and residential buildings designed at this time in America often used isolated classical motifs, such as *urns, a pair of *griffins, or a *swag, set into the stone or brickwork to enliven an otherwise unrelieved surface. Although the general design was plain, such ornament as was used fell into an *Adam style or loose classical vocabulary. A stricter version of classicism was adopted for Italian and German fascist buildings and post-war Eastern European civic architecture. More recently architects have trimmed buildings with classically derived motifs, in the so-called *Post-Modernist phase. *See also* Beaux-Arts style; 'Wrenaissance'.

claw. The claw foot, like the *paw foot and *hoof foot, was used on ancient Greek and Roman furniture. A *dragon's claw or *eagle's talon clutching a ball appears in Chinese art, possibly deriving from the legendary image of the Chinese dragon holding a flaming pearl of wisdom. Ball and claw feet (or talon and ball feet) are a useful device: the claw can be delicately modelled, while the ball provides a steady base for furniture or metalwork pieces; fine examples appear in late 15th and 16th century French gold and silver, and from the early to mid 18th century on English furniture legs. Claws occasionally appear at the base of *herms and sheathed *caryatids in *Mannerist design. Sugar tongs and coal tongs sometimes have claw ends well-suited to the grasping action required. *See also* monopodia.

cloisonné (French, partitioned). In masonry, this form of patterning, achieved by framing stone blocks with brick to give a geometric and polychrome effect, was first mastered in *Byzantine ecclesiastical architecture. It was also found in Carolingian and *Romanesque work, and was favoured by the *Anglo-Saxon

and northern Germanic cultures. In enamel, *cloisonné* produces a glittering, jewelled effect through the use of a gold ground and frame for a design infilled with enamel.

cloudband. Narrow meandering bands of cloud motifs used in Chinese and then in Persian and Turkish ornament, e.g. on carpets, tiles or illuminations, often as a convenient device for unifying sections of decoration. When associated with legendary heroes, religious figures or *angels, it alludes to miraculous powers. It is sometimes formalised into a *meander pattern.

cloven foot. *See* hoof foot.

club. Attribute of Hercules (*see* Herculean decoration). It is often included in *military decorative schemes.

coat of arms. Heraldic insignia deriving from painted surcoats that knights wore over their mail from the beginning of the 13th century. Strictly speaking, coat of arms should refer only to what is borne on a *shield, but it is generally accepted to include both the *helmet (usually shown above it) and the crest. *See also* achievement of arms; heraldic decoration.

Coburg pattern. *See* King's shape.

Cochin, Charles-Nicholas, the Elder (1688-1754). Engraver and publisher who engraved the work of J.A.*Watteau, A. Coypel and B.*Toro, and a quantity of *Rococo ornament including *cartouches, *vignettes, frames, etc.

Cochin, Charles-Nicholas, the Younger (1715-90). The most famous of the Cochin family, and a promulgator of *Neo-classicism, suggesting to craftsmen that 'they will find they need not substitute grasses

claw. 1) Design for Syon House, Isleworth, Middlesex from Robert Adam's Works in Architecture, *1773-79.*
cloisonné masonry. 2) Cathedral of Monreale, Sicily, late 12th century.

and other paltry prettinesses for the modillions, dentils and other virile ornaments.' He published, in association with J.C. Bellicard (1726-86), *Observations sur les antiquités de la ville d'Herculaneum* (Paris, 1754, 1756, 1757; London, 1753, 1756), which provided a selection of everyday utensils that subsequently became motifs for ornament (*see* Herculaneum). He also published ornament such as *Attributs et Trophées de Jardinages* (1771) and made contributions to the development of ornamental typefaces. *See also* personifications; Virtues and Vices.

cock. Motif in Scandinavian, *Celtic, oriental and *Christian art. The Vikings used it as a warring ensign. In *classical ornament, a cock is sometimes depicted drawing the chariot of *Mercury; it may also represent lust. Christian iconography uses it as an allusion to the Denial of Christ by the apostle Peter. Associated with the dawn and therefore the rising sun, it appears in *Apolline decoration: C.*Le Brun used it in ornament for Louis XIV. As a symbol of *day the cock was occasionally used in the decoration of timepieces. Le Brun also used a *French Order, which included the *fleur-de-lis and the cock, for *capitals in the Cour Carré at the Louvre (1671). The cock had long been a national symbol of France, but during the Revolution it was used as an emblem of the new order: e.g. faïence plates decorated with a crowing cock were inscribed '*Je Chante pour la Liberté*' (*see also* revolutionary ornament).

cockatrice. *See* basilisk.

cock beading. A continuous strip of semi-circular *bead moulding used on furniture, e.g. to edge drawers, etc., from the mid 18th century to the early 19th century. When several strips are used together, an effect similar to *reeding is produced.

coffering. Recessed panels, usually ornamented, sunk into a ceiling, soffit, vault or dome to form an overall pattern. Classical Roman precedents were provided by the Basilica of Maxentius and the Pantheon, both much imitated by architects from the *Renaissance onwards. A.*Palladio greatly admired the Pantheon, built 27 BC, the only Roman building dating from this era to survive intact into the 16th century. The motif was taken up widely by 18th century *Palladians

cock. French faïence soup plate, Nevers, dated 1789.

and *Neo-classicists, appearing, for example, in the entrance hall of W.*Kent's Holkham Hall, Norfolk (1734 onwards). Because of its richness and heaviness, coffering was generally applied to large or important spaces – entrances, halls or principal rooms. In the 19th century the application of coffering sometimes became overpowering: a contemporary observer commented of the Great Booking Hall at Euston Station (demolished) designed by Philip Charles Hardwick (1822-92) that it would 'cause the lower part of the apartment to appear based and unfinished.' Coffering was much used in the early 20th century *Baroque Revival.

coffin-end. A *finial in the shape of a coffin for spoons and forks occurring solely in America in the late 18th and early 19th centuries.

coin moulding or **money pattern.** A repeating pattern of overlapping discs used horizontally or vertically, e.g. on *brackets. Like *guilloche and *scale patterns, it tends to occur in heavy *classical styles.

When it occurs in mould-blown or pressed glass, this type of patterning is sometimes known as eye and scale.

Colling, James Kellaway (1816-1905). Influential writer on *Gothic Revival ornament and an admirer of

coffering. 1) Basilica of Maxentius, Forum, Rome, begun 306 A D. 2) Interior of dome, Chiswick House, London, by Lord Burlington, 1725-29.

coin moulding. Door of Midland Bank, Poultry, City of London, by Sir Edwin Lutyens, 1924 (completed 1939).

colonnette. 1) Campanile (Leaning Tower), Pisa, begun 1174. 2) Early 19th century cast-iron porch, Brooklyn Heights, New York.

the work of E.-E.*Viollet-le-Duc. His books include *Gothic Ornaments* (1846-50), *Art Foliage for Sculpture and Decoration* (1865) and *Examples of English Medieval Foliage and Coloured Decoration* (1874). Colling's preoccupation with the importance of the underlying geometry of foliate forms influenced various subsequent strands of decoration, including the work of L.H.*Sullivan and Frank Lloyd Wright in America. In *Art Foliage* (available in America in the early 1870s), he wrote extensively on the *diaper, and his emphasis on 'upright composition . . . flowing upwards and downwards' anticipated the natural forms to be used in *Art Nouveau and *Jugendstil. His examples were drawn from the most important English cathedrals and included tiles, rood screens and enamels as well as purely architectural ornament. He also devised new patterns in the Gothic style.

Collinot, Eugène-Victor (d 1882). French ceramicist who collaborated with the designer Adalbert de Beaumont (d 1869) in the publication of oriental designs. The *Recueil de dessins pour l'art et l'industrie* (1859) offered a selection of Venetian, *Arabian, *Islamic, Chinese and Japanese examples. Later, Collinot produced another series, the *Encyclopédie des Arts Décoratifs de l'Orient* (for which he used de Beaumont's name posthumously as co-author) beginning with *Ornaments de la Perse* (1880) and following with *Ornaments de la Chine* (1882), *Ornaments Arabes* (1883), *Ornaments du Japon* (1883), *Ornaments Turcs* (1883), *Ornaments Vénitiens, Hindous, Russes, etc.,* (1883).

Colonial Revival. This American style ranges from faithful replicas of *Georgian and *American Colonial or *Adam style architecture, to the free interpretation of classical-style buildings as in the *Queen Anne Revival and the *Stick and *Shingle styles of the 1880s and 1890s. The Colonial Revival in its essentials may include a *pedimented porch, a *fanlight and sash windows and became popular from the late 19th century, remaining, like its English counterpart *Neo-Georgian, a standard type of house design until the

J.K. Colling. 'Panel decoration' from his Art Foliage for Sculpture and Decoration, *1865.*

present. The style was disseminated by a large number of well-illustrated scholarly books, many produced in the early decades of the 20th century.

Colonna, Francesco de. *See* Hypnerotomachia Poliphili.

colonnette. Miniature column, of which several are often used in a cluster as ornament on small-scale architectural features such as clerestories, windows and dormers in *Byzantine, late *Gothic, and French *Renaissance styles. Colonnettes also appear on furniture, most frequently in conjunction with *chinoiserie and *Gothic Revival motifs.

Columbani, Placido (b c.1744). Italian designer who worked in England using the ornamental vocabulary of the *Adam style, e.g. *pateras, *husks, *anthemions and *vases. He collaborated with J.*Crunden on *The Chimney-piece Maker's Daily Assistant* (1766). He compiled various *pattern books: *A New Book of Ornaments* (1775), covering designs 'commonly executed in stucco, wood and painting' of the kind typically used on satinwood furniture; *Vases and Tripods* (c.1775), a rather mediocre selection of patterns for these two highly fashionable forms; and *Capitals, Friezes and Corniches* (1776), which was republished by J.A. Heaton in his collection of facsimiles, *Furniture and Decoration in England during the Eighteenth Century* (1892).

column. Primarily a structural form, the column also appears as a purely decorative device in architecture, on furniture and wherever *architectural motifs are

*Placido Columbani. Engraving of *frieze from his* Capitals, Friezes and Corniches, *1776.*

used in the applied arts. Even as decoration the column often conforms to one of the five *Orders. Decorated and ornamental variants include *atlantes,
*banded column, *caryatid, *cippus, *colonnette,
*columna rostrata, *herm, *Osiris pillar, *persian,
*pilaster and *spiral column.

columna rostrata or **rostral column.** This was
originally a Roman monument erected to commemorate naval victory, taking its name from the *rostra* or
prow of a captured ship with which it was embellished.
There is a famous example dating from 260 BC in
Rome. More recently, it has appeared wherever *classical Roman styles have enjoyed a revival and has been
used with a more general maritime or naval significance, e.g. monument to Admiral John Baker in
Westminster Abbey, London (1716), and the pair of
ornamental lighthouses designed by Thomas de Tho-
mon (1754-1813) which stand at the divide of the River
Neva in Leningrad (1806). Rostral columns also appeared as a motif in late 19th and early 20th century
commercial decoration where a business depended
on sea trade, as on the façade of Liberty's store in
London. In Paris, where the ship is the emblem of
the city, the columna rostrata was adopted as the
form for lamp standards in the Place de la Concorde
and near the Opéra.

Colossal Order. *See* Giant Order.

combed decoration or **feathered decoration.** Zigzag,
wavy, festooned or feathery patterns either in glass
or on ceramic slipware. In glass-making, threads of
opaque glass are rolled into the molten body and the
surface is then combed or dragged. Combed decoration appeared on Egyptian core-made vessels
c.1450-1350 BC, on Greek vases c.400-100 BC, and was
revived by 16th century Italian glass manufacturers
(*vetro a pettine*). It later appeared in Victorian Nailsea-
type glass. In ceramics, contrasting slips are worked
into patterns with a brush or stick; the technique was
widely used from the 16th century, especially on folk
pottery, and was most common in the late 17th and

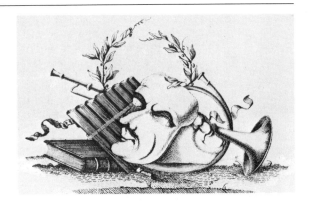

Comedy and Tragedy masks. 1) From W. Richardson's A New Book of
Trophies, *late 18th century. 2) Comédie Française, Paris, rebuilt 1900.
3) Medallion by Hildreth Meière, Radio City Music Hall, New York, c.1940.*

*columna rostrata. 1) 19th century iron light fitting, Place de l'Opéra,
Paris. 2) World War I naval memorial in Plymouth, Devon.*

early 18th centuries. A similar combing technique is
used to produce certain types of marbled paper.

Comedy and Tragedy masks. Conventional emblem
of drama. Masks, one of the attributes of the *Muses
of Comedy (Thalia) and Tragedy (Melpomene), were
used in classical Greek drama to denote the spirit or
type of character played. They were originally introduced to enable actors to play more than one part
and also helped to amplify the voice. In Roman art,
theatrical masks, usually simplified to comic and tragic,
appeared in the wall-paintings of theatres, but also in
private houses, as seen in Pompeii. Since the *Renaissance, this motif, often combined with ancient
instruments such as pipes and *cymbals, has been
widely used in a theatrical context both on buildings
(theatres, music halls, cinemas) and on related ephemera such as posters, tickets and commemorative portraits. Sometimes referred to as scenic masks in the
late 18th and early 19th centuries.

commedia dell'arte. Characters from a form of Italian theatre called *commedia dell'arte* first appeared in ornament in late 16th century Venice (the home of some of the best troupes), either enamelled on glass or as blown glass models made at Murano. Although the numbers of characters in a troupe varied, the most identifiable figures are: Pantalone, the Venetian merchant with dark cloak, long beard, thin red legs and Turkish slippers; the Doctor from Bologna (often called Doctor Gratiano) in a black costume – a short belted tunic over a wide, flowing cape, sometimes with a wide-brimmed felt hat; Harlequin, the comic in a diamond-chequered costume, carrying a wooden sword or stick; Brighella, the villain with an upward-pointing beard and a knife; Pulcinella, who has a hooked nose, hump-back and fat belly (the precursor of the puppet *Punch); the boasting Spanish captain, fashionably dressed with long hair, tricorn hat and sword; Pedrolino or Pierrot (a mainly French development, frequently painted by J.-A.*Watteau) with a white powdered face, wearing a white wide-collared smock and flapping trousers; the much-admired and lovelorn heroine, often called Isabella; the servant-confidante, Columbine.

Although *commedia dell'arte* was played all over Europe the decoration was usually taken from engraved sources: J.*Callot's series of 32 plates published in 1621, *Balli di Sfessania*, was used by Johann Schaper (1621-70) for the figures enamelled on his *Schwarzlot* glass; J.L. Sponsel's *Théâtre des Comédiens Italiens* (1719) was engraved at the Court of Augustus the Strong in Dresden; François Joullain provided illustrations after C.A. Coypel for Luigi Riccoboni's *Histoire du théâtre italien*, which further developed the costumes into familiar types. *Commedia dell'arte* figures occasionally appeared on marquetry and Venetian lacquered furniture, but were most popular as small-scale sculpture in porcelain. Those modelled by J.J. Kändler for Meissen during the 1730s and 1740s were extremely popular and copied by porcelain factories all over Europe. They were then imitated in cheaper, salt-glazed stoneware and earthenware but the fashion had virtually disappeared by the 1760s. T.*Chippendale regarded *commedia dell'arte* figures as a suitable *Rococo subject and incorporated them in designs for a chimneypiece and pier glass.

commemorative decoration. Royal portraits (in Britain, Charles II, William and Mary, and Queen Anne) were used to ornament plates from the mid 17th century, e.g. on Toft ware (slip-decorated Staffordshire earthenware) and English delftware. However, from the end of the 18th century improvements in communications meant that news of nationally important events and people travelled faster and wider, resulting in a great increase in commemorative decoration, at first mainly on ceramic objects, to celebrate royal occasions and personages, military victories and heroes, statesmen, disasters, new building and engineering achievements. As newspapers reached an even wider public, other events, even murders, were commemorated, e.g. the infamous Red Barn Murder of Maria Marten after which models of the barn were produced. New techniques of mass production meant that commemorative ware could be produced fast and at low

commedia dell'arte. 1) Pierrot from Luigi Riccoboni's Histoire du théâtre italien, *1728. 2) German porcelain figure of Harlequin made at Kloster-Veilsdorf, 1764-65.*

prices for a mass market. Wedgwood's creamware, developed in the early 1760s, and Mason's ironstone, which first appeared in 1809, were both well suited to the making of cheap commemorative pieces. Transfer-printing on ceramics was invented in 1756, allowing two men to equal the output of one hundred hand-decorators. Commemorative wallpaper and fabric were also produced by printing. By 1848, ceramic printing in several colours was possible. Commemorative ceramic figures were cast instead of modelled and medals were cast in metal. Once railway travel had made holidays accessible to a large number of people, the souvenir trade developed enormously and a vast range of commemorative objects was produced. Commemorative roller-printed textiles and stevengraphs (silk pictures woven on a Jacquard loom) appeared during the 19th century. *See also* topographical decoration.

commerce. Since Roman times, commerce has been represented by the classical symbols of the *caduceus (attribute of *Mercury, protector of merchants and traders) or the *cornucopia (abundance and prosperity), or by both together. Mercury himself, or his winged helmet, may also appear. These motifs appear on buildings of a general commercial nature, such as

*commerce. Head of *Mercury and wings on P.&O. Building, Trafalgar Square, London, architect A.T. Boulton, 1907.*

stock exchanges, customs houses, banks and markets. The importance of trade in national fortunes and its vulnerability at times of war have led to personifications of *Liberty and *Peace sometimes being used in combination with the *Continents (or corners of the *globe) to emphasise the international aspect of commerce. *Marine and *riparine motifs are reminders that until recently most commercial traffic was water-borne. In the *American Builders' Companion* (1806), A.*Benjamin suggested that a *trophy of commerce be constructed from 'the anchor and rudder of a ship, bales, trunks, cornucopias and other articles of commerce'.

More specific commercial decoration generally consists of motifs denoting particular trades: guilds, trade companies or individual businesses have most commonly been represented by symbols made up from their tools or by elaborate re-workings of medieval pictorial shop signs. The important role played by merchants and the guilds in financing late medieval ecclesiastical buildings led to the incorporation of appropriate emblems of a secular nature in the ornament of churches and chapels. This also extended to buildings under their patronage, schools, almshouses, etc.; *heraldic devices, both of individuals and of merchant companies, were used on *corbels, *capitals, roof *bosses, etc. Buildings concerned with trade in a single product often made extensive use of

*commerce. 1) *Triumphal arch, Rouen, c.1837. 2) East River Savings Bank, Rockefeller Center, New York, 1930s. 3) Frieze of *putti, 123-127 Cannon Street, City of London, architect H. Huntly Gordon, 1895.*

communications. New York Telephone Company, 140 West Street, architects Voorhees, Gmelin & Walker, 1926.

the appropriate motif: e.g. *festoons, *friezes, ornamental ironwork and roundels incorporated bundles of *wheat on corn exchanges, or *hops on hop exchanges and brewery buildings.

During the periods of *classical revival, appropriate themes were drawn from antiquity, e.g. an 18th century scheme for the ceiling of the Draper's Company in the City of London included *Minerva (as patroness of household crafts) in its depiction of spinning and weaving, while the Custom House, New York (by Cass Gilbert, 1907) is ornamented with the head of Mercury, used forty-four times, and depictions of the various races of man.

The use of the manufactured product itself both as an ornamental motif and as an advertisement, became widespread at the end of the 19th and into the 20th century, e.g. the tyres on the Michelin building in London, gramophone needles on the RCA Victor record company's skyscraper in New York. More recently company logos have become important and graphically sophisticated expressions of corporate images. *See also* bee; columna rostrata.

communications. In the early 20th century, a vocabulary of ornament evolved representing the passage of air waves or wire-borne information to symbolise the telegraph and the telephone. The ornament of buildings housing telephone exchanges, radio stations or other centres of communications made full use of such motifs as telegraph wires and *wavescroll forms.

console. 1) 81 Stoke Newington Church Street, London, 1734. 2) Console table, Chiswick House, London, 1725-29.

Even the *grapevine, with its connotations of spreading the word, was used on the headquarters of the Bell telephone company in New York, the Barclay Vesey Building, built 1926 by Voorhees, Gmelin & Walker. Symbols of *time may also be included to allude to the speed with which information passes by these methods. The winged helmet (sometimes with the head) of *Mercury and the *caduceus are occasionally used.

compasses or **dividers.** Instruments of measurement which are common motifs in schemes of *marine decoration and on maps. Compasses also appear as an attribute of Astronomy and Geometry (two of the *Liberal Arts), Maturity (one of the *Ages of Man), and *Justice – hence their appearance in the decoration of objects produced in the course of the French Revolution. *See also* masonic; muses; revolutionary ornament.

Composite Order. *See* Orders.

congelated decoration. *See* icicle; rustication.

console. Ornamental *bracket composed of a *scroll or *volute. *Mannerist examples are often highly exaggerated.
   A console table has one or more legs in the shape of a console supporting it against a wall.

Continents. The earliest imagery of the Continents was taken from Roman coinage, the imperial capital cities, Rome, Constantinople and Alexandria representing, respectively, Europe, Asia and Africa. In the medieval period the Continents were used in religious art, with the three Magi frequently personifying the known continents. The discovery of America, and the publication of Amerigo Vespucci's account *Mundus Novus* (1503), which was rapidly translated into many languages and editions, added the fourth continent to the *Renaissance use of the theme. It reassumed a secular significance from use in cartography and instruments of navigation (the four Continents sometimes replacing the four *Winds, or cardinal directions) to allusions of worldly influence and power in the houses of great dignitaries or at court. 16th century engravings, notably those from C.*Ripa's *Iconologia*, suggested female personifications and the attributes were little altered over the following centuries: Europe, as Queen of the West, had a great horse, and the

symbols of arts and sciences, temporal authority and warfare; Asia was a Turkish princess, with a *camel, a turban or headdress and a censer; Africa, a negress, wore an *elephant headpiece and was accompanied by a *cornucopia, scorpion, snake and *lion; America was represented by an American Indian, bow and arrow, feather headdress and *crocodile. Near contemporary variants, such as that by Martin de Vos (1532-1603), engraved by A. Collaert II (1550-1618), placed Africa upon a crocodile (with an *obelisk in the distance), Europe holds grapes and America is seated on an armadillo. The theme was adopted by the Jesuits in the early 17th century, symbolising their missionary intent. In the 18th century the Continents became a

*continents. 1) Africa, 16th century ornamental panel by Marcus Geerardts. 2) America from C.*Ripa's Iconologia, 1611. 3) Africa on Liverpool Town Hall by John Wood the Elder of Bath, 1749-54. 4) India on a Doulton fountain in the People's Park, Glasgow, 1888.*

standard theme for table ornament, recommended for the dessert course (according to contemporary cookbooks) and sometimes holding receptacles for jellies or sweetmeats (as in a set of Frankenthal figures of c.1765). The theme is used in glass (Bohemian enamelled glass) and silverware as well as porcelain. Meissen used designs by G.-B.*Göz and produced a number of variants on the theme; the Chelsea factory followed them by showing the Continents as *putti. The Nymphenburg factory produced a set of male Continents, also as table settings, c.1763-67. The Ripa iconography was still appearing on mid 18th century tin-glazed earthenware from Frankfurt-am-Main. The subject was also popular for textiles (toile de Jouy, c.1789) but in the 19th century it moved into the realm of public sculpture as a suitable ornament for municipal and government buildings, with its imperial associations. Australasia was a late addition, although discovered in 1771, and often excluded for reasons of symmetry. In the Victorian era Canada, South Africa, India and Australia often replaced the four conventional Continents. As late as 1936 the Copenhagen porcelain factory produced a series of five langorous female personifications of the Continents.

Copland, Henry (fl 1738-c.1753). Furniture designer and engraver who contributed greatly to the development of the *Rococo in England. His first published designs appeared in A New Book of Ornament (1746) and included *cartouche ornament and *rocaille. In 1752 he collaborated with M.*Lock and published another book of the same title containing not only cartouches

corbel. 1) Llanthony Priory, Gwent, 1175-1230. 2) Church of La Trinité, Falaise (Calvados), France, 15th century. 3) Corbel table on the Huis van de Markgraaf, Antwerp, Belgium, 19th century.

Henry Copland. From A New Book of Ornament, *1746.*

and Rococo details, but also some complete designs for woodcarvers: mirrors, tables, sconces, chandeliers, girandoles and stands. This was arguably the most important collection of Rococo designs ever published in English. Copland supplied six previously worked plates of chairs with Rococo *strapwork backs for R.*Manwaring's The Chair-Maker's Guide (1766) and is thought to have worked with T.*Chippendale on some of the designs for The Gentleman and Cabinet Maker's Director (1754, 1755, 1762). His first book was available in America before the Revolution.

copy book. See inscription.

coquillage (French, shell). See rocaille; shells.

corbeil or **corbeille** (French, basket). 18th century term for a popular contemporary motif: a carved *basket filled with fruit or flowers.

corbel. A block, usually of stone, sometimes of brick or iron, supporting a beam or rib in the upper structure of a building (e.g. roof or vault) either internally or externally. Most commonly found in *Romanesque and *Gothic architecture in which the feature first became established, corbels may be plain but are often carved or moulded with *masks or *grotesque masks of humans or animals.

A corbel table is a series of corbels placed just below the eaves.

corbel ring. *See* annulet.

Corinthian Order. *See* Orders.

corn. *See* barley; husbandry; wheat.

corncob. This motif first appeared in Benjamin Latrobe's designs for the Capitol in Washington, D.C., which he was commissioned to rebuild after its destruction by the British in 1814. Corinthian-style *capitals (*see* Orders) were formed from corncobs and tobacco leaves, which subsequently became standard motifs in 19th century American ornament for ironwork, wallpaper, ceramics, furniture detail, etc. In England, Summerly's Art Manufactures produced breadknives with corncob handles in the 1850s – a design that remained popular well into the 20th century.

corncob. 1) 19th century ironwork, New Orleans, Louisiana. 2) American glass flask made at the Baltimore Glass Works, 1840s.

cornflower. *See* Angoulême sprig.

cornice. The uppermost section of the classical *entablature, an obvious place for enrichment. In the 18th and 19th centuries heavy plaster *mouldings were used bearing whatever motif was currently standard. Even quite humble late 19th century domestic villas were given florid cornice ornamentation.

More generally the term is applied to the ornamental feature at the top of a wall or arch, or, internally, at the meeting of walls and ceiling.

corne, à la. Polychrome *Rococo decoration on mid 18th century Rouen faïence, incorporating *cornucopias, *butterflies, *bees and flowers.

cornucopia or **Horn of Plenty.** A goat's horn overflowing with ears of *wheat and *fruit has been a symbol of fertility and abundance since classical times. According to Greek myth, Zeus was once suckled on goat's milk and in gratitude he broke off the goat's horn, declaring that its possessor should always have everything he desired in abundance. In classical decoration, the head of the goat is sometimes included, but in the *Renaissance only the horn appears. The

cornucopia. 1) Italian stone fountain, late 15th century. 2) With banknotes, Martin's Bank, Liverpool, architect Herbert J. Rowse, 1932. 3) Meissen porcelain soup tureen modelled by J.J. Kändler, c.1750. 4) Empire style engraving by Jacob Petit, published 1823. 5) Painted splat on American Hitchcock settee, c.1825-30. 6) American silver tableware, 1887.

cornucopia is used variously as an attribute of *Ceres, Bacchus (*see* Bacchic decoration), *Peace and *Plenty. During the 17th and 18th centuries cornucopias were sometimes combined with the *caduceus, e.g. in *trophies to signify prosperity in the ornamentation of banks, mints and commercial buildings, and might even appear filled with coins or medals. Cornucopias also appear as *volutes and *brackets.

Making use of the association of the cornucopia with food, J.J. Kändler designed for Meissen c.1750 a *finial for tureens of a boy clutching a spilling cornucopia – a motif much imitated in the second half of the 18th century. P.A.L.*La Mésangère designed diningroom chairs with cornucopia arms. Both French *Empire and American *Federal furniture were frequently decorated with cornucopias (often paired, crossed and bound) – the significance of the motif as an allusion to peace, concord and fortune made it a

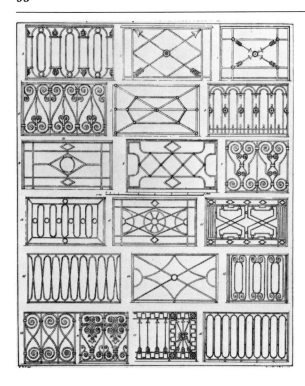

Lewis Nockalls Cottingham. Balcony designs from The Smith and Founder's Directory, *1824.*

particularly suitable symbol for nations making a fresh start. Crossed with *Cupid's arrows and quivers the cornucopia appears in decoration on the theme of *love, as a symbol of fecundity.

corona. Enlarged version of the *fillet, this *moulding is associated with the *cornice.

coronet. In an *achievement of arms, the coronet is placed at the base of the crest. It appears with the family crest as a decoration on small objects to denote ownership, also on picture frames to demonstrate the title of the subject. In British heraldry, dukes, earls, marquesses, viscounts and baronets have coronets composed of different arrangments of strawberry leaves and/or pearls. A so-called ancient coronet is composed of *fleur-de-lis.

cosse de pois. *See* peapod ornament.

Coste, Pascal Xavier (1787-1879). French architect who spent the years 1818-28 working in Egypt on various construction projects. He published *Architecture Arabe ou monuments du Kaire* (Paris, 1837-39) from his own drawings and the book seems to have had an almost immediate effect in France. Léon Vaudoyer's Cathedral in Marseilles (1845) is strongly *Islamic and the two men are known to have been acquainted with each other's work.

cottage orné (French, ornamental cottage). The *cottage orné,* an architectural expression of the *Picturesque, was a rustic style 'cottage' (most were in fact villas)

cottage orné. 1) English earthenware pastille burner, c.1835-40. 2) Old Warden, Bedfordshire, remodelled 1879.

with applied ornament in a fanciful concoction of *Gothic Revival elements, including elaborate *lattice work, verandahs, patterned thatch and ornamental chimneys. The craze for the genre, which was promoted by an enormous number of *pattern books from the late 18th century to c.1840, was largely confined to *Regency England, but its natural successor was the American *Carpenter Gothic style.

In ceramics, *cottages ornés* were modelled in earthenware and porcelain as pastille burners, money-boxes and night lamps by factories such as Rockingham, Coalport, Minton and Spode.

Cottingham, Lewis Nockalls (1787-1847). English architect and antiquary who carried out much restoration work and published a number of *pattern books for ironwork produced by the new cast-iron process. Cottingham's designs reflect contemporary taste for *eclectic styles: *The Ornamental Metalworker's Director* (1823), revised and published in 1824 as *The Smith and Founder's Director,* included stock motifs from 'Grecian, Etruscan, Roman and Gothic schools of Art' as well as examples of ironwork in the fashionable French *Empire style. He later commented that he hoped the directory would help in 'forming correct and tasteful composition, the only way to . . . prevent the inundation of foreign goods.' A further edition of the book was published in 1845 under the title *The Smith's Founder's and Ornamental Metal Worker's Director.* Cottingham also produced *Working Drawings for Gothic Ornaments* (1823), which were rather crude but useful for the less skilled craftsmen labouring on *Gothic Revival buildings with no proper architectural guidance.

counterchange. Interlocking patterns of identical shapes with alternating colours or tones, of which the

*counterchange. *Gyronny pattern on mosaic floor of Roman villa, Lullingstone, Eynsford, Kent, 4th century.*

simplest form is the *chequer. Generally found in tile-work and mosaic during periods of skill in these techniques, e.g. Roman and *Hispano-Moresque work. They appear in early to mid 16th century *pattern books for weaving and embroidery, notably Iseppo Foresto's *Lucidario di Recami* (Venice, 1557). In counter-change or *contrepartie* marquetry, the same shapes were cut from two different coloured veneers or materials, such as tortoiseshell and brass (*see boulle*).

crabstock handles and spout on mid 18th century Staffordshire teapot.

crabstock. Type of ceramic handle or spout made to resemble a twig or branch. This mainly English decoration occurs from c.1750 (an example of the contemporary enthusiasm for *rustic decoration). The body of the piece is usually decorated with leaves and tendrils in relief to match. Common on wares from Leeds, Staffordshire, Liverpool and Derby, and occasionally copied in silverware.

crane. Motif in Roman ornament and medieval church decoration symbolising vigilance. The crane often appears holding a stone in the claw of its raised foot, an allusion to a legend recorded by Aristotle and taken up in medieval *bestiaries that if the crane fell asleep and dropped the stone it immediately woke up again, and was therefore ever watchful. In Chinese art, the crane represented a messenger of the gods, while for the Japanese it symbolised prosperity and happiness. It is a frequent motif in *chinoiserie* and *japonaiserie* schemes, often alongside the *ho ho bird.

crenellated. *See* castellated.

crescent. Ancient symbol of the moon, and attribute of Diana, goddess of the moon, who may be represented with a crescent on her forehead. Diane de Poitiers (1499-1566), mistress of Henri II, modelled herself on the legendary characteristics of the goddess, and the chapel built for her at Fontainebleau is ornamented with crescents.

The crescent is an important emblem of Islam, sometimes combined with a star, and has been used in Western Europe as an ornamental motif whenever things *Turkish (or Ottoman) have been in fashion.

cresting. 1) Hardwick Hall, Derbyshire, 1590s. 2) Wing of Temperate House, Kew Gardens, Surrey, by Decimus Burton, designed 1860-62, built 1896-99. 3) Pennsylvania Academy of Fine Arts, Philadelphia, by Frank Furness, 1876.

crest. *See* achievement of arms; coat of arms; coronet; heraldic decoration.

cresting. Ornamental finish consisting of a regular series of motifs, sometimes pierced for a lighter effect. It is applied to the top of screens, walls and roof ridges in both ecclesiastical and domestic settings. Late *Gothic cresting adopted motifs like *Tudor roses, leaves and miniature *battlements and is often known as *brattishing. *Renaissance motifs included *obelisks and *strapwork. Cresting was a popular embellishment in elaborate 19th century revivalist styles such as *Gothic Revival and *French Second Empire. Mass-produced pierced terracotta tiles and cast-iron ridging finished with cresting were standard forms of decoration for mid to late 19th century terraced housing and villas.

Cresting is also the term applied to the sides, wings, or handles of glass objects, mainly Venetian or *façon de Venise* pieces of the 17th century.

crocket. Small hook-shaped ornament in the form of a bud or curled leaf (occasionally an animal) applied to the edges and outlines of pinnacles, canopies, turrets and *finials. Originally a *Romanesque ornament, the crocket became ubiquitous in early *Gothic architecture, in works reflecting architectural forms (e.g. church furniture and church plate) and subsequently in secular furniture and metalwork. However it was largely abandoned from the mid 13th century as styles became less formal and more naturalistic and elaborate. It was adopted by the early 18th century *Gothick style, as at All Souls College, Oxford, which was built in 1715 by Nicholas Hawksmoor (1661-1736), and featured widely in the *pattern books of B.*Langley,

W.*Ince and John Mayhew in the mid 18th century.
During the *Gothic Revival crockets became, once
more, a popular ornamental motif in architecture,
woodwork and metalwork (e.g. in A.W.N.*Pugin's
ecclesiastical metalwork.).

crocodile. Common motif in ancient *Egyptian art and
ornament – symbol of Sebek, the crocodile-headed
god, also sacred to other gods. It was aptly used to
allude to Nelson's victory at the Battle of the Nile
(1798) in British decoration of the period. The crocodile often appears with Africa in representations of
the *Continents, while the alligator sometimes accompanies America.

crossette, ear or **hawksbill.** Projecting or elaborated
detail applied to the upper corners of doorcases and
window-frames in late *Renaissance and early *Baroque architecture. Sometimes appears in the form
of a *volute.

crown. Ancient mark of honour, achievement or sovereignty in both secular and religious contexts. Its
present form, a royal crown of silver or gold studded
with jewels, probably developed between the end of
the Western Roman Empire and the beginning of the
Middle Ages. Used heraldically it denotes fealty or
possession. The crowns of the royal families of Europe

*crossette. 1) New sacristy of San Lorenzo, Florence, Italy, by
Michelangelo Buonarroti, 1521-34. 2) Palazzo Chigi, Rome, from
Domenico de Rossi's* Studie d'Archittetura Civile, *1655-67.*

are all different and categorised in reference books
such as C.N. Elvin's *Dictionary of Heraldry* (1889). A royal
crown (of Charles II) supported by *cherubs (*see* boys
and crown) occasionally appears as a general motif on
the crests and stretchers of mid 17th century English
chairs and daybeds – conceivably a topical reference
to the Restoration of the Monarchy.

From the Middle Ages *personifications of cities
were often crowned by a circular castellated wall,
known as a mural crown. More recently the motif has
been used in the *coats of arms of county councils.
Personifications of rivers (*see* riparine) and *marine
deities wear a naval crown which incorporates ships
under sail.

Crunden, John (1740-c.1828). English architect and
designer who worked in the *Adam style. He published
Designs for Ceilings (1765), *The Chimney-piece Maker's Daily
Assistant* (1766) with T. Milton and P.*Columbani, and
*Convenient and Ornamental Architecture, consisting of Original
Designs for Plans, Elevations and Sections from the Farm House
to the most grand and magnificent Villa* (1767; frequent later
editions to 1798). He specialised in the design of *fret
patterns, which he described as 'mosaic, gothic, chinese and greek, intended mainly for woodworkers';
these appeared in *The Joyner and Cabinet-maker's Darling,
or Pocket Director* (London, 1760, 1765, 1770) and *The
Carpenter's Companion, containing 32 New and Beautiful Designs
for All Sorts of Chinese Railing and Gates* (1765) on which

*crocket. 1) West front, Nôtre Dame Cathedral, Paris, early 13th century.
2) German pastoral staff in gilt metal, dated 1351. 3) Carving in the
Gothic style, Canterbury Cathedral, Kent, restored 1970s. 4) Stencil
designs from A.W.N.*Pugin's Glossary of Ecclesiastical
Ornament and Costume, *1844.*

John Crunden. 'Grand Mosaik Fret for a Frieze' from The Joyner
and Cabinet-maker's Darling, *1770.*

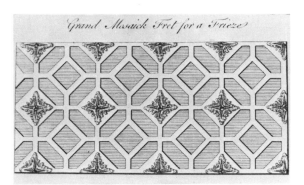

he collaborated with J.H. Morris. Crunden's patterns were influential in America, particularly in Boston and along the North East coast.

crystal. The structure of crystals appealed to the 19th century taste for *geometry and dynamism in natural forms. The snowflake, whose crystalline form had recently been discovered, was employed by L.H.*Sullivan as a hexagonal *diaper on the Getty Tomb (1890) in Chicago.

At the time of the Festival of Britain (London, 1951), crystal structure diagrams drawn by Dr Helen Megaw of Cambridge were used as a basis for designs promoted by the Festival Pattern Group. These repeating symmetrical patterns were taken up by textile, wallpaper, carpet, glass and plastic manufacturers. *See also* molecular structures; Organic Modernism.

C-scrolls and **S-scrolls** were two of the most common abstract forms in *Rococo ornamentation. I.*Ware criticised Rococo decoration in *A Complete Body of Architecture* commenting, 'It is our misfortune to see at this time an unmeaning scrawl of 'C's' inverted, turned, and even hooked together, take the place of Greek and Roman elegance, even in our most expensive decorations. This is not because the possessor thinks there is or can be elegance in such fond weak ill-jointed and unmeaning figures.'

Cubist decoration derived from the irregular geometric forms of Cubist painting that were taken up and modified by *Art Deco and *Modernist designers. The forms translated well into coloured faïence, relief, sculpted and mosaic panels, ironwork for architecture, and even appeared in textiles, rugs and bookbinding. They were most successful on flat, two-dimensional surfaces, although attempts were also made to use the designs on glass, ceramics and jewellery. Cubist designs were most common in France, but spread from there to America and Britain.

The most literal efforts to translate Cubism into architecture were made in Czechoslovakia. There, a group of designers influenced by the *Vienna Secession and the Cubist experiments in Paris ornamented their work with prismatic effects. The principal exponent of the idea was Josef Chochol (1880-1956).

Cufic. *See* Kufic.

cullot or **culot.** 18th century term for a string of *husks, or sometimes the end of a *festoon. *See also* margent.

cup and cover. *See* bulb.

Cupid and **cupids** (Latin, *cupido*, desire). Cupid, the Roman god of love (or Eros, his Greek counterpart) was a widely depicted subject in classical art, and a favourite theme in ornament. He often appears with *Venus (who was considered to be his mother) and may carry a bow, quiver and *arrows (to pierce his victims with love) or a *torch (to set their hearts on fire) and is occasionally blindfold, signifying the blindness of love or the darkness of sin, i.e. sensuality. Cupid playing with the weapons of *Mars or Hercules

C scroll. 1) Carved wood chimneypiece at Stout's Hill, Uley, Gloucestershire, by William Halfpenny, 1743.
*Cupid. 2) French Louis XVI bronze and ormolu mantel clock; Cupid holds an oval relief of himself, and at his feet lie a plumed helmet and shield of *Mars. 3) Engraving from P.*Ayres's Emblemata Amatoria, 1683. 4) Stretcher carved with blindfold cupid firing arrows at a Venus figure on English chair, 1670-75.*

(*see* Herculean decoration) signifies the power of love to overcome strife. Similarly, Cupid crushing the god Pan or standing over a warrior illustrates the quotation from Virgil, 'Love conquers all'. Scenes from the marriage of Cupid and Psyche by the 2nd century Roman writer, Apuleius, are often depicted, particularly in *Renaissance decoration. Like Hercules and Bacchus, Cupid is one of the most widely adopted classical figures frequently appearing, for example, in *emblem books. The engravings of Philip Ayres, *Emblemata Amatoria*, which depicted numerous amorous adventures of Cupid, was first published in 1683; it had simultaneous texts in four languages and was reprinted in 1714, 1725 and c.1750. Cupid with a personification of *Time generally represents the theme of Love triumphing over Time, although the image is sometimes reversed with Time about to cut the Thread of Life and a terrified Cupid dropping his bow and quiver; both themes appear on 18th century French clocks.

During the 18th century cupids became a general motif symbolising *love, often without any reference to specific classical myths, and frequently appeared several at a time in the decoration of bedrooms, bedroom furniture and marriage gifts to symbolise love. Their great popularity in late 18th century decoration led to widespread use of cupid subjects, often deriving from wall paintings at Pompeii and Herculaneum, e.g. the 'sale of cupids' engraved by Carlo Nolli (d 1770) for *Antichità di Ercolano* which appeared on printed cotton and decorated fans. Engravings after A. Kauffman and M.A.*Pergolesi included cupid scenes. In France the type of *putto* that F.*Boucher had made so popular was often converted into a cupid. Victorian cupids were chubby, sentimental infants and almost as popular as *hearts in the ornament of love tokens, valentines, etc. *See also* boxer.

Curvilinear style. The later period of *Perpendicular *tracery, as defined by Edmund Sharpe in 1849.

cushioned frieze. *See* pulvinated frieze.

cusp. In *Gothic architecture, the projecting point where *foils meet in *tracery. Cusps in *Decorated and *Perpendicular architecture frequently have ornamented ends – heads, leaves, flowers or occasionally animals may appear. This detail is also found in furniture, woodwork and metalwork in Gothic and *Gothic Revival styles.

cusping. 1) Gothic Revival choirstall, Church of St Mary, Woolpit, Suffolk. cut card. 2) Silver ewer made in London, 1700-01.

cut card. Decorative technique used on silver which first appeared on mid 17th century chalices as a device to mask the join between bowl and stem. Simple *strapwork and leaf forms cut out and applied to bases, spouts and handle joins and around *finials were fashionable from c.1670 to the early 18th century. Card work was comparatively simple to execute and did not require the silversmith to have skills of casting, engraving or embossing. Huguenot craftsman took up and elaborated the technique, often applying several layers of silver sheets and complex foliate patterns incorporating typical contemporary French motifs such as *lambrequins and *tassels.

Cuvilliès, Jean François de (1696-1768). Architect and designer of some of the finest examples of German *Rococo, sometimes known as François Cuvilliès the Elder to differentiate him from his son, François Joseph Ludwig. He was sent to Paris by the Elector Maximilian Emanuel of Bavaria who had previously employed him as a court dwarf, and returned to Germany having trained in the use of the Rococo style. His early work clearly shows the French influence, as in its free scrollwork, but his finest work, the construction and decoration of the Amalienburg (1734-39) in Nymphenburg shows that he subsequently developed his own considerably more extravagant and mannered style of Rococo decoration.

Engravings based upon designs by Cuvilliès were published from 1737. Over the next twenty years, 74

suites appeared, many of which were well known in England and formative in the development of English Rococo carving. These included general Rococo ornament for *cartouches, panels, *vignettes and *caprices but also furniture which he designed to match and complement the wall decoration and architecture.

Cuvilliès, François Joseph Ludwig (1731-77). Succeeded his father J.F. de *Cuvilliès as architect to the Bavarian court. He also published ornament, but often with a more architectural emphasis: the *Orders, *balustrades, Gothic *niches, monuments. *Vignole Bavarois* (1770), groups of *children and *trophies, relates more closely to his father's work.

cyclopean. Term for huge, irregularly shaped blocks of masonry. It originally referred to pre-classical Greek buildings which were fabled to be the work of a gigantic one-eyed Thracian race called the Cyclopes, although they were in fact constructed by Mycenaean and other primitive Aegean builders of the 13th century BC. Post-Renaissance grottoes and follies were sometimes built in cyclopean style. Joseph Paxton constructed the Cyclopean Aquaduct (known as the Rockworks) in the grounds of Chatsworth, Derbyshire (1839-40).

cyma recta (Latin, *cyma*, wave). Important compound *moulding, combining the *ovolo and *cavetto with the convex moulding below. In section the moulding is a double curve: concave above, convex below. Also known as *ogee moulding.

cyma reversa. The inverse of *cyma recta, with the convex curve above, the concave below. Also known as reverse ogee moulding.

cymbals often appear with drums and tambourines in *Bacchic decoration; also in *trophies and other schemes of ornament on the theme of *music, most commonly in 18th century work.

cyphers. Initials interwoven to form a flat linear design; sometimes letters are reversed to achieve a symmetrical effect. Like *heraldic decoration, cyphers were used as a sign of ownership or of patronage on anything from buildings to personal belongings.

At the end of the 14th century, Charles V of France had his plate and rooms ornamented with a K [Karolus] and the *fleur-de-lis. A portrait (c.1390) of Richard II of England shows how his clothing was embroidered with a design of golden flowers and RR topped by a crown. 15th century ornament in La Sainte-Chapelle, Paris, includes a crowned K on the balustrade to indicate the patronage of Charles VII, the oratory bears LL and a crown for Louis XI. Henry VIII had jewellery designed by Hans Holbein (c.1465-1524) in the form of his initial and he commemorated his marriage to Jane Seymour with a cypher of H and J in the plasterwork of the Great Watching Chamber at Hampton Court, Middlesex.

Louis XIV revived the fashion for cyphers with interlaced Ls and, subsequently, what had previously been a practice confined mainly to rulers and monarchs became widely popular. Patterns proliferated:

cyphers. 1) Pavillon du Roi, Louvre, Paris, built by Claude Perrault for Louis XIV, 1667-70. 2) From A New Book of Cyphers, *c.1760, a reprint of the 1704 work by Colonel Parsons. 3) French monogram brooch, c.1870. 4) Gatehouse of Euston Station, London, architect Stansby, 1869-70.*

S.*Gribelin produced many designs for cyphers, some of which were included in *A New Book of Ornaments usefull to all artists* (London, 1704), and contributed the engravings for *A New Book of Cyphers* by Benjamin Rhodes, 'containing in general all names being interwoven, and reversed, by Alphabet. Being very pleasant for Gentlemen and Ladys, and useful for all sorts of Artists, as Painters, Carvers, Engravers, Chacers, Watchmakers, Imbroderers.' Gribelin also contributed to Colonel Parson's *A New Book of Cyphers; more compleat and regular than any yet extant* (1704). This pattern book is similar to the successful production of Samuel Sympson, *A New Book of Cyphers*, which went into at least three editions (1726, 1736, 1755) and contains every possible combination of two intertwining scrolling letters with flourishes of foliage in the style then popular in both Britain and America.

From the mid 18th century, estate buildings were often identified with a decoratively carved cypher of the owner's initials, a practice that continued through the 19th century.

In the 19th century cyphers became a popular ornament for small personal objects; their design was usually the province of the silver and hardstone engraver and letterpress designer, e.g. F.*Knight, who published several *pattern books on the subject, for example, *Knight's New Book of Seven Hundred and Fifty Eight Plain Ornamented and Reversed Cyphers* (London, 1832), which contained plain scrolled letters based on early 18th century examples. The second half of the 19th century saw a great increase in the use of decorative lettering and cyphers, many of which were extraordinarily elaborate with flourishes, scrolls and many variations in texture, and often *Gothic in inspiration to achieve a grand, *heraldic effect. During the 1870s and 1880s at least three pattern books published by 'heraldic artists' contained designs of immense intricacy and inventiveness: *Monograms and Cyphers* by H. Renoir (London and Edinburgh, 1870-74), *Dictionnaire du Chiffre-monogramme dans les styles Moyen Age et Renaissance et Couronnes nobiliaires* by Charles Demengeot (Paris, 1881) and *Monograms in Three and Four Letters* by J. Gordon Smith (London, n.d.), all of which include especially designed religious monograms for churches and church furnishings, based on the INRI and IHS combinations (*see* Christian motifs).

cypress. Like other evergreen trees, the cypress symbolises immortality and has been associated with *death and mourning since classical times: the Greeks and Romans placed branches of cypress in houses of the dead in the belief that they would protect the body against corruption. It appears in funerary art, and cemeteries are often planted with the cypress. A common motif in Persian carpet patterns, the cypress is one of many plant forms which could have been the basis of elements in *paisley pattern.

damascening. Metal technique originally developed in the Near East (and taking its name from Damascus) in which gold, silver and copper are inlaid into base metal. After the Sack of Damascus in 1401, many metalworkers migrated to Italy, particularly to Venice, where they continued working in their native style, which became known as Venetian Saracenic. Both the technique and the *arabesque patterns were adopted and became fashionable throughout Europe in the early 16th century. At first damascening was used mainly in the decoration of weapons and armour, but soon spread to domestic utensils, caskets, dishes, etc. By the second half of the 16th century, work of this kind was centred in Milan, where craftsmen produced damascened strips to sell to cabinetmakers. Damascening, probably by immigrant Italians, was also carried out in Germany, France and England, mostly on arms and armour.

Having died out in the early 18th century, damascening was revived (originally in Spain) during the first half of the 19th century, mainly for *Renaissance Revival work, although it often consisted of patterning laid on the surface of the objects rather than proper inlay. It was particularly popular in France, where many arabesque designs were republished. Even cheaper methods of producing the fashionable decoration were developed, such as the finish on the Scottish souvenir woodware called 'Scoto-Damascene', which was wood covered with foil and then painted or engraved with the standard designs. Occasionally the black and gold effect created by some damascening was imitated in lacquerwork.

dancette. Term for the *chevron when it appears in *Romanesque architecture.

Daniell, Thomas (1749-1840). English artist who produced primarily *topographical subjects. He collaborated with his nephew William Daniell (1769-1837) on two books that depicted life and landscape in India entitled *Oriental Scenery* (6 vols, completed 1808) and *Picturesque Voyage to India* (1810). The aquatints in these works provided the inspiration for *Indian style architecture as well as acting as a source for the topographical decoration of ceramics by the Swansea porcelain factory, 1817-24.

Dantesque. 19th century revival of medieval styles of architecture current in Italy around the period of Dante's lifetime (1265-1321).

Darly, Matthias (fl 1741-80). English engraver, caricaturist, designer and self-styled Professor of Ornament, whose dictum was: 'On the knowledge of true embellishments depends the improvement of every article.' His book *A New Book of Chinese, Gothic and Modern Chairs* (1751) was the first to include *Gothic Revival furniture designs. Always at the forefront of ornamental fashion, he followed this (in collaboration with George Edwards) with *A New Book of Chinese Designs* (1754), which was 'calculated to improve the present taste, consisting of figures, buildings and furniture, landskips, birds, beasts, flowers and ornaments' and was influential in the development of *chinoiserie*; some of these designs were adapted and used by the publisher Robert Sayer in a *drawing book that was to prove highly popular, *The Ladies' Amusement or Whole Art of Japanning Made Easy* (1760). Darly's next publication, *The Ornamental Architect or Young Artist's Instructor* (1770), presented designs in the classical taste, 'we must own that some of the present Architects of this Nation by their introducing the ornaments made use of by the Ancients have done more good than all the other polite Artists put together'; it includes a range of classical ornament such as *masks, *vases, *tripods, *urns and ball *finials (as well as architectural features) for the use of architects, painters, engravers, carvers, stucco-workers, modellers, potters, ironsmiths, silversmiths, founders, embroiderers, pattern-drawers, tapestry weavers, coach-makers, cabinetmakers, etc. In the 1770s, apart from *A Compleat Body of Architecture* (1773) in which he elaborated on the five *Orders, Darly concentrated on producing ornamental detail in the light *Adam

style, avoiding the kind of patterns that produced 'the monstrous weight that seems to be over our heads in some well-executed ceilings of the Italians.' After *A New Book of Ornaments in the Present (antique) Taste as now used by all Professions* (1772), Darly capitalised on the mania for vases and published at least four collections, *Sixty Vases by English, French and Italian Masters* (1768), *A Variety of Vases and other ornaments* (n.d.), *A New Book of Vases* (c.1770) and *New Vases* (c.1770). Some of Darly's more standard designs were republished in 1892 by J.A. Heaton as a suitable source for the reproduction of 18th century English furniture and decoration.

d'Aviler, Augustin Charles (1653-1700). French architect and author of *Cours complet d'architecture, qui comprend les ordres de Vignole* (2 vols, 1691), which republished designs by G.B. da *Vignola together with contemporary designs. It remained, in various abridged and altered forms, a popular source book through the 18th century and into the early 19th century.

Dawkins, James. *See* Wood, Robert.

day. Like *night, day is usually personified by a female figure, often Aurora or Eos, the Roman and Greek goddesses of dawn. Attributes of day include the *cock, a *flame, the *sun. Italian *Renaissance artists took up the theme of day and night as a humanist symbol of life and death. Personifications of day alluding to the passing of *time appeared in the 17th century, and particularly in the 18th and 19th centuries, on clocks and in the ornament of rooms for day-time use.

Day, Lewis F. (1845-1910). English designer, writer and teacher. With other members of the *Arts and Crafts movement, Day was a founder member of the Art Workers' Guild (1884). He was involved in the establishment of the South Kensington Museum (later the Victoria and Albert Museum) and the School of Design (later the Royal College of Art). A prolific writer on all aspects of ornamentation, he emphasised the importance of selecting pattern and ornament that was appropriate to the material used and to the

Matthias Darly. Engraving from A New Book of Chinese Designs *by Darly and George Edwards, 1754.*

Lewis F. Day. Part of an alphabet designed by Day from his Alphabets Old and New, *1898.*

process of execution, and of creating ornamentation as an integral part of the design rather than as an addition. Although his textbooks were not *pattern books in the strict sense, they were profusely illustrated with historical examples among which he included Japanese work as well as his own designs for stained glass, ceramics, woodwork, textiles, etc. His earliest books were *The Anatomy of Pattern* (1887) and *The Planning of Ornament* (1887). Later, Day explored the motifs and forms that could be taken from plant life, first in *Nature in Ornament* (1896) and then in *Nature and Ornament* (1908-09). In 1902 he published a typically Arts and Crafts work, *Lettering in Ornament*.

death and mourning. The symbolism and imagery of death have given rise to a vast ornamental vocabulary. The personification of death may be a hunter or warrior figure, a symbol such as a *lion, or, more literally, a skeleton. Guardian figures or creatures have been widely used, often winged, e.g. the Christian *angel. The form of the burial place itself may imply eternity or the next world: e.g. the Egyptian *pyramid or *obelisk (both voids within) or the Celtic labyrinth. Early Christians, who had to disguise their beliefs for fear of persecution, tended to borrow cryptic or pagan ornament, e.g. from Etruscan sarcophagi. From the late medieval period two aspects of death were depicted in ornament: on one hand the worldly aspects of life, the achievements of the deceased, and the sorrows of the bereaved (ranks of family mourners known as 'weepers' sometimes appear on *Gothic and Elizabethan tombs), on the other, the passage of the deceased towards a new, mysterious world.

Tombs and memorials tend to reflect contemporary architectural styles, although from the 15th century they were often ornamented with additional motifs: spades, bells, coffins and shrouds, as well as *gison* ornament – crossed bones, *skulls, skeletons, even half-rotted bodies. The figure of Death depicted as a skeleton in a hooded cloak and holding a *scythe and *hourglass first appeared in early 15th century illustrations to the *Triumph* of Petrarch, and was rapidly assimilated into late medieval iconography, particularly in Germany. The figure may also appear with an effigy of the deceased, or with the figure of *Time. Hourglasses, Time's scythe and even clocks are reminders of the transience of life. Suitable Christian motifs such as the *Virtues, the emblems of the Resurrection (fruit and flowers) and those of the Eucharist (the *wheat ear and the *grapevine) are also used. 16th and 17th century *emblem books were important sources.

From the end of the 17th century the cruder references to death began to disappear and decoration became more subtle. The winged *cherub head was universal (sometimes echoed by a skull with bat's wings), but ornamentation was in general *classical: evergreens, especially encroaching *ivy, the lighted *lamp and the flaming *urn (holding the ashes of the dead) signify eternal life; the closed urn and the extinguished *torch, mortality.

In the 18th and 19th centuries, an air of romantic sentimentality pervaded ornament associated with death, and the theme of mourning appeared with

*death and mourning. 1) Bell, hourglass, skull, crossed bones, crossed spade and pick, and coffin on *frieze decorating a grave enclosure, Old High Church, Inverness, 1703. 2) Broken column on 19th century monument, Abney Park cemetery, Stoke Newington, London. 3, 4) 19th century English mourning jewellery with weeping figure and plaited hair.*

increasing frequency. There were weeping willows and *lachrymae* – antique tear vases. Drapery, instead of simply representing a shroud, was used to veil urns, weeping *angels and mourners. Goethe's novel *The Sorrows of Werther* (1774) epitomised the theme and was popular across Europe: the much illustrated scene of Charlotte mourning at the tomb of Werther even appears on Leeds and Staffordshire jugs and mugs. In 1817, the death in childbirth of Princess Charlotte (daughter of the Prince of Wales, later George IV) provoked the production of prodigious quantities of ceramics ornamented with this weeping-at-the-tomb style of decoration. Broken columns and cut flowers, particularly *lilies, on tombs, expressed the idea of death cutting off a life in its prime. Throughout the 19th century, flowers appeared with increasing frequency, most commonly arum lilies, lilies of the valley, forget-me-nots and ivy, sometimes with elaborate emblematic significance encouraged by the publication of such books as Martin's *Le Langage des Fleurs* in France and Belgium and the Rev'd Robert Tyas's *Sentiment of Flowers* and *Language and Poetry of Flowers* in England. In the mid 19th century the fashion for *Egyptian ornament and fascination with the ancient Egyptian cult of death led to the appearance of obelisks and pyramids in many graveyards and on church memorials. With the ascendancy of the *Gothic Revival over *Neoclassicism, the motifs of funerary ornament became overtly Christian, the cross or angels replacing the 'pagan' column, torch or urn.

Mourning jewellery followed fashions set by memorials and tombs, e.g. Stuart necklaces of jet beads interspersed with enamelled skulls, pendants in the form of miniature coffins containing skeletons, and *Georgian weeping willow brooches. The Victorians, who adopted strict procedures that specified type and colour of dress (black, purple, grey and white) and the length of mourning (depending on relationship to the deceased), favoured mourning jewellery containing a lock of the hair of the departed plaited in any of a huge range of patterns. *The Jewellers Book of Patterns in Hair Work, containing a Great Variety of Copper-plate Engravings of Devices and Patterns in Hair Suitable for Mourning Jewellery* (1864) illustrates the favourites: urns, scythes, setting suns, *anchors, *hearts, padlocks, roses, ostrich plumes, *wreaths, yew trees and the serpent swallowing its own tail – a symbol of eternity.

de Beaumont, Adalbert. *See* Collinot, Eugène-Victor.

Theodore de Bry. Two letters from A New Artistic Alphabet, *1596.*

de Bry, Theodore (1528-98). De Bry worked mainly in Strasbourg (1568-90), but also in Liège and Frankfurt, and visited London in the 1580s. He is best known for his topographical engravings of America produced in 1590 to illustrate an edition of *Hariot's Report of Virginia* and based on the navigator and painter John White's *Journal of his Voyage to Virginia* (1581). He also produced a quantity of influential engraved ornament, mostly for goldsmiths and metalworkers (sword hilts, cups, pendants, *cartouches, knife handles), as well as *portrait heads, figure and history subjects within ornamental borders. He was influenced by the work of E.*Delaune who was also working in Strasbourg at the time. Besides typical late *Renaissance forms such as *grotesques and *strapwork, de Bry's work contains naturalistically drawn flowers, insects, birds and small animals reminiscent of contemporary illumination. He produced an early account of oriental life (*see* Turkish style). His sons Johann Theodore (1561-1623) and Johann Israel (d 1611) collaborated with him in his later years.

de Caylus, Comte Anne-Claude-Philippe de Pestels de Lévis de Tubières Grimoard (1692-1765). French antiquarian, traveller and collector who published *Recueil d'antiquités égyptiennes, étrusques, grècques, romaines et gauloises* (7 vols, 1752-67), which contains a vast selection of small household objects as well as the more im-

pressive and better known artefacts of antiquity. His examples came principally from the great private collections and discoveries from new excavations. De Caylus's inclusion of *Egyptian objects and motifs (including *hieroglyphics) was an early and important admission that they should be considered alongside the works of classical antiquity. Though less historically accurate than G.B.*Piranesi, he introduced a large repertoire of new motifs to architects, furniture designers, ceramicists, metalworkers, etc., and was central in the reaction against the *Rococo which led in turn to the sparer Neo-classicism of the *Louis XVI style. His role in the establishment of *Neo-classicism was considerable. The *Recueil* includes lengthy thematic expositions of de Caylus's views about the evolution of styles, including his championing of the Greeks, whose work had, according to him, refined Egyptian and Etruscan art, and was then lost under the debasing influence of the Romans. His opinions influenced the rationalist Abbé Laugier (1713-69) and J.D.*Le Roy and thus contributed to the pure classicism of the *Greek Revival which gathered force after his death. De Caylus himself acknowledged that the designs would serve as source material, as well as having antiquarian interests: '*la gravure les rend communes à tous les peuples qui cultivent les lettres*'. In later volumes, de Caylus added the artefacts of the Gallic tribes and the emphasis from Volume IV onwards shifts to the architectural

Comte de Caylus. Plate from Recueil d'antiquités, *1752-67.*

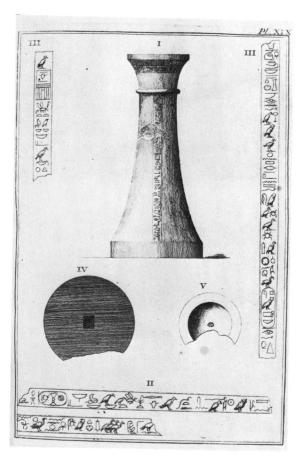

remains of various cultures. Volume VII includes P. S.*Bartoli's engravings of Roman wall paintings. The emphasis on household goods in the volumes led to the influence of the *Recueil* on manufacturers such as the Staffordshire potter Josiah Wedgwood, and allowed an essentially scholarly work to have an extremely far-reaching influence within the European decorative arts.

Decker, Paul, the Elder (1677-1713). German *Baroque architect whose published work is his lasting memorial; he built little. *Fürstlicher Baumeister, oder, Architectura Civilis* (1711; second edition with more plates, 1716) was an enormously important publication, its subject an imaginary palace designed in an amalgam of the styles of J.*Berain and other *Louis XIV ornamentists in France, with German modifications which gave the style more bravura and substance. Decker published engraved suites of ornament for gold and silver objects, for glass, lacquerwork, stucco ceiling ornament, and selections of *emblems and *Muses for application to interiors. His bands of *Laub und Bandelwerk* ornament contain *espagnolette heads,

Paul Decker the Elder. Part of ceiling for audience chamber from his Fürstlicher Baumeister, oder, Architectura Civilis, *1711.*

Decorated. West front of Lichfield Cathedral, Staffordshire, from T. Rickman's The Styles of Architecture, *1848 edition.*

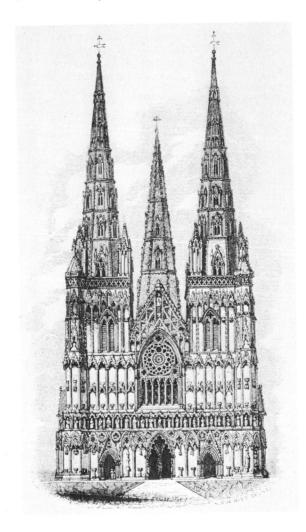

*shell forms, *sphinxes, *monkeys, *serpents, dwarfs in the manner of J.*Callot, *grotesques and *chinoiserie figures; these were widely used, e.g. enamelled on glass. This was collected in the posthumous *Architectura Theoretica – Practica* (1720). Surprisingly, although ornate, the designs never reflected the liking for the exaggerated or the monstrous so common in contemporary German and Flemish designs.

Decker, Paul (fl 1759). Author of two derivative works, *Chinese Architecture, Civil and Ornamental* (London, 1759), which was reworked from M.*Darly, and *Gothic Architecture Decorated* (London, 1759); the latter had *rustic style designs 'many of which may be executed with Pollards, Rude Branches and Roots of Tree.'

Decorated. *Gothic style of architecture that came between *Early English and *Perpendicular and, as defined by the architect Thomas Rickman in the early 19th century, covered the first 80 years of the 14th century. Its characteristics are a developed *naturalism (for example, the simple *dogtooth moulding decoration of Early English architecture was replaced by the more foliate *ballflower), abundant decoration, flowing *tracery with a multiplicity of forms, such as *ogees, *vesica piscis, *mouchettes, *crockets and *arcading, together with *star vaulting. The Continental equivalent of Decorated Style is known as High Gothic.

décor bois. In ceramics, a form of *trompe l'oeil painted decoration that represents a grained wood background with a monochrome (grey, black or red) engraving of a landscape (often in the style of J.A.*Watteau or F. *Boucher), apparently pinned to it. It first appeared

décor bois. French faïence tray, Niderviller, 1774.

on Niderviller faïence c.1770, and probably derived from mid 17th century so-called 'letter-rack' paintings in which prints, letters and other ephemera appear to be stuck behind a lattice of tapes. *Décor bois* was copied by factories in Paris, Brussels and Tournai, and c.1780 at Nymphenburg and also at Vienna, where it was produced alongside patterns imitating shot silk and taffeta. *See also* quodlibet.

décor coréen. Late 18th century name for *kakiemon patterns on French porcelain made at Chantilly between 1725 and 1740. The patterns were taken from a collection of Japanese porcelain (thought to be Korean) owned by the factory's founder, Prince de Condé.

J.L. de Cordemoy. From his Nouvelle Traité de toute l'Architecture, *1706.*

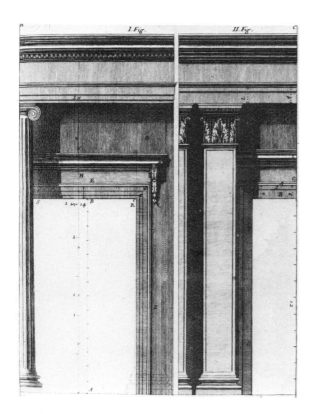

de Cordemoy, J.L. A French priest about whom little is known, but whose book, *Nouveau Traité de toute l'Architecture ou l'Art de Bastir; utile aux entrepreneurs et aux ouvriers* (1706), represents a very early rejection of the excesses of the *Baroque and promoting of *Neo-classical theories. He placed much importance on the need for architecture to reflect its function in its form, undisguised by decorative flourishes. He did not rule out decoration altogether but quoted *Vitruvius's edict that ornament was for public buildings and those of importance; for example, judges' town houses '*doivent être plus spacieuses, plus propres, plus ornées à cause de la multitude du monde qui a affaire à eux*', and he maintained that where ornament was applied, this should be done according to strict rules: *trophies and *vases were suitable for courtyards, *herms and *caryatids for *arcading, and so on; the *Orders should not be used ornamentally, and he considered decoration of a façade to be degenerate. De Cordemoy's theories predated, and appear to have influenced, the architectural writings of the rationalist Marc Antoine Laugier (1713-69), who rejected all ornament.

décor persan, bleu persan or **bleu de Nevers.** In ceramics, a style of decoration consisting of birds, flowers, foliage and insects painted in white, yellow and orange on a blue ground (occasionally white on an orange/yellow ground) which originated at Nevers in the first half of the 17th century and was subsequently widely imitated by other factories. Pierre Custode (d 1656), one of a family of potters who worked at Nevers, was traditionally credited with the introduction of *décor persan*, so-called because it resembled oriental designs.

de la Cour, William (d 1767). French designer and engraver who worked for most of his life in Britain. His *pattern books introduced early instances of *Rococo design to England and included designs for *cartouches, furniture, jewellery and small pieces of goldsmiths' work such as boxes, watchcases, etc. Between 1741, when he published his *First Book of Ornament*, and 1747 he produced seven more pattern books. His *rocaille cartouches are in the manner of the French *ornemanistes* such as J.A.*Meissonier. His designs for furniture tend to be more symmetrical, e.g. he favoured entwined looped *strapwork for chair-backs.

Delafosse, Jean Charles (1734-89). French architect, decorator and professor of design whose ornamental designs contributed greatly to the spread of the *Louis XVI style, a brand of *Neo-classicism sometimes known as the *goût antique*. His *Nouvelle Iconologie Historique* was first published in 1768 with at least five other editions appearing before 1785, including one in Amsterdam (with reworked, more formal plates) and one in Germany; its sub-title indicates the breadth of application '*Attributs Hieroglyphiques . . . composés et arrangés de manière qu'il peuvre servir à toutes Décorations, puis qu'on est le maître de les appliqués également à des fountaines, frontispieces, pyramides, cartouches, dessus-de-Portes, bordures, medaillons, trophées, vases, frieses . . . tombeaux, pendules, etc.*' Particularly influential was his use of thick *swags of tightly packed *laurel leaves, Greek *key pattern and heavy inverted *scrolls. He designed a wide range of

furniture designs, metalwork and *vases. As the title
of the work indicates, Delafosse was greatly interested
in iconographic ornament, and the book includes
*military, *pastoral, *hunting and *fishing, *love and
*music *trophies, as well as designs incorporating
themes such as the *Elements, *Continents, *Seasons
and other *personifications. After the *Nouvelle Iconologie* he published further suites of ornament in the
same vein. Some of his plates, which fitted well with
the *Beaux Arts classicism of the period, were reissued c.1890 in Paris as *L'Oeuvre de Delafosse.*

Delaune, Etienne (1518/19-83). French goldsmith,
medallist, designer and engraver who worked in Paris
and later in Strasbourg and Augsburg. His earliest
engraved ornament, published in 1561, was for a variety of metalwork pieces decorated in the *Mannerist
style of the School of *Fontainebleau with particular
emphasis on the use of elongated female nudes and
*strapwork. During the 1570s, while in Strasbourg
and Augsburg, Delaune published many small-scale
engravings of densely packed *grotesques, *strapwork,

Etienne Delaune. Engraved design for hand mirror, c.1570-80.

*Jean Charles Delafosse. Design for *trophy symbolising Medicine from
his* Nouvelle Iconologie Historique, *1768.*

*fruit and *flowers. These were mainly intended for
gold and silversmiths, enamellers and metalworkers,
but they were adapted for relief work on Rhenish
stoneware mugs and tankards and Limoges enamel.
The decorative themes he followed included classical
mythology such as the Labours of Hercules (*see* Herculean decoration) the *Months, the *Liberal Arts,
battles and *triumphs.

della Bella, Stefano (1610-64). Italian painter and
etcher who also produced ornamental designs, some

*Stefano della Bella. Marine *cartouches incorporating *hippocamps from
his* Nouvelles Inventions de cartouches, *1647.*

of which are clearly influenced by the work of J.*Callot. He worked mainly for the Medici family but from 1639 to 1650 lived in Paris where much of his work was published. His most famous collection, *Raccolta di varii capricii et nove inventione di cartelle et ornamenti* (Paris, 1646), also re-engraved and published in Rome as *Libro di diverse cartelle e scudi d'armi*, is an unusual collection of *cartouches framed and supported by skilfully drawn dogs, horses, bulls, lions and leopards as well as human figures. Some of these designs are asymmetrical and some slightly *Auricular in style. *Ornamenti o grottesche* (c.1640) includes real as well as mythical animals, *camels as well as *sphinxes; *Ornamenti di frege e fogliami* (1646) contains leopards and dogs among *scrolling foliage. Other publications include *Raccolta di vasi diversi* (1640), *Recueil de diverses bacchanales* and *Nouvelles inventions de cartouches* (1647).

della Robbia work. One of the most important contributions to the *Renaissance Revival in England. Approximate imitations of the characteristic tin-glazed earthenware plaques originally made by Luca della Robbia (1400-82) and his family in Florence were produced towards the middle of the 19th century, notably by Mintons and by Doulton & Co. The polychrome stoneware tiles and plaques decorated with *festoons of fruit and flowers and white figures on a light blue ground were intended for both interior and exterior architectural use. Walter Crane wrote of della Robbia work: 'cleanness of surface is in its favour with regard to our black towns; and one would like to see it freely tried, as it would give us *colour* at least.'

de l'Orme, Philibert. Architect who was the first Frenchman to study classical architecture in Rome, c.1533-36. He took a free view of *classicism, recommending the use of new forms and not being bound by Vitruvian principles. He favoured great ornateness in the *Orders, adding his own *French Order, a *banded column, and also one based on the lopped tree trunk, which was derived from earlier sources and called the Rustic Order. In 1547, on the accession of Henri II, he became the official architect to the French court. Almost all of de l'Orme's own work has disappeared except for the Château d'Anet (built for Diane de Poitiers); its gateway is now reconstructed in the courtyard of the Ecole des Beaux-Arts, Paris. His influence on French architecture was through his publications: *Nouvelles Inventions pour bien bastir et à petits fraiz* (2 vols, 1561) and *Traité des Divines Proportions et mesures de l'ancienne et première architecture des Pères du vieil Testament accomodés à l'architecture moderne* (1567; reprinted 1568, 1626, 1628 and 1648). The latter, commonly referred to as *Architecture*, was one of the most practical architectural treatises of the Renaissance, perhaps the reason for its popularity.

demi figure. *See* half figure.

de Montfaucon, Bernard (1655-1741). French antiquary who published the first comprehensive archaeological account of classical antiquities, including buildings, objects and customs: *L'Antiquité expliquée et représentée en figures* (10 vols, Paris, 1719-24); it was translated as *Antiquity Explained and Represented in Sculpture* (5 vols,

Philibert de l'Orme. From his Architecture, *1567.*

London, 1721-25), and a shorter German edition also appeared (Nuremberg, 1757). Though well illustrated it is historically inaccurate, but it proved enormously popular, selling 1800 copies in the first two months after publication and remaining the most important source of its kind until the publication of Abbé *Winckelmann's work later in the century. In 1745, Henry Hoare had seats made for his Ionic Temple of Flora at Stourhead, Wiltshire, that were copied from antique examples illustrated by de Montfaucon. *L'Antiquité* included Egyptian objects (e.g. *canopic jars, mummies) and 'barbaric' designs, as well as an enormous selection of classical objects. Among the engravers who contributed to the work were Giovanni Pietro Bellori (c.1615-1692), P.*Bartoli and Michel Ange de la Chausse. The English edition was arranged with sections covering the Divinities (including 'celestial gifts and graces', *Virtues and Vices, etc.), Ministers and religious buildings (temples, altars, etc.), Greek and Roman customs (dress, contents of houses, sports, games, dancing, hunting, the arts, etc.), military objects, public works, navigation and, in the fifth volume, death. De Montfaucon's coverage of antiquities that were at that time considered to be Etruscan was an important source for the *Etruscan style.

Matthew Boulton bought a copy of the work as late as 1764, and Josiah Wedgwood used *Antiquity Explained* as a source for much of his Egyptian ware produced from c.1770.

dendritic ornament. In ceramics, feathery plant or moss-like markings creating a random or incidental effect and achieved by trailing an acidic pigment over earthenware. It is most common on English mocha ware (so called because it resembles moss agate, mocha stone), often used in combination with bands of pale-coloured slip on jugs and mugs, produced from the late 18th century and during the first half of the 19th century.

D.V. Denon. Ruins of the temple of Hermopolis and various *capitals from his Voyages dans la basse et la haute Egypte, *1802.*

dendritic ornament on mid 19th century English mocha ware jug.

Denon, Baron Dominique Vivant (1745-1825). French collector and antiquarian. He travelled in Russia and southern Italy as a diplomat. In the 1780s and 1790s he published works on Sicily and Pompeii. Of more lasting importance, however, was his journey to the Near East. Denon travelled with a contingent of 160 artists and archaeologists from the Institut des Sciences et des Arts who accompanied Napoleon's military forces to Egypt and Syria from 1798 to 1801. As a result of this visit, Denon produced his classic work on Egyptian art, *Voyages dans la basse et la haute Egypte* (2 vols, Paris, 1802 ; 3 vols, London, 1803; 2 vols, New York, 1803; Florence, 1808). Denon's academic approach to archaeology meant that nothing was unworthy of interest and he illustrated domestic utensils and furniture as well as a wealth of ornamental detail such as *hieroglyphics, emblematic *friezes, *capitals, *sphinxes, etc. The book did much to develop an already growing interest in Egyptian culture, providing an enormously important source for European architects and craftsmen which was much more popularly presented than the official *Description de l'Egypte* (1809-28). Denon's influence on the arts in post-Revolutionary France was considerable: he was Directeur du Musée Central des Arts between 1802 and 1815, and acted as an important arbiter of artistic taste of the age, approving everything made in the Napoleonic court workshops and often supplying his own designs. He owned a famous collection of classical vases which were deposited at the Sèvres factory to serve as examples of a simple classic style. The magnificent *Service Egyptienne* made at Sèvres for the Empress

Josephine in 1812 was painted by Desfontaines with scenes from Denon's *Voyages*. In 1809, bedroom furniture was designed by F.-H.-G. Jacob-Desmalter for Denon, after his drawings of objects at Thebes. Designs loosely derived from Denon's engravings appeared on English transfer-printed ceramics and his name was occasionally used to add authenticity to Egyptian ornament of this type. Not everyone appreciated the charms of the *Egyptian style, however. C.A. Busby in *A Series of Designs for Villas and Country Houses* (1808) stated, 'of all the vanities which a sickly fashion produced, the Egyptian style in Modern Architecture appears the most absurd: a style which for domestic buildings, borders on the monstrous. Its massy members and barbarous ornaments are a reproach to the taste of its admirers; and the travels of Denon have produced more evil than the elegance of the engravings and splendour of his publication can be allowed to have compensated.'

Denon's works provided such an accurate record of archaeological finds that the 19th century Egyptian revival (*see* Egyptian style), which drew heavily on his engravings, achieved an academic respectability comparable with that of the *Greek Revival, although it was never as widely applied.

dentil rim. In ceramics, a decorative edging painted with notches, which is reminiscent of *dentils on a *cornice.

dentils (Latin, *dens*, tooth). Ornamental device consisting of small, spaced blocks running along the lower

*dentils. 1) *Pediment on The Ivy, Chippenham, Wiltshire, c.1730.
2) American maplewood highboy, made in Salisbury, New Hampshire,
c.1775-90. 3) Devonport Town Hall, Devon, by John Foulston, 1824.*

edge of the *cornice, originally used in classical Greek
and Roman architecture. It is similar in appearance
though not in location, to *billet moulding. During
the 18th century dentils appeared on almost every
classical building, whether in wood, stone or plaster.

From the early 17th century dentils appeared on
furniture (bookcases, cabinets, etc.), though not always
in 'correct' architectural positions relating to the use
of the *Orders.

Desgodetz, Antoine (1653-1728). Desgodetz was sent
by the French Académie Royale d'Architecture to
Rome and his study there produced the most accurate rendering to date of Roman classical building.
Les Edifices Antiques de Rome (1682) was dedicated to Jean-
Baptiste Colbert (1619-83), Louis XIV's highly influential Minister of Finance, and was an important
contribution to the classicism of the *Louis XIV style.
It was reissued in 1695 and appeared in a two-volume
English translation in 1771 and 1795 (supplement
added after 1800); it was republished in London in
1848. Desgodetz's work served as the direct source
for many important *Neo-classical buildings, e.g. the
Great Hall at Holkham Hall in Norfolk by W.*Kent
(1734 onwards) in which the colonnade and *entablature came from specific Roman examples illustrated
in the *Edifices*. As late as 1812, Lewis Wyatt (1777-1853)
borrowed directly from Desgodetz for his work at
Willey Park, Shropshire.

deutsche Blumen, German flowers or **Strasbourg
flowers.** In ceramics, naturalistically painted flowers
(e.g. anemones, roses), usually in red, purple and
green, either separate or loosely tied into bouquets,
sometimes with insects among them. *Deutsche Blumen*
all but replaced the earlier vogue for *indianische Blumen. The motif was introduced at Vienna c.1730, but
made famous by the porcelain painter J.G. Höroldt
at Meissen, c.1750-65. *Deutsche Blumen* soon appeared
on porcelain from Stockholm, Venice, Capodimonte,
Mennecy, Dresden, etc., on faïence from Rennes,
Marseilles, Sceaux, Strasbourg, Niderviller, Luneville,
and on opaque glassware from Germany. The flowers
were often painted after botanical engravings such as

those by Johann Weinmann in his *Phytanthoza Iconogra-
phia* (1737-45). By the end of the 18th century, *deutsche
Blumen* were being superseded by more stylised, conventional flower painting, notably at Sèvres.

device. *See* cypher; emblem; heraldic decoration;
impresa; rebus.

Diamant-bückeln (German, diamond bosses). Surface
decoration in the shape of faceted diamonds applied to
17th century German silver. *See also* jewelled strapwork.

diamond-point. *Terminal or *knop of diamond
shape in a pyramid form on silver, brass or pewter
spoons of the late 14th, 15th and 16th centuries.

Diana. *See* crescent; hunting; night.

diaper. Any design of repeated geometric pattern
using a framework filled by such motifs as *lozenges,
squares, *scales or formalised flowers or leaves. The
ease with which diaper ornament can be produced
and its regularity make it one of the most basic and
widely used of all patterns. It is particularly common
in woven textiles where designs are limited to the rectilinear by the warp and the weft. It lends itself to simple

*Antoine Desgodetz. Portico of the Temple of Antoninus and Faustinus,
Rome, from his* Les Edifices Antiques de Rome, *1682.*

diaper. Polychrome tiles, Royal Arcade, Norwich, c.1900.

polychrome effects, as in the widely used *chequer brickwork of *Tudor buildings. Both *chinoiserie and *japonaiserie feature diaper patterns, and they were later enormously popular in Victorian decoration: an overall pattern could be picked up and echoed in fabrics, wallcoverings, furniture, ceramics and floor tiles inside, and in panels of rubbed brickwork or terracotta outside. *Trellis and *lattice are both types of diaper pattern. *See also* counterchange.

Dietterlin, Wendel (1550/1551-1599). German architectural painter whose engraved designs represent a fantastic fusion of the northern European imagination with elements of the Italian *Renaissance and traces of a *Gothic tradition. The *Architectura und Ausztheilung der V Seülen* (from 1593), his sole work, purported to follow the five classical *Orders as described by S. *Serlio, although it contained many examples heavily

Wendel Dietterlin. Engraved design from his Architectura und Ausztheilung der V Seülen, *1598 edition.*

decorated with flamboyant ornament in a *Mannerist style. Dietterlin's amalgam of *strapwork, motifs based remotely on the *grotesque ornament of classical Rome and the Italian Renaissance, and contorted figures – together with much that was idiosyncratic and bizarre in the Northern tradition of the grotesque – was particularly influential in the Low Countries and England. It was difficult to follow Dietterlin's designs to the letter, but the spirit of his work pervades much Elizabethan (*see* Tudor) and *Jacobean ornament. By the late 17th century, however, the term 'ditterling' had become a derisive one.

Volume I of the *Architectura* was published in Stuttgart in 1593, Volume II in Strasbourg the following year. There were editions in German as well as Latin and French parallel texts. In 1598 an enlarged edition with 90 new plates (bringing the total number to 203) was published in Nuremberg. Plates were incorporated in other 17th century treatises and the work was republished in Nuremberg in full in 1655; a facsimile was produced in Liège in 1862. There was never a full English edition although the designs were revived in the *Flemish and *Renaissance Revivals and included in W.B. Scott's anthology *The Ornamentist or Artisan's Manual* (1845). His son, Wendel Dietterlin the Younger, worked in Strasbourg and Lyons as a goldsmith and published engraved grotesques and *peapod ornament. *See also* estipite.

Diocletian or **thermal window.** Semi-circular window, divided into three by two vertical mullions and based on windows at the Baths of Diocletian in Rome. It was a popular motif in *Palladian architecture.

Directoire style. The severe, pared-down *Neo-classical style prevalent in France from the end of Louis XVI's reign in 1795, reaching its peak during the rule of the Directoire (1795-99) and lasting until the burgeoning of the *Empire style. In Directoire furniture, forms tend to be *classical, e.g. *tripods, X-framed stools and chairs, sofas with outward-scrolling ends, but the usually sparse ornament often incorporates *revolutionary motifs such as the *Phrygian bonnet and clasped hands. Later pieces produced during Napoleon's Egyptian campaigns sometimes introduce *Egyptian motifs (e.g. *lotus flower, *sphinx).

Directory or **American Directory** refers to a period in American *Neo-classical design which was based on the French *Directoire style and formed part of the broader *Federal style.

disc moulding. *Romanesque motif consisting of a series of flat disc forms, adjacent but, unlike *coin moulding, not overlapping.

ditterling. *See* Dietterlin, Wendel.

dog. Symbol of fidelity and watchfulness. Sometimes represents smell in the five *Senses. Used on tombs, especially those of women, a dog may represent marital fidelity, as do chained dogs on marriage and mourning jewellery. The *heraldic dog, the talbot, is a common emblem – a stylised creature with a mastiff's body, a hound's head and bloodhound ears.

dog. *Cresting on stone walls surrounding the cour d'honneur, Château de Raray, Ile de France, France, 17th and 18th centuries.

dolphin. 1) *Capital on portal of Vismarkt, Ghent, Belgium, by A. *Quellin the Younger, 1689. 2) American rosewood pier table from the workshop of Charles Honoré Lannuier, c.1815. 3) Waterspout on well head, Steen, Antwerp, Belgium. 4) 19th century lamp standard on bridge at Taunton, Somerset.

Hounds appear in schemes of decoration based on *hunting; they have also occasionally been used to form the handles of mugs and jugs, notably by the American potter Daniel Greatbach (fl mid 19th century), in his work at the Jersey City Pottery and at Bennington. William Hogarth's dog Trump (included in a self-portrait of 1745) was a popular symbol of the spirit of fidelity in the second half of the 18th century, and models made from plaster moulds originally sculpted by L.F. Roubilliac were produced at Chelsea and by Wedgwood and Thomas Bentley. Similarly, *Punch's dog Toby was used ornamentally, e.g. evoking the idea of guard dog on cast-iron doorstops. *See also* seadog.

dog nose. *See* trifid.

Dog of Fo. Chinese mythological animal that is half-dog, half-lion, and used to guard temples and images of Buddha (Fo means Buddha), and precious works of art: hence its appearance as a finial on porcelain vases. Sometimes the animal is playing with a silk ball tied to a ribbon held in its mouth, sometimes it spits flames. Dogs of Fo were frequently used as *finials on Western ceramics of the 17th century.

dogtooth. An elaboration of the earlier *nailhead form, this star-like decoration is carved in relief and used as a repeating *moulding enrichment. It is an *Early English Gothic motif but continued to be used into the 15th and 16th centuries in brickwork and woodwork, and occasionally appears even later. In late Gothic ornament it was replaced by the *ballflower.

dolphin. A motif on Etruscan and subsequently on early Christian sarcophagi. The dolphin is considered

Dog of Fo. 1) *Finial on early 18th century Chinese blue and white porcelain vase.
dog-tooth. 2) Ely Cathedral, Cambridgeshire, 12th century.

King of the Fish, as the *eagle and *lion are thought to be rulers of the birds and beasts. *Christian allegory originally adopted the dolphin from classical art when the Church was still underground. A dolphin with a ship or an *anchor represents the Church guided by Christ. It also came to represent Christ as saviour of souls and as the bearer of souls over the waters of death (reflecting the folk belief that dolphins save shipwrecked mariners). In *classical ornament, the dolphin appears (often with *nereids and *tritons) as an attribute of the Roman god of the sea, *Neptune (or the Greek Poseidon), sometimes twined around the god's trident, and in depictions of *Venus (or her Greek counterpart, Aphrodite) rising from the waves.

One of the most rapidly assimilated motifs of the Renaissance, the dolphin was used with great frequency: as a support – the head forming a base, the tail forming an S scroll above; in the manner of a *grotesque, with the tail transforming into *scrolling foliage; as a formal ornament, e.g. two dolphins symmetrically paired with tails entwined. The dolphin and anchor, adopted by the Venetian printer Aldus Manutius (1450-1515) to illustrate a popular Renaissance maxim, *festina lente* [make haste slowly], subsequently became a favourite typographic ornament.

An obvious component of *marine and *riparine ornament, dolphins appear on ships, bridges, wellheads, fountains, embankments, seaside hotels, fish markets, even on bathroom fittings and drain pipes.

Doric drops. *See* guttae.

Doric Order. *See* Orders.

dove. An attribute of *Venus, and a symbol of *love and constancy certainly since Roman times (doves take only one mate during their lives). In the 18th

dove. 1) French Louis XIV *boulle *cabinet. 2) Enamelled decoration on plate, c.1930.*

century, doves were used in the ornament of furniture and objects given as wedding gifts, usually in pairs, billing, sometimes perched on the bow and quiver of *Cupid.

In *Christian iconography, the dove is a symbol of the Holy Spirit (John the Baptist described the Spirit 'coming down from heaven like a dove') and ornaments tombs and memorials; some medieval Eucharists were in the form of a dove. It represents innocence and baptism and has therefore been used on children's objects, e.g. christening mugs, cradles. With an olive branch in its beak, it is a symbol of peace (deriving from the Old Testament story of Noah's Ark) – a popular image in the 1930s when peace in Europe was felt to be under threat.

Downing, Andrew Jackson (1815-52). American landscape architect, horticulturalist and author of *pattern books in the English *Picturesque vein. *Cottage Residences* (New York and London, 1842; 12 reprints and revised editions before 1887) was followed by *Architecture of Country Houses* (Philadelphia, 1850; 8 further editions before 1865). Both books show buildings derived from English examples but furnished in the French style. Downing was an enthusiastic proponent of the Picturesque and criticised the *Greek Revival for its lack of harmony with nature. He used the designs of others in his pattern books, in particular the work of the influential architect and furniture designer Alexander Jackson Davis (1803-92) whose work encompassed the full range of *eclectic styles, including *Greek, *Etruscan, *Gothic, *rustic and *Empire. He was the architectural partner of C.*Vaux.

dracontine. One of the most common types of *zoomorphic ornament based loosely on *dragon-like creatures. Its sinuous forms were often used as the basis for interwoven patterning in *Celtic and *Viking art. *See also* lacertine.

dracontine. Carved beam on 16th century house at Coggeshall, Essex.

dragon. In Western mythology, dragons are generally evil, destructive creatures with a serpent's body and a fierce head and claws, sometimes spitting fire, often with a forked tongue. Dragons with bat-like wings appear frequently in medieval ecclesiastical art: in wall painting, carved on *capitals and in woodwork, painted on tiles and in illuminated manuscripts; they were probably copied from designs on Eastern silks traded in Europe in the 11th and 12th centuries. Later, *grotesque designs sometimes replaced the dragon's head with that of a woman. Twenty-five types of dragon (all symbolic of evil) appeared in the *bestiaries, including the *salamander and the *wyvern. In legend, dragons are generally malevolent custodians of knowledge, of treasure or even of innocent maidens, and are fought by heroes such as St George and Perseus. For the Celts, however, the dragon was a symbol of chiefdom.

In Chinese art, the dragon has enormous symbolic importance: despite its ferocious aspect it is wholly beneficent and represents supernatural power, fertility, strength, wisdom; it is therefore associated with the emperor. Its appearance varies, but characteristics include: the horns of a stag, the head of a camel, the eyes of a demon, the neck of a snake, the belly of a clam, the scales of a carp, the claws of an eagle, the soles of a tiger, the ears of a cow. Often, the Chinese dragon clasps the 'flaming pearl' of wisdom and enlightenment. It is sometimes used with the *phoenix

dragon. 1) Engraving from A New Book of Chinese Designs *by M.*Darly and G. Edwards, 1754. 2) Decoration on late 19th century building, Barcelona, Spain.*

drapery. 1) San Stefano dei Cavalieri, Pisa, Italy, by G. Vasari, 1596, façade 1606. 2) Late 18th century English silver decanter label. 3) 19th century doorway, Antwerp, Belgium. 4) Wallpaper by Wm Woolams & Co., London, c.1870.

(or *ho ho bird) to represent opposites: Heaven and Earth, the Emperor and Empress. A complex hierarchy of dragons developed, e.g. the Imperial dragon has five claws, the common dragon four, the Japanese dragon three; the hornless dragon lives in the sea, controls the water and symbolises the scholar.

Little of the complex significance of the Chinese dragon was understood by Western artists producing designs for *chinoiserie, but they plundered motifs from Chinese ceramics with impunity: in Germany Meissen produced the Red Dragon pattern c.1730, which was rapidly copied in France at Chantilly and known as the Prince Henri pattern. In England Bow used a dragon in the 1750s and Caughley produced a popular transfer-print called the Broseley Blue Dragon c.1780.

Dragon style. Popular style of ornament derived from *Viking art (in which the *dragon is a central motif). Equivalent to the *Celtic Revival in Britain, it was used on carved furniture and silver during the second half of the 19th century in Scandinavia, particularly Norway. Elements of the style were taken up in Nordic *Art Nouveau.

drake's foot. *See* trifid.

drapery. In *classical and *Renaissance schemes of decoration, a *swag of drapery sometimes replaces the *festoon of flowers that hangs from the horns of a *bucranium or is threaded through the scroll of a

*volute. It may also swathe *masks and heads in *strapwork designed by 16th century French and German *ornemanistes. Admirably suited to the theatricality of the *Baroque, drapery was widely used across Europe from the late 16th to the early 18th century, appearing carved in stone or painted *trompe l'oeil*-style on church domes, hung down the sides of mirrors and windows, etc., sometimes accompanied by *tassels. From the late 17th century it also decorated *apronwork and chimneypieces. Drapery swags were a favourite ornament on American *Federal style chair-backs and on English *Neo-classical furniture in the styles of T. *Sheraton and G.*Hepplewhite.

In early 19th century France and England, real drapery became immensely fashionable in interior decoration, possibly prompted by the development of machinery to weave fabric of much greater width: ceilings and beds were draped like tents, sofas were crowned with hanging fabric, window curtains were extraordinarily elaborate. So great was the enthusiasm that chintzes and wallpapers were printed with drapery motifs and even with elaborate window dressings of blinds and curtaining. *See also* vandycked swags.

drawing books. 18th and 19th century guides for amateurs ranging from instruction in the art of drawing to collections of ready-made compositions, similar to those in *pattern books. Indeed professional craftsmen may well sometimes have consulted this material intended for amateurs, and vice versa. One of the most famous and successful drawing books was *The Ladies' Amusement or Whole Art of Japanning Made Easy* published by Robert Sayer of Fleet Street (1760, 1762, 1775). The 200 plates contained over 1500 designs, many based on earlier work by J.*Stalker and G. Parker, M.*Darly and J.*Pillement; a substantial number were engraved by R.*Hancock who helped himself liberally to fashionable motifs from compositions by J.A.*Watteau, F.*Boucher, Jacopo Amiconi (c.1682-1752), Thomas Gainsborough (1727-88) and Francis Hayman (1708-76). Some of the *Rococo designs, many in the *chinoiserie taste, of *birds, *animals, *ruins, lovers and *fruit appeared in transfer-printed and painted ceramic decoration and on enamels before the publication of the book, suggesting that the designs had previously been published separately. Other examples of Robert Hancock's work are included in *The Artist's Vade Mecum* (1762), Henry Parker's *The Compleat Drawing Book* (1762, 1775) and *The Compleat Drawing Master* (1763, 1770).

Drawing books specialising in botanical designs were popular for ceramics, embroidery, etc. Early examples are A. Heckell's *Lady's Drawing Book consisting of about an Hundred Different Sorts of Flowers* (1753) and Johann Daniel Preissler's various works published in Nuremberg 1734-84. P.-J.*Redouté's work was published in *L'Aquarelle ou les Fleurs peintes d'après la Méthode de M. Redouté* by Antoine Pascal (1836). Drawing books continued to flourish in the 19th century when enthusiasm for amateur decoration was at its height.

Dresser, Christopher (1834-1904). English botanist and designer whose theories, expounded in publications and lectures and demonstrated in his own

Christopher Dresser. 1) English ceramic vase, Mintons, 1867. 2) English cast-iron chair made by the Coalbrookdale Co., c.1875. 3) Design for stained glass window from his Principles of Decorative Design, *1873. 4) English plate produced by the Old Hall Porcelain Co., 1886.*

designs for commercial manufacture, were an important influence on the move away from superabundant *naturalism and towards a functional and organic theory of ornament. His first book was *The Rudiments of Botany, structural and physiological: being an introduction to the Study of the vegetable kingdom* (1860) followed by *The Art of Decorative Design* (1862). His most important works were, however, *The Principles of Decorative Design* (1873) and *Studies in Design* (1874-76). 'By his art the ornamentist may exalt or debase a nation,' Dresser wrote, and he devoted his life's work to establishing a proper basis for ornament, especially in the area of what would now be called industrial design. He was eclectic in his choice of styles although he avoided some: ' . . . with the coarse Assyrian, the haughty Roman and the cold Renaissance I have no kindred feeling,' he claimed in the *Principles*. The historical styles were a tool with which, he considered, designers should 'strive to produce new forms and new combinations in the spirit of the ornament of the past.' Dresser was fascinated by frameworks in the natural world such as plant structure, or even the human skeleton: with the 'friendly aid of natural forces' beauty could be added to the useful, but he disdained the 'deceit' of *trompe l'oeil* techniques such as woodgraining and *marbling.

Dresser was concerned about the debasement of oriental design to meet Western tastes and in 1876-77 he visited Japan, China and the Philadelphia Centennial Exhibition, which included a large number of Japanese exhibits. In 1882 he published *Japan, its architecture, art and art manufactures*, a careful account which put much emphasis on manufacturing processes. He claimed that he wrote for the working man, and believed that manufactured goods should be produced at a price that he could afford.

Dresser's impact was enormous – both through his published work, which reached Europe and America (influencing, for example, L.H.*Sullivan), and through his designs which wholeheartedly embraced mechanical processes and were produced by commercial manufacturers such as the Coalbrookdale ironworks (for whom he designed a number of products from 1871 onwards), Elkingtons, the silver and electroplate manufacturers, the Minton and Wedgwood ceramics factories and many other companies. He did much to elevate the role of industrial designer.

With the aid of science and history, Dresser believed, the grotesque mistakes of the Great Exhibition could be rectified and industrial design would become both ornamental and functional. He considered that ornament should 'appeal to scholarship – to knowledge of what has been done, rather than to any faculty by which distinct originality is evolved.'

drops. 18th century term for *guttae.

Also, the wooden *pendants sometimes carved on the bases of newel posts on Elizabethan and *Jacobean staircases.

drop ornament. *Gothic ornament consisting of a border of *pendants along the inner edge of an arch; it is comparable to *cusping but the drops hang more freely.

Ducerceau, Jacques Androuet (c.1515-84). French architect and *ornemaniste*. He visited Rome in the 1540s and on his return published the first of a large number of engraved works which encapsulated the spirit of the style that came to be known as the French *Renaissance, the bases of which were Italian *Mannerism and its French counterpart, the School of *Fontainebleau. Ducerceau's work constituted one of the few French sources for architecture and decorative motifs in the mid 16th century. Some designs were his own, some copied from the work of Italians such as E.*Vico, A.*Veneziano, S.*Serlio, Polidoro da Caravaggio and Perino del Vaga, and some recorded existing works of architecture. His first architectural publications were *Arcs* (1549), which was dedicated to Henri II and contained fantastic renderings of Roman *triumphal arches and *Temples* (1550). The *Livre d'architecture* (1559), influenced by Serlio, suggested patterns for houses for all ranks of society and contained decorative use of the *Orders which proved to be highly influential. The *Second Livre d'architecture* followed in 1561, and the third in 1576. *Les Plus Excellens Bastimens de France* (1577 and 1579) records, with Ducerceau's variations, the major buildings of the French Renaissance. One of his last books, *Petit Traité des cinq ordres de colonnes* (1583), also covered the five Orders.

Ducerceau was prolific in his publications on ornament, and covered most of the forms and motifs fashionable at the time. His first suite of *Grotesques* was published in 1550 and was again close to the work of Italians such as Veneziano, Rosex da Modena and particularly Vico. The second edition of 1562 had extra plates after *grotesques by Primaticcio. He published a second book of *Grotesques* in 1566, more in the *Fontainebleau style. He followed *Livre contenant passement de moresques* (1563) with a collection of large panels, *Grandes Arabesques* (1566), and one of small panels, *Petites Arabesques*. He also produced designs for *friezes, *cartouches, *balustrades, *caryatids, *herms, *vases, cups, jewellery, church and domestic plate, locks, *fleurons, military *trophies and marquetry. He took some metalwork patterns from the work of Hans Brosamer and P.*Flötner, and his designs were copied and published in Nuremberg and adapted by other French engravers such as H.*Sambin. He produced a collection of furniture c.1560, which was the first to be published in France and correspondingly influential: the basic forms are *classical, but the detail is rich and fantastic with grotesque caryatids, *sphinxes, *harpies, nymphs with elongated necks and limbs, *swags of fruit and flowers, *strapwork and *arabesques.

Ducerceau, Paul Androuet (c.1630-1713). Probably a relative of J.A.*Ducerceau. An *ornemaniste* and goldsmith, he produced ornament for small-scale objects in enamel, marquetry, woven silk or embroidery as well as for larger schemes of decorative painting. He published over twenty collections (usually in sets of six plates) mainly between 1660 and 1680. His ornament consists principally of *scrolling foliage with flowers and birds, *bandwork and *masks.

duck foot, drake foot, Dutch foot or **web foot.** American term for a three-toed foot on 18th century furniture, usually on a *cabriole leg. A typical feature of furniture produced in the Delaware River Valley area.

Durand, Jean-Nicholas-Louis (1760-1834). French academic, architect and theorist who, in his position

Paul Androuet Ducerceau. Engraving of fleurs à la persienne *for embroidery and silks, mid 17th century.*

as professor of architecture at the Ecole Polytechnique, Paris from its foundation in 1795 and in his publications, promoted a version of *Historicism based on a system of bays marked by round-headed arches upon which ornamentation of a chosen historical style could be superimposed. The *Recueil et parallèle des édifices en tout genre, anciens et modernes* (1800), which expounded this theory, was influential, particularly in the development of the *Rundbogenstil in Germany during the second quarter of the 19th century.

Dutch gable. Houses in Grote Markt, Antwerp, Belgium, mainly 15th and 16th centuries, restored.

Dutch gable. The gable ornamented with curved sides, or *volutes, often surmounted by a conventional *pediment, was a common decorative feature of northern *Baroque architecture originating in the Netherlands. There are endless variants of the form, including stepped versions and hipped gables (with the topmost section sloping back). The form travelled to England (particularly East Anglia) in the 17th century.

In the 19th century, the *Flemish Revival made use of highly elaborate Dutch gables, with stepping, series of volutes and the pediment often pushed to an extremity and much reduced.

dwarf. *See* Callot, Jacques.

eagle. From Assyrian times, a symbol of power and victory; the eagle has been considered King of the Birds as the *lion is King of the Beasts. Also an attribute of Jupiter (and his Greek counterpart Zeus), the highest, most powerful god, lord of the heavens, god of rain, storms, thunder and lightning – eagles sometimes appear with emblems of *thunder and lightning grasped in their talons. The legend of Ganymede (the most beautiful of all mortals) being carried off by Zeus disguised as an eagle also makes appearances in schemes of classical decoration. The eagle occasionally represents Sight in ornament depicting the *Senses. In Christian iconography: an eagle fighting a *serpent is an ancient symbol of spiritual victory over sin; it is also an attribute of St John the *Evangelist, sometimes with a pen or inkhorn in its beak; the eagle form of lecterns signifies evangelism.

The standards of Roman legions bore an eagle as a symbol of strength, and many countries have adopted it since as a national emblem. The Holy Roman Empire's emblem was a double-headed spread eagle (symbolising perpetual watchfulness). After the collapse of the Holy Roman Empire in 1805, the double-headed eagle continued to be used as the emblem of

*eagle. 1) 12th century woven silk from Sicily. 2) Medici monument, Piazza Medici Riccardi, Florence, Italy, mid 15th century. 3) English *console table of carved and gilded wood, mid 18th century. 4) American blue glass flask made at Kensington Glass Works, Philadelphia, c.1825-33. 5) Berlin porcelain plate decorated with the Russian Imperial eagle, c.1870. 6) U.S. Administration Building, New York, 1930.*

my wings everything prospers'. In 1815, Samuel McIntire, a cabinetmaker and woodcarver in Salem, Massachusetts, advertised 'eagles from 5 inches to 2ft 6 inches'. More generally, eagles tend to appear wherever a heavy classical Roman style of ornamentation is being used, e.g. topping a gateway or mirror, or supporting a console table, the head in profile, the talons grasping naturalistically modelled rocks.

ear. *See* crossette.

Early English. The first phase of English *Gothic, c.1190-c.1310, as defined by Thomas Rickman (1776-1841) in *An Attempt to Discriminate the Styles of English Architecture from the Conquest to the Reformation* (1817), and clearly illustrated in A.C.*Pugin's *Specimens of Gothic Architecture* (1821-23). Distinguishing features are the pointed arch, simple *tracery forms, a refinement of some *Romanesque motifs, e.g. *dogtooth mouldings and naturalistic foliage carved on *capitals.

In the *Gothic Revival, *Early English style ornament (sometimes called Reformed Gothic) was popular

Early English. North Transept, Beverley Minster, Yorkshire, from T. Rickman's The Styles of Architecture, *1848 edition.*

the Austro-Hungarian Empire until World War I. Among the countries that have adopted the single or double-headed eagle are Prussia, Poland, Nazi Germany, Russia, France under the Napoleonic Empire and the United States of America.

In France, where Napoleon had formally adopted the eagle as a military emblem in 1804, it quickly became one of the key motifs of the *Empire style, often encircled, like ancient Roman examples, in a victor's *laurel wreath. The Americans, anxious after the Revolution to proclaim their patriotism and new nationalism, chose the indigenous bald eagle, although the form chosen was firmly based on the classical prototype with spread wings. It sometimes appears with a striped shield covering its body and either a halo of *stars or starred *banderole in its beak; it may be clutching an *arrow in one talon, and an *olive branch in the other. Occasionally it appears in conjunction with a *cornucopia illustrating the motto 'Under

Eastlake style. 1) American hickory secretaire cabinet in the manner of Charles Eastlake, c.1870. 2) English wallpaper, 1880s.

for longer than the more elaborate *Decorated and *Perpendicular styles. B.J.*Talbert wrote in 1867 that it had 'breadth and simplicity' and William Burges (1827-81) drew on the Early English style for domestic furnishings and metalwork as late as the 1870s.

earth. *See* Elements.

Eastlake, Charles Locke (1836-1906). As an architect and writer on the arts, Eastlake provided an important link between later phases of the *Gothic Revival and the early stages of the *Arts and Crafts movement in England. *Hints on Household Taste in Furniture, Upholstery and other Details*, published in London in 1868, appeared in its first American edition in 1872. The English edition ran to four reprints, the American to six. The book was a mixture of Eastlake's own designs and those of other leading architect designers of the day. In America, Harriet Prescott Spofford, author of a comparable American volume entitled *Art Decoration Applied to Furniture* (1878), remarked, 'not a marrying couple who read English were to be found without *Hints on Household Taste* in their hands'. Motifs from the book such as turned *baluster finials and knobs were soon accepted into the repertoire of American design. Eastlake's wish was to build on tradition and he disapproved of 'this absurd love of change – simply for the sake of change.' He considered that *eclecticism had degraded the decorative arts and that a careful study of selected objects from the past, such as *Jacobean, medieval German and *Early English furniture, would provide a salutory simplicty. He hated the *Rococo. Unlike other theorists of his period, he did not have strong preferences either for hand-crafted objects or for those mass-produced by machines and was prepared to accept both. Before long, the qualities of design that he espoused were (much to his dismay) to become known as the 'Eastlake Style'. Other publications such as Clarence Cook's *The House Beautiful* (1877) helped to promote his influence. In America, the Philadelphia Centennial Exhibition of 1876 was

important in spreading the styles advocated by Eastlake to a wider audience. His name became synonymous with American 'art furniture' (corresponding to English *Aesthetic pieces). The applied ornament was geometric and often incised in thin bandings, on *mouldings, *pilasters, etc. His success in America far outweighed his popularity in England; one English observer thought his work 'suggestive of a cheap style'. By 1886 a contemporary observer noted that in America 'the amplifications of Eastlake's designs continue to be offered to the public, though they have almost ceased to be made in England.'

ecclesiastical hat. Heraldic emblem based on the wide-brimmed cardinal's hat with a network of tassels hanging down on each side: 15 tassels denoted a cardinal, 10 an archbishop, 6 a bishop, 3 an abbot. The shape evolved at the end of the 15th century. It was used (instead of a *helmet) to surmount the arms and decorate the tombs of those churchmen with the right to wear the Pontifical hat in papal cavalcades, i.e. cardinals, bishops and pronotaries. In English heraldry, an ecclesiastical hat appearing above a *coat of arms or as a crest on gates or doors has come to indicate the Roman Catholic church or affiliation to it.

ecclesiastical hat. Early 16th century wall ornament, Mosteiro dos Jerónimos, Belém, Portugal.

echinus. A variant of *ovolo moulding used below the *abacus of a Doric *capital (*see* Orders). It is also the moulding ornamented with *egg and dart situated beneath the cushion of an Ionic capital.

eclecticism. During the 19th century, a highly eclectic attitude to design became popular and the styles of the past were pilfered to provide a vast range of motifs. Unlike *Historicism, which generally involved careful study of the past based on archaeological and scholarly accounts, eclectic design was a much less scrupulous respecter of original integrity of style. Accurate and, often, well-informed though the *pattern books or compilations of O.*Jones, William Bell Scott (1811-90) or H.*Shaw were, they still promoted an anarchic view of design. Shaw offered the best of every style and period 'therefore furnishing hints for a selection of parts which when combined may produce a new arrangement of equal elegance: thus constituting a mass of material from which the artist or manufacturer may derive a succession of entirely normal designs.' In *The Ornamentist or Artisan's Manual* (1845), W.B. Scott drew on work by W.*Dietterlin, J.*Berain,

W. Zahn and 'the best of French and German ornamentists' ranging from the 16th to the 19th century. The same publication offered designs in 'Grecian, Roman, Arabesque, Gothic, Elizabethan, Louis Quatorze and Renaissance' styles and illustrated works from a far wider range than even that list suggests. The eclectic designers also, following the example of the 18th century *Picturesque architects and furniture designers, emphasised the idea of an appropriate style or motif: thus R.*Ackermann's *Repository* in November 1825 showed an episcopal chair 'in the style of Henry VIII [which] may be introduced with propriety into a church, prelate's mansion, or an extensive library.' It was not, however, considered inappropriate to combine the aspects of several styles in a single piece and such catholicism was positively encouraged in the planning of suites of rooms within large country houses, gentleman's clubs or similar grandly conceived buildings. If a house was not large enough for a *Gothic library, then a Gothic bookcase would do: if strength was required, then a seat could suitably be supported by a *lion. Such tips and many others were available from Ackermann's monthly magazine.

New mechanical techniques for the reproduction of stone or woodcarving, fabric printing or electroplating (among many other innovations), and the improved manufacture of certain materials, such as terracotta and *papier mâché*, contributed to the ease with which styles or parts of styles were imitated. C.F. Bielefeld, 'inventor and sole manufacturer' of an 'improved *papier mâché*', claimed that it was ideally suited to the 'exact imitation of the bold florid carvings in such styles as Gothic, Flemish, French, Elizabethan' in *Ornaments in every Style of Design* (1840). Although authors such as C.A.*Chenavard had mixed the Gothic, *Louis XV, *Assyrian, Chinese, *Egyptian and *Greek styles in his *Nouveau Recueil de décorations intérieurs*, he was merely widening the range from that offered by architectural publications of the 18th century such as J.B. *Fischer von Erlach's considerable selection in 1721. Picturesque pattern book authors gathered material from far and wide: R.*Brown's *Domestic Architecture* (1842) was not unique in offering such styles as Moriso-Spanish, Plantagenet Castle, Edward III style and Burmese together with the more common offerings such as Egyptian or Venetian. From around the mid 19th century schools of design and museums of the decorative arts were founded to promote and display the riches of the past. Many objects were exhibited as plastercasts; in London, the Cast Court of what was to become the Victoria & Albert Museum opened in 1873. *International exhibitions also contributed to the wealth of source material available. The official report to the Paris Exposition Universelle, 1878, commented that 'a perfect comprehension of any style and a complete assimilation of ancient techniques have made this exhibition resemble a museum in which an extremely wealthy collector has gathered together the most perfect types of furniture of all ages.' Specific qualities were ascribed to styles deriving from particular countries or periods: productions from the Sèvres factory in 1875 were described as including 'purity and grace from Greece, severity and vigour

from the Etruscans, sparkle and originality from Persia, variety and wonderful colour from the Chinese, the sparkling decor of the Japanese, grace and ingenuity of Arabic art, abundance and richness from the Italians, nobility and distinction from Louis XVI, etc.' Manufacturers were encouraged to select elements from a wide range of styles; designers of interiors laid out suites of rooms as if they were museum settings. *The Decoration and Art Trades Review* (London, 1889) set a competition: entrants were to design a dining room in the medieval style, a drawing room in the *Louis XVI style, a boudoir in the Moresque style and a hall or vestibule in the *Pompeiian style, a scheme that was not at all unusual, especially in America. Harriet Prescott Spofford in *Art Decoration Applied to Furniture* (1878) had firmly counselled the use of Gothic for libraries and *Rococo for parlours – very much as A.J.*Downing and others had advised earlier in the century in line with Picturesque theory.

At the height of the fashion for eclecticism, ornaments and style had become far more important than form. The *Arts and Crafts movement, both in Europe and America, constituted the first strenuous reaction against this tendency. The introduction to the 1887 edition of C.L.*Eastlake's *Hints on Household Taste* suggested that 'the only legitimate use of past styles is such as was made by the artists of the Renaissance.' Further reactions were demonstrated in *Art Nouveau, and, later, in more rigorous returns to functionalism and a rational approach to design.

In America, however, the continuing attraction of stylistic revivals meant that an eclectic attitude to architectural ornament persisted well into the 20th century, despite reactions against it. The Philadelphia architect Frank Furness (1839-1912), and Nicholas Clayton (1849-1916) who worked in Galveston, Texas, both used an imaginative combination of motifs and styles. Ralph Adams Cram (1863-1912), writing of his plans for work at the Rice Institute, Houston, completed 1912, described his search for a 'round arched style based on the Southern development during the eleventh and twelfth centuries of the architecture of the Byzantine and Carolingian epochs. It will bear some resemblance to the early medieval work of Italy, South France and North Spain, and will show borrowings from the East and also from the Spanish missions of Mexico and the Southwest.' Some residential areas in America built in the 1980s still present houses deriving in style from dozens of sources, ranging from Tudor to Spanish.

edge roll. *See* bowtell.

Edwards, George (1694-1773). English ornithologist, caricaturist and illustrator who collaborated with M. *Darly on *A New Book of Chinese Designs*. His *Natural History of Uncommon Birds* (1743-47) was used as a source for porcelain birds modelled at Chelsea in the 1750s.

egg and dart, egg and tongue, egg and anchor or **egg and star.** One of the most widely used classical *mouldings consisting of egg shapes and V shapes, used to enrich an *ovolo moulding such as the *echinus on Ionic *capitals (*see* Orders), and known from its use

egg and dart. 1) Exterior moulding, Layer Marney, Essex, 1520s.
2) Capitals, interior, Polesden Lacey, Surrey, remodelled 1906-08.

on major ancient Greek buildings such as the Erechtheion. A.*Swan, an 18th century carpenter and joiner,
wrote in *A Collection of Designs in Architecture* (1757), 'some
gentlemen forbid it in their houses, being displeased
with its name, and supposing it to represent an unnatural mixture or combination of things which have
no relation to one other viz. eggs and anchors . . . I
would propose to change that unnatural name . . .
into the much more proper and true name of nuts
and husks.' Despite the misgivings of some classically
educated gentlemen, however, egg and dart became
an ubiquitous moulding detail in wood, stone or plaster in *classical style buildings of every description
well into the 19th century, with manufacturers selling
plaster moulding enrichments by length. The inquiry
into the origin of the moulding continued in the 19th
century. O.*Jones suggested somewhat mystifyingly
in *Grammar of Ornament* that the origin of the egg and
dart was a lotus border and alternating bunches of
grapes.

Egyptian style. Knowledge of ancient Egyptian art in
early Renaissance Europe was extremely limited. Roman emperors who had travelled in Egypt brought
back to Rome a few ancient Egyptian artefacts, some
connected with the cult of the goddess Isis. The occasional Egyptian motifs that appeared in *Renaissance art, notably *obelisks, *hieroglyphics and certain
Egyptian gods, derived from this source. The *sphinx
had appeared in the Bestiary of Physiologus (*see* bestiaries) and occasionally re-emerged in decoration from
the late 13th century. The Colonna family considered
that their ancestry derived from Apis and Egypt – the
frontispiece of the Colonna Missal provides a catalogue of the Egyptian motifs known at the period.
The Tabula Bembi or Mensa Isaica (a bronze tablet
inlaid with gold and silver hieroglyphs, gods, etc.)
was discovered pre 1520, and published by E.*Vico in
1559. This and other artefacts found during the Renaissance aroused great interest and engravings of
them by both Italian and foreign archaeologists and
architects ensured that the stock of Egyptian motifs
gradually increased.

Study of Egypt and travel there grew in the 16th
and 17th centuries, but it was not until the second
half of the 18th century that ancient Egyptian art and
antiquities began to make a serious impact on Western
decoration. Influential engraved collections of Greek
and Roman art, which were essential sources in the
development of *classicism, sometimes included a
small section on ancient Egypt. Thus, B.*de Montfaucon's *Antiquité Expliquée* (1719-24) contained illustrations of *pyramids and sphinxes as did J.B.*Fischer
von Erlach's *Entwurff einer historischen Architektur* (1721).
A wider range of ornament appeared in the Comte
*de Caylus's *Recueil d'antiquités égyptiennes, étrusques, grecques,
romaines et gauloises* (7 vols, 1752-67) based on his collection of artefacts excavated from the ruins of Hadrian's
villa at Tivoli; souvenirs of Hadrian's Egyptian campaign were installed in the Capitoline Museum in
Rome in 1748. Illustrated travel books, e.g. Richard
Pococke's *Observations on Egypt* and F.L.*Norden's *Travels
in Egypt and Nubia* (London, 1757), further broadened
the vocabulary. By the mid century, Egyptian motifs
appeared as an exotic ingredient in *Rococo designs.
An early use of Egyptian decoration was by G.B.*Piranesi in the Caffè degli Inglesi in Rome (1765), where
he applied a wide selection of Egyptian detail in a
light, unacademic style; he included engravings of
these designs in his influential *Diverse maniere d'adornare
i cammini* (Rome, 1769). The fact that little was known
or understood of Egyptian architecture allowed an
unsystematic approach to Egyptian ornament. In
1767 Josiah Wedgwood devised a black basalt ware,

*Egyptian style. From G.B.*Piranesi's* Diverse Maniere, 1769.

described by him in 1779 as having 'the appearance of antique bronze, and so nearly agreeing in properties of the basalt of the Egyptians, no substance can be better than this for busts, sphinxes . . . '; he used it for *canopic vases, sphinx spill-holders and inkstands ornamented with *scarabs, *winged discs and *lotus. Wedgwood & Bentley used designs by de Montfaucon as source material. Anton Raphael Mengs (1728-79) produced suitably Egyptian decorations for the Camera dei Papiri in the Vatican (c.1770) and a pyramidic dairy designed by A.J. Carter was illustrated in the *Builder's Magazine* (1774).

During the 1790s, Napoleon began planning his Egyptian campaign. 'The time is not far distant,' he wrote in 1797, 'when we shall feel that, in order to truly destroy England, we must occupy Egypt.' The annihilation of the French fleet by the British at the Battle of the Nile in 1798 gave rise to English interest in Egypt and some whimsical fashions, a crocodile motif, for example, appeared on furniture. C.H.*Tatham published in 1799 a series of etchings of Egyptian artefacts including the sphinxes, lions and idols that could be seen in the Villa Borghese and the Vatican Museum in Rome; these provided a good, archaeologically correct source for designers such as T.*Hope and G. *Smith. Under Napoleon, an information-gathering Institut d'Egypte was set up in Cairo in 1798, which published the exhaustive official account: *Description de l'Egypte* (23 vols, 1809). This, together with the work of D.V.*Denon provided the basis for a much more serious study of the country and its ancient culture. Egyptian-style architecture began to appear. P.F. Robinson's Egyptian Hall in Piccadilly, London (1812) and the interior of the subterranean Egyptian Hall at Stowe, Buckinghamshire (c.1800), modelled on the temple interior of Tintyra, were both based on engravings by Denon, as were numerous designs for the decoration of ceramics, glass, etc. As early as 1809 the writer Maria Edgeworth commented satirically on the style in her novel, *The Absentee*, in which Mr. Soho proclaims: 'You can have the Egyptian hieroglyphic paper with the ibis border to match. The only objection is that one sees it everywhere – quite antediluvian – gone to the hotels even.'

Two themes dominated Western understanding of ancient Egyptian culture: a fascination with the cult of the dead and the process of mummification, and the association of the Egyptian culture with the arcane. As a result the Egyptian style was a frequent choice in the 19th century for cemeteries, and also appeared in the ornament of *masonic lodges and the meeting houses of other secret societies. Egyptian-style decoration even appeared on steam engines, examples of which were shown in the machinery court of the Great Exhibition, London, 1851. The style was popular in the 1830s in America where it was used, for example, by the architect John Haviland (1792-1852) for the New Jersey State Prison, New York

Egyptian style. 1) Oddfellows Hall, Devonport, Devon, by John Foulston, 1824. 2) German sewing machine made by Frister & Rossmann, c.1924. 3) Walnut and marquetry stool, 1920s. 4) American upholstered armchair, 1870. 5) English screen-printed cotton designed by Jenny Lowndes for Warners, 1967. 6) Former cinema, Essex Road, Islington, London, by George Coles, 1930.

City Jail ('The Tombs') and the County Court at Newark, New Jersey, the massive appearance of the style seeming appropriate for secure buildings.

However the general attitude prevailing among architects and designers was expressed by the writer J.C. Loudon: 'Never . . . adopt, except for motives more weighty than a mere aim at novelty, the Egyptian style of ornament.' As one of the many styles adopted by authors of *Picturesque pattern books, Egyptian ornament also occurred in the repertoire of *eclecticism.

The opening of the Suez Canal in 1869 redirected attention towards Egypt and new archaeological discoveries stimulated fresh interest: the discovery of Giza during the 1860s and 1870s resulted in both Liberty & Co. and Tiffany producing Egyptian influenced objects and there was a fashion for Egyptian jewellery. In 1922, the discovery of Tutankhamen's tomb provoked yet another craze for Egyptian ornament, both on small, relatively ephemeral objects and on a grand scale, in the architecture of factories and cinemas. In the case of cinemas, the style was considered appropriately exotic for the newest form of public entertainment. One of the most grandiose examples was Grauman's Egyptian Theatre in Hollywood (1922).

Eisler, Johann Leon(h)art (c.1670-1733). Goldsmith and engraver working in Nuremberg in the early 18th century who produced at least seven suites of ornamental designs for *Laub und Bandelwerk. He also published a collection of *mask designs and *cartouches representing the *Months.

elbows. *See* ancones.

Elements, The Four. Fire, water, earth and air. As a decorative theme it was occasionally used in the *Renaissance, usually represented by the appropriate classical god: Vulcan the smith for fire; *Neptune or a river god for water; Juno (who, as a punishment of Jupiter,

was once suspended from the heavens) for air; a fertility goddess such as *Ceres for earth. An alternative, as in the work of C.*Ripa, was to portray female figures holding suitable attributes: for fire, a flaming head, a *thunderbolt or a *phoenix; for water, *marine beasts such as *dolphins; for air, a chameleon which was believed to live on air; for earth, the scorpion of the Roman agricultural goddess, Tellus Mater, or the castellated (or mural) *crown of Cybele, the Phrygian earth mother.

However, it was in the 17th and 18th centuries that the theme appeared most frequently. Often motifs are whatever the designer's imagination could connect with the Elements; thus on a 17th century Soho tapestry (at Burghley House, Northamptonshire) air is represented by a border of wind instruments. 18th century decorators such as F.*Boucher alluded to the theme by depicting associated activities performed by near-naked *children or elegantly dressed adults: angling (water), horticulture (earth), bubble-blowing or windmill-watching (air). The theme was popular in 18th century France, Germany and Britain as a decoration for enamelled glass and for porcelain figures or as transfer-printed decoration on ceramics. *See also* fire; flames.

elephant. Early legends portray the elephant as a war machine: Alexander the Great used elephants bearing wooden towers in which his soldiers hid when he conquered northern India by his defeat of Porus in 326 BC. This was related in the Romance of Alexander, one of the most widely known and illustrated of medieval stories, and an elephant with a castle on its back subsequently became a frequent medieval motif. In Chinese, Indian and Persian chess sets, the rook was often elephant-shaped. The association of the elephant with victory, perhaps compounded by the exploits of Hannibal, led to decorative schemes in which they pulled the chariot of *Fame. In the *bestiaries, the belief that elephants mate unwillingly led to the animal being used (with or without a castle) as a symbol of the chastity of Adam and Eve, and it appeared carved on medieval misericords, *poppyheads and *capitals. With other motifs derived from the East, elephants were included in designs on 13th century Italian woven silks, which often clearly showed that

Elements. 1) Four Meissen vases modelled by J.J. Kändler representing water, fire, air and earth.
elephant. 2) Elephant and castle motif on 13th century Italian brocade.

elephant. 1) English musical box and clock, mid 18th century. 2) Elephant House, Bronx Zoo, New York, architects Heinz and La Forge, 1911.

Europeans were still unsure of the exact appearance of the beast, although when in 1255 Louis IX of France presented Henry III with an elephant, its journey from Sandwich to the King's menagerie at the Tower of London was well documented by contemporary artists. The ancient use of the elephant as an emblem of kingship was revived by Rosso Fiorentino (1494-1540), who devised a badge composed of an elephant and *fleur-de-lis* for François I. Like the camel, the elephant is often used as a support, a function appropriate to its role as a beast of burden: Archbishop Urso's carved stone throne dating from c.1080 (in Canosa Cathedral, Apulia) is supported by two elephants. The *Hypnerotomachia Poliphili* illustrates an elephant supporting an *obelisk, an idea repeated by the sculptor Giovanni Lorenzo Bernini (1598-1680), who made an elephant base for an ancient Egyptian obelisk which was erected in the Piazza Minerva, Rome. Although J.A.*Ducerceau attempted to design elephant legs for a bed, the animal was more popular as a support for clocks, globes, etc. *Vases were produced at Meissen and Sèvres in the mid 18th century with three elephant heads emerging in tripod form, their trunks forming candleholders. This design (which was probably based on a Chinese Ming original) appealed greatly to the *Rococo taste for the exotic. In representations of the *Continents the elephant is an attribute of Africa, though for the British, the absorption of India into the Empire made it an apt motif of the *Indian style, and revived its connection with a sovereign, in this case Queen Victoria, Empress of India.

Elizabethan. *See* Tudor.

Elizabethan Revival. The Victorians, who associated the reign of Queen Victoria with that of Elizabeth I (1558-1603), revived the 'Elizabethan' style in its own right, rather than treating it as a strand of the *Tudor. The idea of the Elizabethan as a 'national style' together with the Gothic (*see* Gothic Revival) had been fostered before Queen Victoria's accession. In 1835, a Parliamentary Select Committee recommended that the Palace of Westminster be rebuilt in Gothic or Elizabethan style. With the prosperity that came after the breaking of the Napoleonic blockades, Britain

had begun to build up its trade overseas and the confidence of a nation whose economy was based on sea power and overseas colonies was further bolstered by analogies with an earlier epoch of maritime glory and commercial success. The reign of 'Good Queen Bess', regarded as an era of domestic comfort, security and expansion, was an attractive parallel. R.*Ackermann's *Repository* included Elizabethan designs for furniture in 1817. J. Nash's *Mansions of Old England* (1839-49) combined careful topographical observations with scenes of traditional customs, such as Twelfth Night festivities. Other creators of *eclectic design such as H.*Shaw treated the Elizabethan as equal to the Gothic style in importance. In *Details of Elizabethan Architects* (1834) Shaw stated that the style had 'survived the prejudices which first embarrassed its revival: and with all its exuberance and variety of details has been adopted with success in the designs of several considerable mansions recently erected.' He cited original examples throughout his account, in line with the antiquarian approach of the period. The architect Anthony Salvin designed houses in Elizabethan style, such as Mamhead in Devonshire, 1828-30, and Harlaxton Manor in Lincolnshire, 1831-37, complete with Elizabethan suites of furniture. Furniture *pattern books including the Elizabethan style were Shaw's *Specimens of Ancient Furniture* and R.*Bridgens's *Furniture with Candelabra and Interior Decoration* (1838). The Elizabethan Revival consisted chiefly in the use of details: panelling, plasterwork, *heraldic motifs and *strapwork. Many of the motifs were produced with great facility as a result of the development of such techniques as machine carving and of C.F. Bielefeld's new *papier mâché*, which was, he claimed, suited to the 'picturesque and fantastic forms of the Elizabethan style'. Publishers such as John Weale and designers such as Bridgens and Thomas King promoted the fashion and it endured until well after the Great Exhibition (1851). The silverware company Chawmer & Co. first produced an 'Elizabethan' design for flatware c.1850 which had a little interlaced strapwork besides the more usual shells. In the 1920s and 1930s the London firm of Liberty reproduced Elizabethan furniture, and new 'Elizabethan' motifs such as *galleons were incorporated into stained glass doors

*Elizabethan Revival. Table at Leeds Castle, Kent, from H.*Shaw's* Specimens of Ancient Furniture, *1836.*

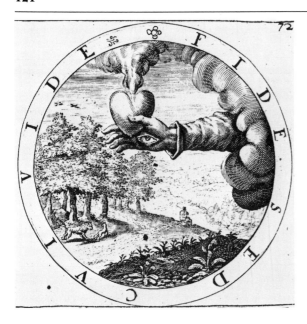

emblem books. 'Give Credit; but, first, well beware, Before thou trust them, who they are' from George Withers's A Collection of Emblemes Antient and Moderne, *1635.*

and windows, fabrics, electric light fittings, etc., to be used in both domestic and public settings, particularly public houses. *See also* Jacobean Revival; Tudor Revival.

emblem books. Books containing epigrammatic mottoes or verses accompanied by emblematic woodcuts or engravings which were fashionable in the second half of the 16th and most of the 17th century. The emblems derived principally from classical mythology – figures of *Bacchus, *Cupid and Hercules (*see* Herculean decoration) were common, and from medieval *personifications and ideas, such as the *Wheel of Fortune, heraldry and *bestiary animals. The first and most influential emblem book was A.*Alciati's *Emblemata* (Augsburg, 1531). It was translated into French, English and Spanish, the number of emblems was greatly increased and the book ran into over 90 editions by the end of the 16th century. Emblem books became known and used across Europe as Renaissance ideas spread, demonstrating a well-developed taste at this period for symbolism and allegory. The cryptic character of some emblematic designs led to a belief that they had originated in Egyptian *hieroglyphics. Subsequent emblem books often borrowed heavily from Alciati; however, emblem writing became a gentlemanly accomplishment and new publications were legion. In France two early and influential collections were *Le Théâtre des bons engins* by Guillaume de la Perrière (1539) and *Devises Héroiques* by Claudius Paradin (Lyon, 1551). The earliest emblem book published in England, Geoffrey Whitney's *A Choice of Emblemes and other Devises, for the most part gathered out of sundrie writers, Englished and Moralized* (1586), used imported plates from, among other sources, Alciati and Paradin. Whitney's introduction describes emblems as ornaments placed upon any surface so as to form a pattern or device, 'such figures or workes as are wroughte in

plate, or in stones in the pavements, or on the waules, or suche like, for the adorning of the place. . .' Another important English book was *Minerva Britanna* by Henry Peacham (1612). Two popular and influential emblem collections were published in 1635: Francis Quarles's *Emblemes Divine and Moral* and George Withers's *A Collection of Emblemes Antient and Moderne*. The illustrations in emblem books were easily accessible sources of decoration reflecting contemporary interest in their selection of emblems, symbols and *personifications. Emblems were particularly popular in embroidery: Mary Queen of Scots used designs from Paradin in her work, and they frequently appeared in tapestries, wall paintings, embroidered hangings and plasterwork. At Hatfield House, Hertfordshire, there is a tapestry of the *Seasons with borders containing 170 emblems, 29 of which derive from Whitney. The gallery ceiling at Blickling Hall, Norfolk (c.1625-35) has motifs adapted from Peacham. By the late 17th century, emblem books were produced for children and, in an increasingly classical age, came to appear unsophisticated and 'medieval'.

Empire style. A *Neo-classical style in French interior decoration, furniture, silver and ceramics that reflected Napoleon Bonaparte's achievements and ambitions for the new empire, his role as a patron of the arts and his own sense of style: 'A King does not exist in nature,' he wrote, 'he exists only in civilisation: there cannot be a King *simple*, he is only a King when dressed.' The establishment of various members of Napoleon's family as representatives of the Imperial government across Europe contributed to the spread of the style. Important designers included C.*Percier and P. Fontaine, the Emperor's own architects, J.C. *Krafft, P.-N.*Beauvallet, C.P.J.*Normand, and P. *La Mésangère. Characteristic elements include: severe rectangular shapes; classical motifs already popular in the *Style Etrusque such as *palmettes, palm-leaf forms, *anthemion, *acroteria, *monopodia, six-pointed *stars, winged *lions and *eagles forming armrests and supports; Roman motifs indicative of Napoleon's eagerness to identify France with the military prowess of the Roman Empire – *wreaths of

Empire style. Early 19th century French cotton made at Jouy.

Empire style. Napoleonic bed from Château de Malmaison (Hauts-de-Seine), France.

*laurel and *oak, lances, *arrows, *fasces, figures of *Victory and *Fame, *griffins, *chimeras, winged *torches, etc.; a large letter N (for Napoleon) sometimes appears, as do the *bee, his personal emblem, and the *swan, that of the Empress Josephine; Egyptian motifs such as *lotus flowers, *scarabs and *hieroglyphics (largely taken from D.V.*Denon's *Voyages dans la basse et la haute Egypte*) celebrate the success of Napoleon's campaign there.

Furniture makers in America, notably the Scot, Duncan Phyfe (1768-84), and Charles-Honoré Lannuier (1779-1814), were strongly influenced by the style. In American Empire style furniture strenuous efforts were made to imitate Greek and Roman originals, most importantly the klismos chair.

encarpa or **encarpus.** 17th and 18th century terms used by architects, carvers, etc. for *festoons of fruit, flowers or foliage.

endive scroll. *See* seaweed.

engine-turned decoration. Curving or geometric patterns incised on metal or clay by means of the machine lathe developed in the late 18th century. Soon engine-turned *chevrons, *chequers, *fluting, even simulations of *moiré* silk and *basketweave patterns were achieved on ceramics and metalwork. The technique was first used by French goldsmiths in the 1760s and quickly adopted by the English pottery manufacturers D.J. & J.P. Elers and, from the 1770s, by Wedgwood.

English Cottage style. 19th century American *Picturesque architecture based on the *cottage orné*.

entablature. A horizontal beam connecting a series of columns and forming the upper part of an *Order. It is divided into the *cornice (uppermost section), *frieze (intermediate) and *architrave (lower), which all bear certain *mouldings and enrichments according to classical conventions.

entrelac (French, *entrelacer*, to interlace). Term sometimes used to refer to the *interlacing ornament of *Celtic Revival and *Art Nouveau stone and metalwork. Occasionally entrelac may refer to *guilloche designs.

escallop. Heraldic term for a *scallop shell. The escallop sometimes has two holes in it indicating its use as a pilgrim's emblem, when it was suspended from a leather thong.

escutcheon. *See* cartouche; shield.

*espagnolette. Engraving by P.A.*Ducerceau, mid 17th century.*

espagnolette. Female mask with a ruff around the head and under the chin, a popular motif in 18th century French decoration particularly during the *Régence. The motif probably developed from the heads with feather circlets that appeared in engraved sources of mid 16th century *Netherlands Grotesque ornament. These, it is suggested, were representations of Mexican headdresses given by Chief Montezuma to the Spanish explorer, Fernando Cortez. Cortez presented them to Charles V and they were subsequently exhibited around Europe, notably in Brussels in 1520. Another suggestion is that *espagnolettes* derived from the Spanish fashion for stiff lace collars. *Espagnolette* heads appear in *boulle* work and in the designs

engine-turned decoration. 1) Early 19th century gold snuff box.
*2) English caneware in *basketweave pattern, Wedgwood, c.1810.*

of D.*Marot, J.*Berain and J.-A.*Watteau, among others. Occasionally a ruff of the same style appears around a dog's head (in the work of N.*Pineau) or a *lion mask. In *Art Nouveau decoration, a variation of the *espagnolette* head has a *swag of drapery replacing the ruff under the chin.

estipite. An elaborately ornamented *pilaster based upon the patterns engraved by W.*Dietterlin and other Northern *Mannerist designers, and adopted in 18th century Spanish *Baroque achitecture. It consists of numerous panels, ornamented with geometric patterns or *cartouches bearing sculpture in low relief, and separated by intermediate *capitals.

estoil. Heraldic *star with six wavy-sided points.

Etruscan style. The ancient civilisation of Etruria centred on Tuscany and part of Umbria in Italy from the 7th century BC until about 200 BC when it was suppressed by the Romans. Until the beginning of serious archaeological research in the 18th century, Etruscan art was considered to be a strand of Roman culture. In the mid 18th century vases that were believed to be Etruscan (but later discovered to be late classical Greek) were unearthed at various sites including Pompeii and Herculaneum. They appeared in engravings by P.S.*Bartoli, and in collections of antiquities published by the Comte *de Caylus and B. *de Montfaucon. These black and red figure vases provided the basis for 'Etruscan style' furniture, interior decoration and ceramics. The style was characterised by the use of red, black and white, and motifs such as *lions, *birds, *sphinxes, *harpies, *griffins, etc., many of which had formed part of the true Etruscan ornamental vocabulary. It was first used from the 1760s in France on *Louis XVI furniture and was quickly adopted in Britain, notably by Robert Adam (*see* Adam

Etruscan style. Painted chimney board for the Etruscan Room at Osterley, Middlesex, designed by Robert Adam, 1777.

style), whose Etruscan Room (1775) at Osterley House, Middlesex, had walls and doors painted with motifs similar to those in Pompeian wall paintings – delicate, airy, circular and lozenge-shaped *medallions suspended from *festoons and *husks. Vertical strips of decoration were composed of *tripods, *urns, leaves, *chimeras and *half figures. The Catel Brothers decorated the painted Etruscan Room in the Kronprinzen-Palais, Berlin, c.1800. Sir William Hamilton's collection of *vases from the tombs of Magna Graecia was bought by the British Museum in 1772 and constituted a valuable source of first-hand information for designers. Josiah Wedgwood, the potter, produced Etruscan ware from 1769 (in *rosso antico* and black basalt ware). From 1786, Etruscan-style porcelain was produced at Naples and at Sèvres, where the factory had a collection of vases that had belonged to D.V.*Denon. By the end of the 18th century, it had been realised that the origin of the vases was Greek, but the form of decoration continued to be described as Etruscan. Etruscan-style pottery, imitating that by Wedgwood, was produced c.1840; glass made by Richardson of Stourbridge was enamelled in Etruscan colours using *palmettes, *anthemions, figurative scenes, etc. Some silver was engraved in the style but was not altogether successful as it lacked the essential colouring. At the beginning of the 19th century, enthusiasm for archaeology grew. Etruscan gold and jewellery were found at Vulci on the estate of Lucien Bonaparte and his wife wore some of the pieces, providing patterns for jewellery in that style. Etruscan metalwork techniques, notably filigree and *granulation, were copied in *Archaeological style jewellery, signalling a keener awareness of the Etruscan culture.

Evangelists, Four. The name derives from the Greek for 'proclaimer of the Gospel'. From the 3rd century the term referred specifically to the four authors of the Gospels: Matthew, Mark, Luke and John. In *Romanesque and *Gothic ecclesiastical ornament, each Evangelist was represented by a winged creature: Matthew by a man, Mark by a *lion, Luke by an ox and John by an *eagle; the wings symbolise divine mission. These four images were based on the beasts described in the Old Testament as surrounding the throne of God in the Apocalypse (Ezekiel 1:5-14 and Revelation 4:6-8). From the Renaissance, the creatures tended to appear with figures of the saints as attributes, rather than alone.

eye. 18th century architectural term for the centre point in the *volute scroll of the Ionic *Order, usually when it is cut in the form of a rose.

eye. 1) All Saints Church, Camden Town, London, architect H. Inwood, 1822. 2) Eye of Horus over door of The Wellcome Building, Euston Road, London, architect Septimus Warwick, 1931.

eye. In ancient Egypt the eye of Horus was an amulet of protection; it appears in 19th century Egyptian-style ornament. The ancient Greeks used the apotropaic eye to ward off evil; good luck charms ornamented with eyes (usually made of glass) are still worn in Greece.

In *Christian iconography, an eye usually represents the eye of God, often in the centre of a triangle representing the Trinity, a device commonly included in *emblem books.

In French and American *revolutionary ornament, the eye represents enlightenment: it appears on the Great Seal of the United States.

eye and scale. American term for *coin moulding when used on mould-blown or pressed glass.

fables. Illustrations of fables such as the Fox and Stork or the Fox and Grapes by Aesop appeared in medieval ecclesiastical art, e.g. carved on misericords and roof *bosses in English country churches. A.A. Filarete (c.1400-70) included images from fables in the ornament of the bronze doors of St Peter's in Rome. An edition of Aesop illustrated with woodcuts was produced by Caxton in 1484; a similar edition appeared in Lyons, c.1490. *Aesop Fabulae*, containing engravings

*fables. 1) The fox and the stork by V.*Solis from* Aesop Fabulae, *Frankfurt, 1574. 2) Plaster decoration, Aesop's fables ceiling, dining room, Áras an Uachtaráin (the former Viceregal Lodge), Dublin, 1751. 3) English display cabinet by Clement Heaton with painted panels illustrating Aesop's fables, c.1880.*

by V.*Solis, among others, was published in Frankfurt in 1574.

In the 17th and 18th centuries, engraved illustrations of fables by Aesop and Jean de la Fontaine (whose first six books retelling many of Aesop's stories were published in 1668) were immensely popular, and many editions appeared across Europe. Perhaps the most notable were a series of engravings by Francis Barlow (c.1626-1702) for a translation of Aesop's fables from the Greek by a Mrs Behn (1666), and the illustrations by J.B. Oudry (1686-1775) to a four-volume edition of *Les Contes de la Fontaine* (1755-59). An Amsterdam edition of the Barlow Aesop published in 1714 describes itself as 'very useful to painters, sculptors, engravers and other artists or amateurs at drawing, who will find animals and birds drawn with exquisite taste and knowledge.' Fables were used extensively as decorative themes in *Rococo ornament. J.J. Kändler modelled sauceboats for Meissen with decorative handles that illustrated the Oak and Reed (1737) and the Eagle's Nest (1742). M.*Lock's *Six Sconces* (London, 1744) and *Six Tables* (London, 1746) and T.*Johnson's *Twelve Girandoles* (London, 1755) adapted engravings by Barlow and incorporated them into Rococo designs. Decoration based on fables seems to have been at the height of its popularity in the 1750s and 1760s and examples exist on plasterwork at Nuthall Temple, Nottinghamshire, at Kirtlington, near Oxford, and at Heythrop and Clandon Park, Surrey, all executed during the 1750s. Barlow's engravings were republished in *Weekly Apollo* during 1752. Chelsea produced porcelain figures of the Fox and Stork in that and the following year. Fables remained popular in ornament well into the next decade and Barlow's work was once again raided, this time by W.*Ince and J. Mayhew for *Picturesque ornament included in *The Universal System of Household Furniture* (1759-62). American furniture and woodwork carved with scenes from fables was produced in the 1760s; an overmantel in the ballroom of the Stedman-Powel House, Philadelphia (1768) depicts three fables including the ubiquitous Fox and Grapes.

During the *Rococo Revival of the 1840s fables occasionally reappeared, particularly on teapots and jugs. *Hints on Household Taste* by C.L.*Eastlake has an illustration of an oak cabinet painted by Clement Heaton (1824-82) with scenes from Aesop's Fables; Mintons produced a series of tiles showing fables designed by Heaton in the *Aesthetic style in 1880.

faceted ornament. *See Diamant-bückeln*; jewelled strapwork; lozenge.

Fame was personified in classical art as a winged female figure in flowing drapery. Typically, the figure was carved on the *spandrels of a triumphal arch. Renaissance examples may carry one or two trumpets to illustrate the spread of fame, or a *palm to signify triumph and victory; occasionally the figure stands atop a globe, to signify world renown. Fame was used to ornament arms and armour, as well as figuring with *Mars in decorative schemes alluding to battle. Representations of famous men (and occasionally women) are often accompanied by Fame, e.g. supporting portrait busts on tombs and memorials or even

Fame. Silver portrait frame made in Paris, 1672.

carved on picture frames. Fame may appear with a similar personification, *Victory, and is sometimes indicated simply by a *laurel wreath.

In the mid 18th century, transfer-printed ceramics were produced in Staffordshire showing Shakespeare and William Pitt accompanied by Fame. A favourite Napoleonic motif, the figure appeared frequently in *Empire ornament, both on small-scale objects, e.g. forming the handle for a sugar bowl, and used architecturally, as on a plaster *cornice. It was included in R.*Ackermann's *Selection of Ornaments* (1817-19).

fan. Both semi-circular and circular fans appear in Chinese and Japanese ornament. A fan shape is one of the main elements in *brocade patterns, and it was an important motif in the 19th century fashion for *japonaiserie*, when real Japanese fans were collected, particularly in England.

Stylised semi-circular fan shapes, often fluted or with a 'writhing' pattern, effectively a half-*patera, were a frequent feature of *Adam style decoration.

'fancy-back' patterns. *See* Hanoverian pattern.

fanlight. A semi-circular light above a door with decorative glazing bars usually radiating from the centre and often elaborated. A useful practical device for admitting light into long, narrow entrance halls, it is highly characteristic of 18th century architecture. *See also* lunette.

Fantuzzi, Antonio (1510-c.1550). Italian who worked with F. Primaticcio at *Fontainebleau, and engraved work by the leading artists of the School in the 1540s. His own *strapwork designs,, typically with nude elongated female figures, were particularly influential.

fan. 1) American brooch in the form of a Japanese fan, made by Tiffany & Co, c.1905.
fanlight. 2) Early 19th century house in Monmouth, Wales.

fan vault. The Divinity School, Oxford (1483), from T. Rickman's The Styles of Architecture, *1848 edition.*

Fantasievögel. *See* birds.

fan vault. In English *Perpendicular Gothic roof vaulting, a complex fan shape formed by the interlacing of ribs, tiercerons and liernes. The late 18th, early 19th century *Gothick style used fan vaulting ornamentally, often where it had no structural function. In the late 18th century, the Coade Manufactory of London produced artificial stone vaulting in a ready-moulded form for instant application. The motif was widely used in the *Gothic Revival.

*fasces. 1) Ornament designed for the Town Hall (now Royal Palace), Amsterdam, by A. *Quellin, mid 17th century. 2) New Town, Edinburgh, 18th century.*

fasces (Latin, bundles). A bound bundle of rods, often enclosing an axe-head, which was a symbol of the authority of ancient Roman Magistrates: the rods (originally birch) denoted their power to scourge, the axe their power to behead. Fasces appear in *military and legal decorative schemes (*see* Justice). Cardinal Mazarin (1602-61) adopted the fasces as his badge and they were carved on the doors of the Palais de l'Institut in Paris built at his instigation. They were a popular component of the *Empire style. In Edwardian *classicism the motif was widely applied, but without symbolism. In the 1930s the fasces became a potent symbol of the fascist movement in Italy, although the motif still appeared without any specific significance in classical schemes across Western Europe, notably on office blocks or department stores.

feather-edged border to English porcelain plate made at Derby, c.1758.

Fates. In Greek mythology, three old women personify the Fates. One old woman (Clotho) spins the thread of life on a distaff or spinning wheel, another (Lachesis) measures it and holds the spindle, the third (Atropos) snips the thread. The theme occasionally appears on 18th century clocks.

Father Time. *See* time.

feathers. The most common ornamental application of feathers is the group of three known as the Prince of Wales feathers. According to tradition, the emblem (three ostrich feathers) was adopted in 1346 by the Black Prince at Crécy from the crest of the King of Bohemia whom he had just killed. Some *Jacobite glass was engraved with three feathers signifying loyalty to the Young Pretender, Charles Stuart.

The motif was used without heraldic significance in the early 18th century, often as a *cresting ornament on mirrors, and appeared in the designs of D.*Marot and J.*Berain. Robert Adam (*see* Adam style) used radiating feathers at the centre of a ceiling design in imitation of the ceiling of the Temple of the Sun, illustrated by R.*Wood in *The Ruins of Palmyra.* At this period a form that partly resembled a feather, partly a *waterleaf (or stiff leaf), was used, particularly several at a time, e.g. on *capitals in classical-style interiors. Hepplewhite introduced a three-feather motif for chair-backs and inlay at the top of table legs, and it was also used by Sheraton.

According to some authorities the use of this emblem in the early 19th century, e.g. on chairs, *pediments, bookcases, bedtesters, indicated support for the Regent and his Whigs (as opposed to the old King's Toryism). American chair-backs decorated with five feathers took up the fashion, while avoiding precise reference to the British monarchy.

A panache is a heraldic device consisting of a circlet of upright plumes arranged in a pyramid shape and borne on a helmet or staff. A similar headdress based on that of the American Indian, also sometimes called a panache, appears as an attribute of America in decorative schemes depicting the *Continents. During the War of Independence, France became an ally of America and adopted certain of the new national motifs, notably the feathered headdress: e.g. panels of the Cabinet du Roi at Versailles were crowned with the motif, which was doubly popular as a result of the cult of the romantic, and particularly the idea of the 'noble savage' as described in the writings of J.J. Rousseau (1712-78).

An *aigrette* was a late 16th, early 17th century head ornament with jewels, enamels, sometimes even real feathers arranged to form feather shapes. *Aigrettes* were again worn during the reign of Louis XV (1715-74), and in the *Regency.

feathered decoration. *See* combed decoration.

feather-edged. In ceramics, a moulded border of a wavy scalloped shape with feathery ribbing. It occurred mainly in the second half of the 18th and in the 19th centuries.

Also, a type of engraved decoration on late 18th century silver.

feather ornament. Type of woodcarving resembling a feather which was used on vertical sections of (particularly English) 17th century furniture.

feathering. A series of *cusps or drops in *Gothic and *Gothic Revival architecture used along *mouldings and around windows, doorways, arches, etc.

Federal style. The predominant style in America from the Declaration of Independence in 1776 through to the early decades of the 19th century. Unsurprisingly, the influence of Britain remained dominant during the early years and the early Federal style is based clearly on the *Adam style, isolated examples of which were beginning to appear just before the Revolution (e.g. the plasterwork of the dining room at George Washington's house, Mount Vernon, Virginia, which was completed in 1775). Particularly suited to domestic buildings, the style is typified by arched windows, *fanlights and delicate columns on the exterior, while the interiors were more richly decorated with *festoons of *husks, *paterae, *rosettes, *urns and *scrolling foliage. Charles Bulfinch (1763-1844), Surveyor of Works for Washington, produced domestic work typical of this style. Parallel with this was the purer *Neo-classical taste of Thomas Jefferson (1743-1826), America's third president. He was the first American statesman to visit France and therefore had knowledge of current European styles. He gathered around him a group of architects and designers, many of whom

Federal style. Florence Griswold House, Old Lyme, Connecticut, 1817.

*Federal style. Brass and giltwood looking glass made in Massachusetts,
c.1790-1810.*

colours, gilt, ornamented and varnished in style only
equalled on the continent . . . real views, Fancy landscapes, flowers, trophies of Music, War, Husbandry,
Love etc . . . window and recess seats, painted and
gilt in the most fanciful manner with and without views
adjacent to this city.' Views of the Hudson River with
New England or New York in the background also
featured. At the beginning of the 19th century the
work of the cabinetmaker Duncan Phyfe (1768-1854)
led the way in the introduction of forms of furniture
based rigidly on Greek and Roman examples: curule
chairs, klismos legs and animal *monopodia were
popular. Many of Phyfe's ornamental details, typically
the cross or lattice-back chairs and *lyre-backed chairs,
came from the *London Chair-Makers' and Carvers' Book of
Prices* (1802, supplement 1808). He also used the *harp
on chair-backs. The influence of French *Empire
designers became gradually stronger, resulting in
heavier detailing and a richer effect, characterised by
the work of cabinetmaker Charles Honoré Lannuier
(1779-1819).

The term American Directoire (or Directory) is
sometimes used to cover the period approximately
1805-30, and American Empire, 1810-30.

femme-fleur or **dream-maiden.** A motif typical of
French *Art Nouveau – a beautiful, sensuous young
woman with flowing hair and half-closed eyes, often
entwined with flowers and tendrils. *Femmes-fleur* appeared on jewellery, light-fittings, vases, paper knives,
even on *keystones. Typical *femme-fleur* figures were
often used in depictions of Leda and the Swan, a recurring subject at the period.

*femme-fleur. 1) Silver mirror back, early 1900s. 2) Art Nouveau
decoration on house in Calle General O'Donnell, Santa Cruz de Tenerife,
Canary Islands. 3) Early 20th century terracotta panel on a hotel,
Plymouth, Devon.*

had trained under the European Neo-classicists, in
order to create buildings for the new capital city,
Washington, and the government buildings for the
new Confederation, which was established in 1788.
Jefferson himself provided the plans for the State
Capitol of Virginia, which showed the first Neo-classical use (apart from garden temples) of a complete
temple form, based on a Roman temple in southern
France, the so-called Maison Carré in Nîmes. Jefferson described it as 'noble beyond expression' and as
'presenting to travellers a specimen of taste in our
infancy, promising much for our mature age.' He
continuously favoured Roman models, as interpreted
by French classicists, e.g. Roland Fréart, a copy of
whose *Treatise* he owned.

In furnishings, the lead at first remained British.
American cabinetmakers followed the *pattern books
of Robert Adam, G.*Hepplewhite and T.*Sheraton,
also T.*Shearer's *The Cabinet-Maker's London Book of Prices*
(1788, 1793) – the result of a collaboration between
several designers. Ornamentation followed fashionable
English examples, although the symbol of Federal
Union, the American *eagle, was proudly inlaid,
carved and painted on many objects. *Baskets of fruit
and *cornucopias were used more widely in this period
than in England. National *topographical decoration
gradually became popular on painted furniture: an
1805 advertisement from a Baltimore cabinetmaker
offers 'Elegant, Fancy, Japanned furniture . . . all

*fern. *Capital, Albert Buildings, Queen Victoria Street, City of London, architect F.J. Ward, 1871.*

fêng-huang. *See* ho ho bird.

ferns were keenly collected in 19th century Britain and grown in conservatories and Wardian cases, becoming a highly popular motif in Victorian ornament, in line with the liking for dense and elaborate natural forms. Scottish souvenir objects were decorated with ferns, e.g. work produced by the Holyrood Glassworks, and 'fernware' – small wooden objects stencilled with fern shapes produced by applying a real leaf and spattering the object with brownish colour. Ironwork garden tables and seats as well as architectural features ornamented with ferns appeared in trade catalogues of cast-iron objects and were exported world-wide. Fern patterns also appeared in glass, textiles and ceramics, including tiles.

ferronnerie (French, ironwork). In ceramics, dense, scrolling patterns of *arabesques and *volutes that appear to be based on ironwork designs. They appeared on mid 16th century tin-glazed ware made in Antwerp but inspired by Italian designs, and on 17th and early 18th century faïence from Rouen, Moustiers and Strasbourg. J.*Berain included *ferronneries* in his designs.

festoon. Loops of fruit and flowers bound together with *ribbons and leaves were common in classical Roman ornament, deriving from the real fruit and floral garlands hung around the *friezes of temples, and therefore often incorporating skulls (*bucrania) and heads (*aegricanes) of sacrificial animals, and ritual instruments such as the *tripod and *candelabrum. It was a frequent decoration on the *metope of the temple frieze. The festoon became one of the key motifs of the *Renaissance, with *rosettes, rings, *lion masks or *putti often replacing the aegricanes and bucrania. In the 16th and 17th centuries, vegetables and shells were often added to the fruit, flowers and foliage. In the 17th century, highly skilled woodcarvers such as the Quellin family in Amsterdam and Grinling Gibbons (*see* Gibbonwork) in England produced fine, elaborately modelled festoons for interiors and furniture, increasing their popularity. For the artisan, there were *pattern books such as Henry Roberts's *A New Book of Festoons after ye Italian Taste* (1670). At the

beginning of the 18th century, heavy and intricately carved decoration, and therefore the festoon, fell from popularity. However it soon reappeared in a much lighter form in *Neo-classical decoration: the *Adam style made much use of it, frequently with the bucranium and/or aegricanes, though often replacing the flowers and fruits with strings of *husks and drops.

*festoon. 1) Ancient Roman *frieze. 2) Silver candlestick by Hendrick Christoph Nicolaas Wiedman, Amsterdam, 1783. 3) Title page of Henry Roberts's A New Book of Festoons after ye Italian Taste, 1670. 4) One East Penn Square, Philadelphia, Pennsylvania, architects Ritter & Shay, 1930. 5) 'Fancy capital' from M.*Darly's Architectural Designs and Ornament, 1770s. 6) Harvard Club, West 44th Street, New York, architects McKim, Mead & White, 1894-1915.*

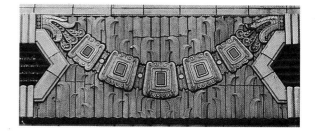

French *Louis XVI decoration favoured thick, loosely hanging, rope-like *swags of densely packed *laurel leaves, as in the designs of *ornemanistes* such as J.C. *Delafosse. *Empire-style festoons tend to be thick, slightly flattened and with *rosettes among the foliage. In the late 18th century, G.*Richardson suggested garlands of fruit and flowers as a suitable ornament for dining-room ceilings. A favourite 19th century use of the festoon was looped around the bottom of a *bracket.

In other media the festoon was infinitely adaptable, changing its character according to the prevailing style, ranging from heavy *Baroque swags deeply embossed and chased on a silver salver to delicately engraved festoons of husks on a Neo-classical sugar bowl, or a light, flowing festoon inlaid on a mid 18th century French *bonheur-du-jour* (lady's work table).

Décor à guirlandes is a painted or moulded decoration on ceramics, a border of festoons around a central panel, introduced notably at Alcora (Spain) and at Moustiers (France) in the early to mid 18th century.

fêtes galantes. Ornamental theme of the *Rococo derived from a mid 18th century style of painting that depicted fashionably dressed men and women in a romantic landscape. Engravings after work by F. *Boucher, J.-A.*Watteau and Nicolas Lancret (1690-1743) were transfer-printed on ceramics, notably by R.*Hancock (who invented the technique) at Bow and Worcester and on Battersea enamel. *Ornemanistes* sometimes produced series of *vignettes of the *Seasons or the *Elements in the style of *fêtes galantes*. The theme reappeared widely in the *Rococo Revival, especially ornamenting hotel and restaurant interiors.

Fiddle pattern. Spoon or fork handles in the shape of a violin, a common form on French 18th century silver. English examples exist from the 18th century but the shape became popular after 1800. Decorative variations include Fiddle Thread (with an engraved line around the edge), Fiddle and Shell (with a *scallop shell), Fiddle Husk (with an elaborately fluted scallop shell) and Fiddle Thread and Shell.

fielded panel. Panel that is raised above its surround and is sometimes decorated, a feature of *classical styles.

fillet. Thin, plain *moulding that often separates two types of decorated moulding. Term also used for the rib-work in *fluting.

finial. Ornament surmounting any prominent terminal. In architecture it might be a *crocket or *fleur-de-lis in the *Gothic style, or a *ballon or astrolabe, even an *obelisk, in a more *classical style. While *pendants ornament hanging features, finials emphasise the prominent elements such as the top of an ornamental gable, or the central point of a pedimented piece of furniture. On silver or ceramics, finials are frequently compact forms such as *acorns or *pinecones, and often double as handles. *See also* knop.

fir-cone. *See* pinecone.

fire may be represented by *flames, by a thunderbolt, signifying Jupiter or Zeus (*see* thunder and lightning), or by the god of fire (the Roman Vulcan or his Greek counterpart, Hephaestos), who is usually shown wearing a short tunic and bonnet and carrying a hammer, tongs and anvil. These motifs most obviously ornament fireplaces, firedogs, mantelpieces, stoves, grates, firebacks, andirons, chenets, candlesticks, gas and oil lamps. However the symbolism of fire has been extremely wide-ranging, representing transformation, purification, strength and religious fervour among other abstract qualities. Mythical animals associated with fire include the *dragon, *griffin, *phoenix and *salamander. *See also* Apolline decoration; Elements.

Fischer von Erlach, Johann Bernhard (1656-1723). Austrian *Baroque sculptor and stucco worker who then turned to architecture (he became Court Architect in Vienna in 1704), mingling his experience of Roman *classical forms with his own South German brand of the Baroque. His *Entwurff einer historischen Architektur* (Vienna, 1721; English edition, 1730) was the first illustrated architectural history and survey to include *Egyptian and Chinese designs. It also contained renderings of Stonehenge and a number of imaginative reconstructions of classical buildings. Although some of his illustrations were based on the observations of well-known published works such as S.*Serlio's *Architettura*, his range was truly eclectic.

J.B. Fischer von Erlach. Collection of Egyptian vases from his Entwurff einer historischen Architektur, *1721.*

fêtes galantes. 1) French agate snuffbox with gold mounts, 1755.
Fiddle pattern. 2) Fiddle Thread and Shell handle on 18th century English silver fork.

Book III comprised his renderings of Arab, Turkish, Modern Persian, Siamese, Chinese and Japanese architecture, and also included a section of *vase designs.

fish and **fishing.** The fish was an early symbol of Christian baptism, and later of Christ himself, appearing on early Christian sarcophagi, lamps, glass and on the walls of catacombs, a symbolic reference which eluded the persecutors of Christians at this early date. Also an attribute of St Peter, the apostle. Three fishes forming a triangle represent the Christian Trinity (see Christian motifs).

Where a fish appears in schemes of decoration depicting the *Months, it refers to Pisces, one of the

*fish and fishing. 1) From Chinese Architecture, Civil and Ornamental, 1759, by P.*Decker (fl 1759). 2) *Trophy from J.C.*Delafosse's Nouvelle Iconologie Historique, 1768. 3) Fish *knop and fishing scenes on French faïence tureen made at the Joseph-Gaspard Robert factory, Marseilles, c.1775. 4) Ironwork fanlight with crozier, fishing rod and mitre, attributes of St Peter, Papal Indulgence Office, Verona, Italy, 1827.*

signs of the *zodiac. In depictions of the *Elements, fish, or sometimes anglers, represent water. *Auricular, *grotto, *marine and *riparine ornament may all incorporate fish.

Like *hunting, fishing was a popular decorative theme in the 18th century, either as an elegantly composed *vignette, such as that by R.*Hancock, 'The Whitton Anglers', which might be transfer-printed on porcelain and enamel, or as a *trophy of rods, net and catch. In the same *Picturesque Rococo vein, fishing was a well-used theme in *chinoiserie, e.g. the fishing parties of mandarins and Chinese ladies under umbrellas designed by J.*Pillement, or variations of the *willow pattern showing fishing. It was an obvious theme for the decoration of silver and porcelain soup tureens, water jugs and, after its introduction in the late 18th century, cutlery specifically made for the eating and serving of fish; a fish slice and fork designed by John Bell (1811-95) for Summerly Art Manufactures depicts freshwater fishing (spiking eel and landing trout) on one handle, and sea fishing (netting fish from the sea) on the other. See also dolphin.

Fitzhugh pattern. In ceramics, a border pattern, usually in underglaze blue (less often in green and iron-red) with *trellis work over which are painted *butterflies, fruit (particularly split *pomegranates) and flowers, and sometimes a *key or *fret patten. It was adapted from export Chinese ceramics of the Ch'ing dynasty by English factories, notably Lowestoft from the 1770s, and subsequently Coalport and Caughley, and appears mainly on plates (where it may be repeated in the centre of the piece), dishes and jars.

flambeau. See torch.

Flamboyant Gothic. In architecture, the French and northern European variant of English *Decorated and *Perpendicular Gothic. Its name derives from the flame-like *tracery with wavy divisions that characterised early Flamboyant Gothic work. The Chapel of St John the Baptist at Amiens (1373-76) has been suggested as the earliest known example, but the style reached its apogee in work in Bohemia, Germany and what is now Poland with mullions and tracery swept into branching formations, knotted and elaborated into a fret-like network of details; vaulting tracery produces star-like patterns of *lozenges and nets further elaborated with *pendants and *bosses. Other characteristics of the style at its fullest include ogival arches, flowing tracery (on windows, walls, arches and balustrades) sometimes depicted quite literally as *tree trunks and branches, *seaweed-like foliage and abundant use of *crockets (on gables, pinnacles, canopies). Flamboyant motifs survived longer in the decorative arts than in architecture: 15th century goldwork (reliquaries and crosses) and wrought ironwork (doors and grills) echoed the architectural motifs. Early 16th century Dutch silver chalices had stems decorated with a Gothic window motif. As in the Decorated style, the liking for naturalistic detail led to minutely sculpted foliage and deeply cut relief work: on the choir stalls at Amiens (1522) for example, holly, thistle, thorns, seaweed, parsley, endive, *grapevine and blackberry are all found.

*Flamboyant Gothic. Church of St Jacques, Dieppe (Seine-Maritime), France. 1) *Rose window, West Front, 14th century. 2) *Blind arcading with *grapevine, Lady Chapel, 15th century.*

flame. An obvious symbol of *fire, particularly in decorative schemes representing the *Elements. It may also symbolise *day. A flaming *torch signifies the fire of love; a flaming *heart represents religious ardour; a flaming *urn alludes to funerary rites. Mythical animals associated with flames include the *phoenix and *salamander.

A stylised flame in the form of a spiral was a popular *finial on 18th century case furniture, particularly in America, where it was sometimes referred to as an auger flame. Also a popular form for *acroteria.

flaming pearl. *See* dragon.

Flemish Mannerism. A northern variant on High *Renaissance styles, in particular Italian *Mannerism and the School of *Fontainebleau, combined with the remnants of the *Flamboyant Gothic of northern Europe. Motifs included *obelisks, *cartouches, *caryatids and *herms, elaborated *pilasters, *strapwork and the bizarre *Netherlands Grotesque ornament. Karel van Mander wrote in 1604 of the Flemish adaptation of Mannerism following the example of Michelangelo: 'to tell the truth this rein is so free, and this licence so misused by Netherlanders, that in the course of time in Building a great Heresy has arisen among them, with a heap of craziness of decorations and breaking of the pilasters in the middle, and adding on the pedestals, their usual coarse points of diamonds and such lameness, very disgusting to see.' The style was influential in England in the mid 16th century, both through the agency of craftsmen from the Low Countries who worked on the great Tudor houses and through the principal *pattern books of engraved

Flemish Mannerism. Huis Rockox, Keizerstraat, Antwerp, Belgium, 16th century.

ornament and architectural motifs, many of which were printed in Antwerp, the publishing centre of Europe for this type of work.

Flemish Mannerism remained confined to the Low Countries and their neighbours. However, much later, elements of the style were enthusiastically taken up in an extravagant version of the *Baroque that developed in 18th century Spain and some of the most ornate and elaborate designs were adopted as the basis for such forms as the *estipite. *See also* W. Dietterlin; E. Hornick; V. Solis; H. Vredeman de Vries.

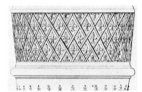

Flemish Revival. Designs from W.B. Scott's The Ornamentist or Artisan's Manual, *1845.*

*fleur-de-lis. 1) On casque from Florence, Italy, 1570. 2) As *diaper on white marble vase for the grounds of Versailles, from J.-F.*Blondel's* Cours d'architecture, 1771-77. 3) Datestone at Penshurst, Kent, built for the De L'Isle family, 1850. 4) Grande Galerie, Louvre, Paris, reconstructed in 19th century.*

Flemish Revival or **Pont Street Dutch.** A simplified version of the *Flemish Mannerist style of architecture that arose in the 1870s and 1880s. Although there are traces of the classical and *Gothic origins of Flemish Mannerism, Flemish Revival buldings tend to emphasise such features as *Dutch gables, panels of rubbed brick, *grotesques and *strapwork. The style was in fact little more than an element within the *Queen Anne Revival in architecture. English architects such as Norman Shaw (1831-1912) and Sir Ernest George (1839-1922) used brick to enliven the elevations of Flemish Revival terraced town houses in the then newly fashionable areas of Kensington and Knightsbridge in London. The style became widely fashionable both in northern Europe and in North America. Hermann Muthesius illustrated a number of Flemish Revival buildings in *Das Englische Haus* (3 vols, Berlin, 1904, 1905).

fleur-de-lis (French, lily flower). Heraldic flower with three petals, a stylised lily. In *Christian iconography it is a symbol of the Virgin Mary, signifying her purity.

According to legend, it was adopted as a symbol of purity by the Merovingian King Clovis on his conversion to Christianity in 493. A popular motif in late *Gothic *tracery, it combined well with the *trefoil, also appearing, for example, on tiles, in *powdered ornament and as a *poppyhead on English country church benchends. Occasionally the *fleur-de-lis* has five petals and resembles the *anthemion. It was taken up in the *Gothic Revival, appearing as a *cresting ornament, on mid 19th century English brick chimney stacks and as a moulded *finial in ironwork.

The *fleur-de-lis* was a central emblem in the royal arms of France from the 12th century and was used in ornament from the Gothic period. In 1793, the Convention decreed that '*signes de la féodalité*' should be removed and use of the *fleur-de-lis* was forbidden in France. When Louis XVIII was restored in 1814, however, he immediately replaced the *eagles and insignia of Napoleon with the *fleur-de-lis* and *helmets. R.*Ackermann's *Repository* of May 1814 describes a fashionable new drapery design: 'azure and white, which may be sprinkled with lilies, are the colours of

floriated merlon. Church of St Peter and St Paul, Lavenham, Suffolk, 15th century.

the legitimate dynasty of France and are beautifully correspondent with the opening season.'

The *fleur-de-lis* was also the emblem of the powerful Italian Farnese family (and appeared on buildings and artefacts as a mark of their ownership or patronage), and of the city of Florence, where it is usually drawn with a small spike on each side of the central petal.

fleurons, printer's flowers, vignettes de fonts or **Röslein.** Single pieces of type cut in decorative shapes, whether floral, geometric or *arabesques, and then used singly or composed to make printed decorative borders on title pages, bindings, etc. Their use was pioneered by 15th century Venetian printers, but they were made popular by Robert Granjon (fl mid-16th century), a Parisian type-founder, printer and publisher who produced fine examples of fleurons from about 1560, adapted from the popular arabesque patterns. After almost one hundred years of popularity they fell into disuse until revived c.1760 by the French type-designer Pierre-Simon Fournier (1712-68), whose type ornaments were copied all over Europe.

Fleuron also refers to a stylised flower form, similar to that in typographic ornament, used in *Gothic and *Gothic Revival architecture, e.g. on *cresting, on tiles and as a *crocket (when it was sometimes called a flos).

fleurons. 1) Around doorway, Church of St Peter, Felsham, Suffolk, 15th century. 2) Designs by Pierre-Simon Fournier, Paris, 1742.

floral ornament. *See* plant ornament.

floriated merlon. In *Gothic architecture, the solid section of a *battlement pierced by a foliate form. This embellishment was popular in the *Gothic Revival.

flos. *See* fleuron.

Floris, Cornelis (1514-75). Architect, sculptor and decorative designer who worked in Antwerp and was, with C.*Bos, the creator of the bizarre *Netherlands Grotesque style, sometimes called 'Floris style'. He first published ornamental designs in 1548, after he had visited Italy. His published designs for cups and jugs (1548) are fantastic *Mannerist confections owing much to E.*Vico. His *grotesques, *Veelderlij Veranderinghe van Grottissen ende Compartimenten,* (1556) and designs for tombs and epitaphs, *Veelderlij Nieuwe Inventien* (1557), contained elaborate and frequently bizarre combinations of *strapwork and semi-human, animal, reptilian and insect forms that became influential across the Netherlands and in Germany and Denmark through Floris's own prints and those of his followers, in particular H.*Vredeman de Vries.

Flötner, Peter (c.1485-1546). Ornamental designer, goldsmith and woodworker, who was probably Swiss in origin but worked in Nuremberg. He produced

Cornelis Floris. From his Veelderlij Nieuwe Inventien, *1557.*

some of the earliest known furniture designs (1533), which were influential, also metalwork decorated with architectural detail such as *columns, doorways and *friezes and general ornament such as *grotesques, *arabesques, profile *medallions, *laurel wreath roundels, *perspective designs, as well as emblematic and allegorical motifs. He was an important figure in the move from *Gothic styles to *classicism during the second quarter of the 16th century, particularly in Germany. Arabesque designs produced by Flötner were republished several times by the Zurich printer Rudolf Wyssenbach (fl.1545-60).

Flowing. Term used until the mid 19th century to describe late *Perpendicular *tracery; it then tended to be called 'Curvilinear'.

flushwork. *Gothic application of knapped flints used in conjunction with dressed stone to produce formal and geometric forms and patterns such as the *lozenge or *chequer and *diaper patterns in general. The feature is typical of 14th and 15th century churches in East Anglia. It became popular again at the height of the 19th century *Gothic Revival, particularly in church restoration. *Proudwork is a variant of this technique.

fluting. Vertical grooves, with a rounded or elliptical section, used on columns in *Graeco-Roman classical architecture. Vitruvius's anthropomorphic explanation was that the flutes were imitating folds in drapery. Fluting is an option in all the *Orders except the Tuscan, in which it never appears. Fluted *pilasters are common, although sometimes only the lower section is carved or depicted (in *trompe l'oeil) in this way. In other applications fluting may be diagonal or curved. Although not an obvious motif for glass, silver and ceramics since it has to be cut, cast or moulded, fluting is widely applied. It is found on 17th and early 18th century silver vessels such as ewers and tankards, late 18th century *Neo-classical pieces and on the bowls (and sometimes the stems) of 18th century wine glasses. Flutes are occasionally square-headed in early 19th century work (as in the work of Sir John Soane) based on this motif at the Temple of Vesta in the Forum, Rome. The lower section of flutes may be infilled, sometimes with cylindrical pieces, to produce *cabled fluting, sometimes more ornamentally (*see chandelles*).

fluting. 1) Grand Central Station, New York, architects Warren & Wetmore, 1913. 2) Square-headed fluting, Tivoli Corner, Bank of England, City of London, architect Sir John Soane, 1795.

flushwork. 1) Chancel exterior, Church of St Peter and St Paul, Lavenham, Suffolk, late 15th century. 2) Cathedral of St James, Bury St Edmunds, Suffolk, rebuilt by Sir George Gilbert Scott, 1865-69.
foil. 3) Transept, Bayeux Cathedral (Calvados), France, 13th century.

foil. The lobed form upon which *Gothic *tracery is based. Foils are separated by *cusps to make up various composite forms: *trefoil, *quatrefoil, *cinquefoil and so on, including multifoil. The trefoil and cinquefoil forms are sometimes used as arches, when the central lobe may be pointed. The quatrefoil, elaborated with barbs, is a form inherited from the ceramic revetments of Spanish and oriental mosques. The foil was widely used, partly because its leaf-like shape was a suitably stylised version of the type of natural foliage (e.g. *grapevine, *ivy or strawberry) so popular in Gothic ornament.

foldage or **foldige.** 17th century terms for foliage, usually in *friezes of *scrolling foliage.

foliage. *See bocage;* leaf ornament; plant ornament; scrolling foliage.

foliate mask. Human face surrounded with foliage and in many cases with leaves appearing to sprout from the mouth and nostrils. The motif appears in Roman art: *acanthus leaves surrounding a *mask that sometimes has staring demonic eyes. It was popular from the 13th to the 15th centuries, principally in England, Germany and France (where it was called a *masque feuillu* or *tête de feuilles*) and found in medieval church carvings decorating *bosses, bench ends, tympana, misericords, *corbels, *spandrels, *capitals and tombs. Often the masks have violent expressions: protruding tongues, fierce teeth, wild eyes and sometimes looks of pain and sorrow which have given them traditional associations with Easter and the Resurrection. The type of foliage used follows the fashion of the period. *Birds sometimes perch among the foliage and blossom. Even after masks had been dropped as a motif in church architecture, they still appeared on tombs and memorials: a very late example is the Sandford-Challoner memorial in St Mary Redcliffe, Bristol, c.1747, which has a foliate *skull. The form has been associated with the Green Man or Jack-in-the-Green, characters of pagan origin who appeared in rural May Day celebrations – the Jack-in-the-Green costume was a wicker framework covered with leaves and boughs that was placed over the head and shoulders of the man or youth. As an element of *grotesque ornament, foliate masks were revived in the second half of the 19th century, e.g. on terracotta panels on buildings.

Fontaine, Pierre François Léonard. *See* Percier, Charles.

Fontainebleau, School of. Style of work by or influenced by a group of Flemish, Italian and French artists

*foliate mask. 1) *Capital, Stokenham Church, Devon, late 14th century. 2) Woodcut attributed to A.*Veneziano, early 16th century. 3) Capital, 19th century commercial building, Inverness, Scotland. 4) English engraved silver tea tray, W.& G. Sissons, Sheffield, 1858. 5) Canterbury Quadrangle, St John's College, Oxford, 1631-36.*

who worked for François I of France. The conversion of his hunting lodge at Fontainebleau provided a focus of artistic activity at a period when the *Flamboyant Gothic had lost its impact and an awareness of the Italian *Renaissance was already growing in France. The project, which began in 1528, involved French and Italian artists and architects including G.B. da *Vignola and S.*Serlio (the latter arrived in 1541), the goldsmith Benvenuto Cellini (1500-71), Rosso Fiorentino (1494-1540) and Francesco Primaticcio (c.1504-1570). It was, above all, the Italians' innovative combination of paint and stucco work in their decorative schemes that was the most influential aspect of the work. These artists brought with them an awareness of the latest manifestation of the High Renaissance, *Mannerism, and an academic approach to *classicism (based on knowledge of actual artefacts). Vignola and Serlio were both authors of important treatises on the classical *Orders and their variations. In ornament, the principal motifs of the School were a complex mixture of *strapwork, *cartouches, scrolls, shields, *caryatids, *half figures and *grotesques. Symbolism and allegory played a major part in the ornamental themes of the School and its followers.

Motifs and decorative schemes were widely transmitted from Fontainebleau through the work of printmakers, the most important of whom (in the field of ornament) was A.*Fantuzzi (c.1508-1550), who took as his material both the complete schemes within François I's palace and the drawings of Rosso and Primaticcio; thus the ornate frames of the gallery became an appropriate engraved border for the

*School of Fontainebleau. *Grotesque ornament by R.*Boyvin, c.1560.*

printed page. Some 16th century French faïence was decorated with Fantuzzi engravings after Primaticcio and Rosso.

The publishing centre of Antwerp, which adopted Mannerism in preference to a purer Renaissance style, published much of the work emanating from Fontainebleau.

Fornordisk. *See* Viking.

fox. The fox appears in illustrations of *fables (notably The Fox and The Grapes and The Fox and The Stork) and of the medieval epic, Reynard the Fox, that decorate medieval illuminations, and wood and stone carving, e.g. on misericords and *capitals. At this period, too, the fox was a favourite animal for satirical comment, e.g. a fox dressed as a friar preaching to geese.

English 18th and 19th century silver stirrup cups, used at hunt meetings, were sometimes made in the shape of fox heads.

A flying fox design (derived from *kakiemon ware) was used on German porcelain made at Meissen in the 1720s. It shows a reddish-brown fox in mid-air above a squirrel and gourd vine. *See also* hunting.

François I. A 19th century revival of the style associated with the reign of François I (1515-47) in France, which, like the Elizabethan period in England, was looked back on as a golden age of prosperity and

François I. 19th century ironwork grille, Paris.

French Second Empire. 1) Philadelphia City Hall, Pennsylvania, architects John McArthur and Thomas V. Walter, 1871-1901. French Order. 2) From Oeuvres de Philibert de l'Orme, *1648.*

artistic endeavour. It formed one strand in the *French Second Empire style. In architecture, it was sometimes known as the Château style being an amalgam of late *Gothic and *Renaissance elements (the latter from the School of *Fontainebleau, François I's own creation) and *Renaissance Revival ornament. Among motifs used were likenesses of François I as *portrait heads in ironwork or carved ornament, and his emblem, the *salamander. Also common were *grotesque forms such as *half figures, scrolling figures, etc.

Free Classicism. *See* classicism.

Free Style. *See* Old English.

French Order. Like the *Spanish and *Britannic Orders, the French Order is a fancy nationalistic creation in which the emblems of France (the *cock and the *fleur-de-lis) decorate a Corinthian *capital (*see* Orders) as, for example, in the Grand Galerie at Versailles. It appeared from the 17th century in France. According to I.*Ware, for whom all that was French was bad, 'the French have attempted a new order idly.'

A more intellectual effort at a French Order was P.*de l'Orme's in which the *banded column was the hallmark.

French Second Empire (1852-70). A period that gave rise to a characteristic style, largely as a result of the patronage of Emperor Napoleon III (President from 1848, Emperor from 1852) and the Empress Eugénie. As an eclectic, widely revivalist style it drew on the *François I style already established in buildings such as the Hôtel de Ville, Paris (Godde and Lesueur, 1837-49) and added further *Baroque elaborations, with heavy and lavish ornaments. Mansard roofs, high *crested outlines and *oeil de boeuf windows, with heavy *rustication, *personifications and *heraldic motifs, appeared on a wide range of buildings – town houses, department stores, hotels, railway stations and the country mansions of the newly rich. The style was applied in northern Europe and, especially, in America. The building which most completely represents the Second Empire style is the extension to the Louvre in Paris by H.M. Lefuel, built from 1853. In 1864, Napoleon III brought the Ecole des Beaux-Arts under state control, giving architectural education a rigidly conformist character. This encouraged a *Historicist outlook based on the minute observation of originals and equally elaborate imaginary reconstructions of these originals.

Furniture of the period was if anything more eclectic in its sources than architecture. Although *Louis XVI was the most widely revived interior style at this time, an over-blown Baroque spirit was dominant in all spheres of design. Work commissioned by the Imperial family borrowed many of the emblems of Napoleon I, such as *bees and elaborated initial Ns. *See also* Baroque Revival; eclecticism; Empire; Gothic Revival; Louis Revivals; Renaissance Revival; Troubadour style.

fret. Geometric pattern in which lines meet at right-angles (occasionally at greater or lesser angles), which may be banded, in a *frieze, used as a *diaper, or compartmentalised. It is suitable for incised, relief or pierced decoration. Early examples exist in *Egyptian, Greek, Roman, Chinese, Japanese, *Celtic, *Romanesque and *Islamic art. In the mid 18th century, the fret was often used instead of the *balustrade. Frets could be broken or continuous, in perspective, and viewed as oblique or square-on. *Pattern book authors supplied fretwork designs in various *Rococo styles. J.*Crunden's *The Joyner and Cabinet-maker's Darling* contained 'Gothic, Chinese, Mosaic and Ornamental frets proper for: friezes, imports, architraves, tabernacle frames, book-cases, tea tables, tea stands, trays, stoves, fenders.' In the 1760s especially, R.*Manwaring, W. *Halfpenny, T.*Chippendale and others rarely omitted fret patterns from their designs. The French term *guilloche* was often used in the 18th century to refer to fret. J.*Gibbs in *Rules for Drawing the Several Parts of Architecture* (1732) shows 'frets or giulochi's' which he describes as 'proper to be placed in Picture-frames, sofites of Arches and Architraves, on faecias and

fret. English wallpaper dado for Royal Pavilion, Brighton, Sussex, c.1822.

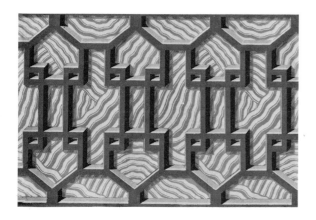

Plinths or Bases, when the root of the members are carved.' During the *Neo-classical period, the straightforward Greek *key pattern fret replaced the more fanciful Rococo frets and was more strictly confined to *borders and *cornices. During the late 18th and early 19th centuries it appeared as a compact border pattern on silver, ceramics and furniture. Many variants appeared in Victorian ornament, and its use was greatly extended: one standard carpenters' manual published in 1853 even included 'fret rails and clock for steamboat cabins'.

Frets confined within circles or *fan-shapes, or used as a ground pattern (rather than as edging patterns) figured in the ornament of *japonaiserie.

In the 17th and 18th centuries the term 'fretwork' was used loosely to define any compartmentalised decoration as, for example, on plasterwork ceilings. By the late 19th century, it had come to mean elaborately ornamental fret patterns cut in wood with a fret-saw. *See also* Chinese paling; interlacing; key pattern; lattice; meander; trellis.

frieze. A decorative band. In *classical architecture it is the section that lies between the *architrave and the *cornice. However, more generally, it describes a strip of decoration of any length. Interior examples may appear over windows or door-cases, on mantelpieces, pier glasses, etc. Ornamentists frequently included designs for friezes of classical inspiration in their work, incorporating such elements as *scrolling foliage, *triumphs, *festoons, sections of *undulate and *vertebrate patterns.

Frieze designs were equally applicable to the ornamentation of furniture, metalwork and ceramics. They provided horizontal decoration on tables, tallboys, bureaux, etc., and were used as *banding on the rims, bodies or bases of plates and vessels. *See also* pulvinated frieze.

fruit. An ornamental motif widely used in periods when *naturalistic ornament is favoured. In periods such as the *Jacobean or early 17th century *classical revivals, fruit ornament became interchangeable with other floral motifs, within a wider vogue for *plant ornament. Fruits, like *vegetables, *shells or even game, are used in highly elaborate carved work, such as that by the Dutch *Quellin family, or *Gibbonwork. The ornate and rotund forms of fruit, especially those such as the *pomegranate or fig in which the seeds are shown bursting forth, were used in *cornucopias, *margents and *festoons in both plaster and wood. *Baskets overflowing with ripe fruits were used in a wide range of applications from stonework terminals on gate piers to small-scale work in silver or ceramics. Fruit combined with flowers and other *Rococo elements often appears entwined around pier glasses or the supports to pier tables and other elaborate giltwood pieces. Fruit lent itself to engraved ornament depicting *Plenty or *husbandry and, in connection with the *Seasons, represents Autumn. Development of scientific botanical illustration from the late 17th century led to painted decoration on ceramics depicting such subjects as rotting or blemished fruit or sliced sections, often with *insects. Exotic fruits were increasingly imported from abroad, and works such as the

Nouveau Livre de trophées de fleurs et fruits étrangers published in the mid 18th century by J.G. Huquier added to the ornamental vocabulary. The nurseryman Robert Furber followed his popular flower catalogue with *Twelve Months of Fruit* (1733), which proved a useful source book for designers. In ceramics and silver, various fruits were a suitable shape to be used as the *knop on a lid. In the mid 19th century Summerly Art Manufactures produced a range of dessert plates, knives and forks ornamented with currants, cherries, filberts, raspberries, strawberries and mulberries. Occasionally specific fruits indicate the use of the object, *apples on cider glasses, *grapevines on wine glasses and decanters. In the early 20th century berry forms were popular, as reliefwork on glass vases and bowls by René Lalique and his imitators, or as coloured patterns on early electric table lamps. *See also* pineapple.

fylfot. *See* swastika.

gadrooning, lobed decoration, (k)nulled decoration or **thumb moulding.** Decoration consisting of a series of lobes, a *Renaissance development of classical *reeding. It was initially used mainly as a border or edge ornament, sometimes diagonally. When used over the whole surface of an object, it may appear vertically, or in diagonal curves to produce a spiralling effect.

Gadrooning first appeared on woodwork and silver but was quickly copied on ceramics, e.g. on late 15th century *Hispano-Moresque earthenware, and became widely used as an emphasising ornament on the bases of vessels. It was popular throughout the 16th, 17th and 18th centuries in woodwork, notably carved on the turned *bulb forms and *mouldings of Elizabethan and *Jacobean furniture, and favoured on late 17th century British and American silver, particularly in spiral form. Some 18th century English and American furniture had gadrooned *apronwork, e.g. on chests-of-drawers, highboys and, as shown in T.*Chippendale's *Director*, on chairs. *Neo-classical forms such as the *urn and *vase (mainly in stone and silver but also in porcelain) were obvious candidates for gadrooning, and were also popular forms for English fonts of the second half of the 18th century.

gaine. 18th century French term for *herm.

galleon. Widely used motif both in *Arts and Crafts work and in the early 20th century *Elizabethan Revival. It seems to have combined the qualities of an interesting, dynamic form (wind-filled sails) with a feeling of nostalgia for the age of the Golden Hind. The Guild of Handicrafts (founded by C.R. Ashbee in 1888) adopted the galleon as a *rebus denoting 'craft' and it frequently marked their work. The motif appears on ironwork (including log bins and fire irons), textiles, tiles and ceramics, in the stained glass of front doors and hall windows of Tudor-style suburban houses built after World War I, even as an electric light fitting.

galletting (French, *galet*, pebble), **garreting** or **garnetting.** Tiny chips of stone or flint pressed into mortar courses, partly for structural reasons but principally as decoration. Characteristic of 14th and 15th century flint churches in Norfolk and of secular buildings in Kent, Surrey and Sussex.

gardening. *See* husbandry.

gargoyle (Old French, *gargouille*, throat). In *Gothic architecture, a waterspout carved in the shape of a (usually grotesque) human or animal head, and terminating a rainwater pipe or duct at roof level or on the parapet of a wall. Gargoyles reappeared in the 19th century on *Gothic Revival buildings.

In classical architecture a *lion's head with a spout directing water through the mouth was sometimes used for this purpose.

garland. *See* festoon.

gaudy Dutch. English ceramic designs produced in Staffordshire specifically for export to America, particularly to the Pennsylvania German communities, c.1810-1830 (*see* Pennsylvania Dutch). The decoration is mainly floral, simply executed in red, blue, and yellow. Some patterns appear to borrow from the English *Imari patterns produced at Derby and Worcester c.1720-1820.

Geminus, Thomas (c.1500-1562). Flemish surgeon and scientific instrument maker who moved to England c.1540. In 1545 he published an edition of Vesalius's *Anatomy* entitled *Compendiosa totius Anatomie delineatio*, which was illustrated with the first copper-plate engravings to appear in England and had a title page decorated with one of the earliest examples of *strapwork and *grotesque ornament. He published the first examples of *arabesque ornament in England, *Morysse and Damashin renewed and encreased Very profitable for Goldsmythes and*

gadrooning. 1) English silver wine cooler, 1809. 2) English silver meat dish, 1830.

gargoyle. 1) Norman Gate, Bury St Edmunds, Suffolk, built by Abbot Anselm, 1120-48. 2) Church of St Mary, Boxford, Suffolk, 1441-69.

gaudy Dutch. 1) 19th century Staffordshire earthenware mug.
Thomas Geminus. 2) Detail from his Morysse and Damashin
renewed and encreased, *1548.*

Embroderars (1548), which were pirated from Italian
engravings. These patterns would also have been suitable as carved or inlaid decorations on furniture.

genii (Latin, *genius*, guardian spirit). The Romans believed that the genius protected man's soul during his
life and conducted it to heaven on his death, an early
pagan equivalent of the Christian *angel. In the 19th
century, the name was used for decorative winged
infants and *putti. *See also* cherub; cupid.

genre pittoresque. *See* Rococo; *rocaille.*

geometric elements. Mosaic, parquetry, and other
inlaid techniques lend themselves to geometric treatments, as do building materials such as tiles, bricks
and slabs of stone. In the 19th century, disenchant-
ment with *eclectic ornament led designers to adopt
the abstract geometrical forms of ancient cultures
such as the *Minoan, *Celtic, or *Islamic. O.*Jones
wrote about the 'Ornament of Savage Tribes', taking
his examples principally from the South Pacific. The
newly founded schools of design considered geometry
to be an essential basis for ornament: D.R. Hay's *Original Geometrical Diaper Designs* (London, 1844) was an
early publication on the subject. Proposition Eight of
O. Jones's *Grammar of Ornament* lays down that 'all ornament should be based upon a geometric construction.'
Designers such as J.K.*Colling, C.*Dresser, E.*Viollet-
le-Duc and L.*Sullivan based their theories of organic ornament on geometric principles, drawing
attention to such forms as the hexagon, octagon and
ellipse in natural forms. In the *Gothic and *Romanesque Revivals, medieval geometrical patterns were
widely admired and published, and appeared in tiling
and in stencilled designs on furniture or wallpaper as
well as in architecture, e.g. polychrome brickwork.

In the 20th century, *Glasgow School and *Vienna
Secession designers depended on sparingly applied
geometric forms used in association with colour both
in architecture and on objects. Frank Lloyd Wright
(1867-1959) generally relied on the careful positioning
of geometric shapes for decoration; his belief in integral design led him to produce polygonal furniture
for a hexagonal house. In the Modern Movement (*see*
Modernist decoration), ornament was largely pre-
empted, but where it did appear it tended to echo the
rectilinear forms of buildings. In *Art Deco ornament,
*chevron, triangle and stepped shapes were important.

Georgian. The period covering the reigns of George I
(1714-27), George II (1727-60), George III (1760-
1820) and George IV, although the period from
c.1800 to 1830 is also sometimes called the *Regency.

The architectural style of the early Georgian period
was *Palladian and the first English translation of
A.*Palladio's *Quattro Libri* appeared in 1715, coinciding
with the beginning of the Hanoverian era. The style
was a restrained form of *classicism, with motifs such
as the *Palladian motif, *triumphal arch or temple
front, and a preference for a correct use of the *Orders. For interiors, a heavier, more ornamental style
was favoured, exemplified by the work of W.*Kent,
using motifs such as *herms, heavily sculpted *eagles
and *dolphins, *masks and *drapery. The domestic
terraced house of the early Georgian period is unrelieved externally apart from the enrichment of the
doorcase, sometimes following the Orders, with a
*fanlight and *pediment above. Reference to an earlier
taste for a more *Baroque style is made with the use
of the *Gibbs surround. Interiors were more ornamental, with moulded *cornices, *fielded panels, and,
by the mid century, elaborated *balusters and chimneypieces, with *volutes and strong mouldings such
as *egg and dart. *Pattern books aimed at craftsmen such as those by B.*Langley, W.*Halfpenny,
J.*Crunden and W.*Salmon, set a seal on the popularity of these motifs. The Georgian style was equally
widespread in American domestic architecture (*see*

Georgian. House, Richmond Green, Surrey.

American Colonial) developing slightly later but following the same pattern books.

The influence of French *Rococo design began to make itself felt in the 1730s and by the middle of the century had become an important element, appearing in the published designs of T.*Chippendale, T.*Johnson, M.*Lock, M.*Darly, W.*Ince and J. Mayhew and others. Ornamental subject matter changed from themes concerned with classical mythology to a lighter and more frivolous vein: *fables, *commedia dell'arte, *fêtes galantes, *singeries, etc. Combined with the *rocaille and asymmetrical scrollwork there was also a fashion for fanciful Gothic forms (see Gothick) and *chinoiserie.

By the middle of the 18th century formal architectural taste had moved to a purer Roman classicism, the *Neo-classical, which was popularised through the enormously widespread fashion for the *Adam style. In America, this period too was echoed in the *Federal style. The external ornament for domestic architecture in the later Georgian period was often in composite stone (rather than wood), typically Coade stone *rustication or *masks. Internally the ornament is usually in plaster, with *reeding, small *lion masks and classical motifs taken from the repertoire of the Adam style such as *paterae, *husks, *rosettes, delicate *scrolling foliage, *urns, *vases and *griffins.

The published designs of G.*Hepplewhite and T. *Sheraton apply this style to furniture. Borrowings from a wider range of sources, Gothick, *Egyptian style, chinoiserie and *Greek Revival in particular were also characteristic and continued well into the *Regency period.

'German Order'. See Britannic Order.

Giant Order or **Colossal Order.** Any *Order where the columns extend the height of more than one storey.

Giardini, Giovanni (1646-1721). Leading Italian goldsmith and metalworker who worked in Rome. He was in charge of the Papal Foundry from 1699 and much of his work was ecclesiastical. His Disegni Diversi, a collection of *Baroque designs first published in 1714, covers in the first section designs for church furniture, e.g. chalices, reliquaries, monstrances, candelabra, incense-burners, and in the second, designs for secular pieces, such as table centrepieces, candelabra, coffee pots, lamps, etc. The designs were republished under the title Promptuarium artis argentariae as late as 1750 by which time they were certainly no longer the novissimae ideae heralded in the foreword of the book. However, perhaps because the church was the most influential Roman patron, Italian silversmiths continued to work in this style for some time, even though the *Rococo was fast gaining popularity in other countries.

Gibbonwork. Woodcarving in the exquisite naturalistic manner associated with the work of Grinling Gibbons (1648-1721), master carver to Charles II, who worked at St Paul's Cathedral, Hampton Court, Windsor Castle, Burghley House and Petworth House. It was also influenced by the Dutch *Baroque style work of the *Quellin family. Motifs include *festoons

Gibbonwork. Limewood carving by Grinling Gibbons, Carved Room, Petworth House, Sussex, 1692.

of fruit and flowers, garlands and *trophies used to frame and ornament pictures, panelling, overmantels, church screens and chimneypieces.

A coarsened version of the style reappeared at the time of the Great Exhibition (London, 1851); an exhibit was illustrated in the catalogue by Wallis of Louth, and it remained in vogue for the English *Wrenaissance (Gibbons had worked for Christopher Wren) in the late Victorian and Edwardian period. As late as the 1920s, Gibbonwork, referred to by one writer as 'dexterous greengroceries', was still appearing in the panelled interiors of, for example, the board rooms of large commercial companies.

Gibbs, James (1682-1754). English architect who was strongly influenced by Italian *Baroque work, after studying under Carlo Fontana (1634-1714) in Rome. Gibbs's work was more exuberant and markedly more ornamental than that of his contemporaries working in the strict *Palladian idiom. His folio publication A Book of Architecture (1728, second edition 1739) was one of the most influential *pattern books of the century. It gave an account of his own works, among them his two great London churches, St Martin-in-the-Fields and St Mary-le-Strand. On the subject of decoration, Gibbs drew attention to the importance of 'a few Ornaments properly disposed . . . for it is not the Bulk of a Fabrick the Richness and Quantity of the Materials, the Multiplicity of Lines nore Gaudiness of the

James Gibbs. Chimneypieces from his A Book of Architecture, 1728.

finishing that give the Grace or Beauty and Grandeur to a Building . . . ' His book was designed to be 'of use to such Gentlemen as might be concerned in Building, especially in the remote parts of the country where little or no assistance for Designs can be procured . . . may be executed by a workman who understands lines.' It was known in America from 1760 and was highly influential both there and in Europe. Among the details included were spires and steeples, *obelisks, chimneypieces, doors, *niches, monuments, *cartouches for monumental inscription, *sarcophagi 'or monumental urns in the Antique Taste' and 54 designs for *vases. His *The Rules for Drawing the Several Parts of Architecture* (1732, 1738, 1753) was both a technical manual and a source of detail, and was a cheaper and therefore more accessible publication than the expensive earlier book. It included suggestions as to the use of *frets and *guilloches. Many of Gibbs's details were lifted by compilers of popular pattern books later in the century. His only work specifically devoted to ornament was *Thirty Three Shields & Compartments* (1731), which featured a variety of *Baroque foliate shields (or cartouches) with *urns, *masks and *putti.

Gibbs surround. Door or window surround named after the 18th century architect J.*Gibbs. It has a triple *keystone that protrudes below the *architrave. The rest of the surround is constructed of alternate large and small blocks comparable to quoining (*see* quoin) with which it may appear.

Gigantic Order. 18th century term used by V.*Scamozzi to denote the Tuscan *Order.

Gillot, Claude (1673-1722), French painter, book illustrator, designer and engraver, who worked in the early *Rococo style in a manner similar to that of G.-M.*Oppenord. *Nouveaux Desseins d'arquebuseries* (c.1720) consists of patterns for gun decoration incorporating such suitable subjects as *gorgon heads and hunting *dogs. Most of his ornamental work was published posthumously: *Livre de portières* (1737), six *grotesque designs centred on classical deities – Bacchus, Diana, *Neptune, etc., as well as several suites of assorted ornamental designs.

Gibbs surround. 1) Doorway to early 18th century stable block, Rousham, Oxfordshire.
Claude Gillot. 2) Designs for gun mounts from his Nouveaux Desseins d'arquebuseries, *c.1720.*

giraffe. In the early 19th century, Mohammed Ali, Pasha of Egypt, presented giraffes both to France and to England. The English animal died but the French one was shown at the Jardin des Plantes, Paris, from 1827 to 1845. A phenomenal interest in the animal, 'giraffomania', gave rise almost immediately to a craze for giraffe ornaments on faïence plates, jewellery, wallpaper, and many other novelty objects in France and Britain.

gladiatorial mask. *See* helmet.

Glasgow School. 1, 2) Glasgow School of Art, architect Charles Rennie Mackintosh, begun 1897 3) Back of chair for order desk, Willow Tea Rooms, Glasgow, designed by Charles Rennie Mackintosh, 1904.

Glasgow School. A group of architects and designers, notably Charles Rennie Mackintosh (1868-1928) with Herbert MacNair (1868-1953), Margaret Macdonald (1865-1933) and Frances Macdonald (1874-1921), who joined forces in 1893. Their work was initially influenced by *Art Nouveau, the work of *Arts and Crafts designers such as Walter Crane (1845-1915) and Arthur Heygate Mackmurdo (1851-1942), and *Celtic and *Viking ornament. However, Mackintosh soon moved away from the elaborately *naturalistic ornament and elongated female figures of French and Belgian Art Nouveau to produce a distinctive style that was characterised by a sparse, linear naturalism based on a theory of organic ornament. Decorative motifs include highly stylised natural forms: *seedpods (apple pips, bulbs, corms), buds, sprouting forms, spreading branches, and simple geometric ornament. Mackintosh also made sparing use of carefully selected classical *mouldings, *bead mouldings and *cyma recta among others. Mackintosh, like his *Vienna Secession counterparts, believed in designing every detail for the interiors of his buildings, including lamps, cutlery, carpets, curtains, door fitments, etc. The Macdonald sisters concentrated on metalwork, leaded glass, embroidery, jewellery and painted gesso panels. The group exhibited in Liège (1895), Venice (1899), Vienna (1900) and Turin (1902) and their work became better known in Europe than Britain, being particularly influential in and around Vienna. It was first published abroad in *Dekorative Kunst* (Munich, Autumn 1898 and Spring 1899), and later in *Deutsche Kunst und Dekoration*. Later work by Mackintosh, with simple geometric inlay used in strips as a moulding or edging device, had much in common with that of Josef Hoffmann (1870-1956) (*see* Vienna Secession). The influence of the Glasgow School was limited – the number of works commissioned was relatively small and their designs were never produced in quantity. Nevertheless they did make an early move away from the use of elaborate ornament, a development that was to culminate in the Modern Movement (*see* Modernist decoration).

globe. The terrestrial globe was used as a symbol of navigation and exploration from the Renaissance. Later it was adopted as a symbol of scientific endeavour, and as an attribute of Geometry and Astronomy in schemes showing the *Liberal Arts. Sometimes personifications such as *Fame or *Justice carry a globe, symbolising universality. An orb topped by a cross is a symbol of the power of a sovereign. It may appear in religious contexts, demonstrating the spread of Christianity, for example.

goose-neck. *See* scrolled pediment.

gorgon. In Greek mythology the gorgons were three fearful women with hair of writhing serpents, and wings, claws and huge teeth. One of them, Medusa, had been a beautiful mortal until she was transformed into a hideous gorgon by the goddess Athena as a punishment. According to legend, Perseus eventually killed her and thereafter Athena wore Medusa's head on her breastplate or at the centre of her shield to frighten the enemy. In ornament only a gorgon's *mask with horrifying expression and piercing eyes is used (sometimes called a Medusa head); often it has wings placed in the snaky hair. Medusa heads decorated arms and armour, doors and gateways. In the *Renaissance and *Neo-classical styles they appear on *keystones and on doorknockers. Illustrations of engraved gems, as in A.F.*Gori's *Museum Florentinium*, provided examples. T.*Hope included a selection of gorgon heads in *Costume of the Ancients* (1809).

gorgon. 1) Early 19th century commercial building, Bonn. 2) On bust of Roman emperor, Chiswick House, London, built 1725-29.

Gori, Antonio Francesco (1691-1757). Italian who, like the Comte *de Caylus, produced large annotated volumes of classical artefacts – gems, coins, statues, *vases, stele, mirrors, sepulchres and sacerdotal instruments such as candelabra, *tripods, sistra, etc. – at a time when most influential publications were concentrating on *classical architecture. *Museum Florentinium* (12 vols, 1731-66) illustrated many objects from the Medici collection and other private Florentine collections. It also included engravings of gems presented according to subject matter, e.g. animals sacred to the gods, fabulous beasts, auspicious animals, superstitious symbols, symbols of the gods, etc., as well as mythological scenes, as did *Thesaurus Gemmarum Antiquarum* (1750), which could be easily translated into metalwork, *cameos, painted furniture, etc. *Museum Etruscum* (3 vols, 1737-43) includes Greek painted vases.

Gothic. An ornamental vocabulary that became progressively more elaborate from the 12th until the early 16th century. It was based on a set of components, which included the pointed arch or *lancet, *foils, *cusping and *arcading; elements such as window *tracery, blind wall surfaces, buttresses and *vaulting were given increasingly complex forms and decorations. In addition, the ornament applied to *capitals,

Gothic. 1) West front, Lisieux Cathedral (Calvados), France, 12th and 13th centuries. 2) Stadhuis, Louvain, Belgium, built 1448-63 by Mathys de Layens, restored 1828-50, 1914, 1976. 3) Carved oak chest, c.1450.

*spandrels, canopies, *niches and porches (and eventually entire façades) grew more *naturalistic. The tendency already apparent in the *Romanesque to depict both ecclesiastical and secular themes in a realistic fashion became more pronounced: flora, fauna, daily tasks and the round of the *Seasons, portraits of masons, clerics or patrons all appear as *corbels or upon capitals. At a time when few people could read, tales and images were depicted with motifs drawn from *sample books, *bestiaries and the artist's own imagination. Formal decoration – *crockets, *stiff leaf and *waterleaf motifs in particular – was either displaced by the accurate depiction of local vegetation or multiplied into dense profusion. The same vocabulary was applied to furniture and artefacts and survived longest in ecclesiastical contexts, for which the style was considered more appropriate than classical motifs with their pagan origins.

The Gothic was widely varied both in regional types and in the increasing sophistication of the style over the centuries. It travelled with the Crusaders to the eastern Mediterranean. In Venice, for example, its combination with the *Byzantine produced a highly original variant of the style. Materials, too, determined the way in which the style developed: in northern Europe, brick was sometimes used in late Gothic buildings, producing a very different effect from examples built in stone. *See also* Early English; Decorated; Flamboyant; Perpendicular; Gothick; Gothic Revival; Manueline; Venetian Gothic Revival.

Gothic cornice. 18th century enrichment composed of a series of openwork *pendant forms arranged horizontally, often producing a lacy effect. It first appeared in the *Gothick and continued to be used in the *Gothic Revival. It appears in cabinetwork and plasterwork, but is also used externally on highly decorated buildings. Later uses of the motif became more

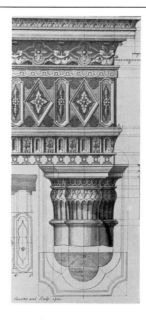 

*Gothick. 1) Design for *entablature dated 1741 from B.*Langley's* Gothic Architecture, *1747. 2) Carved wooden *cornice and panelling, Stout's Hill, Uley, Gloucestershire, 1743.*

Gothic cornice. 1) From Gaetano Landi's Architectural Decorations, London, 1810. 2) Palladium House, Great Marlborough Street, London, by American architect Raymond Hood, with G. Jeeves, 1928.

stylised, as in the 1930s when it appeared as an external *frieze detail, sometimes even two-dimensionally, e.g. as a design on ceramic tiles.

Gothick. An 18th century taste for *Gothic detail which was a strand of the English *Rococo. It preceded the *Gothic Revival, and, in line with the 18th century liking for the *Picturesque, it had little concern with historical accuracy. The Gothic had never been entirely dropped in architecture, seeming particularly appropriate in certain ecclesiastical and academic contexts; it appeared, for example, in the work of such architects as Christopher Wren (1632-1723), Nicholas Hawksmoor (1661-1736) and John Vanbrugh (1664-1726). From the 1740s, however, the style was used in domestic architecture and interiors, often in an attempt to give mansions and houses a spurious air of ancient lineage. B.*Langley's *Gothic Architecture Restored and Improved* (1742) was one of the first *pattern books for the style and included a set of five newly invented *Orders (emphasising the tendency to see Gothick in the light of *classicism). Typical motifs, which were easily assimilated and applied, were pointed and *ogee arches, pinnacles, *crockets, decorative buttressing, *quatrefoil openings, castellated parapets and *fan vaulting. Where the pointed arches and vaulting were purely decorative, and flimsily made in wood and plaster, they could be given more elliptical shapes than the medieval originals. Elaborate plasterwork and mantelpieces, Gothic-style bookshelves and cases, chair-backs with pointed splats, arched *frets and *astragals were designed for Gothick interiors. Lanterns, clocks and metalwork were made to similar designs. Even when precise sources were acknowledged, as at Strawberry Hill, Middlesex (c.1760), where Henry VII's Chapel at Westminster Abbey, Worcester Cathedral and Archbishop Bourchier's tomb were the

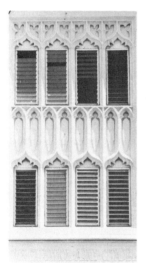

models for chimneypieces, wall *niches or fan vaulting, accurate imitation was still confined to detail, and did not in general affect the choice of structure or materials.

Gothick architecture, which was used especially for incidental buildings such as grottoes, follies, sham castles, garden pavilions and orangeries, reflected both the 18th century fascination with what was seen as the gloomy drama of medieval life – visits to the decaying Gothic ruins that remained after the dissolution of the monasteries were popular – and the fashion for horror, gloom-filled 'Gothic' fiction, such as the novels of Horace Walpole, C.R. Maturin and Ann Radcliffe.

The Gothick has made occasional appearances in the 20th century as a fanciful decorative style, e.g. Rex Whistler's work at Mottisfont, Hampshire. *See also* Castle style.

Gothic Revival. A revival of the *Gothic which began in the late 18th century, and was spearheaded by the publication of numerous antiquarian and topographical writings, many of them under the aegis of the Society of Antiquaries (founded in 1707, formally constituted 1717). By the end of the century the Society was the principal avenue for the publication of scholarly accounts of the Gothic. Men such as John Carter (1748-1817) and John Britton (1771-1857) made accurate records of buildings and their details which provided a source for the next generation of designers. To this information was added a growing interest in the medieval period, a desire for a 'national' style and an attraction to the ecclesiastical connotations of the Gothic. In sharp contrast with the 'crockets by the yard' *Gothick style, there was now a genuine impulse to revive authentic Gothic detail and ornaments in a historically accurate manner. Thomas Rickman (1776-1841) classified the English Gothic into *Early English, *Decorated and *Perpendicular in *An Attempt to Discriminate the Styles of English Architecture from the Conquest to the Reformation* (1817). The decision taken in 1836 to rebuild the Houses of Parliament in London in the Gothic style (chosen in preference to *Elizabethan Revival) gave it both impetus and prestige. Thereafter it was used for many official buildings: town halls, institutions such as hospitals, orphanages, museums and schools (especially after the 1870 Education Act). That the Gothic Revival was of so much greater importance in England than in France or Germany, was partly the result of the lack of a classically based academic architectural education.

On exteriors, terracotta patterning, banded brickwork and polychrome effects produced a richly ornamental result. William Butterfield's *Brick and Mortar in the Middle Ages* (1853) was influential both in Britain and America. The wave of new church buildings, restoration and liturgical change leading to reordering of interiors was to benefit manufacturers

Gothic Revival. 1) Albert Buildings, Queen Victoria Street, City of London, architect F.J. Ward, 1871. 2) 33-35 Eastcheap, City of London, red brick with blue brick and faïence, architect R.L. Roumieu, 1868. 3) Remodelled façade, Duomo, Florence, Italy, architect E. de Fabris, 1871-87. 4) Salvation Army Citadel, Miami, Florida, early 20th century.

such as Minton (tiles), J. Crace (furniture, wallpapers
and fabrics) and John Hardman (metalwork). Various
publications illustrated medieval tiles, e.g. John Gough
Nichol's *Examples of Decorative Tiles, sometimes called Encaustic*
(1845) and Minton's catalogue of 96 replicas of *Old
English Tiles* (1842). The style spread from the Roman
Catholic Church (for which A.W.N.*Pugin worked)
to the Anglican Church where William Butterfield
(1814-1900) was involved with the Cambridge Camden
Society (later known as the Ecclesiological Society).
Butterfield supervised the design of church plate,
entirely in the Gothic style, and his patterns, which
appeared in *Instrumenta Ecclesiastica* (a journal that published work by most leading ecclesiastical artists and
designers of the period between 1847 and 1856), were
disseminated across the British Empire and adopted
by the American Ecclesiological Society.

George Gilbert Scott (1811-78) considered that 'the
great principle is to decorate construction' but the
powerful force of Victorian mass manufacture worked
against the confinement of ornament to specific details
and the Gothic Revival fast became overladen with
spurious decoration. *Papier-mâché*, for example, could
reproduce 'elaborate pinnacles and pendants, rich
corbels and pierced frets of open work, deeply under-
cut rosettes . . . ' In A.W.N. Pugin's Medieval Hall at
the Great Exhibition in London of 1851, even pieces of
machinery were encased in elaborate Gothic ironwork.
Scott's Albert Memorial (1863-72) was considered at
the time as 'the epitome . . . of high Victorian ideals
and high Victorian style'; despite its mixture of styles
in detail the overall conception was unmistakably
Gothic. Later Gothic Revival architects and designers
such as William Burges (1827-81) or George Edmund
Street (1824-81) looked to earlier periods of the Gothic
for their sources, informed by foreign travel and increased scholarship in the subject, and produced work
in a style sometimes known as 'Reformed Gothic'. As
they became sure of their sources, designers felt able
to mingle the Gothic with, for example, the *Romanesque. Ornament became more solid, e.g. *chamfering, geometrical inlay, stump columns enlivened with
painted and stencilled decoration. By 1867 B.J.*Talbert decreed that later Gothic 'with its lavish display
of ornament . . . [was] quite undesirable for Cabinet
work.'

In America the Gothic Revival was more sporadic
and individualistic and lasted longer. *Carpenter
Gothic was a domestic variant, closer to the *Gothick
than to the Gothic Revival. In New York, St Patrick's
Cathedral by James Renwick (1818-95), which was
started 1857-83 and is still under construction, is an
astonishing *pot-pourri* of details culled from British,
French and German Gothic buildings to symbolise
the different countries of origin of the Catholic pop-
ulation. The style was used on university campuses

*Gothic Revival. 1) Episcopal chair, table for a boudoir and drawing room
chair from R.*Ackermann's Repository of Arts, 1825. 2) English oak
and parquetry table, c.1840. 3) *Diaper pattern in Cologne Cathedral,
Germany, from A.W.N.*Pugin's Glossary of Ecclesiastical
Ornament and Costume, 1844. 4) French gold bracelet, c.1845.
5) Austrian carved oak bookcase designed by B. Bernardis and J. Kramer,
from the catalogue of the Great Exhibition, London, 1851. 6) Gilt bronze
mantel clock, made in London, c.1860.*

(alluding to the medieval quadrangles of English colleges in Oxford and Cambridge), churches and some civic buildings, for example, the State Capitol, Hartford, Connecticut (1876-77) by Richard Upjohn (1802-78). At a more humble level, *Upjohn's Rural Architecture* (New York, 1852) provided a *pattern book which illustrated a wooden church, chapel, schoolhouse and parsonage. Showing simple designs with rudimentary Gothic trim, this publication carried the style across America. The Gothic Revival was as widespread in small-scale architecture in America as it was in Britain, even if it was less dour in painted wood than in brick or stone. The Gothic was often applied to skyscrapers, presumably because of the soaring nature of the style, e.g. Cass Gilbert's Woolworth Building in New York (1913), where executives met in a simulated organ loft and the detail – *gargoyles, *crockets, *finials and *corbels sculpted with portraits of patron, architect and others – were all the work of Italian immigrant craftsmen. *See also* Cathedral style; Dantesque; Troubadour style.

Göz, Gottfried-Bernhard (1708-74). German painter and engraver who worked in Augsburg and produced over twenty suites of ornament in the *Rococo style, notably *rocaille* borders framing *vignettes representing allegorical themes such as the *Seasons, the *Senses, the *Elements, and specifically *Christian themes such as the *Virtues and Vices, martyrs, the Virgin Mary, etc. His designs were widely used in the decoration of mid 18th century ceramics and glass.

Graces. The Three Graces, a group of naked or lightly draped female figures, were a symbol of beauty in *Graeco-Roman classicism, and appear, for example, in wall paintings at *Pompeii. They were thought to be attendants of *Venus and shared her attributes – apple, *myrtle and *rose. In the standard iconography they appear with the two outer figures facing forwards and the centre one facing away. They were a popular motif in *classical decoration and in *Neo-classical schemes, especially within the fashionable *tripod format, the three figures creating a tripartite support with their raised arms supporting, for example, a table-top or dish. In the Italian *Renaissance, humanist rationale interpreted the three figures as representing Chastity, Beauty and Love, or, alternatively, as symbolic of three stages in love: Beauty giving rise to Desire, followed by Fulfilment.

The Three Graces are occasionally confused with another classical subject, the Judgement of Paris, in which Paris had to decide between three naked goddesses: Juno (often accompanied by a *peacock), Minerva (with an *aegis) and Venus (with *Cupid).

graining. A *trompe-l'oeil* painted finish used on furniture from the 16th century to simulate grained wood, usually of a fashionable and expensive kind, e.g. rosewood in the early 19th century, bird's eye maple in the mid 19th century.

Graeco-Roman classicism. From the first simple post and lintel structures of 7th century BC Greece to the complex structures of the last years of the Roman Empire around 300 AD, classical Greek and Roman architecture provided an ornamental vocabulary that has been revived constantly. Greek temples, progressively elaborated up to the Hellenistic period of 300 BC, carried ornament in a prescribed position. The Romans elaborated and improvised upon this basis, and added the arch and the vault.

The *Orders (initially codified by *Vitruvius), represented the first system of ornament. The sculptural *frieze and the foliate *capital provided the focus for two principal kinds of decoration in classical ornament: mythical themes and *naturalism. To these were added symbolic objects, e.g. *trophies of war, religion or sacrifice, and household objects, such as the *tripod, *patera or candelabrum. Where naturalistic ornament was concerned the Greeks represented the indigenous plants of the southern Mediterranean relatively formally, while the Romans rendered them in a more representational manner. The *acanthus, *anthemion and the less literal *palmette were the most popular choices, together with the *grapevine and *laurel, and they were used to form *festoons, *rosettes and *scrolling foliage, occasionally with figures, or animals. Roman imperial ambitions introduced further motifs, some based on classical Greek myths, e.g. the *thyrsus and *caduceus, others deriving from the cultures of newly acquired territories. As the range of building types widened in the Roman period, elements that had originally been used purely structurally developed ornamental applications, e.g. the ornamental *column and *pilaster as well as more elaborate combinations of architectural components such as the *aedicule, *triumphal arch motif and *arcading. Graeco-Roman classicism provided a basic source of forms and motifs for countless later styles including *Byzantine, *Romanesque, *Renaissance, *Baroque, *classicism, *Neo-classicism and *Greek Revival.

granulation. An ancient technique of jewellery decoration employed by the Greeks, Romans, Celts and Etruscans, in which minute grains of gold (or silver) were applied, without solder, to an object of the same metal. It was sometimes combined with filigree work. Granulation creates an exceptionally rich effect even when used on thin sheet metal, making it possible to use the minimum of precious metal.

When *Archaeological style jewellery became fashionable in the mid 19th century, attempts were made to copy the technique. Ancient granulation had been achieved without the clogging effect of solder and although the Castellani family of jewellers in Rome had some success using an arsenite flux and a very fine solder, they never equalled the perfection of Etruscan work.

grapevine. A universal decorative form. It appeared in ancient Egyptian art, often combined with the *lotus or *papyrus, e.g. on *capitals or painted on the ceilings of tombs. The Assyrians treated it more formally and symmetrically as a kind of *Tree of Life form, and also, when fruiting, as a symbol of fertility. In classical mythology, the grapevine was sacred to Bacchus (*see* *Bacchic ornament) and to Apollo. It has symbolic significance in *Judaic decoration: the prophet Isaiah described the House of Israel as a Vineyard of the

*grapevine. 1) 16th century screen, Spring Chapel, Church of St Peter and St Paul, Lavenham, Suffolk. 2) American Hotel, Amsterdam, 1920s. 3) Hotel with *Bacchic decoration, Paris, architect Louis Boileau, 1920s. 4) Early 20th century iron grille, New York.*

Lord of Hosts and the men of Judah as the Vine; fruiting vines ornament synagogues, e.g. encircling *spiral columns and Jewish artefacts, and twelve bunches of grapes represent the twelve tribes of Israel. A common element in eastern Mediterranean decoration, grapevines appeared on early Christian catacombs and sarcophagi. They play an important part in *Christian iconography: the vine stands for Christ, the branches for his disciples, the grapes for the eucharistic wine. Use of the motif (often as the more formalised vine-scroll) spread from Syria to Ravenna and then to Christian communities in northern Europe (where vineyards established by the Romans were maintained by the monasteries): early *Celtic crosses were sometimes decorated with grapevines, as were medieval church screens and communion plate. The gathering and pruning of vines are important themes in medieval Books of Hours as a symbol of Autumn; similar scenes or the grapevine itself were later used in decorative schemes showing the *Seasons, particularly in the 17th and 18th centuries. The vine was an important

component of *Renaissance ornament, notably in *scrolling foliage and the *grotesque.

An obvious decoration for wine glasses, decanters, claret jugs, wine labels, grapes and the vine are used in hotels, inns, bars, and dining-rooms. The grapevine is sometimes confused with the *hop plant and *ivy, having similar foliage.

In the mid 19th century flatware handles decorated with vine patterns were popular in Britain and there were many variations including Bright Vine, Trailing Vine, Pierced Vine and Chased Vine; towards the end of the century as the fashion for *naturalism grew, the vine became more entwined and complex, even, sometimes, with the spoon bowl in the form of a large vine leaf.

Grasset, Eugène (1841-1917). French artist, designer, illustrator and writer who was important in the origination and popularisation of *Art Nouveau. His *Ornements Typographiques* (Paris, 1880) was clearly influenced by Japanese design, and it was *Plants and their Application to Ornament*, published first in England in twelve monthly parts (1896-97) and then in Paris as *La Plante et ses applications ornementales* (1898-99), that epitomised current ideas about ornamentation and illustrated in colour how plant forms could be used for ornament in many media: ceramics, glass, furniture, wallpaper, etc. Grasset wrote in 1897, 'Nature is the handbook of design that one should consult, we have only one thing to do, consult present usage, the utility of the objects and ornament them with the help of shapes taken from nature.' (*Revue des Arts Décoratifs*, Vol XVII.) Grasset's selection of plants is typical: it avoids the exotic full-blown flowers used earlier in the century and concentrates on simpler, more delicate species: iris, *poppy, waterlily, columbine, crown imperial, wild geranium, cyclamen, jonquil, snowdrop, lily of the valley, solomon seal, nasturtium, dandelion, wysteria, lilac, chestnut, monk's hood, thistle, periwinkle, buttercup, wild *rose and *chrysanthemum. He also published *Méthode de composition ornementale* (1905) and *Ouvrages de ferronerie moderne* (1906).

Green Man. *See* foliate mask.

Greek key. *See* key pattern.

Greek Revival. A strand of *Neo-classicism that came to dominate European and American design, beginning in the 1750s and enduring almost a century. The monuments of ancient Greece (both in mainland Greece and in southern Italy, the ancient Magna Graecia) were published for the first time in England and France (*see* J.D. Le Roy; J. Stuart and N. Revett) and established a new vocabulary of ornament. A large number of archaeological publications followed, including those sponsored by the Society of Dilettanti such as *Ionian Antiquities* (5 vols, 1769, 1797, 1840, 1881, 1915), the first two volumes of which were by Richard Chandler (1738-1810), and the works illustrating the *vase collections of Sir William Hamilton.

In architecture, the Greek Revival was expressed in purity of form, as promoted by the French rationalists such as the Abbé Laugier, and led to the conscious

'primitivism' of, for example, the architecture of Sir John Soane (1753-1837). Buildings from Leningrad to Glasgow, Berlin to London were built bearing the marks of close attention to the architecture of ancient Greece whilst smaller scale buildings such as the Tower of the Winds or the Lantern of Demosthenes (both in Athens) were reproduced faithfully as garden buildings and eye catchers. The style arrived in America later, not really making an impact until the 1820s, but was no less influential, and the Grecian *Orders and ornament were rarely absent from American *pattern books, appearing as standard detail on relatively humble buildings. The Bank of Pennsylvania in Philadelphia (1798) by B.H. Latrobe (1764-1820) was the first American building to incorporate a classical Greek Order, the Ionic. A.*Benjamin wrote in 1845 that 'since my last publication, the Roman school of architecture has been entirely changed for the Grecian.'

In the decorative arts, the Grecian style lent itself to a lighter treatment and began life mingled within the *Adam style. However, the stricter antiquarian approach promoted in architecture was echoed by the publications of furniture and interior designs by T. *Hope and reinforced by the spare linear depiction of original ancient Greek artefacts by engravers such as H.*Moses or C.H.*Tatham. The sculptor John Flaxman (1755-1826) produced line drawings to illustrate the works of Homer, Virgil and Dante, which were engraved by Thomas Pivoli; Hope admired these greatly. Popular pattern books such as those by G. *Smith and P. and M.A.*Nicholson promoted the Grecian taste, though at this level the concern was with the selection of motifs rather than with absolute authenticity.

By the 1830s and 1840s the Grecian had become just one of many strands within the taste for eclectic design, while in architecture a strong reaction set in. By the mid century, the style that had been taken to symbolise democracy, philosophy and learning, and was thus widely used for university buildings, museums, libraries and seats of government, was viewed as pagan and 'devoid of all life, virtue, honourableness or power of doing good' (John Ruskin in his *Stones of Venice*, 1851-53). The *Gothic Revivalists could find no good words for the Greek Revival, but O.*Jones's view was more balanced: in the *Grammar of Ornament* he observed that Greek Art 'carried the perfection of pure form to a point which has since never been reached; and from the very abundant remains we have of Greek ornament, we must believe the presence of refined taste was almost universal.' *See also* Etruscan style; Federal style; Style Etrusque.

*Greek Revival. 1) Window seat from R.*Ackermann's Repository of Arts, 1809. 2) Borders from Sir William Hamilton's collection of vases, in William Tischbein's Collection of Engravings from Ancient Vases, 1791. 3) English black basalt krater vase, Wedgwood, c.1810. 4) Table from P. and M.A.*Nicholson's The Practical Cabinet Maker, Upholsterer and Complete Decorator, 1826. 5) Garden building, Schlosspark, Klein Glienicke, Berlin, architect K.F.*Schinkel, 1824-35. 6) St Vincent Street United Presbyterian Church, Glasgow, architect Alexander 'Greek' Thomson, 1857-59. 7) English silver milk jug made by Benjamin Smith, 1806. 8) Merchants' Exchange, Philadelphia, Pennsylvania, architect William Strickland, 1832-33. 9) 19th century commercial building, Inverness, Scotland.*

Simon Gribelin. Design from his A Book of Ornaments usefull to all Artists, *1700.*

Gribelin, Simon (1661-1733). French goldsmith, engraver and printseller, who settled in England in 1680. He engraved many important pieces for leading silversmiths in London and published some of the earliest designs for gold and silver in England. *A Book of Severall Ornaments* (1682) contains ornamental panels of *scrolling foliage interspersed with mythical animals, etc. *A Book of Ornaments usefull to all Artists* followed in 1700. *A Book of Ornaments usefull to Jewellers, Watchmakers and all other artists* (1697) provides designs in the form of *friezes, ovals and roundels easily used for watch-cases, boxes, mirror backs, etc. *A New Book of Ornaments usefull to all Artists* (1704) incorporates some previous designs but also includes *cyphers and portrait *medallions among the *scrolling foliage, and motifs clearly influenced by contemporary French decoration: *baldacchino* motifs, *singeries* and *Apolline heads; this book was republished in London c.1760.

Some of Gribelin's leaf and scrollwork patterns were republished in *Knight's Scroll Ornaments* by F.*Knight c.1840.

griffin. Also spelt griffon or gryphon. Mythical animal with the head, wings and claws of an eagle and body of a lion (and according to some sources the beard of a goat). It probably originated in the ancient East; griffins were believed by the Greeks to guard the gold of north eastern Scythia (modern India), and appear, sometimes in pairs, on 12th century woven silks copied from fabrics imported from the East. The griffin appears in a similar form on medieval floor tiles and on 15th century *Hispano-Moresque pottery. It is a common motif (often without wings)

in heraldry where it is emblematic of courage and watchfulness. The griffin was discussed in the *bestiaries and appears in *Gothic church sculpture. In Graeco-Roman mythology the griffin was sacred to *Minerva (and her Greek counterpart Athena). It is occasionally shown guarding the *lyre of Apollo, and through this association became linked with ideas of sun and fire: in *friezes, the griffin often supports the *candelabra and *Neo-classical designers, e.g. J.*Stuart, Matthew Boulton and Josiah Wedgwood used griffins as supports for *torchères*, candelabra, perfume burners and candlesticks. An engraving by G.B. *Piranesi of addorsed griffins with entwined tails represents a popular usage in *Adam style decoration.

grisaille. Figures and patterns painted in shades of black, grey and white on wood, plaster, stone surfaces to imitate stone or marble figure sculpture or relief ornament. During the 14th and 15th centuries, only monochrome shades were used in church decorations during Lent, therefore painted triptych altarpieces often had *grisaille* painting on the reverse which could be folded over the coloured painting; the same effect appears in 14th and 15th century manuscript illumination. *Grisaille* was particularly popular during the *Renaissance and in *Neo-classical styles, which stimulated considerable interest in original classical sculpture and stone engraving. *Grisaille* painting has also been used to imitate *cameo decoration.

griffin. 1) Panel from 1920s commercial building, Philadelphia, Pennsylvania. 2) Byzantine panel built into façade of Cathedral of San Marco, Venice, Italy. 3) 15th century Perpendicular font, Church of St Andrew, Norton, Suffolk. 4) English black basalt candlestick, Wedgwood, late 18th century.

Some 16th century Limoges enamellers, whose designs were based largely on engraved compositions, produced work *en grisaille*.

grotesque masks with a combination of hideous and humorous features were used in *Gothic church architecture, e.g. on *gargoyles, *bosses and *poppyheads, and, particularly in the *Flamboyant Gothic style, on *corbels. The motif was used in the more bizarre manifestations of the High *Renaissance in northern Europe: *Flemish Mannerism and *Netherlands Grotesque. It reappeared in the *Baroque, e.g. on *keystones. 19th century *eclectic styles took it up again; the Martin Brothers, English art potters working at the end of the 19th century, produced jugs and jars with human and bird heads in the tradition of the grotesque mask. *See also* gorgon.

grotesques. System of decoration based on Roman wall paintings that were discovered in 1488 in the buried ruins of Nero's Domus Aurea on the Esquiline Hill, Rome. Contemporary painters made expeditions into the ruins to study the *grottesche*, notably Piero di Cosimo (c.1462-c.1521), Bernardino Pinturicchio (c.1454-1513), Giovanni da Udine (1487-1546) and Raphael (1483-1520) – hence the term Raphaelesques, which was sometimes applied to the decoration. The earliest known engravings of grotesque ornament

grotesques. 1) Mid 16th century wall decoration at Castel Sant'Angelo, Rome. 2) Italian maiolica plate made at Faenza, c.1575. 3) Detail from a 16th century panel representing America by Marcus Geerardts. 4) English earthenware vase by the Martin Brothers, 1886.

*grotesque masks. 1) Engraving by R.*Boyvin from his* Libro di Variate Mascare, *c.1560. 2) Doorway, via Gregoriana, Rome, by Federigo Zuccaro, late 16th century.*

decorated editions of Ovid and Terence published in Venice in the 1490s. The engravings of Marcantonio Raimondi (c.1495-1534) and his school were also important. From 1500 to 1521 both A.*Veneziano and Nicoletto Rosex da Modena (fl 1490-1512) published influential panels of grotesque ornament. *Renaissance designs took some elements of Roman examples – a free, light style of painting, foliate *scrolls incorporating animals, birds and fantastic animals such as *chimeras, *sphinxes and *griffins – and developed them into more ordered structures set within vertical panels and based, for example, on the *candelabra form.

During the 16th century, the use of grotesques spread from painted decoration to ceramics, carved wood, metalwork and tapestry. In Italy it followed the style developed by Raphael and Giovanni da Udine, notably in the *logge* of the Vatican (1518-19). In northern Europe, grotesque ornament was combined with *strapwork (producing a heavier effect) and the bizarre element became increasingly important, culminating in the fantastic design of the *Netherlands Grotesque style. In 1612, by which time the style had reached England, Henry Peacham described this type of decoration in *Graphice*, ' . . . the greater variety you shew in your invention the more you please, but remembering to observe a methode or continuation of one and the same thing throughout your whole work without change or altering. You may, if you list, draw naked boyes riding and playing with their paper-mils or bubble shels upon Goates, Eagles, Dolphins etc, the bones of a Ram's head hung with strings of beads and Ribands, Satyres, Tritons, Apes, cornu-copias, Dogs yoakt, and drawing Cowcumbers, Cherries, or any kind of wild traile or vinet after your owne invention, with a thousand more such idel toyes, so that herein you cannot be too fantastical.' French grotesques followed the Italian models; those designed by J.A.*Ducerceau, *Petits Grotesques* (1550, 1562) and *Grands Grotesques* (1566), depended heavily on the work of E.*Vico. In late 17th century France, there was a revival of interest in Renaissance grotesques and the Vatican decorations were republished, e.g. in a collection after Raphael entitled *Miscellaneae picturae vulgo grotesques in spelaeis Vaticanis* (Paris, c.1660). J.*Berain, a prolific and influential designer, created a light, airy rendering of this decoration, which by the end of the

17th century had confusingly become known as 'ara-besques'. Christopher Wren visited Paris in the 1660s and collected a quantity of engraved patterns which, he noted, would 'give our country-men examples of ornament and grotesks in which the Italians themselves confess the French to excel.' Designs were still based on vertical forms (using as bases *baldacchino motifs or even swings as well as candelabra forms) but lighter scrolls and *bandwork replaced heavy strapwork, and classical motifs such as the sphinx and griffin were joined by children, and *singeries, *commedia dell'arte and *chinoiserie figures. Early *Rococo ornemanistes such as C.*Gillot and Claude Audran III (1658-1734) embraced the grotesque with enthusiasm but the form was on the whole too symmetrical and ordered for the later genre pittoresque.

Towards the end of the 18th century, more grotesque decoration was discovered at *Herculaneum and *Pompeii and in 1774-75 a further sixteen decorated rooms were found at the Domus Aurea, Rome. These finds were extensively published, and painted and modelled 'arabesque' designs became one of the most characteristic elements of European *Neo-classicism. In France, elegant and delicate designs were published by G.-P.*Cauvet, L. Prieur (fl 1765-83), R. de *Lalonde and H.*Salembier. The *Adam style made extensive use of grotesques, primarily as wall decoration.

In the 19th century, chromolithography enabled the first colour illustrations of grotesque decoration to be produced. W. Zahn published illustrations of Pompeii and Herculaneum (1828-59); Prince Albert's adviser on artistic matters, Ludwig Gruner (1801-82), published Fresco Decorations and Stuccoes of Churches and Palaces in Italy during the 15th and 16th centuries (London, 1844; enlarged edition, London and Paris 1854), which aimed (and failed) to introduce the fresco to Britain, and Specimens of Ornamental Art (London, 1850); both publications illustrated the grotesque decorations of Raphael, Giovanni da Udine and Giulio Romano. A good example of a 19th century rendering of grotesque decoration was the painted interior of the London Coal Exchange by Robert Sang (1849, demolished) which placed scenes of collieries and miners among *festoons, *scrolling foliage and *dolphins. Grotesques appeared widely in *Renaissance Revival Schemes; Anton Seder's Die Pflanze in Kunst und Gewerbe (Vienna, 1886) contained designs which, in line with current fashion, incorporated a wide range of plant forms.

grotto ornament. Artificial grottoes created by the Romans were described by L.B.*Alberti in De Re Aedificatoria. The conceit was well-suited to *Mannerist taste, and many grottoes were built during the 16th century, notably in the Boboli gardens in Florence, the Villa Madama in Rome, Palazzo del Tè in Mantua and at Fontainebleau. The required effects were rough, rocky, stalactite and shell-encrusted surfaces over which water cascaded and dripped into pools ornamented with frogs, *fish, snails, snakes, lizards, crayfish. The effect of rocks and stalactites were also used for *rusticated gateways, fountains and garden buildings, and in the late 16th century these elements even appeared in the ornamentation of interiors, ceramics

and metalwork; grotto fauna became part of the general vocabulary of Mannerist ornament. In 1565, the French potter, Bernard Palissy (c.1510-1589), described as 'maker of rustic figures to the King', produced for Catherine de Medici's grotto in the Tuileries ceramic ornaments with mottled glazes that gave a sub-aqueous and slimy effect. The fashion lingered on during the 17th century. John Evelyn wrote in 1657, 'Caves, Grots, Mounts and irregular ornaments do contribute to contemplative and philosophical enthousiasm' (letter to Sir Thomas Browne, 28th January 1657), and into the 18th century, when landscaped gardens, e.g. Stourhead in Wiltshire, c.1748, were not considered complete without a grotto.

Guarini, Guarino (1624-83). Born in Modena, northern Italy, Guarini entered the Theatine Order to train in theology, philosophy and mathematics. Later he turned to architecture and from 1666 remained in Turin, the city with which he is associated. His Architettura Civile (Turin, 1686; two-volume enlarged edition published posthumously, 1737), although crudely engraved, was highly original. It contains drawings of many of his own *Baroque ecclesiastical buildings (in section) as well as countless diagrams and much elaborate ornamentation, including *capitals decorated with *angels, *palm leaves, *lilies and other flowers – all far removed from the classical *Orders. His use of ornamental ribbing in the domes of his churches suggests that he was aware of oriental examples.

grotto ornament with *mask, Vrtba Palace, Prague, 1730s.

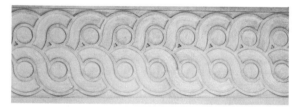

guilloche. 1) Marble fragment, classical period, at Villa Viscaya, Florida. 2) Double guilloche wall moulding, Chiswick House, London, 1725-29. 3) Ormolu band on Louis XVI commode, 1765-75. 4) English silver slop basin made by Boulton & Fothergill, c.1780.

guttae. 1) Renaissance palazzo, Florence, Italy. 2) Parque Güell, Barcelona, Spain, architect Antonio Gaudi, 1900-14.

best known for his survey *Les Maîtres Ornemanistes* (1880), which covers the work of the major European ornamental engravers from the *Renaissance to the end of the 18th century.

guttae. Also known as bells, and, particularly in the 18th century, as *drops or Doric drops, guttae are the element of the Doric *Order thought by some to symbolise the wooden pegs beneath the *triglyph on the *entablature. T.*Hope presented another classical explanation: ' . . . some drops of rain distilled from the ends of the rafters that projected over an architrave so pleased an architect that he added them as ornaments to his Doric triglyph.' The motif was copied on *Neo-classical furniture. An eccentric use of guttae was as feet for tables and chairs, for example, in designs by T.*Chippendale.

gyronny pattern. A triangular equivalent of *chequer pattern that occurs principally in heraldry, but is sometimes found in medieval work, e.g. on tiles.

Haberman(n), Franz Xaver (1721-96). Prolific designer and sculptor, who worked in Augsburg, South Germany. He published a quantity of designs for ecclesiastical and domestic ornament, furniture, metalwork and panelling. He is best known for work in the *Rococo style, which included schemes incorporating the *Seasons and the *Elements; his later work was more in the *Louis XIV style. Haberman's designs were republished several times during the 19th century, by Edouard Rouveyre as *Recueil de motifs et compositions rocailles* (Paris, 1889), in Leipzig as *Rococo Möbel, Rococo Ornamente* (1887-93), and in New York as *Louis XV Collection of Ornaments in the Correct Rococo Style* (1894).

half figure or **demi figure.** Upper half of a human or animal figure, which below the waist or breast metamorphoses into an ornament such as *scrolling foliage. *Grotesque ornament often included such figures, some bizarrely locked into *strapwork bases as in

guilloche. Repeating ornament of *interlacing curved bands, sometimes forming circles that are enriched with *rosettes or other flower forms. One of the most frequently used motifs in *Assyrian ornament and *Graeco-Roman classical ornament. It was revived in the *Renaissance and was a characteristic carved motif on late 16th and 17th century woodwork. It was a constant motif in the *Neo-classical period, in all media. *See also* fret.

Guilmard, Desiré. French publisher, designer and historian of ornament, who from 1839 provided material for the *Historicist movement in France. From 1844 to 1882 he published *Le Garde Meuble Ancien et Moderne,* which annually comprised six instalments each containing three chair, three other furniture and three textile designs. He subsequently published *La Connaissance des styles d'ornementation* (1853; German edition, 1860), which provided documented examples of ornament from the *Romanesque period to the Restoration of the French monarchy in 1818. Guilmard was

*half figure. 1) Palazzo Spada, Rome, 1540. 2) Forming caryatid handle on English silver spout cup, c.1630-45. 3) Engraving of a *cornice from P.*Columbani's Capitals, Friezes and Corniches, 1776. 4) In marquetry on late 18th century Italian commode.*

*Netherlands Grotesque work, others closer to *classical examples with trails of *acanthus leaves.

The half figure is an invaluable form for *brackets, doorknockers, etc. Half-figure handles on metalwork and ceramics are often known as caryatid handles. *See also* herm.

Halfpenny, William (fl 1722-55). Prolific author whose early publications were straightforward builders' manuals, designed as practical architectural guidance

Franz Xaver Haberman. Rococo design, mid 18th century.

in book form. Halfpenny's *Practical Architecture* (before 1724) had run to seven editions by 1751. In his later works he ventured into decorative detail, sometimes with his son John as co-author. The *Modern Builder's Assistant* (1757) included T.*Lightoler's designs for stucco and work by Robert Morris (c.1702-54), which were among the earliest *Rococo designs to be published in England. In *Rural Architecture in the Chinese Taste* (c.1750, second edition 1752), Rococo designs were successfully combined with *chinoiserie; though clearly derivative and with rather crude plates, the book was popular (reprinted 1755) and was known in Germany and America. *Chinese and Gothic Architecture properly ornamented* appeared in 1752. These and other similar publications gave English and American builders a chance to use elements of French Rococo and *chinoiserie* against a background of 18th century *classicism, and helped to make ornament accessible to the builder of urban terraces for the middle classes, where previously it had been the preserve of architects to the landed gentry. *See also* Gothick.

Hall, John (1825-post 1849). Author of *The Cabinet-Makers Assistant* (Baltimore, 1840, second edition 1878), the first furniture *pattern book to be produced in the United States. It claimed to promote 'the most modern style of furniture in an economical arrangement to save labour' and was, in effect, a survey of early 19th century *Federal style furniture. Many designs were deliberately based on single and double *scrolls so that they could be cut with a bandsaw (a steam-driven version of which was introduced in 1878). Hall also produced a series of house designs and a book on hand-railings in 1840.

Hancock, Robert (1730-1817). English engraver and illustrator who, from 1753, pioneered the technique of transfer printing both on enamel at the Battersea enamel factory, London, and on ceramics at the Bow and Worcester porcelain factories. A large number of Hancock's designs incorporated the *Rococo *vignette. Also at the Battersea factory was the French artist and engraver, Simon-François Ravenet (1721-74), through whom Hancock would have known the work of other French Rococo painters and engravers, notably L.P. Boitard, J.-A.*Watteau, F.*Boucher, Nicholas Lancret and J.*Pillement. *See also* drawing books.

hand. In *emblem books, at a time when it was considered sacrilegious to personify God, a single hand denoted the hand of God.

Used on Greek stele, clasped hands appeared as a motif on finger rings in Roman and medieval jewellery and frequently since. The French ornamental engraver Pierre Woeiriot (1531-89) produced designs for them in the late 16th century; they were popular with the Victorians and the Irish Claddagh ring has two hands holding a heart surmounted by a crown, symbolising the care that should be taken of love. During the French Revolution, clasped hands appeared, e.g. on fabrics and ceramics, as a symbol of *fraternité*. In the mid 19th century, a small rounded female hand – a sign of feminine beauty much prized by the Victorians – appeared frequently in ornament:

hand. 1) Mass-produced cast-iron doorknocker on house, Gloucestershire, 19th century.
harp. 2) Harp-back side chair by Duncan Phyfe, New York, c.1800-15.

e.g. on jewellery or as paperweights. Porcelain vases with a supporting hand incorporated into the design were made at the Bennington, Copeland, Minton and Belleek factories, among others. A hand holding a single flower was used in funerary ornament.

In the 1930s, under the influence of Surrealism, hands grew to enormous proportions, e.g. a table was made in the shape of a hand by Costa-Achillopulo, a chair by Salvador Dali. Also in the 1930s a hand wall lamp was made by Nicolas de Molas followed by smaller ornamental pieces: ashtrays, jewellery, even buttons designed for Schiaparelli by Jean Clément.

Hanoverian pattern. Term used to describe the plain, rounded ends to the handles of spoons and forks; mainly used from 1710 to the late 1770s. The form was revived in the 19th century and is still made today. Generally, the pre-1730 examples have rat tails, a tapering ridge extending from the back of the stem on to the bowl of the spoon. Unlike the later pattern, which is known as *Old English, the spoon ends turn down so that, when laid on the table, the back of the spoon bowl faces up. The spoon ends may be further decorated with an engraved line around the edge, known as a Thread, or a feathery effect engraved to resemble miniature *gadrooning, known as a Feather edge. Either of these might be combined with a *scallop shell. The backs of the spoon bowls were also decorated, particularly on teaspoons, from c.1740 until the end of the 18th century. The motifs ranged from scallop shells, flowers, Prince of Wales *feathers, *eagles, political and patriotic emblems, *masonic signs, birds, harvest implements, ships, etc. These 'fancy back' patterns also appear on spoons with Old English and *Fiddle ends.

harp. An ancient musical instrument often used as a symbol of divine *music. It appears, often in the hands of *angels, in ecclesiastical decoration and is also an attribute of David, reputed author of many of the Psalms. According to tradition, it became the badge of Ireland (*see* Irish) after it was adopted by an early king called David. However, it was not generally used in Ireland. In the early 17th century, under James I, it was placed on the royal *achievement of arms of Great Britain.

In the late 18th century, when the harp was enlarged and improved as a musical instrument and

gained in popularity, the shape began to be used in a similar manner to the *lyre on late 18th and early 19th century furniture, mostly in America. Duncan Phyfe (1768-1854), a well-known New York cabinetmaker, probably originated the form, and it is mentioned in the *New York Price Book* for 1817. *See also* Muses.

harpy. A monster with the wings and claws of a bird and the head and breasts of a woman. It appears most frequently in *grotesque ornament, where it is sometimes almost indistinguishable from the Roman form of *sphinx with wings.

hart's-tongue. *See* waterleaf.

Haviland, John (1792-1852). English-born American architect and author of important books in the promotion of the *Greek Revival in America. *The Builder's Assistant* (3 vols, Philadelphia, 1818, 1819, 1821; 2nd edition, 4 vols, 1830) was the first American work to illustrate the specifically Greek as well as the established Roman *Orders. Haviland also prepared the way for the enthusiastic reception that the *Picturesque was to receive, promoting the idea of appropriate architectural and ornamental styles for certain settings.

hawksbill. *See* crossette.

heads. *See* beakhead; boss; cameo; corbel; *espagnolette*; foliate mask; gorgon; grotesque mask; keystone; mask; medallion, personification; portrait head; romayne work.

heart. Symbol of love, both sacred and profane. In *Christian ornament (usually Roman Catholic rather than Protestant), the bleeding heart symbolises the

heart. 1) Winged heart on 15th century Perpendicular font, Church of St Andrew, Norton, Suffolk. 2) Early 17th century English pendant with portrait of Charles I. 3) Roof frame, Glasgow School of Art, architect Charles Rennie Mackintosh, started 1897.

helmet. 1) *Keystone on Berlin Arsenal, 1695 onwards. 2) Minerva from Gaetano Vacani's Raccolta di Antiche Armatura, etc., *1840. 3) Heraldic helmets from C. Demengeot's* Dictionnaire du Chiffre-monogramme dans les styles Moyen Age et Renaissance, *1881.*

Virgin Mary and the sorrows of Christ, and the sacred heart, pierced by three nails and ringed with a crown of thorns, represents the crucifixion. A heart crowned with thorns is the emblem of the Jesuits. The flaming heart is used in both ecclesiastical and secular ornament to denote fervour in love.

Hearts are an ubiquitous folk motif, particularly in central and northern Europe and therefore also in *Pennsylvania Dutch styles in America. Pierced in the backs of chairs, cabinets, etc., they became a popular motif in *Arts and Crafts furniture at the end of the 19th century; they appear frequently, with other simplified forms, in the work of the architect and designer C.F.A. Voysey (1857-1941).

helix (Greek, spiral or tendril). A small *scroll or *volute used on Corinthian *capitals (*see* Orders), where two spring from each of the eight *caulicoli.

helmet. Worn by warriors and heroes, the helmet is an important motif in *military decoration. As an attribute of *Minerva (and her Greek counterpart Athena), goddess of wisdom, benevolence and civilisation, it is used to ornament institutions of *learning and the arts. When the helmet appears with a *shield, it signifies *Mars. Personifications of Faith and Fortitude often wear helmets, as a symbol of preservation and protection. *Heraldic decoration usually presents the range of helmets contemporary with its 14th and 15th century origins. In *Renaissance decoration, when classical styles of armour tended to be used, helmeted warriors within roundels were a popular motif, also a helmet alone (sometimes referred to as a gladiatorial mask) incorporated into a *trophy or *panoply or used as a *finial. Ornamentists of the Northern Renaissance tended to use contemporary

16th and 17th century helmets as well as classical examples. In 18th century *Neo-classical ornament, great care was taken to use helmets that were historically correct: M.A.*Pergolesi included a collection among his engraved ornament, but the most serious attempt at accuracy was made by T.*Hope in *Costume of the Ancients*.

Henri II style. Although the French king Henri II reigned only from 1547 to 1559, his name became associated with a style which showed the growing influence of Italian *Renaissance styles on contemporary French design (as characterised by the work of P.*de l'Orme) and the widened use of *architectural motifs and forms in furniture. The style includes the richly ornate work produced in the Burgundy region, often to the designs of H.*Sambin. *Arabesque patterns were an important element of the style and designs for them were published in quantity. They were used on silver and ceramics, e.g. on Saint-Porchaire earthenware which had patterns of brown clay inlaid into the white body. 19th century imitations of the ware were produced by Wedgwood and Minton in England and at Choisy-le-Roi in France, and called Henri Deux ware.

During the *French Second Empire (1848-70), there was a revival of Henri II furniture. Like its English equivalent, *Elizabethan Revival furniture, it was considered particularly suitable for dining rooms.

Hepplewhite, George (d 1786). Author of *The Cabinet-Maker and Upholsterer's Guide*, first published in 1788 two years after his death. Subsequent editions in 1789 and 1794 were published under the name of his widow, Alice. The *Guide* contains about 300 influential, practical but not innovative designs for household furniture. They are in a severe *Neo-classical style and show a reaction against the highly ornamented and delicate work of the early *Adam style. Bow-fronted furniture and chairs with oval, wheel and shield backs and plain vertical *fluting are characteristic, as are Prince of Wales's *feathers and ears of *wheat decorating shield-back chairs. *Urns, *festoons, *medallions, *rosettes and *vases are typical, as are *pediments topped with urns, *shell and *fan inlay. Although not the height of fashion when published, the designs were widely used in provincial England, and in America Samuel McIntire (1757-1811) of Salem and

George Hepplewhite. Designs for chair-backs from his The Cabinet-Maker and Upholsterer's Guide, *1794.*

John Aitken of Philadelphia are known to have made extensive use of them. Much of the furniture bought by George Washington for Mount Vernon was in the style of Hepplewhite. Some of Hepplewhite's designs were included in the second edition of T.*Shearer's *Cabinet-Maker's London Book of Prices* (1793).

heraldic beasts comprise four types: stylised representations of real animals, such as *stags, *dogs, *lions, porcupines; classical hybrids, such as *griffins or *harpies; fabulous creatures, many from the *bestiaries, such as the *unicorn; creatures devised specifically for heraldic use, such as the enfield (head, hindquarters and tail of a fox, body of a dog, claws of an eagle) or the ypotryll (face of a boar with tusks, curved horns, antelope's body, lion's tail). Typically, heraldic beasts are placed on gateposts, lodges, boundary walls, staircase newel posts, and sometimes, in the manner of supporters, flanking a *shield.

The positions in which creatures are depicted are formalised: couchant, lying with head erect; dormant, lying asleep; naissant, upper half only as though emerging from the womb; passant, walking with one paw raised; rampant, one hind leg on the ground, the others waving fiercely; rampant combattant, two beasts facing one another; rampant addorsed, two rampant beasts back to back; salient, jumping, hind paws on ground, front paws raised; sejant, in sitting position; statant, all four feet on the ground.

The lion sejant became a popular *finial on spoons and tankard handles in late 17th century English silver, and was used without any heraldic relevance, apart perhaps from some general patriotic reference to the emblem of the United Kingdom.

heraldic decoration. Heraldry was a simultaneous development in England, France, Germany, Spain and Italy during the 12th century. It expanded to satisfy the demands for hierarchical *emblems of a feudal society, the complex warring of the Crusades and the rituals of tournament. Apart from representing the bearer and his position in society, the use of *achievements of arms quickly spread to the realm of decoration, where they conveyed pride of ownership or of pedigree. In architecture, heraldic ornament tended to be ostentatiously placed on external features, or on publicly accessible places such as *battlements, doorways, gateposts and fireplaces. Precious possessions such as books, gold, silver and porcelain were similarly decorated and by 1610 the publication of John Guillim's *A Display of Heraldrie* provided easy reference and clear explanations of the rules of heraldry. This was reprinted continuously during the next hundred years and much used in Britain and America. At the same time a code was devised for engraving heraldry on silver whereby different types of cross-hatching indicated different colours, a system that began in Europe and was later adopted in Britain; it was often explained in *pattern books of *cyphers. However, as much French silver and gold plate was melted down to meet the sumptuary laws during the financial crises of Louis XIV's reign (1689, 1700, 1709), it was replaced by faïence dinner services elaborately painted with coats of arms. British and American

*heraldic decoration. 1) English medieval floor tile. 2) *Achievement of arms above entrance, dated 1601, to Montacute House, Somerset. 3) Lid of English portable writing desk, c.1525, lined with leather painted with a heraldic *diaper pattern.*

families at the turn of the 18th century ordered porcelain dinner services from China enamelled with their arms, sending drawings and engravings for the Chinese to copy.

From late medieval times it was customary, on marriage, for the arms of the wife's family to be added to those of her husband and these were often incorporated into the decoration of a marriage bed, new house or refurbished interior. Tombs and tomb structures were an obvious place for heraldic displays of lineage, and *powdered and *diaper ornament were often used to produce the effect of heraldic cloths and draperies. Sometimes the shields were depicted hanging off branches of trees – this may have been a reference to the biblical *Tree of Jesse, though is more likely to have been in imitation of the custom of hanging shields and helmets on trees at tournaments (like the classical *trophy). This style of displaying shields also appears in the borders of early tapestries and precedes the use of heraldic supporters to a shield.

Lavish display and decoration were popular during the *Tudor period. With the demise of the tournament, heraldry's last link with its martial origins was broken but it continued to be used and developed as a code of social status particularly in the staging of funerals, of which Henry VIII's was probably one of the most spectacular examples. It was taken up and adapted in *Renaissance schemes of decoration and the form of the shield gradually evolved into the distinctly unmilitary *cartouche. From the 15th and 16th centuries it became fashionable in Italy and France for quasi-heraldic personal badges to be used, rather than the old family coats of arms; and the use of the *rebus and *impresa spread. In Germany the medieval style of heraldic decoration persisted despite the Renaissance. This was partly due to the fact that Maximilian I, Holy Roman Emperor (1493-1513), had a great nostalgia for the medieval past and, considering himself a worthy successor to King Arthur, continued to hold tournaments long after they had been abandoned elsewhere.

From the 16th century, cities, towns, counties and guilds began to evolve their own achievements of arms, and these became a popular decorative motif on stoneware and glass, particularly in Germany and the Low Countries.

Heraldic ornament has tended to be particularly popular during periods of great social mobility, such as the reigns of Henry VIII, Elizabeth I and Victoria; families who have achieved eminence have often adopted an achievement of arms even if not entitled to do so. Newly acquired coats of arms were usually displayed most prominently. Similarly, heraldic decoration has frequently been adopted by insecure or new leaders to lend weight to their position, e.g. the resumption of the Emperor's emblem by Napoleon III in his restoration of the Château de Pierrefonds. Heraldic design and decoration naturally flourished in the medieval revivalism of the mid 19th century when the concept of chivalry was much admired. The Eglinton Tournament of 1837 in Ayrshire, Scotland, was a typical manifestation of this. During the 19th century, some porcelain factories actually made the production of heraldically decorated ware for London companies, corporations, societies, etc., their main output, so great was the demand, and popular souvenir ware such as Goss China (which carried the arms of scores of British towns) was produced well into the 1930s. See also achievement of arms; emblem books; Gothic Revival; heraldic beasts; military decoration; Troubadour style.

herbals. Like the *bestiaries, manuscript and then printed herbals were an important, early source for representational ornament. Accounts were based on classical texts and covered fabulous plants such as the goose-bearing barnacle tree and the *Tree of Life as well as real species. The earliest known printed herbal was the *Herbarium* of Apuleius Platonicus (Rome, c.1481), which was taken from a 9th century manuscript found at Monte Cassino, Italy. Early, woodblocked illustrations were often botanically inaccurate and drawn diagramatically, and it was not until the appearance of Otto Brunfels's *Herbarum Vivae Eicones* (Strasbourg, 1530) and L. Fuchs's *De Historia Stirpium* (Basle, 1542) that plants were systematically drawn from life. Plates from these two works were pirated and copied for editions of herbals all over Europe. The best-known British example, John Gerard's *The Herball* (1597), contained very few original plates, although it did include one of a potato plant. Floral motifs in embroideries, plasterwork and engraved silver of the late 16th and early 17th centuries show the influence of the woodcut illustrations to the herbals particularly clearly. The *Arts and Crafts designer William Morris (1834-96) owned a copy of Fuchs's publication and his floral designs show the influence of this and other herbals. See also plant forms.

Herculaneum. A Roman city close to Naples, discovered in 1709, which, like Pompeii, had been buried since the eruption of Mount Vesuvius in 79 AD – both cities provided a rich source for late 18th and early 19th century *Neo-classical decoration. As Horace Walpole put it, 'Tis certainly an advantage for the learned world, that this has been laid up so long.' Herculaneum was discovered before Pompeii; work began on the site in 1738 under the sponsorship of Charles VII, King of Naples. It was excavated at intervals until 1820 and publications documented the finds as they occurred. *Le Antichità di Ercolano* (9 vols, 1757-92) was published under the aegis of the supervisory body for excavations, the Accademia Ercolanese (founded 1755). The engravings were much copied, and reprints, abridged for popular use, soon appeared, despite attempts to prevent this. In London the work was available from 1776, in Italy from 1789. Of the original volumes, five were concerned only with the paintings (1757, 1760, 1762, 1765, 1779), one with small bronzes (1767), one with statues (1771) and one with lamps and candelabras (1792). A further volume dealt with wall and floor decoration. C.-N.*Cochin the Younger published another account of the artefacts found in Herculaneum as early as 1753 in London and 1754 in Paris. The discoveries were highly influential because they revealed the details of daily life and domestic environments in a Roman city; hitherto only the grandiose temple architecture and ornament of Rome had been known. At first the Naples porcelain factory used motifs taken from pieces excavated at Herculaneum only for important royal gifts, such as the service made 1785-87 and given by Ferdinand IV of Naples to George III, but by the 1790s they were used more widely. Whole rooms were decorated in 'Herculaneum style'; the so-called 'Herculaneum dancers' (in fact taken from a *Pompeian scene of dancing nymphs) were an immensely popular theme. Plaster and porcelain *medallions decorated with such Roman themes were essential ingredients of the *Adam style and its European equivalents. Furniture designers of the *Empire style and German *Neo-classicists such as K.F.*Schinkel borrowed motifs from the *Antichità*, and publications such as W. Zahn's *Die schönsten Ornamente und merkwürdigsten Gemälde aus Pompeji, Herkulanum und Stabiae* (parallel texts in French and German, Berlin, 1828-59). The latter is a magnificent example of chromolithography and exemplifies the early 19th century concern with historical accuracy. Zahn claimed that his work had 'the exactitude which science demands', and O.*Jones admired it greatly. In the mid 19th century souvenir items were made for visitors to Herculaneum and Pompeii often decorated with copies of the frescoes (carefully avoiding the erotic subjects). *Archaeological jewellery was produced accurately copying the original pieces found. See also grotesques.

Herculean decoration. 1) The Fourth Labour of Hercules, the destruction of the Erymanthian boar, by Marcus Geerardts, 16th century. 2) French steel sword hilt, chiselled in relief with the Labours of Hercules, c.1760-70.

Herculean decoration. The Greek hero Herakles, more generally known by his Roman name, Hercules, was the personification of strength and courage. He is generally depicted bearded and muscled, wearing a *lion's pelt around his body with its head as a helmet, and carrying a knotted club which sometimes appears with more conventional weapons in schemes of *military decoration. The Twelve Labours of Hercules was a popular theme in *Renaissance ornament, taken up particularly by influential 16th century engravers such as H.*Aldegrever and E.*Delaune. The most frequently illustrated Labour is Hercules fighting with the Nemean lion. The remaining Labours, which appear more rarely in ornament, are: the fight against the Lernean hydra; the capture of the Arcadian stag; the destruction of the Erymanthian boar; the cleansing of the stables of Augeas; the destruction of the Stymphalian birds; the capture of the Cretan bull; the capture of the mares of the Thracian Diomedes; the seizure of the girdle of the Queen of the Amazons; the capture of the oxen of Geryones in Erythia; the fetching of the golden apples of the Hesperides; and the bringing of Cerberus from the lower world.

Herculean decoration, signifying strength, appears on arms and armour, in military *trophies and in other schemes of decoration alluding to military exploits, and even on objects such as nutcrackers. The figure of Hercules is sometimes used as a support, as at the Hofburg Palace, Vienna, where the doorways are flanked by Herculean figures, each portraying a different Labour. At Ely House, Dublin (1777), Hercules stands at the foot of the stairs as a newel post whilst the Labours, on metal panels, ascend the stairs. The mask of Hercules, draped in a lion pelt and suspended from lion's paws was used in the late 17th and early 18th centuries, but fell into disuse with the coming of *Neo-classicism.

herm, hermes, term or **therm.** A male or female bust, usually armless, sometimes with *volutes in place of arms, surmounting a pillar or pedestal which tapers towards the base. Feet, not necessarily human or relating to the figure at the top, often appear at the bottom of the pedestal. The form derives from the wooden posts topped with a carved head of Hermes

(*see* Mercury) that were used as milestones or to mark boundaries in ancient Greece. During the *Renaissance, herms were often used as garden ornaments, e.g. in the gardens of the Palazzo Farnese at Caprarola, Italy (1547-49) planned by G.B. da *Vignola. They also appear in the form of handles or free-standing as for candlesticks. Pairs of male and female herms were popular in *Baroque decoration; particularly eccentric examples appear in Joseph Boillot's *Nouveaux Pourtraitz et figures de termes pour user en architecture* (Langres, 1592), which had animal heads paired according to the antipathy between them as indicated in the *Historia Naturalis* of Pliny. The richness of these 16th century designs was particularly suited to woodcarving, and herms were much used on furniture and elaborate fire-places, often in contemporary costume. A hermetic column is one where there is a carved head in place of the more usual *capital. *Mannerist architecture used them to support the *entablature, and some designers of the Northern Renaissance (e.g. H.*Sambin) even produced elaborately conceived variations to complement each of the five *Orders. Used as a supporting part of a structure, herms are sometimes referred to as sheathed *caryatids or caryatid terminals. Herms were not widely used in the *Rococo, but they reappeared, mainly on silver and furniture (sometimes elongated for use on legs) in the 18th and early 19th centuries. John Carter's *The Builder's Magazine* (1774) suggested them as a suitable decoration for theatres.

Hermes. *See* Mercury.

herringbone. In architecture, a simple pattern of opposed diagonals that is also a tensile structural device. One of the most effective forms of *geometric decoration, herringbone brickwork is found in *Anglo-Saxon architecture and, applied with elaborate finesse, in *Tudor and Elizabethan work. Also used in stone and slatework.

heroes. *See* Worthies.

Hiberno-Romanesque or **Hiberno-Saxon** (*Hibernia*, Latin, Ireland). A style of architectural ornament in Ireland that was at its height in the first half of the 12th century. It was then superseded by *Early English Gothic. As in the Continental *Romanesque style, ornament was profuse, *naturalistic and often quite crude. Foliate forms such as vinescrolls (*see* grapevine) and *acanthus were introduced. Church portals, for example, tended to be thickly clad in this ornament, often with various geometric and abstract *mouldings, e.g. *chevron, *cable, *billet. Symbolic and emblematic figures, both *Christian and secular, were sometimes included. By the 13th century the style had faded out, to be replaced by a rather weak version of the *Gothic. *See also* Celtic Revival; Irish.

hieroglyphics. Picture characters evolved by the ancient Egyptians. By the 5th century BC the knowledge of their decipherment had been lost and the mystery was not resolved until 1822. Successive Roman emperors brought home from their forays into Egypt

herm. 1) With Ionic *capital on early 16th century chimneypiece, Compton Wynyates, Warwickshire. 2) Oude Handboog Huis, Antwerp, Belgium, 1582. 3) Garden ornament, Chiswick House, London, 1725-29. 4) Designs by J.*Le Pautre emblematic of Venus and Mars, c.1668. 5) Garden front, Sans Souci Palace, Potsdam, East Germany, sculpted by F. Glume, 1745 onwards. 6) Oriental Institute, Oxford, carving by W. Aumonier, architect Basil Champneys, 1883-96. 7) 16th century Italian bronze candle snuffers. 8) Late 18th century Egyptian style fireplace, Belton House, Lincolnshire. 9) Late 19th century shop, Paris.

*obelisks and other artefacts engraved with hieroglyphics and set them up in Rome. These objects stimulated interest in Egyptian art during the *Renaissance. So impenetrable did hieroglyphics seem that they were regarded by some as magical symbols, which if understood would reveal fundamental mysteries of the universe. In 1419 an Italian, Christoforo de Buondelmonte discovered a 5th century Greek text, the so-called Horapollo, on the island of Andros in the Aegean, which purported to be an explanation of the meaning of hieroglyphics. It was known in an Italian version in 1471 and first published in modern Greek in 1505, but later proved to be an inaccurate and fanciful account, dating from a period when knowledge of hieroglyphics was already lost. L.B. *Alberti discussed the explanations in *De Re Aedifica-*

toria and adopted the winged eye as his personal emblem with the motto *Quid Tum*. Donato Bramante planned to ornament the Belvedere in the Vatican with them. Some artists 'invented' meaningless hieroglyphics, e.g. those in the woodcuts in the **Hypnerotomachia Poliphili* (1499). By the mid 16th century genuine hieroglyphics were being engraved and published (though still not understood), notably a vast compilation by Piero Valeriano entitled *Hieroglyphica* (1556), which was dedicated to Duke Cosimo de Medici and in 70 years had run to eleven editions. *Vestustissimae Tabulae Aenae Hieroglyphica* by E.*Vico (1559) was a collection of engravings of the Tabula Bembi or Mensa Isaica, a bronze tablet inlaid with gold and silver and covered with hieroglyphics and representations of Egyptian gods. Its origins are unknown, but it appeared before 1520 and was an influential source of *Egyptian motifs before the opening up of Egypt in the 18th century; it was republished with new engravings by Lorenzo Pignoria in 1669.

In 1799 Napoleon's soldiers discovered the Rosetta Stone, which led to the deciphering of hieroglyphics for the first time. However, this did not inhibit the continued use of imaginative renderings of hieroglyphics as a popular ornament, even on dress fabrics

hieroglyphics. From the title page of A.*Kircher's Obeliscus
Flaminius, *Amsterdam, mid 17th century.*

(illustrated in the fashion magazine, *La Belle Assembleé*,
June 1829). *See also* Egyptian Revival.

High Gothic. *See* Decorated.

Hindoo or **Hindustanee.** 19th century terms for
*Indian style.

hippocamp. A fabulous creature from classical art,
with the head and forelegs of a horse and the tail of a
fish. An element in *marine ornament, often shown
drawing the chariot of *Neptune. *See also* sea horse.

Hispano-Moresque. Style clearly influenced by *Islamic forms and motifs resulting from the domination

hippocamp. 1) Panel on a marine theme by P.A.*Ducerceau from the series
Panneaux d'ornements servant aux peintres, sculpteurs et
autres, *c.1650. 2) Surmounting the entrance to Glasgow Fish Market,
architects William Clarke and George Bell, 1873.*

of Spain (particularly the southern part of the country)
by the Moors from the 8th century until their defeat
in the 15th century and subsequent expulsion in 1610.
In architecture, early work corresponding to the
*Romanesque is referred to as *Mozarabic; later ex-
amples, in which the fusion of elements from the two
cultures is more developed (14th century), are known
as *Mudejar. Hispano-Moresque pottery, produced
from the 13th to the 15th centuries and widely admired in Europe at the time, combined glazing and
lustre techniques and motifs such as *Kufic inscriptions, boldly painted animals and scrolling acacia
leaves from the East, with *Gothic motifs, *heraldic
beasts such as *lions and *griffins and contemporary
motifs such as Portuguese ships from Europe. The
Arabs introduced silk weaving into Spain in the 8th
century and soon a thriving export trade developed
based in Almeria. No early silks survive that can def-
initely be ascribed to Spain; however the Mudejar-style
silks produced in the 15th century have striking and
original designs with a combination of Islamic and
*Gothic motifs.

Historicism. In the 18th century the *Picturesque
enthusiasm for a mixture of styles led to much experi-
ment and imitation of historical styles without much
concern for authenticity, in a spirit of *eclecticism.
From the 1830s a more scholarly attempt was made
to understand and represent the styles of the past.
Archaeological and topographical academic studies, the
foundation of museums and educational institutions
devoted to design, and the travels and researches
of individual architects greatly increased the stock of
accurate information. The choice of architectural
styles was no longer simply between the *classical and
the *Gothic but accommodated the *Byzantine, *Romanesque, *Moorish and *Egyptian. Ornament was
crucial, often offering the clearest indication to the
public of the intended style of the building. Certain
styles were deemed appropriate to certain functions,
much as the *Orders were held to suit different types
of buildings. Thus the Italian *Renaissance was felt to
be appropriate for museums, the French Renaissance
(or Château style) evoked a spirit of luxury and was
thought suitable for hotels and department stores, castellated structures suggested prisons, and *Venetian
Gothic was used for commercial premises (reflecting
the reputation of the Venetians as famous traders).
Historicist jewellery of the period was inspired by
ancient Greek and *Etruscan jewellery (*see* Archaeological), *Anglo-Saxon and *Celtic designs or even by
pieces that appeared in Holbein portraits.

ho ho bird (Japanese, *hō-hō*, phoenix). Mythical bird,
Japanese equivalent of the Chinese fêng-huang. It is
said to eat nothing living and is a symbol of fire. It
appeared in 16th century Italian *grotesque ornament,
and in the 18th century was enthusiastically adopted
as a *chinoiserie* motif, e.g. in woodwork, plasterwork,
ceramics. It has a long beak, crest, claws, flowing tail
and curving neck and is often rendered as an amalgam of pheasant, phoenix, bird of paradise, stork
and heron.

hollow chamfering. *See* cavetto moulding.

hom. *See* Tree of Life.

honeycomb vaulting. *See* stalactite work.

honeysuckle. Although this flower has been cited as the source for the most widely used of classical floral forms, the *anthemion, the honeysuckle in its freer, naturalistic form has also been a long-serving motif. Its long stalks and tendrils decorated with attenuated trumpets provide a useful scrolling form. In the catalogue of the Coade Manufactory, which sold mass-produced artificial stone ornament in the late 18th century, a distinction is drawn between 'Greek honeysuckle' (i.e. anthemion) and 'honeysuckle'.

hoof foot, pied de biche or **cloven foot.** The cloven hooves of goat or ram were sometimes used to terminate *cabriole legs in Roman furniture. Hoof feet were a popular device in the late 18th and early 19th centuries, first in France, then in England, when they were often called *pieds de biche*. Sometimes a piece of furniture with a hoof foot has a ram's head (or *aegricanes) or *satyr *mask elsewhere in the general design.

*hoof foot. 1) English jasper ware *tripod vase made by Wedgwood, 1789. 2) American curule form stool by Duncan Phyfe, c.1815-20.*

Hope, Thomas (1769-1831). Influential English collector and patron of the arts; a member of the Society of Dilettanti. In 1807 Hope published *Household Furniture and Interior Decoration*, which illustrated the formal rooms he had created at his homes in London (Duchess Street) and Surrey (The Deepdene) as settings for his collections of ancient Greek, Roman and Egyptian artefacts, which were complemented by meticulously researched and designed reproduction furniture. Hope had travelled extensively in Greece and the Eastern Mediterranean as well as France and Germany and was well acquainted with the pioneering *Neoclassical works of G.B.*Piranesi, J.D.*Le Roy, Abbé *Winckelmann and the Comte *de Caylus as well as those of R.*Wood, J.*Stuart and N. Revett and Robert Adam (*see* Adam style). He also studied D.V.*Denon's archaeological accounts of ancient Egyptian sites. Central to Hope's work were a concern for authenticity (he never mixed the *classical and *Egyptian tastes) and a belief that furniture and interior architecture should be integrated and complementary. He also subscribed to the *Picturesque theory that ornament should be appropriate to the function of a room. Thus a sideboard in a dining room was ornamented with *Bacchic decoration and attributes of *Ceres and

the cellaret beneath it was in the form of an *amphora.

Hope's influence was wide. Few pieces of furniture were made to his specific design but other *pattern books, notably those of G.*Smith, contain more workable designs based on Hope's ideas: typical motifs were *lyre-shaped supports, *tripod forms, cross-framed chairs, ram's head *finials, *lion *monopodia, *pinecones, *volutes, and Egyptian *hieroglyphics and *winged discs. Hope disapproved of this use of his work. In 1805 he wrote to Matthew Boulton that he had 'endeavoured to make himself master of the *spirit* of the Antique. That consequently imitating me was only imitating the imitator and that he would do better still by applying at once to the fountain-head, to those sources of beauty which lay open to everybody.' He continued: 'Beauty consists not in ornament it consists in outline – where this is elegant and well understood the simplest object will be pleasing; without a good outline, the richest and most decorated will only appear tawdry. Ornament can only be of use after we have sufficiently surveyed and dwelt upon the perfection of the whole, to make us find new pleasure in examining the detail. But for that reason it should always appear to be subordinate, particularly in objects of utility.'

Thomas Hope. Grecian dress from Costume of the Ancients, *1809.*

In 1809 he published *Costume of the Ancients*, a characteristic plea for accuracy in depicting the Greek and Roman ways of life. The book, with engravings by H.*Moses, provided a comprehensive catalogue of detail for ordinary British craftsmen who had little chance of seeing 'distant originals'. Many of the plates were republished by Gaetano Vacani as *Raccolta di antiche armatura, maschere, istrumenti musicale ecc.* (1840). A cabinet made by Holland & Sons as late as 1870 has female figures taken from the book within veneered oval panels.

Hoppenhaupt, Johann Michael (1709-69). German designer and woodcarver whose published engravings are typical of the German *Rococo style developed under the patronage of Frederick the Great. Both Johann Michael and his brother, Johann Christian (1719-86) settled in Berlin on the accession of Frederick and worked on the furniture and decoration of his Potsdam and Berlin palaces. Although Johann Christian was appointed Directeur des Ornements it was his brother who, for several years after his retirement from the court in 1750, published designs for furniture, chimneypieces, clock-cases, sedan chairs, consoles, pier glasses and chandeliers. Typical of these designs are elaborately detailed twiggy plant forms, *rocaille, flower sprigs, and areas of *icicle motif. Great care was taken to ornament and shape the furniture so that it matched the wall decoration. The spindly inward-turning feet characteristic of his furniture were later copied by Berlin cabinetmakers.

hops were grown in Germany and the Low Countries in the late 15th century, but it was not until the 17th century that they were widely cultivated in England and used as a decorative motif. They generally appear in the ornament of public houses and breweries and on beer glasses. Like the *grapevine the hopvine was a popular motif in 19th century cast-iron work and plasterwork, lending itself to decorative schemes where it could twine abundantly across ceilings, often supported by *trompe l'oeil* *trellis work.

Hornick, Erasmus (d 1583). Flemish goldsmith and designer who worked in Nuremberg and between 1562 and 1565 published a large number of designs for jewellery and metalwork: small objects such as needle-cases, cutlery, small arms, tableware, etc. Hornick worked in the *Renaissance style with the characteristic *strapwork, *arabesques and *masks. He also published, c.1565, extravagant *Mannerist designs for *vases and ewers, some decorated with strapwork containing fleshy objects, and some formed of fantastic Bosch-like animals deriving from the vocabulary of *grotto ornament.

horn. Celtic gods were thought to be horned; the Vikings decorated their helmets with horns. An attribute of Pan and *satyrs in *classical art, the horn symbolises the phallus and thus fertility. It appears in *Bacchic decoration again as a phallic symbol but also as a drinking horn. These pagan associations led to the idea of a horned devil in *Christian art. *Judaic decoration may include the ram's horn, the shofar, which, according to Jewish law, will be blown by God on the

*Johann Michael Hoppenhaupt. Design for a Rococo *console table, published c.1750.*

Day of Redemption. In medieval iconography a horn may represent the *wind. 17th and 18th century decoration used it to signify wind or air in schemes of the *Elements. *See also* antlers; cornucopia.

Horn of Plenty. *See* cornucopia.

horse. The motif of four horses harnessed abreast and drawing a chariot, a quadriga, appears in *Graeco-Roman classical architecture, notably surmounting *triumphal arches as a symbol of victory. A three-horsed version is a tririga, a two-horsed one, a biriga.

The winged horse appeared on *Etruscan funerary objects and in early Christian catacombs, signifying the swift passing of life and journeys into the next world. Pegasus, the winged horse of classical mythology, occasionally appears in ornament, sometimes associated with the *Muses because of the legend that, with a stamp of his hoof, he created for them the fountain or spring of inspiration, Hippocrene, on Mount Helicon. *See also* centaur.

horseshoe arch. *Islamic form, used in *Hispano-Moresque and *Saracenic styles in which either a rounded or a pointed arch springs inwards at the impost. The shape, based on the oriental *crescent, appears at the entrance of mosques. It is the single most recognisable form in 18th and 19th century *oriental revival styles.

In the 19th century a rather esoteric *Picturesque use of the horseshoe arch was as the entrance to a blacksmith's forge. The line of the arch appealed greatly to *Art Nouveau designers, and A.*Mucha and his followers used it in their decorative work.

A real iron horseshoe is sometimes placed over an arch or a doorway as an emblem of good luck and protection.

hound. *See* dog; hunting.

hourglass. Symbol of *time, emphasising the transitory nature of life and therefore implying *death. An hourglass is often carried by personifications of Death or Time. It was a common motif on 18th century memorials and tombs, sometimes equipped with *wings to emphasise the swift passing of life.

Hourglass pattern. *See* King's shape.

Huet, Christophe (1700-59). French *Rococo artist best-known for his *singerie* designs. He decorated rooms at the Château de Chantilly and the Château de Champs in Brie with a curious combination of fashionably dressed monkeys and mandarins and produced two collections of engravings: *Singeries, ou différentes actions de la vie humaine représentées par des singes* and *Nouveau Livre de singeries* (c.1755). The aim of these publications appears to have been as much satirical as decorative and included scatological scenes. Monkeys hunting, falconing, painting and sculpting were used in marquetry decoration and porcelain painting. Huet's *Trofées de chasse* (Paris, 1757), published in the same year in London as *A New Book of Hunting Trophys*, also contained monkeys, as well as designs composed of dead game and hunting horns hanging from ribbons. The English edition indicates the growing fashion for ornamentation with *trophies, describing its plates as 'properly adapted to the new method of ornamenting rooms and screens.'

Huet, Jean Baptiste (1745-1811). The nephew of C. *Huet. French painter and designer of wallpaper and *toile de Jouy* (a printed cotton fabric) for which, in 1781, he created patterns consisting of *vignettes depicting *rustic idylls. In the same year he published at least two further collections of vignettes. His later textile designs were more *Neo-classical in flavour. He also published panels of *grotesques, designs for upholstery, *trophies, and, like his uncle Christophe Huet, a few *singeries.

hunting. From the late 14th century hunting and hawking were the chief recreations of the ruling classes.

horseshoe arch. 1) Forge, Ford village, Northumberland, 1860s. 2) Window, Calle General O'Donnell, Santa Cruz de Tenerife, Canary Islands. 3) Window, Waalse Kaai, Antwerp, Belgium. 4) Masonic Temple, 135 West 55th Street, New York, architect H.P. Knowles, 1924.

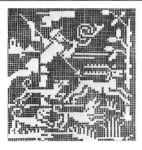

*hunting. 1) Cutwork design depicting stag-hunting from F. di *Vinciolo's* Les Singuliers et Nouveaux Pourtraicts pour toutes sortes d'ouvrages de lingerie, *1587. 2) *Trophy from S.*della Bella's* Ornamenti o grottesche, *c.1640. 3) Belvedere House (now College), Dublin, by Michael Stapleton, 1786. 4) English pottery terrine festooned with dead game and vines, 19th century.*

Valuable objects, principally tapestries and metalwork, were decorated with scenes of the chase. The legend of St Eustace (who was converted to Christianity while out hunting by the sight of a white stag with a crucifix shining on its antlers) was a popular subject in the ornament of ecclesiastical buildings, particularly in France. From the beginning of the 15th century treatises on hunting were produced which contained detailed descriptions of the pursuit of different animals, providing useful sources for decorative schemes. One of the earliest printed hunting manuals, *Venationes* (1578) by the Flemish artist Giovanni della Strada, included scenes involving elephants and ostriches. A later example is F.*Barlow's *Several Wayes in Hunting* (c.1675), which contained engravings of fox hunting, fishing, otter hunting, pigeon shooting, deer hunting and rabbiting that were the basis for the plaster ceiling at Denham Place, Buckinghamshire, c.1693. The British passion for hunting was even celebrated indoors, with hunting *friezes decorating often the grandest rooms, e.g. a stag-hunting frieze in the Great Chamber at Hardwick Hall (1590-97). Although hunting was also the official pastime of the French court throughout the 17th and 18th centuries its translation into decoration was more elegant and less literal: the tapestries depicting the *Chasses de Louis XIV*, with beribboned *trophies of hunting horns, idealised pieces of dead game, and classical allusions to Diana, goddess of hunting, were all preferred to more mundane portrayals. A bed for a hunting lodge in the *pattern book of P.A.L.*La Mesangère has Diana within a *wreath and hounds intertwined with horns.

In 18th century England and Germany a keen demand for 'sporting prints' developed and these provided the patterns for the engraving of powder horns, inlaid stocks and engraved barrels of sporting guns, drinking horns and even the decoration of chintzes and ceramics. Special dinner services for hunting lodges were made at the Meissen and Vienna porcelain factories in the mid 18th century, but it is unlikely that all the tableware decorated with hunting themes was for such specific use. English hunting scenes appear on early 18th century Creil pottery, and dead game in the style of J.B. Oudry appears on French porcelain. In 1744 I.*Jones and W.*Kent submitted designs to the Prince of Wales for a chimneypiece ornamented with *masks, brushes, stirrups, bridles and hunting horns. A typical source entitled *New Invented Borders for Rooms etc of Field Sports*, engraved by Merke after R.B. Davis, was published in London in 1810.

During the 19th century hunting became a more widely popular sport and references to it increased: stirrup cups in the form of a *fox mask or hound's head, and sporting jewellery, e.g. cuff links, cravat pins and brooches decorated with representations of gundogs, hounds, hunters or game birds. Spode produced dishes with adaptations from *Oriental Field Sports* by Captain Thomas Williamson, illustrated by S. Howitt, between 1810 and 1835. Flatware designed on hunting themes was produced by the silversmith Paul Storr (1771-1844) and the firm of Rundell, Bridge & Rundell to designs by Thomas Stothard: boar hunts, fox hunts and stag hunts were crammed in relief decoration along the handles. Many of the designs continued to be produced into the late 19th century. In the mid 19th century Richard Redgrave designed ceramic handles for table knives and forks produced by Summerly Art Manufactures ornamented with fish, fowl and game.

husbandry has a wide and ancient repertoire of associated motifs. Attributes representing fertility and fruitfulness such as the *cornucopia were borrowed from the classical vocabulary of *Bacchic decoration and the attributes of *Ceres. Figures personifying the *Seasons are usually linked with the processes of cultivation, as are the Labours of the *Months (and *zodiac signs). *Wheat, barley, *hops, rice, *olive and the *grapevine, among other crops and vegetables,

are all celebrated in ornament, reflecting the central importance of husbandry in daily life over the centuries. The tilling of the soil often appears in the ornament of *Romanesque and *Gothic churches and cathedrals as well as in illuminated manuscripts – agriculture and gardening were central to life in most monastic establishments.

From the 18th century, there was a tendency fostered by the Romantic Movement to glorify rural life and rustic pursuits became part of the repertoire of *pastoral ornament. The *Picturesque attitude to landscape endorsed this attitude with such ideas as the *ferme ornée*, an ornamental farm designed for show rather than food production. In 1830, Sèvres produced a '*Service de la culture des fleurs*'. The new landed class of the late 18th century, however, took a more matter-of-fact view of agriculture using farm implements in *trophies as ornament in a classical format. Garden furniture and buildings echoed the trend and a farmer's gravestone of 1813 at Redbourne, Hertfordshire, showed a wheatsheaf, harrow, handmill, sieve, sickle and rake. In the 19th century, agriculture became more mechanised and less ornamental, but gardening, seen as a lady-like occupation, remained a suitable subject to incorporate within decorative schemes.

*husbandry. 1) Engraving by A.*Quellin, mid 17th century. 2) Design for a garden seat from the third edition of T.*Chippendale's Director, 1762. 3) Resting reapers by F.L. Coates of Lambeth on the Corn Exchange, Sudbury, Suffolk, 1841.*

early source for *Renaissance decoration, and their influence lasted into the 17th century. Nicola Pellipario (fl 1510-42), the most famous Italian ceramic painter of his age, used the illustrations from the *Hypnerotomachia* extensively in his work at Castel Durante, Fabriano and Urbino. A second edition was published in Venice in 1545, and in 1546 a French edition appeared with new illustrations based on the originals. The lion's *paw feet, the *portrait heads and more complicated motifs such as *sirens and *scrolling foliage were clearly shown and copied. The book was reprinted in Britain in 1888; a note by its editor J.W. Appell pointed out that 'if the Dream of Poliphilus displays little or no merit as a romance, it nevertheless is a work full of curious details for the architect, and suggestions for the ornamentist.' The book design and illustration of Charles Ricketts (1866-1931) and Charles Shannon (1863-1937) were clearly influenced by the work.

icicles. A standard representation of water in ornament, icicles appeared as a form of *rustication called congelation on fountains and in *grotto ornament from the 16th century. Use of the motif extended to *Rococo style ornament, often carved in giltwood with elements of *chinoiserie; it appears, for example, in designs by T.*Chippendale. In America, the term denotes a particular style of wooden inlay in the *Federal style: a series of inverted triangles normally running vertically down furniture legs.

*husk. 1) Logge of Basilica, Vicenza, Italy, designed by A.*Palladio, 1546, built 1549-1616. 2) Early 20th century commercial building, Bonn. 3) Wrought iron stair balustrade, Claydon House, Buckinghamshire, c.1768. 4) English silver covered cup made by Boulton & Fothergill, 1777. 5) 19th century commercial building, Liverpool, England.*

Hypnerotomachia Polyphili. 1) Woodcut illustration, 1499.
*icicles. 2) Chinoiserie pier glass frame from T.*Chippendale's Director, 1754. 3) Grotto erected in the gardens of Viscaya, Miami, Florida, early 20th century. 4) *Keystone, New York Yacht Club, West 44th Street, architects Warren & Wetmore, 1899.*

husk or **bellflower.** A stylised, bud-like motif popular in the late 18th century, particularly in *Adam style or *Federal style ornament, when it was nearly always used in a string or *margent and almost completely replaced early, more floral *festoons. Federal style examples, popular on furniture, were usually referred to as bellflowers. The Coade Manufactory in London produced artifical stone husks in foot lengths to be used as desired on interiors and exteriors. The ornament was equally popular in wood, stucco, stone, marble, metalwork and ceramic painting. Sometimes a series of husks were alternated with beads and sometimes they were graduated in size: e.g. a string of husks inlaid down tapering furniture legs would narrow correspondingly.

Hypnerotomachia Poliphili. A curious allegorical work by a Dominican monk, Francesco de Colonna (1433-1527), published by Aldus Manutius in Venice in 1499. Illustrated with extremely accomplished woodcuts by an unknown artist, it depicts ancient edifices, *pyramids, *obelisks, temples with gates, columns, altars, fountains and architectural fragments, in fact the whole range of *classical architecture and decoration. These illustrations were an important

Imari pattern. A general, rather vague term referring both to the original 17th century Japanese patterns on Imari porcelain (so called because it was shipped from Imari for export to Europe) and to the later 18th and 19th century imitations of the designs produced by European factories. Sometimes loosely referred to as *japan patterns. Predominantly dark red and dark blue, these elaborate patterns are composed of flowers, *vases, *birds and figures. During the late 18th and early 19th centuries the designs were widely copied in Europe particularly at the Worcester, Minton, Derby and Spode factories, and given names like Derby Japan, Spode Japan and Old Imari.

imbrication. See scale pattern.

immortelle, Blaublümchenmuster or **Strohblumenmuster.** Ceramic pattern of small blue flowers derived by Meissen decorators from late Ming porcelain and used from the 1720s to 1800. Adopted and used in underglaze blue on a fluted surface by 1790 at the Royal Copenhagen factory, where it is still in production. Also copied at Lowestoft and Worcester (where it was known as the Royal Lily pattern).

impresa. A pictorial device or *emblem, often with an accompanying motto or verse, invented for an individual and alluding to character, position or occupation. Impresas were popular in Italy and France from the early 16th century and throughout the 17th century and were adopted by ecclesiastics, judges, lawyers and artists as well as the nobility. Famous examples include the *salamander of *François I of France and the *crescent of Diane de Poitiers. In decoration they were used in a similar manner to heraldry, except that they signified ownership by an individual, rather than a family.

Published collections of impresas such as Ieronimo Ruscelli's *Le Imprese Illustri* (Venice, 1566) and Lucca Contile's *Ragionamento Sopra la Proprietà della Impresa* (Pavia, 1574) would have encouraged the fashion, and suggested ideas to those inventing their own. Impresa designs were sometimes included in emblem books; one of the few collections published in England was Henry Peacham's *Minerva Britanna, or a Garden of Heroical Devices furnished and adorned with emblems and impresa's of sundry natures, newly devised, moralized and published* (London, 1612), in which he suggests, for example, three interlocking garlands of *laurel, *oak and *olive for Henry, Earl of Southampton to represent, respectively, his learning, his prowess in war and his marriage. *See also* rebus.

Ince, William (fl 1758-1803). English cabinetmaker who was co-author, with his partner the upholsterer John Mayhew (d 1811), of *The Universal System of Household Furniture* (1759-62). The book, which had parallel texts in French and English, was widely used by American cabinetmakers. Published serially and with similar designs, it was a strong rival to T.*Chippendale's *Director*, attempting to be more comprehensive by the addition of a metalwork section with designs for stoves, fenders and grates. There are some designs in the *Rococo manner, such as those adapting F.

Impresa for Count Scipio Porcellaga from Ieronimo Ruscelli's Le Imprese Illustri, *1566. The island in a stormy sea indicates the steadfast character of the user.*

*Barlow's illustrations to Aesop's *fables, but generally the designs are symmetrical: flat *strapwork decoration arranged in loops and scrolls, sometimes countersunk and sometimes carved in open-work *tracery. The designs for *frets contained both *Gothick and *Rococo elements. Ince also contributed to *Household Furniture in the Genteel Taste for the year 1760* by A Society of Upholsterers, Cabinet-Makers etc.

indianische Blumen, Indian flowers or **fleurs des Indes.** By the 18th century, oriental porcelain was highly prized in the European market. It was therefore not surprising that the new porcelain manufactory at Meissen decorated its ware with an amalgam of oriental flower motifs, deriving mainly from the stylised Chinese *famille rose* and *famille verte* and the Japanese *kakiemon designs. This so-called *indianische Blumen* pattern, which included flowers such as *chrysanthemums and peonies that were scarcely known in

William Ince. China shelves in the chinoiserie *style from his* The Universal System of Household Furniture, *1759-62.*

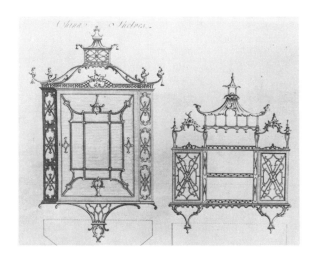

Europe, was first used at Meissen in the mid 1720s and was then widely imitated by other porcelain factories such as Strasbourg, Bristol, Derby and Plymouth until the second half of the 18th century. It was also used on some opaque German glassware which provided a cheap substitute for porcelain. Meissen abandoned the motif in the 1740s in favour of the more realistic and recognisable European flower motif, *deutsche Blumen.

Indian mask. Alternative term for *espagnolette* head, particularly when the feathers resemble an Indian headdress.

Indians. From Filippo Morghen's Viaggio dalla Terra alla Luna, *late 1760s.*

Indians. Depicted as semi-clothed native figures, Indians were occasionally introduced into *Rococo decorative schemes as a change from the ubiquitous Chinamen. But it was the idea of the Noble Savage created by romantic works like *Paul et Virginie* (1789) by Bernardin de Saint Pierre that caused the figure of an 'Indian', a racially indeterminate native of the Americas, Asia or the South Seas, to be widely introduced into ornament, as a symbol of liberty and unfettered humanity. These figures appear on printed textiles, wallpapers (Dufour produced a 'Paul et Virginie' paper in 1823-24) and transfer-printed on ceramics, the designs deriving in most cases from popular engravings. A more accurate depiction of the North American Indian became a popular theme in 19th century *American ornament. *See also* revolutionary ornament.

Indian style. The influence of the Indian sub-continent on the decorative arts and architecture of the West falls into two main categories. The British had been trading in India since the early 17th century under the aegis of the East India Company and imported Indian cottons and silks clearly influenced British textile patterning (*see* chintz; paisley; Tree of Life).

But in a second wave of interest, dating from the decline of the Mogul Empire and the corresponding rise in British influence in India, the emphasis was on a variant of the Picturesque *orientalism much in vogue in architecture and interior design from the late 18th century. Also known as the Hindoo style, it was, to begin with, an amalgam of both Mogul and Hindu architectural detail, sometimes combined with other styles, such as the so-called Hindoo Gothic. George Dance's South Front of the Guildhall, London (1788) is an example of the latter. Interest in India at this period was confined to Britain, since other European countries had no comparable commercial links with the sub-continent. Nevertheless, even in England Indian or Hindoo style lagged well behind other styles in popularity. At the end of the 18th century, in line with the general move towards a more scholarly and accurate rendering of foreign architecture and antiquities, topographical artists produced illustrated travel books on India. William Hodge's *Selected Views of India* (1785-88) and T. and W.*Daniell's *Oriental Scenery* (1795-1808), in particular, provided sources for a wide range of ornament: for example, the Monopteros pattern (circular temple buildings in a wooded landscape), transfer-printed on pearl porcelain by Spode (c.1810-35) and at Swansea (1817-24), was adapted from plates in the Daniells' book.

Indian-style architecture, still vaguely construed, was taken up for garden buildings or pavilions, though less readily than the other oriental styles. Thomas Daniell himself designed a garden temple at Melchet Park (1800) in honour of Warren Hastings (1732-1818), Governor-General of the East India Company from 1773. Patrons of Indian-style architecture were often those who had returned from service in the Colony. Warren Hastings's own house, Daylesford in Gloucestershire (1790-96), included *caryatids in the form of Indian women. Sezincote House (c.1805), also in Gloucestershire, which was built by Samuel Pepys

Indian style. 1) Sezincote House, Gloucestershire, architect S.P. Cockerell, c.1805. 2) Verandah, Brighton Pavilion, Sussex, architect John Nash, 1815-22. 3) Great Hall, Elveden Hall, Thetford, Suffolk, enlarged and redesigned by William and Clyde Young, from 1899.

Cockerell, for his brother Sir Charles, was the only thorough translation of the style into country house design. It had features like *lattice work, 'chatris' (corner turrets) and a 'chiyjah' (a heavily projected and ornamented cornice); its authenticity of detail can probably be ascribed to the close connection of Thomas Daniell with the project, though the interior does not continue the Indian effect either in plan or in detail. T.*Hope had an Indian drawing room in his Duchess Street mansion and published it in *Household Furniture and Interior Decoration* (1807), although apart from the paintings by Daniell that it housed, its relationship to India was tenuous. In the early Victorian period, the craze for Indian-style architecture waned. One problem, according to O.*Jones, was the lack of accurate archaeological information, with which it might have become clear 'how far it is entitled to take rank as a really fine art, or whether the Hindoos are only heapers of stones, one over the other adorned with grotesque and barbaric sculpture.'

Nevertheless, India's importance within the British Empire together with new commercial opportunities ensured that India soon re-emerged as an artistic influence, at least in the decorative arts. After the Great Exhibition in London in 1851, the Committee spent £1276 on Indian items, which were later displayed in the future Victoria and Albert Museum. Owen Jones, a member of this committee, wrote in his *Grammar of Ornament* of 'the gorgeous contributions of India . . . uniting the severest forms of the Arabian art with the graces of Persian refinement.' Such virtues were to be lauded at a time when British design had, in the view of many, lost all sight of such disciplines. The Indian style gained renewed popularity upon the declaration of Queen Victoria as Empress of India in 1877; she herself had a Durbar Room designed at Osborne House, on the Isle of Wight. Ironically, cast ironwork (which as the landscape gardener Humphry Repton had earlier observed lent itself to fine Indian designs) in the Hindoo style was exported from British foundries such as Macfarlane's of Glasgow for the new structures of imperial India – banks, shops and railway stations. The interest was kept alive by events such as the Delhi Durbars and continuing close connections through the Colonial Service and Indian Army until 1947. *See also* bell; elephant; Continents.

inscriptions were commonly used on Roman architecture, particularly monumental inscriptions along the *friezes of temples and *triumphal arches, often providing information about the building or an event its erection commemorated, but also acting as ornament. During the medieval period, when few people could read, inscriptions were rare and their place was taken by elaborate pictorial carvings and graphic representation: e.g. the cathedral door (equivalent to the inscribed temple portico) might be richly sculpted or cast with stories and figures from the Old and New Testaments. The growth of printing and engraving during the 15th century stimulated learning and provided craftsmen with models from which to work. Many 16th century ornamental engravers produced decorated *alphabets which were used to inscribe mottoes, legends, quotations from songs and poems and the moral sayings which decorated interior walls,

inscriptions. 1) 'Watch and Pray – Live Well and Die Well' on English oak coffer, dated 1659. 2) ' Chant Sacre' on French silver waist clasp by E. Becker, 1898; the other half bears ' Chant Profane'. 3) 'Time and Tide Wait for No Man' on English clock by C.F.A. Voysey, c.1900.

tapestries and metalwork. Copy books were also a source for craftsmen, e.g. *The Waye to Fayre Writing for the more ready use and help of sundry artefices that work in metal, stone, timber, silkcloth, tapestry etc.* (London 1586-87). *Scrolls and *cartouches were designed to contain inscriptions. The *heraldic motto became increasingly popular and appeared in key positions over doorways, gateways, fireplaces, etc. By the turn of the 17th century heraldic mottoes or initials and dates were appearing pierced in parapets or roof *balustrades where they dominated the whole building, as at Castle Ashby in Northamptonshire and Felbrigg Hall in Norfolk. Inscriptions gradually spread to the decoration of smaller domestic objects: sets of tablemats and plates, each decorated with a different couplet of a poem, were produced, e.g. the Delftware 'Merryman' plates or grace plates, which appeared from the 1670s until the 1740s. French faïence factories such as Nevers produced decoratively inscribed plates, known as *faïence parlante*, which carried maxims or witticisms. During the 19th century inscriptions indicating the function of a building like 'Magistrates Court' and 'Public Baths' were often elaborately decorated with tiling, moulded terracotta, or carving and surrounded by cartouches or appropriate symbols. During the *Gothic Revival there was a fashion for more whimsical inscription, e.g. A.W.N.*Pugin's 'Waste not Want not' bread plate for Minton (c.1850) and 'Venez lavez' on a washstand by William Burges (1880). Emile Gallé (1846-1904) went further and decorated vases and furniture known as *meubles parlants* with quotations from Victor Hugo, Paul Verlaine, Maurice Maeterlinck, William Morris and John Ruskin. In 1889 he exhibited a florally decorated vase with the

Verlaine quotation, '*Je récolte en secret des fleurs mystérieuses.*' See also Kufic.

insects tend to be most suitable as motifs in small-scale ornament, e.g. jewellery, painted ceramic decoration, embroidery and lace. Carefully observed and drawn beetles, *butterflies, moths and flies were painted along the margins of 13th and 14th century illuminated manuscripts, sometimes with a *trompe-l'oeil* shadow, so that they appear to have strayed on to the page. This *naturalism remained popular in the decorative arts – dresses in Queen Elizabeth's wardrobe for her progresses were said to be embroidered with 'worms of silk of sundry colours . . . with spiders, flies and roundels, with cobwebs . . . workes of snails, worms, flies and spiders'. 17th century natural history collections gave rise to carefully drawn illustrations which were an important source for craftsmen, e.g. Thomas Johnson's *A Booke of Beasts, Birds, Flowers, Fruits, Flies and Wormes exactly drawn with their lively colours truly described* (1630). But it was Thomas Moffet or Muffet (1553-1604) who produced the first collection devoted entirely to insects, *Insectorum Theatrum* (published posthumously, in Latin, 1634, 1672), based on unpublished material collected by Conrad Gesner for *Historia Animalium* (1551-58) and including illustrations of flies, mosquitoes, wasps, bees, moths, butterflies, caterpillars, grasshoppers, winged beetles, stag beetles, earwigs. Moffet's book was published in English in 1658 as *The Theatre of Insects*, and was later added to Edward Topsell's *The History of Four Footed Beasts*. Late 17th and early 18th century *chinoiserie decoration often incorporates dragonfly-like insects of unnaturally large size, and J.*Stalker and G. Parker included several examples in their *A Treatise of Japanning and Varnishing*. Robert Hooke's invention of the compound microscope in the 1660s and the publication of *Micrographia* (1665), which illustrated insects in enlarged detail, provided useful source material for artists. As interest in botany and horticulture grew during the second half of the 18th century, a large number of plates illustrating plants and *fruit were produced, many of which included insects. Just as the fruit might be sliced to show the arrangement of the seeds, so it was sometimes arranged to show blemishes, diseases and even the insects that had caused them. This aspect of botanical illustration was chiefly influential in ceramic painting. The mid 19th century enthusiasm for naturalism meant that the insect again became a popular motif: a book published in France, *L'Insecte* by A.A. Michelet, specifically advocated the insect as a source of inspiration for designers, particularly goldsmiths and jewellers, and insects remained fashionable in jewellery design for the rest of the century. Transparent *plique-à-jour* enamelling was revived in the 19th century and the colourful dragonflies, butterflies and more fanciful insects devised by the *Art Nouveau artists René Lalique (1860-1945) and Philippe Wolfers (1858-1929) exploited its qualities perfectly in their jewellery. L.C. Tiffany (1848-1933) made coloured glass leaded lamps with insects included in the design. In their wake followed many imitations. The ironwork balconies of the London School of Tropical Medicine and Hygiene (1927) incorporate appropriate insects including the disease-carrying mosquito and cockroach. *See also* bees; scarab.

Instruments of Christ's Passion. Objects from the story of the crucifixion of Christ: thirty pieces of silver, the scourge with leaded thongs, pillar and cord, reed sceptre, crown of thorns, nails, seamless robe, dice, sponge, lance, ladder and winding sheet. These are sometimes carried by *angels, or may surround sculptures and other depictions of Christ. During the 15th century when the fashion for *heraldic decoration was at its height, the Instruments were often placed on the shield and called the *arma Christi* with angels used as supporters. The motifs appear grouped at the base of the cross in depictions of the crucifixion, or where an allusion to Christ's Passion is intended, particularly in the ornamentation of tombs. Found most frequently in pre-Reformation British and 16th century Italian and Spanish religious art.

insects. 1) Late 16th or early 17th century embroidery. 2) Dragonfly and reed design from M.P. Verneuil's L'Animal dans la décoration Paris, 1897. 3) Handle on an Italian writing table by Carlo Bugatti, c.1905. 4) Early 20th century Danish silver brooch by Eric Magnussen.

interlacing features in the ornament of most cultures, usually as a development of the *cable or plait. It is sometimes referred to as entrelac. (For rectilinear rather than curved interlacing *see* Chinese paling, fret and key pattern.) *Graeco-Roman interlacing tended to be used in a band as a progressive ornament, with symmetrical curves often around regularly placed knobs or eyes, e.g. the *guilloche, which appears in its most elaborate form on mosaics. In *Celtic, *Anglo-Saxon, Scandinavian and Frankish art, interlacing is one of the most conspicuous decorations incorporating angular bends and often being expanded in a free-flowing manner to fill the required space. *Byzantine and *Romanesque interlacing, while using more even and regular patterns from classical prototypes, also incorporates angular bends.

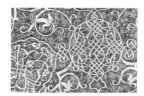

interlacing. 1) Font, Church of St Michael, Castle Frome, Somerset, c.1140. 2) Early 16th century Venetian Saracenic dish. 3) English silver jewel box by Alexander Fisher, c.1900. 4) Design for needlework from N.*Zoppino's Esemplario di Lavori, *1529.*

In Europe, complex interlacing patterns were also copied from Eastern examples such as those found in *Moorish architecture, Coptic textiles and the so-called Venetian Saracenic metalwork produced by oriental craftsmen in Venice. Panels, often circular, of fluent and intricate interlacing deriving from these sources were published in the early 16th century; the patterns are sometimes called knotwork, a reference to their looped and knotted appearance. Early examples were engraved by Albrecht Dürer in 1505 (he had journeyed to Venice from Germany that year) and by N.*Zoppino in his collection of patterns for lace and embroidery, *Esemplario di Lavori* (Venice, 1529). Inter-

lacing was difficult to adapt to heavier media, such as stone carving and wood inlay, and was probably most frequently used for engraving on metalwork and for textiles. Combined with foliage, it formed the basis of *strapwork patterning in the highly popular *arabesque designs. Simplified interlacements provided the patterns for the layout of knot gardens, which were popular in the 16th and early 17th centuries. All but the simple guilloche style of interlacing deriving from antique examples were dropped from use with the increased influence of *classicism in the 18th century. But the 19th century revival of historical styles resulted in their reappearance, particularly from the mid-century, with the increasingly frequent publication of *Arabian, *Hispano-Moresque and *Persian artefacts and architecture, and the *Celtic Revival. Some *Art Nouveau and *Jugendstil decoration uses rich and complicated interlaced forms.

international exhibitions. National trade fairs were first organised in the late 18th century. Several were held in Paris from 1797 in a post-revolutionary attempt to boost the sales of the former royal manufactories of Sèvres, Gobelins and Savonnerie. But the Great Exhibition, held in the Crystal Palace, Hyde Park, London, in 1851, was the first truly international exhibition 'of the works of Industry of all Nations'. There were almost 14,000 exhibitors from the British Isles and Empire and 6,500 from other foreign countries. Because of the immense size of the display, the tendency was for each exhibit to attempt to outshine the next, and the overall effect was of debased design and gross ornament. Many of the exhibits were illustrated or listed in the *Industrial Arts of the 19th century at the Great Exhibition 1851* (two volumes) published by Matthew Digby Wyatt. The cosmopolitan atmosphere at the fair was well in keeping with contemporary taste for *Historicism and *eclecticism. The Great Exhibition provided a showcase for recent developments in mass-produced domestic ornament, with technological achievements in industry rather badly represented. 'The ornamental so largely prevails to the exclusion of the useful,' commented the jury of selectors sourly, and went on to remark that there was 'no fitness in surrounding the frame of a pier glass with dead birds, game, shell-fish, nets and so on . . . nor is it clear why eagles support a sideboard or dogs form the arms of an elbow chair,' yet this type of ornament was 'the ruling vice of the exhibition'. The 1893 World's Columbian Exposition in Chicago, which set its own architectural style, 'Neo-Classical Florentine', provoked a similar comment from L.H.*Sullivan: 'damage wrought by the World's fair will last for half a century . . . if not longer.' The influence of exhibitions was through their displays, and through related publications such as catalogues which insured that they also acted as forums for the exchange of ideas, styles and methods of manufacture. Colonial powers could include products from their dependencies: Indian wares, for example, were important in the British Empire displays. Commercialisation ensured that items exhibited reached an increasingly wide public. The London International Exhibition of 1862 gave prominence to the *Arts and Crafts and *japonaiserie styles; the Exposition Universelle in Paris in 1855, 1867 and then at eleven-year intervals competed with such exhibitions as the Weltausstellung (1873) in Vienna, the Manchester Jubilee Exhibition (1887) and the highly important Philadelphia Centennial Exhibition (1876) in which the Americans were given a panoramic view of European progress in the arts and industry as well as a survey of artistic trends in their own country. The 1900 Exposition International in Paris promoted the commercial possibilities of *Art Nouveau just at the moment when its freshness as a new style was waning. The Exposition of Modern Decorative Arts held in Turin in 1902 deliberately excluded objects in imitation of historical styles and set out to promote Art Nouveau in Italy; the German and Dutch sections of the exhibition were impressive and the influence of the *Vienna Secession strongly in evidence. The Louisiana Purchase International Exhibition, which took place in St Louis in 1904, was a forum for promoting American Arts and Crafts work, particularly ceramics. The Exposition des Arts Décoratifs Industriels (1925) was an important vehicle for *Art Deco (and gave the style its name), whilst the Exposition Coloniale, Paris (1931) included art from French African colonies, inspiring an interest in ivory

international exhibitions. Porte d'Orsay entrance to the Exposition Internationale des Arts Décoratifs et Industriels Modernes, Paris, 1925.

and exotic woods. More recently, International Exhibitions in New York (1939-40), Brussels (1958), Montreal (1967), and Osaka (1970) have illustrated the weakening influence of these displays on design.

Ionic Order. *See* Orders.

Irish ornament consists of elements from the *Celtic Revival and a repertoire of romantic and nationalistic motifs and symbols. The shamrock, a specifically Irish emblem, first appeared in the *Tudor period. Like the *fleur-de-lis* it could be used to represent the Trinity (*see* Christian ornament), and so was also the symbol of St Patrick. By the early 19th century it was appearing in *Neo-classical ornament, e.g. on the 'Greek Chair' designed for the Theatre Royal in Dublin. In the late 1850s and early 1860s, the Belleek factory produced porcelain decorated with a shamrock on a wicker background. The Irish *harp was included in the arms of Ireland from the reign of Henry VlII and has remained a popular decorative motif. During the 19th century, the Irish wolfhound became as important an emblem in Ireland as the *stag in Scotland. Another national motif, the round tower, was used as a *finial or as machicolations along a parapet, as a table pedestal or added as an architectural detail in its own right, as at E. Godwin's Dromore Castle (1868-70), Co. Limerick. The popularity of such motifs at the period was ensured by the Irish exhibits at the Great Exhibition (London, 1851), which included such oddities as upholstered furniture and pillows in the shape of shamrocks, a chair of bog yew with wolf-hound armrests, the figure of Hibernia 'with accessories of wolf-dog, harp etc.', leprechauns and scenes of early Irish history, and by further displays at the 1853 Dublin Exhibition. Commemorative ware was decorated with local scenes and antiquities in wooden inlay (Killarney work), and other souvenirs (even jewellery) were made of bog oak. In the 1920s, however, the Irish Free State rejected much of this imagery as backward-looking and out of tune with the newly formed, fiercely independent nation. *See also* Hiberno-Romanesque.

Islamic or **Mohammedan** ornament evolved in line with the ruling in the Koran that no human or animal forms may be represented; symbolism is also forbidden. The principal buildings of the Islamic city are religious: mosques, schools, hotels for pilgrims and baths all promote the observance of Islam and are ornamented with related motifs. As Islam spread, it absorbed into its basic formal and highly elaborate ornamental vocabulary certain motifs from the Sassanian Persian, ancient Greek and Roman, early *Christian and *Byzantine cultures. Many patterns were dense and repeating, sometimes regulated by linear scrolling forms. Other complex elements – drop-like forms, inscriptions in *Kufic script, *interlacing of ever-greater intricacy – gave rise to the *arabesque. The overall effect of Islamic ornament is of profuse ornamentation with few surfaces left plain. Decoration such as *stalactite work or *damascening became accepted in the West as the epitome of *oriental styles. Islamic forms were disseminated far beyond the Arab world, notably with the Moors into Spain, where the *Hispano-Moresque style was created, into Asia with the Mogul Empire, where it was combined with the arts of the Hindu peoples, and north east to Soviet Central Asia, via Persia. The Seljuk and Ottoman influence was felt wherever the power of the Turkish Empire extended, further enriching the repertoire of Islamic art. The Crusaders came back to Europe bearing Islamic artefacts, in particular textiles. Trade links with the Near East grew through, for example, the Levant Company chartered by Queen Elizabeth I in 1581 (operating from Constantinople and Aleppo). Later, the reports of an increasing number of travellers, who, from the early 18th century, extended the Grand Tour from classical Europe to Asia Minor and Egypt ensured that what became known as *Arabian or *Saracenic style was influential in Western countries. *See also* Indian style.

ivy. A popular motif in Greek and Roman ornament, particularly in the decoration of ceramics. Ivy was considered sacred to Bacchus and is therefore an integral part of *Bacchic ornament. As ivy holds fast to whatever it grows upon, it came to symbolise fidelity,

Iznik. 1) Decoration on French faïence vase by Théodore Deck, 1862-67. ivy. 2) Pierced stone balcony, Grosvenor Hotel, Victoria, London, architect J.T. Knowles, 1860. 3) Granite ornament on apartments in Gramercy Park, New York, 19th century.

*Jacobean. 1) Exterior stonework, Audley End, Essex, built 1603-16.
2) Silver gilt steeple cup dated 1613 and engraved with *fish and *shells.
3) Wooden *herm from Chastleton House, Oxfordshire, built 1602 onwards.*

friendship and even marriage. Being evergreen it also stood for immortality and eternal life. It was frequently used in *Gothic *naturalistic decoration with other *trefoil-shaped leaves. In the 18th century its association with *ruins made it an ornament well-suited to the *Gothick taste for images of rustic decay. Like much dense evergreen foliage, ivy was popular in 19th century gardens, and, suiting the Victorian taste for lush, naturalistic ornamentation, it was useful for cast-iron balconies and garden furniture. In America, ivy was a favourite plant form in the *Gothic Revival and appeared, for example, incised on stone lintels or even garlanding gaslights.

Iznik or **Isnik**. In ceramics, a type of decoration that originated on wares made at an Ottoman pottery centre of the same name, c.1490-c.1700. The main characteristics of this ornamentation are long, curling serrated leaves (often known as *saz* leaves), stylised flowers based on roses, tulips and carnations, *palmette shapes, *arabesques and thin spiralling stems. The colouring is cobalt blue, turquoise, green, purple, black and a sealing wax red. Although pieces travelled to the West earlier, the style was not particularly influential until the awakening of interest in the Near East in the mid 19th century. Imitations were made in France from the late 19th century, and several art potters, notably William de Morgan (1839-1917), produced designs inspired by the style.

Jack-in-the-Green. *See* foliate mask.

Jacobean. Period covering the reigns of James I and Charles I, 1603-49. Early Jacobean work by craftsmen and architects continued to use the *Flemish Mannerist details characteristic of late *Tudor work. In brick the *diaper and *chequer patterns of the Tudor period were still popular, but architectural outlines became more varied through the use of *Dutch gables and 'fancy' chimneys. Gradually these enrichments gave way to more *classical and symmetrical schemes often based on *Renaissance precedents, although the *Orders were frequently misused. Characteristic features include *jewelled strapwork, stiff *herms on chimneypieces or at entrances, *obelisks, *balustrades, *niches and elaborately moulded panels. Oak furniture and panelling were richly carved with *lunette forms, interlaced *arcading, *scoop and *guilloche bands and mouldings and *gadrooning; *balusters were elaborated into *bulb and *twist turned shapes. There was also extensive use of *heraldic, *military and emblematic motifs. In textiles the enthusiasm for *naturalism led to the use of carefully observed flowers and plant forms, and motifs such as the *Tree of Life were borrowed from the newly available oriental *chintz patterns. Plasterwork, often framed by *strapwork, also introduced natural forms such as *pomegranates and *thistles.

Jacobean Revival. In its first phase, during the 1820s and 1830s, this style was not usually clearly distinguished from *Tudor or *Elizabethan Revival ornament, and certain motifs (tall, crested backs to chairs, spiral twists on legs and stretchers) were applied to objects considered to be representative of those periods. However, in the later 19th century, the Jacobean style gained favour on its own account, and several influential designers, e.g. B.J.*Talbert, adopted it. Some furniture designs are included in Adolf Jonquet's *Original Sketches for Art Furniture, in the Jacobean, Queen Anne, Adams and other styles* (1879, 1880). In architecture, it was combined with the *Queen Anne Revival which tended to simplify the design: Norman Shaw's New

Jacobean Revival. Former railway station, Maldon, Essex, 1846.

Zealand Chambers, London (1872-73) is a good example of the meeting of the two styles. In the early 1900s, furniture and interior decoration was heavily influenced by the Jacobean Revival. Major manufacturers such as Waring & Gillow produced copies of originals, e.g. 'Knole settees'. However, the return to *chintz patterns, often with bold *Tree of Life patterns, was the most pervasive aspect of the Jacobean Revival. With black and white Tudor gabling and Elizabethan or Jacobean style electric light fittings, furniture and fabrics, the beneficiaries of the English inter-war housing boom opted for a strong, if confused, flavour of 16th and 17th century England. *See also* Old English.

Jacobite ornament. Supporters of the Royal House of Stuart – James II who abdicated in 1688, the 'Old Pretender' James Edward (1688-1766) and the 'Young Pretender' Charles Edward (1720-88) – devised a series of undercover emblems with which to proclaim their loyalty. Until 1745, the *rose (representing the English king) was most commonly used, with mottoes such as *Fiat* (let it be done), *Redeat* (may he return) and *Audentior Ibo* (I will go more boldly). After the failed uprising in 1745, motifs became still more discreet: a rose with one or two buds (to represent the English crown and the two Pretenders), the Scottish crown, *thistle, cobwebs, *bees, blackbirds, *oak leaves, stars, jay and portraits of the Young Pretender. These motifs were engraved mainly on goblets and drinking glasses (for toasting the Stuarts), but also sometimes appeared on small personal objects such as snuffboxes.

Jamnitzer, Wenzel (1508-85). Virtuoso engraver and glass enameller who worked in Nuremberg and was the author of an important 16th century source book on *perspective, *Perspectiva Corporum Regularium* (1568).

japan patterns. Rich designs for ceramics which were developed, mainly in England, in imitation of Japanese *Imari patterns (which were considered typically Japanese) with additions from Chinese porcelain. They featured, in general, flowers and foliage, usually based on *brocade patterns, and were mainly coloured dark blue under the glaze overlaid with iron red enamel and gilt. They were popular in the late 18th century: the 1769 catalogue of the Worcester factory advertised 'Old Japan Fan', 'Old Mosaic Japan' and 'Japan Sprig'. The style returned to fashion in the mid 19th century, notably at Derby, which in 1847 advertised for 'twenty good enamel painters who can paint different Japan patterns'.

Japanese pie ornament. *See* kikumon.

japonaiserie. Until the mid 19th century trade with Japan was strictly limited, and its artistic influence in the West was felt only in ceramic decoration, notably the *japan patterns which were copied from the relatively few pieces imported by the Chinese and Dutch through Nagasaki, and the *brocade and *kakiemon patterns. In 1858 America negotiated trading rights with Japan. Europe rapidly followed and Japan's long-cherished isolation was over. The art that arrived in

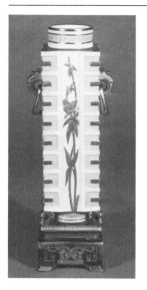

*japonaiserie. 1) English porcelain vase, W. Brownfield & Sons, 1875.
2) English porcelain vase, Royal Worcester, 1878. 3) English
electroplated coffee set, James Dixon & Sons, c.1885.*

Europe, ceramics, enamels, prints, bronzes, brocades,
swords and sword furniture, provided an entirely
new approach to design and decoration and was
quickly admired by leading architects in America,
England and France, remaining a strong influence
until the end of the century. Samuel Bing, owner of
the shop 'L'Art Nouveau' in Paris, described it in 1888
as 'a fresh form of art, quite startling in its novelty . . .'
and referred to 'the marvellous fertility of that Japanese imagination which has formed an endless variety
of brilliant designs all bearing the stamp of the purest
and most ingenious taste.' Japanese art was admired
by practitioners of the *Aesthetic movement for its
simplicity, and by medievalists and the *Arts and Crafts
movement for its status as the product of a non-indus-
trialised, craftsman-oriented society. Early influential
exhibitions of Japanese art included one in London
in 1862 organised by Sir Rutherford Alcock, British
Consul to Japan from 1859, and one in Paris in 1867.
The great demand for Japanese goods grew during
the 1860s and 1870s as knowledge of Japan spread
from the artistic *avant-garde* to the general public, and
was met by importers such as the firm of Liberty in
London. As the craze grew, the Japanese began to

supply cheap goods produced specifically for the
Western market. This is reflected in the difference
between the early Japanese-influenced work of E.W.
Godwin (1833-86) – simple furniture (known as *Anglo-
Japanese), wallpaper, textiles and tiles decorated with
flat Japanese patterns taken from original sources –
and the later mass-produced pottery and porcelain of
the 1880s smothered in every conceivable Japanese
motif: *blossom, *bamboo, *birds, *frets, *chrysanthemums, *kikumon and *fans, all arranged in asymmetrical compositions which designers quickly adopted
as typical of Japanese art. Designs in the Japanese
style appealed to decorators because of their relative
simplicity: their clear definition and often two-dimensional nature made them easy for stencilling,
painting, etc. By the end of the 1870s, *japonaiserie*
had spread to all branches of architecture and the
decorative arts in England, America and France: e.g.
silver designed by C.*Dresser and made by firms such
as the American Gorham Corporation and Elkington
& Co. in England, jewellery by L.C. Tiffany, *cloisonné*
enamels by A. Falize, architectural metalwork designed by T. Jeckyll for the iron founders Barnard,
Bishop & Barnard of Norwich, and ceramics by Worcester, Mintons and Wedgwood. To meet the demand
for information and patterns there was an onrush of
illustrated books, either setting out to show the finest
examples of Japanese art, which were rarely represented in national museums, or presenting a selection
of Japanese motifs. Among these were Sir Rutherford
Alcock's *Art and Art Industries of Japan* (London, 1878), *A
Grammar of Japanese Ornament and Design* (London, 1880)
by Thomas W. Cutler, D.H. Moser's *Book of Japanese
Ornamentation* (London, 1880) which contained designs
for the use of signpainters, decorators, designers and
silversmiths, and books by G.A.*Audsley and C.
*Dresser. In France, *L'Art Japonais* by Louis Gonse was
published in 1883 and Samuel Bing's *Japon Artistique*
(published simultaneously in England as *Artistic Japan*)
appeared between 1888 and 1891. Many of these
works were expensively produced editions with elaborate chromolithographic plates; cheap design books
were produced at the peak of the Japanese craze in
the late 1880s in London by B.T. Batsford, e.g. *Japanese Encyclopedias of Design*, and in Paris by Charles Gillot,
Documents Japonais pour le Dessin Industriel. See also komai.

jewelled decoration. In ceramics, a jewelled effect
achieved with drops of coloured enamel on a gold or
silver foil ground, which was pioneered at Sèvres,
c.1780. It was revived on porcelain produced at Worcester during the 1860s when the effect was produced
by incorporating blobs of colour into the body and
then firing the piece. Jewelled glassware is decorated
in a similar way, with drops of coloured glass applied
when molten. Early examples exist from 4th and 5th
century Egypt, Cyprus, Gaul and Rhineland. This
style of decoration also appeared on 16th and 17th
century Antwerp (Flemish) glass and 18th century
German glass. 'Jewel and eye' describes the same decoration with tiny dots of molten glass applied to the
larger drops.

jewelled strapwork or **strap and jewel.** A late 16th
century, early 17th century elaboration of *strapwork

in which increasingly intricate banding was ornamented with studs or *lozenges, which were faceted to represent jewels (sometimes referred to as *prismatic ornament). This reflected the liking for a richly textured and patterned design in the Italian *Renaissance, although jewelled strapwork was particularly characteristic of the Northern Renaissance. It became popular again from the 1830s, in the *Elizabethan and *Jacobean Revivals.

Johnson, Thomas (d 1644). Prominent member of the Society of Apothecaries and Botanists who published the first local catalogue of plants in Britain and an enlarged edition of Gerard's *Herball* (1636). His natural history collection *A Booke of Beasts, Birds, Flowers, Fruits, Flies and Wormes* . . . (1630) included material taken from the work of other artists and became a popular source book for *insects, *plants and *animals.

Johnson, Thomas (1714-c.1778). London woodcarver and designer who introduced and popularised the most elaborate of English *Rococo designs, which derived largely from the work of French *ornemanistes* such as J.A.*Meissonier and B.*Toro. Typical motifs include *dolphins, exotic *birds, *cornucopias and Rococo scrollwork enclosing such scenes as cows grazing, dogs baiting bulls, swans in front of a ruin. Johnson's woodcarving designs for essentially decorative pieces are composed of light scrollwork and *rocaille* with many *rustic details, and were apparently almost impossible to execute. Some of them include creatures from Aesop's *fables and *chinoiserie* figures. His first publication was *Twelve Girandoles* (1755), followed by designs issued in monthly instalments, 1756-57. The complete collection was published as *One Hundred and Fifty New Designs, consisting of Ceilings, Chimney pieces, Slab Glass and Picture Frames etc . . . the whole well adapted for Decorating all kinds of Ornamental Furniture in the Present Tastes* in 1758 and again, with one further plate, in 1761. An additional collection of designs, *A New Book of Ornaments*, was published in 1760 and included designs for chimneypieces which merge with the overmantel scheme of mirror and candelabra. There are no complete copies extant but some plates were republished in the 1830s and 1850s by J.C. Weale (who claimed that they were the work of T.*Chippendale) to meet the market for *Rococo Revival designs; Johnson's influence is clear in the inclusion of Rococo carvers' pieces in the third edition of Chippendale's *Director*. Johnson's patterns were also known and imitated in America, usually becoming popular there roughly ten years after their publication in Britain. His last publication, *New Book of Ornaments . . . design'd for tablets and frizes for chimneypieces; useful for youth to draw after* (1762), was less exuberant and moved to more standard *scrolling foliage, *rustic scenes, etc.

Jones, Inigo (1573-1652). English architect who visited Italy probably before 1603 and again in 1613. There he met V.*Scamozzi and became acquainted with the work of A.*Palladio. On his return he worked for the Crown from 1615 until the Civil War broke out in 1642, and during that period designed the first strictly *classical buildings in England, the most famous examples of which are the Queen's House, Greenwich

(from 1616) and the Banqueting House, Whitehall (1619-22).

18th century architects and designers working in the *Palladian style much admired Jones's work, engravings of which were published by W.*Kent, J.*Vardy and I.*Ware. Lord Burlington (1694-1753), who was prominent in promoting the style, bought Jones's collection of Palladio drawings c.1720.

Jones, Owen (1809-74). Architect, ornamentist, designer, teacher and theorist whose *Grammar of Ornament* (folio 1856, quarto edition of 1868 reprinted until 1910) was the most important work on historical ornament of the 19th century. He travelled extensively in Egypt, Turkey and Spain during the 1830s, and was a member of the group of designers who helped organise the Great Exhibition in London (1851) and set up the Museum of Manufactures at Marlborough House which later became the Victoria and Albert Museum. Jones's designs appeared in the *Journal of Design and Manufactures*, founded in 1849 by Henry Cole (1808-82), but it was in the *Grammar* that his grasp of styles of ornament was fully expounded, making the book a crucial tool for designers, not least because it had an appreciation of the foreign styles shown at the Great Exhibition at a time when knowledge of foreign

Owen Jones. Egyptian ornament, 'Conventional representation of actual things on the walls of the temples and tombs' from his Grammar of Ornament, *1868 edition.*

and exotic arts was still minimal. The book contained 3000 colour illustrations culled from many sources and reproduced as chromolithographs. It explored previously unconsidered areas of ornament such as primitive art, and the choice of colour was as important and influential as the use of abstract forms (Jones was responsible for the contentious colour schemes used at the Crystal Palace). Jones's most important source was the Orient: Chinese (*see* chinoiserie) and Far Eastern, *Persian, *Indian and Arabic styles (*see* Arabian) were all included; *Islamic decoration provided rich examples of geometric design subsequently applied to inlay, tiling, etc. His hope was that he could arrest the tendency to *Historicism *per se* and 'awaken ambition to find a better style'. He considered that the decorative arts 'arise from and should be attendant upon architecture' and that geometric construction should underlie design 'so that the whole and each particular member should be a multiple of some simple unit'. From the 1840s he designed tiles and mosaics, for Mintons and Maw & Co. *Designs for Mosaic and Tessellated Pavements* (1842) contains his own geometric designs and *Encaustic Tiles* (1843) gives ancient examples. Other publications included *Examples of Chinese Ornaments* (1866-67) based on objects in the South Kensington Museum in London and in other collections: here he changed his view of Chinese art as expressed in the *Grammar*, finding it no longer odd or unimaginative, as before. *Plans, Elevations, Sections and Details of the Alhambra* (1842-45; reprinted 1877) had given rise to work of his own in *Moorish style and he decorated the Khedive's palace in Egypt. He also designed a *Pompeian room (c.1860) probably based on W. Zahn's fine colour publications of *Herculaneum and *Pompeii. *One thousand and one initial letters* (London and Leipzig, 1864) reveals Jones's interest in medieval manuscripts.

Owen Jones was enormously influential in Europe, and his essays were widely translated and published, e.g. in César Daly's *Revue* in France. C.*Dresser was a fervent Jones disciple, republishing the 'propositions', a list of practical points to assist designers, in the 1880s. Even in the early 20th century American designers such as L.H.*Sullivan were still following the basic prescriptions of the *Grammar*, though their interpretations were often strikingly idiosyncratic.

Judaic decoration is principally based on the sacred utensils of Jewish liturgy. The most common is the *menorah, the seven-branched candlestick (sometimes with tongs and snuffers); the gabled ark of the Covenant containing the torah (the scrolls of law); the shofar (the ram's horn); the incense shovel; the vase containing manna; the citrons and the *palm branch, symbol of Judah, abundance and redemption. These motifs appear on objects important in the Jewish faith such as Passover and Sabbath plates, Hannukah lamps, marriage certificates, glass, wine cups, etc. Scenes and figures from the Old Testament, particularly themes involving Moses, Aaron, David, Solomon and Judith, are also used in ornament; the sacrifice of Isaac is often used for the decoration of silver plates used in the ceremony Pidyon ha-Ben, during which the father places a coin on the plate for the redemption of his newly born son.

Jewish tombs are often decorated with two hands raised in blessing, the thumb and forefinger touching. Series of twelve symbols representing the tribes of Israel are important in synagogue architecture, and on early buildings motifs such as the signs of the *zodiac were used for the same reason. During the 19th century, when Jewish communities in Western Europe grew rapidly, many Jewish public buildings, synagogues, Jewish schools and institutions were built, usually in an Eastern style that avoided allusion to the *classical style of the Romans who had caused the Exodus, or to the *Gothic style with its affinity to Christianity. The *Byzantine Revival was particularly popular.

Judgement of Paris. *See* Graces.

Jugendstil. A predominantly German manifestation of *Art Nouveau, named after the magazine *Jugend* (published in Munich from 1896 to 1914), which illustrated work designed in the style and was influential in Germany, Austria and Scandinavia. Art guilds were set up in Munich and Dresden: the Münchener Vereinigte Werkstätten für Kunst im Handwerk (1897) and the Dresdener Werkstatte für Handwerkskunst (1898). Prominent practitioners of Jugendstil included Otto Eckmann (1865-1902), E.M.A. Endell (1871-1925), Herman Obrist (1863-1927) and Richard Riemerschmid (1868-1957).

Jupiter. *See* eagle; fire; thunder and lightning.

Justice. This female personification, one of the *Virtues, represents the administration of law or justice, and ornaments law courts, town halls, objects produced by newly liberated nations, even, rather whimsically, weighing machines. The figure usually holds a sword, emblem of her power, and *scales, emblem of her impartiality; she sometimes appears standing on a *globe to emphasise the universality of justice and law. After the *Renaissance, the figures was often shown blindfolded, another sign of impartiality. The *fasces or other measuring instruments such as plumb rules, *compasses, and set squares sometimes replace the scales.

kakiemon. Western term for a style of decoration copied from Japanese porcelain imported to Europe in the late 17th and early 18th centuries and made by

Justice. 1) Wooden door, Palais de Justice, Cherbourg (Manche), France, c.1800. 2) Justice and Faith transfer-printed on a late 19th century weighing machine.

William Kent. English giltwood *console table, c.1700-50.

keel moulding. So-called because it resembles the keel of a ship, this moulding has a sharp edge and curved profile.

Kent, William (1685-1748). English architect and publisher of a number of influential compilations who, although a *protégé* of the architect Lord Burlington (1694-1753) and thus close to the mainstream of *Palladianism, retained a kind of *Baroque classicism in

kakiemon. Flying Fox and Squirrel pattern on French porcelain dish made at Chantilly, c.1730.

Jugendstil. 1) Doorway to apartment block, Prague, 1900s. 2) House doorway, Bonn, c.1900. 3) Iron railings in the Schwarzenburg Platz, Vienna, c.1900.

the famous Japanese porcelain maker Sakaida Kakiemon (1596-1666) and his successors. The principal motifs are birds, flowers like the *chrysanthemum and prunus *blossom, and animals, sometimes fantastic, such as *dragons, usually surrounded by a floral or *diaper border. Colours are iron-red, bluish-green, light blue and yellow on a white ground. Kakiemon decoration was used by German, French and English porcelain manufacturers who produced different variations, many of which have specific names, e.g. Bursting Pomegranate, Squirrel and Banded Hedge, Wheatsheaf, Quail, Prince Henri, Gourd Vine, Flying Fox and Squirrel, Hob in the Well, Chinese Sage Story, Quail and Millet, Lady in a Pavilion, Sir Joshua Reynolds pattern, Red Dragon. The main factories producing kakiemon ware were Bow, Chantilly, Chelsea, Meissen, Mennecy and Worcester.

his designs for interiors. Kent greatly admired I.*Jones and published *Designs of Inigo Jones* in 1727, with subsequent editions in 1735, 1770 and 1785; the book was available in America after 1775. Kent's own work was influential, mainly through its publication in compilations by J.*Vardy and I.*Ware. He was the first English architect to make a regular practice of designing furniture to match his interiors; many of the *eagles, *dolphins, *cherubs and *sphinxes that support his pieces have a strongly sculptural feel reminiscent of Inigo Jones's work.

key pattern. 1) American silver soup tureen made by William Forbes, c.1830. 2) 19th century Greek Revival commercial building, Liverpool.

key pattern. One of many variations on the *fret, the key pattern is an important and widely used *classical motif of interlocking right-angled and vertical lines, sometimes intermittently broken but more often applied as a continuous pattern. It is sometimes varied by the insertion of *paterae or *rosettes within the squares created by the design or by doubling the lines to produce a perspective effect. The best known variant of the pattern is Greek key, which appears frequently in Greek and Roman art and in much classically inspired ornament. In the medieval period the key form was taken up as part of a general interest in *labyrinth and *interlacing forms.

keystone. Central stone of an arch, originally the crucial wedge in the construction, but often applied as a purely decorative feature, e.g. on door or window surrounds. It may be ornamented, e.g. with vermiculated *rustication, *masks or *portrait heads. The use of a head on the keystone was promoted by architectural treatise writers: Sir Henry Wotton (1568-1639) wrote of the desirability of 'some brave *Head* cut in fine *Stone* or *Marble* for the Key of the *Arch*.' In the 17th and 18th centuries the keystone was often elaborated with a scrolling *bracket. Where it is placed over a doorway, a motif which has associations with protection such as a *gorgon or *lion may be chosen. Sometimes, as in the *Gibbs surround, multiple keystones are used to produce a relief effect. *Oeils de boeuf* are frequently ornamented with four regularly spaced keystones, when they may be called keyed-in windows. A dropped keystone, which projects below the door or window frame, was a characteristically

unsettling *Mannerist device, popularised by Giulio Romano (1492 or 1499-1546). In the 19th century, the keystone was occasionally treated as a visual pun, with a key incised into the central block.

In the 18th century, sagitta (or saetta) denoted a keystone – an allusion to the arrowhead shape of a functional keystone.

kikumon or **Japanese pie ornament.** A formalised *chrysanthemum with sixteen petals and central calyx that was originally a heraldic device in Japanese ornament. A symbol of Imperial power, the kikumon was used in the design of fabric for Imperial robes and in *Imari ceramic patterns. It was imitated in the

*keystone. 1) Campanile of Sta Maria Formosa, Venice, Italy, 16th century. 2) Entrance to covered market, Inverness, Scotland, 1890. 3) Female *mask with wreath of corn ears, Berners Hotel, London, built 1909. 4) Art Deco doorway, Lower Broadway, New York. 5) 19th century bank building, Eastbourne, Sussex.*

*kikumon. 1) English cast brass fireplace surround made by Barnard, Bishop & Barnard and designed by Thomas Jeckyll, 1873. 2) *Frieze on bank building in Saffron Walden, Essex, architect Eden Nesfield, 1874.*

West on *japan-patterned wares and late 19th century *japonaiserie* objects.

King's shape. In flatware handles, a softened version of the *Fiddle pattern dating from the early 19th century. It was used in many decorative variations throughout the century, particularly as heavier and more elaborate patterns became fashionable.

There are several common variants on the shape. In King's pattern, where the handle end is a *scallop shell or husk, the rim has a slightly scrolled band, a double *anthemion marks the point where the stem meets the broadened end, and another anthemion masks the junction between the base or heel of the handle and the spoon bowl or fork. Queen's pattern is a late 19th century variation which differs only fractionally from King's: the shell on the end is convex instead of concave. Hourglass pattern is the same as the King's pattern except that an hourglass-shaped motif replaces the double anthemion. The popular Coburg pattern, designed by Paul Storr c.1810, incorporates a *scale pattern, shell end, and scallop shells of decreasing size down the stem of the handle.

Rarer variants include the Double Shell and Laurel (laurel band down the stem), Bacchanalian, Staghunt, Foxhunt, and variations on Vine patterns; 'Elizabethan' pattern and 'Rococo' pattern followed during the revivals of these styles.

Kircher, Athanasius (1601-80), German scholar, mathematician and Jesuit priest. In 1635 he settled in Rome, where he became increasingly interested in archaeology. Although he never travelled there, his contemporaries considered him to be the world expert on Egypt. He wrote extensively on Egyptian culture, even theorising on the meaning of *hieroglyphics.

Two of his books had fine and detailed plates illustrating Egyptian antiquities, many of which were part of his own collection: *Obeliscus Pamphilius* (Rome, 1650) and the later and more elaborate *Oedipus Aegyptiacus* (3 vols, Rome, 1652, 1653, 1654). Besides Egyptian mummies, *canopic jars and *sphinxes, they also had engravings of *obelisks, showing each of their four sides and the hieroglyphics that appeared on them. The work also illustrated such famous Egyptian artefacts as the Tabula Bembi (engraving after E.*Vico). J.B.*Fischer von Erlach used some of the plates from *Oedipus Aegyptiacus* as a basis for invented designs for Egyptian vases in *Entwurff einer historischen Architektur* (1721).

Drawing on information from Jesuit missions to China, Kircher published *China Illustrata* (Amsterdam, 1667), which contained descriptions of the people, buildings and landscapes of China and provided an early source for *chinoiserie* decoration.

Knight, Frederick. 19th century compiler of at least nine *pattern books, most of which were reprinted several times during the 1820s, 1830s and 1840s. He concentrated on patterns for *heraldic crests, *cyphers and *alphabets, evidently directed principally at silversmiths and metalworkers. He also provided designs for vases and *tazze* in the *Rococo Revival style, many taken from original sources such as the work of J.A. *Meissonier, J.*Le Pautre and J.F.*Cuvilliès.

knop. A swelling formed in glass blowing that appears on the stem of drinking glasses and goblets. Knops became popular, especially in Britain, after the development of lead glass in the late 17th century and remained a common form of glass decoration in the 18th century. They appear in a wide variety of similar shapes: tyre, egg, cylinder, *acorn, mushroom, cone, drop, cushion, annular and ball. 'Tears' of air were often blown into the knops. *Baluster glasses have

King's shape. English silver flatware. 1) Coburg pattern, made by Paul Storr, early 19th century. 2) King's husk pattern, c.1820.

combinations of several forms of knops down their stems.

Also, the cast *finial at the end of a spoon handle, for example, on *Apostle spoons, *lion sejant spoons or seal tops, common in the 15th, 16th and 17th centuries.

In metalwork and ceramics, knops often act as handles on the lids of chocolate cups or tureens, appearing in a multitude of forms: *heraldic beasts, flowers, *eagles, figures, *cornucopias; sometimes, on tureens for example, particular vegetables, fruit, game or crustaceans, suggest the contents of the vessel.

knot. A heraldic motif by virtue of the fact that some of the earliest and simplest family badges were made by tying a length of cord which was then stitched on a surcoat. Variously tied knots appear in the heraldic devices of the British families of Bourchier, Bowen, Cavendish, Heneage, Hungerford and Stafford.

An obvious symbol of two people joined together in *love, the knot has been frequently used as an ornament for love tokens and on objects made to commemorate a marriage, e.g. engraved glass marriage goblets made by Giacomo Verzelini (1522-1606). Love knots, usually two strands following the same line, appeared frequently on 19th century sentimental jewellery. The single-stranded 'widow's knot' was popular at the time for mourning jewellery, sometimes accompanied by such apt inscriptions as 'Fast Though Untied'.

knotted column. A column with a knotted shaft. Sometimes two or more columns are laced or knotted together. The form is found in late *Byzantine and *Romanesque architecture, usually in small-scale work.

knotwork. *See* interlacing.

knulled decoration. *See* gadrooning.

knurl foot, knulled foot, Spanish foot or **whorl foot.** Furniture foot formed of an inward-turning scroll and resembling a semi-flexed fist resting on its knuckles; used across Europe in the late 17th century and first half of the 18th century. A *scroll foot usually scrolls outwards.

knurled ornament. Strips of connecting rings forming a pattern similar to *beading. The form appears on *Federal style furniture but was not widely used on English pieces.

komai. Silver patterned in imitation of the Japanese komai technique during the fashion for *japonaiserie. Its irregularly shaped geometric sections, each decorated with a different *scale, *fret or *geometric pattern, creates an overall patchwork effect. Original komai patterning was achieved by combining silver with other metals, but as British hallmarking laws forbade this, the imitation ware, which appeared from the 1870s, was made from silver only. The Birmingham silver manufacturers, Elkington and Co., were possibly the first to use the patterns. In America, the Gorham Corporation and the American Silversmiths Company both used komai decoration on silver tableware.

knop. 1) Dutch porcelain, Amstel, c.1800
knotted column. 2) Byzantine doorway, Dome of the Rock, Jerusalem.

Krafft, Johann Carl or Karl (1764-1833). Author of a number of *pattern books. The most influential was that engraved by Pierre Nicolas Ransonnette (1745-1810), *Plans, coupes, élévations des plus belles maisons et des hôtels construits à Paris et dans les environs* (Paris, 1802). This chronicles the change in Parisian domestic architecture from E.L. Boullée's Hôtel de Brunoy (1772) to designs by Pierre Gabriel Berthault for the Princesse de Courlande's Turkish boudoir (1801). The preface was in French, English and German and the excellent presentation of the material, with plans, sections, and elevations as well as details and furniture designs, made the book influential in the development of the *Empire style. It contained work by the leading *Neo-classicist architects in France, including Claude-Nicholas Ledoux (1736-1806) and Jacques-Germain Soufflot (1713-80). Krafft was also responsible for a number of other publications aimed at a wide market and dealing with technical information as well as with designs in contemporary style. The *Plans, coupes, élévations de diverses productions de l'art de charpente* (1805) includes a range of primitive rustic huts in fashionable taste, with variations in the *Gothick style. The *Orders de Paestum et Toscan* are presented, also in wood, and to demonstrate his eclecticism in *charpenterie légère*, he includes examples of the Chinese, *Turkish, Gothic and *Moorish styles. Krafft's publications were also influential in the early 19th century *Greek Revival in America. The *Traité sur l'art de la charpente* (Paris, 1819-22) has a trilingual text and contains designs for carpentry.

Krammer, Gabriel (fl 1598-1606). Cabinetmaker, engraver and designer in the *Flemish Mannerist style who worked in Prague. His designs followed the work of W.*Dietterlin and H.*Vredeman de Vries. They include fantastic architectural elements such as *cornices, doors, windows, *caryatids, altars, arches and *perspective designs, which were mostly too fanciful to serve any structural purpose, but were useful for decoration, as well as furniture designs and *Baroque *cartouches and *strapwork. Predominant motifs in Krammer's work include *grotesques, *jewelled strapwork and, peculiar to his output, wolf heads. His two main collections of engravings were *Architectura von den fünf Seulen sambt ihren Ornamenten und Zierden* (Prague, 1599; reprinted five times before 1611 in Nuremberg and Cologne) and *Schweiff Büchlein Mancherley Schweift* (Prague, 1602, 1611).

Kufic or **Cufic inscriptions.** Kufic script was in common use during the first centuries of Islam, and, although it was later replaced by the flowing nashki script, it remained in use for formal decorative *inscriptions, e.g. on ceramics and carpets, often giving details about the object's manufacture or citing verses from the Koran. On buildings, inscriptions explained the purpose of the building or perpetuated the memory of the founder. Many Early Christian, *Byzantine and Crusader buildings captured in the Middle East by Arab victors were transformed into Islamic places by the simple expedient of setting into the masonry stonework panels of Koranic inscriptions. Kufic characters appear in *Byzantine manuscripts, in Greek church decoration, in Spanish *Mozarabic work as in the Great Mosque at Cordoba (765-88), and in silk produced by Byzantine weavers in the mid 12th century at Palermo, Sicily.

Soon, European craftsmen began to apply Kufic inscriptions, apparently without realising that the 'pattern' was in fact a script. 14th century Italian silk weavers, who took many motifs from Byzantine and oriental work, jumbled and repeated the script along the borders of silk cloth. Spanish metalworkers imitated earlier Moorish pieces engraved with Kufic script

*Gabriel Krammer. *Grotesque *strapwork supporting figures and pediments from his* Schweiff Büchlein, *1611 edition.*

and produced decorative but unintelligible results. Kufic characters appear on 14th and 15th century *Hispano-Moresque buildings decorated in the *Mudejar style in southern Spain, and also on buildings in Sicily. 15th century Hispano-Moresque pottery is sometimes decorated with the script, e.g. the benediction 'alafia'. Kufic inscription patterns occasionally appear in France, and even, in rare instances, in England: the Winchester Bible has illuminations decorated with Kufic characters.

During the 19th century, Kufic script was accepted as part of the vocabulary of ornament for the *Moorish and *Turkish styles. Sources such as *L'Art Arabe* (1869-77) by A.C.T.E.*Prisse d'Avennes contained clear reference to the script. In architectural interiors it fitted well as a continuous decorative band on borders, and it was extensively used on metalwork objects.

kylin or **ch'i-lin.** Chinese mythological animal with a single horn on its head, flaming shoulders, the body and legs of a deer or *stag and a bushy tail; sometimes confused with the *Dog of Fo. It appears on Chinese ceramics and metalwork, and attempts were made by 19th century Western decorators to copy it, as in two designs produced by Worcester porcelain manufacturers: the *Bishop Sumner pattern, and the 'Kylin Pattern', which had four sections containing two kylins and two oriental tables with plants.

kylin. German porcelain saucer dish made at Meissen, c.1735.

labarum. The Roman imperial standard, originally surmounted by an *eagle, but after the Emperor Constantine's conversion to Christianity, topped by a chi-rho symbol (composed of the first two letters, ХР, of the Greek work for Christ). Post Renaissance decoration tended to use the eagle version, usually with other Roman *military equipment, in *trophies and *panoplies. It was an important feature of Napoleon's *Empire style, e.g. as a wall ornament, often in interiors where the style of decoration mimicked the inside of a military *tent.

label, drip mould or **hood mould.** In architecture, a functional ledge or *moulding which deflects water from the window opening and is sometimes ornamented. It often appears as a right-angled moulding, the ends decorated with an ornamental motif known as a label stop, though it might also take the form of a furled ribbon, for example. A feature of *Tudor and *Tudor Revival styles.

label. Hôtel Escoville, Caen (Calvados), France, 1809.
label stop. Church of La Trinité, Falaise (Calvados), France, 15th century.

Label also refers to the rectangular shape, sometimes with tab-shaped ends, that was used by the Romans as a ground for *inscriptions, and revived as an ornamental feature in the *Renaissance and in the *Neo-classical styles of the 18th and 19th centuries.

labyrinth. 17th and 18th century term taken from topographical use to describe *interlacing or *fret patterns.

lace pattern. A type of woven design fashionable in England in the 1690s and 1720s in which compartmented forms (a development from the symmetrical

Minard Lafever. Corinthian Order, the Monument of Lysicrates, Athens, from his The Modern Builder's Guide, *1833.*

*pine and *pomegranate forms of the *Renaissance) surround a large central floral motif in a *diaper pattern that often resembles lace or net.

The Doulton pottery company created patterns on their *chiné* ware by impressing real lace on the damp clay surface (1886-1914).

For lace glass *see latticinio.*

lacertine ornament. (Latin, *lacerta*, lizard). In *Celtic and *Viking art, a type of ornament incorporating a two- or four-legged creature with ears, biting snout and tail, which often transforms into *scrolling foliage. Like the *dragon (*see* dracontine ornament), it was used in metalwork, carving and illuminated manuscripts. It gradually disappeared from late Celtic ornament, surviving only in medieval woodcarving.

Lady and Squirrel pattern. A Chinese motif used on Western *chinoiserie* ceramics that consists of a woman seated within a trellised arbour with a squirrel crawling along its top.

Lafever, Minard (1797-1854). American author of a number of popular architectural works that concentrated on the *Greek Revival (a style which was adopted considerably later in America than in Europe). The *Beauties of Modern Architecture* (New York, 1835) offered a historical background for 19th century revivalist styles and had appeared in five editions by 1855. *The Modern Builder's Guide* (New York, 1833) was also reissued regularly until 1855.

lag and feather. Popular banding pattern on English ceramics used, particularly by Wedgwood, in the late 18th and early 19th centuries. It imitates, two-dimensionally, the *fluting and *husks used in *Adam style metalwork.

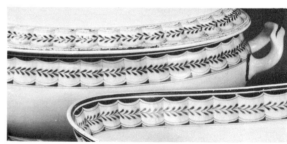

lag and feather. 19th century English Queen's ware made by Wedgwood.

La Joue, Jacques de (1686-1761). French painter and engraver of *Rococo ornament in the *genre pittoresque* style, much influenced by J.-A.*Watteau and F.*Boucher, particularly in his work incorporating figures. His decorative designs were published in Paris during the 1730s and pirated collections appeared in Augsburg in the 1750s. The designs were in general based on the *cartouche and intended to suit certain themes, such as the *Seasons and the *Liberal Arts; they were used in ceramic decoration, printed textiles, marquetry, etc. La Joue also published designs and *vignettes of fantastic architecture (*Livre de douze* *morceaux de fantaisie*), *vases and *rocaille; also a *Livre de buffets* with designs for elaborate Rococo furniture (1735).

Lalonde, Richard de (fl 1780-90). French decorator and designer who worked in the *Louis XVI style producing designs for interior architectural details, furniture, fittings and metalwork. These appeared in a series of publications called *Cahiers du livre d'ameublemens* (c.1780-85). His work is somewhat unusual for a French designer in that the drawings are exactly dimensioned so that they can be used as instructions for the manufacture of both joinery and ornament; even the smallest details are specified, e.g. fingerplates, door knobs, furniture legs. He also published *Différentes Grilles pour les châteaux, les choeurs et les chapelles de communion* (1789) and *Cahier d'orfévrerie* (1789). Lalonde used both a heavy Roman style of ornament, with *fasces, *spears and *helmets, and a lighter style with swagged *drapery and elaborate, small-scale *mouldings.

Some of Lalonde's smaller decorative details were later published by Edouard Rouveyre as part of his series *L'Art Décoratif appliqué à l'art industriel* (Paris, 1889).

lamb. One of the oldest and most frequently used symbols of Christ, representing, as the Paschal Lamb, his sacrifice on the cross, and alluding to the ceremony of the Jewish Passover that traditionally involved a sacrificial lamb. It appears widely in ecclesiastical embroidery, mosaics and stone and wood carving, sometimes with a cross. A lamb supporting a pennon or flag with its foreleg is the emblem of St John the Baptist. The Apocalyptic Lamb has a book and seven seals. The Lamb of God standing on a hill from which four streams are flowing represents the Christian Church and the four gospels.

During the 19th century the lamb or sheep was used in a secular context, often in tiling or ironwork, as a realistic motif in the decoration of meat markets and butchers' shops.

lambrequin (French, heraldic mantling). A short *swag or apron imitating woven fabric, with a looped lower edge which may be scalloped, fringed or tasselled. A popular element of *grotesque decoration, it appears frequently in the work of Netherlandish ornamentists

lambrequin. 1) Engraved on French silver-gilt covered cup by Pierre Lasalle, 1706.
Pierre La Mésangère. 2) Sofa design from Collection de meubles et objets de goût, *1802-35.*

Richard de Lalonde. Engraved design for lock plate, c.1785.

of the mid 16th century (e.g. in metalwork, carved wood). Lambrequins, often combined with *espagnolette heads, were an important element in J.*Berain's designs, and in the *style rayonnant faïence decoration subsequently influenced by his work. They were again popular in the early 18th century, appearing particularly in France, in ormolu as furniture mounts, and in plasterwork. *See also* vandycked swag.

In the 19th century, lambrequin described a decorative panel of fabric pinned along a mantelshelf.

La Mésangère, Pierre Antoine Leboux (1761-1831). French publisher whose *Collection de meubles et objets de goût* was issued in instalments between 1802 and 1835 as a supplement to his *Journal des dames et des modes*. These engravings provided cabinetmakers and craftsmen with up-to-date designs in the *Empire style, and in some cases with simplified versions of specific pieces made by C.*Percier and P. Fontaine for Napoleon. Long after the French Empire had ceased to exist, La Mésangère's work perpetuated a watered-down version of the Empire style which was popular in France, Italy, Germany and Austria into the mid 19th century. His designs combined *Egyptian motifs, such as *winged discs and winged Egyptian heads, with elements from the *Style Etrusque such as *lion masks, *monopodia, flaming *torches and *chimeras.

lamp. Lamps appear in ornament as a symbol of enlightenment, and of immortality on tombs and memorials. In the 18th century a lamp was also occasionally used, particularly in America, as a *finial on *urns or *vases. In both cases the form derives from the oil lamps traditionally used in Mediterranean countries. *See also* torch.

lancet. A thin pointed window in *Gothic architecture, so-called because its shape resembles a lance head.

Langley, Batty (1696-1751). Prolific English author of architectural *pattern books, often in collaboration with his brother Thomas, an engraver. He appears to have been a jack-of-all-trades; he even made a kind of artificial stone. Although something of a plagiarist (usually of designs from foreign publications), Langley had a wide knowledge of pattern-book literature. His attempts to present the *Gothic to a new public were not particularly scholarly; however, *Ancient Masonry* (2 vols, 1734-36) was an extensive theoretical and practical survey using plates from works by J.J.*Schubler, J. *Tijou and H.*Vredeman de Vries among others. His *Gothic Architecture* (1747) was the reissue of *Ancient Architecture Restored and Improved . . . entirely new in the Gothick Mode . . .* (1741-42), and the change of title was significant: he tried to graft the elements of the Gothic (as he understood it) on to a *classical framework, even going so far as to invent five Gothic *Orders. But among artisans and craftsmen, the most popular of his books was *The City and Country Builder's and Workman's Treasury of Designs* (1740, first recorded in America in 1754), which included a number of designs taken from J.*Gibbs's *Book of Architecture*. Like the *Builder's Jewel* (first issued in 1741; first recorded in America, 1755; published Boston, 1800), it ran into countless editions. The range of application for the designs, from pulpits to clocks, sundials to chimneypieces, meant that there was something for every builder. The book was particularly influential in American domestic architecture.

languet (French, *langue*, tongue). U-shaped or tongue-shaped repeating pattern used on woodwork, e.g. panels or chests, and sometimes found on *friezes or *mouldings. It originally appeared in *classical decoration, and subsequently in *Neo-classical styles.

lappet. Repeating pendant motif, similar to the *lambrequin, and used as a border decoration, originally on Chinese ceramics and embroideries. It was later adopted in *chinoiserie* schemes.

lattice. Openwork decoration in wood, stone or metal. The diamond-shaped leading of early glazed windows (late 16th century) was known as 'lattice-work'. T. *Chippendale used carved lattice work on furniture, along seat rails, on stretchers, ornamental *brackets or even shaped into *scrolled pediments, particularly in conjunction with *chinoiserie* motifs. More elaborate lattice or *fret patterns formed glazing bars on late 18th and early 19th century bureaux and bookcases. Metal lattice, sometimes with tiny *rosettes at each overlap and set over pleated silk, was a popular treatment of cabinet or chiffonier doors in *Regency furniture. Wooden Arab lattice screeens, known as *mushrebîyeh* work, originally used for privacy and to filter harsh sunlight, ornamented many 19th century *oriental style interiors in Europe. *See also* key pattern; meander; trellis.

latticinio. Style of glass decoration developed in Venice in the 16th century in which threads of opaque,

Batty Langley. 'Common or garden chimney pieces' from his The City and Country Builder's and Workman's Treasury of Designs, *1740, engraved by Thomas Langley.*

milky coloured glass are embedded in clear glass to form a variety of patterns. Glassware produced in this way is called *vetro da trina* (lace glass). The different effects are called: *vetro a retorti* (twisted thread), *vetro a reticello* (threads criss-crossed to form a network), and *vetro a fili* (spirally patterned). It remained a popular decoration in Italian glass up to the mid 18th century and was revived in the 19th century. The same method of decoration appears in the stems of 18th century English and Dutch wine glasses, where it is usually referred to as opaque twist.

Laub und Bandelwerk (German, foliage and bandwork). Late *Baroque combination of bands interlaced with flowers and foliage. Mainly used in early 18th

*lattice. 1) Garden seat from T.*Chippendale's* Director, *1762 edition. 2) Sezincote House, Gloucestershire, architect S.P. Cockerell, c.1805.*

*Laub und Bandelwerk. From J.J.*Baumgartner's* Neues Teil Buchel von Laub und Bandelwerk, c.1725.*

century German and Austrian interior decoration, though similar effects did appear in French work. The designs were developed from the work of J.*Berain, compressing what was a major feature of the *grotesque into a border decoration. *Laub und Bandelwerk* patterns were published by J.C. Weigel of Nuremberg, notably those by Paul *Decker the Elder, J.-L.*Eisler and J.J.*Baumgartner, who contributed *Gantz Neu Inventiertes Laub und Bandelwerck* (Augsburg, 1727). The ornament was frequently engraved on glass, and painted on porcelain (particularly at the Vienna, Meissen, Dorotheenthal and Bayreuth factories), but it was also applied to interior wall panels and plasterwork.

laurel or **bay.** The bay is the European or true laurel. In *Graeco-Roman classical ornament, the laurel symbolised renewal, resurrection, glory and honour. As an evergreen it also signified eternity and thus was used on memorials or monuments. Achievements in the ancient world were marked with the presentation of a laurel *wreath – the poets Virgil and Petrarch and battle heroes or conquerors like Julius Caesar

are depicted wearing laurel crowns. (The words laureate and *baccalauréat* commemorate the practice in modern language.) The military connotations of laurel have led to its frequent use in *military architecture and decoration, e.g. on war memorials or on commemorative china, for instance, the Berlin porcelain made for Frederick the Great (1712-86).

The simple and distinctive shape of laurel leaves made them a favourite motif in *festoons, garlands, and in a thick, bound form as in a *torus moulding. The base of Trajan's column carries a *pulvinated frieze of bound laurels and the motif has appeared regularly since Roman times, particularly in *Neoclassical styles. The Greek name for laurel, Daphne, alludes to the legend in which Apollo pursues a nymph and then loses her when she is transformed into a bush, reputedly the laurel (*see also* Muses).

Laurel berries are often incorporated into a band or *frieze of laurel leaves (in the same way that *acorns appear with *oak leaves, or olives with *olive leaves).

leaf ornament appears most frequently as a *moulding or *diaper pattern, but also as a suitable motif for a *capital, possibly alluding to the column as a tree trunk. Foliate capitals have been widely used – the *Egyptian capital uses *lotus leaves; Greek and Roman Corinthian and Composite capitals (*see* Orders) have dense *acanthus foliage; *Decorated and late *Gothic capitals are *naturalistic in style. In *friezes and *moulding detail, leaves may be packed into a classical *wreath form, or used as *scrolling foliage, or appear as repeating ornament interspersed by other forms, e.g. *egg and leaf, and leaf and dart mouldings. The small leaf of the *laurel (or bay) could also be used as a type of *scale pattern: the roof of the Choragic Monument of Lysicrates (334 BC) in Athens was widely imitated, for example on the headquarters of the *Vienna Secession (1898-99) by Josef Olbrich (1867-1908), where metal foliage covered the dome in a dense mass. *Pattern books were produced giving guidance on the

leaf ornament. 1) English silver hot water jug with spout formed by leaves. 2) Palazzo de Turismo, Piazza del Duomo, Milan, Italy, 1930s.

*laurel. 1) English jasper ware vase, Wedgwood, c.1770. 2) Wooden *moulding, Cobham Hall, Kent, remodelled by James Wyatt, 1790s.*

more unfamiliar types of foliage, e.g. Giovanni Battista Mutiano's *Il Primo Libro di fogliami atiqui, con la regula delle foglie maestri per imparar a spicigar detti fogliami* (1571). I.*Ware, in *A Complete Body of Architecture*, encouraged imaginative use of leaf forms within classically inspired architecture: ' . . . foliage is an excellent antik of sculpture and there is a source of endless variety in it, for half the beauties of nature are not exhausted . . . why should not the ingenious carver add to them truth and a greater variety when the models are so properly thrown before him?'

By 1822, the principal leaves considered appropriate for ornamental use by R.*Brown were the acanthus, *grapevine, *ivy, laurel, lotus, *oak, *olive, *palm, *parsley, *thistle, and *waterleaf. During the *Gothic Revival, a theory was elaborated that connected the choice of foliage with the *Seasons and also, rather obscurely, with the various periods of Gothic development: *Early English, spring-like, half-opened; *Decorated, summer, recognisable plants, strong growth; *Perpendicular, autumn, more stem and bough, fewer leaves. Foliage was an important ingredient of *Art Nouveau, and of *Art Deco work in which predominantly oval leaves were sometimes combined with fruit and flowers. Leaves have sometimes been used as forms for dishes and bowls: innumerable factories produced ceramics and metalwork in the form of cabbage or vine leaves during the 19th century. *See also* mitre leaf; raffle leaf; stiff leaf.

learning. In classical Greece, the *Muses were the personifications of learning. *Minerva, goddess of the arts, is also important in this context. In *Christian decoration, the four *Evangelists and the doctors of the Church represent ecclesiastical scholarship; in secular contexts, the *Liberal Arts appear, headed by Philosophy. All of these figures have special attributes, some obvious, such as the book, pen, and ink horn, others which became motifs symbolising learning in their own right, notably the *owl, symbol of wisdom and an attribute of Minerva, which appears constantly in the ornament of 19th century libraries, schools and museums. At Regent House, Trinity College, Dublin (1752), a mortar-board is incorporated into the plasterwork. Other motifs include *masks of *Mercury, the *alphabet, which he was said to have

Jacques Le Moyne de Morgues. Pea and raspberry from his La Clef des champs, *1586.*

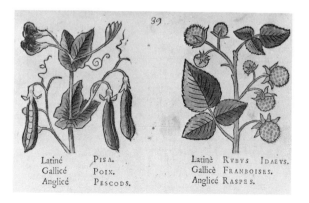

invented, series of *portrait heads of the great figures of literature, the sciences and the arts, and improving *inscriptions. The classically inspired *laurel wreath of academic excellence is frequently found on the *friezes of university buildings.

Le Blon, Michel (1587-1656). Goldsmith and engraver, son of a Flemish settler in Frankfurt. He worked in Frankfurt, Amsterdam and London, engraving ornament mainly for metalwork: *Versheyden Wapen-Schilden* contains heraldic shields for use on silver, and *Eenvoldige Vruchten en Spitsen* (1611) includes decorated *alphabets. Le Blon published a series of designs based on *scrolling foliage with animals and birds for knife handles, plate borders, swords, watch-cases, etc. He also produced designs for *arabesques in silhouette.

Le Brun, Charles (1619-90). Painter and designer who presided over the development of French *classicism and became the arbiter of *Louis XIV taste and style, employing many of the more prominent artists and craftsmen of the time in his role as head of the royal manufactories, and overseeing all those designs that he did not provide himself. He combined the skills of architect and designer, holding posts both as Directeur des Bâtiments and Directeur de la Manufacture Royale des Meubles de la Couronne at Gobelins. Many of the ornamental motifs he used derived from his personal observations on Roman art, particularly those forms which suited his symbolic style such as military *trophies and *marine decoration. Roman mythology provided themes for particular rooms, e.g. the Pavillons du Jardin de Marly, the Pavillons de Jupiter, . . . de Minerve, . . . de Mars, . . . de Venus, etc., all carefully designed with appropriate attributes. These 'classical' schemes were combined with *Baroque scrolls and forms. The six volumes of Le Brun's engraved designs concentrate on the architectural aspects of his work: *triumphal arches, pavilions, fountains, staircases and trophies of arms, but he was also responsible for designs for tapestries, furniture, sculpture, architectural decoration, goldsmiths' work, gondolas, carriages and door furniture.

Le Fèbvre, François. 17th century French goldsmith and jewellery designer who published an influential source for *plant ornament, *Livre de fleurs et de feuilles pour servir à l'art d'orfevrerie inventé par François Le Febvre maître orfèvre à Paris* (1635, 1645, 1665).

Le Jeune, Antoine. *See* Pierretz, D. Antoine.

Lemersier, Baltasar. 17th century French engraver known for his patterns for *peapod ornament.

Le Moyne de Morgues, Jacques (d 1588). French artist who was an early traveller to America and author of a *pattern book frequently used by embroiderers, *La Clef des champs* (London, 1586). It has parallel texts in Latin, German, French and English, and contains a series of simple woodcuts illustrating animals, fruit and vegetables. Unlike other contemporary collections, it does not portray mythical *animals alongside known domestic ones, although it does include animals not native to Europe which would have been known only from menageries (e.g. the *camel) or from representations on oriental artefacts. The plants are drawn in a simple, formal but accurate style. Le Moyne suggests that the book is suitable for those wanting 'good and honest things'.

Le Muet, Pierre (1591-1669). French architect who produced a volume of designs for town houses, *Manière de bien bâtir* (1623; enlarged edition including designs for larger houses, 1647; English edition, 1670), which was influential because it included engravings of interior decoration together with elevations. The only earlier precedent had been J.A.*Ducerceau's work of 1559. Le Muet also produced a version of the first book of A.*Palladio, the part of the work devoted to the *Orders, which was widely known in France and England.

Leoni, Giacomo (c.1686-1746). Venetian architect, who worked in England and published the first English edition of A.*Palladio's works and L.B.*Alberti's treatise on architecture.

Le Pautre, Jean (1617-82). One of the most prolific and influential of all ornamental designers and engravers, Le Pautre published over one thousand designs for ornament, mostly between the late 1650s and the late 1670s. He engraved much of C.*Le Brun's

Jean Le Pautre. Engraving from his Les Cabinets, *c.1670.*

work at Versailles which was subsequently used as a blueprint for *Louis XIV interior design in France. Many of his designs were republished (some almost immediately) in England, the Netherlands and Germany, often in pirate editions, and, even though the schemes were not necessarily adhered to in their entirety, the details were copied throughout Europe. Le Pautre covered almost every aspect of interior decoration and furnishings in his work: *lambris* (wall panels), chimneypieces, ceilings, coving, *cornices, alcoves, *friezes, picture frames, *vases, *trophies, furniture, keys, andirons. He also published a number of designs for church furnishings. In keeping with their *Baroque style, his designs included many motifs and themes from classical mythology, *atlantes, *caryatids and rich *scrolling foliage. He categorised some of his designs as *à l'antique, à la romaine, à l'italienne, à la française* and *à la moderne*. His brother Antoine (1621-91) was a successful architect.

Le Pautre, Pierre (c.1648-1716). Son of J.*Le Pautre. In 1699, he became Dessinateur et Graveur du Roi et Sculpteur des Bâtiments du Roi. Under the architect Jules Hardouin Mansart (1646-1708), Le Pautre's designs for apartments at Versailles and other palaces were widely copied. Like his father, he produced engravings of interior design schemes, chimneys, wall elevations, doorways, etc. He was an important influence in the transitional process from the heavy *Louis XIV style associated with C.*Le Brun to the early *Rococo style. He extended the work of J.*Berain by taking his two-dimensional *arabesque patterns and giving them a more sculptural treatment on wall panelling, where they frequently overran the frames into the surrounding space. Le Pautre was a contemporary of D.*Marot, and a comparison of their work demonstrates the differences in approach between the French and Dutch or English decorative styles at the time.

Le Roy, Julien David (1724-1803). Frenchman who preceded J.*Stuart and N. Revett in the publication of examples from ancient Greek architecture. His work, though less accurate than that of Stuart and Revett, was to have a greater influence in the early *Greek Revival. Le Roy had visited Athens only briefly

Julien David Le Roy. The Erechtheion, Athens, from his Les Ruines des plus beaux monuments de la Grèce, *1758.*

and his texts leant heavily on the work of Jacques Spon (*see* Stuart, J.), and were thus of less interest in archaeological terms, *Les Ruines des plus beaux monuments de la Grèce* (1758) was republished in two volumes in 1770, by which time the fashion for Greek styles was growing. Differences in approach between Le Roy and Stuart and Revett provoked considerable disagreement between them, resulting in Le Roy's riposte in 1767: *Observations sur les édifices des anciens peuples, précédées de réflexions préliminaires sur la critique des ruines de la Grèce, publiée dans un ouvrage anglois* [by J. Stuart] *intitulée 'Les Antiquités d'Athènes' et suivies de recherches sur les mesures anciennes.*

lesene. Plain stone *pilaster, with neither base nor *capital, applied as a thin strip decoration to the exterior of *Anglo-Saxon buildings. It is sometimes called a pilaster strip.

Liberal Arts. The seven subjects which were the basis of classical learning and subsequently of European scholarship in the Middle Ages. Each was personified by a female figure with appropriate attributes, sometimes accompanied by a famous practitioner of the art: Grammar (Priscian or Donatus) with two pupils or, from the 17th century, shown watering plants; Logic (Aristotle) with serpent, scorpion, viper's nest, lizard or scales or flowers; Rhetoric (Cicero) with sword, shield, book or scroll; Geometry (Euclid) with compasses, terrestrial globe, set square, ruler; Arithmetic (Pythagoras) with tablet, abacus, ruler; Astronomy (Ptolemy) with celestial globe, compasses, sextant, armillary sphere; Music (Pythagoras or Tubal-cain) with small organ, viol, lute, swan. The theme appears in *Romanesque and *Gothic ecclesiastical ornament, particularly on tombs and pulpits, sometimes in conjunction with the *Virtues, often in the decoration of places of *learning, institutions, etc. Series of engravings of the subject were published in the 15th and 16th centuries, but the theme rarely appeared thereafter.

Liberty. Personified by a female figure, Liberty was a popular theme in the Italian *Renaissance, often used with personifications of *Peace, *Justice and *Plenty in the decoration of civic buildings and seats of government or administration. The figure of Liberty has tended to be an important element in *revolutionary ornament or in newly founded or independent states, particularly France and America. Benjamin Henry Latrobe (1764-1820) devised decoration for the House of Representatives, Washington, that incorporated the heroic figure of Liberty. *Liberté, Fraternité* and *Egalité* appeared widely as the emblematic virtues of Republican France. Attributes of Liberty include the *Phrygian cap, a sceptre and, perhaps best known of all, the flaming *torch, as held by the Statue of Liberty (a gift from France to America, erected 1885) on Liberty Island in New York Harbor.

lightning. *See* thunder and lightning.

Lightoler, Timothy (fl 1755-75). English woodcarver who contributed designs to *The Modern Builder's Assistant* (1757) in collaboration with John and William *Halfpenny and Robert Morris. Lightoler's designs

lesene. 1) Church of All Saints, Earls Barton, Northamptonshire, late 10th century.
lily. 2) Terracotta panel on house, Chelsea Embankment, London, architect E.W. Godwin, 1876-78.

showed the most advanced *Rococo style in the compilation, and their light touch was reminiscent of work in the French manner.

lily. The white, trumpet-shaped flower of the Madonna lily is an ancient symbol of purity. In *Christian iconography it is primarily associated with the Virgin Mary, although it is also the attribute of other saints, and appeared from the *Renaissance in depictions of the Annunciation. In the 19th century it became one of the most common motifs of the *Aesthetic movement.

Arum lilies, water lilies and lilies of the valley were the kind of stiff, waxen, rather exotic blooms beloved by the Victorians and they appeared on many objects. However their main use was still in funerary decoration as symbols of piety and innocence; sometimes, more than one sort of lily is used on a single memorial stone. The water lily was particularly favoured for the decoration of water jugs and its sinuous form later made it a popular motif in *Art Nouveau designs.

lily leaf. *See* waterleaf.

lily pad decoration. Like *prunts, this decoration is achieved by applying lumps of molten glass to glass

lily pad decoration on American glass pitcher, c.1840-60.

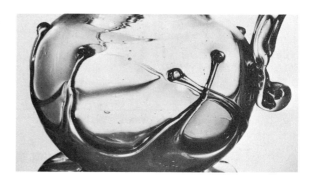

vessels, and then drawing the blobs upwards and tooling them into shapes, in this case resembling lily pads. A typical device on early 19th century American glass produced in New Jersey, although it was originally associated with the work of Caspar Wistar (1696-1752).

linenfold. Decoration evolved by woodcarvers in the late 15th century and used exclusively on wooden panelling and furniture. With regional variations, it appeared first in the Low Countries and then in France, England and Germany. Like other *Gothic motifs, it fell from favour in the *Renaissance. The 19th century name 'linenfold' suggests that it imitated cloth hanging in folds on the walls, although there is no evidence of this as a form of decoration and its origin remains obscure. It is more likely that it arose in imitation of the wall paintings depicting verses and inscriptions on scrolls which were fashionable in the mid 15th century. Its French name, *parchemin plié*, alludes to this explanation. It may also be an elaboration of the practice established during the 13th century of lining rooms with tongue and groove boarding.

During the 19th and 20th centuries a rather lifeless version of linenfold was revived in machine carving on *Tudor Revival woodwork. *See also parcheman.*

lion. In most cultures the lion is regarded as King of Beasts and symbolises strength, courage, pride, fortitude and majesty. In Islamic and Egyptian myth it is believed to protect against evil, and lion sculptures keep watch at doorways or by steps and gateways. In Assyrian art the striding warrior lion is winged. The battle between the lion and an adversary, usually a *serpent, is an ancient image, symbolising the fight between good and evil (*see also* eagle). In some cultures the beast is associated with the omnipotence of the *sun, his mane replaced by sunrays. On Greek stele the lion commemorates dead warriors, and in early Christian art it came to symbolise Christ's resurrection. In the *bestiaries a tale was recounted of newly born lion cubs which lay dead for three days

*lion. Engraving of design by A.*Quellin for the Town Hall (now Royal Palace), Amsterdam, mid 17th century.*

until their father brought them to life by breathing on their faces. Christian legend also suggests that the lion sleeps with its eyes open, giving it the attribute of vigilance and spiritual watchfulness. The lion has been a much favoured emblem, a winged lion for St Mark the *Evangelist, for example, most famously represented in Venice. A crouching lion was often used as a base for medieval and early *Renaissance pulpits (a motif of *Lombardic ornament in particular), and also as a base for thrones: the Coronation Chair (1300) in Westminster Abbey is supported by four lions. Paired, seated lions is a motif with its origins in oriental silks, the source of its frequent use in 14th century Italian textiles, which in turn led to the appearance of the lion as a *heraldic beast.

The lion skin or pelt is a frequent addition to *trophies and arises from *Herculean myth, often implying the hero overcoming death. It is also used, combined with a *lion mask, in a *swag or *cartouche form applied as a surround to a window.

The lion of *Baroque and early 18th century ornament is an exuberant, realistic beast with a heavy mane (sometimes its ferociousness is accentuated almost to caricature). The years 1720-35 are sometimes known as the 'lion period' in English furniture because of the frequent use of lion masks on arms and front legs, often with *paw feet. Some pieces even had lion's hair represented on the *cabriole legs. In the late 18th and early 19th centuries, *Neo-classical restraint tempered the use of lion motifs, although *monopodia were frequently found on *Regency chairs. At this period the lion tended to appear in a more Egyptian, cat-like form, as exemplified on the Fontana dei Termini, Rome, which was drawn by C.*Tatham in the 1790s, and engraved in *Architectural Ornament*. Neo-classical designs included a lion ridden by a *cupid (a popular *Empire motif) or by a *dove (used for example by M.A.*Pergolesi).

The lion's significance as a symbol of victory and its heraldic aspect made it a favourite emblem of imperial regimes: it was used frequently on objects or buildings associated with the heyday of Queen Victoria's Empire. In his *Handbook of Ornament* (1888), L. Meyer commented that 'in the present day the lion enjoys the lion's share in decoration.' In the 20th century the lion has reappeared in revivals of *classical, *Egyptian and *Assyrian styles. *See also* chimera; Continents; Dog of Fo; zodiac.

linenfold. 1) South door, Church of St Peter and St Paul, Lavenham, Suffolk, late 15th century. 2) The Vyne, Hampshire, 1520s.

*lion mask. 1) Residential building, Potsdam, East Germany, by Georg Christian Vuger, 1785. 2) Classical stone fragment in garden, Villa Viscaya, Miami, Florida. 3) Canterbury Quadrangle, St John's College, Oxford, 1631-36. 4) Hôtel de la Monnaie, Paris, 1772-75. 5) Corn Exchange, Sudbury, Suffolk, 1841. 6) *Bracket on French Second Empire commercial building, Paris. 7) Residential building, Bonn, 1920s or 1930s.*

lion mask. A frequent motif in Chinese, Persian and *Graeco-Roman classical decoration that is ubiquitous during periods of *classical revival. It appeared widely in medieval and *Renaissance ornament, e.g. on *bosses, *corbels, *gargoyles, *rosettes, and as a *keystone during the *Neo-classical period. A lion mask used at the centre of the *abacus is a feature of the so-called *Spanish Order mentioned by I.*Ware, who considered the lion mask to be as important an ornament as the human head. A lion head with a ring

in its mouth was used as a handle on ancient Roman furniture and the motif has reappeared repeatedly in this form, also as a doorknocker. In Venetian and *façon de Venise* glass, *prunts were moulded in the form of lion masks and applied to pieces, probably an allusion to the emblem of Venice, the lion of St Mark. The motif is frequently applied to early to mid-18th century furniture, e.g. decorating a *cabriole leg, or acting as a support for an arm rest. A lion foot, or *paw, even a lion pelt may appear in conjunction with the mask, often to a quite different scale.

lobed decoration. *See* gadrooning.

Lock, Matthias (fl 1724-69). Master carver and the first English designer to grasp the complexities of the French *Rococo style and convert it into designs for structurally sound furniture. His work included elements of *chinoiserie, architectural fantasies and *rustic decoration. His first book, *A New Drawing Book of Ornaments, Shields, Compartments, Masks* (1740), was one of the earliest collections of *rocaille motifs published in England. He followed it with *Six Sconces* (1744), *Six Tables* (1746) and, in collaboration with H.*Copland, the important and influential *A New Book of Ornament* (1752), in which *chinoiserie* was a predominant theme. In 1768 and 1769, he republished the designs for tables and sconces and designs from the Copland book in addition to collections on foliage, pier-frames, ovals, etc. Like many Rococo designers of the period, his patterns were republished in the 19th century as a source for the *Rococo Revival. The connection between his work and French design was by then accepted, although his work was mistakenly believed to represent the *Louis XIV style. M. Taylor of London published Lock's designs c.1838 as a *Collection of Ornamental Designs* 'applicable to furniture, frames and the decoration of rooms in the style of Louis 14th'. Similarly, J. Weale republished some in *Old English and French Ornaments* (1858-59).

Loir, Alexis (1640-1713). Engraver and goldsmith, the younger brother of Nicolas Loir (1624-79); they both worked in the Baroque *Louis XIV style. Alexis published his own designs, for *friezes, panels and ceilings, as well as for smaller objects such as *guéridons* buffets, braziers, and also engraved his brother's designs, which included *putti, carriages, panels and fans.

Lombardic. An important variant of the *Romanesque style peculiar to Lombardy and the area around Milan, now part of northern Italy, where an abundant supply of clay led to roughly formed and profuse ornament, much of it in terracotta. Its form and detail were based on northern *Celtic forms transmitted through Christian manuscripts and portable objects, rather than on *classical antecedents. Realistic scenes from daily life were depicted, and grotesque, exaggerated types of figure sometimes appeared, e.g. crouching human figures as supports for pillars (especially in porches) are characteristic, as well as *lions and *griffins.

In the early 20th century there was a Lombardic Revival in America, as the style was thought suitable for Roman Catholic churches.

Long Eliza pattern. Originally a Chinese motif composed of elongated female figures, it was adapted for use as a pattern on 17th century Dutch delftware. The name is an English corruption of the Dutch term *lange Lijzen*. Occurs on Dutch and English delftware and on mid 18th century Worcester porcelain.

long and short work. Primitive type of *quoin in which irregular horizontal stonework strips alternate with long thin vertical sections, emphasising the corner of a building in *Anglo-Saxon and early *Romanesque architecture.

long and short work. 1) Church of All Saints, Earls Barton, Northamptonshire, late 10th century.
*lotus. 2) From Temple of Dendur, Egypt. 3) Oddfellows Hall, Devonport, Devon, architect John Foulston, 1824. 4) English circular table, early 19th century. 5) Brighton Pavilion, Sussex, architect John Nash, 1815-22. 6) Stencilling on English ebonised wardrobe designed by C.*Dresser, c.1879.*

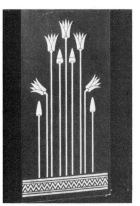

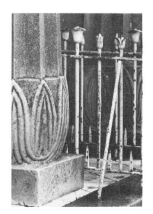

lotus. The formalised flower, buds and leaves of the lotus have all been widely used as motifs in ornament, originally in Egyptian art, then in *Egyptian revivals, and more generally during the early 19th century. The leaf, in particular, was used as a repeating ornament along *friezes, *mouldings or around *capitals.

In ancient Egypt, the lotus was a symbol of fertility and regeneration, as well as being closely identified with death: the soul of the departed was thought to enter the calyx of the lotus flower, and guests at funerals were presented with bouquets of lotus. It was also widely adopted as a symbol of the sun in Egypt, Assyria, India, China and Japan, because of its property of opening and closing with the rising and setting of the sun. In 1891, W.H. Goodyear published his elaborate *The Grammar of the Lotus*, subtitled 'A development of sun worship', in which he strove to identify the lotus as the key to the entire *classical ornamental vocabulary. Although Goodyear's main theory is far-fetched, his book provides a useful catalogue of the many ways in which the plant is used in ornament: the flowers are sometimes closed, sometimes open, and appear with stalks and foliage or alone. On early 19th century furniture, lotus leaves sometimes encircle the pedestal of a table or chair legs. The lotus appeared widely in 19th century funerary ornament, e.g. on cemetery gates, monuments, etc., its stiff forms making it a particularly suitable motif for ironwork. C.*Dresser, like many, approved of the rigidity of line and severity of the form as an antidote to the overblown *naturalism of mid 19th century decorative themes. *See also* persic column.

Louis XIV style. Louis XIV succeeded Louis XIII in 1638 and reigned until 1715. The sudden flowering of decoration and architecture during this period was due to the unprecedented patronage of Louis XIV, his court and administration, when they moved from Paris to Versailles, where the palace, its furnishings and grounds were designed to proclaim the glory of the King. Earlier in the century, Flemish craftsmen had been brought to France by Henri IV to work on the Louvre, and the great collectors and patrons Cardinals Richelieu and Mazarin both employed Italian cabinetmakers, as did Marie de Médicis, Henri's second wife, so that the existing style was based on a combination of *Flemish Mannerism and Italian *Baroque. Jean Baptiste Colbert (1619-83), who succeeded Mazarin as the King's Minister of Finance, established state patronage of the decorative arts at Gobelins with the Manufacture Royale des Meubles de la Couronne in 1662. This gave work and stimulus to both native and *émigré* craftsmen. An Académie Royale d'Architecture was also established which encouraged the accurate study of *classical buildings in Rome. The director of the Manufacture Royale was C.*Le Brun, who was also Directeur des Bâtiments; the restrained classical style which he imposed on all the works under his command gave architecture and decoration a unity that had not been achieved elsewhere. Le Brun did not publish many designs himself but the prolific work of J.*Le Pautre disseminated his style and it was taken up by contemporary craftsmen such as A.C. Boulle (*see boulle*). Towards the end of the

Louis XIV style. From J.*Berain's Ornemans, *late 17th century, republished 1711.*

reign, is generally referred to as the Régence and, in essence, was the first sign of the Rococo in France.

Louis XV style. Louis XV succeeded his great-grand-father in 1715. For the first six years of his reign, the country was in the care of a Regent, the Duc d'Orléans, hence the so-called *Régence style. This developed into a full-blown *Rococo style, which was anti-classical and frivolous, aiming to give an impression of lightness and movement rather than dignity. The leading *ornemanistes* of the period were N.*Pineau, J.A.*Meissonier and G.-M.*Oppenord. But the style had its opponents, in C.-N.*Cochin (1715-90), the architect J.G. Soufflot (1713-80) and the Comte *de Caylus. By the late 1750s, their influence began to be felt and a move was made towards a more rectilinear style with heavier, more solid ornamentation, based once again on *classical themes, despite the fact that the King and his influential mistress, Madame de Pompadour, continued to prefer the Rococo.

Louis XVI style. Louis XVI reigned from 1774 until the Revolution in 1792 and the style named after him clearly shows the re-establishment of the *goût antique* or *Neo-classicism. The style did not depend on court patronage, but was much more generally adopted. Designers whose engraved designs typified and disseminated the style were C.*Delafosse, R. de*Lalonde and J.F.*Neufforge. *Boulle* work returned to fashion once again and a great deal of furniture was made according to the designs of A.C. Boulle; characteristic ornament included heavy *swags, many composed of leaves rather than flowers, *trophies, *bead moulding, crumpled *ribbons, oval *medallions, squared *volutes, *fluting, Greek *key and *wavescroll patterns. By the end of the reign, simpler and more classically correct forms were becoming popular.

Louis Revivals. These 19th century revivals, which were popular both in Europe and in America, were generally referred to as Louis Quatorze, Louis Quinze and Louis Seize. Designers were often confused as to the exact original period of the styles they wished to

century, after the death of both Le Brun and Colbert, the edge was taken off the dignity and grandeur of the style and a new, lighter approach to decoration appeared, typified by the designs of J.*Berain. This style, which was prevalent during the last few years of Louis XIV's reign and the early years of Louis XV's

Louis XV style. French kingwood and tulipwood commode by Claude Charles Saunier, c.1755.

*Louis XVI style. Engraved design for grate by R. de *Lalonde, c.1780.*

Louis Revival. 'Louis Quatorze Drawing-Room Stove-Grate' exhibited by William Pierce of London at the Great Exhibition, 1851.

imitate, and therefore *Rococo Revival designs, for example, are often erroneously described as Louis Quatorze or even more vaguely as 'Old French'. From the 1820s until the end of the century, Louis Revival styles were particularly favoured for ladies' drawing rooms and bedrooms, as indicated by the frequent use of the French words *boudoir* or *salon* to describe them. During much of the 19th century, 18th century French furniture in this style was enthusiastically collected and reproduced.

In America the attraction of the pre-Revolutionary styles associated with the French monarchy was at its height among the fabulously wealthy on the East Coast in the late 19th and early 20th centuries. William K. Vanderbilt's summer residence, Marble House (1888, completed 1892) by Richard Morris Hunt in Newport, Rhode Island, had a dining room based on the Salon of Hercules at Versailles, and his favourite motif, the *Apolline mask (alluding to Louis XIV) appears repeatedly together with a cypher of wv. Mrs Hermann Oelrichs had an immense ballroom at Rosecliff, Newport (completed 1902) designed to resemble the Grand Trianon, Versailles. An innovative and restrained version of Louis Revival styles was pioneered by Ogden Codman in the 1890s. Furniture and wall decorations were based on Louis XVI *Neo-classical examples with cool colouring and little gilding. In 1897 Codman published *The Decoration of Houses*, co-authored by the novelist Edith Wharton who gave him some of his earliest commissions, which clearly demonstrated a move away from the gilded excess of the early Louis styles to a simpler, more elegant rendering.

love. During the Middle Ages the popular theme of courtly love appeared in the ornament of secular buildings and objects, usually in the form of scenes representing episodes from well-known courtly love poems such as Tristan and Iseult. These sometimes appeared in an ecclesiastical context as examples of the worldly counterpart of the spirit of divine love, e.g. on *bosses and misericords (as at Lincoln and Chester cathedrals), and tiles. Tombs and funerary ornaments often bore allusions to conjugal love.

With the *Renaissance, study of classical mythology led to a widening of the ornamental vocabulary of love and the use of such motifs as *Venus, her son *Cupid with his bow and quiver of arrows, *doves (sometimes called lovebirds), Hymen, the god of marriage with his torch and bridal veil, and *triumphs of love. *Satyr masks and goat heads alluded to lust – these motifs were dropped by the more prudish ornamentists of the late 18th century. The Aldobrandini Marriage, an early 1st century Roman frieze showing preparations for a wedding, and named after Cardinal Aldobrandini who acquired it in 1605, became a favourite model for classical depictions of love, and was reproduced by Mrs Coade, inventor of a stone aggregate used in ornament, in the second half of the 18th century. In the 18th and 19th centuries decoration alluding to love tended to be confined to beds, marriage chests, bedroom furniture and love tokens – usually jewellery or jewel caskets – and women's furniture such as toilet tables, work tables and objects given as wedding gifts.

The *heart is the most commonly used symbol of love. Heart-shaped brooches first came into fashion in the early 14th century; after the Renaissance they were often shown pierced with Cupid's arrow. The theme of binding two people together is demonstrated by the love *knot, shackles, chains, padlocks and buckles, mostly popular in the late 18th and 19th centuries. Lovers gave each other gifts on Valentine's Day from the 16th century and Valentine's Day cards were sent as early as the late 18th century. But it was the Victorians who explored the theme of love more thoroughly than any other age with the commercialisation of Valentine's Day and the mass production of love tokens, mostly in the form of silver jewellery. *Myrtle and the red *rose are emblems of *Venus and therefore have a long history as the floral emblems of love; mistletoe, a parasitic plant, signifies dependence and its use in ornament appears to date back to the 17th century. The immensely popular, sentimental 'language of flowers' books, mostly compiled in England and France in the early 19th century, considerably widened the range of floral love emblems: the forget-me-not stood for 'true love'; the pink convolvulus, 'worth sustained by judicious and tender affection'; the *ivy for friendship, fidelity and marriage; the daisy for 'I share your sentiments'; the pansy for 'you occupy my thoughts'.

*Inscriptions of love have long been used in the ornamentation of jewellery and love tokens, from the 14th century *vous estes ma joy moundeine* (you are my earthly joy) to the popular Victorian *mizpah* (an allusion to the Bible reference, 'And Mizpah; for he said, The Lord watch between me and thee when we are absent from one another.' (Genesis 31:49).

The *unicorn was used as a symbol of the beguiled lover after its appearance in Richard Fournival's *Bestiaires de l'amour* dating from the early 14th century. In *Christian iconography it is associated with the Virgin Mary and therefore represents purity in some schemes of decoration alluding to spiritual or religious love.

lovebird. When *doves appear in a decorative context in pairs they are often referred to as lovebirds, particularly in schemes of decoration on the theme of *love.

lozenge. Like the *diamond, the lozenge is used as a ground for other patterns, or as a *diaper pattern, or as a single motif as in *jewelled strapwork. In *Romanesque and *Romanesque Revival decoration it is used like the *chevron or zigzag pattern. Lozenge-shaped compartments appear in *net vaults. In heraldry, the arms of a spinster or widow are contained in a lozenge.

lunette. Semi-circular or crescent-shaped area on a wall or vaulted ceiling which may be plain, decorated or form an opening. Lunette windows are characteristic of late 18th and early 19th century architecture. In domestic American architecture they sometimes appear on *pediments and gable ends. The glazing bars may be arranged vertically as in a *Diocletian window, or radiating from the centre of the base as in a *fanlight, or in other patterns.

Also, the carved semi-circular ornament used in a series to form a band and sometimes infilled with *acanthus-type foliage that was a common decoration in 17th century woodcarving. It reappeared in the *Jacobean Revival.

lunette. 17th century English oak press.

Lutma, Johannes (1587-1669). Dutch silversmith who worked in Amsterdam from the 1620s in the *Auricular style. His designs were published in *Veelderhande Compartimente Getekent* (1653) and *Versheide Snakeryen* (1654). His son, also called Johannes Lutma (1624-89), continued the Auricular tradition and published *cartouches in *Einige Nieuwe Compartimente* (n.d.).

lyre. An instrument dating back to antiquity which appeared as a decorative motif in *Neo-classical ornament. Its invention was credited to *Mercury who was said to have put strings over the shell of a tortoise, but its main decorative use is as an attribute of Apollo, god of song and music, sometimes combined with an *Apolline mask, for music rooms, music stands, etc. Lyre-shaped clocks, first made in France in the late 18th century and subsequently copied in America, alluded to Apollo's role as god of the sun (the movement of the sun indicating the passing of time). Used on a writing table, the lyre alludes to another invention of Mercury, the *alphabet. A lyre-back chair was designed by J.B. Séné in the mid 18th century, but it was in the early 19th century that the form became widely popular in Europe and America for chair-backs and table legs. F.H.G. Jacob-Desmalter (1770-1841), a French furniture maker in the *Empire style, supplied

*lyre. 1) Engraving from G.-P.*Cauvet's* Recueil d'ornements à l'usage des jeunes artistes, Paris, 1777. 2) On *urn, The Casino, Marino, Dublin, architect Sir W.*Chambers, 1758 onwards. 3) Early 19th century German silk brocade. 4) Ventilation grille, concert hall, Cherbourg (Manche), France, architect Charles de Lalonde, 1880-81. 5) Pedal attachment on English Broadwood piano, c.1880.*

lyre-back chairs for the Music Room at the Tuileries in 1806, about the time that the chair and cabinetmaker Duncan Phyfe (1768-1854) started making them in America. Good examples of lyre-backs are illustrated in the 1817 *New York Book of Prices for Manufacturing Cabinet and Chair Work*.

machinery motifs. Decorative motifs based on machine parts were used by a group of French jewellers and silversmiths working in the *Modernist style. At the end of the 1920s, a group including Raymond Templier (1891-1968), Jean Desprès (b 1899), Gérard Sandoz (b 1902) and Paul Brandt produced highly finished work in silver, platinum, white gold, jet and enamel that incorporated exposed screw-heads, articulated links and sections resembling ball-bearings and girders.

Maenads. *See* Bacchic decoration; thyrsus.

Magot. *See* pagod.

maidenhead. Terminal for a silver spoon in the form of a (sometimes crowned) female head and bust, popular in the late 15th, 16th and 17th centuries. The figure may represent the Virgin Mary.

mandorla. *See* vesica piscis.

Mannerism. Mid 16th century style which, by extending and playing upon some of the *classical conventions established during the Italian *Renaissance, introduced a highly ornamental flavour into architecture and the decorative arts, and was the precursor of the *Baroque. In sharp contrast to the academic approach of architects such as A.*Palladio or V. *Scamozzi, classical rules in the hands of Michelangelo or Giulio Romano seemed to exist only as a basis for improvisation. Thus, in architecture, Mannerist motifs such as dropped *keystones, vast scrolling *brackets or *Orders embedded in walls serve no structural function whatsoever, and therefore both derive and depart from the established canon. In the more exuberant ornament which appeared in the work of the School of *Fontainebleau or the *Flemish Mannerists, some motifs were taken to extremes: *pattern books, originating almost entirely in northern Europe (e.g. by H.*Vredeman de Vries, W.*Dietterlin and S.*Serlio), extended the range of possibilities and took the style to England, where it became popular in plasterwork, woodwork, metalwork, stonecarving and in a newly invented material, stucco (which came into use c.1520). Mannerism sometimes produced a highly theatrical effect in which an abundance of ornament – *herms, *swags, *cartouches, *strapwork, in particular – was plastered liberally over every surface. Looking back at the style in 1604, Karel van Mander wrote that Michelangelo had provided the impetus for Mannerism: 'in architecture beside the old common manner of the ancients and Vitruvius, he has brought forth other new orders of cornices, capitals, bases, tabernacles, sepulchres and other ornaments, wherefore all architects that follow after him owe him thanks for his having freed them from the old bonds and knots, and given them free rein and licence to invent something beside the Antique.' Although the Italian Mannerists depended heavily on the grammar of classical antiquity, in northern Europe the remnants of late *Flamboyant Gothic were woven into the style. Soon the Northern Mannerists took an increasingly independent stance (*see* Netherlands Grotesque), and the style became considerably more bizarre than it was ever to be in its country of origin.

In the decorative arts, the rich and extravagant Mannerist style, which had its origins in Florence and Fontainebleau in the 1530s and 1540s, appealed mainly to the kings and princes of Europe. A number of virtuoso goldsmiths began to work in the style, often travelling from court to court to do so, partly as a result of the greatly increased supply of gold and silver from the New World and the upsurge in enthusiasm in artefacts made from the metals. Mannerist styles in metalwork survived well into the 17th century.

Engravings by R.*Boyvin and the Italian A.*Fantuzzi were highly influential in dessiminating the early Fontainebleau style of Mannerism, and included a typical repertoire of motifs: strapwork, cartouches as an ornament in themselves, slender, naked female figures, *caryatids, *grotesques, *masks and *chimeras. The lack of rational construction in Mannerist design coupled with a plethora of ornamentation fast became popular with German, Flemish and, to a lesser extent, English goldsmiths. Highly decorated cups and vases incorporating rare metals, woods, shells, hardstones, precious and semi-precious stones were popular. Elaborate designs were engraved by E.*Hornick, C. *Floris, V.*Solis and Matthias Zündt of Nuremberg (fl 1551-70).

François I set up a temporary tapestry factory in the Galerie François I at Fontainebleau for the weaving of a series of hangings reproducing integrated schemes of frescoes and plasterwork by Rosso Fiorentino (1495-1540) and Francesco Primaticcio (1504-70). The tapestries themselves soon became an influential source for the Mannerist style. Elaborately carved furniture and woodwork was produced; its most famous exponent was the Burgundian furniture-maker and woodcarver H.*Sambin. Certain extreme manifestations arose from the style such as *grotto ornament and the *Auricular style.

Some elements of Mannerist design reappeared in late 19th, early 20th century revivals such as the *Baroque Revival and some of the more imaginative renderings of classicism.

mantling. *Drapery, *lambrequin, *vandycked swag, etc., used as a surround or background for *shields in *achievements of arms and *heraldic decoration.

Mannerism. French cabinet made at Lyons, 1550-1600.

Manueline style. 1) 17th century doorway, Church of St Francis of Assisi, Goa, India. 2) Abbey of Batalha, Portugal, mid 15th century.

Manueline style. Portuguese late *Gothic style of architecture, named after King Manuel I (1495-1521) and consisting of a combination of the twisted and soaring forms of *Flamboyant Gothic and the ornate, encrusted decoration known in Spain as *Plateresque. In probably the most elaborate exercise in the style, the Convent of Christ at Tomar in Portugal, a single window is carved into innumerable forms: *marine motifs (knotted *rope, cork floats, billowing sails, capstan, seaweed, anchor chains), Manuel's personal *emblem, the armillary sphere, and his personal decorations, the ribands of the Order of the Garter and Golden Fleece. The marine motifs were intended to reflect the glory of Portugal's long history of seafaring. Manueline architecture also has a strong oriental feel, as shown, for example, in the dense *tracery of the Royal Cloister at Batalha. This derives mainly from the Islamic influence of Spain's Moorish architecture and from Portuguese involvement in the Indian subcontinent from the early 16th century.

A Neo-Manueline style appeared in the second half of the 19th century and was favoured for grandiose buildings, among them Lisbon railway station, King Fernando II's Pena Palace at Sintra and the Buçaco Palace, near Coimbra.

Manwaring, Robert (fl 1760-79). English cabinet-maker who worked in London and published three *pattern books concentrating on chairs: *The Carpenter's Compleat Guide to the whole system of Gothic Railing* (1765); *The Cabinet and Chair-Maker's Real Friend and Companion* 'containing upwards of 100 new designs for all sorts of chairs' (1765), which popularised chair-backs with flat *interlacing patterns; and an innovative book of *rustic designs – *The Chair-Maker's Guide, being upwards of 200 new and genteel designs* 'for Gothic, Chinese, ribbon and other chairs . . . many of the rural kind may be executed with rude branches or limbs of trees' (1766).

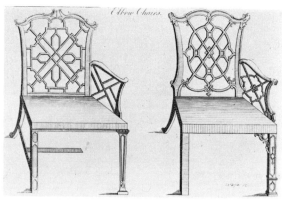

Robert Manwaring. From his The Cabinet and Chair-Maker's Real Friend and Companion, *1765.*

marbling. *Trompe-l'oeil* decoration imitating marble, alabaster, basalt or *verde antiche* painted on surfaces of furniture and walls, columns, etc., in Europe from the 17th to the 19th centuries, especially in Italian or Italian-influenced architecture as a cheap alternative to the real material, but also because of a general liking in *Baroque design for painted wall decoration.

In ceramics, marbled effects are achieved by mixing different coloured clays, slips or glazes. 1st century Roman and Chinese T'ang period (618-907) potters mixed different coloured clays; the technique was used by J. Dwight (1637-1703) at Fulham in the late 17th century and by J.F. Böttger (1682-1719) at Meissen. Early 18th century Staffordshire solid agate ware mixed white, brown and blue-stained clays and was copied by Wedgwood and then by some French and German factories (e.g. Apt, Douai, Orléans, Königsburg). An alternative method of achieving a marbled effect on ceramics was to spatter different coloured glazes on to the body and then to comb or sponge them together to simulate marble. Several factories did this including Wedgwood and the American factory of Bennington in Vermont.

*dolphins, *nereids, *tritons and *mermaids. In the *Renaissance, engravings of classical myths such as the Battle of the Tritons and Sea Gods, and the Triumph of Galatea (depicted as a sea nymph, riding on a shell pulled by hippocamps, tritons, dolphins, etc.) were popular. The flora and fauna of the sea provide further motifs: *shells, crustaceans, *seaweed, coral, *fish. Sea monsters deriving from travellers' tales appeared occasionally in Elizabethan ornament, e.g. a combined fish and dog creature on a plasterwork ceiling at Audley End, Cambridgeshire. The *Rococo period made especially inventive use of marine forms.

The only motif to survive from ancient Roman seafaring is the *columna rostrata. In the Middle Ages,

*marine decoration. 1) English silver soup tureen and stand by Robert Garrard the Younger, 1824-25. 2) Huis der Onvrije Schippers, Koornlei, Ghent, Belgium, 1740. 3) Stone *mouldings in Neo-Manueline style, Buçaco Palace Hotel, Coimbra, Portugal, 1887-1907. 4) New York Yacht Club, West 44th Street, architects Warren & Wetmore, 1899.*

*margent. 1) Chiswick House, London, built 1725-29. 2) Edinburgh New Town, late 18th century. 3) *Festoons and margents of *laurel on 19th century commercial building, Liverpool, England.*

Marbled paper was used by French bookbinders for endpapers early in the 17th century, but was not widely adopted in book production until fifty years later. In 1625, Francis Bacon described marbled paper thus: 'The Turks have a pretty art of chamoletting of paper which is not with us in use. They take divers oyled colours and put them severally in drops upon water lightly and then wet their paper (being of some thickness) with it, and the paper will be waved and veined like Chamolet or Marble.' In fact it is more likely to have been a German invention. Imitation marbled paper was printed in the 19th century, and hand-made marbled paper has remained popular for high-quality book-binding.

margent. A strip of leaf and/or flower forms hanging downwards (sometimes from a ring held by a *lion mask), this decorative device developed from the *festoon with which it often appears. Both ornaments were common in the 17th and 18th centuries. A margent was used to emphasise vertical elements such as window frames or ornamental panels in architecture, and the slender panels on table legs, chair legs and chests. A.*Swan illustrated a selection of margents in Volume II of *Collection of Designs in Architecture* (1757).

marine decoration. Much of marine decoration derives from classical mythology. Popular subjects include: the bearded Roman sea god *Neptune (or his Greek counterpart, Poseidon) carrying a *trident and accompanied by his wife, Amphitrite, *hippocamps,

the *nef, a model ship made of precious metal, was popular throughout Europe. The growing interest in boat-building and navigation and the subsequent exploration and seizure of new territories from the 15th to the 17th centuries were reflected in the architectural decoration of the time: for example, Belem, outside Lisbon (Portugal), from where Vasco da Gama sailed, has a *Manueline cloister ornamented with *rope, armillary spheres and marine and tropical vegetation. Motifs deriving from the art of navigation include: *compass, *anchor, astrolabes, plumb lines, etc. A. *Benjamin's suggestions in 1806 for a *trophy of navigation included 'anchors, cables, rudders, mariners' compass, speaking trumpet, quadrant and pendant.' Marine decoration is often used to allude to the involvement of an individual or an organisation with the sea: it may appear on the frame around a sailor's or explorer's portrait, on his memorial or on his house; it decorates houses and buildings in ports, defence ministries, naval headquarters, Admiralty buildings, and commemorates naval exploration and victories, shipping offices, seaside resorts and docks. Marine motifs also appear as part of a more broadly based vocabulary of ornament associated with water, on fountains, grottoes, even in bathrooms.

In the early 20th century, as seaside holidays became popular and affordable for increasing numbers of people, motifs like *shells, *waves, *sea horses, seagulls and yachts became popular on mementoes from the new seaside resorts and were used on textiles, wallpapers, etc. Having been most popular in the 1920s and 1930s, this style of decoration emerged again in the late 1940s and early 1950s – a reflection of the opportunities for seaside holidays after World War II.

Marot, Daniel (1663-1752). French engraver and designer. As a Huguenot exiled from France in 1685, he took his knowledge of the contemporary *Louis XIV style (as shown in the work of J.*Berain and his former teacher J.*Le Pautre) to the court of William of Orange in Holland and later to the King and Queen Mary in England. He worked on the interior decoration and garden design of their palaces at Het Loo in Holland and Hampton Court in England and evolved an individual *Baroque style showing a particular concern for the overall design, which was complemented by the skills of his fellow Huguenot craftsmen: upholsterers, carvers, gilders, silversmiths, etc. Although Marot's influence was already spreading before the publication of his designs, *Oeuvres de Sieur Marot* (1702, second expanded edition 1712) confirmed and extended it. These designs were wide-ranging: suites of furniture and upholstery, curtains and pelmets, parterres, ceilings, chimneypieces, pier glasses '*à la manière de France*', vases, clock-cases, gates, even carriages. His elaborately upholstered state beds with their fringed, swagged and tasselled testers were much copied. Among Marot's published engravings were designs for cabinets that were mounted on small brackets around fireplaces, overmantels or *cornices for the display of the fashionable blue-and-white Chinese porcelain. These became so popular that they actually stimulated the production of new blue-and-white vases to *chinoiserie* designs in England and Holland. Marot

created a distinctive style, particularly in furniture, and his influence lasted until the onset of *Palladianism both in England and in America.

Marot, Jean (c.1619-79). An architect who engraved two volumes summarising the achievements of French architecture in the first half of the 17th century. D.*Marot was his son. *L'Architecture Française* (c.1660), sometimes referred to as the '*Grand Marot*', contained work by leading French architects such as Salomon de Brosse (1571-1627), Louis le Vau (1612-70), Nicholas-François Mansart (1598-1666) and Antoine Le Pautre (c.1617-82), elder brother of J.*Le Pautre. Although largely devoted to plans and elevations of important palaces, *châteaux* and *hôtels*, it also included tombs, *arcs de triomphe*, ceiling details, a handful of Italian buildings including Michelangelo's work from 1539 at the Piazza del Campidoglio, Rome, as well as an imaginary Roman temple reconstruction, and the Temple of Baalbec. The *Recueils d'architecture* (c.1670), known as the '*Petit Marot*', gave a similar account of domestic and ecclesiastical architecture, though on a smaller scale, and was thus less useful for ornament. However, Marot did publish several series of engravings illustrating specific ornamental details such as *vases.

Mars. Roman god of war who is sometimes included in schemes of *military decoration, and usually depicted as a young warrior with *helmet, *shield, breastplate, *spear, sword and occasionally a halberd. According to legend, Mars fell in love with *Venus: *Cupid is therefore sometimes shown playing with his armour, illustrating the notion that even strife may be overcome by love. Mars is sometimes shown with *Minerva, goddess of wisdom, who brings to war the virtues of prudence, courage and perseverance – an antidote to the destructive powers, thus representing *Peace.

*Daniel Marot. Engraving of *cornice designs, late 17th or early 18th century.*

Jean Marot. 1) Engraving of lion and unicorn vase, c.1660-70.
*masks. 2) *Bacchic mask enamelled on glass vase by Eugène Rousseau, late*
*19th century. 3) *Keystone, 1930s commercial building, Paris. 4) 19th*
century apartment building, Amsterdam. 5) Doorcase, 81 Stoke Newington
*Church Street, London, 1734. 6) From M.*Darly's A New Book of*
Ornaments, 1772. 7) Fountain, Stazione Centrale, Milan, Italy, 1930s.

martlet (French, swift). Heraldic bird with tufts of feather replacing shanks or legs, possibly because swifts are usually in flight (they even mate on the wing), so perhaps were thought to have no legs at all.

mascaron (French, grotesque mask). *See* grotesque.

masks representing the heads of humans, gods, goddesses, animals, birds or monsters are a universal decorative motif. They were common in ancient Greek and Roman art, though usually in the form of a god or goddess appropriate to the context of the decoration or the function of the piece or place they ornamented: e.g. the head of Bacchus, Silenius or a *satyr on a wine vessel (*see* Bacchic decoration), or the head of a *gorgon on a breastplate. In *Romanesque architecture, the mask appears frequently as the central motif on stone *capitals with foliate decoration springing from, or surrounding it, and also as a *corbel, *label stop or *keystone. The *Renaissance use of animal heads as decorative masks derived from classical examples, the most common being the *lion, followed by the ram (*see* aegricanes), goat, panther and *tiger. Animal masks were particularly popular in the ornament of *Neo-classical furniture and silver, often combined with *monopodia. Masks of all descriptions are a central feature in *grotesque ornament. In *Gothic architecture, a mask functioning as a waterspout or *gargoyle is a favourite device. Sometimes, contemporary personalities' faces appear in architecture: e.g. master masons were immortalised as corbel stones on Gothic cathedrals, and in the 18th, 19th and 20th centuries human faces, sometimes remarkably life-like, sometimes fashionably idealised, frequently appear. M.*Darly, in the *Ornamental Architect* (1770), stated the usual positions in which masks were found: keystones were the most obvious place, where they could 'be used to great advantage among many ornaments such as the tops of festoons, middle of frames, in consoles, ceilings, etc. They are pleasing ornaments when well designed and executed'. *See also* bucranium; Comedy and Tragedy masks; foliate masks; grotesque masks; portrait heads.

masonic emblems. Motifs that derive from the myth and symbolism in masonic ritual and are used to decorate objects belonging to freemasons and to ornament their meeting places. The origins of freemasonry lie in the medieval craft guild of stonemasons, and many of the emblems represent their working tools. For freemasons these have since acquired particular meanings: the set square and compasses, united to regulate lives and actions; the level for equality; the plumbline for justice and uprightness of life and action; the drawing or tracing board for divine laws and moral plans; the rough ashlar for man in his primitive state; the perfect ashlar for a life spent in acts of piety and virtue; the open bible (called the volume of sacred law) and the blazing sun, stars, moon, and the globes indicate enlightenment; four tassels decorating the corners of the Lodge stand for Temperance, Fortitude, Prudence and Justice. Other emblems are the beehive (*see* bee) for thrift and industry and Jacob's ladder to represent the connection between heaven and earth, God and man.

masonic emblems. 1) English freemason's jewel, c.1800. 2) 19th century English transfer-printed mug.

Masonic decoration also includes *Egyptian elements such as *obelisks, *pyramids and *hieroglyphics, which are partly an allusion to the legend that tells of Euclid of Alexandria working out the formula for successful masonry (supposedly already demonstrated in the construction of the Temple of Solomon and the Tower of Babel), and partly an indication of the absorption by freemasons of the tenets and interests held by the Rosicrucians, a society of mystics and alchemists which devoted its studies to the arcane mysteries of Egypt. Meeting places of the masons and other secret societies such as the Oddfellows (records of the latter started in 1745) were sometimes built entirely in the Egyptian style.

Masonic ornament on glass and ceramic objects was most common in the late 18th and early 19th centuries: there are German enamelled beakers, American flasks, English transfer-printed pottery, probably all used for eating and drinking at masonic gatherings, and also masonic chairs and other items of furniture. During this period, the masons were often associated with liberalism and even suspected of taking part in subversive activities. And indeed many of the masonic emblems resemble *revolutionary motifs, especially those relating to equality and justice, e.g. the open bible transformed into a book of law or constitution.

matsu-no-ke. *See* pine tree.

matting. Textured surface on metalwork, produced by hammering with a punch. 17th century drinking vessels have bands of matting, possibly to disguise the dulling effect that fingermarks have on polished metal. Matting was used continually until the 19th century, often as a background for other decorative effects such as chasing.

Mayer, Luigi (d 1803). Draughtsman whose watercolours were reproduced in a series of volumes, *Views in Egypt, Palestine and the Ottoman Empire* (1801-10), which were used as source books for *topographical decoration, in particular as an early authoritative source on *Egyptian antiquities.

Mayhew, John. Upholsterer and business partner of W.*Ince with whom Mayhew produced an influential

collection of designs entitled *The Universal System of Household Furniture* (1759-62).

meander or **maeander.** *Progressive ornament consisting of winding lines, either curving, e.g. the *cloudband, or geometric, e.g. *key and *fret patterns. Some forms, such as the *wavescroll, are known as spiral meander. This type of ornament is used in wood or stone for *friezes, flat *mouldings, or, in ceramics, for the rim or base of a piece.

matting. 1) English silver goblet, 1657.
medallion. 2) Exterior of Palazzo di Giustizia, Rome, 1889-1910.

medallion. Circular or oval decorative device usually bearing, as the term suggests, a portrait or some other subject in light relief. Popular in *Neo-classical decoration where medallions appear particularly frequently in plasterwork, silver, porcelain and textiles.

medicine. Various motifs appear in the ornament of buildings and objects associated with the profession of medicine. They include the *rod of Aesculapius (in which two intertwined serpents denote the forces of sickness and health), surgical instruments and aids such as the lancet and leech, and the eye and hand, signifying the skills of the surgeon. Occasionally the figures of Aesculapius and his daughter Hygeia (sometimes referred to as his wife) appear, as on the College of Surgeons, Dublin (1806). The red and white barber's pole (representing bandaging applied before blood-letting, with the gilt knob standing for the brass basin) originally indicated a barber surgeon's practice, but became the sign of the barber alone after the separation of the two professions in 1745. A long-necked, round-bottomed medicine flask signifies the profession of a chemist, as do the pestle and mortar, a reference to the apothecary pounding his own remedies. The French engraver M. Gravelot included a *personification of medicine in his *Almanach Iconologique* (1765): the figure has a flaming torch of observation and a lancet, 'most essential of her instruments', and is accompanied by a dog, indicating gentleness. In the 19th century, concern about hygiene and research into tropical diseases produced more motifs (*see* insects) that were used on hospitals, hospices, research institutions, etc.

Medieval style. This primarily English style appeared alongside the 18th and 19th century *Gothic Revival.

Juste-Aurèle Meissonier. Engraved designs for snuffboxes, c.1730-50.

Medieval style. 1) English stoneware jug by William Ridgway, c.1848.
2) English earthenware tile panel by Morris & Co., 1870s. 3) English
transfer-printed and painted tile by W.W. Copeland & Sons, c.1878.

It consisted of a range of images evoking a romanticised view of the domestic and secular arts of the Middle Ages in contrast to the purely *Gothic in which ecclesiastical and *naturalistic motifs were dominant. In the words of C.L.*Eastlake, 'It was the love of medieval lore, of Old English traditions, of border chivalry, which, by the magic power of association, led the more romantic of our sires and grandsires first to be interested in Gothic architecture and then to discern its beauties.' In the early 1800s, romantic historical fiction, particularly the novels of Walter Scott (*see* Abbotsford style), stirred this nostalgia, and legends such as King Arthur, and Tristan and Iseult became highly popular themes in the decorative arts, as they had been in the Gothic period itself: 14th century French ivory jewel boxes were often ornamented with the figures of Sir Lancelot, Sir Gawain and Sir Galahad, or with scenes from their adventures. Tennyson's poetry, events such as the Eglinton Tournament (1839), and the paintings of the Pre-Raphaelites (some of whom, e.g. E. Burne-Jones, decorated actual pieces of furniture) reinforced the fashion for medieval subjects in ornament. Panels for furniture and tapestries, e.g. those produced by William Morris's workshop at Merton Abbey in the 1880s, had designs incorporating damsels in loose robes, *fleur-de-lis, *millefleurs, *unicorns and motifs associated with *heraldic decoration.

The French version of this enthusiasm for medieval styles and decoration was the *Troubadour style. *See also* Cathedral style; Dantesque.

Medusa. One of the three *gorgons; used particularly in *classical *military decoration.

Meisson(n)ier, Juste-Aurèle (1695-1750). Italian-born designer, silversmith and architect who moved to Paris in 1720, succeeding J.*Berain as Architecte-dessinateur de la Chambre et du Cabinet du Roi in 1726. His engraved patterns show him to be, with N.*Pineau, a leading artist in the *genre pittoresque* phase of the *Rococo. His ornamental designs, composed of *rocaille, scrollwork, waterjets, flowers and curling *acanthus, were much copied. They were published in sets between 1723 and 1735, and are for interiors, furniture and silver or gold objects such as boxes, salts, tableware, candlesticks and sword-mounts. To demonstrate the asymmetrical nature of his designs, Meissonier sometimes illustrated three views of the same piece, as in *Chandelière de sculpture en argent* (1728), as an aid to the craftsman working in this new, rather unusual style. His collected works, *Oeuvre de Juste Aurèle Meissonier*, were first published in 1734 with several subsequent editions. Meissonier's influence is most evident in the design of ormolu mounts on *Louis XV furniture and on French silver and gold. His designs were also popular in Germany; some of those for interiors were reworked in a lighter vein by German Rococo designers, and elements from his work for silver translated well into designs for German hard-paste porcelain. Meissen used them for the Swan Service (1737-41), as did the Chelsea and Longton Hall porcelain factories in England. His *naturalistic decoration, e.g. *fish and *vegetables among the *rocaille* on a soup tureen, was widely imitated in both silver and porcelain. Many of Meissonier's designs were republished at the time of the 19th century *Rococo Revival in Paris by E. Rouveyre in his series *L'Art Décoratif appliqué à l'Art Industriel* (1888); they were also republished in Frankfurt in the same year.

melon bulb. *See* bulb.

menorah. This seven-branched candelabrum is an ancient symbol of Judaism, and now the national emblem of Israel. Like most stylised branching forms, it is often considered to derive from the *Tree of Life. In Jewish ritual it is placed in front of the sanctuary and represents the light of God and judgement. It is particularly associated with Hanukkah – the mid-winter festival of lights. As a decorative motif it is used as a general symbol of the Jewish faith and appears on the entrances to synagogues and Jewish schools, on

mermaid. 1) Carved mermaid with comb and mirror on medieval house, Caen (Calvados), France. 2) P. & O. Building, Trafalgar Square, London, architect A.T. Bolton, 1907.

Mercury. 1) French Louis XIV Boulle cabinet, early 18th century. 2) Post office, Kew, Surrey, 1930s. 3) British Empire Building, Rockefeller Center, New York, 1930s.

glass, amulets, medals, wine cups, Passover dishes, etc., and on gravestones. *See also* Judaic decoration.

Mercury. The principal role of Mercury (and his Greek counterpart Hermes) was messenger and herald to the gods. Thus, he is god of eloquence, travel and commerce, and his head was carved on milestones and boundary posts, later on doorways and gateposts (*see* herm). Mercury and his attributes – a petasus (a broad-brimmed winged hat), winged sandals and the *caduceus – appear on buildings and objects connected with travelling (e.g. Milan railway station), *commercial enterprise (banks, office buildings), communications (post offices), and, as he was considered to have invented the alphabet, the written word (e.g. libraries, writing tables). More rarely, Mercury appears in contexts reflecting other beliefs about him: that he was the inventor of the *lyre, numbers, astronomy, weights and measures, the art of fighting, gymnastics.

merlon. The solid section of a *battlement. Decorative variations include *floriated merlons and *swallow-tail merlons.

mermaids combine the characteristics of classical *nereids and *sirens with the fish tails of *tritons and the luxuriant hair, mirror and comb of *Venus (or her Greek counterpart Aphrodite). By the early Christian era, mermaids had been established as a separate species and were included in early natural histories, such as those by Pliny the Elder and Plutarch. They were thought to be seductive, vain creatures, and appear in medieval iconography as symbols of lust and temptation, notably in church carvings of the period, e.g. *bosses, pew ends, *gargoyles, misericords, etc. They are sometimes depicted triumphantly holding

a *fish, which represents a captured Christian soul. Although mermaids usually have a single tail, they sometimes have a double one, splayed outwards in medieval work, but elegantly twisted in 18th century representations which often appeared as a variant of the fashionable *half figure. They were popular in *emblem books and in *heraldry: some families were keen to claim descent from mermaids as folklore decreed them to be excellent and fertile wives. By the end of the 17th century they mainly appeared in *marine decoration, although in the late 19th century mermaids were again used as motifs in their own right, reflecting contemporary interest in folklore and mythology. In the late 1940s and 1950s they reappeared, part of a general enthusiasm for marine decoration.

merman. *See* triton.

*metope. 1) With various symbols, St Carolus Borromeüskerk, Antwerp, Belgium, by Pieter Huyssens, 1615-25. 2) With *rosettes, David Hume's monument, Calton Old Burial Ground, Edinburgh, by Robert Adam, 1777.*

metope (Greek, *meta*, between, *ope*, opening). In *classical architecture, a thin rectangular panel which can be plain or decorated with a sculptured relief. It is virtually the only space allowed for decoration in the Doric *Order, and appears in the *frieze alternating with the *triglyph. Forms such as the *bucranium, *centaur and *wreath are popular enrichments for the metope.

military decoration ornaments weapons and armour; military establishments such as barracks, arsenals, guard rooms, the officers' mess; the appurtenances of military men and heroes, their houses, their tombs, even the frames around their portraits; and memorials to war dead. In architecture, it appears principally on gateways, railings and gates, overmantels, halls and staircases. During the 17th and 18th centuries, it was sometimes used to imply family history and pedigree. In the *Renaissance (and frequently since then), ancient Roman arms and armour were the most common form of military decoration, usually appearing in *trophies and in *friezes. Frequent motifs include the cuirass (modelled to the shape of a human torso), scale armour, greaves, *shield, *helmet, *pelta, *spear, short sword, dagger and pike. The motifs used by the Romans on their arms and armour – the Medusa head (see gorgon), *laurel wreaths, *thunderbolts, *lion and *eagle heads – were also incorporated. Personifications of *Fame and *Victory were natural additions to the repertoire, as were references to *Mars, god of war, and Hercules, personification of might and power (see Herculean decoration). Classical prototypes were easily available on *triumphal arches, Trajan's Column in Rome, etc.

In the 16th and 17th centuries, the vocabulary of military ornament widened considerably as the theme extended to contemporary military kit: uniforms, cavalry equipment, the instruments of martial *music, particularly drums, flags, and standards, armour and the most important contribution to the development of warfare, firepower. A typical example of these new motifs is the Porta dei Bombardieri (1687) in Verona: in place of columns, gun barrels rest on military drums, and there are, in addition, powder barrels, coils of rope and engineers' tools. Ornamentists would often produce patterns specifically devoted to the theme, e.g. J.*Le Pautre's *Trophées d'armes antiques et modernes* and H.*Vredeman de Vries's trophies that are classical in form but include boots, bridles and flintlock guns. G.F. Riedel (1724-84) also produced a suite of designs for military trophies which included imaginary relics of 'guerres antiques' with Turkish and Crusader arms and armour. The dead and vanquished might also be included: *keystones of the late 17th century arsenal in Berlin depict dying warriors; J.*Barbet devised a military chimneypiece supported by captive prisoners (see persians).

An inappropriate subject for the *Rococo style, military decoration returned to favour with the *Neoclassical style, e.g. the earliest known work by Claude-Nicholas Ledoux (1736-1806), the Café Militaire, Paris

military decoration. 1) From *Hypnerotomachia Poliphili, *Venice, 1499. 2) From H.*Vredeman de Vries's* Panoplia, *1572. 3) French commode in mahogany with gilt metal mounts, 1786. 4) 'A Camp Bedstead' from R.*Ackermann's* The Repository of Arts, *1825. 5) Mannerist *herms designed by Heinrich Muntinck, 1604. 6) From the Comte *de Caylus's* Recueil d'antiquités, *1752-67.*

*military decoration. Bank of Ireland, Dublin, 1729 onwards, *panoply carved by Thomas Kirk.*

(1762), was decorated with bound *fasces surmounted by *helmets. Attempts were made at accurate representations of antique arms and armour with the aid of such publications as T.*Hope's *Costume of the Ancients.* Military motifs were frequently used in the decorative schemes produced for Napoleon, and were among the most popular of the *Empire style. Cannons formed bedposts, stools resembled military drums and wallhangings were suspended from pikes. The decoration of the Salle du Sacre, Versailles, included a range of tunics and shakos, bayonet and cannon. R.*Ackermann's *Repository* suggested in 1819 the following decoration for a drawing room: 'the piers may be embellished with busts of our most illustrious military and naval commanders, sustained by pedestals decorated with appropriate trophies or designs, commemorative of their individual achievements.' By the next decade there was a growing interest in the *Medieval style and chivalry, and Samuel Rush Meyrick provided an important illustrated survey, *A Critical Inquiry into Ancient Armour as it existed in Europe, but particularly in England, from the Norman Conquest to the reign of King Charles II* (London, 1824).

The full range of military ornament has continued to appear on war memorials, in cemeteries and on buildings associated with militaristic regimes.

millefiori (Italian, thousand flowers) or **mosaic glass.** Flower-like decoration in glass achieved by bundling together canes of coloured glass and then cutting off cross-sections to embed in clear glass. This technique, probably developed by the Romans, is known to have existed in Alexandria in the 1st century BC. It was revived in 16th century Venice decorating the bases of small bowls, vases, bottles and jugs and in paperweights. *Millefiori* reappeared in France, Bohemia, England and America during the 19th century, chiefly in paperweights.

millefleurs (French, thousand flowers). Flower-studded backgrounds, particularly on medieval tapestries depicting the Virgin and Child or scenes of courtly love or *hunting. An aspect of the strong vein of *naturalism in the 14th and 15th centuries, typical flowers include anemones, pinks, columbines, *roses and violas. It was revived in the 19th century *Medieval style.

Millefleurs may also refer to the decoration consisting of tiny painted or moulded flowers on certain types of Chinese and Meissen porcelain.

Minerva. The Roman goddess of wisdom and patroness of all arts and trades. Her Greek counterpart is Athena. She sometimes appears as the rational, and therefore peaceful, antidote to *Mars, or as a symbol of good government. Minerva and her attributes, the *owl and the *helmet, are favourite ornaments for libraries and learned institutions.

Minoan forms appeared occasionally in early 20th century architecture and decorative schemes in the wake of Arthur Evans's excavations at Knossos, Crete, between 1900 and 1908. His revelations of a civilisation dating from 2000 BC, contemporary with that at Mycenae on the Greek mainland, fired the imagination of designers tired of the familiar sources of historical ornament. Characteristic features include stubby columns with heavy *capitals and downward-tapering, baseless shafts (reflecting the concerns of a period reacting against excessive decoration). Motifs were largely stylised *marine subjects.

Mission style. Late 19th, early 20th century American style, principally of furniture. Essentially functional, its decoration is confined to emphasising and revealing constructional devices such as mortice and tenon joints, pegs, etc. There is minimal ornament in the form of mother-of-pearl, inlaid metals, usually pewter, and fretwork in simple shapes vaguely reminiscent of *Art Nouveau designs.

Mission style. American library table by Gustav Stickley, c.1906.

The style evolved from a combination of influences, principally the work of the Shaker religious community (from 1850) and the English *Arts and Crafts movement – the latter was particularly evident in the work of the Roycroft Craft Community and Gustav Stickley's Craftsman Workshop, both in New York. Furniture designed by the architect Frank Lloyd Wright (1869-1959) and the Buffalo furniture maker Charles Rohlfs (1853-1936) was also important in the development of the style. In California the architects and brothers Henry and Charles Sumner Greene worked in a variation of Mission style; however, their furniture was produced exclusively for the houses they built around Pasadena, 1907-09.

Mitelli, Agostino (1609-60). Italian painter and etcher based in Bologna. His ornamental designs concentrated mainly on the *cartouche, although he also produced patterns for *scrolling foliage, *vases, *grotesques, *brackets and *capitals in two collections: *Disegni et Abozzi* (1636) and *Freggi dell'Architettura* (1645). Fundamentally *Baroque, Mitelli's work also shows the influence of the *Auricular style – he devised some unusual asymmetrical cartouches (published in Bologna in 1636 and 1640, and reprinted 1642 and 1664), which were to become a feature of much later

millefiori. 1) 19th century French glass paperweight.
*Agostino Mitelli. Design for *cartouche, c.1640.*

Rococo ornament. Some of his work was later re-issued in London as *Designs for Ornament*.

mitre leaf. Contemporary term for 18th and early 19th century *moulding enrichment consisting of a leaf split at the base, and used in architecture, woodwork and silverwork. It is sometimes used with *beading, when it is called bead and leaf.

Modernismo. Spanish term for *Art Nouveau, a favourite style of ornamentation in Spain and Portugal for commercial buildings, hotels, offices and apartment blocks from the 1890s to the early 1900s. Antonio Gaudi (1852-1926), one of many architects and designers in Spain who moved from *eclecticism to Art Nouveau at that time, was the most extreme and idiosyncratic exponent of the style, and worked in and around Barcelona.

Modernist decoration. Although the Modern Movement specifically repudiated the use of ornament as an adjunct to functional design in architecture, those buildings designed with an eye to earlier Expressionist principles often incorporated a small degree of ornament, in general confined to *friezes or entrances. Equally, many buildings designed loosely under the Modern Movement allowed the occasional touch of levity, usually schematised *geometric or abstract patterns that were easily produced by mechanical process. Most motifs were based on broadly *classical ornament, thus *coin moulding, *fluting and the *wavescroll are often recognisable, although elements from early decorative vocabularies, such as *Anglo-Saxon *nebule or *chevron ornament, also appeared. Simple devices were used in new ways, as in stepped *mouldings, dramatically emphasised *keystones, or the insertion of luminous or coloured materials (glass, foil, chrome) to introduce textural or tonal contrasts. Some Modern Movement buildings had interiors that veered toward *Art Deco, e.g. the Daily Express Building, London (1931), by Ellis & Clarke with Owen Williams.

Styles of interior furnishing were developed according to the same purist, rationalist tenets as the architecture. The simplicity of much of the design had been anticipated in the later work of *Arts and Crafts and *Glasgow School designers in Britain, the *Mission style in America, and in Europe by the Bauhaus, itself the outcome of earlier ideas expressed by the *Vienna Secession. Angular, geometric, unadorned forms and an emphasis on the quality and the texture of the material used rather than its embellishment were typical: tubular metal, chrome, glass, wood veneer and leather were all popular. Just as the Arts and Crafts movement had sought to reveal the hand-crafted nature of its artefacts in its sparse ornament, so Modernist decoration highlighted industrial processes and origins. Although the work of some Modernist style artists was hand-crafted, e.g. the lacquer of Eileen Gray (1879-1976) and Jean Dunand (1877-1942), the silver and jewellery of Raymond Templier (1891-1968) and Paul Brandt, most designs were intended for manufacture. Famous examples are the furniture of Le Corbusier (1887-1965) and

the chairs of Mies van der Rohe (1886-1969) which went into production in the late 1920s. It was the handmade jewellery however, that made use of *machinery motifs such as screw-heads, ballbearings, etc.

Textile design, particularly for rugs, was the only area where decoration and colour flourished. Patterning was, in the main, abstract, geometric and *Cubist-inspired. Good examples are the work in England of Marion Dorn (1900-64) and her husband Edward McKnight Kauffer (1890-1954) for the Wilton Royal Carpet Factory in Wiltshire from 1928, and in France the designs of Jean Lurçat (1892-1966) and Sonia Delaunay (1885-1979), who published her abstract designs in *Compositions Couleurs Idées* (1930).

The purist, rationalist approach of Modernism was most successfully adopted in Scandinavia, and the Stockholm exhibition of 1930 was the culmination of the trend. *See also* revolutionary ornament.

modillion. First Bank of the United States, Philadelphia, Pennsylvania, by Samuel Blodgett, 1795-97.

modillion. The *bracket or *console in the Corinthian and Composite *Orders that supports the upper section of the *cornice; often used in pairs. The modillion also appears in interior schemes and on doorways, its *classical placing forgotten, though it usually still serves a structural function.

molecular structures. Patterns consisting of thin tubular lines, usually black, terminating in primary-coloured blobs or balls. Like *crystals, they were part of the post-war search for new forms of ornament. Their origin in scientific observation meant that they were associated with modernity and progress. They appeared at the very end of the 1940s and with increasing frequency during the 1950s: the 'Abacus' screen by Edward Mills at the Festival of Britain in 1951 was a particularly well-known example; furniture featuring tubular metal with plastic or wooden balls was also common, and a variety of manufacturers adopted the style of decoration for textiles, glass, ceramics etc. The 'Atomium', an enormous architectural structure which dominated the 1958 Brussels World Fair, was one of the last examples of the fashion for this form.

Mondon, Jean (fl 1736-60). Prolific designer in the *Rococo style, many of whose patterns were published in both Paris and Augsburg. His first suite, *Premier Livre de forme rocquaille et cartel*, was published in 1736 and was possibly the first time that *rocaille* had been used to describe this form of Rococo ornament. At least five subsequent collections also covered *rocaille* forms, incorporating fashionable French figures, *Figures de Mode* and *Figures Françaises*, as well as an early instance of Rococo **chinoiserie*, *Figures, oyseaux et dragons chinois*. Characteristically for the period, Mondon also designed ornament within Rococo *cartouches on the themes of the *Continents, and the four times of day (morning, midday, afternoon and evening), and several collections of *trophies.

money pattern. *See* coin moulding.

monkey. In early medieval Christian iconography the monkey represented the devil. Later, with an apple in its mouth, it symbolised the fall of man. Gradually it became a symbol of luxury and vanity, satirising the follies of man. St Bernard of Clairvaux (1091-1153) specifically deplored the 'unclean apes' represented in the extravagant and grotesque imagery of Cluniac monasteries. It was a commonplace decoration by the end of the 14th century, first on ecclesiastical and then on secular buildings, usually illustrating stories and *fables. A monkey pillaging the goods of a sleeping pedlar recurs in illuminated manuscripts, on misericords, in wall painting and metalwork, but the story of which it is an illustration has been lost. Monkeys appear in *grotesque decoration, particularly 16th and 17th century German and Dutch work, and, combined with *arabesques and *scrolling foliage, they became a particularly popular ornament in France at the turn of the 18th century. *Singeries, which showed monkeys engaged in human activities, were an important strand in *Rococo decoration. Ornament illustrating the *Senses sometimes uses a monkey to represent taste.

monogram. *See* cypher.

monopodia. Form taken from classical Roman art consisting of a head, usually of an animal, from which a disproportionately large leg or foot emerges. Used similarly to the *caryatid, as a support, primarily in furniture but also in metalwork. *Mannerist examples sometimes appear with human *masks but the foot, which may be a *claw, *paw or *hoof, often does not match the head. The form was much favoured by J.*Stuart, T.*Hope, C.*Percier and P. Fontaine and their followers in the early 19th century for chair or table legs, usually with a mask and foot of the same animal, most commonly the ram, *lion or *eagle.

Monopteros pattern. *See* Indian style.

Months. The cycle of the months was a frequent subject in the decoration of illuminated manuscripts of the Christian calendar and medieval Books of Hours. Each month was represented by the labour or pleasure particularly associated with it, e.g. wine-making in September, seed sowing in October, feasting in January and hawking in May. In addition, the appropriate sign of the *zodiac might be included, indicating the month during which the sun entered into a particular zodiacal sign. Each month also had associations with classical mythology which were frequently incorporated: Janus, the two-faced god for January; *Venus and *Cupid for February; *Mars for March; Rape of Europa (Jupiter disguised as a bull abducting a girl) for April; Castor and Pollux drawing Venus's chariot for May; Phaeton for June; Hercules in a lion-skin for July; Triptolemus for August; *Ceres for September; Bacchanalia (*see* *Bacchic) for October; Nessus the *centaur for November; Ariadne milking a goat with the infant Jupiter beside her for December.

This decorative theme was periodically revived, particularly during the 18th century when thematic groupings such as the *Elements and the *Seasons were popular.

moon. The moon, either full or crescent-shaped, appears in decoration alluding to *night (e.g. in bedrooms, on cradles, etc.) The *crescent moon, a symbol of the Ottoman Empire, is used in *Turkish style decoration. It is also sometimes an allusion to Diana, goddess of the moon.

Moorish style. A 19th century revival of *Hispano-Moresque styles in architecture and the decorative arts. Like **chinoiserie* and *Indian style, Moorish elements had been popular from the mid 18th century, particularly for incidental buildings such as summerhouses. In 1815 J.C.*Murphy published an account of Moorish architecture in Spain, but it was O.*Jones who really brought the style to prominence. In collaboration with Jules Goury (1803-34), a French architect he had met in Egypt in 1832, Jones published *Plans, Elevations, Sections and Details of the Alhambra* (1842-45; reprinted 1877), which illustrated profuse ornament combining formalised foliage with abstract and geometric patterns to give an effect well in tune with the fashions of the day. In 1843, Jones demonstrated his attachment to the style by producing Moorish designs for the ceilings and the exterior (the latter in cement) of 8, Kensington Palace Gardens, London. The idea was sufficiently novel to prompt the commissioners responsible for the designs on the site to state: 'We do not feel that we ought to object to the

monopodium. 1) *Griffin on English giltwood *console table, c.1820.
Months. 2) December, French wallpaper panel by Dufour et Cie, 1808.

Moorish style. Apartment building, Roemer Visscherstraat, Amsterdam, c.1900.

peculiarity of the proposed Moresque enrichments though hitherto not much adopted in this country.' For the Alhambra itself, Jones had the highest praise; '[it is] at the very summit of perfection of Moorish art, as is the Parthenon of Greek art. We can find no work so fitted to illustrate the grammar of ornament as that in which every ornament contains the grammar in itself.' It demonstrated that the Moors 'decorate construction, never construct decoration'. Jones's illustrations were reconstructed exactly in the Crystal Palace and from there this exotic style, and already made fashionable by the paintings of the time, spread to jewellery and domestic interiors. During the 1870s and 1880s, the French jewellers and silversmiths Falize Frères (founded c.1860) produced Moorish-influenced work decorated with *Kufic inscriptions, and the glass-maker Joseph Brocard made imitations of the richly enamelled mosque lamps. In the late Victorian period a publication on household decorations observed how 'exceedingly suitable rich oriental furniture and hangings are to our chilly comfortless climate.' Late 19th century American wallpaper manufacturers produced so-called 'Moorish' papers in garish colours with patterns represented as three-dimensional designs.

The Moorish style continued to be used in architecture, particularly for buildings connected with entertainments, theatres, exhibitions or cinemas; the Alhambra Theatre (demolished 1936) in Leicester Square, London, and the Horticultural Building at the Philadelphia Centennial Exhibition (1876), were good examples. Characteristic features of the style include the *arabesque, *horseshoe arch and *honeycomb vaulting. *See also* oriental.

moresques. Contemporary term for formal foliate patterns used in intertwining and *interlacing designs in the second half of the 16th century. They are more commonly referred to as *arabesques.

mosaic. Originally, a design made up of small pieces of coloured glass, stone or ceramic. Some *Archaeological style jewellery was decorated with miniature panels consisting of tiny sections of coloured glass and stone in imitation of Roman and *Byzantine architectural mosaics. Earlier examples (from 1820) usually depicted classical buildings, inscriptions, etc., but by the mid-century the method was also used for more decorative designs incorporating animals, flowers, etc.

Mosaic also refers to the decoration of glass objects with small sections of vari-coloured glass. Like *millefiori, mosaic glass existed in Roman times and was later revived in Venice and then across Europe.

*Scale pattern was sometimes referred to as mosaic in the 18th and 19th centuries, and J.*Crunden used the term to describe his *fret patterns.

Moses, Henry (1782-1870). English engraver working in the spare, linear *Greek Revival style popular in the early 19th century (similar to C.*Normand's work for C.*Percier and P. Fontaine). Moses engraved the plates to T.*Hope's *Costume of the Ancients* (1809) and published a similar book himself, *Designs of Modern Costume* (1812, 1823). His *Collection of Antique Vases, Paterae, Tripods, Candelabra, Sarcophagi etc* (London, 1814; Italian translation, Milan, 1824) was a useful source for the Greek Revival style.

motor cars. 'Road Way', cotton print from the Second Cotton Printing Factory, Serpulkhov, Russia, 1930.

motor cars. Like *railway trains in the 19th century, and, more recently, *aeroplanes, motor cars and their fitments have been used in ornament, usually on garages and buildings associated with the manufacture of cars or related products, e.g. the Chrysler Building in New York which has an automobile motif picked out in brick on its exterior and repeated in the interiors designed by W. Van Alen. The Michelin Building (1910) is decorated with faïence panels and motifs alluding to the joys of motoring and even

mouchette. 15th century French carved walnut cabinet.

uses *pulvinated friezes as a visual pun on the rubber tyre. In the first half of the 20th century, particularly the 1920s and 1930s, the new shapes and styles of cars, especially racing cars such as the Bluebird, were commemorated with novelty items such as teapots and cigarette lighters.

motto. *See* impresa; inscriptions; rebus.

mouchette. *Gothic *tracery motif consisting of curving, flame-shaped sections with *cusping. It originally appeared in *Decorated Gothic work but in the late 18th and early 19th centuries appeared in small-scale *Gothic Revival metalwork as well as architecture.

mouldings. Thin bands of stone, wood, plaster or metal, used in innumerable different combinations to ornament walls, ceilings and any junction between surfaces which needs disguise and/or elaboration. Mouldings may have a flat or curved surface. They are sometimes plain but provide a perfect ground for enrichment, ranging from simple *geometric forms to complex *naturalistic or stylised detail. 18th and 19th century mouldings were infinitely varied – their production made simpler by improved methods of manufacture and more sophisticated wood-turning equipment and casting methods. Different architectural styles produce identifiable styles of moulding, but pure *classical mouldings (Roman, *Renaissance and early 18th century) followed strict rules as to their proper use in relation to the *Orders and each other.

Specific types of moulding appear as individual entries in this book. Classical examples include: astragal, bolection, cavetto, cyma recta/reversa, fillet, ogee, ovolo, scotia and torus. Enrichments and later variants include: bead and reel, bead and spindle, beading, billet, cable, chevron, coin, disc, egg and anchor, egg and dart, pulvinated frieze, ribbon and rosette, ribbon and stick, waterleaf. Glossaries of different dates give almost endless variations of nomenclature – these are the most widely used.

Moyr Smith, J. English designer, whose history of interior decoration, *Ornamental Interiors* (1887), contained designs for the *Aesthetic taste and *Renaissance Revival, among other contemporary styles.

Mozarabic. Period contemporary with the *Romanesque when *Islamic styles were integrated with the European architecture of southern Spain to create *Hispano-Moresque styles. Motifs such as the *horseshoe arch gave the buildings a Moorish flavour, despite their Christian context. *See also* Mudejar.

Mucha, Alphonse (1860-1939). Czechoslovakian artist working in Paris from 1887, whose lithographic posters (especially of the actress Sarah Bernhardt from 1895) made his particular brand of *Art Nouveau graphics highly popular. His favourite themes were women and flowers, his style was an amalgam of influences, including the work of E.*Grasset, Japanese woodcuts, *Byzantine and *Islamic ornament and mosaics.

During the 1890s he published postcards and *panneaux décoratifs* – long, narrow, ornamental posters of

*mouldings. 1) Below *pediment on façade of Chiswick House, London, by Lord Burlington, built 1725-29. 2) 'To Draw the Eggs and Darts for the Embellishment of the Ovolo' from M.*Darly's The Ornamental Architect, 1770. 3) From R. de *Lalonde's Bordures à l'usage des artistes, c.1785.*

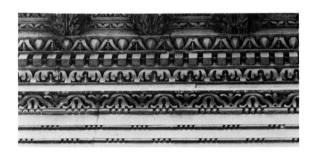

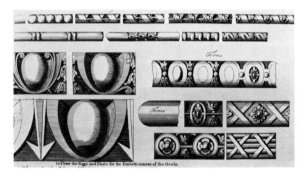

Alphonse Mucha. 1) Lily design from Documents Décoratifs, *1902. Muses. 2) Erato and Urania from G.*Richardson's* Iconology, *plate first published 1776.*

sinuous young women illustrating various themes: the four *Seasons (1896), four flowers, rose, carnation, lily, iris (1897), four arts (1897). These included characteristic forms and motifs – flowing locks of hair, the *horseshoe arch form, *crescents, *interlacing, *Celtic *arabesques.

In Mucha's own words, ' . . . my art, if I may call it that, crystallized. It was *en vogue.* It spread to factories and workshops under the name *style Mucha.*' Such was its popularity that he produced a catalogue, *Documents Décoratifs* (Paris, 1902), that illustrated his designs for cutlery, jewellery, combs, glass, lace, furniture, bookjackets, bindings, lettering, fabric, friezes, wallpaper and carpets, and must have been invaluable to manufacturers wanting to imitate the Mucha style. *Figures Décoratifs*, which adapted the female figure to a variety of decorative poses, followed in 1905, but by this time Mucha's impact was waning. His work was much admired and emulated in America.

Mudejar. Term in *Hispano-Moresque architecture denoting the application of entirely *Islamic forms to Spanish buildings. The style continued during the late medieval period, lasting until the Moors were finally banished from Spain in 1610. Motifs include cusped *Saracenic arches, *stalactite work, a kind of *strapwork and *Kufic inscriptions, as well as dense, abstract *arabesques. Spanish-influenced Latin American countries adopted a version of the Mudejar style in the 16th to 18th centuries. *See also* Moorish; Mozarabic; Plateresque.

mural crown. *See* crown.

Murphy, James Cavanah (1760-1814). Irish antiquarian who at a very early date published works on the *Islamic-influenced architecture of the Iberian peninsula. He started with the cathedral at Batalha in Portugal, and then turned his attention to Spain. *Arabian Antiquities of Spain* (London, 1815) was prepared during his stay in Spain between 1802 and 1809 and published posthumously. Though not always accurate, it was important in opening up Moorish Spain to a wider public and O.*Jones owed Murphy a considerable debt when he published his own work on the Alhambra.

Muses. Nine goddesses and companions of Apollo, each with her own sphere of influence in learning and the arts. Their attributes vary according to the period, but, after the *Renaissance, often followed the designs laid down by C.*Ripa: Calliope – epic poetry and eloquence (tablets, stylus, books and laurel crown); Clio – history (book, scroll, laurel crown, trumpet of fame); Erato – lyric and love poetry (tambourine, lyre, swan, triangle, viol); Euterpe – music and lyric poetry (flute or double pipe); Melpomene – tragedy (horn, tragic mask and a weapon: sword, dagger or Herculean club, and sceptre or crown); Polyhymnia – heroic hymns (small organ, lute); Terpsichore – dancing and song (viol, lyre, harp); Thalia – comedy and pastoral poetry (scroll, viol, mask); Urania – astronomy (globe and compasses).

The Muses were a popular ornament in the 17th and 18th centuries, tending to be used as a group in the decoration of interiors, e.g. the plasterwork reliefs of the Music Room, Lancaster (c.1730-40), or individually to proclaim the purpose of a building such as a theatre or concert hall. During the 18th century, depiction of the Muses was altered and simplified to suit contemporary culture. An interior of the Hôtel de Soubise in Paris (1737) is decorated with the figures of Tragedy and Comedy, Painting and Poetry, History and Fame, Geography and Astronomy and M. Gravelot's *Almanach Iconologique ou des Arts pour 1765* gives extensive details on the personification of artistic pursuits, e.g. Architecture, ' . . . the seriousness of her expression pronounces her usefulness and her nobility is shown by her leaning against a column. In one hand she holds a groundplan and compasses for working out proportions and in the other a plumb line showing that she believes in the principle of solidity required in her work. Vitruvius' treatise leans against the pillar, also a ruler, set square and chisel by which civil or military buildings achieve their characteristics.' He also included Painting, Sculpture, Dance, *Music, Medicine.

Not all personifications of the Muses were so complicated. In the late 18th century reclining females were mass-produced in composition stone and appropriate attributes could be attached to create the Muse of your choice. A set of Muses designed by J. Flaxman (c.1775) were cast and produced in large numbers to add to the low relief plaster decoration of the *Adam style: they were copied from the Apotheosis of Homer relief in the British Museum. One of these sets decorated a mantelpiece at Monticello, Virginia, the house (built 1769) owned by Thomas Jefferson (1743-1826), third President of the United

States. During the 19th century the figures continued to appear, although mainly on public buildings and losing favour to more literal schemes of *personification, e.g. decorating a museum with figures of great artists of the past. *See also* Comedy and Tragedy masks; horse.

music. As a decorative theme, music is most commonly suggested by *trophies composed of instruments, with the selection varying according to the type of music most suited to the context of the decoration. For the *classical, the *lyre and flute, the sistrum, syrinx (pan-pipes); for *military music, kettledrums and fifes; tambourines, pan-pipes and cymbals (as in *Bacchic ornament) signify light amusement and dancing; pastoral simplicity is suggested by bagpipes and flutes, sacred music by harps and portative organs. M. Gravelot, in his instructions for the *personification of music (1765), makes the following comment: 'Around her lie instruments, a variety to show the different characteristics of music; hautbois give the idea of playful airs, the guitar suggests love music and the harp sacred music. As for the violin, the spirit of concerts, it embraces them all.' I.*Ware, in *A Complete Body of Architecture* (1756), recommended music trophies for their graceful shape, considering the French horn 'an agreeable object', the flute and hautbois having 'nothing inelegant'.

Orpheus and Apollo often appear in ornament on a musical theme: Orpheus for the power to charm even inanimate objects with his music and Apollo as god of song and music, often with his instruments,

*music. 1) *Cartouche on violin-makers' house, 12 Neruda Street, Prague, c.1730. 2) *Trophy from P. Charpentier's* Second Livre de differens trophées, *mid 18th century. 3) Late 18th century Coade stone *urn, Wimpole Hall, Cambridgeshire.*

the flute and lyre. In schemes of decoration representing the *Senses, hearing is sometimes depicted by the playing of music. The academic approach to *classicism of the late 18th and early 19th centuries resulted in a more systematic cataloguing of ancient instruments, as shown by those illustrated in T.*Hope's *Costume of the Ancients.*

In ecclesiastical schemes, *angel musicians are frequent, but the instruments rarely appear on their own.

Often combined with the *Muses, *Comedy and Tragedy masks or personifications of the *Liberal Arts, musical themes aptly decorate musical instruments (especially keyboard) as well as music stands, music rooms, ballrooms, concert halls, opera houses and theatres. By the late 19th century, however, classical figures representing music were replaced by likenesses of famous composers, as on the tiled panels at the Criterion Theatre, London.

mutule. Small *bracket or block used as a repeating motif and supporting the *cornice of the Doric *Order (commemorating the beam ends of the wooden temple).

myrtle. Evergreen shrub sometimes confused with the *olive because of the similar appearance of the leaves. One of the attributes of *Venus and the three *Graces, it was adopted in the Renaissance as a symbol of everlasting *love. It also signifies marital fidelity.

nailhead. Small, pyramid-form used in relief as a repeating motif in a similar manner to *dogtooth ornament. A popular *Romanesque and early *Gothic enrichment, it also appeared in 18th and 19th century *Neo-Norman stonework.

From the 16th century decorative nailheads were sometimes used to attach upholstery to furniture, and might be multiplied for ornamental effect, particularly on 17th and 18th century furniture. *See also* prismatic ornament.

naturalistic ornament tends to appear after periods of intensely stylised ornament. Roman and *Byzantine work made greater use of naturalism than the *Romanesque did. However the Romanesque period was followed by the early *Gothic period (from the late 12th century), when craftsmen in stone, metal and illumination produced bravura work demonstrating their ability to recreate objects, motifs and events in a highly literal form.

Decorative carving and illumination of extraordinary naturalism appeared in Gothic buildings and manuscripts first in France and then in Germany and England, mainly in monastic centres, where the contemplative life of the closed orders allowed careful study of nature. Gradually, misrepresentation promulgated by the *bestiaries and *herbals was replaced by accurate observation of plants and animals and sometimes of scenes of contemporary life (*see* husbandry). *Crockets, *capitals and *friezes were decorated with carefully observed and recognisable plants, animals and birds. At Rheims Cathedral in northern France the capitals are carved with buttercups, wild and cultivated *grapevines, *roses, *ivy, rue, wild strawberries, wallflowers, thistles and branches of *olive, poplar, maple, elm, *laurel, pear, chestnut and *oak. Similar work appears in Germany at Nuremberg, and in England at Southwell Minster, Nottinghamshire and St Frideswide in Oxford. Naturalistic decoration remained important in the English *Decorated Gothic and later European Gothic styles, and in northern Europe it was still used even after the arrival of *Renaissance ornament.

*Mannerist artists such as the French potter Bernard Palissy (c.1510-90) and the German goldsmith Wenzel Jamnitzer (1508-85) produced *grotto ornament with lizards, snakes, frogs and weeds (Jamnitzer even cast them in metal from life). English embroiderers strewed *insects and flowers on Elizabethan clothes.

When not bound by strict *classical fashions, the decorative artist would automatically turn to nature for inspiration, and in any case classical forms often failed to provide the desired prototypes for decoration of porcelain, silver, textiles and other media.

In the mid 19th century, a more literal, 'scientific' naturalism appeared, helped by new techniques such as electrotyping which could exactly reproduce natural forms. Richard Redgrave described it in his *Report of the Juries of the Great Exhibition*: 'There has arisen a new species of ornament of the most objectionable kind . . . This may be called the natural or merely imitative style . . . Thus we have metal *imitations* of plant forms with an attempt to make them a strict resemblance, forgetting that natural subjects are rendered into ornaments by subordinating the details to the general idea, and that the endeavour ought to be to seize the simplest expression of a thing rather than to imitate it . . . Ormulu stems and leaves bear porcelain flowers painted to imitate nature, and candles are made to rise out of tulips and china asters, while gas jets gush forth from opal arums . . . enormous wreaths of flowers, fish, game, fruits etc. imitated *à merveil*, dangle round sideboards, beds and picture frames . . . In fabrics where flatness would seem most essential, this imitativeness is often carried to the greatest excess; the carpets are ornamented with waterlilies floating on their natural bed . . . ' In addition scientific and educational advances led to an expectation that decorators and designers would depict nature with absolute accuracy; nowhere is this more evident than in the ornament applied to institutions built to further the study of natural history, like museums and university buildings such as the Natural History Museum, London (1873-81), which is ornamented with all manner of creatures; the keeper's quarters are decorated with the domestic cat. O.*Jones concluded the *Grammar of Ornament* with 'Leaves and Flowers from Nature' offering naturalism as an alternative to *eclecticism and *Historicism, and A.W.N.*Pugin stated in *Floriated Ornament* (1849) that 'the natural outlines of leaves, flowers etc. must be more beautiful than any invention of man.'

naval decoration. *See* marine decoration.

naval crown. *See* crown.

nebule, nebulé or **nebuly** (Latin, *nebula*, cloud). Rounded zigzag ornament (*see* chevron) used on stone

*naturalistic ornament. 1) Stone *frieze in Clock Court, Hampton Court Palace, Surrey, improvements by Sir Christopher Wren, 1689-94. 2) Italian porcelain dish made at Nove, c.1820.*

*mouldings on the exterior of *Anglo-Saxon buildings, and later in wood, brick, plaster, etc.

nef (French, ship). An impressive centrepiece in the form of a fully-rigged ship was a popular subject for late Gothic goldsmiths in France and Germany; often the ship was a salt, an important piece of tableware that marked the place of the host at table. By the 16th century, the form was used in a variety of ways: Venetian glassblowers produced nef ewers and German goldsmiths used the nef as the case for a clock. In 1754, Sèvres designer Jean-Claude Duplessis (d 1774) revived the form for one of the manufactory's most prestigious vases, a *pot-pourri* vase in the form of a *vaisseau à mât*. Nefs also appeared as elaborate porcelain and silver tureens and as fountains. Copies of medieval nefs were made in the 19th century across Europe.

Neo-classicism. The mid 18th century return to the repertoire of *Graeco-Roman classicism both in the loosest sense, as in the *Adam style, and in the strictest sense, as in the *Greek Revival. It was, in part, a reaction against the excesses of the *Rococo. A good guide to the progress of the new enthusiasm is offered by the development of the Society of Dilettanti, founded in London (1732) for those gentlemen who had

Neo-classicism. 1) The Casino, Marino, Dublin, by W.*Chambers, 1758 onwards. 2) Incised ornament, Sir John Soane Museum, Lincoln's Inn Fields, London, 1812 onwards.

Neo-classicism. English jasper ware vases, 'Sacrifice to Ceres' and 'Chariot of Venus', made by Wedgwood, 1790.

undertaken the Grand Tour (of the great classical sites of Europe). According to rules established in 1734, members could propose only the names of those they had met in Italy; by 1747 Avignon had been added and in 1764 the category extended to the 'Classic Ground' (Greece). The Society was not only a meeting place for artists and patrons but also sponsored the publication of several important volumes on architecture and antiquities, and visits to specific sites in Greece and Asia Minor. The toast of the Society was to 'Grecian Taste and Roman Spirit', heralding the growing acceptance of Greek models.

Not all those who subscribed to Neo-classical ideals were to favour Greece, however: W.*Chambers fulminated at length against what he termed 'the *gusto greco*'. An enormous body of published material, based on archaeological investigation at a variety of classical sites (especially those at *Pompeii and *Herculaneum), and on the catalogued collections of travellers and scholars, provided the basis for Neo-classical ornament. Notable French contributions included the theoretical writings in the mid-century of C.-N.*Cochin the Younger and the Abbé Laugier (1713-69)) and the architectural masterpiece of Jacques-Germain

Soufflot (1713-80), the Panthéon in Paris (built 1757 onwards). Classical travel and publications such as those by J.D.*Le Roy and M.J. Peyre (1730-85) began to shift the emphasis of French Neo-classicism towards the Greek. *Précis et leçons d'architecture* (1802-09) by the rationalist J.N.L. Durand led to a particularly stark form of classicism. In Germany, where a translation of Durand's work appeared, the Neo-classical arrived later and was typified by the work of K.F.*Schinkel, who was a whole-hearted Greek Revivalist. The *Empire style, which embraced a Roman style of ornament, was to a considerable extent a reaction against this, and heralded a renewed interest in the ornamentation of both exteriors and interiors. Extensive libraries such as that of T.*Hope give an indication of the range of accessible material known internationally, which allowed designers to draw upon source material without necessarily being familiar with ancient sites or original artefacts.

Neo-classicism reintroduced a distinct range of classical ornamental motifs including the *anthemion, *palmette, *vase or *urn, mythical creatures such as the *sphinx and *griffin, formal patterns such as *scrolling foliage and *candelabra forms, *key patterns and a range of *moulding enrichments taken from the *capitals, *entablatures and bases of the various *Orders. This range of decoration was also applied in the decorative arts, for example, on the now simplified rectangular lines of furniture; antique shapes such as vases and urns now predominated in ceramic and metalwork design.

A loose interpretation of Neo-classicism provided the basis for the French *Louis XVI style and the *Style Etrusque. However, Sir John Soane (1753-1837) gave a typical Neo-classicist's view of ornament in the introduction to his *Plans, Elevations and Sections of Buildings* *erected in the Counties of Norfolk, Suffolk etc* (1788). He wrote of 'the absurdities daily intruded on us for French refinement . . . Ornaments are to be cautiously introduced . . . used as tend to shew the definition of the edifice, as assist in determining its character and for the choice of which the architect can assign satisfactory reasons.'

Neo-classicism in America followed the European model, slightly belatedly. It fell into two periods, the *Federal style and the Greek Revival. The two are sometimes hard to differentiate, and American Neo-classicism in general is quite varied and individualistic, according to the preferences of the architects concerned. Thomas Jefferson (1743-1826) had *Palladian models in mind when designing Monticello (1769) in Virginia. Jefferson and B.H. Latrobe (1764-1820) were responsible for the design of the Virginia State Capitol (1785-96) in a sternly Roman vein which was to be the model for a number of such buildings, including the Capitol in Washington. Jefferson's interest was in French Neo-classicism and he borrowed from the *pattern books he owned, whilst Latrobe, an Englishman, who had been educated in Germany and knew France and Italy well, provided first-hand experience of European models. The architect Charles Bulfinch (1763-1844) and woodcarver Samuel McIntire followed European patterns closely. Subsequent phases of Neo-classicism in America, however, were much more independent and Latrobe's work, for example, follows the spirit of the designs of Claude-Nicolas Ledoux (1736-1806) rather than imitating them directly. The Greek Revival was followed by the *Picturesque, *Historicism and *eclecticism, as American architects and designers increasingly borrowed from all sources and periods.

Neo-Georgian. A revival of certain elements of the *classical styles in *Georgian domestic architecture. It developed as a more sophisticated version of the *Queen Anne Revival with references to the French *Louis Revivals. In America the style was more wholeheartedly adopted, as *Colonial Revival. In Britain and the Dominions, Neo-Georgian was in evidence from the last two decades of the Victorian era but achieved maximum popularity in the early 1900s. There were variants until the late 1930s in the work of designers such as Oliver Hill (1887-1968), who embraced other styles too, but perfectly interpreted a light Adam style interior vocabulary when it seemed appropriate.

Neo-Georgian has remained a popular style for suburban housing developments, despite often illiterate use of classical detail or ornamental motifs. The recent introduction of vast ranges of polystyrene *mouldings has facilitated the use of ornament, and the debasing of the style in both America and Britain has tended to give the term Neo-Georgian a distinctly pejorative ring.

Neo-Manueline. *See* Manueline.

Neo-Norman. Widely used, if historically inaccurate, term describing the revival of both *Anglo-Saxon and *Romanesque forms and ornament. The first

Neo-Norman. St George's Congregational Church, Thornton Hough, Cheshire, architect J. Lomax-Simpson, 1906-07.

work in this style was the rebuilding by S.P. Cockerell of Tickencote Church in Rutland (now Leicestershire), which demonstrates a spirit of *Picturesque romanticism informed by late 18th century antiquarianism. The style was mainly applied to church restorations, which were often virtual reconstructions, and the building of a handful of full-scale castles, such as Penrhyn or Arundel, in which the full repertoire of Romanesque forms and motifs was called upon: stubby *arcading, simple *geometric ornament such as *chevron, heavy columns, round-headed *arches and *net vaults. The style was also adopted, though infrequently, in Ireland and in America, where S.*Sloan, author of a book describing various *Historicist styles of architecture, included an example in Neo-Norman style.

Neptune. The chief Roman sea god, whose Greek counterpart was Poseidon. He rides a shell-shaped chariot drawn by *hippocamps; his attributes are a trident to cleave rocks and stir the waters, and *dolphins, symbolic of his power to calm the sea. He may be accompanied by *tritons and *nereids, and is often crowned to indicate his dominion over the waters. A

*Neptune. Picture frame from T.*Chippendale's Director, 1762 edition.*

central motif in *marine ornament, the figure is a frequent choice for the ornamentation of fountains, salt cellars, public baths, etc. The *mask of Neptune is often applied to *keystones of waterside or mercantile buildings.

Despite his appearance in ornament as the main sea god, Neptune, strictly speaking, ruled only the Mediterranean. Oceanus ruled the water that was believed to encircle the earth and therefore became associated with the Atlantic Ocean.

nereids. Sea nymphs, one of the categories of nymphs of classical mythology, who were said to be daughters of Nereus, the Old Man of the Sea. They sometimes appear in *marine decoration as the attendants of *Neptune and his wife Amphitrite – also a nereid, or as the female counterparts of *tritons, with whom they share certain attributes: oars, conch shells and *hippocamps.

Netherlands Grotesque. A particularly bizarre style of *grotesques combined with *strapwork that was produced by mid 16th century *Flemish Mannerist designers, such as C.*Bos, C.*Floris and H.*Vredeman de Vries. A characteristic feature of the style is strapwork entrapping figures rather than supporting them. Plasterwork, metalwork and woodcarving in the Netherlands, Belgium, Scandinavia and England were decorated in this style. The *espagnolette, which became a popular motif in 18th century French decoration, first appeared in Netherlands Grotesque ornament.

net vault. Vault with ribs that form *lozenge-shaped compartments. A northern European development of net vaulting of much greater elaboration is found in late 15th century *Flamboyant Gothic buildings.

Neufforge, Jean-François (1714-91). French architect, sculptor, engraver and prolific designer, who worked in Paris. His *Recueil Elémentaire d'architecture*, which appeared in eight volumes between 1757 and 1768 and contained a total of 900 plates, demonstrates a clear move away from the *Rococo and towards *Neoclassicism. The publication was influential, setting the tone for the development of the *Louis XVI style. Each volume contained interior and exterior architectural details as well as furniture designs for sofas,

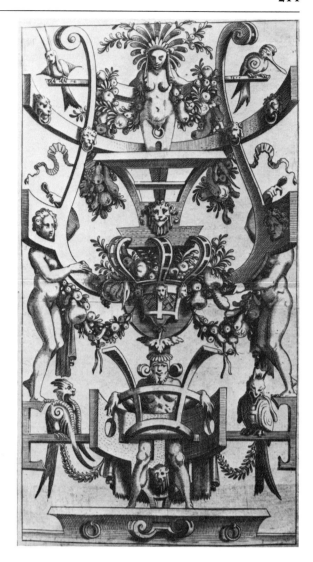

*Netherlands Grotesque. Design for panel of grotesque ornament by C.*Bos, c.1550.*

Jean-François Neufforge. 'Canapé, Sopha or Lit de repos' from his Recueil Elémentaire d'architecture, 1757-68.

cupboards, clocks, consoles, commodes, etc. In 1772, Neufforge produced a supplement of metalwork designs: grilles, doors, balconies. The interior designs are marked by cumbersome rectilinear forms incorporating heavy *mouldings, particularly *guilloche, *gadrooning, *coin moulding and *egg and dart. Exterior designs have an equally heavy emphasis with varieties of *rustication. Neufforge included many circular forms, notably *rosettes and *pateras, thick *swags of drapery and *festoons of tightly packed leaves. Robert Adam (*see* Adam style) borrowed some of Neufforge's details.

niche (Italian, *nicchio*, shell). Semi-circular arched recess, a favourite architectural motif in *Graeco-Roman classicism, often with a *scallop shell head, and originally built to contain a statue, fountain, etc. It appears, for instance, in profusion in the temple at Baalbec (2nd and 3rd century AD). As a small-scale motif, it ornamented sarcophagi, where it often contained figures and scenes behind a screen of *colonnettes. Use of the niche continued into early Christian and *Byzantine ornament, appearing in ecclesiastical metalwork as well as on funerary objects and in architecture. The *Gothic niche, with its pointed head, used in all aspects of ecclesiastical architecture, furnishing and artefacts, was elaborated with a profusion of detail, on canopies and in *tabernacle work. The plainer treatment of the niche in the *Romanesque and *Lombardic periods was revived in the *Renaissance, when the round-headed niche was used more subtly, for example, alternating with fenestration, as in Donato Bramante's Tempietto in Rome (1502). From the late 17th century, the niche was used in *Neo-classical style screens or garden walls, often containing an *urn, *vase, statue or bust. During this period, the shell-headed niche was also widely adopted in interior woodwork, used as a corner cupboard or even as a seat. *See also* aedicule.

Nicholson, Peter (1765-1844) and Michael Angelo (1796-1842). Father and son, authors of innumerable *pattern books and technical manuals which were influential during the 19th century when historical styles, still loosely *classicist, were being translated into the increasingly complex language and techniques of the age. The work for which they are mainly known is a joint effort, *The Practical Cabinet Maker, Upholsterer*

*niche. 1) 15th century apse, Duomo, Florence, Italy. 2) Ionic and Corinthian niches or buffets from B.*Langley's The City and Country Builder's and Workman's Treasury of Designs, 1740.*

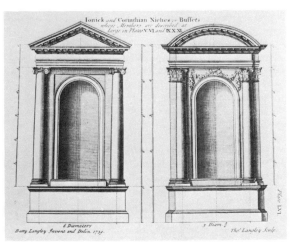

and Complete Decorator (1826), which contains mainly *Greek Revival designs.

Nieuhof, Jan (1618-72). Dutch traveller and writer, whose account of the Dutch Embassy to the Emperor of China in Peking, *Atlas Chinensis*, was an important early source for *chinoiserie. The engravings, by Wenceslaus Hollar and others, illustrated Chinese figures and buildings such as temples and *pagodas which were used as patterns for japanning, and on gold and ceramic objects. It was first published in Amsterdam in 1665 (later editions, 1670, 1673); it appeared in England in 1669 and was translated into several languages.

Jan Nieuhof. Chinese Men from Atlas Chinensis, *1665.*

night is usually personified by a veiled female figure, the veil sometimes scattered with stars. Sometimes the figure holds two children, one black (death), the other white (sleep). Occasionally in the *Renaissance the children were replaced by black and white rats, symbolising the destructive aspect of time passing. A more elaborate image of night shows a masked woman, intended as a symbol of the deceit and vice that occur under cover of darkness.

*Personifications of day and night were popular in the Italian Renaissance. Michelangelo's figures on the tomb of Lorenzo di Medici in Florence (begun 1520) were well-known examples, which led to the imagery being associated with funerary monuments. In the late 18th and early 19th centuries there was a resurgence of interest in the theme fuelled particularly by the Danish *Neo-classical sculptor Berthel Thorvaldsen (1768-1844), who produced plaques of Day and

night. Plaque after B. Thorvaldsen on the tester of a state bed exhibited by Faudel & Phillips at the Great Exhibition, London, 1851.

Night which were manufactured in plaster and had a considerable vogue, even extending to Berlin woolwork in the mid 19th century. Day was represented by a female figure bearing flower garlands with, on her shoulders, a boy carrying a flaming torch; Night was a melancholic female figure with two small boys on her shoulders (Sleep and Death) and an owl in the distance.

The theme of night figures in the decoration of cradles, beds and bedrooms and, together with representations of day, may ornament clocks. The motifs associated with it (sometimes overlapping with those for *death and *time) include the *crescent moon (attribute of Diana – goddess of the *moon), *owl, black wings, *poppies, *masks and the extinguished flame (an inverted *torch).

Nilson, Johann-Esaias (1721-88). German painter and engraver, who worked in Augsburg and Nuremberg, and was one of the principal exponents of the German *Rococo. Most of his ornament, produced during the 1750s, was based around the *rocaille *cartouche and such themes as the *Seasons, science, agriculture, *music, etc., although he engraved a few *chinoiserie designs. Much of his work was used for German porcelain decoration, e.g. at Ansbach and Kiel.

nipt-diamond-waies. *Diaper effect on glassware (e.g. drinking glasses, bowls, jugs) devised by the English glassmaker George Ravenscroft (1618-81) in the 1670s, whereby glass strands were either applied or mould-blown and pincered together to form diamond shapes on the surface of the glass.

Norden, F.L. (1708-42). The first European to travel far up the Nile, whose account was illustrated by engravings which were to be important sources in the vogue for *Egyptian decoration. His findings were published from 1741, but most fully as Travels in Egypt and Nubia (2 vols, 1757).

Norman. Frequently used but misleading name for English and northern French *Romanesque architecture.

Norman, John (1748-1817). Englishman who compiled the Town and Country Builder's Assistant (Boston, 1786), the second architectural *pattern book to be published in America, which included examples from the work of A.*Swan, W.*Pain and I.*Ware.

Normand, Charles Pierre Joseph (1765-1840). French architect and prolific designer and engraver. He was a member of the French Academy in Rome until it closed at the outset of the French Revolution. His best known work is the Nouveau Parallèle des Ordres d'Architecture des Grecs, des Romains et des Auteurs Modernes (Paris, 1819, 1825, 1828, 1852). It was published in London in 1829 in a translation by A.C.*Pugin with two additional plates; a German edition was published in Potsdam in 1830. In a single volume, Normand illustrated *Graeco-Roman classical architecture and details as well as the work of A.*Palladio, V.*Scamozzi,

G.B. da *Vignola, P.*de l'Orme and Jean Goujon (c.1510-68). It was only by study of this large selection of renderings of the classical, commented Pugin, and 'by learning to compare and to analyse them [that the architect] will exercise his judgment and mature his taste, discover how to modify and adapt.' Normand's main works on style and ornament were Nouveau Recueil en divers genres d'ornemens et autres objets propres à la décoration (Paris, 1803, 1828), a selection of designs for *vases, panels, bas-relief, furniture, *friezes etc., in the *Empire style of C.*Percier and P. Fontaine; Normand engraved the plates for their Recueil de décorations intérieurs (1801). His Recueil Varié de plans et de façades (Paris, 1815), suggested various motifs for town and country houses and public buildings. With P.N.*Beauvallet, he published Fragmens d'ornemens dans le style antique (Paris, 1820), and finally in his unchanging and by now rather outdated Empire style, Le Guide de l'ornemaniste ou de l'ornement (Paris, 1826), in which he pointed out that the architectural ornament it offered could easily be adapted for use on furniture.

Norse. See Viking.

nulling. See gadrooning.

nymph. In Greek mythology, nymphs were lower rank female divinities representing various aspects of nature: *nereids were the nymphs of the sea; naiads – the nymphs of fresh water (often appearing in *riparine ornament); dryads – tree nymphs; oreades – the nymphs of mountains and grottoes. Depicted as beautiful, naked or lightly clad young women, they were used in ornament relating to their particular sphere of nature. Specific nymphs from mythology were sometimes used: Amalthea, who nursed the infant Zeus with goat's milk, was depicted in the decoration of Marie Antoinette's dairy at Versailles. The companions of Diana were nymphs and so they sometimes appear in decorative schemes featuring the *moon goddess.

In the 18th and early 19th centuries, dancing maidens, dressed in flowing and revealing draperies and generally described as nymphs, were a frequent ornament in their own right. They often derived from classical originals, usually in reliefs or wall paintings, e.g. the famous Roman relief once at the Villa Borghese in Rome recorded by the engraver P.S.*Bartoli in Admiranda Romanorum Antiquitatum (1693), which had dancers linking hands in a chain, and later provided the inspiration for Wedgwood's most popular relief decoration, the Dancing Hours, modelled by John Flaxman in 1778. Such figures would often be used in threes (sometimes an allusion to the Three *Graces) to encircle the stems of tazze, *urns, candelabra, etc. See also siren.

oak. According to classical myth, the oak was sacred to Jupiter. It was also considered sacred by the Druids. In Roman society, oak leaves, like *laurel leaves, were bound into *wreaths, and presented in recognition of civic virtue, notably for the saving of a life. In *Renaissance and, later, *Neo-classical decoration, oak leaves appear in wreaths and *pulvinated friezes, often scattered with *acorns.

A common tree across Europe, the oak, its branches, leaves and acorns all appear in *naturalistic decoration, particularly the *Gothic. During the Renaissance, the oak was chosen as the *impresa of the powerful Della Rovere family who lived in Rome (Italian, *rovere*, oak) and it thus appears on much of the work commissioned by the popes of that family, Julius II (1443-1513) and Sixtus IV (1414-84), as well as on *maiolica* from Urbino and Castel Durante where the factories were patronised by the family; the arrangement of leaves and acorns on this porcelain is sometimes called cerquate.

The oak tree or its leaves may imply steadfastness when ornamenting buildings of authority or uniforms. In *marine contexts, as on uniforms of the British navy, oak may also allude to the timber from which ships were once made.

obelisk. First erected during the Egyptian Middle Kingdom (2130-1580 BC), obelisks were the sacred symbol of the sun god of Heliopolis and usually stood in pairs at temple entrances, their four sides incised with *hieroglyphics. They were a source of fascination and speculation in Europe for centuries: the Roman Emperors brought at least twelve obelisks to Rome, some of which survived and were still much admired in the *Renaissance. Antonio Pisanello's medal of

*obelisk. 1) From *Hypnerotomachia Polyphili, 1499. 2) Oude Handboog Huis, Grote Markt, Antwerp, Belgium, 1582. 3) Obelisk of Marcus Aurelius from J.*Fischer von Erlach's Entwurff einer historischen Architektur, 1721. 4) Mannerist *pediment, Grtba Palace, Prague, c.1631.*

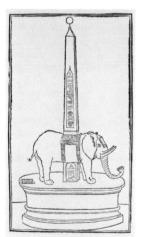

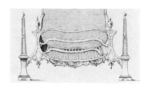

*obelisk. 1) Imaginary scene with ruins by V.*Solis, mid 16th century.
2) Oak newel post, Chastleton House, Oxfordshire, 1602 onwards.
3) Stove grate from T.*Chippendale's Director, 1762 edition.*

John Paleologus (1438-39) shows obelisks in the background. Antonio Aveline Filarete (c.1400-69), in his *Trattato d'architettura* (written 1461-64, but not published until the 19th century), deals at some length with the subject. During the 1580s, obelisks were re-erected in several Roman squares. By the end of the 16th century, they had become immensely popular as *finial ornament, sometimes pierced or elaborated, and the fashion lasted into the mid 17th century. Detailed engravings of obelisks were published by A.*Kircher in *Obeliscus Pamphilius* (3 vols, Rome, 1650) and *Oedipus Aegyptiacus* (Rome, 1652, 1653, 1654). Used, for example, on *Dutch gables, or combined with *balustrading, they were particularly predominant in German architecture and figured frequently in contemporary *Mannerist *pattern books such as those of W.*Dietterlin. Obelisks were also popular in the Netherlands and Britain, although there was no attempt to decorate the sides with copies of hieroglyphics, so the form was often simply given a ball top and mounted on scrolled bracket feet. It also appeared on silver standing cups (known as steeple cups) echoing current vogues in architecture. During the 18th century, the free-standing obelisk appeared as a garden ornament in landscaped grounds and parks. The earliest English example was probably that erected by the architect Nicholas Hawksmoor (1661-1736) in the marketplace at Ripon, Yorkshire. These obelisks, however, tended to be placed on substantial pedestals in the manner of those in Rome and were therefore often considered more Roman than Egyptian. By the early 19th century, knowledge of Egypt was more widespread and the obelisk was used in its original pedestal-free form. Although they had had no place in funerary ornament in ancient Egypt, by the end of the 18th century they had become popular tomb or memorial motifs in

Europe, possibly because of knowledge of the Egyptian cult of death.

oculus. A small round window, sometimes specifically one in the top of a dome.

oeil de boeuf (French, bull's eye). A circular or oval window or opening, often punctuated by four *keystone forms. It may also have decorative glazing bars. A feature of French 17th century architecture, often piercing the attic or a mansard roofline, it reappeared in the 19th century revival of the *French Second Empire style.

oeil de boeuf. 1) Attic window from early 18th century palace, Potsdam, East Germany. 2) Bury St Edmunds Railway Station, Suffolk, 1847.

oeil de perdrix (French, partridge eye). Ground *diaper pattern devised for French porcelain made at the Vincennes and Sèvres factories in the 1750s. It consists of small dotted circles, often gold, enclosing white on a blue and turquoise background. Great admiration for Sèvres porcelain in mid 19th century Britain led to the imitation of the pattern on Coalport and Minton ceramics and on opaque blue Bristol glass.

oeillets. In medieval architecture, pierced circular apertures in *battlements or fortifications, believed to have been for the firing of missiles. Oeillets were revived for purely decorative use in the *Castle style.

ogee. Combination of a concave and convex line, producing a serpentine shape, either as a *moulding (an S form in cross section) or as an elaborated pointed arch. It is particularly characteristic of the *Venetian Gothic Revival, *Gothick and *Gothic Revival styles, although ogee forms appeared in textiles from the 12th century. In the 18th century the word was some-

ogee. Early 19th century Picturesque cottage, Marford, Clwyd.

times written as o--g. A nodding ogee is an arch in which the head projects. *See also* cyma recta/reversa; keel moulding.

Old English. 19th century term coined to describe the revival of vernacular forms in an architectural style which ran concurrently with the *Queen Anne Revival. It reflected an interest in the 1860s in traditional architecture and marked the beginnings of concern about restoration and preservation. The architectural ornament of this style, one of the currents within the *Arts and Crafts movement, was based on traditional forms: patterned tile hanging, leaded windows and simple embellishments of rubbed or cut brick or terracotta. The inspiration for the style came from the buildings of Kent, Surrey and Sussex; it was considered an appropriate rural equivalent of the urban Queen Anne style. Richard Norman Shaw (1831-1912) and William Eden Nesfield (1835-88) were notable designers in the Old English manner. In the 1880s and 1890s the distinction between Old English and Queen Anne styles became less marked and a new term, Free Style, began to be used. In America, the *Colonial Revival had much in common with Old English and followed a similar path towards a more inventive application of its stylistic elements in what is now known as *Shingle style.

Old English pattern. Plain rounded ends to spoons and forks, a later development (starting in the 1770s) of *Hanoverian pattern. The spoon end is turned in the opposite direction to the spoon bowl, so that the spoon is laid on the table bowl upwards – as with modern spoons. The shape remained popular in the 19th century and has been revived during the 20th century.

Variations include Old English Bead (popular in the 1780s and the late 19th century), which has a rim of *beading around the handle; Old English Thread (late 18th century) is edged with a thin line; Featheredge (late 18th century) is engraved with a feathery effect resembling miniature *gadrooning. Old English Shell (1780s and Victorian) has a scallop shell at top of the handle.

A variation of Old English pattern called Admiralty, in which handles were engraved with a crown and anchor, was produced during the first half of the 19th century for the Royal Navy.

Old French style. Early 19th century term for *Rococo Revival.

Oleaginous style. *See* Auricular style.

olive. Easily confused, in its decorative form, with the *laurel or bay, and indistinguishable from the *myrtle. The olive was sacred to the Roman goddess *Minerva (and her Greek equivalent, Athena). A crown of olive was the highest award at the Olympic games, as a symbol of immortality, fruitfulness and plenty; the leaf itself signified renewal of life. As a Mediterranean species, it is more common in the ornament of countries in that area than in northern Europe where the *oak is often used in its place. In *Christian iconography an olive branch and a *dove (an allusion to the Bible story of Noah), symbolises peace.

Onslow pattern. On spoon and fork handles, a scrolled end with two outward turning *volutes. It appeared on British silver, c.1760, and was used throughout the *Regency period. A pattern known as Albany or Queen Anne, which is based on Onslow, appeared in the mid 1880s.

opaque twist. *See latticinio.*

open pediment on English mid 18th century carved wooden doorcase.

open pediment. *Pediment with a break at the apex of the triangle, whereas a *broken pediment has a break in the base: the two are often confused. A typically *Baroque device transforming a simple, *classical shape into a highly ornamental form, it appeared in many variations often with much elaboration. *See also* scrolled pediment.

Oppenord(t), Gilles-Marie (1672-1742). Architect and prolific designer who settled in Paris in 1698. He had studied in Rome, where he had been influenced by the Italian *Baroque (particularly the work of Francesco Borromini) and by the grottoes in Italian gardens. Oppenord worked on the design of interiors and was under the patronage of the Duc d'Orléans, Regent of France from 1715 to 1723. His work was in the early *Rococo or *Régence style, although a few of his *cartouche designs moved towards the *genre pittoresque.* Many of Oppenord's designs did not appear until after his death, when they were engraved and published by J.G. Huquier. His work covered a wide range of interior detail: *mouldings, panels, chimneypieces, *pilasters, *friezes, furniture, clocks and cartouches, and appeared in three series as advertised in the journal, *Mercure de France: Livre de différents morceaux* known as *Le Moyen Oppenord* (1737-38), *Livre de fragments d'architecture* known as *Le Petit Oppenord* (1742-48), and *Oeuvres* known as *Le Grand Oppenord* (1748-51). Some of the designs were republished in the series *L'Art Décoratif appliqué à l'art industriel* in 1888, the time of the *Rococo Revival in France.

orchid leaf or **octopus leaf.** Fleshy leaf form with rounded lobes in *Romanesque architecture.

Orders. The Orders constitute the basis of *classical architecture. Each Order consists of a *column supporting an *entablature, with a *capital, an *abacus and base, sometimes including a *pedestal or *plinth. *Vitruvius described three Orders, Doric, Ionic and Corinthian, and mentioned a fourth, the Tuscan. He described them in terms of human characteristics: male and female, sturdy or tall, etc., thus introducing a frame of reference that was interpreted with great licence by late 16th century and early 17th century designers, culminating in the work of, for example, W. *Dieterlin. In the 15th century, L.B.*Alberti identified and codified the five Orders: Doric, Ionic, Corinthian, Tuscan, and a newcomer, the Composite, although it was S.*Serlio who first illustrated them, in 1537.

The Doric Order was associated with mainland temples and those in the west of the country in 6th century Greece. The Greek version of the Order, which was quite different to the Roman variant, had no base, and both its proportions and ornament (on both capital and entablature) are much more circumscribed, giving a purer effect overall. Nevertheless, within the Greek Doric there was a development over a period until an exampl such as the Temple of Zeus at Olympia of c.460 BC perfected the type. Vitruvius considered the Doric to be a 'male' Order, and this view persisted. V.*Scamozzi renamed it the Herculean Order. The 17th century commentator Sir Henry Wotton described it as follows: 'The *Dorique Order* is the grandest that hath beene received into civill use . . . a little trimmer than the *Tuscan* . . . save a sober garnishment now and then of *lions' heads* in the *Cornice* and of Triglyphs and Metopes alwayes in the frize . . . rarely, chaneled and a little light sculpture about the . . . *Necke* under the *Capitall'.* More refined than the

*Orders. From S.*Serlio's* Architettura, 1619 edition.*

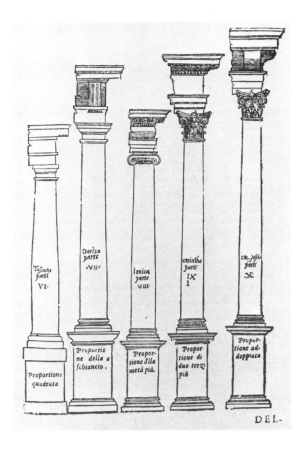

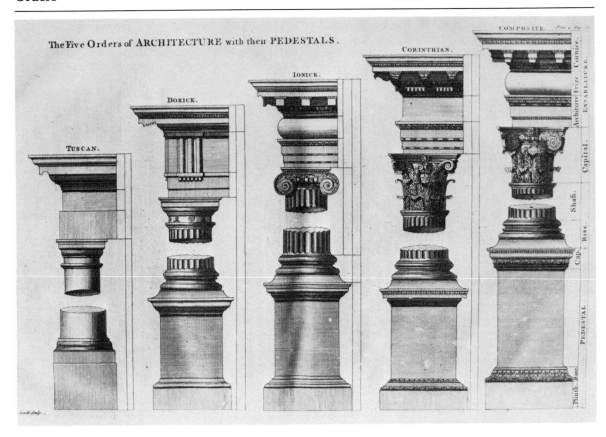

Orders. The five Orders with their *pedestals from I.*Ware's A Complete Body of Architecture, 1756.

Tuscan, the Doric was nevertheless seen as the tough Order, suitable for what Sir John Summerson has termed 'extroverted male saints' or military structures. In addition to the characteristics above, the Doric Order introduced *mutules and *guttae and a capital with a simple cushion-like abacus. It was little used in the Renaissance; rare examples such as G.B. da *Vignola's Palazzo Farnese at Caprarola were borrowed by I.*Jones for his work at Greenwich and published by *pattern book authors such as G.*Edwards and M.*Darly. A Doric column used for the Flamborough Head lighthouse by Samuel Wyatt in 1806 was perhaps the ultimate development of a single column form. The late 18th and 19th century application of the Doric was largely the Greek version of the Order, much purer and quite different to the Roman variant.

The Ionic Order was the Order adopted in eastern parts of 6th century Greece (the Doric being used elsewhere). In its developed, Roman form, its distinguishing features are a capital formed of *volutes and *dentils on the *cornice. (A capital with crude, bolster-like volutes and no additional *mouldings is known as an Aeolic capital.) Its elegance, according to Vitruvius, gave it 'feminine' characteristics, and Sir Henry Wotton described it as follows: '[it] doth represent a kinde of Feminine slendernesse . . . not like a light Housewife, but in a decent dressing, hath much of the *Matrone* . . . Best knowne by his trimmings,

for the bodie of this *Columne* is perpetually chaneled, like a thicke plighted Gowne. The *Capitall* dressed on each side, not much unlike womens Wires, in a spirall wreathing, which they call the *Ionian Voluta*. The *Cornice* indented. The *Frize* swelling like a pillow; And therefore by Vitruvius, not unelegantly tearmed *Pulvinata*.' Scamozzi described the Ionic Order as 'a medium between the strong and the rich' (i.e. the Doric and the Corinthian). Edwards and Darly, reflecting well-established 18th century practice, mention that the Order 'is generally employ'd in Halls of Justice, in Colleges, Librarys or in the kind of Structures that have any relation to Arts, Letters, etc. It may be employed with propriety in the Appartments alotted to the Ladies or in places consecrated to Peace, Tranquillity etc.' In a strictly classical treatment of buildings of more than one storey, the Ionic, 'adorning the second Story', is placed above the Doric, which is used for ground floors. Rationalist theorists of the Orders deduced that the Ionic represented the adorned tree trunk, and that the Ionic volute derived from the ram's horns used to ornament temples.

The Corinthian Order, last comer in the pantheon of the three original Greek Orders, was first adopted in the late 5th century BC. It is, however, the heavily foliate Roman example that has provided the prototype for the Corinthian capital in classical revivals: it consists of *acanthus leaves, arranged in two rows, with the stalks (*caulicoli) also emphasised. Though it was seen by Vitruvius and his adherents as a 'virginal' Order, attitudes had changed sufficiently by the 17th century for Sir Henry Wotton to observe that the

Corinthian is 'laciviously decked like a Curtezane' with 'In the *Cornice* both *Dentelli* and *Modiglioni*. The *Frize*, adorned with all kinds of *Figures* and various Compartments at Pleasure. The *Capitall*, cut into the beautifullest leafe, that Nature doth yeeld . . . As *Plainenesse* did Charactarize the *Tuscan*, so must *Delicacie* and *Varietie* the *Corinthian* Pillar, besides the height of his Ranke.' The ornamental nature of the Order was emphasised by the elaboration of the entablature with a variety of mouldings, and it was favoured for small-scale uses ranging from the *colonnettes on Early Christian sarcophagi to 17th and 18th century candlesticks. In I.*Ware's words, this 'is the Order to which recourse is usually had for giving the utmost elegance to a building. It is remarkable that the ruins of *Palmyra* are all *Corinthian* except two . . .'

The Tuscan Order is the most basic of the five Roman Orders, a stubby column without ornamentation, derived from an ancient Etruscan temple. Sir Henry Wotton described 'a plain, massie, rurall Pillar, resembling some sturdy well-limmed labourer, homely . . . the *Tuscan* is of all the modest Pillar, and his principall Character *Simplicity*.' Inigo Jones used it for St Paul's, Covent Garden (1630) but it was to become the Order associated with simple rural buildings (emphasising the *rustic aspect) or, as suggested by S. *Serlio, with fortification and prisons. *Rustication was often applied to buildings using the Tuscan Order.

As its name implies, the Composite Order combines elements of two other Orders, the Ionic and the Corinthian. Omitted by Vitruvius, it had evolved in the last phase of Roman classicism and achieved importance only after the publication of L.B.*Alberti's treatise in the late 15th century. It was regarded by the theorists in an unfavourable light, as a compromise solution, a cheap amalgam. Sir Henry Wotton put it trenchantly, ' . . . this Pillar is nothing in effect, but a *Medlie*, or an *Amasse* of all the precedent *Ornaments*, making a new kinde by stealth, and though the most richly tricked, yet the poorest in this, that he is a borrower of all his Beautie . . . to know him will be easie by the verie

*Orders. Composite *capitals by Paul Vredeman de Vries, c.1600.*

mixture of his *Ornaments*, and *Cloathing*.' Edwards and Darly gave a number of variations on the type but with a caveat, ' . . . some must never be us'd in regular architecture, but may be occasionaly used in Scenery and fancied compositions.' The Composite Order was viewed as theatrical, and not to be taken seriously. Also known as the Roman or Italian Order and, by Scamozzi, as the 'Heroic' Order.

The Renaissance interpretation of the five Orders was based on examples of classical Roman architecture, e.g. the Colosseum in Rome which uses the three principal Orders in the correct sequence, storey by storey, with the Doric at the bottom. This application became standard not only in architecture but also in furniture and the decorative arts. Various authors of treatises and pattern books provided inventions and adaptations of the Orders during the 16th, 17th and 18th centuries. Serlio's work, *Architettura*, was the first to be concerned with the ornamental detailing of buildings, followed by those of Vignola, A.*Palladio and Scamozzi; there was also a steady stream of new translations and editions of Vitruvius. Many pattern books, notably those by *Flemish Mannerist designers such as Dietterlin or H.*Vredeman de Vries, grafted onto the established Orders a wealth of ornamentation on capitals, mouldings, column shafts, *pilasters and bases, as well as fanciful *caryatids, atlantes and *herms, applied more or less at the whim of the individual author. Each country produced its own crop of editions of the treatises, e.g. that by J.*Shute in England or Jean Bullant (1555-80), whose *Règle Générale des cinque manières* (1564) was influential in France. From the 16th century the Orders were treated as a set of rules made to be broken: the *Mannerist use of *Giant Orders, running the full height of a façade, or the various specially concocted Orders, such as Jacopo Sansovino's Rustic Order (banded Doric, used on the Venetian Mint, 1537) or P.*de l'Orme's French Order for the Tuileries (also given horizontal features) diversified the classical vocabulary with constant innovation. However, I. Ware commented, 'The original orders have something great and noble in them but there is nothing but quaintness and fancy ill-employed in these.

Ornemanistes produced much work on the decorative application of the Orders, e.g. J.A.*Ducerceau's *Petit Traité des cinque ordres* (1583) was echoed two centuries later by T.*Chippendale, who included in the *Gentleman and Cabinet-makers' Director* eight plates on the proportioning of the Orders as a necessary background to cabinet-making, together with perspective renderings.

With each revival of *classicism, the Orders were returned to their basic formulae, only to be further diversified at will, as in B.*Langley's spurious set of Gothic Orders, or the American Order instigated in the late 18th century by Benjamin Latrobe for the Virginia State Capitol. W.*Chambers's *Treatise* was probably the definitive 18th century publication on the subject. With the *Greek Revival, further 'pure' versions of the Orders were used, identified always as 'Greek' Doric, Ionic or Corinthian. In the most ascetic and abstract renderings of *Neo-classicism, the Orders were dropped altogether. However, their enduring importance as the basis for classical architecture is demonstrated by the fact that the treatise by C.*Normand

*Orders. Corn *capital and tobacco capital designs by Benjamin Latrobe for the United States Capitol, Washington, D.C.*

(1765-1840), published in Paris in 1819, and translated and added to by A.C.*Pugin in 1829 as *A New Parallel of the Orders*, included Greek, Roman and Renaissance Orders and was in use in British architectural schools in 1942 in an edition 'brought up to date in line with the current architectural educational requirements.' The longest-lasting adherence to the Orders was at the French Beaux-Arts School of Architecture, which continued to train its architects in the full academic classicist system until 1968. *See also* American motifs; Attick, Britannic, French, Spanish and Texan Orders.

Organic Modernism. Asymmetrical, amoeboid shapes, sometimes with holes, were used in *Post War architecture and decorative art in Britain. The style derived from the work of artists and sculptors such as Salvador Dali, Jean Miro and Jean Arp, and was sometimes referred to as Organic Modernism. New techniques in pre-cast concrete, plywood and injection-moulded

Organic Modernism. 'Surrey', a wool, cotton and rayon fabric designed by Marianne Straub for the Festival of Britain, 1951.

plastic manufacture all allowed for the flexibility in design (e.g. multi-directional curves) necessary for these soft, flowing shapes. Examples include chairs made by Charles Eames (1948), glass designed by Alvar Aalto (1947) and silver designed for the Danish firm of Georg Jensen in the early 1950s. One of the most popular amoeboid shapes played on the form of an artist's palette and was often used for table tops.

oriental. An 18th century catch-all term to cover Eastern styles of ornament. The confusion over different styles is typified by the title of Jean Antoine Fraisse's *Livre de desseins chinois tirés de Perse, des Indes, de la Chine et du Japon* (1735). Later, however, efforts were made to distinguish particular strands of the oriental, for example *Arabian style, *chinoiserie, *Indian style, *japonaiserie, *Moorish style, *Persian style and *Turkish style.

A satire on the vogue for the oriental in *pattern-book design was advertised by Robert Sayer, the London publisher, in 1755, under the title 'Country Five Barr'd Gates, Stiles and Wickets, elegant Pig-styes, beautiful Henhouses, and delightful Cow-cribs, superb Cart-houses, magnificent Barn Doors, variegated Barn Racks, and admirable Sheep-Folds: according to the Turkish and Persian manner; . . . To which is added, some Designs of Fly-Traps, Bee Palaces and Emmet Houses, in the Muscovite and Arabian Architecture: all adapted to the Latitude and Genius of England. The whole entirely new, and inimitably designed in Two Parts, on Forty Pewter Plates, under the immediate Inspection of Don Gulielmus De Demi Je ne Sçai Quoi, chief Architect to the Grand Signior.'

os de mouton (French, ram's horn). A pronounced *volute, used to finish the end of a chair arm, which first appeared in the 17th century.

Osiris pillar. Column in the figure of the ancient Egyptian god of nature, Osiris, which is used similarly to the *caryatid or *persian in classical Greek architecture. It appeared in ancient Egyptian architecture, and was popular in the *Egyptian style, especially in cemeteries, e.g. on mausolea.

Ottoman. *See* Turkish.

ovolo moulding. Convex *moulding (usually a quarter of a circle in section), often enriched with *egg and dart or similar ornament.

owl. As an attribute of the goddess of learning, *Minerva (and her Greek counterpart, Athena), the owl appears principally in the decoration of libraries, writing tables, etc., sometimes with a *laurel wreath or perched on a pile of books. In this context, it was recommended by R.*Brown and C.*Dresser, among others. A nocturnal bird, it sometimes represents *night and therefore sleep. In medieval iconography the owl was sometimes used as a symbol of the Jewish people, a reference to the owl preferring darkness to light, as Judaism was regarded as opposing the new light of Christianity. The Bestiary of Physiologus (*see* bestiaries) contains a description of the owl being mobbed by other smaller birds and this image is occasionally found in medieval decoration, e.g. on misericords or roof *bosses.

ox head. *See* aegricanes; animal; bucranium.

pagod, Poussah or **Magot.** Small fat figure inspired by Pu-T'ai, the Chinese god of contentment. Chinese and Japanese examples in porcelain, ivory and wood were copied by 18th century European porcelain factories such as Chantilly, Mennecy and Meissen, and appeared either as free-standing figures or as part of a *chinoiserie* landscape. Sometimes the figure had a hole in its mouth or head so that it could be used as an incense or pastille burner.

pagoda. A common motif in *chinoiserie*. Pagodas, with their upturned eaves, *fretwork *brackets and decorative *finials and *pendants, were repeatedly illustrated in descriptions of China, from J.*Nieuhof's *Atlas Chinensis* (1665) to the later and more precise work of W. *Chambers's *Designs of Chinese Buildings* (1757). They were occasionally used as finials on *chinoiserie* furniture and even appeared hung with *bells as a kind of canopy forming the top of a china cabinet (illustrated in

*pagoda in Kew Gardens, Surrey, by Sir W.*Chambers from G.L. Le Rouge's* Jardins Anglo-Chinois, *1774-89.*

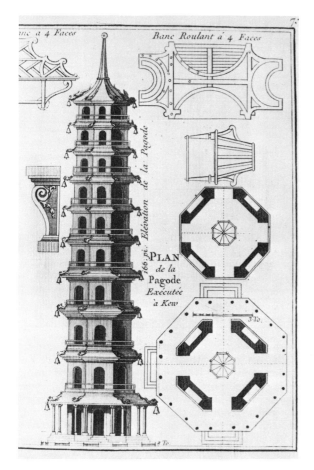

*pagod in J.*Pillement's* A New Book of Chinese Ornaments, *1755.*

the third edition of T.*Chippendale's *Director*), a four-poster bed or a Chinese lantern; a silver *épergne* made 1762-63 by Thomas Pitts I has a pagoda canopy hung with bells. As an architectural form the pagoda was used for ornamental garden pavilions. Chambers's pagoda in Kew Gardens, Surrey, erected in 1757-62, was printed on cotton produced by Collins Woolmers in 1766, and subsequently became a fashionable motif for wallpapers known as 'pagoda papers'.

Pain, William (c.1730-c.1790). English author of numerous *pattern books aimed at builders, who described himself as an 'architect joiner'. Some of his publications ran into several editions and most were widely known in America, although American editions did not appear until much later in the century. *The Builder's Companion and Workman's General Assistant* (1758) went into three editions and dealt with the house ' . . . from the Plan to the Ornamental finish'. Books such as *The British Palladio* (1786), a collaboration with his son James, illustrated a selection of the type of ornament regarded as important on standard late 18th century terraced housing and included *frets and *guilloches, *Gothick columns, *open pediments with 'bustos and shells', Venetian seats and *trellising. Windows, chimneys, *mouldings, *cornices and staircases were the areas of the house considered suitable for these decorative touches. Pain addressed himself to 'masons, bricklayers, plasterers, carpenters, joiners . . . and gentlemen' and the material, presented in the form of large, easily copied designs, was, by the standards of the time, extremely conservative.

paisley. Pattern developed from formalised representations of *pinecones, and infilled with small, incidental

paisley. Scottish woven shawl, early 1830s.

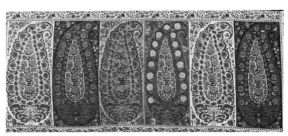

motifs found in Indian textile design. The precise derivation of this form, found throughout the Orient and sometimes known as a boteh, is obscure. Its function is as a kind of all-purpose, stylised vegetation, equally distantly resembling the *palm, almond, *cypress and other plant forms that figured in Eastern art; Hindu and Moghul designs often incorporate the pattern.

In Britain it was taken up after appearing on a certain type of embroidered Kashmiri shawl much favoured by Queen Victoria. Fabric patterned with the motif quickly became fashionable around the mid 19th century and was produced in quantity, notably at Paisley, a wool-weaving town in Scotland. It was also adopted in France at the same period.

Palladianism. An early 18th century *classical revival based on an admiration of the buildings and published works of A.*Palladio. Palladio's own architecture, together with his observations on Roman and *Renaissance buildings brought classicism to a wide audience in Europe and eventually in America. It was still, however, classicism without reference to ancient Greece. The Palladians' attitude to ornament can be gauged from the words of Robert Morris (1701-54), an influential architect and theorist of the movement, who wrote, 'If you will be lavish in ornament, your structure will look rather more like a fop, with a superfluity of gaudy Tinsil, than a real Decoration.' Decorum and convenience dictated the limits. The seminal work for the English Palladians was Giacomo Leoni's English translation of Palladio's *Quattro Libri*, entitled *The Architecture of A. Palladio, revis'd, design'd and publish'd by Giacomo Leoni, a Venetian*, which had a text in English, French and Italian. As the first reissue of the work for almost a century, with high-quality engravings instead of woodcuts, the book had a great impact. It coincided with the publication by Colen Campbell (1673-1729) of Volume I of *Vitruvius Britannicus*, a *résumé* of modern architecture which, by promoting the work of Palladio and I.*Jones, aimed to undermine the hold of the *Baroque in architecture (a style described as 'affected and licentious'). Further volumes followed in 1717 and 1725, and it was reissued in 1731. The book gained Campbell the support of Lord Burlington (1694-1753), patron, amateur architect and publisher. It

also prompted William Adam (1689-1747), father of Robert and James, to prepare a *Vitruvius Scoticus* in 1727, although it did not appear in print until 1812.

Further publications that supported the return to relatively academic classical architecture included W.*Kent's *Designs of Inigo Jones* (1727), financed by Lord Burlington, who also published drawings by Palladio from his own collection as *Fabbriche Antiche Disegnate da Andrea Palladio* (1730). Palladianism travelled to Russia with Charles Cameron (c.1740-1812) and Giacomo Quarenghi (1744-1817), both of whom worked for Catherine the Great, whilst in Prussia, Frederick the Great commissioned a number of Palladian-inspired villas in Potsdam in the 1750s.

Thomas Jefferson (1743-1826) supported the style in America, in particular with his own house, Monticello, in Virginia (1769 onwards). From the 1740s Palladianism was highly influential in *American Colonial and early *Federal style architecture. Because of the shortage of stone, a wooden façade was sometimes cut and sand-painted in imitation of ashlar and *quoins, since the clap-board finish did not lend itself to a classical elevation. Motifs most commonly associated with Palladianism include the *Palladian motif (or Venetian window), temple-front porticos, *coffering, heavy *rustication and the use of *Giant Orders.

Palladian window. Mid Georgian house, Long Melford, Suffolk.

Palladian motif, Palladian window, Serliana or **Venetian window.** A window or archway with three openings, the central one a wide arch, the side ones narrower and usually flat-topped. It was first taken from the work of Donato Bramante (1444-1514), popularised by A.*Palladio, and illustrated by S.*Serlio in his *L'Architettura*. In the 18th century it became a hallmark of *Palladian architecture.

Palladianism. Chiswick House, London, by Lord Burlington, 1725-29.

Andrea Palladio. Logge *of the Basilica, Vicenza, Italy, designed by Palladio 1546, built 1549-1616.*

Palladio, Andrea (1508-80). Italian architect trained as a sculptor and stonemason, who influenced the course of Western architecture to the extent that *Palladianism is an architectural term in its own right. Palladio was known through his own architectural work, and, more widely, as the author of a treatise which followed *Vitruvius and L.B.*Alberti in codifying *classical architecture, drawing on both Roman and Italian *Renaissance precedents. In 1556, Palladio advised Daniele Barbaro on the reissue of Vitruvius's treatise and provided illustrations. His own *I Quattro Libri dell'Architettura* was published in Venice in 1570; a second edition appeared in 1581, another in 1601 and many more subsequently. The four books covered the *Orders, domestic buildings (including Palladio's own designs), public buildings (most Roman, but including his own Basilica at Vicenza from which the famous *Palladian motif came), and Roman temples (including Donato Bramante's Tempietto at San Pietro, Montorio, Rome, 1502). It was a more accurate account than the treatises either of G.B. da *Vignola or S.*Serlio, both of which were known in France and

England as well as in Italy. Palladio's book was soon known to architects outside Italy, well before translations and reissues began to proliferate. I.*Jones's copy, later bought by Lord Burlington (1694-1759), bears Jones's annotations and gives a fascinating indication of his own architectural ideas.

The first complete English edition of *I Quattro Libri* appeared in 1715-20 in two volumes produced by Giacomo Leoni (c.1686-1746). Entitled *The Architecture of A. Palladio, revis'd, design'd and published by Giacomo Leoni, a Venetian*, it had a text in English, French and Italian introduced by Nicholas Dubois (c.1665-1735) and was a somewhat individual interpretation of the original. A strictly faithful edition, using exact reproductions of the Palladio plates, was published in 1738 by I.*Ware. Under the aegis of Lord Burlington (1694-1753), *Palladianism, which promoted a faithful rendering of the architectural precepts of the man who gave the movement its name, was enormously influential. However, B.*Langley, in his introduction to the *Treasury*, commented on the large folios of grand buildings 'which to workmen are of little Use, and as those Books are of large Prices, beyond the Reach of many Workmen and too large to Use at work: I have therefore for the common Good, extracted from the works of that great Master Palladio, all that is useful to workmen.' Another English edition, consisting of the first

*Andrea Palladio. The Pantheon, Rome, from I.*Ware's 1738 edition of* Four Books of Architecture.

book only, was produced by Godfrey Richards and was supplemented by a section by P.*Le Muet on doors and windows. This version of Palladio was first recorded in America in 1744 and became well known there.

palm. This tree, indigenous to much of Asia and Africa, has been widely used as a decorative motif since classical times, its appearance varying with each ornamental style. In ancient Egyptian architecture, the palm was used as a *column, with a banded shaft representing the trunk and the leaves tight-packed to form a *capital.

The palm's connotations of oriental exoticism made it a popular motif in the *Rococo. Combining well with *chinoiserie* motifs, it endured into the light *Neoclassicism of the *Adam style, e.g. palms form the bedposts on the great bed and the matching *torchères* that Robert Adam and J. Linnell designed for Kedleston in Derbyshire, c.1765. Cast-iron columns at the Brighton Pavilion (c.1815) in Sussex are topped with copper palm leaves. It appeared in the early and mid 19th century *Egyptian style, and again in the 1920s and 1930s.

Traditionally associated with triumphal processions, the palm was used at the first Olympic Games, and figures in the story of Christ's entry to Jerusalem. It is an emblem of *Fame and *Victory and, with this connotation, appeared as a surround for portrait *medallions (often with two fronds crossed) or in *cartouches. In Louis XIV's Galerie des Glaces at Versailles, the usual *acanthus capitals were replaced by palm leaves. It also took on the religious significance of victory over death (the martyr's palm), and has appeared in Christian funerary ornament since early times. The commentator Franz Sales Meyer, author of *Handbook of Ornament* (1888; second edition 1892), wrote that its symbolism of eternal peace 'has secured for the Palm leaf a place in modern art on tombs and similar monuments.' It is also a frequent *heraldic emblem, sometimes appearing in place of *mantling on engraved silver.

*palm. 1) *Cartouche from J.*Gibbs's A Book of Architecture, 1728. 2) Palm trunk support for Chinese tea house at Sans Souci, Potsdam, East Germany, 1754-57.*

*palmette. 1) Etruscan sarcophagus, now in the museum at Volterra, Tuscany, Italy. 2) Etruscan style English parcel gilt amphora made by Robert Hennell, 1870. 3) Stencilled ornament on early 19th century villa by K.F.*Schinkel, Glienicke, Berlin. 4) Incised ornament on Vincent Street Church, Glasgow, architect Alexander Thomson, 1859. 5) Early 19th century American stool by Duncan Phyfe. 6) *Frieze, Bar Association of the Bar of the City of New York, West 44th Street, New York, architect Cyrus L.W. Eidlitz, 1895.*

Palm fronds, particularly the long, flat type with curving tips, were also more generally used in 18th century ornament for capitals and *mouldings.

Delian palm refers to the palm that appears in Greek and Roman ornament, often in the context of *Apolline ornament.

palmette. Widely used motif based loosely on a formalised *palm leaf, often used in conjunction with the *anthemion, the two forms sometimes appearing almost indistinguishable, particularly when they are rendered in a relatively florid style. An ubiquitous form in *classical decoration from the Etruscan period through to 20th century classical revivals, the palmette has been interpreted with anything from extreme simplicity to great ornateness, according to the style in which it appears.

pampre. 19th century term for ornament composed of *grapevine leaves and bunches of grapes.

panache. *See* feathers.

pancarpi. 18th and 19th century term for a *festoon of flowers.

panoply (Greek, *panoplia*, complete armour). An array of uniform, armour and weapons arranged in an ornamental group. This motif appears widely on such structures as palaces, *triumphal arches or barracks to signify military splendour. It has its origins in ancient Rome and when it was reintroduced in the late Renaissance the accoutrements tended still to be those of Roman warriors rather than of contemporary soldiers. Often used as sculptural ornament on parapets, panoplies appear widely as carved and painted decorations in the houses of military heroes. *See also* military decoration; trophy.

papyrus. One of the motifs taken from ancient Egyptian art and architecture. It is frequently confused with the *lotus as the buds of both plants were similarly depicted. O.*Jones stated in his *Grammar of Ornament* (1856) that the papyrus was a typical Egyptian ornament. This view was also held by C.*Dresser, who, in *The Principles of Decorative Design*, suggested that as the earliest Egyptian buildings would have been constructed from bundles of papyrus reeds, it was natural for Egyptian *capitals to be decorated with papyrus, although, W. Goodyear claimed in *The Grammar of the Lotus* (1891) that all Egyptian decoration was based on the lotus. R.*Brown remarked in 1830 that the papyrus was an eminently suitable 'botanical enrichment' for writing tables.

parapet ornament. *See* acroterion.

Parasole, Isabetta/Elisabetta/Isabella Catanea (fl 1595-1616). Italian designer whose patterns for different types of lace were published in three collections, *Specchio delle virtuose donne* (Rome, 1595), *Studio delle virtuose dame* (Rome, 1597), and *Fiori d'ogni virtu* (Rome, 1610); the latter was published in 1616 under the title *Teatro delle nobili et virtuose donne* and ran into several editions. At the end of the 19th century Parasole's books were republished in facsimile in Berlin and London.

parcheman or **parchment panel.** Early 20th century term for a 16th century development of *linenfold panelling, in which the carved 'folds' swell in and out to incorporate *grapevine stems, foliage, etc. Used on furniture of panel construction in England and the Low Countries.

parchemin plié. *See* linenfold.

Parker, George. *See* Stalker, John.

*panoply. 1) From the Comte *de Caylus's* Recueil d'antiquités, *1752-67.
2) Parapet from Christopher Wren's work on the Clock Court, Hampton Court Palace, Surrey, 1689-94.*
*papyrus. 3) *Capital from the reconstructed Egyptian Temple of Dendur, Metropolitan Museum, New York.*

parsley. Foliage used in *Gothic *naturalistic ornament (especially in the French *Flamboyant style. It appears in 18th and early 19th century *pattern books such as A.*Benjamin's *American Builder's Companion*, where it is offered as an option between the extremes of the highly serrated *acanthus leaf and the straight-edged hart's-tongue fern called a *waterleaf. R.*Brown referred to 'a double parsley leaf, which is very intricate but rich and beautiful' (1822).

pastoral. A highly romanticised view of the simplicity and natural charm associated with the countryside that became a popular theme in early 18th century literature and painting, partly as a result of the view of classical Arcadia popularised by late 17th and early

parcheman. Carved wooden panel from Cothele, Cornwall, early 16th century.

18th century painters, which provided a range of 'pastoral' motifs: Arcadians hunting, attending cattle, or worshipping Pan with musical instruments. These themes appeared on tapestries, silk, ceramics and enamel.

Pastoral decoration was most popular in France from the 1730s. Leaders in fashionable taste such as Madame de Pompadour and Queen Marie Antoinette toyed with the pastoral and the *rustic. At Versailles, Marie Antoinette's Petit Hameau (1783) was self-consciously designed in a style reminiscent of buildings in Normandy and consisted of dairies, cowshed, mill, aviary and farmhouse. Madame de Pompadour kept fowl and cattle at the Grand Trianon and farmyard poultry were included in the gilded *frieze decoration of the Pavillon de Jeu at the Petit Trianon. *Fêtes champêtres* were a popular court entertainment, with actors performing supposed country dances and leading around spotlessly clean flocks of sheep. F.*Boucher produced designs for tapestry entitled *Nobles Pastorals* and *Fêtes de Village*. Porcelain factories produced figures of peasants. Engraved *vignettes (sometimes called *bergeries*) were published of milkmaids, haymakers, shepherds and rural lovers, and copied on ceramics, enamel, glass and textiles. The characters in pastoral scenes were idealised, beautiful, young and the settings often distant, e.g. Boucher's *Fêtes de village à l'italienne*. *Ornemanistes* devised a range of pastoral trophies that incorporated farm implements, basketry, peasant food such as root vegetables and cheeses and pastoral instruments such as castanets, pipes and bagpipes. A change in the political climate and the advent of a strict *Neo-classicism in France led to the disappearance of pastoral decoration. In England pastoral elements developed into a taste for the *Picturesque.

pastoral column. An element of 18th century *rustic work. J. Carter's *Builder's Magazine* (1774) describes a pastoral column as having shaft imitating a tree trunk, complete with bark and knots, supposedly suited 'for gates of parks and gardens'. *See also* tree.

patera (Latin, dish or wine holder used in religious ceremonies). Oval or circular form usually decorated with a formalised flower or *rosette and/or *fluting. From the 18th century pateras were almost always designed as rosettes, and the two terms were used interchangeably. Pateras were widely used in *Neoclassical ornament, applied to *friezes, *archivolts, *spandrels, soffits and *coffering: Sir John Soane (1753-1837) included them in many of the interiors he designed. Manufacturers of plaster *mouldings and cast ironwork produced innumerable variations of the motif, and an oval brass plate embossed with a patera became a standard shape for brass furniture handles. In late 18th and early 19th century houses, a patera often formed the centre point of the ceiling in standard plaster moulding detail, and this was later adapted as the light point for gas or electric fittings or as a disguise for ventilation ducts.

paternoster. *See* bead and reel.

pattern books. Collections of ornamental designs by artists and architects produced for the guidance of

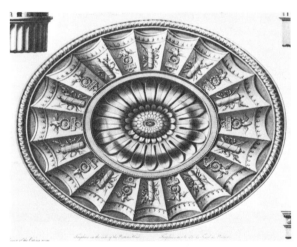

pastoral. 1) Mid 18th century French design for a pastoral *trophy, engraved by P. Cherpitel.
patera. 2) 18th century wooden door, Neruda Street, Prague. 3) Ceiling beneath portico, Osterley House, Middlesex, by Robert Adam, 1763-80. 4) Patera incorporating military trophies and *labara, designed by Robert Adam for the Porter's Hall of a house in St James's Square, London, from his Works in Architecture, 1773-79. 5) Late 18th century bank building, Philadelphia, Pennsylvania.

builders and craftsmen of all kinds from the 15th to the 19th century. They first appeared as a result of the use of woodcuts in printing, and were greatly improved during the second half of the 15th century by the process of engraving, which allowed finer detail to be reproduced. Although many patterns were bound as books (whether expensive folio editions produced for wealthy patrons or small cheap books for craftsmen), some engraved ornament was sold in collections of six to twelve loose sheets, often known as suites or *cahiers*. One of the earliest known dated pattern books was a collection of geometric and foliage designs for needlework by H.*Schönsperger, published in Augsburg in 1523. Within a few years, this book had been reproduced in printing centres all over Europe, by Peter Quentel in Cologne (1527), Willem Vorsterman in Antwerp and G.A.*Tagliente in Venice.

Apart from the designs for embroidery and lace, most of the early patterns, such as those by H.*Aldegrever, the *Beham brothers and A. Altdorfer, were aimed at metalworkers and goldsmiths, as the techniques of producing engravings and working with metal were closely allied. Early printed publications on architecture were in general treatises, the most well known of which was that by *Vitruvius. Patterns for furniture, interior and exterior detail appeared from the late 16th century, initially in the work of engravers such as W.*Dietterlin, H.*Vredeman de Vries and H.*Sambin.

In general, the effect of pattern books was to disseminate new forms and styles from the artistic centres to provincial areas and from country to country. Their multiplicity meant, for example, that the newfound *Renaissance motifs or later, the complexities of *Rococo designs, were incorporated relatively quickly into ornament across Europe. Pattern books were economically designed to show as many variations on a theme as possible, e.g. one plate showing six alternative *caryatids, a chimneypiece divided in half to show two treatments, and some contemporary pieces make it evident that craftsmen occasionally copied indiscriminately from the page.

The 18th century was perhaps the heyday of the pattern book when styles in ornament changed rapidly and a large number of highly skilled craftsmen

were continually meeting the growing demands for fashionable buildings and furnishings from an increasingly affluent middle class. Successful architects, cabinetmakers and designers were also learning to profit by offering their designs to a wide audience. M.*Darly described his *Ornamental Architect* as 'most essential to Artists, Manufacturers and Mechanics... the Professions, Architects, Painters, Engravers, Carvers, Stucco-workers, Potters, Ironsmiths, Silversmiths, Founders, Embroiderers'-pattern-drawers, Tapistry weavers, Coach makers, Cabinet Makers and numbers of other ingenious professions.' Early *American Colonial ornament was utterly dependent on imported skills and designs in pattern books.

From the second quarter of the 19th century, coverage in pattern books shifted towards *Historicism and an *eclectic view of styles, often collating illustrations of ornament from all seriously considered cultures, as in O.*Jones's work. 16th, 17th and 18th century designs were republished in facsimile, e.g. Ovide Reynard's *Ornements des Anciens Maîtres des XV, XVI, XVII and XVIII siècles* which was published in 20 parts between 1844 and 1845 (*see also* Rococo Revival).

By the end of the 19th century, pattern books were relatively scarce, apart from the work of the *Audsley family, E.*Grasset and A.*Mucha. *Art Nouveau and *Art Deco were transmitted far more quickly and effectively via the new international illustrated art magazines and journals, which from the 1890s published photographic half-tone illustrations. The frequency of *international exhibitions, increased travel and the wide publication of illustrated art journals and catalogues meant that the pattern book became largely obsolete.

paw. Like the *claw and the *hoof, the paw usually appears at the base of a furniture leg. Classical examples include *lions' paws used to support stone sarcophagi or forming the bases for bronze candelabra. The form was revived in the *Renaissance. *Mannerist engravers such as H.*Sambin and J.A.*Ducerceau designed furniture with paw feet at the base of grotesque supporting figures. Popular on the front legs of early to mid 18th century English chairs, the allusion was occasionally carried further up the furniture leg with a furry hock or knee. *Monopodia frequently feature paws, often accompanied by *lion masks.

A pelt with paws and a lion mask hanging from it was an element of *Herculean decoration. In the *Baroque repertoire it appeared as a motif surmounting doors and window frames.

Peace. Important personification in *Graeco-Roman classicism. Usually female, her attributes include a *palm frond (also an attribute of *Victory), an *olive branch or crown, a *dove, and sometimes a collection of arms strewn on the ground, indicating the cessation of war; the figure sometimes carries a *torch, to set fire to the weapons.

Personifications of Peace and Good Government often appeared together, particularly in the civic-minded Italian *Renaissance, as did Peace and *Plenty (when the *cornucopia is often present) and Peace and *Liberty. Personifications of Peace appear on

Peace burning the implements of war. English jasper ware clock-case made by Wedgwood, c.1802.

peacock. 1) American Favrile glass vase, Tiffany Glass and Decorating Company, c.1900. 2) Marquetry design on late 19th century mahogany wardrobe. 3) Doorway, Westminster Cathedral, London, architect John Francis Bentley, 1895-1903.
peapod ornament. 4) Early 17th century engraving by Pierre de la Barre.

*commemorative ware, on memorials to statesmen and on civic buildings. The dove and olive branch were used as an emblem of peace on the back of tea-spoon bowls (so-called fancy-back spoons) in the 18th century. *See also* Minerva.

peacock. The bird or its distinctive feathers appear in Roman, *Persian, Indian and *Byzantine ornament. In Byzantine art the peacock sometimes represents the Empress. In Roman mythology, the peacock, which was sacred to Juno, was believed to have incorruptible flesh: it was thus a symbol of immortality and often appeared combined with the *grapevine and *acanthus. In *Christian iconography it is a symbol of the Resurrection of Christ, and hence of immortality. The eyes in the tail feathers led to their adoption as symbols of foresight.

A popular motif in oriental textiles, the peacock came to be used, via the silk route, on early Italian woven silks, probably the source of the peacock pattern for lace in F. di *Vinciolo's *Les Singuliers et Nouveaux Pourtraicts* (1587). Peacock feathers were used in the *scale patterns on late 15th century Italian *maiolica* made at Faenza, supposedly as a compliment to Cassandra Pavone (*pavone* is the Italian for peacock), mistress of Galeotto Manfredo, Lord of Faenza. Delftware apothecary jars of the mid 17th and 18th centuries are often ornamented with two peacocks facing each other, probably signifying longevity and immortality.

In the late 19th century *peacocks, and particularly

their feathers, became recurrent motifs in the *Aesthetic movement as symbols of beauty. The challenge of reproducing the iridescent blue/green colours was met in glass by Tiffany & Co., in ceramics by William De Morgan (1839-1917), in enamel by the Guild of Handicrafts (founded by C.R. Ashbee in 1888) and in fabric by the London store of Liberty & Co. – the Liberty 'peacock and peony' design was the most successful produced before 1930.

peapod ornament or **cosse de pois.** An early 17th century style of ornament, half-way between *arabesque patterns and naturalistic flower decoration, the dominant feature of which is sprays of graduated dots similar to peas. The foliage is often presented in bouquet form. Intended principally for jewellery settings and enamel watch-cases and pendants, the pattern was popular in France and northern Europe. The style was propagated by the engraved patterns of J. Toutin (1619), Jacques Hurtu (1619), Peter Symony in *Tabulae Gemmiferae* (1621), Antoine Hedouyns (1623, 1633) and Baltasar Lemersier (1625, 1626), among others. Examples of most of these engravers' work were reprinted by O. Reynard in *Ornement des anciens maîtres* (1844-45) and may have had some influence on the designs of the enamels made in the mid 19th century.

pear-drop. Small, pear-shaped pendant handle (usually brass) for a drawer or cupboard door in late 17th century furniture.

pear-drop moulding. Alternative American term for *Gothic cornice.

pearling. *See* beading.

pedestal. The section below the base of a *classical column.

pediment. Triangular gable end form taken from the classical temple. It is used widely and in many variations

pediment. 1) The Register House, Edinburgh, by Robert Adam, 1774-92.
*2) *Scrolled pediment on mid 18th century Dutch walnut armoire.*

as an ornament: above doors, *niches, *aedicules, chimneypieces, windows, or on furniture, usually in an 'architectural' position. The most common forms of pediment are: *broken pediment, *open pediment, *scrolling pediment, *segmental pediment. However, the foreword to B.*Langley's *Builder's Jewel* described 'fourteen varieties of raking, circular, scrolled, compound and contracted pediments'.

pelican. The pelican-in-her-piety, nourishing her young with blood from her own breast, became a symbol of Christ's work and resurrection and was defined in the *bestiaries. *Emblem books presented the motif as a symbol of redemption, sacrifice and atonement. The pelican appeared frequently from the 13th century on illuminated manuscripts, seals, misericords and later on memorial tablets and tympana. It was used, appropriately enough, in the decoration of the 16th century colleges of Corpus Christi in Oxford and Cambridge. Occasionally, the pelican is used as a lectern; in *Gothic Revival ornament, it appeared as a potent ecclesiastical symbol of medieval times, though it tended to be rendered naturalistically.

Pellegrino, Francesco (d 1552). Italian artist who worked at Fontainebleau with Rosso Fiorentino (1494-1540), R.*Boyvin and Léonard Thiry (c.1500-c.1550). He published one of the first books of *arabesque ornament in Europe and the first in France, *La Fleur de la science de pourtraicture* (Paris, 1530), which contained designs for both the simple foliate arabesques or moresques, and those combined with *bandwork.

pelican. 1, 2) 15th century misericord with inscription In omni opere memento finis *[In all undertakings, remember the end] and font, Church of St Andrew, Norton, Suffolk. 3) English encaustic tile by the Campbell Tile Co., c.1885.*
Francesco Pellegrino. 4) Design from his La Fleur de la science de pourtraicture, *1530.*

pelta. 1) Naval Ministry, Avenue Octave, Paris, early 20th century. 2) Above door of R.A.C. Building, Pall Mall, London, architects Mewes & Davis with E. Keynes Purchase, 1908-11.

pelta (Latin, *pelta*, light leather shield). Pelta ornament usually appears as an overall *diaper pattern and variant of *scale ornament consisting in a series of linking convex and concave shield shapes, similar to the pelta shield. Of classical origin, this form of patterning became popular in *friezes and wall decorations, appearing in *Early English Gothic work in the west of the country. The shield shape was revived from the 18th century in *Neo-classical ornament both as a motif in its own right and as a repeating ornament. Robert Adam (*see* Adam style) used it in friezes, *trophies and *arabesque compositions and as a scale pattern. In the *Empire style it was used as a chair-back form.

pendant. An ornamental projection or terminal hanging from a canopy or ceiling. Treated in a similar fashion to the *finial, it is used both in architectural ornament and in woodwork. It assumed particular

*pendant. 1) Mid 15th century cloister in the Manueline style, Batalha, Portugal. 2) From St Stephen's Chapel, Palace of Westminster in H.*Shaw's* The Encyclopaedia of Ornament, *1842. 3) Canopy of English Jacobean oak settle. 4) House in Petersfield, Hampshire, 1613.*

importance in highly decorated styles, such as *Perpendicular or *Flamboyant Gothic vaulting, together with naturalistically carved or moulded motifs. In 16th and 17th century plasterwork or stucco the simple conical *bosses of early work are pulled into richly wrought forms, pierced, carved or incised. In furniture, ornamental pendants are associated particularly with the rich carpentry of the *Jacobean period, and reappeared in 19th century *Jacobean Revival work, both in wood and in plasterwork ceilings. *See also* stalactite work.

pendant frieze. *See* Gothic cornice.

Pennsylvania Dutch (corruption of *Deutsch*). Folk style of ornament introduced by German settlers into 18th century America, mainly East Pennsylvania. This strain of decoration, with its brightly painted simple motifs: *hearts, animals and birds, geometric shapes and flowers, particularly *tulips, continued through the 19th century and was used on furniture, ceramics and chalkware, and enamelled on glass tumblers, jugs, etc., e.g. those produced in the late 1760s and early 1770s at Henry William Stiegel's glassworks in Manheim, Pennsylvania.

Percier, Charles (1764-1838) and **Fontaine,** Pierre (1762-1835). French architects and designers who

Charles Percier and Pierre Fontaine. Emperor's Throne from the Palais des Tuileries in their Recueil de décorations, *1812.*

were the main creators of the *Empire style. After visiting Italy in the 1780s and 1790s and absorbing and admiring Roman and *Renaissance architecture, they published *Recueil des palais, maisons et autres edifices modernes dessinés à Rome* (1798). Their first important commission was to convert Malmaison (1799) for Josephine Bonaparte, and from this point they became the arbiters of style under Napoleon. They restored many royal palaces stripped at the time of the Revolution: the Tuileries, Saint-Cloud, Compiègne, the Louvre, Versailles, Rambouillet. Percier and Fontaine also designed furniture, silver, textiles and details for Napoleon's two most self-aggrandising events: his Coronation (1804) and his marriage to Marie Louise of Austria (1810). In 1801, they published *Recueil de décorations intérieures comprenant tout ce qui a rapport à l'ameublement*, which contained 72 detailed plates illustrating a selection of interior designs for the Emperor and other clients and can be seen as a summary of their styles. The book was reissued in 1812 and 1827 in Paris and in an Italian edition (with additions by the Italian architect Giuseppe Borsato) in 1843. The influence of Percier and Fontaine spread throughout Europe and many of their commissions came from outside France. Their basic architectural style was strictly *classical, though it tended to draw upon Roman examples (the Imperial epoch) rather than Greek. For Napoleon, they produced schemes incorporating symbols of military power: *laurel wreaths, Roman imperial *eagles, *torches, winged figures of *Fame and *Victory and military *trophies. They were also careful to use appropriate decoration: *poppies and stars for a bedroom, a *trident and *sea horses on a washstand. On the whole they avoided human figures, preferring legendary creatures from classical myth such as the *sphinx and *chimera, and animals like eagles, *swans, *lions, etc. Their style was easy to follow: much of the ornament was shallow and applied, e.g. cast metal motifs for mahogany furniture, plaster ornament for *friezes, gilt metal on marble and extensive use of drapery.

Pergolesi, Michel Angelo (fl 1760-92). Italian artist and designer, brought from Rome to London by the Adam brothers (*see* Adam style). He worked in their team of decorators from the 1760s, e.g. on the long gallery at Syon House, Middlesex. Pergolesi published *Designs for Various Ornaments* in suites of five plates from 1777 until 1792; the final four plates were published posthumously in 1801. Designs are for ceilings, furniture, chimneypieces, *cornices, *pilasters and wall schemes, as well as ornamental details such as *vases, *rosettes and decorative bandings based on *frets and floral motifs. He also incorporated engravings after decorative paintings by Giovanni Battista Cipriani (1727-88) and Angelica Kauffmann (1741-1807) for painting on ceilings and wall panels. The whole series constitutes a complete catalogue of the Adam style and its range of motifs. His *Original Designs in the Etruscan and Grotesque Style* was published posthumously in 1814.

Some of Pergolesi's designs were republished by J.A. Heaton in 1892 in *Furniture and Decoration in England in the Eighteenth Century*, described as 'a good hunting ground for designers today'.

Perpendicular Gothic. The final stage of English Gothic, equivalent to the continental Flamboyant style and identified as Perpendicular by the architect Thomas Rickman (1776-1841) in his publication *An Attempt to Discriminate the Styles of Architecture in England* (1817). Perpendicular ornament shows a greater vertical emphasis and is more complex than the earlier *Decorated style. Typical motifs include elaborate vaulting patterns, in particular the *fan vault (introduced in the mid 14th century), and the *ogee form and *Tudor flower. The complexity and elaborateness of the style, as exemplified in the Henry VII Chapel at Westminster Abbey, irritated early classicists of the 17th century. John Evelyn referred to the 'sharp *Angles, Jetties*, Narrow Lights, Lame *Statues, Lace* and other *Cut-work* and *Crinkle-Crankle* . . . *Turrets and Pinnacles*, thick set with *Munkies* and *Chimeras*' as not worthy of 'the name of *Architecture*'. Sir Christopher Wren called the chapel 'a nice piece of embroidery work'. In domestic use Perpendicular was rather restrained and merged into the *Renaissance interest reaching England during the late *Tudor, early Elizabethan period. 18th century *Gothick, typified by Horace Walpole's Strawberry Hill at Twickenham, Middlesex, was loosely based on the Perpendicular style. As in the revival of *classical styles, it was the later, more ornamental aspects of Gothic that were copied at first; the purer earlier forms were to appeal to the more serious late 19th century *Gothic Revival.

Perrault, Claude. *See* Vitruvius.

Michel Angelo Pergolesi. Set of furniture and wall decorations dedicated to the Duke of Northumberland, late 18th century.

Perpendicular Gothic. 1) Church of St Mary, Taunton, Somerset, from T. Rickman's The Styles of Architecture, *1848 edition. 2) South porch, Church of St Peter, Felsham, Suffolk, 15th century.*

persian. The male version of a *caryatid. According to *Vitruvius, persians commemorate a group of slaves (renowned for their valour), who were taken captive in the long Persian-Greek wars (Battle of Marathon, 490 BC). Caryatids were also captives during the same hostilities, hence their pairing in ornament. W.*Chambers, in his *Treatise on Civil Architecture*, describes the distinction as it seemed appropriate to 18th century designers: 'male figures may be introduced with propriety in arsenals, or galleries of armour, in guard rooms, and other military places; where they may be represented under the figures either of captives, or of martial virtues; strength, valour – e.g. Persian slaves.'

*persian. 1) From Fra Giocondo's edition of *Vitruvius's* De Architectura, *1511. 2) Engraved designs by J.B. Cipriani, late 18th century.*

Persian style. In the general confusion over the precise sources of *Islamic and Far Eastern styles, 'Persian' was often used to describe a range of *oriental motifs. The confusion was increased by the fact that China had been an important influence on Persian art from the 12th century and Chinese motifs such as *dragons and *cloudbands became assimilated into the Persian repertoire. Shah Abbas I (1588-1628) of the Safavid dynasty encouraged Persian skills in ceramic tiles,

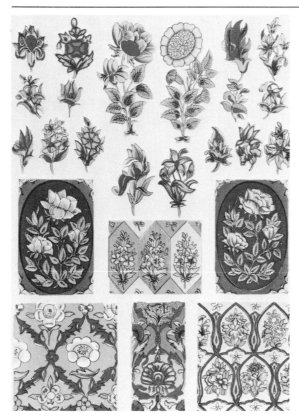

Persian style flowers from O.*Jones's Grammar of Ornament, *1856.*

textiles and book illustration and opened up contact with the West. Persian work of this period was much admired and copied for its highly skilled depiction of flowers, trees and animals. 17th century Persian hunting, garden and vase carpets were scattered with animals such as antelopes, gazelles, boars, tigers, and flowers, including tulips, hyacinths, roses, iris, carnations, cypress trees, weeping willows and birds.

Décor persan is the ceramic decoration composed of foliage, flowers, birds and insects that was painted in white and yellow on a blue ground and first appeared on the tin glazed earthenware of Nevers in the mid 17th century; it was widely imitated by other factories. In 18th century textiles a 'Persian' print is a small flowery pattern on a darkish, often buff-coloured ground.

In the 19th century, O.*Jones dismissed Persian art as inferior to *Arabian and *Moorish, but did recommend its treatment of flowers and animals, suggesting that this 'conventional rendering of natural flowers' would greatly improve British floral wallpapers and carpets (*Grammar of Ornament*). The French potter and designer E.-V.*Collinot picked out the same sort of Persian ornament in *Ornements de la Perse* (1880). In the mid 19th century, the carpet manufacturers of both Kidderminster in England and Beauvais in France produced work based upon original Persian carpets.

persic column. An adaptation of the Persian columns common in the architecture of Persepolis and Isfahan fashionable in 19th century *Egyptian ornament. It

has a bell-shaped *capital and base, both of identical size and ornamented with *lotus leaves. Persic columns appear in the furniture designs of G.*Smith and R. *Ackermann, among others.

personifications existed in *classical art, architecture and literature, e.g. the female figures of *Fame and *Victory, and personifications of cities and rivers (*see* crown). They became important in medieval decoration, often used by the Christian Church in its teachings. The *Virtues and Vices – which derive from the writings of the first Christian poet, Prudentius (b 343 AD) – appear on a 12th century portal at Aulnay in France. On a portal at Amiens Cathedral (c.1225), the Christian Virtues appear as seated women holding shields bearing their emblems. Medieval personifications were not exclusively Christian – Henry III (1207-72) is recorded as having the chimney-hood of the Queen's Chamber at Westminster aptly decorated with the figure of an old man to represent Winter.

During the *Renaissance, personifications were widely used and endlessly interpreted: e.g. figures representing the *Ages of Man, the *Seasons and the Times of Day all imply the passage of *time, and were thus considered apt decoration for tombs. Equally, personifications of Virtues were used to surround many Italian Renaissance tombs, their presence alluding to the character of the deceased: Fidelity, Simplicity, Vigilance, Industry, Fortune, etc. C.*Ripa's *Iconologia* was perhaps the most important contemporary source of personifications for the craftsman and architect. Running into many editions (and translated into seven languages by the 18th century), Ripa was endlessly plundered by later authors, for example Henry Peacham who, in *The Gentleman's Exercise* (1612), a 'handbook for painters', professed his aim 'according to truth to portract and express Eternitie, Hope, Victorie, Pietie, Providence, Vertue, Time, Peace, Concord, Fame, Common Safetie, Clemencie, Fate, etc.' The intricacy of the rationale behind the use of personifications matched the interest during the 16th and 17th centuries in *emblems, devices, *rebuses and *impresas.

During the 18th century, many of the medieval representations were redrawn by engravers, but some, such as the *Liberal Arts, fell from popularity and were replaced by more modern figures. A series of ornamental personifications, mainly engraved by C.-N.*Cochin the Younger and H.F. Gravelot, and published under the title *Almanach Iconologique* (1764-78) covered the following themes: the Arts, including Military, Medicine and Navigation; Sciences, including Chemistry, Botany, Microscopy, Mechanics, etc.; Virtues; *Muses; *êtres métaphysiques*, including Nature, Instinct, Memory, Theory, Society, Doctrine, Imagination, etc.; *êtres moraux*, including Intelligence, Nobility, Glory, Fame, Abundance, Fidelity, Glory, Friendship, etc.; Elements; Parts of the World (*see* Continents); and Seasons.

Such figures appeared mainly in architectural decoration particularly on the exteriors of public buildings, often alluding to their functions. Personifications were also used to ornament ceramics, glass, furniture and textiles, but in the later period a specific theme or

personifications. 1, 2) Beauty and Eternity from C.*Ripa's Iconologia, *1611 edition. 3) Chastisement from the 17th century entrance to a prison, the Rasphuis, Amsterdam. 4) Painting and Sculpture from G.*Richardson's* Iconology, *1779.*

perspective. The scientific study of the visual rendering of distance and space introduced in *Renaissance painting and architecture, notably in the work of Paolo Uccello, Andrea Mantegna, L.B.*Alberti and Donato Bramante, was echoed in the decorative arts.

Much of the engraved instruction in the art of perspective was used as a source of patterns for *intarsia* work, which appeared widely on wall panels, choir stalls, altars, cupboards and grand doors. The Library of the Palazzo Ducale, Urbino (1465-79) and the monastery at Monte Oliveto Maggiore, Siena, have early and important Italian Renaissance examples.

Perspective decoration also became extremely popular among *Mannerist designers in northern Europe and the illusionistic effects of distance, angles and space (**trompe-l'oeil*) were explored to the full by virtuoso woodworkers. Numerous sources were published, including Albrecht Dürer's *Undererweysung der Messung* (1525), Jean Cousin's *Livre de Perspective* (Paris, 1560), W.*Jamnitzer's *Perspectiva Corporum Regularium* (Nuremberg, 1568), the distorted, unrealistic forms of Lorenz Stöer's *Geometria et Perspectiva* (Augsburg, 1567), and the work of H.*Vredeman de Vries. The English inlaid wooden chests, sometimes known as Nonsuch chests and possibly made by immigrant craftsmen, represent an application of this work. Painted work (when feigning architecture, known as *quadratura*) in *niches, cupboards and on screens known as *devant la cheminée* (which gave protection from draughts) extended the use of perspectival decoration into domestic interiors of the late 17th and early 18th century. Some perspectival ornament was taken directly from architectural pattern books, e.g. G.B. da *Vignola's *Cinque Regole* was used in this way. But the popularity of the genre led to the publication of books that clearly aimed to show the potential of perspective as a device in decoration. Jean Dubreuil produced an important source, *La Perspective Pratique* (1642-49; second edition 1651), which was published in England by R.*Pricke as *Perspective Practical* in 1672, 1679 and 1698; there were

perspective. 1) Relief carving by Tullio Lombardo on the exterior of the Scuola Grande di San Marco, Venice, Italy, c.1490. 2) Marquetry perspective on the door of a 16th century Italian walnut press.

subject was more likely to be represented by a *trophy than by a personification.

The 19th century taste for moral or didactic decoration made use of personifications to this end. The anonymous *An Iconology, or a Collection of Emblematic Figures Moral and Instructive* (London, 1832) contained a fraction of the range of personifications offered by Ripa, and tended to concentrate on the more worthy subjects. Apart from the usual range of Virtues, Muses, Senses and Rivers, Patriotism was a new addition and Benevolence was given an importance it would not have had in earlier iconologies.

In the 20th century the device has, surprisingly, survived, particularly in commercial contexts when it is often used to advertise the business followed in the buildings, e.g. the helmeted winged figure (the Spirit of Power) above the main entrance of the Niagara Mohawk office building in Syracuse, New York (1930s).

many subsequent editions, and the work was known in America by 1741. A.*Pozzo, an architect and *Baroque designer, created elaborate interiors in which perspectival renderings in various media achieve sumptuous effects. His high-quality engraved designs, a synthesis of *trompe-l'oeil* paintwork and stucco within a framework of quite ordinary paint and stucco, were published in *Perspectiva Pictorum et Architectorum* (1693 and 1702), which ran into numerous editions and was translated into several languages in the early 18th century.

petal diaper. *See* scale pattern.

phoenix. A mythical bird of Egypt, referred to by classical authors such as Herodotus (c.485-c.425 BC) and Ovid (43 BC -c.17 AD), which was said to have lived for many hundreds of years, and finally burned itself to death on an altar fire; three days later a young phoenix arose from its ashes. The early Christians adopted the phoenix as a symbol of immortality and, specifically, of the resurrection of Christ. It was used in funerary sculpture, mosaics and manuscripts. It was a common motif in medieval emblems and allegorical decoration because the story of the phoenix had so many applications, e.g. the renewal of love, childbirth. Important in heraldry, the phoenix was incorporated into the badges of both Henry VII and Elizabeth I.

The phoenix appears in 18th century decoration, although usually in its almost unrecognisable *chinoiserie* form, the *ho ho bird, often placed on *rockwork or a twiggy branch rather than in flames. The Nymphenburg porcelain factory used a phoenix rising out of flames on a food warmer, c.1760. Buildings reconstructed after fire are sometimes ornamented with

*phoenix. 1) On *pediment, St Paul's Cathedral, London, by Christopher Wren, symbolising rebuilding after the Great Fire of 1666. 2) Exterior of house, Woodbridge, Suffolk.*

the bird, as at St Paul's Cathedral, London. After America had attained independence, the phoenix became a suitable emblem for the new nation and it was popular in England and America during the late 18th and early 19th centuries, e.g. surmounting looking-glasses and on door-cases.

Philadelphia Chippendale. *See* Chippendale, Thomas.

Phrygian bonnet or **Phrygian cap.** Conical headgear, a symbol of *liberty: an allusion to the freeing of Roman slaves, when they were ceremonially capped. Used as a decorative motif on objects produced in post-Revolutionary France and, to a lesser extent, in America. It was often stuck on the end of a pike and crossed with patriotic flags and weapons. It appeared on American textiles and wallpapers produced to commemorate the centenary in 1876 of the Declaration of American Independence.

Picturesque, The. An 18th century taste that sought to emphasise the connection between nature (selected or rearranged to reflect the ideals of the theorists) and built forms, such as the *cottage orné, particularly in the context of landscaped gardens and parks. It was a product of early 18th century romanticism, which was in its turn based upon classical Arcadia as rendered by late 17th century painters.

In ornament, it led to a fondness for *topographical decoration, *pastoral and *rustic themes, and *fêtes galantes, and in architecture, the theatricality of the *Castle style, the *Gothick, and a liking for atmospheric scenes set, for example, among *ruins.

The Picturesque, expanded in the 19th century as an aesthetic concern, underlay the tastes for *eclecticism, a repertoire of styles judged appropriate for certain building types, and some of the more fanciful aspects of the *Gothic Revival. Countless Picturesque *pattern books appeared in the first half of the 19th century providing eclectic designs for rural buildings and introducing a range of ornamental detail such as carved *bargeboards, *finials and *pendants, elaborated verandahs, porches and balconies, all of which were echoed in the American *Carpenter Gothic style. The American architect A.J.*Downing produced pattern books based on English Picturesque design.

pie ornament. *See* kikumon.

piecrust. Scrolled, scalloped rim applied mostly to English furniture (especially tables) and silver (particularly salvers). A popular ornament in the mid 18th century when it fitted the *Rococo predilection for

piecrust. English silver salver, 1735.

curving outlines, it also provided a useful raised rim. Piecrust ornament was revived and frequently used in the 19th century.

pied de biche. *See* hoof.

Pierretz, D. Antoine (fl c.1640-50). French architect, engraver and ornamentist in the *Louis XIV style. He published *Livre d'architecture de portes et de cheminées* (1647) and *Divers Desseins de cheminées à la royalle* (c.1650), which contained chimney designs of the pyramidal hood type (predating the classical rectangular chimneypiece that appeared later in the century). He also published a more general book of motifs fashionable at the time: *Recherche de plusieurs beaux morceaux d'ornemens antiques et modernes, comme trophées, frises, masques, feuillages et autres* (1648), a collection of designs for *Tabernacles, autels epitaphs*. He also illustrated Primaticcio's *grotesques at Fontainebleau under the title *Feuillages Modernes*. His son Antoine Le Jeune (fl c.1660-66) published ornament for metalwork, *Livre Nouveau de serrurie*, as well as *Livre de vases et ornements*, which included decorative borders for looking glasses.

pilaster. Flat, rectangular column form, one of the elements of *classical architecture which was enthusiastically readopted in the Italian *Renaissance. The function of the pilaster is only superficially that of support but it usually appears with an *entablature and flattened versions of the appropriate *capitals. It conforms to the system of the *Orders, but is generally associated with the more decorated types, with pronounced, tapering *reeding, *fluting or other decoration such as *chandelles or *cabled fluting on the shaft. Sir Henry Wotton (1568-1639) wrote that pilasters 'must not be too tall and slender, lest they resemble *Pillars*, too *dwarfish* and grosse, lest they imitate the *piles* or Peeres of Bridges: Smoothnesse doth not so naturally become them, as a Rusticke *Superficies*, for they ayme more at *State & Strength* than *Elegancie*'; although this is an accurate account of the Elizabethan pilaster, the classical version is usually treated in a lighter, more decorative fashion than Wotton's observation might suggest.

The pilaster doubles as a buttress in 16th century French buildings – this usage was emulated in the 1570s at Kirby Hall, Northamptonshire, but it was gradually flattened to mere surface decoration, until by the early 19th century it appeared in the *Greek Revival work of architects such as Sir John Soane, as a series of lines incised on otherwise unrelieved surfaces, only slightly resembling the pilaster form, and acting as a mere hint of ornament. Pilasters are sometimes used in the manner of a *Giant Order, running the height of more than one storey of the building.

A pilaster that does not conform to the Order of the building in general is known as an *anta – it is usually placed on a corner or projection, e.g. on a portico or at either end of a row of columns. A pilaster form with neither base or capital is called a *lesene or pilaster strip. *See also* chaînes.

pillar and arch. Standard trade description of an 18th century wallpaper pattern consisting of a round-headed arch supported by a pair of pillars or columns.

*pilaster. 1) *Giant Order pilasters on Palladian villa, Vicenza, Italy. pillar and arch. 2) American wallpaper fragment from a house in Haddam, Connecticut, c.1794-1800.*

It is generally used as a framing device. Pillar and arch patterns attained great popularity in America in the late 18th and early 19th century centuries.

Pillement, Jean (1727/28-1808). French painter and designer who worked in France, London, Spain, Italy, Portugal and finally Poland where, in 1767, he held the position of Premier Peintre du Roi de Pologne, Stanislaus August. He had similar status at the court of Marie Antoinette from 1778. He was a prolific designer in the light *Rococo style and incorporated many fantastic *chinoiserie motifs. His patterns have been identified on lacquered and marquetry furniture, silver, enamels, textiles, japanned tinware, porcelain and earthenware.

Pillement appears to have published at least 23 suites of ornamental designs between c.1755 and 1774, many in both London and Paris. He specialised in *chinoiserie*: *A New Book of Chinese Ornaments* (1755), *Livre de chinois* (1758), *Cahier d'oiseaux chinois* and *Etudes de différentes figures chinoises* (1758) being only a few.

Pillement was born in Lyons and some of his flower sprig designs are similar to those used in Lyons silk. Apart from naturalistic flowers he also devised fantastic and exotic blooms, e.g. *Recueil de nouvelles fleurs de goût pour la manufacture des étoffes de Perse* (1760), *Fleurs Persannes* (1760), *Recueil de fleurs de caprice* (1760) and *Fleurs de fantaisie dans le goût chinois* (1760). In England Pillement's work was widely used and influential, unsurprisingly, as he offered a wide range of subjects in the fashionable French Rococo style. *The Ladies Amusement or the Art of Japanning Made Easy* 'drawn by Pillement and other Masters' was first published in 1758, with a second edition in 1762, and reached a relatively wide audience. Pillement proffered advice on the use of his highly fanciful designs: 'for instance, if the scene be *European*, in the body of your Design place no exotic nor preposterous object', but in the case of Indian or Chinese subjects ' . . . greater liberties may be taken, because

Jean Pillement. 1) Engraving from The Ladies' Amusement, *1762. 2) Swedish faïence soup tureen with decoration after Pillement, made at Rörstrand, 1767.*

luxuriance of fancy recommends their Productions more than Propriety, for in them is often seen a Butterfly supporting an Elephant, or Things equally absurd: yet from their gay Colouring and Airy Disposition seldom fail to please.' Pillement added that his designs 'enabled any One (tho' unacquainted with Design) to embellish a plain surface with Ornaments superior to those we purchase at so great an Expence from *India* and elsewhere . . . ' An American reissue of 1959 had a note stating ' . . . Modern manufacturers of fabrics, textiles, silks, carpets, wallpapers and also interior decorators will also find the Ladies Amusement of the utmost interest and importance.'

pine. A decorative amalgamation of the ogival forms of the *pinecone and *pineapple used with additional flowers and foliage to create an effect that sometimes resembles Indian *Tree of Life textile patterns. Pines were a dominant element in the design of 15th and 16th century European textiles, particularly damasks and cut velvets. Although they fell from favour in the 17th century, patterns appeared up to the 20th century, their use extending to flocked wallpaper, which imitated cut velvet. *See also* paisley.

pineapple. Ancient symbol of fertility, particularly in the Middle East, and, from the late 17th century, a symbol of hospitality in Europe and subsequently, America, hence its use on gate piers, guest beds and bedrooms, at points of entrance and as a centrepiece in tableware. Charles II was presented with the first pineapple grown in England by John Rose, the royal

gardener, and thereafter it was cultivated as an exotic fruit.

In ornament it was often confused with the *pinecone (known in the 17th century as a 'pinappel'). Decorated silver cups for display were common gifts in the 17th century and in Germany they were often made in the form of pineapples (*Ananaspokal*), with the stem in the shape of a tree trunk or figure. A suitable form for a *finial, it appears frequently in *Rococo furniture, e.g. on the crest of a *pediment on a gilt mirror (c.1755) at Castle Howard, Yorkshire, on the state bed designed by G.B. Bovra, c.1752, at Stowe House, Buckinghamshire. The ceramics manufacturer Josiah Wedgwood produced 'pineapple ware' – tableware in the form of pineapples – c.1760, taking advantage of his newly developed solid green and yellow glazes.

Pineau, Nicolas (1684-1754). One of the leading exponents, with J.-A.*Meissonier, of the late *Rococo style (incorporating *rocaille curves and scrolls with flowers, *shells, *putti, etc.), in other words, the *genre pittoresque* that was fashionable in France during the 1720s and 1730s. Pineau trained as a sculptor and architect in France and, early in his career, worked in Russia. After his return to Paris in 1726 he rapidly became one of the most fashionable interior designers in a style that was to remain prevalent until the last quarter of the 18th century. The architect J.F.*Blondel, who borrowed freely from Pineau's designs in his *De la distribution des maisons de plaisance* (Paris, 1738), described the effect of Pineau's work (wall panels and furniture) for the Duchesse de Mazarin at the Hôtel Mazarin: 'Symmetry is banished, the composition and elegance of the ornament has never been more satisfying – amusing ideas which the magic of mirrors repeat and multiply to infinity.' Engravings of Pineau's designs were popular – suites for *cartouches, chimneypieces, panels, mirrors, *console tables, *torchères, vases, etc., – and his work was pirated by many other authors. During the 1740s, in England, B. and T.*Langley published Pineau's designs for console tables as their own 'after the French manner', and in Germany the

*pine. 1) 14th century Sicilian woven silk. 2) 16th century velvet damask hangings from H.*Shaw's* The Encyclopaedia of Ornament, *1842.*

designers, particularly those working in the *Neo-classical style, adopted the pinecone from Egyptian and classical sources as, for example, in designs for chairs by both C.*Tatham and T.*Hope. The *thyrsus, often shown in *Bacchic ornament, has pinecone terminals.

pine tree. An important motif in Japanese decoration, the pine tree is one of the Three Friends of Winter; the other two are *bamboo and plum *blossom. It frequently appears in *chinoiserie and *japonaiserie. In the mid 1920s, the English glass artist, Frederick Carder (1864-1963), created a range of decoration at the Steuben glassworks, New York, based on the gnarled pine tree branch and called by its Japanese name, *matsu-no-ke*.

Pine trees and other coniferous trees were also used in a style of *pastoral ornament that was popular in the mid 19th century, e.g. the Sèvres porcelain *service forestier* is bordered with pine.

Piranesi, Giovanni Battista (1720-78). Italian architect, archaeologist, art dealer and engraver who pursued an individual but highly influential path in the development of *Neo-classicism. Although until the mid 1760s he stoutly defended the functionalism of Roman architecture and ornament, he then changed course, promoting its imaginative richness – he regarded the narrow precepts of *Vitruvius as obstacles to creativity. Piranesi increasingly advocated the re-assembling of fragments of the past into new forms and many of his engravings combined antiquarianism and artistry to full effect. He went on to suggest that the bases of modern ornament and design should lie not merely in Greece and Rome, but also in *Etruscan and even *Egyptian precedents. Piranesi's publications and engravings were widely known, especially

*pinecone. 1) Frontispiece from the Comte *de Caylus's* Recueil d'antiquités, 1752-67. 2) *Finials on 'Grand Antique Chair' from C.H.*Tatham's* Etchings Representing Fragments of Grecian and Roman Architectural Ornament, 1806. 3) The Orangery, Castle Ashby, Northamptonshire, architect M.D. Wyatt, 1861-65.*

pineapple. 1) Early 17th century German silver gilt Ananaspokal. *2) Ham House, Surrey, 1637. 3) English earthenware teapot, Wedgwood, c.1755-65. 4) Queensware centrepiece, Wedgwood, c.1774. 5) Base, English silver pier table by Andrew Moore from Windsor Castle, Berkshire, c.1700.*

Augsburg publisher J.G. Merz republished a number of Pineau's suites of designs in the 1750s. Like the work of many other Rococo *ornemanistes*, his designs were republished by Edouard Rouvèyre in Paris in 1889.

pinecone or **fir-cone.** Sometimes called a fir-apple or pinappel. In Egyptian funerary art, the pinecone was used as a symbol of fertility and regeneration (e.g. in the Hall of Osiris, Denderah). It appears in Assyrian art with the *Tree of Life motif. A similar motif has been found on Etruscan tombs. The pinecone rarely appears in medieval and *Renaissance ornament in Europe. Sir Christopher Wren (1632-1723) used it as an alternative to the *acorn for *finials, and it has since proved a highly popular ornament for finials, *pendants and *knops. Used on top of doorways, gate-posts, mirrors, bureaux, etc., it has often been confused with the *pineapple. Early 19th century

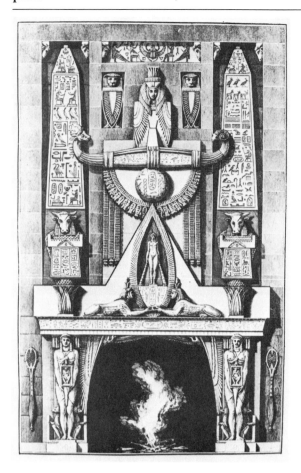

Giovanni Battista Piranesi. 1) Egyptian fireplace from Diverse Maniere d'Adornare i Cammini, *1769. 2) Vase from the Circo di Caracalla, Rome.*

to patrons of architecture and architectural students in Rome in the 1760s. He dedicated *Il Campo Marzio dell'antica Roma* (1762) to Robert Adam (*see* Adam style), and other leading collectors were mentioned in his works, either as owners of the objects illustrated (many of which had passed through his hands in his role as a dealer) or as dedicatees, and, often, subscribers. His first important publication was an account of late Roman work, *Antichità Romane de' tempi della Repubblica* (1748), although his first suite of engravings, *Prima*

parte di architettura e prospettive (1743), an account of late Roman work, had been surprisingly *Rococo in spirit. Particularly influential in the area of architectural detail and ornament were *Antichità Romane* (4 vols, 1756), *Della Magnificenza ed Archittetura de' Romani* (1761), *Vasi, Candelabri, Cippi, Sarcophagi* (engraved sheets, 1768; bound edition, 1778), and in 1769 his most important work for interior decoration, *Diverse Maniere d'Adornare i Cammini*. Sources for *Diverse Maniere* included Roman sarcophagi, *friezes from the Temple of Antoninus, and Faustina, *trophies from the base of Trajan's column, details from *triumphal arches, reliefs from *stucchi* in Roman tombs, and, most originally, Egyptian designs. It also contains his decorations in the *Etruscan style for the Church of the Knights of Malta, S. Maria del Priorato (Aventine Hill, Rome), Piranesi's only architectural work, rebuilt 1765. Piranesi designed wall paintings in a loose rendering of the Egyptian style for the Caffè degli Inglesi (an English meeting place in Rome), also providing *Pompeian murals and mosaic floors in line with the fashions of the time. Two plates were published in 1769 with *An Apologetical Essay in Defence of the Egyptian and Tuscan Architecture.*

The *Diverse Maniere* was a highly influential source for many of the most important decorative schemes of the late 18th century and, in its themes, of inestimable importance to early 19th century European and American *eclecticism. Though Piranesi's work showed a *Baroque type of *classicism, his wide-ranging source material was novel and in sharp contrast to the purist attitudes of the *Greek Revival designers of the late 18th and early 19th centuries. Specific examples of this influence include motifs such as *griffins seated back to back with their tails entwined, used by François-Joseph Bélanger (1744-1818) in his decoration of the Bagatelle in the Bois de Boulogne, Paris, a little *château* built for the Comte d'Artois (brother of Louis XVI and the future Charles X) in 1779. Robert Adam's decoration of the 1770s and 1780s (*see* Adam style) owed a heavy debt to Piranesi for ideas such as Etruscan rooms. Despite his many followers, Piranesi also had his detractors. His undermining of Vitruvian classicism attracted the accusation from C.H.*Tatham that by 'rejecting with disdain the constraints of minute observation, he has sometimes sacrificed accuracy to what he conceived the richer productions of a more fertile and exuberant mind.' In addition, the designs were 'too voluminous and expensive for general circulation; and hence their utility must be confined to a few, while the want of that assistance they are capable of affording must be felt and lamented by many.' In 1789, long after his death, his sons took the plates to Paris and successfully republished his work there, reflecting the renewed interest in classicism evinced by the new regime.

plaid. *See* Scottish ornament.

plant forms are perhaps the most universal theme in ornament. Each culture has its own repertoire, with the plants often having symbolic importance and frequently being stylised almost beyond recognition. Ornament in *Graeco-Roman classicism used garlands, *festoons, foliage (especially the *acanthus leaf) on

plant forms. 1) Late 16th century English linen embroidered with black silk. 2) Manueline foliate *mouldings, Mosteiro dos Jeronimos, Belém, Portugal, early 16th century. 3) Late 17th century English or Dutch carved boxwood frame in the manner of Grinling Gibbons. 4) Jacobean carved panel, Chastleton House, Oxfordshire, 1606. 5) Petites Fleurs Arabesques, ou semences de bouquets pour les etoffes *by P.A.*Ducerceau, c.1700.*

*capitals, and *friezes of *scrolling foliage. *Gothic architecture made broader use of plant motifs, which were often highly *naturalistic, and they appeared on *mouldings and *crockets, in particular.

Textile design has always made extensive use of plant motifs, particularly of floral subjects. At first, patterns were restricted by weaving techniques and the size of printing blocks, but there was still a substantial variety of patterns. Medieval tapestry used clumps of *millefleurs, early *Renaissance damasks and velvets employed a wide range of symmetrical designs based on stylised *pomegranate and *pine forms. At first, the *herbals were the only source of botanical illustrations, but gradually *pattern books became important (*see* Le Moyne de Morgues, J.).

In metalwork and jewellery the graphic possibilities of engraving made plants a rich and important vein in decoration, in stylised 17th century *peapod ornament as well as in naturally depicted flowers. The range and toning of colours that it was possible to produce with enamelling made this another obvious medium for the use of plant motifs.

Throughout the 17th century, knowledge of plants grew, and collections of rare specimens were made. Plant and flower engravings provided a wealth of sources for ornamental craftsmen, and interest in botany grew. In France, Henri IV purchased a garden and plant collection started by Jean Robin in Paris, which was the basis for the Jardin du Roi (later the Jardin des Plantes) and in 1608 *Le Jardin du Roi* was published with engraved plates by Pierre Vallet (1575-1642), who was described in the book as Embroiderer to the King. Many rare and newly introduced species such as *tulips were included in this book, and it was suggested that the illustrations, apart from their value as a botanical record, would be useful to embroiderers, painters, illuminators and tapestry weavers. For most of the 17th century, naturalistic renderings of flowers were common. Flower painting, particularly in Holland, was enormously popular, and pattern books, sometimes focusing on specific plants, proliferated. Important designers in this area included Nicolas Guillaume de la Fleur (d 1670), whose suites of flower designs were published in Rome, Paris and Amsterdam, and Jean Baptiste Monnoyer (1635-99), who was himself a flower painter and produced designs in which the flowers were arranged in baskets, vases, garlands and bound sprays. Sometimes the patterns were aimed at specific craftsmen: François Lefebvre, a Paris goldsmith, published *Livre de fleurs et de feuilles pour servir à l'art d'orfevrerie* (1635, 1639), which was engraved by Balthasar Moncornet (d 1688) who also engraved *Livre Nouveau de fleurs très utiles pour l'art d'orfevrerie* (1645, 1665) and *Ornements de joaillerie* (1665). Lefebvre also published Jean Vauquer's suites entitled *Livre de fleurs propres pour orfevres et graveurs* (1680). P.A.*Ducerceau's *Bouquets propres pour les etoffes de Tours* (c.1660-70) was for woven silk designs, and *Livre de fleurs, feuilles et oyzeaus* (1656) by Guillaume Toulouze was aimed at embroiderers. The range of flowers was wide, but among the most popular were tulips, narcissi, snake head and crown imperial fritillaries, crocuses, lilies, orchids, roses, pinks, clematis and campanula. At the end of the 17th century extravagant scrolling foliage and *baskets of fruit and flowers were very popular.

In Britain, the arrival of *William and Mary from Holland in 1688 increased the influence of Dutch painters of flowers, and floral designs appeared in marquetry on chests, desks, cabinets, and later longcase clocks. A new and important influence in plant ornament also appeared at this time from the East. Chinese lacquer and ceramics were imported in quantity, and in their wake there developed a vein of exotic, sometimes fantastic, flower ornament, as Western craftsmen attempted to copy unfamiliar flowers such as the *chrysanthemum painted by the Chinese. **Chinoiserie* designs also imitated the oriental compositions of flowers and plants towering over tiny figures and animals. By the *Rococo period of *chinoiserie*, some purely imaginary flowers had been devised, such as the 'umbrella flower' concocted by J.*Pillement. Chinese *famille rose* and Japanese *kakiemon patterns were widely imitated.

Towards the middle of the 18th century, there was a general move in plant decoration away from exotic plants and a new enthusiasm for simpler, often wild

plant forms. 1) Flowers for September from Robert Furber's The Flower Garden Display'd, *1732. 2) Umbrella flowers from J.*Pillement's* Fleurs Idéales, *1770. 3) English cotton fabric designed by J.S. Wheelwright for Warner & Son, 1929.*

be instructed in designing, colouring and shadowing of natural flowers and ornaments', an indication of the importance attached to this type of natural decoration at the time.

In the mid 1750s, Chelsea produced a range of plates known as Hans Sloane Botanical which were adapted from the illustrations in Philip Miller's *Figures of the Most Beautiful and Uncommon Plants* (1752). Copenhagen's Flora Danica plates, produced from 1790, were decorated in a similar manner using the *Flora Danica* (published 1761-1871) as their source. Even seed catalogues were used for reference: the Kensington nurseryman Robert Furber produced a catalogue of his stock entitled *Twelve Months of Flowers* (1730) with engravings after Pieter Casteels, which were republished six times between 1740 and 1760. An abridged edition of the catalogue called *The Flower Garden Display'd* was described at the time as 'very useful, not only for the Curious in Gardening, but the Prints likewise for Painters, Carvers, Japaners, etc. also for Ladies as Patterns for working and painting in watercolours; or furniture for the closet.' As there was a precedent for the use of naturalistically rendered plants in Roman art of the Augustan period, they were considered acceptable in *Neo-classical ornament, although they had to be accomodated within the formal restrictions of *pateras, narrow friezes, *rosettes and the *Orders, and tended to be plants such as marguerites, *roses, *palms, and *laurel. The *Empire style, however, abandoned plant forms in favour of militaristic motifs and mythical beasts.

The Victorian enthusiasm for brightly coloured and over-blown flowers was clear in the outburst of naturalistic plant ornament in the mid 19th century. According to the Jury of the Great Exhibition, London, 1851, 'the task is to cover the surface almost entirely with large, coarse flowers: dahlias, hollyhocks, roses, hydrangeas, or other which gave scope for strong or vivid colouring, and which are often magnified by the designer much beyond the scale of nature.' Droopy, bell-like flowers such as lily of the valley, convolvulus, snowdrops and harebells were also popular.

From the 1820s a large number of books were published on 'floral emblems' and 'flower language'. Every plant was invested with some symbolic meaning, often on fairly tenuous grounds, e.g. the poppy, known to induce sleep, represented consolation. Thomas Miller, in the *Poetical Language of Flowers* (1855), suggests moss for Maternal Love: 'soft, green velvet covering of many a spot which would otherwise be brown and barren; it grows around and shelters the stem of many a delicate flower, which would otherwise perish, and gives warmth to many a chilly nook; and so may fancy stretch, link by link, until it traces in it a resemblance to Maternal Love'.

In the second half of the 19th century, William Morris (1834-96) and the *Arts and Crafts movement led the move back to simple, uncomplicated flowers, as illustrated in medieval *herbals, which Morris had studied extensively. His designs include columbines, poppies, honeysuckle, pinks, anemones, marigolds, daisies, jasmine, etc. Morris advised designers to 'be shy of double flowers . . . choose the old china aster with

flowers to produce naturalistic sprigs and fronds with uncomplicated blooms, which were equally popular as motifs on furniture mounts, porcelain, plasterwork, *boiseries*, silver and in silk design. Marie Antoinette's bedroom at the Petit Trianon, Versailles (1768), was decorated with a typical selection: daisies, stocks, violets and anemones. Also popular were larkspurs, roses, carnations, *poppies and cornflowers (*see* Angoulême sprig). In 1756, a contemporary writer on 'the designing and drawing of ornaments, models and patterns' suggested that those intending to pursue the art of decoration should go first to drawing schools and then be placed with a flower painter 'where they may the yellow centre, that goes so well with the purple-brown stems and curiously coloured florets, instead of the clumps that look like cut paper, of which we are now so proud.' The *Aesthetic movement also espoused simple flowers and plant forms such as *sunflowers; the Guild of Handicrafts adopted the pink as an emblem. Towards the end of the 19th century, *Art Nouveau architects and designers turned towards roots, buds and *seedpods for a new vocabulary of shapes and motifs that would fit the dynamic lines of the style's ornament. Emile Gallé (1846-1904) considered that the only natural ornament for wooden furniture was vegetal motifs, preferably suggestive of lines of natural growth. Like his mid-century predecessors, Gallé enjoyed appropriate ornamentation: a dining table decorated '*aux herbes potagères*', for example. Like Morris, Gallé chose the plants that were growing around him in the French countryside: cow parsley, mistletoe, sycamore, waterlilies. The work of E.*Grasset, M.P. Verneuil's *Etude de la plante, son application aux industries d'art* (Paris, 1901) and E.A.*Séguy's *Les Fleurs et leurs applications décoratives* used a wide selection of plants, often with a bias towards sinuous forms, such as passion flowers, poppies, wisteria and waterlilies. The English designer and teacher L.F.*Day was a great exponent of exploring new areas of plant ornament: 'the rose has been variously treated, but comparatively little use has been made of the fruit, or of the thorns, or of the broad stipules at the base of the leaves. We have to be grateful when the buds, with

*plant forms. 1) French Art Nouveau bed with inlaid wooden decoration made by Perol Frères, c.1900. 2) Engraved silver cigarette case made at the Wiener Werkstätte, 1920s. 3) Textile design by E.A.*Séguy from his* Bouquets et frondaisons, *1925. 4) English silvered wood cabinet designed by Serge Chermayeff, 1930s.*

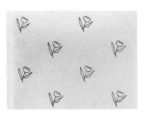

their boldly pronounced sepals are, once in a way, tuned to ornamental account.'

Stylised flowers were a predominant theme in *Art Deco ornament, although they tended to be confined to festoons, garlands or baskets in the classical manner, or to be used to produce a densely packed effect. Favourite forms included tightly packed rosebuds and composites such as marguerites, daisies and zinnias, as in E.A. Séguy's *Bouquets et frondaisons* (Paris, 1927).

*Modernist decoration ousted the plant from ornament. But the work of Frank Lloyd Wright (1869-1959), much influenced by earlier designers such as L.H.*Sullivan, demonstrated the use of plant ornament in a formalised but still decorative manner. More naturalistically rendered floral decoration returned to the provinces of textiles, ceramics and jewellery, but rarely strayed into furniture or architecture.

Plateresque (Spanish, *platero*, silversmith). Highly decorated style adopted in 16th century Spanish architecture. Motifs were *classical and *Renaissance forms sometimes intricate enough to recall metalwork in the *Mudejar style. Decoration was applied somewhat indiscriminately to the exterior and interior walls of late *Gothic buildings. The ornament is usually concentrated in doorways, open upper storeys and *cresting, *finials, *arcading, stairways and ceilings. Contemporary and comparable to *Lombardic Renaissance decoration in Italy or the *Manueline style in Portugal, the style combined the overall ornamentation introduced in the *Hispano-Moresque period with ostentatious ornament, indicative of Spain's newfound wealth in the Americas. The style had an echo in the *Churrigueresque style of the *Baroque period. It reappeared in late 19th century America as one of the strands in the *Spanish Colonial Revival.

Plenty. Personification that first appeared in the *Renaissance. It was popular in the 18th and 19th centuries in Europe and America, often accompanied by symbols of fertility, *cornucopias and sometimes the figure of *Peace. An appropriate figure for use on markets and commercial buildings.

The word Plenty, with a cornsheaf below it, is used as a decorative motif on fancy-back spoons (*see* Hanoverian pattern), usually teaspoons.

plinth. The square base of a *column or *pedestal.

plume. *See* feathers.

pomegranate. As a symbol of fertility and fecundity, because of its many seeds, the pomegranate is an ancient motif in oriental and *classical decoration. Its Christian significance is as a symbol of chastity (seeds enclosed within the fruit), or of the Church. It appears in many media, e.g. early 15th century Italian textiles (derived from Eastern *Tree of Life patterns) and 17th century woodcarving and plasterwork. When used in silver, it occasionally forms a ball foot (usually on tankards). It was also used, like the *boteh in *paisley designs, as a repeating motif in formalised vegetal patterns. Depicted as an open fruit, its seeds exposed

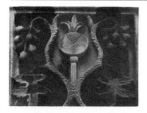

pomegranate. 1) Byzantine fragment, Cathedral of St Mark, Venice,
Italy. 2) Carved wooden doorcase, Paycocke's House, Coggeshall, Essex,
c.1500. 3) Plaster ceiling, Chastleton House, Oxfordshire, 1606.
4) Plasterwork at a late 19th century public house, Dulwich, South London.

and surrounded by leaves and tiny blossoms, the pomegranate was a favourite *Jacobean motif in stone
and wood but especially in plasterwork, and as such
enjoyed a revival in the late 19th century *Jacobean
Revival.

It was the *impresa of the Holy Roman Emperor
Maximilian I (1459-1519), the badge of Catherine of
Aragon and the emblem of the Spanish province of
Granada (granada is Spanish for pomegranate).

Pompeian style. Pompeii (known as Città until 1763)
was discovered in 1748 and excavated from 1755.
When details of the contents of this sizeable Roman
town in southern Italy were published, together with
information about *Herculaneum, they were a revelation to architects, designers, engravers and craftsmen. Pompeii was an important primary source of
information about Roman domestic surroundings
and artefacts, because examples had been preserved
in outstanding condition by the lava from Mount
Vesuvius that had engulfed the town in 79 AD. The
frescoed wall decorations were to provide the chief
inspiration, with delicate motifs such as *nymphs,
*candelabra and *grapevines framed in fragile *trel-
lising and *grotesques. Their forms and clear, deep
colours were to inspire many a 'Pompeian Room' and
to establish a vogue lasting almost a century. Mosaics
and stuccoed ceiling ornament were also influential.
The excavations of Herculaneum and Pompeii were
as important to interior designers as publications of
classical Greek buildings were to architects at the same
period. G.B.*Piranesi used Pompeian motifs in his
Diverse Maniere. A full and accurate description of
Pompeian discoveries was provided by Sir William
Gell (1777-1836) and J.P. Gandy (1747-1850) in Pompeiana; the Topography, Edifices and Ornaments of Pompeii

(1817-19); another edition appeared in 1821, a French
edition in 1827, and a revised version with new finds
in 1832. Gell, famed for his earlier publications on
Greek sites, was converted to a preference for Roman
*classicism and on settling in Italy he decorated a room
in a Pompeian-cum-Etruscan style. W. Zahn's publication (see Herculaneum) was greatly admired by O.
*Jones, who eulogised the free-hand, sketchy technique
of the designers, ' . . . which has never been accomplished in any restoration of the style'. *Adam style
decorators scattered their interiors with medallions
and plaques filled by dancing nymphs ('Herculaneum
dancers'); delicate frameworks of loops of *husks or
exquisite borders echoed those used to compartmen-
talise Pompeian decoration. Pompeian interiors were
popular over a long period in England, from the
Pompeian Hall (c.1782) by Joseph Bonomi at Great

Pompeian style. 1) Side of a Cubiculum from Sir William Gell's
Pompeiana, 1817-19. 2) Pompeian ornament from O.*Jones's
Grammar of Ornament, 1868 edition.

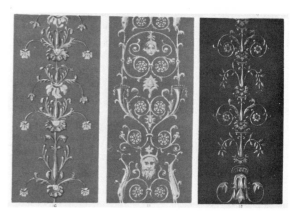

Packington, Warwickshire, to a scheme at Ickworth, Suffolk, dating from as late as 1879. Prince Albert's Garden Pavilion at Buckingham Palace also adopted the style.

The French equivalent of *Pompeiana* was a book by Charles François Mazois (1783-1826) called *Les Ruines de Pompeii* but only four volumes of a projected series were published, in 1809, 1811, 1824 and 1838. The Grand Salon of the Petits Appartements of Marie Antoinette at Versailles (1783), as well as the cups, saucers and milk bowls for her Laiterie de Trianon (1788), were carried out in Pompeian style. From the mid 1780s French manufacturers followed the royal example.

In Germany K.F.*Schinkel used Pompeian decoration, notably at the Glienicke, Berlin, a landscaped area of park and villas with incidental buildings where exterior walls were enlivened with such schemes. Leo von Klenze (1784-1864) designed the Hofgarten Arcade in Munich (from 1826) in a similar vein. The motifs of the style were soon mass-produced, especially the nymphs and *bacchantes: a silver plaque bearing such figures was produced in electrotype in Britain, Germany, France and America, with a design that was registered as late as 1876.

Pont Street Dutch style. *See* Flemish Revival.

poppy. Well known as an opiate from classical times and therefore the attribute of Hypnos, god of sleep, of Morpheus, god of dreams, and of *night. In ornament, poppy flowers and seed pods were particularly popular for the decoration of bedrooms, beds and tombs. The motif was used frequently by C.*Percier and P.*Fontaine and subsequently recommended by T.*Hope, R.*Ackermann and R.*Brown. The decorative potential of the flower was fully exploited in *Art Nouveau, and appeared in most collections of plant ornament at the time, such as E.*Grasset's *Plants and their Application to Ornament* (1896).

poppyhead. Carved *finial on pew ends, characteristic of 15th century ecclesiastical interiors. Poppyheads are generally carved with stylised foliage (the *fleur-de lis lends itself well to the form), but they may also be in the shape of more naturalistic plants, figures or animals.

poppyhead. Carved bench ends. 1) Church of St Andrew, Norton, Suffolk, 15th century. 2) Church of St Margaret, Cley, Norfolk, early 16th century.

*portrait heads. 1) Early 16th century stone carving on Church of St Saveur, Caen (Calvados), France. 2) Engraving by Adriaen Collaert with portrait of the Roman Emperor Tiberius set within grotesque *strapwork, late 16th century. 3) Building in Trinity Street, Cambridge, England, c.1860.*

portrait heads. Classical portraits, often in profile, on *cameos, gems, coins and medals were the origin of this popular *Renaissance motif, which quickly spread from Italy across Europe. There were many engravings of portrait heads, usually set within a roundel. Early examples are included in the *Hypnerotomachia, and in illustrations to works that originally appeared in the 14th century such as Petrarch's *Trionfi* (Venice, 1500, 1523, 1545), Giovanni Boccaccio's *De Casibus Virorum Illustrium* and Jacob Mazocchi's *Illustrium Imagines*. Specific *pattern books of portrait heads quickly followed: E.*Vico engraved *Primorum XII Caesarum Verissimae Effigies, Omnium Caesarum Verissimae Imagines ex Antiquis Numismatis Desumptae* (1553) and an early non-Italian work in this style, A. Gessner's *Imperatorum Romanorum Omnium Orientalium et Occidentalium Verissimae Imagines* (1559). Portrait heads were also incorporated in panels of *scrolling foliage, *strapwork, *arabesques and *grotesques, particularly by Dutch and German ornamentists, such as Lucas van Leyden (fl 1468-1533) and the *Beham brothers. During the second half of the 16th century, they frequently appeared engraved on metalwork, carved on furniture and applied to the exterior of buildings. The earliest examples in Britain were terracotta Caesar heads, the work of an Italian craftsman, which ornament the Tudor wing of Hampton Court Palace, Surrey, commissioned by Thomas Wolsey, Cardinal and Lord Chancellor under Henry VIII. During the 17th century, Roman emperors' heads quite frequently decorated Caroline houses, applied directly to walls set within *niches or on small *scrolled pediments, emphasising their classical Italian design. Soon, instead of classical heroes, figures from more recent European history were used; V̄.*Solis, for example, produced a series of the Kings of France. Portrait heads gradually fell from favour although they were readopted, particularly in cameo form, wherever *classicism appeared. In the 19th century they were again revived, usually on the exterior of public buildings, depicting great men of the past (e.g. Shakespeare, Newton, Handel), although also accompanying contemporary figures. Often the selection reflected the purpose of the building, e.g. artists on art galleries, scientists on technical schools. *See also* romayne work.

Post-Modern. Term recently coined to cover the tendency, in architecture at first, to reject the plain, unadorned forms of the Modern Movement and later *Modernist work. From the mid 1960s onwards American and European architects began to look for historic references and a new repertoire of forms for their buildings. Tradition and the *classical repertoire were both invoked: ornament such as false *pediments or *keystones, the *ribbon garlands on Michael Graves's Portland Public Building (1982) and the sun motifs scattered throughout Charles Jencks's house in West London demonstrate a reaction against the dourness of the preceding period, rather than a style in its own right.

Post War. The functionalism of the Modern Movement in architecture and associated design, followed by the drabness of the war years, meant that, by the late 1940s and early 1950s, designers were ready for a return to the ornamental. The reaction was summed up by designer Geoffrey Boumphrey, writing in the magazine *Contact*, in 1949: 'After years of austerity I feel a need for ornament, gaiety and pattern.' The *classical shapes and forms which had been favoured in

Post War. Page from Joan B. Priolo's Designs and How to Use Them, *New York, 1956.*

the 1930s were ignored in favour of the novel. Ornament was to draw on such themes as advanced science, nuclear physics, *crystals and *molecular structure. It also drew upon the expressive amoeboid shapes of contemporary painting and sculpture (*see* Organic Modernism). Various forms of revivalism also became evident: the folk art of fairground and circus, Victoriana (vintage cars, penny-farthing bicycles, ballooning), but above all the revived possibilities of foreign travel which made topography and, in particular, popular symbols of France (pavement cafés, artists in berets, the Eiffel Tower) or Italy (Venetian gondolas, the Leaning Tower of Pisa) widely used themes in ornament. Seaside or *marine subjects were popular, probably because of the large number of people able to take holidays after the years of wartime austerity. The 1951 Festival of Britain concentrated the attention of the public on design in a light-hearted event intended to lift the Post War mood of austerity. However these escapist themes did not endure much past the mid 1950s.

*powdered ornament. Patterns for powdering from A.W.N.*Pugin's* Glossary of Ecclesiastical Ornament and Costume, *1844.*

powdered ornament. Decoration originating in medieval *heraldic ornament. Small decorative devices, typically *fleurs-de-lis, *stars and flower sprigs are scattered evenly over a surface. Powdered ornament reappeared in the 19th century *Gothic Revival, often stencilled. Designs were produced by C.*Dresser and the *Audsley family, some using *japonaiserie motifs, although these tended to be placed more formally than they would have been in the original Japanese designs.

In heraldry, this form of ornament is known as semé, semy, aspersed, replenished, strewed or poudré decoration.

Pozzo, Andrea (1642-1709). A lay brother in the Jesuit order and an architect, Pozzo was best known as a painter of illusionistic ceilings (*see* perspective). Much of his life was spent in Rome, though he moved to Vienna in 1702. Through his *Perspectiva Pictorum et Architectorum* (2 vols, Rome 1693 and 1702), his influence in spreading the Italian *Baroque was considerable. His work was translated into English, German and Flemish and there was a manuscript version of the book in Chinese. Apart from the designs concerned with perspective, there are also flamboyant designs for altars, tabernacles and temporary structures.

Pricke, Robert (fl 1669-98). London bookseller and publisher of a number of anthologies of French and Italian engraved ornament in *pattern book form. The need for such borrowing from continental Europe illustrates the paucity of English material at this period, when there was hectic building activity following the Restoration of the Monarchy in 1660 and the Great Fire of London in 1666. Examples of his publications include *Ornaments of Architecture* (1674), *The Architect's Storehouse* (1674) and work by the artists J. and P.*Le Pautre, J.*Marot, D.A.*Pierretz, A.*Mitelli, S.*della Bella, J.*Barbet, P.A.*Ducerceau and P.*Le Muet. *Ornaments of Architecture* and *The Architect's Storehouse* were produced as companion volumes and dealt with architectural detail and ornament, including *heraldic motifs, *festoons, funerary monuments and *inscriptions.

Prince Henri pattern. *See* dragon.

prismatic ornament. 20th century term for simple, three-dimensional geometric forms in low relief, a widely used decorative effect in architecture. Common variations include *jewelled strapwork, *lozenges and chamfered *rustication. Prismatic ornament was one of the few types of embellishment to be used on the relatively undecorated buildings of the 1920s and 1930s.

Prisse d'Avennes, A.C.T.E. (d 1879). French engineer who, from 1830, was employed permanently in Egypt. His interest in archaeology led him back to France in 1844 to begin work on a series of publications, illustrated with the highest quality coloured chromolithographs, including *Les Monuments Egyptiens* (1847) and *L'Histoire de l'art égyptien* (2 vols, 1858-77). However, by far his most important work was *L'Art Arabe d'après les monuments du Cair depuis le VIIe siècle jusqu'à la fin du XVIIIe siècle* (1869-77). Prisse d'Avennes was one of the few Westerners who had actually gained access to *Islamic interiors, and he included detail such as *Kufic inscriptions, *stalactite work, *mushrebîyeh* screens and elaborate geometrically patterned wall tiles, that he had observed first-hand. The general effect was an authentic one that in general escaped fashionable 19th century *Arabian style designers who were interested in a general effect rather than archaeological or historic accuracy. He also illustrated carpets, ivories, damascened metalwork and arms and armour. Despite the fact that *L'Art Arabe* was incomparably better researched than other publications on Islamic art, e.g. the early works of P.-X.*Coste and O.*Jones, it appeared too late to be widely influential. However William Burges's Arab Hall at Cardiff Castle, Wales (1881) closely followed certain of Prisse d'Avennes's illustrations and included stalactite work, *trellis screens and Kufic inscriptions.

prismatic ornament. 1) Cobham Hall, Kent, late 16th and early 17th centuries. 2) House in Roemer Visscherstraat, Amsterdam, c.1900. 3) Late 19th century villa, King William district, San Antonio, Texas.

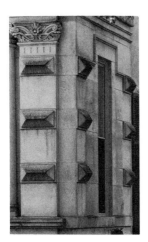

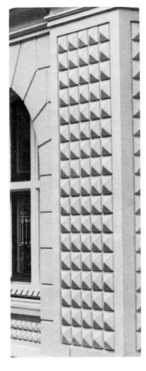

A.C.T.E. Prisse d'Avennes. From L'Art Arabe, *1869-77.*

progressive ornament. An uninterrupted strip or band of ornament e.g. *wavescroll, *key or *guilloche patterns.

protomai. *Capital with *half-figures, often animals, projecting from its four corners. Widely used in *Romanesque architecture.

proudwork. Similar to *flushwork, but with the stone in higher relief than the flint. It is less frequently used, but appears mainly in ecclesiastical architecture, especially *Perpendicular Gothic and *Tudor.

prow. The projecting prow of a classical vessel appears multiply on the *columna rostrata, and is also an ornamental motif in its own right, in schemes of *marine decoration and, in particular, where there is an association with *commerce. The ship is the emblem of the city of Paris and thus the form appears widely in Parisian ornament. Its protruding shape makes it a suitable architectural embellishment, in effect a highly elaborate *keystone, over prominent gateways or doorways.

prow. 19th century commercial building, Liverpool, England.

prunt. Ornamental blob of glass particularly characteristic of 15th century German drinking glasses. Applied when molten, the glass prunt is then shaped. It may be pulled into a large spike as on a tumbler called an *Igel* (German for hedgehog) or drawn into a more squat spike as on the so-called *Krautstrunk* (German for cabbage stalk). Prunts may also be press-moulded to make blackberry or medallion shapes. *See also* lily pad.

Pugin, Augustus Charles (1762-1832). Father of A.W.N. *Pugin, whose various antiquarian publications, largely on *Gothic architecture, were the starting point for his son's involvement with the architecture and ornament of that period. Two of his more important titles were *Pugin's Gothic Ornaments Selected from Various Buildings in England and France* (London, 1831; new edition 1916) and *A Series of Ornamental Timber Gables from Existing Examples in England and France* (1839). *See also* Ackermann, Rudolph.

Pugin, Augustus Welby Northmore (1812-52). A pioneering propagandist for the *Gothic as the true Christian architectural style, Pugin was also adamant that ornament should be 'honest' to the underlying structure, i.e. that it should be an embellishment rather than a disguise. Early work (which he later regretted) consisted of helping his father design furniture for Windsor Castle, prints of which were published in R.*Ackermann's *Repository* in 1827. *Gothic furniture in the style of the 15th century* (1835), *Designs for Iron and Brass Work in the style of the XV and XVI centuries* (1836), *Designs for*

Gold and Silversmiths and *Details of Ancient Timber Houses of the 15th and 16th centuries* (1836) were later produced in a collected edition as *Ornaments of the 15th and 16th centuries* (Edinburgh, 1904). These publications established Pugin's reputation as a designer. They were reissued in France in the 1850s and gained a further boost in Britain in the 1890s as a result of the *Arts and Crafts movement, whose members appreciated their authenticity. Pugin's early sources for the Gothic style were the 17th century illustrators David Loggan and Wenceslaus Hollar, and he based his decoration on actual medieval examples in his possession, e.g. 14th century manuscripts, casts of Gothic sculptures. *The True Principles of Pointed or Christian Architecture* (1841; French edition 1850) in which he expounded his view of the Gothic as the ecclesiastical style *par excellence* established Pugin as a theorist and polemicist. He had prepared the ground with *Contrasts, or a Parallel between the Architecture of the 15th and 19th century* (1836; second edition 1841) in which he employed contrasting illustrations to show a medieval scene with a skyline pierced by a filigree of spires, against the chaos and ugliness of a modern townscape. The *Glossary of Ecclesiastical Ornament and Costume* (1844; second enlarged edition 1846) extended the theme to the smallest detail of church furnishings, once again to demonstrate the important Catholic tradition in art. *Floriated Ornament* (1849, 1875) was largely taken from a late 16th century botanical volume, *Eicones Plantarum* (1590) by Jacobus Theodorus. In its theories about the geometrical forms in plants that can be found to justify the use of *naturalistic ornament, Pugin predated the ideas of J.K.*Colling, C.*Dresser and L.*Sullivan. Leaves or flowers flattened and extended to a two-dimensional form demonstrated marked geometrical structures, he believed. The book was an important source for the American *Gothic Revival, and was used, for example, by the architect P.B. Wight (1838-1925). The influence of Pugin in the *Gothic Revival and other 19th century design movements (including the Arts and Crafts movement) was immense, through his publications, as well as through his own multifarious activities as architect, designer of church plate and ecclesiastical

A.W.N. Pugin. Borders for altar cloths from Glossary of Ecclesiastical Ornament and Costume, *1844.*

furnishings, interior designer and antiquarian (as when he turned to original 15th century fabrics for patterns). At the Great Exhibition (London, 1851), Pugin displayed many of his designs and supervised the Medieval Court which contained some of the best (and also some of the worst) expressions of the Gothic Revival. He was an eloquent defender of simplicity and fitness for purpose, 'upholsterers seem to think that nothing can be Gothic unless it is found in some church. Hence your modern man designs a sofa or occasional table from details culled out of Britton's cathedrals . . . we find diminutive flying buttresses about an armchair, everything is crocketted with angular projections, innumerable mitres, sharp ornaments and trivetted extremities. A man who remains any length of time in a modern Gothic room, and escapes being wounded by some of its minutiae, may consider himself extremely fortunate.' Ironically, he had himself first supplied many of the motifs and details that were now scattered at random across the parlours and hall-ways of Victorian suburbia. However the emphasis in his own work was always upon a relative balance between the size of the building (or artefact) and its details. Like George Moller, a German authority on the Gothic, his main concern was with unity of style, purpose, structure and decoration.

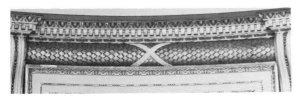

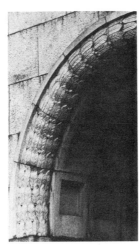

*pulvinated frieze. 1) Cross-bound with ribbon over doorway, Chiswick House, London, built 1725-29. 2) *Triumphal arch into Russian War Cemetery, Berlin, late 1940s. 3) Around door, Bracken House, Cannon Street, City of London, architect Sir Albert Richardson, 1956-59.*

pulvinated frieze or **cushioned frieze.** In *classical ornament, a fat, convex frieze, often decorated with bound *laurel leaves, *oak leaves or other vegetation, and usually used in short sections, either vertically or horizontally.

Punch and Judy. British development of *commedia dell'arte characters as puppets that first appeared in the early 18th century. A satirical humorous weekly paper, *Punch, or the London Charivari*, was started in 1841, and the figure of Punch and his family, including the dog Toby, was used on the magazine's masthead. During the second half of the 19th century, the characters appeared in ornament, e.g. as cast-iron doorstops, spoon *finials, etc.

purfled (French, *purfiler*, to decorate with a border). 18th century *Gothick ornamental effect – a ruffled or curved band that appeared on furniture and in architecture and resembled drapery, embroidery or lace work.

putto. 1) Plaster ceiling, 85 St Stephen's Green, Dublin, by the Francini Brothers, 1739. 2) Doorcase, Florence, Italy. 3) Dining-room fireplace, Polesden Lacey, Surrey, remodelled 1906-08.

putto. Small, chubby infant widely used in ornament, deriving both from angelic spirits (*see* cherubs) and from the attendants of *Cupid (or Eros). An endlessly used motif from the *Renaissance, most commonly shown playing among *scrolling foliage or appearing as a supporter of *festoons and *swags and in panels of *grotesque ornament. The *putto* was a popular motif in the second half of the 19th century, particularly in the *Renaissance Revival, sometimes appearing, rather unsuitably, in the manner of a *caryatid.

pyramid. Form associated with ancient Egyptian royal tombs. It was known in Italy in the *Renaissance, being used by Lorenzo Ghiberti (1378-1455) on a panel showing the Gates of Paradise on the Baptistery in Florence (c.1435), and discussed by L.B.*Alberti in

pyramid. From J.B.*Fischer von Erlach's Entwurff einer historischen Architektur, *1721.*

his treatise. In the 16th and 17th centuries the form was an object of curiosity and was sometimes given a 'scientific' explanation, as in John Greaves's *Pyromido-graphia* (1646). With the resurgence of interest in Egypt in the 18th and 19th centuries, and a more accurate knowledge of the original Egyptian pyramids from the work of D.V.*Denon and others, the pyramid was treated in Europe virtually as the emblem of Egypt, often appearing with the *obelisk in ornament. In the 19th century it was frequently used in funerary decoration.

quadratura. *See* perspective; *trompe l'oeil.*

quadriga. *See* horse.

Quaint style. *See* Art Nouveau.

quatrefoil. Four-lobed *Gothic *tracery form, en-larged to dramatic effect in Venetian Gothic, e.g. on the Ca' d'Oro, in Venice, c.1425-c.1440. It was some-times formed by adding *cusps to a *lozenge shape. The barbed quatrefoil was produced by cutting back the cusp and thus producing two smaller, deeper cusps. The form possibly originated in the ceramic revet-ments of Spanish and oriental mosques. Although a Gothic form, the quatrefoil survived into the *Renais-sance in Italy. *See also* cinquefoil; foil; trefoil.

quatrefoil. Window in tower, built 1903, of Church of the Holy Trinity, Long Melford, Suffolk.

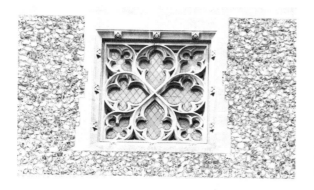

Quatremere de Quincy, Antoine C. (1755-1849). French scholar, archaeologist and classicist. He was editor of the *Dictionnaire d'architecture* (1795-1825), in which he defined ornament as raising 'that which had originally been dictated by necessity to the realms of pleasure'. In his *De l'Architecture Egyptienne* (1803), he gave a scholarly account of Egyptian artefacts, and also outlined his theories on ornament, commenting that it 'adds to the sensation or impressions already produced by the object itself'. He believed that the Egyptians had possessed the most developed idea of decorative art, with their elaborated *capitals, ceilings, *cornices and *entablatures as well as *hieroglyphics, *sphinxes and *obelisks, although he also considered there to be an absence of taste which led to exagger-ation and an accumulation of ornament. Quatremere de Quincy, like the earlier Abbé *Winckelmann, was important in establishing the theoretical background to the *Empire style and *Neo-classicism popular in early 19th century France. He was permanent secretary of the influential Institut des Beaux-Arts in Paris and managed to survive all the revolutionary upheavals of the time.

Quattrocento. 19th century term denoting the 15th century Italian *Renaissance style. In the *Renaissance Revival, the term was frequently applied to work imi-tating that of the Florentine Renaissance.

Queen Anne. Two-handled silver cup made by the Huguenot silversmith Philip Rollos, London, 1713.

Queen Anne. The reign of Queen Anne (1702-14) was, in stylistic terms, a period of transition from the fundamentally *Baroque tastes of the *Restoration and *William and Mary towards a *classicism of a much simpler order. It affected furniture, silver and metal-work and, in particular, architecture, in which the term betokens restraint and domestic-scale design, a combination which proved highly attractive in later revivals, both in Britain and in America. Motifs such as *dentil *cornices and stone *quoins, with elaborated *consoles supporting a canopy over the door were characteristic of smaller Queen Anne country houses. Terraced houses in the city were plainer still, though they might have a carved *scallop shell above the door as a flourish. However, the period also saw, by contrast, the highly flamboyant approach apparent in the Bar-oque palace at Blenheim, Oxfordshire (begun 1705) by John Vanbrugh (1664-1726) and the six London churches (begun 1711) by Nicholas Hawksmoor.

In the decorative arts, the French influence was less prevalent during the war of the Spanish Succession (1701-13). Ornamentation was simpler: plain veneers replaced marquetry and parquetry, *cabriole legs and ball and *claw feet were used in preference to carved stretchers and spiral turning, and chairs and bureaux were often crested with a simple scallop shell. In silver design the plainer shapes and *mouldings introduced by Huguenot silversmiths were influential.

Queen Anne Revival. From the 1860s, a search for a style without specific associations led a number of young English designers to examine the simpler domestic architecture and decoration of the 17th and 18th centuries. It represented in part a conscious reaction against the *Gothic Revival, and partly a reaction against strict academic *classicism. Elements taken loosely from the classical style: *broken pediments, *pilasters or *niches were used at random to enliven surfaces of buildings or furniture. Because its sources were various, and several of the architects who designed in the Queen Anne style also worked in a more vernacular vein (the so-called *Old English or Free style), the purists were highly critical; an author in the magazine *Decoration* wrote in 1886 that it was 'all things to all men . . . pure English, pure Flemish, pure Italian.' It was sometimes referred to as 'late Elizabethan'. Practitioners such as Richard Norman Shaw (1831-1912) or William Eden Nesfield (1835-88) used the ornamental vocabulary of the *Aesthetic movement and gradually extended the scope of the style from the field of domestic buildings into that of public commissions and larger scale works. In designs for woodwork illustrated in magazines and *pattern books such as A. Jonquet's *Original Sketches for Art Furniture, in the Jacobean, Queen Anne, Adam and other styles* (London, 1879). Queen Anne coexisted with many other styles, combining broken pediments, incised decoration in the style of C.*Eastlake and turned *balusters with elaborate overmantels and corner cupboards upon which

Queen Anne Revival. Houses, Bedford Park, West London, 1875 onwards.

stood the blue and white china and other ornaments of the *Aesthetic interior.

The style was also taken up by American architects who combined noticeably English features such as ornamental oriel windows, pronounced gables, high decorative chimneys and moulded brickwork with elements that were more specifically American in origin: elaborately turned wooden balustrading on balconies, porches and verandahs (developed from *Carpenter Gothic) and decorative wooden shingles, which replaced the English tile-hanging. The circular turret was also a particularly popular motif, appearing frequently on both individual and terrace or row housing. In America the style was watched with interest and there was much exchange between it and the *Colonial Revival.

Queen's pattern. *See* King's shape.

Aert Quellin. Design for ornamental window for Amsterdam Town Hall (now Royal Palace), engraved by Hubertus Quellin, 1655 or later.

Quellin, Quellinus or **Quellien,** Aert or Artus (1609-68). Eldest of an important family of Dutch architects, Artus Quellin was a sculptor by training. He is best known for the rich and *naturalistic decoration on the interior and exterior of Jacob Van Campen's Amsterdam Town Hall, built 1648-55. These ornamental schemes were published as part of the comprehensive record of the architecture and decoration of the building, *Afbeelding van 't stadt huys van Amsterdam . . .* (plates by his brother Hubertus with text in Latin, Dutch and French, 1655 onwards; reissued 1719). These designs influenced contemporary Dutch *Baroque furniture and represented the type of decoration that came to England when William of Orange ascended the throne in 1688. Grinling Gibbons (1648-1721) worked with Arnold Quellin, his son, and the Quellin influence thus lay directly behind the ornament of many late 17th century buildings in England, including St Paul's Cathedral (*see* Gibbonwork). The hallmarks of the style are densely packed fruit, vegetables, *shells, game, etc., worked into *trophies, *swags, *festoons and carried out with almost obsessive verisimilitude.

quilling. White opaque glass combed into *festoon shapes on a coloured glass vessel. Popular on 19th century English Nailsea-type glass.

quiver. *See* arrow; Cupid.

quodlibet (Latin, what pleases) or **quodlibetz.** Type of *trompe-l'oeil* decoration in ceramics: a selection of odds and ends – usually letters, scissors and playing cards, painted with shadows on dishes and trays to look as if they have been carelessly dropped there. Popular in the mid 18th century, first at the Meissen porcelain factory and then at Royal Copenhagen.

quoin (French, *coin*, corner). Emphasis given to the corner of a building consisting of alternate long and short horizontal blocks let into the structure or strips of a facing material applied to it. Quoining is carried out in a contrasting material or picked out with some elaboration, most commonly *rustication, and is an important decorative feature in *classical architecture where play of texture and materials are a major ingredient within the overall simplicity of elevations. *See also* long and short work.

quoin. 1) House in Hemingford Road, Islington, London, c.1840.
2) Early 20th century commercial building, Philadelphia, Pennsylvania.

raffle leaf. 18th and early 19th century term describing a development of the *acanthus into a freely flowing, asymmetrically curving leaf that was the basis of much *Rococo decoration, often forming the characteristic *C and S scrolls. Many *pattern books included examples, e.g. M.*Lock's *The Principles of Ornament, or the Youth's Guide to Drawing of Foliage* (c.1765) and N. Wallis's *A Book of Ornament in the Palmyrene Taste* (1771), which mentions 'Pannels, Pateras and Mouldings with the Raffle leaves at large.' R.*Brown, in his *An Elucidation of the Principles of Drawing Ornaments* (1822), stated, 'foliage ornament is composed of leaves only, the subdivisions of a leaf are called plants, and the small external divisions raffles . . . ' W.*Ince and J.I. Mayhew, in their *Household Furniture* (1759-62), describe the ability to draw the raffle leaf as 'extremely necessary to bring the hand into that freedom required in all kinds of ornament, useful to carvers, cabinet makers, chasers, engravers, etc.' *See also* scrolling foliage.

ragged staff. Heraldic motif of a lopped tree.

railway motifs became popular in Britain from 1825 when George Stephenson's steam locomotive first ran from Stockton to Darlington. At first they tended to appear on *commemorative ware, such as a cast-iron doorstop of 1825 in a locomotive shape or an English chintz of the 1830s emblazoned with the termini of the time, Lime Street in Liverpool, Euston in London, etc. *Wheel shapes were used as *brackets on cast-iron canopies; winged wheels represented the power of steam locomotion. The railway companies used their monograms and *cyphers to decorate iron seats. Parisian goldsmiths in the early 1860s manufactured *bijoux chemin de fer* (as well as *bateaux à vapeur*) decorated with screws, rivet, nails, locks and padlocks (*see also* machinery motifs). As the century progressed, the production of ephemera incorporating railway motifs grew: there were locomotive-shaped coffee pots, sets of plates with the great stations of the world on them, railway games, and a wide range of commemorative ware. Sometimes heads or busts of railway engineers and designers appeared on panels or as *capitals on buildings in the *Gothic manner. Main-line termini were often ornamented with stirring *personifications, either representing the cities in which they were situated or principal destinations (e.g. the Gare du Nord in Paris is crowned with a figure of Paris, the Gare de l'Est with a figure of Strasbourg), or alluding to good relationships between countries, particularly in continental Europe where networks linked many countries within short distances. Railway workshops were ornamented with sculpted panels of locomotives and railway hotels combined the ornamental vocabulary of steam train travel with that of *topography.

ram. *See* aegricanes; Bacchic; bucranium; hoof.

Ranson, Pierre (1736-1819). French painter and designer, working in Paris. From 1780 he was designer at the Aubusson carpet manufactory. The engraved ornament in *Nouveau Recueil de jolies trophées* (1775) was in a light *pastoral style, with informally arranged flowers, intertwined *ribbons, *trophies of *love,

*raffle leaf. 1) 'A Systematical Order of Raffle Leaf from the Line of Beauty' from W.*Ince and G. Mayhew's* The Universal System of Household Furniture, *1759.*
Pierre Ranson. 2) From his Premier Cahier de groupes de fleurs et d'ornemans, *c.1780.*

railway motifs. 'Tunnel', cotton print from the F. Zinovev Factory, Ivanovo, Russia, late 1920s or early 1930s.

*music and *hunting and was intended for *boiserie* panels, furniture, etc. The style was well suited to embroidery, and Ranson designed a collection of embellishments for coats and waistcoats. In 1778 he published *Oeuvre contenant un recueil de trophées, attributs, cartouches, vases, fleurs, ornemens, et plusiers desseins agréables pour broder des fauteuils*. He also published designs for *cyphers. Many of his engravings were published in Germany.

Ransonnette, Pierre Nicolas. *See* Krafft, Johann Carl.

raphaelesques. 19th century term for *grotesques, so called because the painter Raphael (1483-1520) was, with Giovanni da Udine, among the first to revive Roman grotesques in his decoration of the Vatican *logge* (1518-19).

Raynerd, D. Co-author with A.*Benjamin of the *American Builder's Companion* (1806).

rebus. A non-heraldic badge, the components of which pun on the name of the bearer. Rebuses were popular

raphaelesques. 1) Embossed leather wall covering at Royal Holloway College, Egham, Surrey, 1879-87.
*rebus. 2) *Pilaster with falcon's head, Palazzo Falconiere, Rome, by Francesco Borromini, mid 17th century.*

in the 15th and 16th centuries and were particularly favoured by ecclesiastics who did not bear arms, e.g. Bishop Alcock had a *frieze of cocks and globes carved in his chantry at Ely Cathedral (c.1500) and Abbot Islip had the *cornice of his chantry chapel at Westminster decorated with an eye and a slipped tree (c.1530). Personal badges and *heraldic decoration were popular in decoration during this period, and the rebus was commonly used to ornament both secular and ecclesiastical buildings and possessions. Italian *Renaissance families decorated their palaces with rebuses, e.g. the bats of the Pipistrelli family who lived in Florence (*pipistrello*, Italian, bat) and the falcon heads of the Falconieri in Rome.

Red Dragon pattern. *See* dragon.

reeding. Parallel *mouldings, the convex equivalent of *fluting. Reeding was particularly fashionable from the end of the 18th century and throughout the first half of the 19th century. It is found on fireplace and door surrounds and was popular in furniture design; T.*Sheraton, for example, frequently used reeded columns, legs and supports. Silver of the period often has reeded rims, foot rings or edges.

Reed and tie, or reed and ribbon, where the reeding is loosely bound together with criss-crossed ribbons, was an elaboration on this popular ornament, for example, in the work of the English silversmith Matthew Boulton (produced in the 1770s and 1780s), or as a cast brass edging on furniture. T.*Shearer included it as an ornament for chair legs in *The Cabinet-Makers' London Book of Prices* (1788). The American cabinetmaker Duncan Phyfe (1768-1854) further varied the design by tying the reeding together at intervals.

In Edwardian architecture, reeding appeared as a roof ridge detail, and was often used to emphasise the line of French Château-style mansard roofs.

*reeding. 1) English silver candlestick made in Sheffield by Henry Tudor and Thomas Leader, 1791. 2) Reed and tie *moulding on English silver spoon made in Birmingham by Boulton & Fothergill, 1774.*

Régence. A style in French furniture and interior decoration which dominated French taste from approximately 1710 to 1730; it is named after the period between 1715 and 1723 when the Duc d'Orléans was Regent to Louis XV. The style is characterised by a move away from the heavy academic *classicism exemplified by the court style of Louis XIV which was first apparent in the work of J.*Berain. Régence is generally seen as the first phase of the Rococo, preceding the *genre pittoresque*. The ornamental subject matter became increasingly frivolous: Watteau-esque *fêtes galantes* replaced the earlier grand mythological scenes, and *singeries* and *chinoiseries* appeared, sometimes within the framework of the revived *grotesque. The principal Régence *ornemanistes* were G.M.*Oppenord and, to a lesser extent, C.*Gillot, some of whose designs were published posthumously.

Regency. Literally the period when the Prince Regent ruled in place of his father, George III, 1811-20. However, in the arts it is an imprecise term usually taken to cover the period from the late 1790s to the end of George IV's reign in 1830.

Regency style in the decorative arts was broadly *classical, drawing heavily on the French *Empire style and the *Style Etrusque (although Napoleonic devices do not appear). Elements of *Greek Revival and *Gothick styles are also used, as well as *Egyptian

*Regency. 1) English painted and gilded window seat, c.1805. 2) House close to Brighton Pavilion, Sussex, c.1815-20. 3) Design for window draperies by John Stafford of Bath from R.*Ackermann's The Repository of Arts, 1819.*

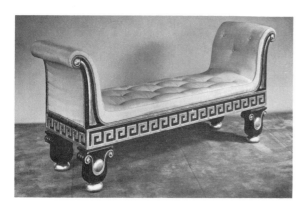

motifs (the result, indirectly, of Napoleon's Egyptian Campaign and Nelson's victory at the Battle of the Nile) and *chinoiserie. T.*Sheraton's work epitomises the style, both in form (e.g. sabre legs and X-shaped supports) and ornament (e.g. animal motifs, usually *masks and *monopodia of *lions, *griffins and *dolphins). T.*Hope's archaeological designs illustrated the growing tendency to borrow carefully and accurately from classical sources; they were later popularised by G.*Smith who produced simpler versions of the designs, thus rendering Hope's style more accessible to craftsmen. Ceramics used classical subjects for decoration, though often rendered rather more heavily than in the earlier *Neo-classical and *Adam styles.

There is no Regency style of architecture as such – classical, *Gothic and the eclectic styles of the *Picturesque all made their appearance. Carlton House, with extensions and alterations by Henry Holland (1745-1801) and Brighton Pavilion by Holland and John Nash (1752-1835) represent Regency taste at its most elaborate, under the patronage of the Prince Regent. A less extravagant, more general rendering of Regency appeared in elegant town villas with bowed fronts, ornamented with delicate cast-iron work from *pattern books such as those by L.N.*Cottingham. Cast stone composition, produced by the Coade Manufactory, took the place of stone sculpture.

reglet or **riglet.** Flat, narrow, plain *moulding, thinner than the *fillet, often used to separate decorated mouldings or other ornamental details.

relieving arch. An additional plain arch placed above an arch or lintel providing extra support and simple ornament. It is a frequent device in *Neo-classical buildings where ornament has been kept to the minimum.

relieving arch. St Anne's Church, Newcastle-upon-Tyne, by William Newton, 1760.

Renaissance. The Italian Renaissance marked a reappraisal of the vocabulary of *Graeco-Roman classicism, largely on the basis of the architecture and artefacts surviving in Italy from ancient Rome. The first glimmerings of the style, the so-called Proto-Renaissance, were perceptible in the late 11th century, and centred on Florence; the Baptistery is an example. Subsequently, the Renaissance proper developed in

Florence and the principal towns of Tuscany and Umbria. Secular, humanist interests and a new intellectual curiosity, which dominated the Italian Renaissance from its beginnings, provoked the gathering together of a large repertoire of forms and meant that a wide selection of sources was available to artists. Engravings and access to collections of bronzes, gems, and medals belonging to men like Lorenzo di Medici and Pope Paul II fuelled the return to classical designs. Archeological finds, such as the *grotesque ornament in the Golden House of Nero, also contributed to the fund of material.

The early Renaissance, in the 14th century, mingled classical forms with relics of the *Gothic style. In the early 15th century the treatment was still light, as in the *arcading and roundels of the *logge* of Filippo Brunelleschi's Ospedale degli Innocenti in Florence (1419). As the century progressed, however, the style became heavier and more ornate, with naturalistic, Roman-influenced *acanthus leaves, *scrolling foliage, *rustication, *swags and *festoons used frequently. The effect, even in textiles or embroidery, was sculptural, depending on techniques such as *grisaille*. Other standard Renaissance motifs and features were *putti*, *dolphins, decorated *pilaster panels, *pateras, and *scallop shells. Classical architectural motifs re-entered the realms of ornament: round-headed *niches, *pediments, temple fronts, *aediculés, etc. The various stages of the Renaissance can be seen in the changing approach to the classical idiom: the adoption of a strict architectural vocabulary with associated ornament in the early 15th century was followed by a systematic elaboration of all these elements until the work of Michelangelo and Giulio Romano (e.g. Palazzo del Te, Mantua, 1526-41) introduced *Mannerism in which the rules existed only to be departed from. This development marked the beginning of a move towards what was to become the *Baroque.

The use of different materials in the various areas of the Italian peninsula led to wide regional variations:

Renaissance. 1) Palazzo Strozzi, Florence, Italy, begun by Benedetto da Maiano, 1489 onwards. 2) Sculpted panel of Autumn by Jean Goujon, Hôtel (now Musée) Carnavalet, Paris, mid 16th century. 3) Bureau des Finances, Rouen (Seine-Maritime), France, built by Roulland le Roux, 1509-10.

Renaissance. Design for silver cups by Hans Brosamer c.1545.

the black and white marble used as geometric patterning, such as in L.B.*Alberti's S. Maria Novella, Florence (1456 onwards) or the Lombardic work on the façade of the Certosa in Pavia (1456-72) in which the local clay was utilised for complex terracotta ornament.

The early 16th century, or High Renaissance, was to be the most directly influential period outside Italy. The classicism of A.*Palladio became the inspiration for early 18th century classical architecture throughout Europe and North America.

The Renaissance travelled outside Italy by various means. These included French incursions into northern Italy with the invasion by Charles VIII of France in 1494, Italian artists going to work at *Fontainebleau and, above all, the engraved treatises and publications which served as the most direct link with classical antiquity and the Renaissance. In northern Europe the influence of the Renaissance was heavily coloured by the tendency towards Mannerism and the continued influence of late Gothic. The real impact of the Renaissance in England and Holland, for example, was not to be felt until well into the 17th century.

Renaissance Revival. Though less widely followed than the *Gothic Revival, this was one of the major strands of 19th century *Historicism in Europe and America. The revival of the Italian High Renaissance *palazzo* style reintroduced the motifs of *rustication, *pilasters and *classical ornamental motifs, becoming progressively more elaborate between the 1830s and 1850s. Sir Charles Barry's gentlemen's clubs in London (Traveller's, 1829, Reform, 1837) were one manifestation of the style, whilst much later, in New York,

Renaissance Revival. 1) English tazza by Charles Toft in Minton's Henri II ware, 1875-80. 2) Late 19th century office building, 19 Eastcheap, City of London. 3) English Cellini pattern silver ewer by Stephen Smith & Son, 1885. 4) House in Antwerp, Belgium, 1908.

McKim, Mead and White's Villard Houses (1884) and University Club (1899) followed the same lead. In America, the *Beaux-Arts training of many architects, together with the establishment of the American Academy in Rome (1846), promoted the choice of European classical prototypes. The Renaissance Revival was viewed as an appropriate style for important town houses and the new public libraries. For interiors, various Renaissance styles were used: J. Moyr Smith in *Ornamental Interiors* (1887) stated that in England 'at the present time the Italian and Flemish Renaissance style seem to be in the ascendancy for dining room and library decoration.'

In America, the Renaissance practice was followed of craftsmen working in *ateliers* (a parallel with the Gothic Revivalists who were to promote the medieval guild system). Throughout Europe and America specific types of ornament were copied, e.g. *grotesques after Raphael, and *della Robbia work for both interior and exterior decoration, which allowed the use of historically accurate, smaller scale ornament to complement the styles chosen for architecture. A particularly elaborate application of the style was at The Breakers, Newport, Rhode Island, designed by Richard Morris Hunt (1827-95) and completed in 1895, the exteriors inspired by 16th century Italian palaces, the interiors ornamented with, for example, *grisaille* panels showing the *Elements and the *Muses. The Vanderbilts even adopted a family emblem of three acorns and oak leaves in the manner of Italian Renaissance families. The Victorian enthusiasm for rich carving on panelling, overmantels, etc., as well as furniture, was facilitated by the development of woodcarving machines in the 1840s and led to the return to the sculptural effects of the Renaissance. Jewellers, too, turned their attention to the production of Italian Renaissance work, closely copied from originals. Other Renaissance Revivals were based on the Renaissance style of the particular country: the French Renaissance, or Château style, was applied both in France and in England and America (especially for great country houses, hotels and office chambers). Dutch, Austrian, German and *French Second Empire architects returned to their own national Renaissance styles as alternative to the Gothic Revival, e.g. buildings on the Vienna Ringstrasse and the Paris boulevards of Georges-Eugène Haussmann (1809-91). *See also* François I style; Rundbogenstil.

repeating ornament. A pattern that can be limitlessly extended because its basic motif can be endlessly repeated, e.g. *diaper, *chequer. Usually used for the decoration of flat surfaces or as a ground pattern.

Restoration. The styles current in Britain from the restoration of Charles II to the throne in 1660 after the Commonwealth until the flight of James II in 1688 when William and Mary arrived from Holland. Charles II and his followers had spent their exile in Holland and France and on their return brought with them a taste for Continental fashions. *Baroque motifs of twisted and *spiral columns, sculptural and heavy supporting figures, high *cresting, scrolling *acanthus, *feathers and fringes were all popular. Motifs such as

revolutionary ornament. Russian porcelain plate, The Victory of Labour 1917-20, by Rudolf Fyodorovich Vilde, 1920.

*boys and crowns, used on chair-backs or as a stretcher embellishment, were direct references to the Restoration. Elaborate and rich finishes were favoured, such as gilding, silvering, lacquer, floral marquetry and parquetry and finely detailed carving as in the work of Grinling Gibbons (*see* Gibbonwork).

Architecture of the period demonstrated the acceptance of *classicism, as typified by the work of Hugh May (1622-84) and Sir Roger Pratt (1620-84), in symmetrical 'villas' with *pediments, hipped roofs and often full-height *pilasters. Their work was followed by that of William Talman (1650-1719) and, of course, Sir Christopher Wren (1632-1723) who, after the Fire of London (1666), received an unprecedented professional opportunity, that of rebuilding London. While he was well-versed in contemporary French and Dutch classicism, his designs for St Paul's Cathedral are a monumental affirmation of the hold of the Italian *Renaissance on the imagination of the greatest English architect of the period. However, more typical of the Restoration is Belton House, Lincolnshire (begun 1685), with its hipped roof, cupola and balustraded parapet disguising the richness of the interior.

reticulated or **reticular pattern.** Network of *lozenge shapes, or square pieces set diagonally in masonry.

In ceramics or glass, a net or web-like pattern of interlaced lines.

Revett, Nicholas. *See* Stuart, James.

revolutionary ornament. After the American Declaration of Independence in 1776, there was little to mark the event except commemorative portraits of General Washington (sometimes surrrounded by the equilateral triangle signifying the equality of the three orders), the weapons of war which had helped to win

independence, and a carefully chosen national emblem, the bald *eagle. In 1876, centennial celebrations of Independence were marked with souvenir textiles, wallpapers and ephemera, which used some of the symbols of equality and liberty made popular during the French Revolution.

In post-revolutionary France, ceramics, textiles and furniture were decorated to suit the new political climate. From 1789, symbols of Republican, rather than Imperial Rome appeared: pikes, *fasces, civic *wreaths of *oak. Other motifs included the eye, as a symbol of enlightenment; the compasses, the level and the equilateral triangle, representing the equality of all men and justice for all; the open book, symbol of the new Constitution; the cock crowing 'Liberty', the bird escaping from the cage, and the tricolour ribbons and cockade (flowers coloured red, white and blue – poppy, daisy and cornflower – were also often used). Once the political situation had stabilised in Republican France, the new theories were formally applied to decoration: in 1794, instructions were given to the Savonnerie carpet designers 'not to employ any human figures, since it would be revolting to tread them underfoot under a government that had recalled Man to his dignity.' Accepted figures were mythical Roman *chimeras, *centaurs, *tritons, etc.

In the early 20th century, post-revolutionary Soviet Russia largely rejected the classical vocabulary of ornament that was associated with Imperial Russia, and new motifs were introduced suggesting that social, economic and technical progress was proof of the efficacy of the revolution. Constructivist motifs, followed by more eclectic patterns extolling the virtues of technology, were widely applied in textile design in the 1920s and 1930s. Motifs of *aeroplanes, tractors, even electric light bulbs were used in repeating patterns, often of considerable ingenuity. In addition, the emblem of the new order, the hammer and sickle, was widely applied, even, sometimes, overlaid on pre-revolutionary ceramic blanks that had been partially decorated in traditional style. *See also* Liberty.

ribbon. Often used in conjunction with other ornament, particularly classically derived motifs such as the *bucranium, *laurel and *oak *wreaths and fruit and flower *festoons. They are also used to bind together and suspend *trophies and *margents, sometimes following antique examples by ending with a knot or *acorn-like knob.

From the mid 18th century, ribbon appeared as an ornamental motif in its own right. It was sometimes used as a replacement for *bandwork, as a framing device for other elements of decoration. The silky, waving quality of ribbon is much emphasised, together with a variety of knots and bows, and it appears in gold, marquetry, painted decoration, woven silk and printed cottons, often combined with bunches of flowers. The freer treatment of ribbon in the *Rococo is clear in J.*Pillement's engraved patterns, *Six Noeuds de rubans* (1770) and the designs of P.*Ranson. T.*Chippendale designed ribbon-back chairs for the 1754 *Director* which demanded that wood be carved to look like fluttering silk. Ribbon tied in a bow with deep crinkling was one of the most frequent motifs in all

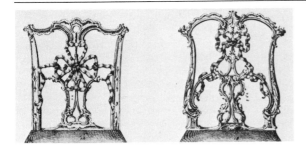

ribbon. 'Ribband Back Chairs' from T.*Chippendale's Director, 1762 edition.

media in the *Louis XVI style and was revived in the mid 19th century. A decoration combining different coloured ribbons in an interlaced design called *à rubans* was used at Sèvres in the 18th century. Generally, from the 18th to the 20th centuries, ribbon motifs have been most popular in textiles, also appearing on wall paper. For ribbon-like form in ironwork *see* bent ribbon.

ribbon mouldings sometimes appear alone but are often combined with other motifs, e.g. ribbon and rosette, which has *rosettes scattered among intertwined ribbons; other variations include ribbon and stick (ribbons entwined round a stick), ribbons with *reeding, or ribbons with knots or *labels. Ribbon mouldings were popular in the 18th and 19th centuries for furniture and on plaster and woodwork in principal interior locations, where they were frequently used to emphasise a central field of panelling, or to run as one of numerous *mouldings on the *entablature.

ribbon mouldings. Ribbon and stick on late 18th century English jasper ware cup made by Wedgwood.

rice leaves and grains. An ornamental motif in southern rice-growing areas of America, rice leaves and grains were used particularly as carved detail on early 19th century furniture, in a similar manner to the bunches of wheat ears common on Hepplewhite-style furniture.

Richardson, George (c.1736-c.1813). English draughtsman and designer who worked for the Adam brothers (*see* Adam style). His *Book of Ceilings* (1776, further edition in 1793) is of considerable importance, and was dedicated to Lord Scarsdale for whom he had worked at Kedleston, Derbyshire. His designs 'in the style of the Antique Grotesque' were from 'Homer, Virgil, Ovid and Iconology of Cavaliere Ripa'. He also produced a two-volume English edition of C.*Ripa's

George Richardson. Panels from his A Collection of Ornaments in the Antique Style, *1816.*

seminal work *Iconology or a Collection of Emblematical Figures* (1779-80), which he described as 'an assiduous study of allegory . . . the most effectual means of rendering the ornaments that adorn the sides and ceiling of the apartments of the great expressive and significant; it would enable the artist to suit his decorations to the place he designs to embellish . . . ' The book contains 424 new designs, which, while being in the fashionable Adam style, remain true to Ripa's original descriptions. He published further books on chimney-pieces (1781), the *Orders (1787), *vases and *tripods (1793), *capitals and *friezes from the antique (1793), and, most ambitiously, the *New Vitruvius Britannicus* (2 vols, 1802-08 and 1808-10, an attempt to emulate Colen Campbell's earlier work (*see* Palladianism). *A Collection of Ornaments in the Antique Style*, which stemmed from a revival of 17th century *classicism and showed the influence of French design, was co-authored by his son William who published it in 1816 after his father's death. J.A. Heaton, in the introduction to his reissue of 18th century furniture patterns in 1892, wrote that there was 'not a foolish or impracticable design in the book and most address themselves to a middle class public rather than to the millionaire.'

rigaree marks. *See* trailed decoration.

riglet. *See* reglet.

rinceau. French term used in England in the late 18th century for *scrolling foliage (usually composed of *acanthus leaves) in carved, moulded or painted decoration.

Ripa, Cesare. (c.1560-pre 1625). Author of *Iconologia*, a sourcebook of *personifications which was immensely influential from the beginning of the 17th century until the late 18th century. The first edition of 1593 (published in Padua) was unillustrated, but gave descriptions of over 800 allegorical figures of the *Virtues and Vices, Arts, Humours, *Elements, celestial bodies, Italian provinces and rivers (*see* riparine). These were drawn from ancient Egyptian, Greek and Roman and *Renaissance sources, both textual and pictorial. According to Ripa's introduction, the book had a wide range of application, being suitable for 'orators and poets' as well as for engravers, designers of emblems, painters, sculptors and architects. A new edition of 1603 included a number of woodcut illustrations, though a large number of emblematic figures remained unillustrated. The *Iconologia* ran into numerous editions – even within Italy there were four published in Padua, two in Venice – and was translated into many languages throughout the century and into the next. French and Dutch editions appeared simultaneously in Amsterdam and Paris in 1644. It subsequently became known in England and was influential in the *Jacobean period, for example for masque costume. Henry Peacham drew on the work in his *Minerva Britanna* (1612) and *The Gentleman's Exercise* (1616). The first English edition of Ripa's *Iconologia* appeared in 1709.

G.*Richardson, in his *Iconology*, drew on about half of Ripa's original descriptions, providing 424 contemporary designs for them in the fashionable *Adam style, and covered 'Elements and Celestial bodies, Seasons and Months of the Years, Hours of Day and Night, Quarters of the World, principal Rivers (including figures for London and the Thames), Four Ages, Muses, Senses, Arts, Sciences, Dispositions and Faculties of the Mind, Virtues and Vices.' The subscription list included architects: the Adam brothers,

Cesare Ripa. 'Matrimony' from the 1611 edition of his Iconologia.

Sir W.*Chambers and George Dance; decorative painters: G.B. Cipriani, Antonio Zucchi and Biagio Rebecca; engravers: Francesco Bartolozzi, Charles Grignion; the silver manufacturer, Matthew Boulton; the porcelain manufacturers, Messrs Duesbury; the cabinetmakers T.*Chippendale and W.*Ince; as well as builders, coachpainters, a japanner, carvers, statuary manufacturers, a modeller and seal engraver – an indication of the importance of the work as a source for *Neo-classical decoration.

riparine ornament. Sculpted panel, Reichstag, Berlin, 1919.

riparine ornament takes as its theme the river gods and spirits of the water. In *classical ornament these figures are represented crowned with reeds, often leaning against an *urn from which water is flowing. *Personifications of famous rivers were a popular theme in the *Renaissance. C.*Ripa included descriptions of sixteen in his *Iconologia* of 1593: Italian rivers such as the Tiber, Arno and Po; rivers from classical mythology and history such as the Styx, Acheron, Achelous and Cocytus; and exotic rivers such as the Nile, Tigris, Danube, Niger, Indus and Ganges. In his *Iconologia* of 1779-80, G.*Richardson added the Plate and the Thames – a resplendent *Neptune-like figure in a naval *crown. Occasionally the *Continents are represented in ornament by personifications of appropriate rivers. In the 19th century R.*Brown suggested river nymphs as a suitable ornament for mirrors, alluding to the similarity between glass and the surface of water. But the main applications of riparine ornament, which includes bullrushes, *swans, frogs and *fish, are on water gardens, riverside buildings, seats, lamps, pumps and fountains. *See also* dolphin; marine.

rising sun. *See* sun.

rocaille (French, rockwork) or **Muschelwerk** (German, shellwork). One of the most important decorative forms of the *Rococo, particularly characterising the *genre pittoresque*. Deriving from the rock and shell forms that made up *grotto decoration, the dynamic asymmetrical shapes, some rocky and jagged, some soft and almost *Auricular, provided a perfect background for other Rococo motifs. The silversmith Nicholas Sprimont (c.1716-71), later director of the Chelsea porcelain factory, developed a method of casting *rocaille*

decoration from real shells. Early engraved patterns
for *rocaille* were published by G.-M.*Oppenord and J.-
A.*Meissonier during the early 1720s. A large number
of engraved *rocaille* patterns were published, perhaps
reflecting the difficulty experienced by craftsmen in
producing this abstract form with its unfamiliar asym-
metricality. They were especially popular in France
and Germany where over 80 engravers, among them
J.W.*Baumgartner, G.B.*Goz and J. Wachsmuth
(1711-71), published designs incorporating *rocaille*
patterns, principally in Augsburg. One of the most
prolific designers of *rocaille* was J.*Mondon, who was
also the first to use the word *rocaille*. His work was
published in Paris from 1736 and frequently republished in Germany during the 1750s. Among his *rocaille*
designs were suitably outlandish figures, mostly
Chinese, though some with touches of Egyptian and
*Turkish costumes or style, and the combination of
these styles became frequent thereafter. The Slodtz
brothers, René Michel, called Michel-Ange (1705-64),
Paul Ambroise (1702-58) and Antoine Sébastien (1694-
1754), each of whom took on the post of Dessinateur
de la Chambre et Cabinet du Roi at some time, also
published a quantity of designs. J.-A. Meissonnier's
silver designs were influential in the work of English
goldsmiths from the 1730s (particularly the immigrant
Huguenots who were sensitive to French styles). But
it was not until the 1740s that English designers, notably M.*Lock, T.*Copland and T.*Johnson, began
to produce fully fledged *rocaille* ornament principally
aimed at the woodcarver.

rockwork. Both real and imitation rocks were used in
*grotto decoration. However, this form of decoration

*rockwork. Early 18th century doorway at the Clam-Gallas Palace,
Prague, with sculptural additions, possibly by M.B. Braun.*

*rocaille. 1) From J.*Mondon's Quatrième Livre de formes ornées
de rocailles, cartels, figures, oyseaux et dragons chinois,
1736. 2) Doorway in Antwerp, Belgium.*

was applied more widely in the *Baroque styles and
in the early 18th century, e.g. in carved giltwood or
ormolu at the base of *console tables or on top of
pier-glass mirrors, often as a perch for an *eagle.
Rockwork was considerably elaborated with the advent
of the *Rococo, when it was subsumed into *rocaille*.

Rococo. A style devised by the French that spread
throughout Europe in the early 18th century. Its early
manifestations coincided with the death of Louis XIV,
thus appearing symptomatic of a relaxing of the exces-
sively formal atmosphere that had pervaded Versailles,
but it also owed something to *Baroque and *Auricular design. The heavy classicism of the *Louis XIV
style gradually gave way to a lighter, airier and more
frivolous style of decoration. Motifs were neither from
the antique nor nationalistic. Colours were gayer,
woods were lighter coloured and the exotic was an important element: *chinoiserie, *Turkish figures, *Indians
and *singeries were combined with naturalistic sprigs
of foliage and flowers and the more abstract but essentially Rococo forms of *rocaille, *icicles and *grotto
ornament. The most instantly recognisable feature of
Rococo decoration is scrollwork, with *C scrolls and
S scrolls usually forming the framework from which
other motifs emerge. The early Rococo style (often
referred to as the *Régence) is characterised by the
use of *scallop shells, *diaper patterns, *bandwork,
*espagnolette heads and light scrollwork; it tended to
retain much of the symmetry of the earlier period,
and silver bore engraved patterns. The designs of J.
*Berain are typical. By the 1720s, the Rococo in France
was developing into a more extravagant style which
was markedly asymmetrical and in which all angles
are softened, curved or curled; *rocaille* was highly characteristic of this phase, which presented craftsmen
working in wood, plaster, metal and stone with highly
challenging tasks. A mass of engraved ornament was
published, much of it based on the supremely popular
*cartouche form, often in conjunction with thematic
ornament such as the *Elements, the *Seasons and
Aesop's *fables. Important figures among Rococo

ornemanistes were G.-M.*Oppenord, J.-A.*Meissonier, B.*Toro, N.*Pineau, J.*Pillement, J.F.*Cuvilliès, F.X. *Habermann and J.M.*Hoppenhaupt. From c.1730, this later phase of the Rococo, sometimes called the *genre pittoresque* or *style pittoresque*, spread rapidly across Europe, finding particular popularity in Germany and Austria. It was best suited to interior decoration, and designers produced overall schemes including complementary designs for wall panels, ceilings, furniture, chimneypieces and overmantels. In ceramics, the development of hard-paste porcelain provided a good medium for the crisp scrolls and curls of Rococo work as produced by the Meissen, Frankenthal, Nymphenburg and Chelsea porcelain factories. Similarly, the development of *papier-mâché* and greater sophistication in the use of plasterwork made it possible to reproduce designs for gilded ornament around mirrors, for example, faster and more easily than they could be carved in wood. In Britain, *émigré* Huguenot silversmiths and goldsmiths were quick to adopt the style of their native France. The novelty of the Rococo in England is indicated by a letter written in 1769 describing the plasterwork at Claydon House, Buckinghamshire: 'Mr Lightfoot's design for finishing the great Eating Room shock'd me so much and is so much the ridicule of all who have seen or heard of it . . . With regard to the Saloon and the Drawing Room, they are not so bad, and their absurdities might be easily remedied.' Current anti-French feeling was at the root of much of the British disapproval of the style. I.*Ware described it as 'a caprice of France', and the French as 'frivolous people whom we are apt to imitate'. All this may have contributed to the success of the *Gothick at the time. In the mid to late 18th century, the Rococo was largely ousted by *Neoclassicism, but lingered on in some parts of Europe into the 1790s. Its impact in America was even more limited than in Britain, although Rococo designs were sometimes included in architectural pattern books, e.g. plates by T.*Lightoler were included in W.*Halfpenny's *A Modern Builder's Assistant* (1742).

Rococo Revival. The restoration of the Bourbon monarchy in France, 1815-24, provided the initial impetus to look back to the *Rococo, which had been the prevalent style during the reign of the 18th century monarchs and offered the greatest contrast to the severe, classical, rather militaristic flavour of the *Empire style. From the late 1820s Rococo Revival designs were a popular choice in Britain, America, Germany and Austria. The style was considered particularly suitable for the decoration of women's rooms, boudoirs, bedrooms and drawing rooms, the emphasis being on delicate gilt scrolls and curves. The style was variously referred to as Old French, Louis XIV, Louis XV, Louis XVI, French Modern and French Antique. 18th century French furniture was keenly collected and copied, and *pattern books such as F.*Knight's *Fancy Ornaments* (London, 1834) were published. However, much of the demand was met by republishing

Rococo. 1) Plasterwork, 20 Lower Dominick Street, Dublin, by Robert West, 1755. 2) Design for panel by F.X.*Habermann, mid 18th century. 3) French faïence soup tureen made at Sceaux, c.1755.

original engravings by 18th century Rococo designers, such as T.*Chippendale, M.*Lock, T.*Johnson, M. *Darly, etc., although often with some disregard for their real authorship. For example, John Weale published in 1834 *Chippendale's One Hundred and Thirty-three Designs for Interior Decoration in the Old French and Antique Style* in which the designs were in fact by T.*Johnson. Another popular compilation produced by Weale was *Old English and French Ornaments* (1858-59), described as 'elaborate examples of hall glasses, picture frames, chimney pieces, stands for china, clock and watch cases, girandoles, brackets, grates, lanterns, ornamental furniture, ornaments for brass workers and silver workers, rich ornamental ironwork patterns, and for carvers and modellers.' Many details were cast in composition stone, metal or plaster because, even by the 1830s, the carving required to produce exact replicas was too costly and elaborate a proposition.

In America, the style was well suited to the newly discovered furniture-manufacturing techniques practised by makers such as John Belter, Charles Baudoine and Joseph Meeks, whereby laminated rosewood was steamed in moulds to achieve curved and scrolling forms combined with flowers, birds and grapes. Soon, however, these makers developed a style of their own, far removed from the Rococo originals; chair-backs and *cresting rails were pierced to achieve a lighter effect, but they never approached the delicacy demanded in the original 18th century carved pieces. In spite of this, the complexities of Rococo designs continued to be adapted to the new technical methods of moulding, casting and machine carving, and pieces were produced in quantity.

By 1860, the Rococo Revival had largely fallen from fashion, although it did have another limited burst of popularity in the 1880s and 1890s, particularly among a small but wealthy group of bankers which included the Rothschild family. The Rococo was regarded as a *style de luxe* and was used to create such an atmosphere, as at the Ritz Hotel in London. Edouard Rouveyre, the Paris publisher, responded by republishing patterns by G.-M.*Oppenord, F.X.*Haberman and J.-A. *Meissonier. By reintroducing an asymmetrical style in the 19th century, the Rococo Revival can be seen as having, to some extent, prepared the ground for *Art Nouveau.

Rococo Revival. 1) Papier-mâché designs from C.F. Bielefeld's Ornaments in Every Style of Design, *1840. 2) Rosewood chair by John Henry Belter, New York, 1845-55.*

rod of Aesculapius. 1) Apothecary's sign, Volterra, Tuscany, Italy. 2) Bronze lamp fitting, Wellcome Building, Euston Road, London, 1931.

rod of Aesculapius. A staff entwined with serpents. Aesculapius was the Greek god of healing and his shrines often harboured sacred snakes. The two serpents twined round the rod were thought to represent the opposing forces of sickness and health. The rod of Aesculapius appeared as a *Neo-classical motif and was popular in the *Empire style. As a universally recognised symbol of *medicine it is found on chemists' shops, hospitals, etc.

The rod of Aesculapius closely resembles the *caduceus, which combines a staff and entwined serpents with wings and is an attribute of *Mercury.

roll moulding. A simple, semi-circular *moulding. Roll-and-fillet is a variation of roll moulding but with a square *fillet added.

rollwork. Term sometimes used for *strapwork.

Romanesque. As the name suggests, this is a style that reverted to precedents set by *classical Roman architecture. As a style that dominated Europe throughout the 11th and 12th centuries it took many forms and absorbed many influences. Thus in England, the Romanesque contained frequent reminders of a *Celtic and *Viking past, whilst in southern France, Lombardic Italy and Spain, where Roman originals were nearer to hand, classical references were more direct. Romanesque ornament consists of architectural motifs including round-headed arches and *arcading, *colonnettes, *niches, *brackets, twisted columns as well as patterns introduced by the materials themselves (e.g. banded brickwork or marble). *Mouldings are ornamented with geometric forms such as *chevron, *lozenge, *bead, *cable and *billet motifs. *Beakheads on the voussoirs, *corbels and *label stops introduced the heads of birds, beasts and imaginary monsters. The style is marked by a fresh approach in which ornament is less confined to specific elements than an overall scheme. The iconography is derived from pagan themes, many of them reinterpreted and invested with a Christian or biblical significance. Oriental subject matter is frequently used, coming from Byzantine precedents or via the Crusader contacts with the East that were made from the 11th century. Figures of humans and beasts, figured *capitals and columns, sequences of *personifications (such as the *Virtues

and Vices) and secular accounts such as the Deeds of Arthur ornament ecclesiastical buildings in profusion. Many of the motifs and forms used in the decorative arts, notably in metalwork, particularly *champlevé* and *cloisonné* enamel, and carving, are derived from architectural uses, e.g. reliquaries in the form of cruciform churches. Motifs based on nature are usually stylised, the most common being *scrolling foliage and the *palmette. The influence of *Viking work can be seen in the Romanesque of northern Europe with the use of *zoomorphic or biomorphic figures, *interlacing and the fusion of abstract with remarkably naturalistic forms.

Although the term Norman has been popularly used to describe the English variation of Romanesque, it is inaccurate both in historical period (*Anglo-Saxon elements are strongly present in the geometric patterning of Romanesque ornament) and geographical location.

Romanesque Revival. An influential strand of *Historicism that varies widely according to its source. German Romanesque was the basis for the *Rundbogenstil, and many *Beaux-Arts trained architects turned to a French Romanesque vocabulary, especially in America. From the 1860s a number of scholarly books on the period were published in Europe and, later, in America, indicating in detail the ornamentation associated with the style. Some architects familiarised themselves

*Romanesque. 1) Norman Gate, Bury St Edmunds, Suffolk, built by Abbot Anselm, 1120-48. 2) *Capital from Sé Velha Church, Coimbra, Portugal, c.1162. 3) English ivory book cover, early 12th century. 4) Church tower, Cunault (Loire), France, 11th to 13th centuries.*

Romanesque Revival. 1) Romanesque House, Nîmes from H. Revoil's Romanesque Architecture in the South of France, New York, 1880s. 2, 3) Baptist Church, Frogmore Street, Abergavenny, Wales, 1877.

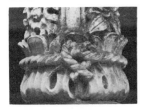

rope. 1) Base of Neo-Manueline column, Palace Hotel, Buçaco, Coimbra, Portugal, 1887-1907. 2) 19th century building in Louvain, Belgium. 3) 1930s apartment block, Paris.

with the period by carrying out restoration work, much as the architects of the *Gothic Revival were to do. Paul Abardie (1812-85) had worked on Angevin Romanesque churches before designing the Sacré Coeur, Paris (1874-91), in which he used a combination of *Byzantine and *Romanesque elements. Romanesque was a popular historical style since it combined certain elements of *classicism, in particular the round arches, with the possibilities of *naturalistic ornament. Alfred Waterhouse (1830-1905) exploited these characteristics in his Natural History Museum, London (1873-81). In America, the Romanesque Revivalists distinguished between continental European Romanesque and British *Anglo-Saxon and Romanesque styles. The most distinguished and influential American architect to adopt the Romanesque style was Henry H. Richardson (1838-86). His interpretation comprised a rough stone masonry surface with a heavy horizontal emphasis, arched window openings and doorways, the use of short, stumpy columns and often a single tower form. One of his most admired buildings was Trinity Church, Boston (1872). This style was frequently used where ideas of strength and seriousness of purpose were to be conveyed, e.g. on court houses, schools and university buildings. *See also* Neo-Norman.

Romantic Classicism. *See* Beaux Arts; Baroque Revival.

romayne work. 16th and 17th century term for profile heads set within roundels. *Renaissance examples included famous Roman emperors, etc., as well as contemporary figures, engraved or carved in the manner of heads on coins or medallions. They sometimes appear among *scrolling foliage. The motif was used on late 16th and early 17th century English furniture, and, occasionally, in church panelling. *See also* portrait heads.

rope appears in *cable moulding in a highly formalised representation, but it may also be realistically

reproduced with knots, bows and frayed ends, usually when alluding to *marine or naval themes.

ropework. *See* cable moulding.

rose. Motif that varies from the simple wild rose to the full, many-petalled bloom of the cultivated rose. The wild rose was used in medieval heraldry and *millefleurs. In *Christian iconography the rose is an attribute of the Virgin Mary; she is sometimes depicted surrounded by them (a rose without thorns, i.e. sinless). The rose garden is a symbol of paradise and appeared on tombs in Roman catacombs. Also, a red rose may symbolise martyrdom and a white rose, piety. In classical mythology, the rose is an attribute of *Venus and her handmaidens, the Three *Graces; Cupid was said to have given a rose to the god of silence, Harpocrates, in order to bribe him not to betray the amours of Venus.

*rose. 1) *Knop on silver teapot by Valentijn Casper Bömke, Amsterdam, 1769. 2) Designs based on the wild rose from E. *Grasset's Plants and their Application to Ornament, 1896-97. 3) Early 20th century carved stone shop façade, Budapest. 4) Figure with roseball, silver-painted wood inlaid with coloured glass, inside door of cabinet for 14 Kingsborough Gardens, Glasgow, Scotland, 1902.*

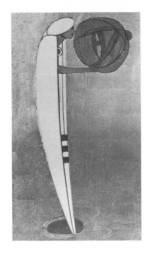

The rose has traditionally been associated with secrecy (hence the phrase *sub rosa*): 16th century confessionals are sometimes decorated with roses and they were used as a *Jacobite emblem, e.g. on drinking glasses.

18th century French *ornemanistes* used little stems of *noisette* roses informally woven into garlands, *festoons and bunches on porcelain, and in ormolu furniture mounts, woven and printed textiles, etc. The guelder rose ornament (German, *Schneeballen*) on 18th century Meissen porcelain consists of tiny blooms modelled and applied to the surface of the vessel, sometimes combined with *grapevines. Victorian and Edwardian decoration favoured the larger, plusher cabbage roses and hybrid tea roses developed at the end of the 19th century. The *Arts and Crafts movement characteristically took up the medieval briar rose; it sometimes appears as a motif in rubbed brick panels set into garden walls, often springing from a vase.

Formalised, tightly budded roses, sometimes called roseballs, were used by the *Glasgow School, and adopted by Charles Rennie Mackintosh (1869-1928) as his personal device. Roseballs were taken up in the work of some *Vienna Secession artists. They reappeared in the work of *Art Deco designer Paul Iribe (1883-1935) and became a dominant motif in French ornament of the 1920s.

roseball. *See* rose.

rosette. Circular, formalised flower ornament, although rosette often loosely describes any circular ornament with elements radiating from its centre. It often enriches a *patera form. A universal decorative motif, it appeared on objects associated with the goddess Inanna in Mesopotamia, c.2500 BC, and was a much-used form on the funeral *stele* of classical Greece. It was a frequent motif in *Romanesque architecture and passed into the standard *classical repertoire from the early *Renaissance. A convenient enrichment in architecture, furniture and metalwork in progressive ornament such as *guilloches, *ribbon mouldings or *frets or to cover the joins on *lattice patterns, the motif may also be used as a central ceiling ornament, sometimes as a surround for a light fitting.

rose window. A late *Gothic circular window that is divided into segments with *tracery elaborated into *foils, bearing an obvious similarity to a petalled flower. It is similar to the earlier *wheel window which was divided up with radiating bars.

Rosman, N. 17th century Dutch author of *Neuw Zirat-Büchlein* (1627), a book of designs in the *Auricular style.

rostral column. *See* columna rostrata.

Ruga, Pietro. Early 19th century disseminator of the *Empire style in Italy. When Napoleon occupied Italy, his Imperial Government established Bonaparte residences in many of the important towns on the peninsula; the Empire style was thus widely known and adopted. Ruga's *pattern book (which owed much to

*rosette. 1) From R. de *Lalonde's* Modillons et rosacées, c.1785. 2) From Cobham Hall, Kent, alterations by James Wyatt, 1790s.

C.*Percier and P. Fontaine) was called *Invenzione diverse de mobili, utensili sacri e profani raccolte ed incise in 100 tavole* (Milan, 1811, 1814, 1817).

ruins appeared in engravings in 16th and 17th century studies of *Graeco-Roman classical architecture, particularly in the sections dealing with *perspective. Thus ruined classical architecture (usually imaginary) seen through an arch became a popular subject for inlaid wood decoration. One collection of designs was V.*Solis's reissue in 1555 and 1565 of Léonard Thiry's *Fragmenta Structurae Veteris* (Orleans, 1550), which consisted of entirely invented material, but claimed to depict genuine Roman ruins.

Schwarzlot, or black enamel decoration on late 17th and early 18th century German porcelain, frequently depicted ruins, probably in imitation of contemporary engravings. But it was G.B.*Piranesi's etchings which, above all, prompted the idea of *Picturesque ruins. Paintings of great buildings of the time in a state of ruin became fashionable, e.g. a depiction of the Louvre by Hubert Robert (1733-1808). In England, fashionable architects built mock *Gothic ruins in the corners of the parks and grounds of country houses, e.g. at Kedleston Hall, Derbyshire, by Robert Adam and Pitzhanger Manor, Middlesex, by Sir John Soane. The ornamental *vignette encircled by a *cartouche, an especially popular motif in the *genre pittoresque* phase of the *Rococo, often depicted a fantastic architectural ruin; there are good examples in J.F. de *Cuvilliès *Morceaux de caprices* (1745). The designs were reproduced on printed cottons, pottery, porcelain, enamels and in painted wall decoration. Picturesque decay was in vogue for a considerable period of the 18th and 19th centuries and, like the cracked ancient bas reliefs and imitation tables that Piranesi used (especially on the title pages of his publications), the Romantic idea of impermanence and ivy-covered mounds of stone became highly popular, appearing in a much-used *drawing book called *The Ladies Amusement. See also* broken column; rustic; rustication.

Rundbogenstil (German, round-arched style). Style of architecture prevalent in Germany in the 1830s and 1840s in which the use of arches was a dominant feature, although the stylistic basis could equally have been *Byzantine, *Romanesque, Florentine *Renaissance or classical Roman. It was employed by Leo von Klenze (1784-1864) and Friedrich von Gartner (1792-1847) in particular, and seems to have been inspired by the Romantic Classical theories of J.-N.-L. *Durand.

Runic. Term loosely applied, especially in the 19th century, to *Viking and *Celtic styles.

running dog. *See* wavescroll.

Ruprich-Robert, Victor-Marie-Charles (1820-87). Holder of the influential position of Professeur de Composition et d'Histoire de l'Ornement at the Ecole Impériale et Spéciale de Dessin, Paris. His *Flore Ornementale* (1866; published as *Ornamental Flora* in London in 1876) and articles published in César Daly's *Revue Générale de l'architecture* (e.g. Vol XI, 1853; Vol XXVIII, 1870) demonstrate how plant forms can be adapted for ornament. The *Revue* also contained contributions from O.*Jones (in translation), but Ruprich-Robert was rather dismissive of Jones's work, commenting that he produced 'above all a history of ornament . . . plant drawings taken from life . . . that are picturesque, accidental and natural: but this is not of itself ornament.' Ruprich-Robert's own contribution was a kind of pseudo-scientific approach to nature; he was particularly interested in the formation of *crystals and illustrated snowflakes. He was also intrigued by the *seed-pod and in this respect was an important influence on L.H.*Sullivan.

Russian. In the late 18th and early 19th centuries, increased foreign travel and the historical connection between France and Russia led to a vogue in Europe (but particularly in France) for decorative schemes including painted wall panels, tapestries, ceramics, using Russian costume scenes and motifs. For example, at Gobelins a series of tapestries entitled 'Jeux Russes', and at Beauvais, 'Fêtes Russes', were produced. In 1812, Napoleon's Russian Campaign (like his Egyptian Campaign a few years earlier) promoted interest in the country and the knout, a kind of Russian scourge, sometimes appeared in *trophies of war. In England, Staffordshire pottery with Russian motifs was also produced at this time.

rustic. Like *pastoral decoration, rustic ornament was a strand of the 18th century liking for the *Picturesque. The particular architectural expression of the style was the *cottage orné. Most commonly, rustic embellishment simulated anything connected with the *tree: bark, lopped branches, twigs, roots, even roughly hewn logs, and it worked most successfully when applied to incidental and intentionally rural buildings, such as grottoes, 'root houses', garden houses and dairies. Inevitably, garden furniture was produced in the style. R.*Manwaring's *The Cabinet and Chair-Maker's Real Friend and Companion* (1765) included a number of chair designs 'supposed to be executed with the Limbs of Yew, Apple or Pear Trees, ornamented with Leaves and Blossoms, which if properly painted will appear like Nature.' Similar rustic designs appeared in Charles Over's *Ornamental Architecture in the Gothic, Chinese and Modern Taste* (1750s), which was known

rustic. 1) Late 19th century American cast-iron seat. 2) Mid 19th century lodge at Kenmore Perth, Perthshire.

in America. William Wright published *Grotesque Architecture or Rural Amusement* (1767) illustrating *rockwork, grottoes and elaborate fountains using rustic detail. Another typical publication was *Ideas for Rustic furniture proper for garden seats, summer houses, hermitages, cottages etc.* published by I.& J. Taylor in the 1790s and reissued in 1835; the designs were much used in 19th century cast-iron manufacture, an important vehicle for the spread of styles as pre-fabricated parts were sent across the British Empire to Australia, the Far East, India, etc.

During the 19th century, rustic embellishment, particularly in the form of branches (e.g. as bench legs), was thought ideal for the gardener's cottage, potting shed, park lodge and the impedimenta of the garden.

rustication. Architectural feature consisting of heavy masonry blocks, decorated or plain, with deep joints – a textural device usually reserved for exteriors and in classical use confined to the lowest levels of the building. In Roman architecture its heaviness denoted security, thus the Castel S. Angelo, Rome (originally Hadrian's mausoleum, built 135 AD, and converted to a citadel and prison in the 5th century) had rustication applied to doors, windows and the bases of walls, gateways and entrance lodges. This use reappeared in the Italian Renaissance, when the motif was also used as a sophisticated modulation for wall surfaces, either as an overall ornament or for certain vertical features, *chaines and *quoins in particular. Rusticated columns became an important feature of *Mannerist and *Baroque architecture. Giorgio Vasari (1511-74) described them as the Rustic Order after he had seen those applied by Jacopo Sansovino to the Venetian Mint (1537). Many authors of *pattern books, e.g. S.*Serlio, explored the possibilities of rustication, elaborating the form to the limit. In Spanish *Plateresque decoration the individual blocks were given further surface ornament and on occasions the chamfering whittled away the surface to a sharp, diamond form (e.g. Casa de Los Picos, Segovia, c.1550). Rustication was also used in *trompe l'oeil* decoration: the Banqueting House, Whitehall (1581), which was demolished to make way for I.*Jones's Banqueting Hall, was painted 'with a worke called rustike, much like to stone'. Rustication in the 18th and 19th centuries was used both as a classical motif and as a romantic allusion to *ruins. It is an obvious device for *grotto ornament, although the pock-marked natural surface

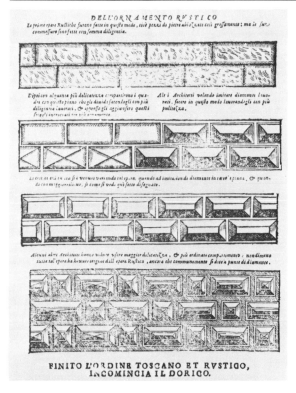

rustication. 1) From S.*Serlio's Architectura, 1537-47. 2) Palazzo Pitti, Florence, Italy, 1458 onwards. 3) Chiswick House, London, by Lord Burlington, built 1725-29.

of tufa, frequently used in this context, gave the same effect.

The elaboration of the form led to a number of specific variations during the Renaissance, especially in the 16th century. They include banded rustication in which only the horizontal joints are exaggerated; chamfered rustication in which the edges are cut back to back to emphasise the joints; diamond-pointed rustication, cut in on the four sides to produce pointed forms (see dogtooth; nailhead); frosted or congelated rustication giving the effect of water (see also icicles); rock-faced rustication, in which the surface is rough and randomly chiselled; vermiculated rustication (or *vermiculation), in which the effect is that of worm

tracks. In *Renaissance Revival architecture, rustication was sometimes employed, as it had been originally, to give an appearance of security, in this case to bank and government buildings. County Hall, London (1911-22) emulated the great rusticated 'water gates' used on W.*Chambers's Somerset House across the river (1776 onwards) that had, in their turn, been based on the engravings of G.B.*Piranesi.

rustick work. 18th century term for *rustication.

sabre. See sword.

sagitta or **saetta** (Italian, arrow). 18th century term for a *keystone, an allusion to its wedge shape.

Saint-Aubin, Charles Germain. (1721-86). French textile designer who published a book of engravings featuring anthropomorphised *butterflies and two sets of designs for *cyphers.

salamander. 1) François I Revival doorway, Alwyn Court, West 58th Street, New York, architects Harde-& Short, 1909. 2) Top of dormer window, probably from the Château de Chambord (Loire), France, built for François I, early 16th century. 3) French enamelled cast-iron stove, late 19th century.

salamander. A mythical beast resembling a newt or lizard (though it sometimes appears rather dog-like), which, according to the *bestiaries, could breed and exist within *flames, and also had the power to extinguish flames. It was adopted as a Christian motif representing enduring faith (which could not be consumed by the fires of temptation) and was used particularly for the decoration of fonts as a symbol of baptism by fire and water. It was used as a *heraldic motif to suggest bravery and courage despite the fires of affliction. François I of France (1494-1547) adopted the salamander as his *impresa and it decorates his royal buildings; it was a prominent motif in the 19th century *François I Revival. Sometimes it appears as an attribute of *fire in schemes of decoration involving the *Elements. A later application was in the decoration of fireplaces, andirons, firebacks, etc. 19th century French cast-iron or enamelled stoves were sometimes ornamented with salamanders.

Salembier, Henri (1753-1820). French ornamental designer who published work between 1777 and 1809 in typical *Louis XVI style. Apart from designs for furniture-makers and goldsmiths, e.g. *Tables, feux et ornements* (1778) and *Modèles de dessins d'orfevrerie* (1809), he is best known for his panels of *grotesque ornament.

Salmon, William (c.1703-79). English carpenter and joiner whose publications borrowed the systems of ornament formerly available in more academic form, as original *classical treatises, and made them available in simplified manuals for the builder. Titles include *Palladio Londinensis, or the London Art of Building* (1734, 1738, and many subsequent editions), *The Builder's Guide and Gentleman and Trader's Assistant* (1736) and *The London and Country Builder's Vade Mecum* (1745). These works were continually reissued into the 1770s and were well known in America, arriving there as early as the mid 1750s.

Sambin, Hugues (c.1520-1601). French architect, engraver and cabinetmaker who worked in Dijon. His *pattern book, *Oeuvre de la diversité des termes, dont on use en architecture, reduict en ordre* (Lyons, 1572), was particularly influential in French furniture of the period 1580-1600. Sambin used the work of J.A.*Ducerceau and H.*Vredeman de Vries as a starting point for his columnar figures, developing richer and more inventive versions, some of which are far removed from the traditional descriptions of *caryatids and *atlantes, which he grouped into six *Orders (one of his own invention). For example, for the Tuscan Order he invented *rustic figures, bristling with twigs and crawling with insects and reptiles; for the Composite Order he abandoned the convention of a single figure in favour of a pillar swarming with dancing *satyrs, goats and *putti. He also incorporated figures from classical mythology such as Hercules and the multi-breasted Diana of Ephesus into his designs. His male and female pairs of *herms are typical of his *Mannerist approach.

samorodok (Russian, nugget). Technique used on late 19th century Russian metalwork to give silver or gold an uneven, crinkled appearance. The effect was produced by heating the metal almost to melting point and then allowing it to cool. It was mostly used on pieces with flat surfaces, such as cigarette and card cases.

sample books. Sketch books of motifs used by the masons of Gothic Europe. Before printed material was available, these books, together with illuminated manuscripts (including the *bestiaries), were the only form of dissemination of motifs in the *Gothic style. Villard de Honnecourt's famous early 13th century sample book included beasts, foliage, everyday events, *personifications (Pride, Humility, the Church Triumphant), and symbolic motifs such as the *Wheel of Fortune.

Facsimile editions of Villard de Honnecourt's work were published in the 19th century, providing an important source for the *Gothic Revival: J.B.A. Lassus's *Album de Villard de Honnecourt* (Paris, 1858) was published the following year in an English edition as *Fac-Simile of the Sketch Book of Wilars de Honecort* with notes by Lassus and additional text by Rev. R. Willus.

Saracenic. Originally, the style of architecture and ornament that resulted from the meeting of Islam in the Near East and North Africa with existing Christian styles during the 7th century crusades. The Saracenic combined with the *Byzantine and influenced *Romanesque work in areas such as Sicily where the different cultures met and mingled. 'Venetian Saracenic' describes the type of metalwork made by Moslem craftsmen in 15th and 16th century Venice (*see* arabesque).

As a revivalist, exotic style of the late 18th, early 19th century, 'Saracenic' covered *Indian or *Arabian style work and had no particular claim to derive from the ornament of a specific region or century – the dome of the stables at Brighton Pavilion (1804) by William Porden (1755-1822), an important example of Saracenic style, contained ornaments and drawings by Decimus Burton (1800-81) which were described

*Hugues Sambin. 1) *Herm for the Composite *Order from Oeuvre de la diversité des termes, 1572.*
*satyr. 2) 16th century house, Rouen (Seine-Maritime), France. 3) *Masks from P.A.*Pierretz's Recherche de plusieurs beaux morceaux d'ornemens antiques et modernes, 1648. 4) English green jasper ware ewer, c.1800. 5) Design for *grotesque ornament by R.*Boyvin, c.1560.*

as 'Saracenic work from India'. The style still had a following when the Philadelphia Centennial Exhibition (1876) was mounted – the Horticultural Hall by Herman J. Schwarzman was described as being in polychrome Saracenic style. *See also* Islamic.

sarcophagus. Like the *urn, the sarcophagus appears as a literal motif in funerary ornament. It was taken up by *Neo-classical and *Greek Revival styles and appeared as *acroteria and along parapets, particularly on mausolea.

The shape was also used at the same period for wine coolers and log boxes, although often only distantly resembling the original form: T.*Sheraton in *The Cabinet Dictionary* (1803) describes wine coolers being 'in some faint degree, an imitation of the figure of these ancient stone coffins, on which account only the term can with any colour of propriety, be applied to such wine systems.'

satyr. A creature from classical mythology with goat-like hairy legs, cloven hooves, a tail, a man's torso and bearded face, and horns. As attendants of Bacchus (*see* Bacchic ornament), satyrs are sometimes crowned with *ivy and may carry the *thyrsus, grapes or pitchers of wine. As spirits of fertility, they bear *cornucopias and baskets of fruit. Often used to represent untamed nature, licentiousness and lust, as their leering expression indicates, they occasionally appear on such furniture as marriage coffers.

In the medieval and Renaissance periods, the satyr was regarded as a figure of evil, indeed the image of Satan with hooves and cloven feet derives from this source. By the 17th century the satyr had become an acceptable figure in ornament, though often reduced to a *mask. The motif was popular in the *Louis XIV and *Louis XV styles. In the third edition of the *Director* there is a design by T.*Chippendale for a 'toylet table' ornamented with satyrs – probably an allusion to the myth of *Venus surprised by satyrs while at her toilet. A popular ornament for furniture mounts in the 18th century, satyr masks appeared most aptly on wine coolers, table and chair legs and sideboards.

scale pattern, imbrication or **petal diaper.** Ornament of overlapping, scale-like shapes. Usually used as a *diaper pattern, sometimes in pierced form. The classical application of scale pattern was as roofing – one of the best-known examples is the Choragic Monument of Lysicrates in Athens (334 BC). The motif appeared frequently in *Graeco-Roman classical architecture and subsequently in Italian *Renaissance work. Where a scale pattern is used in a military context, it may allude to the pattern of Roman armour; more frequently it is based on fish scales or, alternatively, on densely packed foliage. When tiles, wooden shingles and slates are used as wall cladding they may be cut or manufactured to form scale patterns, sometimes alternating with *lozenges or other geometric forms.

Scale pattern has frequently been used as a ground pattern and border decoration on both glass and ceramics. It appears enamelled on Murano glass of the late 15th and early 16th centuries and on Italian *maiolica*

scale pattern. 1) Floor tiles in Romanesque church at Cunault (Loire), France, built 11th to 13th centuries. 2) Early 19th century window, Glasgow, Scotland. 3) Late 19th century terracotta panel, Thetford railway station, Suffolk. 4) Italian maiolica drug-pot made at Deruta, 1502.

of the same date. It was used in a more delicate form on porcelain of the second half of the 18th century: e.g. moulded in relief on ware from St Cloud and enamelled on pieces from Meissen, Vienna and Berlin. In Germany scale pattern is sometimes referred to as *Mosaik*. The pattern also appears as a heavy classical motif in woodwork as a surface decoration, e.g. carved, and sometimes pierced, on furniture in the style of W.*Kent. *See also* pelta.

scales. Motif symbolic of the weighing of good against evil, and truth against falsehood, therefore appearing in decorative schemes on the theme of *justice and law (and thus a common embellishment on courthouses, etc.) and in association with Logic in depictions of the *Liberal Arts. In *Christian iconography it is an attribute of St Michael (for the weighing of souls). It is also a symbol of equality in *masonic and *revolutionary ornament, and is one of the *zodiac signs, Libra.

scales. Palazzo di Giustizia, Rome, 1889-1910.

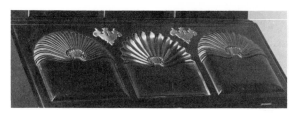

*scallop shell. 1) *Niche, St Carolus Borromeüskerk, Antwerp, Belgium, by Pieter Huyssens, 1615-25. 2) *Cresting on early 18th century English lacquered chair. 3) Niche, St Paul's Cathedral, London, by Sir Christopher Wren, 1675 onwards. 4) Mahogany secretary attributed to J. Goddard, made in Newport, Rhode Island, 1760-75. 5) *Aedicule, The Great Temple, from R.*Wood's The Ruins of Baalbec, 1757.*

scallop shell. This semi-circular, ribbed form has had many applications. It was used as decoration for an apse, squinch, *aedicule or *niche head in ancient Greek and Roman architecture. The form continued in *Byzantine art and frequently reappeared in the *Renaissance and in all subsequent *classical revivals, from the early Tempietto (built 1502) by Donato Bramante (1444-1514) in Rome, to the Viceroy's house in New Delhi (built 1913-31) by Edwin Lutyens.

The scallop form is equally suitable as a *cresting detail and has appeared in many contexts from gravestones to state beds. Its period of greatest popularity as a general motif was the late 17th century (it was typical in the ornament of D.*Marot) and first half of the 18th century throughout Europe, e.g. in *Laub und Bandelwerk borders in Germany, on W.*Kent-style furniture in England and in *Régence plasterwork in France. It was a standard ornament for the knee of a *cabriole furniture leg, on the apron or the back of a chair in the early 18th century. It was also widely used in ceramics and silver: on boxes, dishes, flasks, even as a spoon bowl. It is one of the most persistent ornaments on flatware, appearing in *Hanoverian pattern, *Old English pattern, *Fiddle pattern, *King's pattern and *Coburg pattern. The more elaborately fluted scallop shells were sometimes referred to as husks (as in the early 19th century pattern known as Fiddle Husk).

The scallop was used as an apt form for drinking fountains, holy-water stoops, basins, soap dishes and salt dishes. A set of scallop shell chairs and tables were made in the 19th century for the royal residence in Greenwich.

The use of the scallop shell as a Christian symbol of pilgrimage originated in the 12th century, when pilgrims travelling to the shrine of St James of Compostela in Spain wore his emblem, a scallop, on their hats, cloaks and bags. The heraldic scallop (or escallop) often has two holes pierced in the beak of the shell, a reference to the cord on which the pilgrims wore them.

Scamozzi, Vincenzo (1552-1616). Italian architect and follower of A.*Palladio, who presented Palladio's theory of the *Orders in a solidly academic manner. His *Dell'Idea dell'architettura universale* (Venice, 1615) was translated into English by William Leybourn from an intermediate Dutch edition and published as *Mirror of Architecture* (London, 1669); it ran to several editions and was frequently revised, appearing at roughly ten-year intervals up to 1721, when it was still regarded by classicists as a seminal work. The book was well known in America after c.1750.

Scamozzi's variant of an Ionic *capital came to be known as a 'Scamozzi capital' and his term for the Tuscan Order, the *Gigantic Order, was widely used in the 18th century. Scamozzi preferred to keep ornament to the essentials, and was critical of what he regarded as

Vincenzo Scamozzi. Tuscan colonnade from Dell'Idea dell'architettura universale, *Venice, 1615.*

ASPETTO DEL COLONNATO TOSCANO

'enchanting and delightful palaces which were only for effeminate men . . . the architects ruined the fathers of the families who had them built.'

scarab. A symbol of the sun, life and regeneration for the ancient Egyptians, this winged beetle later appeared as a symbol of good fortune in other Mediterranean countries. With or without its wings outstretched it was one of the motifs taken up by the 19th century *Egyptian and *Archaeological styles, particularly on necklaces, bracelets and belts.

scenic masks. 18th and early 19th century term for *Comedy and Tragedy masks.

Schinkel, Karl Friedrich (1781-1841). Berlin-based architect and designer whose individualistic rendering of *Neo-classical motifs was widely influential. His *Technische Deputation für Gewerbe: Vorbilder für Fabrikanten und Handwerker* appeared in two volumes, the first 1821-30 and the second 1830-37; the latter included designs for iron railings, goblets, lamps, picture frames, upholstered furniture and glass. Like designs in the *Biedermeier style, which Schinkel sometimes approaches, his work shows an entirely individual adaptation of classical motifs rather than a zealous concern with antiquarianism. Architectural designs were published as *Sammlung architecttonischer Entwürfe* (1819-40) and in English as *Collected Architectural Designs* (1823-38). His sparing use of Neo-classical detail and his careful application of ornament accurately based on classical prototypes, e.g. the Four *Winds scheme on the Schloss Tegel, Berlin, or the winged *Victories in a *frieze on the Neue Wache [New Guard House], Berlin, was to influence *Greek Revival architects such as Alexander 'Greek' Thomson (1817-75) of Glasgow and practitioners in America. Although much of Schinkel's work was Greek Revival in style, some was *Gothic Revival (including some fine brick churches) and he even made use of *Pompeian decoration.

Schönsperger, Hans or Johann (fl 1520-30). Designer of an early *pattern book for embroidery, *Furm oder Modelbüchlein* (Augsburg, 1523), followed by two others, *Ein new Modelbuch* (1524) and *Ein ney Furmbüchlein* (1529). These were later reproduced in French and Italian pattern books, such as those of G.A.*Tagliente.

Schübler, Johann Jakob (1689-1741). German mathematician, inventor and furniture designer. He published books on *perspective and carpentry, but his most successful and influential work was the *Werck*, published in parts c.1715-c.1730. Each set of six plates covered a different subject, such as canopied beds, cabinets, chimneypieces, writing desks and dressing tables, clock-cases, tables and chairs, *vases and garden ornaments. The designs reflected contemporary taste in Germany for a heavily detailed *Baroque style with many *scrolls and *volutes. Many of his designs verged on the fantastic and were dominated by gadgetry, such as devices for reclining chairs, and dining tables incorporating dumb waiters and fountains; his most extreme designs were *Nützliche Vorstellung* (Nuremberg, 1730). However, at least twenty editions of his

scarab. 1) Oddfellows Hall, Devonport, Devon, architect John Foulston, 1824. 2) English gold scarab beetle brooch, c.1870.

work are recorded. B.*Langley used a table design from the *Werck* in his *The City and Country Builder's and Workman's Treasury* (1740).

scoop pattern. Horizontal progressive ornament consisting of sections of vertical *fluting with curved closed ends; sometimes one end is flat. Much used in *Jacobean and later woodwork, and revived in the 19th and 20th centuries.

scotia. A deep-cut concave *moulding, made up of two cavetto mouldings of different sizes, resulting in a projecting lower edge, used for example at the foot of a column between two *torus mouldings.

Scotic. Loose 19th century term for *Celtic, *Hiberno-Romanesque and *Anglo-Saxon work.

Scott, William Bell. *See* eclecticism.

Scottish Baronial. Style adopted at a period contemporary with the *Jacobean Revival in England. It

*scoop. 1) *Frieze ornament on mausoleum, Calton Hill burial ground, Edinburgh.*
Scottish Baronial. 2) Aigas House, Inverness-shire.

combined the medievalism of traditional fortified architecture with the irregular outlines favoured by designers in the *Picturesque and *eclectic modes of the early 19th century. Scottish Baronial was in effect a regional and belated version of the *Castle style, applied largely to country houses. The principal features are a profusion of turrets, *battlements and heavily hewn stonework. The best-known designer in this fashion (which he used together with a wide variety of alternatives) was William Burn (1789-1870).

Scottish ornament. Apart from the politically and religiously loaded symbolism of the *Jacobite era, the use of Scottish motifs did not begin in earnest until the 19th century, when a sudden interest in Scotland developed, fuelled by the popularity of the novels of Walter Scott, the poetry of Robert Burns, the interest of the Romantics following the publication of the counterfeit Ossianic myths, the *Picturesque liking for dramatic scenery and Queen Victoria's decision to build Balmoral Castle and to take holidays there.

The Royal retreat to the Scottish Highlands led to the popularity of tartan plaids, not just as a pattern for textiles, but also, for example, for wooden souvenirs called Tartan ware printed with tartan patterns and produced for tourists from the 1860s. The *thistle, emblem of Scotland, and the Scottish dagger, the *skean dhiu*, appeared in jewellery and in cast-iron railings and other artefacts. A silver candelabrum made by G.R. Elkington (1801-65), which was based upon a design by the Prince Consort and shown in 1862, consisted of thistle candleholders, swags of plaid and *Celtic *interlacing patterns. It was set with cairngorms and its base consisted of stags' heads, standing on stag's feet. *See also* Abbotsford style.

scroll. Based on a C-curve, the scroll is a basic element in *Graeco-Roman classicism (and in *classical revivals), used singly or as a repeating ornament with scrolls either flowing in the same direction or facing each other. It was dominant in *Celtic and *Viking work. Both the *Baroque and *Rococo styles depended heavily on curving forms and a wide variety of scrolls developed as a result, among them the *arabesque, *cloudband, console, *C-scroll, *scrolled pediment, *scrolling foliage, *volute and *wavescroll.

scroll moulding or **edge moulding.** A variation of *roll moulding whose shape resembles a loosely rolled piece of paper.

scrolled heart. Repeating pattern used as border or *frieze decoration in *classical and *Neo-classical ornament. Though the form is heart-like, it is in fact made up of two facing bands of *wavescroll. It is a typical *Adam style ornament.

scrolled, swan-neck or **goose-neck pediment.** In America, **bonnet-top** or **bonnet scroll pediment.** *Open pediment in which the two sides are formed of S-shaped scrolls pointing inwards. Mainly used for smallish details, e.g. on door-cases, it was popular in the *Baroque style, and later, in the 18th century, as *cresting for tallboys, bureaux, long case clocks (*see*

*scrolled pediment. 1) Chimneypiece designs from J.*Gibbs's* A Book of Architecture, *1728. 2) American mahogany highboy, made in Philadelphia, c.1760-75. 3) Doorway in Wolstraat, Antwerp, Belgium.*

also whales' tails) and for the early 19th century American shelf clocks known as pillar-and-scroll clocks.

scrolling foliage combines *naturalistic forms in abstract curving lines and is eminently adaptable to many media and many uses. Its origins probably lie in the Alexandrian Greek usage of the *grapevine, when it was employed to create dynamic and rhythmic patterns. The form was absorbed into the vocabulary of *classical ornament, in which it was most commonly composed of the *acanthus. In the late Roman period the foliage tended to be more lavish and drooping, the ornament more complex and in deeper relief. The *Byzantine use of the motif gave it a spiky shape. Scrolling foliage was popular throughout the *Romanesque period and was among the most widely applied motifs in the *Renaissance. Benvenuto Cellini (1500-70), in his autobiography, drew attention to the variety of ways in which the ornament was rendered: 'It is true that in Italy we have several different ways of designing foliage; the Lombards, for example, construct very beautiful patterns by copying the leaves of briony and ivy in exquisite curves, which are extremely agreeable to the eye; the Tuscans and the Romans make a better choice, because they imitate the leaves of the acanthus, commonly called bear's foot, with its stalks and flowers, curling in divers wavy lines; and into these arabesques one may excellently insert the figures of little birds and different animals, by which the good taste of the artist is displayed.' German engraved ornament varied the foliage further, with many artists such as H.*Aldegrever using fig leaves, and others, e.g. Daniel Hopfer (c.1470-1550), producing a leaf with a more spiky, *Gothic feel. Scrolling foliage was a standard detail in 16th century engraved ornament and *pattern books when it seems to have been used mainly on *friezes, decorated *brackets

scrolling foliage. 1) Late 16th century enrichment to columns, Duomo, Pisa, Italy. 2) Engraving by A.*Veneziano, early 16th century. 3) Silver candelabrum by Anton Hendrik Paap, Amsterdam, 1787. 4) Late 19th century dock sheds, Antwerp, Belgium.

and handles (being suited to curved elements), and on *pilaster shafts and panels in a variant of the *candelabra form. Gradually, scrolling foliage became incorporated into larger schemes with other motifs such as *grotesques, birds, *putti, *sirens or *dragons. Still extremely versatile, it was used either as a spare linear ornament or as a thickly packed, dense motif. The development of scrolling foliage provides a good indication of the changes wrought in universally popular classical ornament over different periods. Designers explored its full potential, experimenting with different types of leaf or flower according to contemporary tastes, as in J.*Le Pautre's *Rinceaux de différents feuillages* (1660).

In the 18th and 19th centuries, the ornament was variously referred to as broccoli, *parsley, *raffle leaf or *rinceau*. The Victorians adopted scrolling foliage as the perfect vehicle for the much-favoured full-blown naturalism of the period. As tastes changed, the motif was retained but became increasingly stylised or dependent on Renaissance prototypes.

scythe or **sickle.** Attribute of Father *Time, who is also known as The Reaper [of Life], the association probably arising from the close similarity between the Greek words for time, *chronos*, and the god of agriculture, Cronos. Used in the ornamentation of timepieces, and in decoration associated with *death and mourning, the scythe alludes to the sense of time cut short. The personification of Death as a skeleton often carries a scythe.

The scythe or sickle may also represent harvest time, e.g. in *trophies for *husbandry, and Summer in schemes of the *Seasons. The sickle appears in some early 20th century Russian ornament, with the hammer, as an emblem of the Revolution.

sea-dog. An Elizabethan concoction – a fantastic beast with the head and forelegs of a dog and a fish's tail, used as a support on elaborate pieces of furniture of the period; it also appeared in plasterwork.

sea horse. Animal whose scrolling shape sometimes appears in *marine ornament and is occasionally used as a motif in the *Rococo, an apt contribution to *rocaille or *grotto ornament. Like other marine subjects, e.g. *shells, *waves and seagulls, sea horses were popular in 1920s and 1930s ornament. *See also* hippocamp.

seal-top. Flat circular *finial placed on an oval, circular or polygonal *baluster forming a typical English spoon-end from the late 15th century to the mid 17th century. Occasional 17th century examples are hexagonal, often marked with a monogram, initials or a date.

Seasons, The Four. A decorative theme from classical times. The Seasons are usually represented as *personifications, Spring with flowers and garlands, Summer with sheaves of *wheat, Autumn with a fruiting *grapevine and Winter, thickly wrapped against the cold, sometimes with a bundle of faggots. The theme was popular in medieval decoration, particularly in *naturalistic ornament, often combined

scrolling foliage. 1) 19th century ironwork, entrance to Hapsburg Garden, Vienna. 2) Wrought iron hinge and closing ring formed of bracken and hart's tongue fern from J.K.*Collings's Art Foliage, 1865.

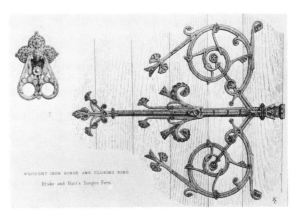

seaweed. 1) Lady Chapel, Ely Cathedral, Cambridgeshire, 1320s onwards.
seedpod. 2) Formalised honesty seedpod on English bowl in Liberty Tudric
pewter designed by Archibald Knox, c.1905.

The Four Seasons. 1) Engraving by J.*Le Pautre for *herms representing
the Seasons in the classical pantheon as Saturn (Winter), Bacchus
(Autumn), Ceres (Summer) and Flora (Spring), c.1760. 2) German
porcelain figures symbolising Spring, Autumn, Winter and Summer,
modelled by J.J. Kändler, Meissen, c.1750.

with representations of the Labours of the *Months.
The Renaissance revived *classical representations:
Flora or *Venus for Spring, *Ceres for Summer, Bacchus for Autumn (see Bacchic decoration) and Boreas
(the North Wind) or Vulcan (the Roman god of fire)
for Winter. The iconography of the Seasons may be
combined with the four *Ages of Man, thus Spring
represents childhood, Summer, youth, Autumn, middle age and Winter, old age. The Seasons sometimes
decorate painted clock faces, signifying the passing of
*time, but are also an obvious subject for ornament,
sculpture and buildings in gardens and parks. Common in the 18th century when thematic series in decoration were particularly popular, they appeared as
sets of *caryatids, porcelain figures, in tapestries, enamelled on opaque white glass, transfer-printed on
enamel and porcelain, and in plasterwork. During
this period, they were sometimes represented by pastimes, e.g. courting or bird-snaring for Spring; bathing
or harvesting for Summer; grape-gathering for Autumn; skating or playing indoors for Winter. Four-
part themes were particularly appropriate to domestic
interiors, being applied to the four walls of a room.
See also zodiac signs.

seaweed. Seaweed occasionally appears in *marine
decoration but the term usually describes a seaweed-
like effect. Thus, seaweed foliage is the term some-

times used for the foliage on *crockets and *capitals
of *Decorated and *Flamboyant Gothic architecture.
    Seaweed (or endive scroll) marquetry refers to a type
of patterning based on *moresque designs that appeared in late 17th century English woodwork, particularly on long-case clocks, tables, etc.
    A thin, branching twig-like pattern used as a ground
pattern in the late 18th and early 19th centuries for
ceramics and textiles was referred to by some porcelain manufacturers as 'seaweed' or 'fibre'.

Second Empire. See French Second Empire.

seed-pods. Popular decorative motifs symbolising
fecundity, growth and life: the *peapod and *pomegranate bursting asunder to display their seed-filled
contents were widely used in plasterwork and woodwork throughout the 17th and early 18th centuries.
Rather too vulgar for *Neo-classical sensibilities, the
form was readopted by late 19th century designers
(in tune with contemporary botanical investigations)
as much for its significance as a symbol of force and
vitality as for the geometric possibilities of its form.
*Glasgow School designers adopted the apple pip,
bulbs and corms. The winged sycamore seed-pod
and the oval, silvery pod of the honesty plant were
much used at the turn of the century, particularly in
metalwork and jewellery, the latter in fashionable
and appropriate materials: silver, pewter, enamels
and moonstones. Louis Majorelle (1859-1926) used
honesty for a forged iron banister; Archibald Knox
(1864-1931) used the same motif on a range of 'Tudric'
pewter for Liberty & Co. (c.1905).

segmental pediment. *Pediment in the form of a
segment of a circle, which, like its triangular equivalent,
may be *open or *broken. See also scrolled pediment.

Séguy, E.A. Compiler of *pattern books containing
colour illustrations of repeating designs, that were
used mainly by textile manufacturers but were broadly
suitable for any two-dimensional application. His early
books were in the *Art Nouveau style, with designs
based on *plant forms, e.g. Les Fleurs et leurs applications
décoratives (1901-03). Gradually, however, he adopted
a more *Art Deco style, as in Primavera (1913), Floréal
(1914), Samarkande (1920), Suggéstions pour étoffes et tapis
(1923), Bouquets et frondaisons (Paris, 1925; New York,
1926), Papillons (c.1927), Insectes (c.1928), Prismes (c.1930).

Senses, The Five. Usually represented by female *personifications pursuing an occupation connected with each sense: for example, Hearing is shown playing music; Smell holds flowers; Taste is eating, usually fruit; Touch may be holding or have something soft or sharp, e.g. an ermine or a hedgehog; Sight looks into a mirror. The Senses appear on the Anglo-Saxon Fuller Brooch (now in the British Museum) and in the 14th century wall painting at Longthorpe Tower near Peterborough, where each Sense is represented by an animal: monkey – taste, vulture – smell, spider's web – touch, boar – hearing, cock – sight. The theme was employed in both *Gothic and *Renaissance work. Later, the designs often derived from sources such as C.*Ripa's *Iconologia*. The senses appeared in plasterwork in the early 17th century and the theme was popular among *Rococo *ornemanistes*: porcelain figures were produced, e.g. those modelled by J.J. Kändler and J.F. Eberlein for the Meissen factory, c.1745, and *vignettes were engraved and enamelled on German and Bohemian glass.

Serlio, Sebastiano (1475-1554). Italian architect who joined the court of François I and worked in France from 1540. He is best known for the publication of *Architettura* (between 1537 and 1547). The work was

*segmental pediment. 1) From R.*Pricke's* The Architect's Storehouse, London, 1674. 2) Over window on 19th century commercial building, Liverpool, England.
E.A. Séguy. 3) From his* Bouquets et frondaisons, *1925.*

*Sebastiano Serlio. Corinthian *Order chimneypiece from Book IV of his* Architettura, *1537.*

the first architectural treatise to depend upon lavish and properly arranged illustrative material, rather than upon its written or intellectual content (see *Vitruvius and L.B.*Alberti). It was published as a series of volumes, confusingly appearing out of numerical order. First was Book IV, dealing with the *Orders and their ornamentation, together with variations taking in such detail as *rustication. Then came Book III, in 1540, which showed classical Roman architecture and works by Donato Bramante (1444-1514) and Raphael. Both these books were published in Venice and quickly ran into further editions, including French and Dutch translations of Book IV in 1545 and 1549 respectively, and a French translation of Book III in 1550. The remaining books were all first published in France and showed the French influence in the increasingly *Mannerist style of the illustrations. Books I and II were published as one volume with a text in both Italian and French, so too was Book V. The five books were first issued in one volume in 1566, with the *Libro extraordinario* appended. This was a treatise on doorways, with 50 plates, which, in the 1600 edition, and thereafter, was known as Book VI. The true Book VI remained in manuscript and was first published, in facsimile, in the 20th century. Book VII was published posthumously in Frankfurt by Jacopo de Strada, and an intended Book VIII on military buildings was never completed or published. The first English translation of the complete *Architettura* appeared in 1611, taken from the Dutch translation and called *The Book of Architecture*; however, the Frankfurt edition had been available in England and the large number of illustrations meant that the work had for some time been readily accessible to architects even if they could not read the text. Serlio, whose work, even at its most ornamental, was a far cry from the excesses of the late 16th century Northern Mannerists, provided a guide which the Elizabethans embraced with enthusiasm. It appeared before most English architects had begun visiting Italy to view classical examples for themselves, and suggested the superior claims of a classical vocabulary of architecture to builders and designers still steeped in the *Gothic. According to one historian, the *Architettura* became the 'architectural bible of the civilised world'. Authors of later treatises such as J.*Shute were heavily indebted to Serlio.

Serliana. *See* Palladian motif.

serpent. Motif used with widely varying symbolism in the ornament of many cultures. In early oriental and Greek myth, the serpent was a force of evil. In Christian symbolism, it represents temptation (a reference to the Bible story of Adam and Eve in the Garden of Eden) and thus sin and heresy. The battle between the *eagle and the serpent, or the *lion and the serpent, has appeared in countless images over the centuries, usually illustrating the battle between good and evil, or, more specifically, Christianity and heretics of various sorts.

However, the serpent also appears as a symbol of wisdom, twined around the tree of knowledge and used, for example, on the frame of a portrait of Benjamin Franklin (1706-90). The serpent biting its own tail represents eternity, and is much used in mourning jewellery and around the dial of clocks. It appears on christening cups to suggest longevity. Two serpents twined around the *rod of Aesculapius represent the opposing forces of sickness and health.

The 9th century Celtic Book of Kells represents the earth, one of the *Elements, with serpents. In *Viking decoration, formalised serpentine ornament is much used, together with *zoomorphic, *lacertine and *dracontine forms, as a kind of scroll or tendril form, often with the tails knotted.

Symbolism apart, the serpent was a decorative form which was practical as a handle; Roman originals were copied by 16th century engravers such as E.*Vico and readopted in the 18th century. They were used by Sèvres (applied in ormolu) in the 1760s, and by Josiah Wedgwood and Matthew Boulton in the 1770s. The motif was sometimes elaborated, with double snakes tied with ribbons or entwined. Snakes are found curled around *lion *monopodia (a reference to their legendary conflict) and appear within *tripods (as illustrated by T.*Hope in *Costume of the Ancients*). At Kilmainham Gaol, the Dublin County Prison (1796), chained serpents ornament the *tympanum. In jewellery, the snake form has been used for bracelets and rings from early times, sometimes twining up the length of the fore or upper arm or finger, sometimes as a single band. In the 19th century a more *naturalistic approach often led to the ornamentation of such

serpent. 1) Lion mask and serpent fountain, Italy. 2) English jasper ware vase, Wedgwood, c.1785. 3) Iron doorstop, Italy. 4) Door-knocker, Hôtel des Monnaies, Paris, 1771-75. 5) Cobra, Royal Holloway College, Egham, Surrey, architect W.H. Crossland, 1879-87. 6) Banding on entrance to Castelo da Pena, Sintra, Portugal, by Baron von Eschwege, c.1840.

bracelets with precious stones for the eyes and enamelling or *pavé* stone settings for the scales. R.*Brown, in his *Rudiments* (1830), took a stand on the literal usage of serpents in ornament: 'the modern upholsterer and cabinet-maker now apparently try how disgusting and preposterous, as well as hideous, they can render their appartments, by the introduction of serpents and other reptiles to which we have natural antipathy.' Despite these words, the Great Exhibition catalogue (1851) shows a wide variety of objects entwined with snakes, among them a carved sideboard by Messrs Poole & MacGilvray, London, and a wire flower table by John Reynolds of London, in addition to ceramic and metalwork vases and jewellery. *See also* caduceus; gorgon.

shaft ring. *See* annulet.

shamrock. *See* Irish.

Shaw, Henry (1800-73). English antiquary, draughtsman and illuminator. An early contributor to the field of published *Historicist ornament, Shaw specialised mainly in *Gothic, *Elizabethan and *Jacobean architectural detail and decoration of illuminated manuscripts, thus providing source material for the Victorian revivals of these styles. *Details of Gothic Architecture* (1823) included examples from various cathedrals and churches, chiefly carved foliage. *Examples of Ornamental Metalwork* (1830) consisted mainly of existing work, but also contained some Gothic designs devised by Shaw himself. *Illuminated Ornaments Selected from Manuscripts and Early Printed Books from the Sixth to the Seventeenth Centuries* (1833) included borders, *arabesques and initials from a variety of rare manuscripts reproduced for the first time, many in colour. In 1834 he published *Details of Elizabethan Architects*, a secular companion to his earlier Gothic Details. *Specimens of Ancient Furniture* (1836) illustrated furniture and metalwork from medieval times to the late 17th century, and *Specimens of Tile Pavements* (1858) provided specifically non-architectural prototypes for the *Gothic Revival. Shaw's best known work was *The Encyclopaedia of Ornament* (London, 1842; reprinted Edinburgh, 1898). This anticipated the many *pattern books of historical ornament that appeared after the Great Exhibition in London in 1851. It included colour plates and covered styles of ornament up to the 17th century in carving, stained glass, ironwork, painted tiles, needlework, lace, velvet, jewellery and bookbinding. Shaw's last three books concerned themselves with providing specimens of lettering and illumination, which was undergoing a revival during this period for letter heads, subscriptions and presentations. He published *Alphabets, Numerals and Devices of the Middle Ages* in 1845, *The Handbook of Medieval Alphabets and Devices* in 1853 and finally *A Handbook of the Art of Illumination* in 1866.

Shearer, Thomas. Assumed to be a working cabinet-maker, Shearer's name is known only from the signature on most of the plates in *The Cabinet-Makers' London Book of Prices*, first published in 1788. Issued as a trade manual with tables of prices, it costed separately the

Thomas Shearer. From his The Cabinet Makers' London Book *of Prices, 1788.*

*Henry Shaw. Late 13th century *bosses from Southwell Abbey and Westminster Abbey in his* The Encyclopaedia of Ornament, *1842.*

furniture and their additional ornamentation such as 'plinthing, therming, pannelling, or putting corner strings in different sorts of legs and claws, veneering, planting on, and working astragals of different descriptions, cross-banding etc.' A wide range of cabinet pieces in common and popular production were illustrated, making the catalogue influential both in Britain and in America (*see* Federal style). An enlarged second edition, published in 1793, contained some designs by G.*Hepplewhite, and a similar third edition appeared in 1803. The work was superseded in 1811 by *The Cabinet-Makers' Union Book of Prices* by which time Shearer's predominantly *Neo-classical designs had been dropped.

sheath. A decorative device, typical in *scrolling foliage, that provides a mask or casing for the joint between *acanthus leaves or *grapevine leaves and their stalks. The *papyrus flower is also depicted springing from a sheath of casing leaves. Sheaths also appear on *herms, at the point where the human bust and ornamental support meet. It was referred to in the 18th century as a vagina.

shells. Large and exotic shells were highly prized from the time that travellers first began to bring them to Europe. From the medieval period to the 17th century, they were frequently elaborately mounted in gold and silver, sometimes to form salts, standing cups or ewers, particularly during the *Mannerist enthusiasm for curious and exotic objects. *Grotto ornament, another manifestation of Mannerist taste, also used shells, real or modelled, of all species.

The use of a shell as an apt form for a salt cellar remained popular long after the fashion for mounting real shells had declined. Shell forms both in ceramics and silver also had other uses, especially during the 18th century: spiral shells such as the nautilus formed tureens, sauceboats, etc., flat shells made dishes and

shells. 1) Design for ewer by C.*Floris, after 1540. 2) Design for salt by Paul Flindt incorporating nautilus shell, *hippocamp, *dolphin and *Neptune, Nuremberg, Germany, 1594. 3) *Vermiculation effect with shells on a *quoin, late 17th century house in Rouen (Seine-Maritime), France. 4) Fish and shell garland on Irish silver sauceboat by Thomas Williamson, c.1750. 5) Shell-headed canopy on 18th century hôtel, rue de Grenelle, Paris. 6) *Capital, New York Yacht Club, West 44th Street, architects Warren & Wetmore, 1899.

plates, and Wedgwood used bivalve shell shapes for pickle or preserve dishes. *Rocaille decoration combined well with shell forms. In the late 18th and early 19th centuries a single spiral shell was a common design on inlaid wood furniture or as an ornament for bathrooms (an early example is Louis XVI's Chambre des Bains at Compiègne, rebuilt from 1751). The Belleek porcelain factory produced a range of shell forms with an iridescent mother-of-pearl glaze in the 1860s (which has since been revived). Shells in a simplified form based on a wood-block impression were a popular motif for textiles in 1930s, as well as for the printed paper covers and endpapers of books. *See also* marine decoration; scallop shell.

Sheraton, Thomas (1751-1806). English furniture designer, cabinetmaker and draughtsman, who advertised himself as teacher of 'perspective architecture and ornaments'. His first *pattern book exemplified the late 18th century taste for *Neo-classical furniture design and presented it so as to make the manufacture of every detail comprehensible to craftsmen. The book was popular in America and, with G.*Hepplewhite's designs, provided a basis for the early *Federal style. The Boston cabinetmakers John and Thomas Moore Seymour produced typical interpretations of Sheraton. *The Cabinet-Maker and Upholsterer's Drawing-Book in three parts* plus its *Appendix* and *Accompaniment* was published in London, 1791-94. It had 700 subscribers, but additional demand was such that a second edition was published later in 1794, with nine further plates. A third edition appeared in 1802. The book was well adapted to the new fashion for marquetry or painted decoration after carved decoration fell from favour in the 1760s. Sheraton made varying use of ornamental motifs from the *Adam style: *urns, *vases, *pateras, *festoons of *husks, *ribbons and flower garlands together with *stringing and banding and geometric patterns that emphasised the quality of the woods. The forms are relatively simple with a rectilinear emphasis: square-backed chairs infilled with vertical bars, and square, tapering legs often with reeded and caned work. He also used brass galleries on tables and desks and lyre-shaped end supports, both features influenced by the markedly French-style work of Henry Holland (1745-1806), who had just finished the decoration at Carlton House, London, for the Prince Regent. Sheraton's book gave general advice, e.g. that furniture for the dining room 'should be substantial and useful things, avoiding trifling ornaments and unnecessary decorations', as well as detailed suggestions, e.g. that drawing-room chairs could be 'finished in white and gold, or the ornaments may be japanned (painted with a ground colour of black, cream or green).'

Sheraton's second pattern book, *The Cabinet Dictionary* (1803), included several elements taken from the *Louis XVI style: *colonnettes, feet like spinning tops, spiral *fluting and ribbon borders. There is also clear evidence that he had absorbed the new influences which were to be the basis for the *Regency fashion: the large-scale scrolls and *volutes introduced by C.H. *Tatham, increased use of animal motifs (terminals in the form of *aegricanes, *dolphins, *claw and paw

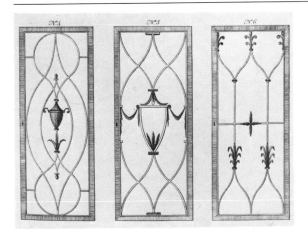

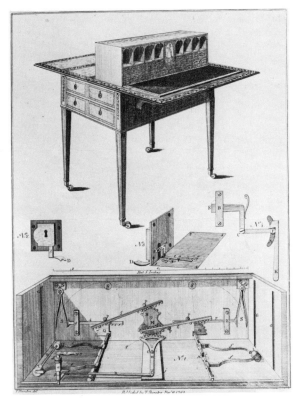

Thomas Sheraton. 1) Doors for Bookcases. 2) A Harlequin Pembroke Table. Both from his The Cabinet-Maker and Upholsterer's Drawing-Book in three parts, *1793.*

feet and *lion masks). His last work, *The Cabinet-maker, Upholsterer and General Artist's Encyclopedia*, was begun in 1804, but on Sheraton's death in 1806 only 30 of the projected 125 parts had been completed. However, he had already included details of *Egyptian style ornament, which was soon to become popular. In the late 19th century and during the 20th century, Sheraton's early designs were frequently reprinted, and not merely as documents of historical curiosity: Charles M. Stow, in the introduction to an American reprint of 1938, described the publication as 'a real service to the cause of beauty in the American home'.

shield. The ancient Greek crescent-shaped shield, the *pelta, was used in *Graeco-Roman classical ornament and reappeared in *Neo-classical decoration. A motif based on the medieval shield, which was triangular or spade-shaped, is common in *heraldic decoration. The shapes of tilting or jousting shields used in tournaments, with a deep notch for a spear on one side (usually the right), began to make an appearance at the end of the 14th century. In the 16th century, the introduction of firearms made the shield a redundant means of defence. However, in ornament the form remained, was soon elaborated with *strapwork, scrolls and *mantling, and ultimately evolved into the *cartouche. Shield-shaped cartouche forms were also used as lockplates and name plates; these were particularly common in the *Gothic Revival because of their chivalric and medieval associations. *See also* aegis.

Shingle style. American equivalent of the *Old English vernacular revival in England. The 1876 Centennial celebrations directed the attention of designers and architects towards early Colonial houses. From 17th and early 18th century houses on the New England seaboard, they took the wooden shingle cladding, gambrel and salt-box roofs and combined these with elements of the currently fashionable *Queen Anne style, such as dormers and oriel windows. In some cases the woodwork was increasingly elaborated with patterned shingles, *lattices, grilles and *balustrading.

shofar. *See* Judaic.

Shorleyker, Richard. Compiler of *A Schole House for the Needle* (1624, 1632). Shorleyker described the patterns it provided as 'sundry sorts of spots, as Flowers, Birds and Fishes etc . . . [which] will fitly serve to be wrought, some with Gould, some with Silke, and some with Crewell.' Despite the patterns' suitability for the then fashionable monochrome or blackwork embroidery, usually stitched in isolated spots or subjects, they do show a move towards designs suitable for the flowing wool crewel work which was soon to become more popular than blackwork. Some designs in the collection had already been published, notably those by J.*Sibmacher, F. di *Vinciolo and P.*Flötner. The original designs were typical of late *Tudor and *Jacobean embroidery decoration, incorporating flowers such as the wild strawberry, rose and pansy, and birds like the *peacock, often formalised and almost heraldic in flavour.

Shute, John (d 1563). English painter, architect and author of *The First and Chief Groundes of Architecture* (1563), which was the first architectural *pattern book, and the second engraved book, published in England. There were four plates and one woodcut illustrating the *Orders. Largely based on the work of *Vitruvius and S.*Serlio, it was extremely popular (reprinted 1579, 1584, 1587). Shute had been sent to Italy by the Duke of Northumberland in 1550 but the experience did not make his observations any more accurate. The title page shows Italianate *grotesques, the text is attractively vague and *classical elements are freely

John Shute. The Ionic *Order from his The First and Chief Groundes of Architecture, *1563.*

embellished. Of the Composite Order, he wrote 'as touchinge the bodye of the Pedestall they have garnished it beautifully after diver sortes'. However Shute was the first English writer to name and describe the classical Orders and he carefully described the *frieze decoration of the Doric Order: 'Betwixte the two Triglyphos you shall set Methopa . . . and in that square shall be made a bulles hed, his hornes bound about with rybandes garnished with branches, flowers and jewelles, hanging at the endes of the Ribandes. In every second Methopa out to be made a faire basone or flat place, the which inwardely should be garnished but I am not able to set fourth the bewtye thereof in so small a figure.' Shute originally gathered the subject matter for the book 'for my private commoditie', exploring the sources available in Latin, Italian, French and 'Douche'. There were no further original architectural pattern books in England until 1715.

Sibmacher, Johann (d 1611). Nuremberg engraver best known for his designs for weaving, embroidery and *reticello* lace. His two famous collections were *Schön Neues Modelbuch von allerley lustigen Modeln neu zunehen, Zuwurchen -un Zusticken* (Nuremberg, 1597) – a pattern book of all kinds of amusing and original designs for sewing, tapestry, weaving and embroidery – and *Neues*

Modelbuch (1601, five editions by 1604). The patterns ranged from friezes to single motifs such as figures in contemporary costume. Their influence extended far beyond Germany and many of the designs appeared in other published collections, e.g. those of J.*Boler and R.*Shorleyker. The most important later edition of Sibmacher was an enlarged and revised *Neues Modelbuch*, published in three parts in Nuremberg, 1666-67. German facsimiles of the book were published in 1866 and 1877. Sibmacher also engraved books of heraldic ornament, one small and one large collection, both entitled *Wappenbuch* and published in Nuremberg, one in 1596, the other in 1605 and 1609.

sickle. *See* scythe.

singerie (*singe*, French, monkey). A style of decoration developed from the *grotesque in the 17th and 18th centuries that consisted of monkey figures, usually mimicking human habits and pastimes, placed among *scrolling foliage and light *bandwork. J.*Berain produced famous designs for *singeries*, which are characteristic of the lighter decorative touch heralding the *Régence (or early *Rococo) and marking the end of the *Louis XIV style. A.C. Boulle used Berain's *singerie* designs for marquetry (*see boulle*): a toilet mirror decorated with them was perhaps an intentional allusion to the monkey as a symbol of luxury and vanity. Claude Audran III (1658-1734) painted an arbour with monkeys eating at table at the Château de Marly (1709), but the most famous examples are those by C.*Huet at Chantilly in which he mixed fashionably dressed monkeys with *chinoiserie mandarins. A popular series of monkey musicians modelled by J.J. Kändler at Meissen c.1750 were traditionally thought to represent the Dresden Royal Orchestra, but it is more likely that they were another manifestation of Rococo *singeries*; the figures were widely copied in Europe, notably at Vienna, Chelsea and Derby. Although *singeries* were rare in England, compared to France and Germany, the so-called Monkey Room at

Johann Sibmacher. Geometric designs for needlework from his Schön Neues Modelbuch, *1597.*

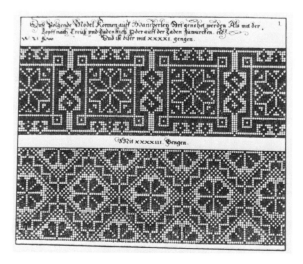

singerie. 1) 'Le Maître de cors de chasse' from C.*Huet's Singeries, ou différentes actions de la vie humaine représentées par des singes, c.1755. 2) German porcelain plate, probably painted by C.G. Albert, Fürstenberg, c.1770.
skull. 3) Memento Mori emblem from Geoffrey Whitney's A Choice of Emblemes, 1586. 4) Carved window bracket, late 17th century Baroque church, Rome.

Kirtlington Park, near Oxford, was modelled by the French artist J.F. Clermont in 1745. He dressed the creatures for *hunting and grouped them in scenes signifying the Four *Seasons, thus combining three current fashionable subjects at once. *Singeries* reappeared in the 19th century as part of the revival of 18th century taste.

siren. According to legend, the sirens were sea nymphs until the Greek goddess of love, Aphrodite, turned them into maidens with the feet and feathers of birds, whose beautiful singing could lure sailors to their deaths. In decoration, they often have fish tails like *mermaids. A standard motif in *marine ornament used, for example, on fountains.

skeleton. *See* death and mourning.

skull. A symbol of mortality, worldly vanity and the transitory nature of life, the skull appears in moralistic and funerary art (*see* death and mourning). It seems to have been little used in Europe before the 15th century when it became a *memento mori*. It was popular from the 16th century in German and Flemish engravings and it appears as an ornament wherever reference is made to death, mortality, life's brief span, etc. In French engraved Books of Hours skulls appear as border ornament. The skull was a popular form for watches made in Switzerland, France and Germany in the 17th century, the lower jaw opening to reveal the dial. Skull beads were incorporated into mourning jewellery of the period. In early 16th century England, the skull often decorated tombstones but, in common with most figurative work, such imagery was suppressed during the Puritan regime. By the 18th century, it was again frequently used on tombs and monumental wall tablets, becoming as common as the *hourglass or *scythe with which it sometimes appeared. As a *heraldic ornament on tombs and funerary monuments, it could, when it replaced the *shield, signify the end of a family line. Sometimes the skull is combined with cross-bones, or with skeletal bats' wings in a macabre imitation of the winged *cherub's head.

slip. A sprig of foliage with flowers and/or fruits, the stem diagonally cut to form a 'heel'. An embroidery motif popular in the 16th and 17th centuries, it was also used on plasterwork.

slipped in the stalks, slip-top or **slipped-end** all describe a diagonally cut end used on six-sided spoon handles – a popular device occurring principally in the early Stuart period.

Sloan, Samuel (1815-84). Philadelphia-based architect and author of three *pattern books that reflected the *Historicist vein in mid 19th century American architecture. *The Model Architect* (Philadelphia, 1852; three editions in the 1860s and a final one in 1873) was followed by *City and Suburban Architecture* (Philadelphia, 1859 and 1867), which included a *Romanesque Revival ornamental store front, an Italianate bank, a 'mercantile building' in *Neo-Norman style and *Renaissance Revival department stores. Sloan also illustrated a range of Minton tiles, used in Britain for 'upwards of 500 churches . . . 700 mansions and conservatories', as well as ornamental chimney tops and garden *vases. *Homestead Architecture* (1861, 1867, 1870) concentrated on Italianate villas, in tune with the *Picturesque mood of contemporary domestic building.

Smith, George (fl 1804-28). English furniture designer and practising cabinetmaker, whose first *pattern book, *A Collection of Designs for Household Furniture and Interior Decoration* (London, 1808), presented, in its 158 aquatinted hand-coloured plates, the full development of *Regency style. The range of designs was eclectic but they were practical and therefore easily assimilated

George Smith. Pier glass and side table from A Collection of Designs for Household Furniture, 1808.

Virgil Solis. 1) Imaginary ruins. 2) Ewer in the form of a snail. Both mid 16th century.

by other cabinetmakers in Britain and America. Smith presented a wide range of pieces, both grand and simple, in the Greek, Roman, Egyptian, Gothic and Chinese styles. He also included schemes for whole rooms. He was greatly influenced by T.*Hope, using many of his motifs, though with none of Hope's archaeological seriousness. He also adopted elements from the work of T.*Sheraton and C.*Percier and P. Fontaine. His second book, *A Collection of Ornamental Designs after the Manner of the Antique* (London, 1812), concentrates on the Greek style, and is again heavily dependent on Hope's work. The flexibility with which he presents designs for borders is typical: they are 'capable of being executed in carpetting, paper or silk; they might also be cast and finished in ormulu or bronze.' Smith's constant emphasis on Greek motifs above all others was an important contribution to the survival and popularity of the *Greek Revival style in the early 19th century. Finally, he published *The Cabinet-Maker and Upholsterer's Guide* (London, 1826-28). As well as containing new furniture and interior designs, this included essays on perspective, geometry and ornamental drawing. The designs, mostly Greek, but also Egyptian, Etruscan, Roman and French, mark the end of the Regency style and begin to show the heaviness of the Victorian. Some of his work was published by R.*Ackermann in the *Repository*.

snake. *See* serpent.

snowflake. *See* crystal.

Solis, Virgil (1514-62). An extraordinarily prolific designer of ornament who worked in Nuremberg and Augsburg as a painter and engraver. The influence of his woodcuts, etchings and engravings was wide ranging. Although primarily used by German silversmiths, they spread across Europe, even appearing engraved on English silver. Many of his designs were specifically for metalwork, some of them relatively simple to meet the new demands from the middle class for gold and silver objects. He published 24

etchings of cups that could be taken apart for use as candlesticks, salts, wine-tasters, etc. His patterns (incorporating *peacocks, *monkeys and *lions) are in the *Flemish Mannerist style with *arabesques, *grotesques and *strapwork. Solis also produced fantastic designs for ewers and *vases incorporating typically *Mannerist *grotto motifs such as snails, frogs and *insects, as well as hunting scenes and allegorical subjects such as the *Ages of Man. His book illustrations for the Bible, Ovid's Metamorphoses and Aesop's *fables were also plundered by craftsmen for the ornamentation of plasterwork, reliefs on stoneware, inlay, woodcarving and enamelled glass. Some of his arabesque designs were republished in the 19th century, e.g. by Ovide Reynard in Paris (1844-45) and must have been useful source material for the *Renaissance Revival.

Solomnic pillar. *See* spiral column.

Sondergotik. German term for all the late *Gothic styles from 1300 beginning with the *Perpendicular in England.

spade. *See* death and mourning.

spandrel. Triangular section on each side of an arch, e.g. over a doorway, that may be used as a decorative ground. Spandrels often bear paired figures, such as

spandrel. 1) Cranes on bank doorway, Saffron Walden, Essex, architect Eden Nesfield, 1884. 2) Globe on early 20th century office building, Lower Broadway, New York.

*angels, *Victories, *cherubs, etc., or symmetrical designs.

Spanish Colonial. From the late 16th century the southern and western states of North America were colonised by Spain, which led to the importation of Spanish styles of architecture in the Colonial period. The most important early buildings were the mission churches which followed the elaborately ornamented *Plateresque and *Churrigueresque styles, but also, sometimes, showed the influence of the simply shaped Indian *adobe* buildings.

In the late 19th century the style was revived, particularly in California and Florida to the south west of the country, based not only on this early ecclesiastical architecture but also on the low, white stucco domestic buildings of the Spanish Mediterranean with their arched *logge*. Often, Spanish elements were mingled with *Moorish or Italian *Baroque features, giving an eclectic effect. An influential source for the style was the ten-volume reference work *Spanish Colonial Architecture in Mexico* by Sylvester Baxter (1902). He was assisted in preparing the material by the architect B.G. Goodhue (1869-1924), who designed a number of buildings in the style, culminating in his work as architect for the Panama-Pacific Exposition (San Diego, California, 1915). This reinforced the influence of the Spanish Colonial Revival, which enjoyed great popularity in the 1920s.

Spanish Colonial Revival. Spanish-Mexican Baroque on Smith Western Bell Telephone Building, San Antonio, Texas, architect I.R. Timlin, 1931.

Spanish foot. *See* knurl foot.

Spanish Order. A variation on the Corinthian *Order, mentioned by I.*Ware, in which the rose that is usually found on the *abacus is replaced by a *lion mask.

spear or **lance.** Although this weapon was functionally redundant by the 16th century, it was retained for ceremonial use, often with a small flag or *tassel below the spearhead. Used in groups bound together like *fasces, or single, spears are obvious motifs for *military decoration, *trophies and *panoplies. However, they appear most frequently in the ornamentation of iron railings, gates and balconies – a suitable motif for the symbolic protection of property.

spear. 19th century cast iron railings, Glasgow, Scotland.

sphinx. In ancient Egypt the sphinx was a royal and religious symbol appearing as a giant sculpture and never as ornament; the Egyptian sphinx had the body of a recumbent lion, usually with the head of a reigning pharaoh (androsphinx, emblematic of intellectual and physical power), but sometimes with the head of a ram (criosphinx, emblematic of silence), a hawk or falcon (hierocosphinx, emblem of the sun). The ancient Greek sphinx had a woman's head and breasts, a lion's body (sometimes wings) and was regarded as a source of enigmatic wisdom. The Romans adopted the Greek prototype, with or without wings, and treated the sphinx more decoratively, e.g. with the body sometimes trailing off into *scrolling foliage.

The Egyptian sphinx was scarcely known in Renaissance Italy, although Pope Sixtus IV who founded the Capitoline Museum at the end of the 15th century did exhibit two basalt examples there. The Roman sphinx was the source of those incorporated into *grotesque ornament in both northern and southern Europe. Its female beauty was emphasised and certain 18th century French examples were supposedly given the faces of court beauties, often with their necks lengthened for elegance. The original function of sphinxes as guardians of temples and tombs was reflected in their use during the Italian Renaissance as supporters for sarcophagi (in the same manner as crouching *lions) and in their frequent appearance from the *Baroque period as garden ornaments on terraces, steps and gate posts. Later they appeared as firedogs: the French *ébéniste* and sculptor Charles Cressent (1685-1758) designed some on which the

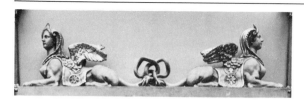

sphinx. 1) Overmantel in marble, wood and plaster by Benjamin Carter, c.1750, from Northumberland House, The Strand, London. 2) English jasper ware candlestick, Wedgwood, c.1785. 3) Garden ornament at Chiswick House, built 1725-29. 4) From G. *Richardson's A Collection of Ornaments in the Antique Style, 1816. 5) Illingworth Mausoleum, Undercliffe Cemetery, Bradford, Yorkshire, c.1854.

sphinxes lounge on ormolu scrolls and fondle monkeys and kittens. In the *Neo-classical period, they supported chair arms, *vases and side tables, and also figured as architectural *brackets, e.g. in *Adam style work. A more Egyptian-looking sphinx, with characteristic headdress and often wings, was a common motif in the early 19th century, sometimes in groups of three as a *tripod base.

spindles. Wooden rods, circular in section and either of constant diameter or slimmer at each end than in the middle, they resemble spindles and are turned on a lathe. Used principally for the decoration of chairbacks (spindle backs were common on 18th century country-made chairs) they also appeared in galleries on the tops of cabinets and desks. In the 19th century, spindles were sometimes alternated with pierced *baluster-shaped splats in chair-backs. The device was revived by the *Arts and Crafts movement, as on William Morris's Sussex Chair.

spiral. *See* interlacing; shells; trumpet pattern.

spiral column or **twisted column.** Also known as the Solomnic column or Solomnic pillar after the famous Colonna Santa, preserved in St Peter's, Rome, said to be one of the brass pillars of Solomon's Temple, but in fact a 4th century *Byzantine column.

Spiral columns are a common feature of *Judaic

ornament, particularly framing the Ark of the Covenant, and appear widely on decorative objects in Jewish ceremonial, e.g. on Hannukah lamps and in Hebraic texts, sometimes wreathed with *grapevine.

Spiral columns were used, sometimes paired, in *Romanesque architecture (borrowed from Byzantine usage), e.g. in cloisters. They appeared in *Flamboyant Gothic style work as *colonnettes and nave columns. However, it was in the early 16th century that the twisted column became widespread. Engravings after Raphael's tapestry cartoons showing Christ at the Temple were well known and disseminated the spiral column as an acceptable feature of Christian architecture. Raphael's pupil, Giulio Romano, used twisted fluted columns in the Palazzo Ducale at Mantua (1538-39) to contrast with the heavy *rustication ornamenting it. Spiral columns, often wreathed in foliage, later became associated with *Mannerism.

G.L. Bernini (1598-1680) chose spiral columns to support his *baldacchino over the High Altar at St Peter's in Rome (1633), and they became a much exploited feature of the *Baroque, especially for altar pieces and church porches in Spain (*see* *Churrigueresque style), Italy, Austria, Germany and England.

*Cable moulding, when extended into a thin shaft or colonnette, can appear as an attenuated type of twisted column.

spiral meander. *See* meander.

spiral turning. *See* twist.

split baluster. Small wooden *baluster split vertically in two that was applied, several at a time, to furniture. This form of decoration was common on 16th and 17th century English furniture, and was subsequently used in America.

spool turning. Ornamental turned decoration on furniture rails or legs composed of linked spool shapes. It is similar to *bobbin turning, but flatter with shorter sections, creating the effect of cotton reels strung

spiral column. Italian Renaissance gilt copper reliquary casket made in Florence, 1446.

together. Common on 17th century English furniture and 19th century American furniture.

S-scroll. *See* C-scroll.

stag. An attribute of Diana (and her Greek counterpart Artemis), the goddess of hunting, who transformed Actaeon into a stag. Used in decorative schemes alluding to the legend, sometimes with Diana carrying a bow and quiver or spear. Diane de Poitiers, mistress of Henri II of France (1519-59), identified herself with the goddess Diana and the Château d'Anet, built for her by P.*de l'Orme (1548), was ornamented with stag motifs. A stag with a crown around its neck was, in any case, one of the emblems of the French royal family from the reign of Charles VII (1403-61), and had been a frequently used emblem in *heraldic decoration throughout Europe. In Britain, until the 18th century, stags were more commonly hunted than the fox, and they remained a popular quarry in northern Europe throughout the 19th century. They were therefore a frequent motif in *hunting themes and the decoration of hunting lodges, stables, etc.

In Britain a general enthusiasm for things *Scottish and the great success of animal painters such as Edwin Landseer (*Stag at Bay*, 1846, *Monarch of the Glen*, 1851) led to a rush of stag's head decoration: e.g. cast-iron garden ornaments, *finials to park gateposts, cast-iron *vases from Coalbrookdale, damask table cloths and Berlin embroidery as well as furniture and fitting, were manufactured from *antlers. The *Gothic practice of using antlers to form candelabra was revived in 19th century Germany and subsequently whole suites of furniture were produced from antlers. *See also* Herculean; kylin.

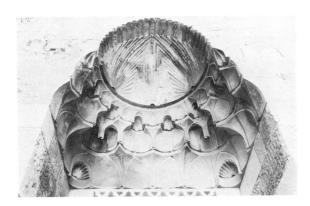

stalactite work. Mihrab in the Dome of the Rock, Jerusalem.

stalactite work or **honeycomb vaulting.** Decorative treatment (often without any structural justification) of domed ceilings, pendentives or squinches, so-called because of the *pendants that terminate each of the corbelled squinches making up the pattern. It is ubiquitous in *Islamic architecture, where it is called *muqarnas*, in *niches and alcoves such as the *iwan* or *mihrab* or as a ceiling in a free-standing pavilion, e.g. for a fountain or washing-place. This decoration became the hallmark of 19th century revivals of the variously

titled *Arabian, *Moorish and *Turkish styles: a particularly fine, late example is the Moorish smoking room at Rhinefield House, Hampshire, c.1890, by Romaine Walker and Tanner.

Stalker, John and **Parker,** George. Their *A Treatise of Japanning and Varnishing* (Oxford, 1688) provided 24 engraved plates of designs and proved to be a welcome source for European copiers of the rare and expensive pieces of Chinese lacquered furniture that became fashionable during the last quarter of the 17th century. Japanning was an occupation undertaken by amateurs (mostly women) as well as craftsmen, and patterns for it were extremely popular. Stalker and Parker provided the full range of *chinoiserie* motifs: temples, *cranes, *insects and *bamboo, Chinamen with umbrellas and children with kites, *blossom and rocks. The designs reproduced the unrealistic scale of Chinese work, e.g. the insect appeared larger than a man's head, although in the introduction, Stalker and Parker claimed to have improved this aspect: 'Perhaps we have helpt them a little in their proportions, where they were lame or defective, and made them more pleasant, yet altogether as Antick. Had we industriously contriv'd prospective or shadow'd them otherwise

John Stalker and George Parker. Chinoiserie *designs for cabinet drawer fronts from their* A Treatise of Japanning and Varnishing, *1688.*

than they are, we should have wandered from our Design, which is only to imitate the true genuine Indian work'. The patterns were for the decoration of 'tables, stands, frames, cabinets, boxes etc.' The authors described the designs as 'delightful and ornamental beyond expression . . . Ancient and Modern Rome must now give place; the glory of one country, Japan alone, has exceeded in beauty and magnificence all the pride of the Vatican at this time, and the Pantheon heretofore . . . Japan can please you with a more noble prospect.' [Their use of the words 'Indian' and 'Japan' demonstrate the great confusion over Eastern origins at the time.] Apart from being a useful source of patterns for lacquerwork, they were also used by silversmiths for engraving, particularly on small pieces such as toilet sets.

star. A motif that is the logical result of linear or geometric styles and techniques, occurring, for example, in *vaulting, tiling and cut glass. It appears frequently in *Islamic styles. The six-pointed star, commonly known as the shield or star of David, is an Islamic motif, first taken into *Judaic symbolism in the 12th century and becoming the emblem of Judaism (replacing the *menorah) in the 16th century.

The star became a popular *Regency motif, particularly on furniture, where its use is thought to have originated in the ornamented metal bolt-heads used on *classical furniture to lock together wooden joints. Both T.*Hope and G.*Smith included applied metal stars in their designs and they became a generally popular motif of the period.

In America, a star signified each state that joined the Federal Union, and although they were primarily used on the national flag, stars spread to more general decorative contexts in the early years of Independence.

In heraldic use the star in some form constitutes part of the insignia of every order of knighthood and recipients of honours such as the Order of the Garter would often decorate their rooms or furnishings with the Garter Star to celebrate, e.g. the Earl Temple had it depicted in plasterwork on the ceiling at Stowe, Buckinghamshire, in 1760. The Irish Knights of St Patrick (now obsolete) also used the Garter Star insignia.

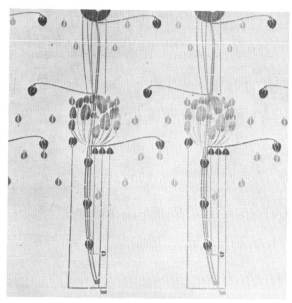

*stencilled decoration. 1) From W. and G.*Audsley's Polychromatic Decoration as Applied to Buildings in Mediaeval Styles, 1882. 2) Wall decoration, Cloister Room, Ingram Street Tea Rooms, Glasgow, Scotland, designed by Charles Rennie Mackintosh, 1900.*

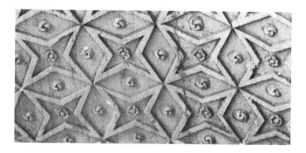

star vault. Decorative rendering of star vault on soffit of arch, Kirby Hall, Northamptonshire, additions from 1630s.

star vault. Vault composed of an elaborate arrangement of ribs and intermediate ribs forming an intricate star shape. Characteristic of *Flamboyant Gothic structures, it was later used purely decoratively.

stencilled decoration. A type of ornament that was widely used (especially in America) in the 18th and 19th centuries. In the late 19th century stencilling became particularly popular, as it lent itself well to the effects required by *japonaiserie and for the geometric shapes and *powdered heraldic ornament of the *Gothic Revival. The *Glasgow School architect Charles Rennie Mackintosh (1868-1928) used stencilled upholstery fabric.

Such fashionable use of stencilling led to imitations of the effects it created of solid blocks of colour and crisp lines. The New York design magazine, *The Craftsman*, published by Gustav Stickley (1857-1946), illustrated from 1903 fabrics by the London firm of Liberty, ceramics by Maurice Dufrène (1876-1955) and wallpaper by C.F.A. Voysey (1857-1941), all of which affected a stencilled appearance. *Pattern books for stencilling were produced, one of the earliest being M.P.*Verneuil's L'Ornementation par le pochoir (1898).

G.A. and B. Audsley (*see* Audsley family) published *Artistic and Decorative Stencilling. A Practical Manual on the Art of Stencilling on Paper, Wood and Textile Fabrics for Home Adornment and Articles of Dress* in 1911 when the fashion was already beginning to fade.

Stick style. In American architecture, a form of ornamentation popular in the second half of the 19th century. It involves the structure of the house being expressed on the exterior by the application of wooden struts (or 'sticks') over the clapboard cladding and creating a half-timbered effect. This form of decoration is usually accompanied by gabled roofs and similar angular woodwork on porches and can be seen as a development of *Carpenter Gothic.

stiff leaf. Stylised, three-lobed leaf used in *Gothic ornament, often forming the foliage of the *crocket. It frequently appears on the *capitals and *bosses of *Early English buildings.

Stiff leaf also refers to a long, strap-like, feather-shaped leaf that is used primarily in *Neo-classical ornament (*see* waterleaf).

*stiff leaf. 1) *Capital on bookcase, Library, Polesden Lacey, Surrey, remodelled 1906-08. 2) Office building, King Street, City of London, architect Humphrey Hopper, 1936.*

stile Liberty. Italian term for *Art Nouveau.

strap and jewel. Term for the ornamentation of split *balusters and *bosses sometimes applied to 17th century furniture. *See also* jewelled strapwork.

strapwork. Ornament consisting of twisted and intertwined bands (based on leather strips or ribbons). An early version of strapwork is found in *Mudejar ceiling decoration (e.g. at Aljaferia, Saragossa, dating from 1492) but its real popularity arose in the Northern *Renaissance and the School of *Fontainebleau in the 16th century. It was adopted by engravers (becoming virtually *de rigueur* for the *cartouche) and spread into every branch of the decorative arts, often combined with *arabesques. There are examples in the ceiling decoration for Wolsey's Room at Hampton Court Palace, Surrey (1521), and in France in Rosso Fiorentino's high-relief plasterwork at Fontainebleau (1531). It also formed the framework for Northern Renaissance *grotesques of the type pioneered especially by C.*Floris and C.*Bos, in which strapwork surrounds figures and animals. There was hardly a

*strapwork. 1) Stonework, Audley End, Essex, 1603-16. 2) Designs from G.*Krammer's Schweiff Büchlein, 1611 edition. 3) Scottish silver hot water jug, Glasgow, 1860.*

book of ornament engraved in northern Europe in the second half of the 16th century or the early 17th century that did not include strapwork in some form. It was used studded with *rosettes, *pyramids, discs, pellets, *nailheads and 'jewel' *lozenges (*see* jewelled strapwork). It could be incised on metalwork, carved on wooden panels, moulded from plaster and stucco, or pierced, as for a stonework parapet or wooden stair-rail. In the early 17th century the form became increasingly elaborate, far exceeding its original function as a border detail, with the intervening patterned space often becoming entirely subservient to scrolling, tendril-like strapwork, represented either three-dimensionally or flat. Even the early 18th century *pattern-book designers used versions of strapwork – B.*Langley in *A Sure Guide to Builders* (1729) used it on columns 'after the old Grecian and Roman manner'. Some 17th and 18th century renderings of strapwork, often referred to as *bandwork, were not at all angular and appeared combined with elements such as scrollwork and foliage.

In England, strapwork once again regained importance in the *Elizabethan and *Jacobean Revivals from the 1830s, when it was used on panelling and as *cresting on screens and parapets. *See also* bandwork; *Laub und Bandelwerk.*

streamlining. The study of aerodynamic design arose in the wake of the invention of the petrol-powered internal combustion engine and the electric motor. Locomotives designed in 1914 by Ernst Neumann of the Deutscher Werkbund had flared edges to funnels, domes and cabs, however most of the pioneering work was done in the late 1920s by the American stage designer and architect Norman Bel Geddes (1893-1958). Not only did he streamline moving, speeding objects such as ocean liners, motor cars, coaches, aeroplanes and locomotives, but he transferred the forms and lines to radio cabinets, cameras, telephones, even scent bottles. American designers such as Henry Dreyfuss (1903-72), Raymond Loewy (b 1893) and Walter D. Teague (1883-1960) all followed Geddes's lead. From America, the curved shape, parallel lines and speeding *wing motifs spread to Britain and Europe and were used as an indication of modernity on objects such as electric fittings and buildings such as cinemas. The use of brilliant materials (e.g. chrome) emphasised the lines of the ornament. The Coca Cola Bottling Company corporate offices in Los Angeles, designed by Robert W. Derrah 1935-37, were given a streamlined appearance with curved corners and horizontal line detail. Streamlined ornament was particularly used for factories, possibly to create an image of speed and efficiency.

striae or **striges** (Latin, *stria*, groove). The channels in *fluting on a column that appear between the ribs or *fillets.

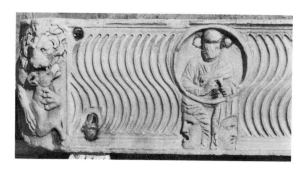

strigillation on ancient Roman sarcophagus, Borghese Gallery, Rome.

strigillation. Curving, fluted pattern named after the strigil, a grooved instrument used by the Romans for removing oil from the body after ceremonial anointment. It was commonly used on Roman sarcophagi, and was revived in the 18th and 19th century *Neoclassical ornamental vocabulary. In ancient *classical use, it was also sometimes used to allude to water, in particular the rivers of the afterlife.

string course. Horizontal band of *moulding used on the exterior of a building, indicating interior floor levels. Often decorated with carved mouldings or projections, or in brickwork, with a change of pattern or colour.

stringing and banding. Decorative technique in cabinet-making, involving the insertion of thin lines of contrasting wood, usually emphasising the lines of the piece, e.g. around the edges of tables or drawers, often appearing as a *trompe-l'oeil* *moulding. It was especially popular in the late 18th century when satinwood veneer, which provided an easy ground for the

device, became fashionable. It appeared on American furniture made in New England where the stringing was frequently composed of a small geometric pattern. During the *Regency period brass strips were often used instead of wood. *See also* banding.

Strohblumenmuster. *See immortelle.*

Stuart, James (1713-88) and **Revett,** Nicholas (1720-1804). Two of the most important illustrators of the buildings and ornament of classical Greece. Stuart, an architect, spent four years (1751-55) with Revett in Athens preparing drawings, plans and elevations of principal monuments, which were published as *The Antiquities of Athens* in four volumes; the first appeared in 1762, the second in 1790, the third in 1795, and the fourth not until 1816. It was the first volume, concerned more with the decorative aspects of the Greek style than the structural, that became the most popular. The importance of the publication lay in the fact that it took an archaeological approach to ancient sites and buildings, in contrast to earlier accounts of Greece such as that by Jacques Spon (1647-85), whose *Voyage d'Italie, de Dalmaties et du Levant* (3 vols, 1678-80) included a handful of sketchy and imprecise renderings of the major monuments.

Stuart's own designs for interiors at Kedleston Hall, Derbyshire (1757), and at Spencer House, London (1759), were possibly the first *Neo-classical interiors in Europe with *Pompeian motifs, for he had visited Pompeii in 1748, the year excavation began. The Doric Temple at Hagley Hall, Worcestershire (1758), was a pure *Greek Revival building and he built replicas of the Tower of the Winds and the Lysicrates Monument at Shugborough in Staffordshire (1764-70). It was his own application of motifs, often exact replicas from his published works, which added weight to his influence. He was a close friend of the ceramics manufacturer Josiah Wedgwood and gave him advice on the correct form and ornamentation for many of the firm's productions.

J.D.*Le Roy published his *Les Ruines des plus beaux monuments de la Grèce* in 1758; it was produced at great speed, and though better known was less accurate than the *Antiquities*. In the words of Stuart, 'Le Roy, though an ingenious author, is well known to have visited Greece in the most rapid and cursory manners.' Stuart and Le Roy engaged in extensive criticism of each other's works.

The partnership between Stuart and Revett did not last – Revett felt Stuart had taken more than his fair share of the glory and sold him his interest. Revett set out again with Richard Chandler (1738-1810) and others to collect material from Greece and Asia Minor for the Society of Dilettanti's publication *Ionian Antiquities* (5 vols from 1769). *The Antiquities of Athens* came into its own in the early 19th century with the fashion for the pure *Greek Revival; there were further English editions in 1825-30 and in 1849, and a German translation was produced in Darmstadt, 1829-33.

stump tracery. Late *Flamboyant Gothic feature in which ribs in a vaulting system are arbitrarily cut off, resembling the stumps on a lopped *tree.

Style Etrusque. As in the English *Etruscan style, Etrusque is a misnomer, stemming from the belief that certain painted vases unearthed at classical sites such as *Pompeii and *Herculaneum were Etruscan; they were in fact Greek. The term was often applied fairly indiscriminately to signify a light, *Neo-classical style using motifs such as *festoons, *husks, *anthemions, *monopodia, winged *lions, *eagles, flaming *torches and *chimeras.

style 1925. French term for *Art Deco.

style rayonnant or **décor rayonnant.** A type of ceramic painting first devised at Rouen in the late 17th century and popular until c.1730-40, by which time it had been used on faïence by, among other factories, Moustiers, Nevers, Marseilles, and on porcelain at Copenhagen, Rörstrand, Ansbach, St Cloud, etc. The patterns, which on plates and dishes radiate inwards from richly decorated borders, are a combination of *lambrequins, *ferronnerie, *scrolls and *festoons, the whole influenced by engraved embroidery designs and, possibly, by decoration on imported Chinese blue-and-white porcelain. At the start of the 18th century, orders from the French government to melt down silver and gold plate gave faïence manufacture a boost and elaborate ornamentation such as *style rayonnant* became popular.

Sullivan, Louis Henry (1856-1924). Prominent American architect who, like the commentator on architectural design Adolf Loos (1870-1933), had an ambivalent attitude to ornament. In 'Ornament in Architecture' (an essay published in *Engineering Magazine* in 1892) he wrote, 'ornament is mentally a luxury, and not a necessary . . . it would be greatly for our aesthetic good if we should refrain entirely from the use of ornament for a number of years', and he described buildings as 'comely in the nude'. Despite these words, which must be taken less as a theory than as a reaction against the *Historicism still raging across Europe and America in the last decade of the 19th century, Sullivan's own use of ornament was an important part of his architecture. He viewed the geometry of *seed-pods and the *crystal, for example, as appropriate ornamental forms. His *A System of Architectural Ornament* (1924) is full of annotated drawings indicating the struggle between organic and inorganic forms. On the Getty Tomb (1890), he used a *diaper of hexagonals, based on the snowflake diagrams of V.-M.-C. *Ruprich-Robert. On the Wainwright Building, St Louis (1890), he used the exploding seed-pods of the maple, with the influences of both *Romanesque and *Gothic low relief foliage carving in evidence. For Sullivan, the reinterpretation of natural forms outside the constraints of Historicism was essential. He was influenced by the work of many botanists, e.g. Asa Gray's *Elements of Botany* (1836), as well as the numerous 19th century publications on *naturalism and *plant forms in decoration. Sullivan wrote of the 'spirit of ornament' and stated that a 'decorated structure, harmoniously conceived . . . cannot be stripped of its system of ornaments'. He believed that ornament should be utterly integral to structure. On this basis,

'the possibilities of ornamentation . . . are marvellous.' He concluded, 'America is the only land in the whole earth wherein a dream like this may be realised: for here alone tradition is without shackles.' O.*Jones influenced both Sullivan and his sometime partner Frank Furness (1839-1912). Sullivan in his turn passed on his ideas to Frank Lloyd Wright (1867-1959) and the Prairie School of architects.

sun. Many ancient motifs represented the sun, for example the *swastika, the Egyptian *sun disc, and the *wheel. The *lion, *eagle and *phoenix have also at various times and in various cultures symbolised the sun. The classical sun gods, Apollo, Mithras and Helios were all depicted with sun beams radiating from their heads, as were deified Roman emperors; the Christian halo, which appeared in about the 5th century, originally derived from this source. From the *Renaissance, sun rays sometimes surrounded the heads of royal figures, e.g. Louis XIV (*see* Apolline decoration).

The sun surrounded by rays (also called sunburst, sun-in-splendour, sun-in-glory) was a popular *Baroque motif. In a religious context it often appeared

sun. 1) Clock, campanile, *Sta Maria Formosa, Venice, Italy, 16th century. 2) 18th century ironwork, Versailles, France. 3) St Carolus Borromeüskerk, Antwerp, Belgium, by Pieter Huyssens, 1615-25. 4) Trellised pavilion, Sans Souci, Potsdam, East Germany, c.1750. 5) Carpenter Gothic house, Galveston, Texas.*

with a *dove, symbolising the Holy Spirit. But it also had many secular applications, e.g. as a gilded surround for a mirror, clock or barometer and as a central point for ceiling decoration (sometimes in the 19th century decorating a light fitting). The sunburst was also popular on early 19th century American mould-blown glass flasks. It was later a favourite motif in *Art Deco.

Formalised sunrise (or sunset) motifs with radiating stripes representing the rays were widely popular in the 1920s, frequently appearing in stained glass on windows, doors and *fanlights, on garden gates and on manufactured goods such as radio sets.

sun disc. Ancient Egyptian symbol representing the sun god Re (or Ra). The *serpent that often appears around its perimeter is the sacred Uraeus, worn on the headdress of Egyptian gods and kings (thought to be sons of Re) as a protection against evil. The motif was taken up in the 19th century *Egyptian Revival. *See also* winged disc.

sunflower. A symbol of gratitude, constancy, remembrance and the art of painting, the sunflower has been a popular motif in the decorative arts since the 17th century. In England, the Chelsea porcelain factory produced dishes and lidded pots in sunflower form c.1752-55. By 1830 R.*Brown was referring to the vulgarity of the sunflower, ' . . . although we frequently see it introduced'. By the middle of the 19th century the sunflower had spread beyond the confines of Pre-Raphaelite paintings (William Morris, Rossetti and Burne-Jones all included it) into decoration. It was a key motif for the *Aesthetic movement, and its architectural equivalent, the *Queen Anne Revival of the 1870s-90s. It appeared in rubbed brick and moulded terracotta, either as a repeating pattern or, more naturalistically, growing from a pot, or even as cut blooms in a vase. Sunflowers were used by Eden Nesfield (1835-88) at Kinmel Lodge, Clwyd (1868), and by Norman Shaw (1831-1912) at the Royal Geographical Society, London (1874), in both cases in terracotta panels set into brickwork. At the Philadelphia Centennial Exhibition (1876), the English exhibit included a sunflower-patterned quilt, an *appliqué* curtain and cast and wrought-iron railings made of a succession of sunflower blooms (by Barnard, Bishop and Barnard of Norwich). A memorial glass made by René Lalique for the founder of Boots the Chemist (as a symbol of remembrance) had a design based on sunflowers. By the late 19th century, the proliferation of sunflowers in ornament was sufficient to provoke a writer to refer to the 'sickening repetition of the sunflower in all sorts of decorative work as though it were the sum total of all beauty'.

swag. Often denotes the same motif as *festoon – a pendant garland composed of any combination of flowers, fruit and vegetables, leaves or shells – but it may also, unlike festoon, describe a loop of *drapery, even a drape of *Herculean *lion pelts. Originally a *classical motif, it was taken up in *Neo-classical styles in both architecture and the decorative arts, especially ceramics and silver. *See also* vandycked swag.

sunflower. 1) English cast and wrought iron sunflower designed by Thomas Jeckyll and made by Barnard, Bishop & Barnard, Norwich, 1876. 2) Gilded decoration on marble exterior of Karlsplatz underground railway station, Vienna, by Otto Wagner, 1898. 3) Jugendstil house on Kaiser Friedrichs Promenade, Bad Homburg, Germany. 4) Neo-classical marble fireplace, Polesden Lacey, Surrey, remodelled 1906-08.

swag. 1) Apron ornament on 19th century Neo-classical building, Paris. 2) Beneath window in Chiswick House, London, built 1725-29. swallow-tail merlon. 3) Templeton's Carpet Factory, Glasgow, Scotland, architect William Leiper, 1889.

swallow-tail merlon. Raised portion of a *battlement consisting of two right-angled triangular sections facing each other to leave a V-shaped space. This early Italian *Renaissance motif was widely adopted, especially in Eastern Europe.

swan. Common *heraldic device in the medieval period: a number of families used it to indicate their supposed descent from the Swan Knight of medieval romance,

swan. 1) Swiss gold pendant depicting Leda and the Swan, c.1905. 2) Chair-back from R.*Ackermann's The Repository of Arts, *1824. 3) Dutch porcelain vase made at Amstel, c.1800. 4) Leda and the Swan on 1220 Avenue of the Americas, Rockefeller Center, New York, 1930s.*

among them the de Bohun, Beauchamp, Courtenay and Beaufort families. During the 15th century it was also the badge of the Prince of Wales. Like many heraldic devices, the swan was frequently used to ornament tiles, plasterwork, tapestries, jewellery, etc.

In classical legend, the myth that the swan sings just before its own death made it an occasional attribute of Apollo in his capacity as god of music (*see* Apolline decoration), and of the *Muses Erato and Clio. Swans pull the chariot of *Venus and so appear in schemes of decoration relating to her and/or *love. A popular motif in the *Empire style, C.*Percier and P. Fontaine used it in work produced for the Empress Josephine, whose device was a black swan, probably chosen because of its allusion to Venus. In J.C.*Krafft's designs for Mme Récamier's bed, gilded bronze swans form the bed-posts. Also popular in the *Biedermeier and *Regency styles, the swan head and neck were used as a curving *finial for chair arms and bed ends. The classical myth of Zeus in the form of a swan falling in love with Leda found great popularity in *Art Nouveau work, with the swan appearing sinuously entwined with an archetypal, dreamy-looking, long-haired girl.

Swan, Abraham (active 1738-68). English carpenter and joiner who published a number of architectural works aimed at the working builder and craftsman, rather than the architect/patron, which were highly popular in America. *The British Architect or the Builder's Treasury of Stair-cases* was published in 1745 and was in a fourth edition by 1758. It appeared in Philadelphia in 1775, the first architectural book to be printed in America, although the British edition had been known there since 1762; a second edition was published in Boston in 1794. Swan felt that staircases were ideal features for ornamentation and that they had been neglected by A.*Palladio, V.*Scamozzi and G.B. da

*Vignola. He concentrated on *brackets and *consoles and his designs generally have a *Rococo flavour, though the exteriors of his buildings are mainly *Palladian in feel. *A Collection of Designs in Architecture* (2 vols, 1757) was followed by the popular *One Hundred and Fifty New Designs for Chimney Pieces* (1758; four editions by 1768), in which Swan advised builders to 'convert even the conduits of soote and smoacke into ornaments'. The second volume of the *Collection* shows rooms with 'their decorations, viz. Bases, Surbases, Architraves, Freezes and Cornices, properly inriched with foliage, frets and flowers in a New and Grand Taste'. The importance of the underlying design of the room or building is emphasised 'for if the original Design be bad, superadded Ornaments will make the whole to appear rather awkward than graceful, like a Clown in a laced Waistcoat . . . a Multitude of ornaments stuck on, as we sometimes see, without Meaning, breeds nothing but Confusion . . . '. However, in spite of these remarks, Swan's own designs were derivative and flimsy, his publications typical of the flood of architectural handbooks available to the mid 18th century builder or carpenter.

Abraham Swan. *Rocaille mirror design, mid 18th century.

swan-neck. Alternative term for *scrolled pediment. Also a type of curved hanging brass handle, usually on drawers, introduced c.1760.

swastika (Sanskrit, well-being). An ancient diagrammatic representation of the sun's course and the rotation of the heavens, which has appeared in many variations and in most cultures (especially those of the East). The *Anglo Saxon fylfot [four feet], which sometimes has human legs bent at the knee forming the four radiating spokes, is one version. Much of the swastika's original significance as a pagan symbol

swastika. Roman mosaic pavement, Kourion, Cyprus.

remains obscure, but it has been widely used as a symbol of prosperity and revival, e.g. on early Greek jewellery, pottery, mosaics and on Etruscan burial urns. In Christian symbolism it was adopted as a cross form and appears on early gravestones, particularly *Celtic. In Chinese porcelain, border patterns based on swastikas are common, combining well with *key patterns. The swastika as a symbol of revival perfectly fitted Hitler's ideal of German nationalism during the 1930s.

sword. The sword is a common heraldic emblem: crossed swords (*in saltire*) are used by families with military associations, but also in the ecclesiastical coats of arms of church militants; a Claymore sword has a basket-shaped hand guard; a seax was an Anglo-Saxon weapon with a broad, curved, notched blade. The sword also appears as a symbol of authority (e.g. the sword of state) and as an attribute of *Justice.

In general ornament the sword is mainly used together with other weapons in *military schemes, especially in Roman military *trophies and *panoplies. Much French *Empire style ornament had a militaristic flavour and classical X-framed stools were made with sabre-shaped legs.

tabernacle work. Late *Gothic elaboration of ornamental carving consisting of *finials elaborated with *crockets, pinnacles, *cresting, etc., which was used in canopies on screens, *niches, stalls and elsewhere in ecclesiastical interiors of the 14th and 15th centuries. It reappeared in the *Gothick, e.g. in the canopies over mirrors in the Gallery by John Chute at Strawberry Hill, Middlesex, built in 1760 for Horace Walpole – the details were copied from the 15th century tomb of Archbishop Bourchier in Westminster Abbey.

tabernacle work. 16th century Spring Chapel, Church of St Peter and St Paul, Lavenham, Suffolk.

tablet flower. Variation on the *ballflower but with four wide petals. It was used in similar instances, e.g. as a *moulding enrichment in English *Decorated Gothic architecture.

Tagliente, Giovanni Antonio. Tagliente produced one of the earliest dated *pattern books, *Essempio di Recammi* (Venice, 1527 and 1530), with woodcuts that were intended for embroidery and weaving but would also have been used for metalwork, painted decoration and marquetry. Tagliente included the first *arabesques and *interlacing designs to appear in a pattern book, as well as an *alphabet, birds, beasts, stylised flowers and ships and a few designs from a pattern book of an even earlier date, H.*Schönsperger's *Furm und Modelbüchlein* (Augsburg, 1523).

Talbert, Bruce James (1838-81). Important English architect and furniture designer whose work was influenced by the *Gothic Revival pioneered by A.W.N. *Pugin, and applied by such architects as William Burges (1827-81) and William Butterfield (1814-1900). These and other architects were involved in the design of furniture and interior decoration, but it was Talbert's *Gothic Forms Applied to Furniture, Metal Work and Decoration for Domestic Purposes* (1868) which provided extensive details of Gothic geometric patterns, polychrome designs, simple formalised leaves and flowers and *chamfering, etc., for use by commercial manufacturers, thus making the style more accessible to popular taste. He wrote, 'where a repetition of 16th or 17th century work is desired it is easier to obtain furniture corresponding, but it is more difficult to procure that which shall be in keeping with the purer early styles.' His second book, *Examples of Ancient and Modern Furniture, Metal Work, Tapestries, Decorations etc.* (1876), was intended as a supplement to the first and contained the original introduction (with additional comments on the revival of the 'so-called Queen Anne style') with plates which Talbert described as Jacobean, Flemish Renaissance, Classical and Carolian [sic]. Despite its title, the Jacobean style room includes *japonaiserie motifs. Perhaps the most important innovation in Talbert's work was the simple, geometric inlay, which was to be influential in later furniture design.

talbot. *See* dog.

talon and ball. *See* claw.

tambour (French, drum) or **bell capital.** 18th century terms sometimes used for Corinthian and Composite *capitals (*see* Orders).

tassel. The tassel has had a surprisingly wide application in ornament. An obvious accompaniment to *drapery and *lambrequins, it also appears in military *trophies, on flags and standards. A typically Dutch motif of the early 18th century combined the tassel with the *scallop shell (possibly echoing the use of the scallop as a pilgrim's emblem). Tassels were sometimes carved on late 18th century furniture, e.g. chairs produced 1760-70 in Philadelphia had a tassel replacing

*tassel. 1) Marble fireplace, Chiswick House, London, built 1725-29.
2) American wallpaper, c.1860. 3) Gate, Midland Bank, Poultry, City of London, architect Sir Edwin Lutyens, 1924 (completed 1939).*

the central splat, an adaptation of the ribbon-back chair. In the late 18th and early 19th centuries, drapery and *passementerie* [tassels, fringes and braids] became ever more elaborate. This was reflected in ornament: ormolu tassels ornamented furniture, printed tassels appeared on wallpaper. Later, *Art Deco made full use of the motif: necklaces were hung with silken tassels, furniture had tassel handles, and they even appeared carved in wood (e.g. as furniture feet) and in architectural stone carving.

Tatham, Charles Heathcote (1772-1842). English draughtsman and architect. Tatham worked in the office of Henry Holland (1745-1806), who sent him to Rome for three years (1794-97) so that he could study and make drawings of classical Greek and Roman ornament which Holland then incorporated into his designs. Tatham published one of the most accurate collections of classical detail, *Etchings of Ancient Ornamental Architecture drawn from the Originals in Rome and other parts of Italy* (1799). There were subsequent editions in 1803, 1810, 1826 and 1843, which helped to keep the classical style alive in the face of the growing popularity of the *Gothic Revival and other *Historicist styles. A German edition of the book was published in Weimar, in 1805. Tatham's approach was strictly archaeological – he considered that G.B.*Piranesi's treatment had been too imaginative. In the intro-

duction, Tatham stated, 'The works of the Ancients are *A Map to the Study of Nature*; they teach us what objects we are to select for imitation, and the method in which they may be combined with effect. All natural objects are not ornamental . . . ' Designers such as T.*Hope borrowed motifs from Tatham's etchings, and many of these later formed part of the general range of *Regency ornament. Tatham published a second series, *Etchings, representing Fragments of Antique Grecian and Roman architectural ornaments; chiefly collected in Italy, before the late revolution in that country, and drawn from the originals* (London, 1806; reissued with first series in 1826). In 1806 he also published *Designs for Ornamental Plate* with detailed and finely finished ornament and a massive effect far removed from the light *Adam style. Regency silversmiths such as Paul Storr (1771-1844) and Benjamin Smith (fl 1791-1822) led the fashion in this new style and produced silver wine coolers based on an etching by Tatham of a *vase in the Villa Albani.

telamon. Figure of a man used, like *atlantes or *persians, to support the *entablature. The name derives from that of the Greek hero, Telamon, father of Ajax, and one of the Argonauts.

tendril. The curling tendril form of creeping plants is much used in both *naturalistic and stylised foliate ornament. In classical decoration, the tendril is combined with the *anthemion and/or the *palmette in *scrolling foliage. It reappeared in Italian *grotesque ornament of the 16th century, especially with the *grapevine. It was widely used in *Celtic ornament but as a kind of spiral, its linear form being well suited to formal designs. *Art Nouveau and associated styles adopted the floating tendril form from its usage in *Viking and Celtic art.

tent. A popular form for 18th century garden buildings (seats, pavilions, etc.) where an exotic or oriental impression was intended, e.g. Charles Hamilton placed a 'Turkish tent' in the ornamental garden he created in the 1750s and 1760s at Painshill, Surrey. The military theme of much *Empire decoration led to the tent form being used, often in association with *spears and lances, for beds and even entire rooms. The tent also appears in funerary ornament, either to represent a warrior's tent in battle or to suggest, by the drawing back of drapery, the passing of souls from one world to another.

Charles Heathcote Tatham. Klismos stool from the front and in profile, one of a group of 'Antique seats from originals at Rome' from his Etchings of Ancient Ornamental Architecture, *1799.*

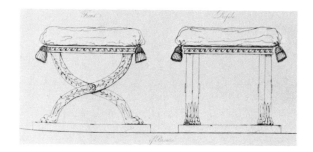

term or **terminus.** *See* herm.

Texan Order. In America, the use of the 'Lone Star of Texas' as a motif was the invention of Nicholas Clayton (1849-1916), an Irish-born architect who worked in the booming cotton town of Galveston, Texas, from the mid 1870s. The star, together with the *olive and *oak branches that figured in the state arms, was used wherever the ornamental schemes on his buildings allowed.

Texier, Charles Félix Marie (1802-71). French archaeologist who made a number of government-sponsored journeys to the Middle East between 1833 and 1837. His observations, with much detail and fine chromolithography, were published as *Description de l'Asie Mineure* (3 vols, Paris, 1839-49) and *Description de l'Arménie, la Perse et la Mésopotamie* (2 vols, Paris, 1842). Texier received the Gold Medal of the Royal Institute of British Architects in 1864 and his work was well known to devotees of *Islamic art and ornament.

therm. *See* herm.

thermal window. *See* Diocletian window.

thistle. Motif most commonly associated with *Scottish decoration, following its adoption as the national emblem by James III, King of Scotland (1460-88). It appears in *Jacobean plasterwork dating from after the Act of Union (1603), and was frequently used on objects decorated in support of the *Jacobite cause. A thistle has sometimes been used as an alternative to the *acanthus because of the similarity of its foliage and the fact that it was a more familiar plant in northern Europe. It was widely applied as a *finial on 18th and 19th century cast-iron railings as an alternative to the *spear or arrow head. It was a popular motif among the promoters of late 19th and early 20th century theories of organic ornament. *Art Nouveau artists of the Nancy School, such as Emile Gallé (1846-1904), particularly favoured the thistle form.

Silver mugs of a vaguely thistle-head shape were produced in Scotland in the late 17th century and are known as thistle cups.

*thistle. 1) Late 19th century cast-iron *capital on balustrade, Glasgow, Scotland. 2) 19th century commercial building, High Street, Inverness, Scotland, modernised 1920s.*

thunder and lightning. In classical myth, thunder and lightning are associated with Jupiter (and his Greek counterpart, Zeus), overall ruler of the sky. Jupiter's weapon is a thunderbolt – usually shown as a spiral roll representing thunder, sometimes gripped in the

thunder and lightning. 1) In talons of Prussian eagles supporting medallion of Frederick the Great, Berlin Arsenal, built from 1695. 2) Ironwork at Charlottenburg, Berlin, 1695 onwards.

talons of an *eagle, another attribute of Jupiter. It may be accompanied by zig-zag, forked or arrow-headed forms that represent lightning-flashes. Other pictorial symbols of thunder and lightning include a trident, an axe and a hammer.

These motifs have sometimes been used in decorative schemes to imply power and enlightenment. They were liberally applied to the possessions of Frederick the Great, King of Prussia (1740-86), e.g. on the *metopes of the Arsenal in Berlin, and C.*Percier and P. Fontaine used them widely in their Napoleonic decoration.

The spiral thunderbolt may also stand for *fire in decorative schemes illustrating the *Elements, and as an ornament for fireplaces. A motif of two spiral thunderbolts, crossed, with an arrow, was popular in panels of 19th century cast-iron railings. Towards the end of the 19th century, lightning symbols, together with coils of wire, were used to represent the telegraph (*see also* communications), and electricity, appearing, for example, on generating stations.

thyrsus. Staff with a *pinecone at one end, often entwined with *ribbons and/or *grapevine or *ivy leaves. It appears in *Bacchic decoration as an attribute of Bacchus, *satyrs and Maenads (or Bacchantes). From the late 18th century it was used as a general motif, e.g. as a curtain rail or on a looking-glass frame, often in rooms used for dining.

tiger. An important symbolic animal in ancient Chinese art, where it represented the western quarter of the world, and in Japanese art. The tiger appears in *kakiemon ceramic patterns, such as the Tiger and Wheat-sheaf pattern (also known as Korean tiger) used at the Meissen and Chelsea porcelain factories. Plymouth and Worcester porcelain decorators used a pattern known as Bengal Tiger, which showed a tiger with its body curved around a tree.

Like leopards and panthers, tigers sometimes appear in *Bacchic ornament, drawing the chariot of Bacchus. The concept of the tiger as a wicked and man-eating beast grew up as a result of the British presence in India; stories filtered home of Sir Hector Monro's son being eaten by a tiger, and of the passion for tigers of Tipu Sultan, the arch-enemy of the British who was finally killed in 1799. Thereafter, tigers appeared in popular British art as evil, man-eating beasts. Tiger-hunting was a popular sport for the Europeans in

India, and was frequently depicted on objects commemorating life under the Raj.

Tijou, Jean (fl 1689-1712). French Huguenot craftsman who worked in wrought iron and came, via the Netherlands, to England during the reign of William and Mary. *A New Booke of Drawings Invented and Desined by John Tijou* (1693) had a French and English text and illustrated Tijou's own work. It was the first collection of ironwork designs to be published in England and was a major source for the wrought ironwork that had virtually disappeared in England after the late *Gothic period and was now re-emerging. Tijou's designs were strongly French in style, resembling the work of J. *Berain and D.*Marot, with a *Baroque profusion of detail which was usually considerably simplified when the objects were actually produced. In England, Tijou's own ironwork attracted the notice both of other blacksmiths and of more general observers. Celia Fiennes, a late 17th century traveller and diarist, noted that at Hampton Court Palace 'on the gate is Lyon, Unicorn and flower potts, the Starre and Garter and Draggon, the Thistle and Rose carv'd'. At Burghley House, near Stamford, Lincolnshire, she saw 'all sorts of leaves, flowers, figures, birds, beasts, wheat.' Other motifs included *eagle heads, *scallop shells, *masks, *heraldic motifs and a full selection of allegorical emblems. The designs in Tijou's books were for 'several sorts of Iron worke as Gates, Frontispieces, Balconies, Staircases, Pannells etc. of which the most part hath been wrought at the Royal Building of Hampton Court and to severall persons of Qualitye Houses'. *A New Booke of Drawings* was widely pirated; Louis Fordrin produced the *Livre de serrurerie de composition angloise* (Paris, 1723) and influenced the design of much wrought ironwork in France and England until a simpler, more *classical approach was adopted in the late 18th century. *See also* Langley, Batty.

time. Often personified by Father Time, an old man who was sometimes winged and almost naked. He carries a *scythe and an *hourglass, and, more rarely, a crutch, *scales or a *serpent with its tail in its mouth. An obvious choice for the decoration of clocks, clocktowers, watches, tombstones and memorials and mirrors (the latter reflecting the signs of the passage of time on the face of the onlooker). When allegorical ornament was most popular, from the 16th to the 18th centuries, Father Time also appeared in more sophisticated schemes, e.g. on a plasterwork ceiling combined with *personifications of Industry and Idleness to demonstrate the rewards and punishments of time spent well or badly. From the late 17th century, particularly in France, complex combinations of Father Time and *Cupid decorated clock-cases, the most usual was 'Love triumphing over Time', which has Cupid flying cheerfully atop a clockface while Father Time lies dejected below it. Sometimes the theme is reversed: Father Time flies on top of the clock about to slash the Thread of Life of the terrified Cupid dropping his quiver and bow on the rock below. Further and more complicated ornamental references to man's mortality were sometimes made on clocks, e.g. the English silversmith Matthew Boulton (1728-1809)

Jean Tijou. Bracket from A New Booke of Drawings, *1693.*

produced the 'Minerva' clock-case, which shows the goddess of wisdom unveiling a plaque depicting Prudence making a libation to Time and pointing to the 'flying moments', while a boy sits nearby reading John Gay's appropriately moral lines about time, or, in other versions, Virgil's lines on the brevity of life.

A French printed cotton of c.1800 has a design titled 'Friendship has no fear of time' and shows Cupid rowing Time towards a Temple, and Time then rowing Cupid away.

References to time may also appear in schemes depicting the times of *day, the *Seasons, the *Months of the year (usually shown by the Labours), the signs of the *zodiac and the *Ages of Man. *See also* death and mourning; Venus.

topographical decoration. Early topographical ornament was primarily an indication of ownership, whether by an individual or family or by the state or empire, and appeared mainly on small, portable objects, notably ceramics. In England the Derby factory, for example, produced a set of dessert plates depicting the Cavendish family seats for the 6th Duke of Devonshire, c.1830. Many other landowners had similar sets. The territorial ambitions and acquisitions of expansionist heads of state have often been commemorated in ornamental form: Napoleon's Egyptian and Russian campaigns both led to the representation of scenes from these countries and the application

*time. 1) Gilded figure of Time, with serpent of eternity around his *scythe, supporting dial of 18th century French clock. 2) Wings of time, Broadcasting House, Langham Place, London, architects Val Myers and Watson-Hart, 1931.*

of engravings from D.V.*Denon's work, for example, to Sèvres plates.

The fashion for travelling on a grand scale in the 18th and 19th centuries led to the production of souvenir wares, particularly depicting well-known picturesque locations such as Switzerland, North Wales or Vesuvius. The sources for this type of decoration were usually engravings in travel books that were easily accessible and much copied by decorators. Thus Spode in the early 19th century adapted plates from *Oriental Scenery* by the joint authors T. and W. Daniell and used the exotic *Views in Egypt, Palestine and the Ottoman Empire* by L.*Mayer for its transfer-printed Caramanian pattern, 1810-35.

Topographic subjects also appear as *commemorative ornament, e.g. to mark an engineering feat such as the opening of a new building, railway line or bridge. The Sunderland Pottery produced vast quantities of ware showing the cast-iron bridge over the River Wear from its opening in 1796, and transfer prints of the bridge continued to be used throughout the 19th century. An American teapot made c.1836 by Tucker Hemphill commemorated progress in the new nation by illustrating the Philadelphia Waterworks next to a primitive frontier dwelling. It was also a suitable vehicle for the expression of national pride – the natural phenomenon of the Niagara Falls appeared in Parian ware.

Some topographical ornament evolved simply as a result of curiousity about far-away and exotic places. The Frog Service, made 1773-74 by Wedgwood for Empress Catherine II of Russia, consisted of 952 hand-painted pieces in monochrome of English abbeys, castles and houses. Wedgwood instructed his decorator: 'Dare you undertake to paint the most embelish'd views, the most beautiful Landskips, with Gothic Ruins, Grecian temples and most Elegant Buildings with hands who never attempted anything beyond Hut and Windmills, upon Dutch tile at three halfpence a doz!' The *Rococo and *Gothick styles both made use of imaginary scenes of exotic places, but with *Neo-classicism and a growth of antiquarian interest, topography was to become an important and exacting art of decoration in which historical accuracy was important. 'Scenic' wallpapers, which had in the Rococo period shown imaginary scenes, *paysages*, ruins, etc., now incorporated views of existing landscapes and buildings. *See also* railway motifs; Post War.

Topsell, Edward (d 1638). Author of two natural history books, *The Historie of Four-footed Beastes* (1607) and *The Historie of Serpents* (1608), the plates of which were an important source for representations of animals, both real and imaginary.

torch. Classical Greek symbol of life, and therefore when inverted and extinguished symbolic of *death; a frequent ornament on tombs and memorials. A flaming torch (or *flambeau*) is also the attribute of Eros, the god of *love, *cupids, Hymen, the god of marriage, and *Venus, and signifies, in general, the fire of love. Like the flaming *urn and the *lamp, the torch appears as a *finial in architecture and furniture. The *Baroque architect Filippo Juvarra (1678-1736)

torch. 1) Relief of flambeaux *and cords on English jasper ware* jardinière, *Wedgwood, c.1790. 2) Crossed torches on the Guardian Royal Exchange Assurance Group Building, King William Street, City of London, architect H.L. Anderson, 1921.*

used the torch as a repeating motif along the roof line on several of his buildings. It was a particularly popular motif in the *Empire style, often for gilt mounts on furniture, although P.*La Mesangère included among his designs table legs in the form of torches. They were also often combined with *wings, another favourite motif of the period. The torch motif sometimes appears as a symbol of enlightenment and knowledge, e.g. on late 19th and early 20th century schools, libraries, etc. In the 1920s and 1930s, the ancient torch was a popular form for electric light fittings.

Jean Bernard Honoré Toro. Engraved design, 1710s.

Toro or **Turreau,** Jean Bernard Honoré (1672-1731). French sculptor and ornamental designer in the *Rococo style. His engraved ornament published between 1716 and 1719 (sometimes signed Tarot or Taureau) shows an early move towards the asymmetrical style of late *Rococo design and included *Cartouches nouvelement inventés, Livres de tables de diverses formes, Desseins arabesques à plusieurs usages* and *Trophées nouvellement inventées.* Toro's work greatly influenced the work of both French designers, such as N.*Pineau, and Englishmen such as T.*Johnson, who was acquainted with the English editions of Toro's work such as *Masks and Other Ornaments* (1745). Typically, for the period, his designs concentrated on *cartouches, *trophies, *friezes, *vases and *masks. A contemporary observer commented in the *Journal des Savants* (1716) that 'these compositions are the newest, most varied and the best taste that have yet appeared.' Some of Toro's designs continued to be published after his death.

tortoise. One of the most important animals in ancient Chinese art, the tortoise represents the northern section of the world. It is also held to have supported the world during the creation, possibly the reason for its use in 17th and 18th century Western ornament as a decorative foot or support on anything from clocks to fountain basins.

torus. Semi-circular convex *moulding used frequently at the base of columns, etc., with the same profile as the *astragal, but thicker. It may be enriched with bound *laurel leaves, plaiting or *reeding.

town canopy. French *Romanesque motif of small arcaded buildings used around columns or over sculpted memorials. In French *Gothic architecture it was adapted to form *capitals, the perspectival rendering being reduced to *arcading with schematic towers. There are examples at Chartres (the Portail Royal) and on the South Door at Rheims cathedral. Although they had disappeared as architectural embellishments

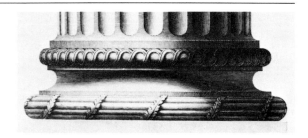

torus mouldings on base of column for the Saloon at Luton Park House, from the Adam Brothers' Works in Architecture, *1773-79.*

*town canopy. 1) From Notre Dame de Paris, begun 1163. Restored in the 19th century by E.-E.*Viollet-le-Duc.*
tracery. 2) Balcony of house, Icod de los Vinos, Tenerife, Canary Islands.
3) Flamboyant Gothic window, Church of La Trinité, Falaise (Calvados), France, rebuilt 15th and 16th centuries.

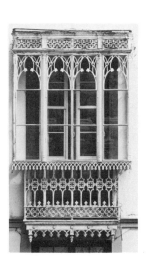

by the late 13th century, town canopies survived on tomb slabs, and in glass painting and goldsmiths' work, appearing, for example, as censers. E.-E.*Viollet-le-Duc revived the motif in his work at the Château de Pierrefonds (1863-70).

tracery. In *Gothic architecture, an ornamentation of the upper portion of windows, consisting of ribs springing from mullions, and usually composed of *cusps and *foils. Tracery became increasingly elaborate through the successive periods of the Gothic, and subsequently in the *Gothick and *Gothic Revival. It has even been given the form of branches and tree trunks, notably in the *Flamboyant Gothic style. *See also* blank tracery; mouchette; rose window; wheel.

trail. 18th and early 19th century term for a repeating ornament of leaves, flowers and *tendrils, as in *scrolling foliage.

trailed decoration, trailing or **threading.** One of the simplest methods of decorating glassware, in which molten threads of glass are applied to a vessel. It was used by ancient Roman and Egyptian glassmakers, and was a common form of glass ornamentation until more mechanical methods of decoration, such as moulding, cutting and etching, were developed. Chain trailing involves two intersecting threads; in snake trailing, the threads wave in a serpentine pattern; chequered trailing has horizontal threads inserted in a vertically ribbed mould so that the indentations break the trailing. Rigaree marks occur when the glass threads are impressed by a wheel making a series of parallel notches.

tree. The tree has enjoyed a symbolic status in architecture as a result of the theory that the basis of *Graeco-Roman classical architecture lay in the primitive wooden temple, and, further back still, in the rustic hut. In both *Renaissance and *Gothic architecture, the analogy between column and tree trunk was given a literal rendering: Donato Bramante, in the Canons' Cloister at S. Ambrogio, Milan (from 1492), used a series of columns carved as tree trunks complete with lopped branches. In Prague, at the Hradshin, the Cathedral Oratory (1480s) uses the same device in the *Flamboyant Gothic style, with columns and *stump tracery metamorphosing into tree trunk and branches. Window *tracery also lent

tree. 1) Rustic column from P.*de l'Orme's Architecture, 1567.
2) Stained glass window, Royal Arcade, Norwich, Norfolk, by J.G.
Skipper, early 19th century. 3) English Consolette radio made by Ekco,
1931. 4) Art Nouveau decoration, 14 rue d'Abbeville, Paris. 5) English
silver and enamel chalice.

itself to decorative treatment based on a stem and branch, often taking the theme of the *Tree of Jesse.

Increasing naturalism in the 16th century produced examples such as Hans Witten's 'tulip' pulpit at Freiburg (1510) in which the steps are supported by lopped tree 'trunks, complete with roots spreading below, or work in the Spanish *Plateresque or Portuguese *Manueline styles. At the early 16th century Convento de Cristo, Tomar, the roots spill on to the windowsill below the tree form tracery. The lopped column, sometimes even having roots and branches, is a favourite *Mannerist device and appears in *pattern books by H.*Vredeman de Vries and W.*Dietterlin, for example, depicted variously as a *herm or *triumphal arch.

18th century academic classicists, particularly the French rationalists and their followers, returned to the idea of the primitive hut as the starting point of architectural history. Thus the *rustic hut, in the form of a garden temple, pavilion or any of a wide range of

incidental rural buildings, was often ornamented with bark-covered wooden columns, as in Sir John Soane's dairy at Hamels Park, Hertfordshire (1781-83). The tree trunk became one of the most commonly used devices of *Picturesque and *pastoral buildings, and in the early 19th century split twigs were often used as superficial ornament on gardeners' cottages, summer houses or even mere garden sheds.

From the mid 18th century, furniture, such as that illustrated by P.*Decker or R.*Manwaring, also adopted the forms of branches; a pier glass and console table, probably designed and made by M.*Lock for Corsham Court, Wiltshire, use the tree as a support for the table and embellishment for the mirror. T.*Chippendale encircled mirrors with naturalistic branches. Victorian cast-iron garden furniture used particularly gnarled and twig-like decoration. In ceramics, *crabstock designs echoed the fashion. Oriental styles of architecture in the late 18th and early 19th centuries suggested the *palm trunk as a suitable column, as used at the *chinoiserie tea room by Johann Gottfried Büring at Sans Souci, Potsdam (1757). Stylised trees with almond-shaped leaves, often used in the form of a *frieze with the foliage interlacing tree with tree, were popular in both *Arts and Crafts and *Art Nouveau ornament, for example, the stone panels on the Bishopsgate Institute, London, by Harrison Townsend (1894).

Tree of Jesse. Motif based on the scriptural story of Jesse's dream as given in Isaiah 11:1, 'There shall come forth a rod out of the stem of Jesse and a Branch shall grow out of his roots.' It occurred first in the 11th century and appeared frequently on *Romanesque artefacts, in illuminated manuscripts, sculptured panels and stained glass windows, usually representing the supposed lineage of Christ. In the *Gothic period, highly elaborate stone *tracery sometimes took the form of the branches of a tree, with the surrounding glass depicting representations of figures (prophets, saints or fathers of the church) or symbols. Sometimes Christ and the Virgin are represented, but rarely personified. Late and complex variations of the Gothic, such as the *Flamboyant style, used the tree more literally. It may also appear as an elaboration of *scrolling foliage or of simple *spirals or *tendrils. In some variants, the Tree of Jesse takes a *candelabra form. It endured as a decorative and symbolic form in church architecture across Europe into the 17th century.

Tree of Life. The idea of a tree form symbolising the life force was common to a number of ancient oriental cultures. The *Assyrian (then Persian) hom had a relatively rigid form, whilst the Indian variant was more serpentine. The idea of a central stem or trunk with foliage of some formalised kind is the common element, but by the time the 17th century English pattern known as the 'Tree of Life' had emerged, its origins were entirely obscured.

In this form, the sinuous stems and *tendrils, together with fanciful flowers and exotic fruit such as the *pomegranate, were woven around motifs such as birds of paradise or butterflies and used particularly in crewel embroidery of the period. The motif is highly characteristic of *Jacobean decoration, and 19th century *Jacobean Revival chintzes almost inevitably used it. In the early 19th century, the Coalport porcelain factory produced a range known as Indian Tree which was based on the Tree of Life form.

trefoil. Circle with three *cusps forming a three-lobed motif – an important element in *Gothic decoration. Like other tripartite devices, the trefoil has sometimes been used to symbolise the *Christian Trinity. The trefoil (like the *quatrefoil and *cinquefoil) was widely used in simple, geometric *Gothic Revival designs of the 1860s, appearing in metalwork, furniture inlay, stencilled wall decoration, etc.

In *heraldic decoration, the trefoil has a short stalk.

trefoil. Balcony of gatehouse to ruins of Abbey of Jumièges (Seine-Maritime), late 19th century.

treillage (French, trellis work). An elaboration of trellis work that is constructed with false perspective, so as to give an illusion of a building, *niche or archway. B.*Langley in his *New Principles of Gardening* (London, 1728) illustrated 'Temples of Trelliss work after the Grand Manner at Versailles.' Other examples include *treillage* niches creating garden screens at Sans Souci, Potsdam and a Chinese aviary and Tuscan doorways at Dropmore in Buckinghamshire.

trellis. Criss-cross support for plants. It appears frequently in depictions of gardens in medieval illuminated manuscripts. From this source it reappeared in the 19th century *Medieval style, a strand of the *Arts and Crafts movement, used as a formal ground pattern, e.g. on William Morris's Jasmine Trellis wallpaper, 1868-70. More literally, a design of trellis with hops appeared on Worcester porcelain. *Regency ironwork balconies and verandahs, often used to support growing plants, were produced in trellis form c.1770-80. As a light-hearted motif for painted decoration or wallpaper, the trellis has proved enduringly popular: from the painted ceiling of the breakfast room (1812) at Sir John Soane's own house in Lincoln's Inn Fields to designs on modern mass-produced wallpaper. *See also* lattice.

trident. *See* Britannia; marine decoration; Neptune; thunder and lightning.

trifid, trefid, trefoil, pied-de-biche or **split-end.** Decorative terminal used on spoons and forks from c.1660 to the early 18th century. The lobed end is notched and hammered out to make a tripartite splay, sometimes with tiny triangular projections between the *foils. The dognose, a rounded variation with less

pronounced notches, appeared in the *Queen Anne period.

Also, trifid and trefid denote a furniture foot characteristic of early 18th century American pieces made in Philadelphia that was sometimes known as a drake's foot.

triglyph (Greek, three channels). Grooved blocks that alternate with the *metope on the *frieze of the Doric *Order. One theory of the origin of the Doric Order suggests that the triglyph commemorates the ends of the timber cross members in the wooden prototype of the classical temple.

*triglyph alternating with *cherubs' heads on *metope, St Mary-le-Bow, Cheapside, City of London, by Sir Christopher Wren, 1670-80.*

tripod. The classical tripod (three legs, usually terminating in animals' feet, supporting a bowl) was used for domestic items, in religious ceremonies and rituals, and as a prize for athletic and literary achievements. Adaptable to many uses both as a form (candelabra, small table, washbasin, pedestal, plant stand, flower vase or tea urn) and as a motif the tripod became a favourite motif for architects and designers in the early years of 18th century *Neo-classicism. An example is a perfume burner made c.1760 by the English silversmith Matthew Boulton for Kedleston Hall, Derbyshire. J.*Stuart and Robert Adam were among the first to use the form in England. In France tripods were called *athéniennes* because of their inclusion in a painting by the Neo-classical artist Joseph Le Vien

treillage. 1) Cabinet de treillage de M. Prince de Schwarzenberg from G.L. Le Rouge's Jardins Anglo-Chinois, 1774-89.
trellis. 2) English wallpaper designed by William Morris, 1864.

tripod. 1) Ancient bronze tripod owned by the King of Sicily by G.B.*Piranesi. 2) Decorative panel from G.-P.*Cauvet's Recueil d'ornements à l'usage des jeunes artistes, *1777.*

called *La Vertueuse Athénienne*. The French favoured a design with a *serpent coiling around the legs to reach the bowl, and this usage had spread to England by the 1770s. Tripods were also used two-dimensionally, e.g. in wall painting and as chair-backs. Early engraved patterns for tripods appear in Stuart and Revett's *Antiquities of Athens*, in Volume II of the Comte *de Caylus's publication and in G.B.*Piranesi's work. They remained a popular form in the *Empire style, but then faded from fashion.

triquetrac or **triquetra.** Triangular motif of interlaced *crescents, producing a three-lobed form much used in *Celtic art, sometimes representing the Trinity in *Christian iconography.

triskele. Y-shaped sun form signifying the rotation of the sun in ancient Greece and adopted in *Celtic ornament and other pagan cultures. Similar in its symbolic significance to the *swastika, it is sometimes formed from three animal legs or human legs, as in the emblem of the Isle of Man.

Triton and **tritons.** In classical myth, Triton was the son of Poseidon and Amphitrite. Half-man, half-fish, he rides over the sea on *sea horses or sea monsters and blows on a conch shell to soothe the waves; he is sometimes shown holding an oar. He generally appears in decoration on a *marine theme.

Tritons are also minor sea deities, a variation on mermen.

triumph. In classical Rome, victorious military leaders were drawn in procession through the city on decorated chariots. This idea was revived and expanded from the early Renaissance: princes and potentates staged 'classical' triumphs for themselves, e.g. in 1443 Alfonso of Aragon entered Naples in a Roman chariot followed by decorated triumphal cars. Triumphs were extended to allegory – Dante (1265-1321) described

Beatrice in such a procession in *La Divina Commedia* – but the spread and popularity of the subject was prompted by illustrated printed editions of the poem *Trionfi* by Francesco Petrarch (1304-74), which appeared from 1488, and describes the subsequent triumphs of Love, Chastity, *Death, *Fame, *Time and Eternity, whose chariots are usually drawn by white horses, *unicorns, oxen, *elephants, *stags and *angels, respectively. These themes were a popular decoration for panels on *cassone*, tapestries and ivories. There were also specific triumphs for the gods of classical mythology, such as Bacchus (*see* Bacchic decoration), Diana, *Ceres, Jupiter, etc., and themes such as the *Virtues and Vices, *Justice, the Christian Church, riches, poverty, etc. The triumphal procession was revived as an ornamental subject in the *Neo-classic period, the *frieze shape fitting well into the decoration of a mirror, mantelpiece or overmantel.

triumphal arch. 1) From the Château d'Anet, late 1540s, now in the Ecole des Beaux Arts, Paris. 2) From Book III of S.*Serlio's Architettura, *1540.*

triumphal arch. In ancient classical architecture, a freestanding form through which military victors and heroes passed. It was widely adopted by *classicist designers as a motif for gateways to houses and gardens, though now incorporated into the façade itself, as well as being used for altars. From its wide representation in engraved ornament, it became one of the commonly used architectural elements in ecclesiastical plate, funerary monuments, jewellery and on the title pages of books. It is often used in *intarsia* work

triton. From Mosteiro dos Jerónimos, Belém, Portugal, early 16th century.

for furniture and wallpapers and also appears as an element in large-scale furniture, such as court cupboards. As a door form it implies the principal point of entry; in interiors it is used to emphasise the importance of the room (as in the hall at Blenheim Palace, Oxfordshire). Originally consisting of a single arch (e.g. the Arch of Titus, Rome), the triumphal arch is given further complexity with double and then triple openings, a form that is echoed in the *Palladian motif. P.*de l'Orme's doorway from the Château d'Anet (1547) is one of the finest examples of the type. Triumphal arches came to England via 16th century French *pattern books. Robert Smythson (1535-1614), for example, made full use of the classical, grandiose entrance in 1585 at Burghley House, near Stamford, Lincolnshire. Following the example of the actual triumphal arch, the motif used as a doorway is often ornamented with sculptural groups, *spandrel figures representing *Victory or *Fame, or military *trophies. See also aedicule.

trompe l'oeil (French, trick of the eye). Form of decoration used to imitate a surface or texture, or to create in two dimensions an impression of three-dimensional objects or patterns. Plain wood, stone or plaster are transformed with *marbling, *graining or *grisaille. Quadratura represents architectural views in *perspective, creating the illusion of distance. *Décor bois and *quodlibet give the impression that objects are

trompe l'oeil. Sgraffito ornament, Schwarzenberg Palace, Prague, by Augustin Vlach, 1543-63.

lying on surfaces: 15th century illuminated manuscripts sometimes have flowers, insects and jewellery apparently carelessly scattered across their margins. Some mid 18th century German porcelain had designs of painted flowers with shadows, ombrierte *deutsche Blumen, that were later copied in England, notably at Chelsea.

trophy. This form has its origins in the celebration of military victory. The Greeks hung the arms of the defeated enemy on an oak tree to commemorate victory, and the Romans created artificial stone or bronze trophies. It differs from a *panoply, in which the weapons are heaped. A translation from Virgil describes the composition of a trophy: ' . . . they fix'd the shining armour on,/the mighty spoil from some proud warrior won./Above the crest was plac'd, that dropped with blood,/A grateful trophy to the warlike god./His shattered spears stuck round. The corselet too,/Pierc'd o'er in places, hung deformed below./ While the left side his massy target bears – /The neck the glittering blade he brandished in the wars.' Revived in the *Renaissance, trophies were naturally used to decorate buildings connected with war and victory: barracks, arsenals, *triumphal arches, and arms and armour themselves. The practice of depicting ancient Roman armour in trophies persisted and patterns appeared in the mid 16th century by engravers such as E.*Vico, and R.*Boyvin. The engravers of the Northern Renaissance gradually added contemporary armour and weapons to military trophies, although the ancient examples remained more common.

In the 17th century, the popularity of the trophy as an ornamental motif began to grow, spreading first into allied themes such as *hunting. By the 18th century, it was one of the commonest motifs and, particularly in France, was elaborated to cover any number of themes, e.g. *husbandry, theatre, *fishing, astronomy, *love, the sea, the sciences, the *Seasons, *pastoral life and *music. In ecclesiastical decoration, for example,

trophy. 1) Engraving of design by A. *Quellin, published 1665-69.
2) French design representing Music by P. Cherpitel, mid 18th century.

a trophy might combine censers, candles, snuffers, aspergils, psalters and lecterns. Engraved designs for trophies proliferated and almost all ornamentists of the period produced some. The use of trophies soon spread from purely architectural decoration (exterior and interior) to textiles, embroidery and marquetry. 18th and 19th century *Neo-classicism returned to the military-oriented trophy, albeit sometimes a rather debased version of it. A.*Benjamin in the *American Builder's Companion* (1806) gives an indication of the seriousness with which the trophy was treated at that time, 'A hall, saloon or staircase ought to exhibit something of . . . solidity and strength. Therefore trophies of different kinds may be introduced.' Trophies, usually military, were a popular ornament on early 20th century commercial buildings in the *classical style. *See also* heraldic decoration; panoply; Victory.

Troubadour style. French style that used the loosely *Gothic elements which had characterised the *Gothick in 18th century England, and reflected the general interest of 19th century ornamentists in the medieval period. The impetus came from the Napoleonic court where, alongside the *Egyptian and *Greek elements of the *Empire style, the Empress Josephine introduced a Gothic gallery at Malmaison (1805) and F.H.G. Jacob-Desmalter (1770-1841) made Gothic church furnishings for the chapel of the Petit Trianon, Versailles (1804). The publication of early manuscripts, stained glass and other medieval artefacts gathered momentum. A.W.N.*Pugin's earlier English *Gothic Revival books in French editions appeared subsequently and were important sources for the style. With the Restoration of the Bourbon Monarchy in 1814 and the personal patronage of the Duchesse de Berry, the Gothic was accorded high esteem in France. It had always carried monarchical associations, being the style of La Sainte Chapelle in Paris (1243-48), where marriages of the French royal family took place, and of the Basilica of S. Denis, the mausoleum of French royalty, from the mid 13th to the end of the 16th century. The Troubadour style was essentially light-weight and mid 19th century interest in accurate renderings of Gothic buildings meant that a more academic interest in the period was soon to overshadow it.

trumpet pattern or **blind trumpet.** *Celtic motif consisting of curvilinear trumpet shapes (usually two or three), the spaces between them filled with sinuous forms. Found in metalwork, stonecarving and manuscripts.

trumpet. Motif that often accompanies personifications of *Fame, as well as representations of the *Winds, and the *Elements (representing air). It also appears in decorative schemes on the theme of music.

Tudor describes the period 1485-1603 during which the last vestiges of *Perpendicular Gothic gave way to a style loosely based on continental *Mannerism, particularly the version that had developed in the Low Countries. Engraved books of ornament were the principal source of motifs although foreign craftsmen working in England were also influential. In the

Elizabethan period the Northern *Renaissance vocabulary of *strapwork, *jewelled strapwork, elaborated *pendants and *finials, *parcheman, *grotesques and *herms was adopted, although in architectural ornament the decoration was usually limited to the entrance porch and parapets on the exterior, and to chimneypieces, plaster ceilings and household artefacts in the interior. *Flemish Mannerism was the dominant influence, but motifs from the School of *Fontainebleau as well as from the purer Italian Renaissance, and relics of English native ornament (such as *nailheads) were also evident. *Gothic devices such as returned *labels over doors and windows, *tracery and *pendants were either abandoned or adapted. Among the most widely used *pattern books were those of H. *Vredeman de Vries, which, though Flemish, specifically stated that styles could be 'accommodated to national needs' and W.*Dietterlin, whose name gave rise to the 'ditterling' ornament associated with the period and criticised by later classicists as decadent. Silverware was usually highly ornate, woodwork gadrooned or with deeply carved repeating ornament, textiles tended to adopt bold patterns, showing plants, animals, knotwork (*see* interlacing) and sometimes mythological or biblical scenes. During the Tudor period increasing prosperity and the growth of the new merchant classes meant that fashionable architecture and fine things were no longer the exclusive province of the exceptionally wealthy – the decorative arts flourished and ornament gradually spread into relatively modest dwellings.

Tudor Revival. A strand of 19th century *eclecticism that combined a rather mild version of the *Gothic Revival with motifs taken from the domestic architecture of the *Tudor period. Often the ornamental characteristics of Tudor, Elizabethan and *Jacobean periods were mingled (giving rise to the terms Tudorbethan or Jacobethan) and *pattern-book authors frequently included all three, as well as the unspecific 'Old English' style. In Lewis Wyatt's *A Collection of Architectural Designs* (1800), as in many *Picturesque collections of cottage designs of the period, the various terms were used fairly indiscriminately. Motifs included *diaper-patterned brickwork, furled, bannerlike *labels, *Tudor roses, elaborate half-timbering,

Tudor Revival. Thornton Hough, Cheshire, 1890s.

mullions, and, in interiors, hammerbeam roofs, *linen-fold panelling and stained glass.

The 20th century Tudor Revival, preceded by some very careful Tudor-style work in late 19th century country house design, was somewhat frivolous. Leaded fenestration and fake half-timbering were complemented by manufacturers of interior furnishings such as Liberty of London, who advertised in the 1930s that, 'whether it is to be Tudor, Jacobean, Adam or some other bygone period . . . Liberty will gladly wait upon you.' The shop sold oak furniture, panelling and suitable fabrics to set off the style, and its own premises, built in 1924, are an example of the decorative possibilities of the Tudor style applied conscientiously but out of context.

Tudor flower. Stylised tripartite flower, similar to a *trefoil, but with its lobes resembling the petals of a *Tudor rose. A motif used in *cresting or *brattishing in English late *Gothic and *Tudor work.

Tudor rose. *Heraldic motif symbolic of the re-establishment of the Tudor monarchy at the end of the Wars of the Roses in 1485. It is made up of the white rose of Lancaster superimposed on the red rose of York, therefore appearing to have two rows of petals. Tudor roses were widely applied to buildings, furniture, textiles and metalwork. They were a popular motif in the 19th century *Tudor Revival.

tulip. Indigenous to the East, the tulip is said to have first become known in the West when the Holy Roman Emperor Ferdinand I of Austria received a gift of tulip bulbs from the Sultan of Turkey in 1554 (*see* Turkish style). The plant was cultivated in Augsburg, and the first Western illustration of a tulip appeared in Conrad Gesner's *De Hortis Germaniae Liber* (Augsburg, 1561). The tulip was adopted in German decoration and appears, for example, on late 16th century Saxon pottery. Emigrants from Germany took the motif to America and it eventually became typical of *Pennsylvania Dutch decoration; their ceramics, for example, became known as tulip ware. The tulip was first cultivated in Holland c.1570, and in England c.1577. In Holland C.*van de Passe I published several plates of tulips in *Hortus Floridus* (1614), which was published in England the following year. Propagation centred on Holland from the early 17th century, the speculation in bulbs reaching epic proportions during the years 1634-37. This popularity was reflected in the use of the tulip as an ornamental motif in the early to mid 17th century on Dutch pottery, lace, marquetry, silver, ironwork. The craftsman could not usually observe the flower first-hand, but he could depend for reference on the 'tulip books' put out by bulb dealers.

turkey. *See* American motifs.

turtle-back. Patterned ornamental *boss in wood or stone typical of *Jacobean ornament.

tun. The traditional Bordeaux wine barrel is an important motif in *marine decoration, used to allude to commerce. The form is also widely used as a *rebus, punning on the final syllable of many English proper names, e.g. Sutton, as at Sutton Place, Surrey.

Turkish or **Ottoman style.** The style identified as Turkish in Western Europe was in fact a fusion of elements from the *Byzantine Empire, the Seljuk Islamic period (roughly equivalent to early and middle *Gothic in Europe) and the Ottoman Empire.

An engraved account by J.T.*de Bry entitled *Leben und contrafetten der Turckischen und Persischen Sultanen, von Osmane, an biss auff den ictz tregierenden Sultan Muhumet II* (1596) is evidence of early Western interest in the Ottoman Empire. In the 17th and 18th centuries, oriental carpets in general were often called 'turkey carpets', although genuine Turkish carpet patterns were more schematic and geometric than Persian designs.

Decorative motifs particularly associated with Turkish art are the *tulip (symbol of the House of Osman), *arabesques, spiralling motifs similar to the Chinese *cloudband (also known as Mohammedan scrolls), the so-called *quatre-fleurs* style (naturalistically depicted carnations, hyacinths, roses and tulips), the 'saz' style (long, pointed, serrated leaves with stylised, circular, elaborate flowers), the *crescent and the turban.

Contact between the court of Louis XIV and that of the Ottoman Empire led to French interest in Turkey from the late 17th century. Count Charles de Ferriol's *Les Différents Nations du Levant* (Paris, 1714) was the source for Meissen porcelain figures of Turks modelled in the 1740s, and subsequently copied in England at Bow, Derby, and Longton Hall in the 1760s. *Cabinets turcs* or *boudoirs* ornamented with crescents and turbans were designed at the Hôtel Beauharnais, Paris (mid 18th century) and Fontainebleau (1775). Gobelins produced a tapestry series showing Turkish scenes (1781-84). The Empress Josephine had a Turkish bedroom at Fontainebleau (1806), in which the bed fringe was woven with crescents and stars. As the enthusiasm for *oriental styles grew, Turkish ornament was often used as an alternative to, or in conjunction with *chinoiserie. In England, W.*Chambers included a Turkish mosque among the buildings he designed for Kew Gardens (from 1757).

Turkish style. 1) Jug from Jules Peyre's Orfèvrerie, bijouterie, nielle, armouries, etc., *1845. 2) Wall tiles in the 16th century Palais d'Ismayl Bey from A.C.T.E.*Prisse d'Avennes's* L'Art Arabe, *1869-77.*

Serious collecting of Ottoman textiles and ceramics developed from the mid 19th century and Turkish style ornament became more closely based on genuine Ottoman artefacts, although it was often still only vaguely identified. O.*Jones, in the *Grammar of Ornament*, described it as a modification of the *Arabian style. The intertwined floral patterns, pointed serrated foliage and stylised flowers of *Iznik pottery were taken up by the potter William De Morgan (1839-1917) and commercial tile manufacturers. The French potter and designer, E.-V.*Collinot illustrated Iznik designs in his *Encyclopédie des arts décoratifs de l'Orient* (Paris, 1880s).

The new smoking rooms that appeared in fashionable mansions after 1850 were frequently decorated in Turkish style – sometimes the gentlemen even took to wearing the fez. E. Julienne in *L'Orfèvrerie Française* (1864) illustrated cigar holders ornamented with Turkish figures; an English electroplate tobacco jar (c.1853) has a crouching turbanned figure as a *finial. Public baths and bathrooms, as well as Turkish baths, were ornamented in Turkish style, e.g. that designed for a Parisian courtesan at the Hôtel Paira, Paris (1855-65). The Turkish Bazaar at the Philadelphia Centennial Exhibition (1876) had rooms arranged for low-level seating, with cushions, low stools or pouffes, jewel-coloured fabrics and brasswork, and the London shop Liberty & Co. displayed imported oriental wares in a setting designed to resemble a Turkish harem.

Tuscan Order. *See* Orders.

twist. A spiral effect, usually in wood or glass. In woodwork, the spirally turned *baluster, furniture leg and stretcher were popular in the mid 17th century, corresponding to the fashion for the *spiral column in architecture. As wood-turning techniques became more sophisticated, elaborate versions were devised: the double twist (sometimes called the barley sugar twist), double open twist and triple twist. In the early 19th century, spirally turned work was thought (erroneously) to be typically Elizabethan, and was used by *Tudor and *Elizabethan Revival designers such as R.*Bridgens, not least because it could be effectively and quickly produced by machine.

In glass, twist patterns are a popular decoration for stems, notably of early 18th century wine glasses. The twists are achieved with opaque or coloured glass, or by the introduction of lines of air, or a combination of both. There are many terms applied to these effects in glass: cable, colour, corkscrew, cotton, double series, enamel, gauze, incised lace, mercury, mixed, multiple series, outlined, single series, tape, tartan, thread and triple. *See also* cable moulding.

tympanum. In architecture, a block (usually stone) within the *pediment or over an arch which forms the ground for sculptural or relief ornament.

undulate band. Strip of ornament in a continuous waving form, e.g. *wavescroll or *scrolling foliage, in which the main line or stem curves gently from side to side. *See also* vertebrate band.

unicorn. Fabulous creature which was a symbol of purity in Egypt and Persia long before its appearance in Christian and medieval art. In the Bestiary of Physiologus the animal was interpreted as a monstrous beast that bellowed, had elephant's feet and a horn four feet long – a description which appears to be a confusion with the rhinoceros. However, the creature represented widely in the medieval period and since is a delicate beast, a bearded deer or horse with a single spiral horn and a lion's tail.

In *Christian iconography, the unicorn is a symbol of purity and chastity, associated particularly with the Virgin Mary. In the *Bestiaire de l'Amour* by Richard de Fournival (early 14th century) it was established as a symbol of the beguiled lover in medieval courtly love. An important heraldic beast, it sometimes represents the ideal knight. It is also the emblem of Scotland and is therefore incorporated in the arms of Great Britain. Its horn was said to be the antidote to any poison and this legend led to the appearance of the creature in the trade signs of apothecaries.

Unteutsch, Friedrich. 17th century German cabinet-maker who published designs in the *Auricular style.

urn. The urn is usually distinguished from the *vase by its lid, but is also represented as a pitcher. It ranges from a relatively squat shape to the attenuated Greek form. Symbolising *death and mourning, both in its emptiness, possibly denoting loss, and as an allusion to its more literal funerary function as a receptacle for ashes, it has been used since classical times as a motif on monuments to the dead. Sometimes it has *flames issuing from it, more rarely the figure of the deceased is shown rising out of it. The lid of the urn is usually elaborated with a decorative *finial or *knop, a useful feature when the urn appears, for example, as a coffee pot, mustard pot or church ampulla. In architectural ornament, urns (sometimes topped by a

*undulate band. 1) *Frieze below *cornice on 19th century commercial building, Liverpool, England.*
unicorn. 2) Bench end, Church of St Andrew, Tostock, Suffolk, 13th and 14th centuries. 3) 15th century font, Church of St Andrew, Norton, Suffolk.

urn. 1) Funerary urn, Calton Old Burial Ground, Edinburgh, late 18th century. 2) Fireplace, Polesden Lacey, Surrey, 1906-08. 3) Hôtel de la Monnaie, Paris, 1772-75. 4) Burton's store, Tunbridge Wells, Kent, 1930s.

flame) appear in interiors above chimneypieces, on exteriors as *cresting details, on parapets, or as *acroteria. Also popular as a finial on cast-iron railings.

Vallet, Pierre (1575-c.1647). French engraver of a much-used early 17th century source book for *plant ornament.

van de Passe, Crispin I (c.1565-1657) and his son, Crispin II (c.1597-post 1666). Engravers and print-sellers, based first in Cologne and then in Holland. Among the wide range of engravings they produced was a collection of furniture designs, *Oficina arcularia in qua sunt ad stectantia diversa eximia exempla ex varijs autoribus collecta* (first published in Utrecht in 1621 by Crispin I, with a second revised edition published by Crispin II in Amsterdam in 1642 and 1651). Other members of the family worked and sold the prints in Paris and England. The designs, which were in a relatively sophisticated Northern *Renaissance style and probably illustrated existing pieces, appear to have been widely known.

vandycked swag. 19th century term for a loop of drapery with a scalloped lower edge. It is similar in form and use to the *lambrequin, and was named after the indented lace collars in portraits by Anthony van Dyck (1599-1641). A frequent feature of *Netherlands Grotesque ornament, combined with *strapwork.

Vardy, John (d 1765). English architect in the Office of Works who worked with W.*Kent. As a result of this

professional connection he produced *Some Designs of Mr Inigo Jones and Mr William Kent* (1744), which included 17 of Jones's designs, mostly for chimneypieces, and 36 by Kent for metalware, vases, candelabra, furniture and incidental buildings. As the only contemporary engraved source of Kent's design work outside architecture, Vardy's work was an important publication, attracting much interest.

vases. In periods of *classical revival, no other classical artefact has been as popular as the vase. Engraved series of vases were legion, based on a mixture of famed classical prototypes, initially, Roman examples such as the Medici and Borghese vases (so-called after their Renaissance owners), and subsequently, as a result of 18th century archaeological work, Greek vases. *Neo-classical variants were sometimes imaginative reworkings of the type, but there were also numerous mass-produced copies of originals. The vase form, with its thin neck and base, graded shape (allowing for a rich selection of *mouldings), handles and rim was a perfect vehicle for ornament.

The ornament applied to antique vases provided an unending source of motifs for the later generations of copyists and craftsmen. E.*Vico produced a series of volumes, *Sic Romae antiqui sculptores ex aere et marmore faciebat* (Rome, 1534), which gave a typically *Mannerist rendering of the possibilities offered by the vase form, with the bodies of the vases disguised beneath intricate arrangements of animals and plants. Many publishers, especially in the Netherlands, drew on the fantastic designs of Polidoro da Caravaggio, whose contorted rendering appealed to the *Flemish Mannerists. Such invention was not usually intended to be translated directly on to actual vases but provided suggestions for the vase motifs used in wall paintings, metal or ceramics, engraved frontispieces, etc.

*vandycked swag. 1) Exterior, Audley End, Essex, early 17th century. vases. 2) From J.B.*Fischer von Erlach's Entwurff einer historischen Architektur, 1721. 3) From J.*Gibbs's A Book of Architecture, 1728. 4) Public garden, Icod de los Vinos, Tenerife, Canary Islands.*

The growth in popularity in France of the vase as an ornamental motif can be gauged from D.*Guilmard's *Maîtres Ornemanistes* – 14 sets of designs were recorded in this publication during the reign of Louis XIV, 12 in the reign of Louis XV and 52 in the reign of Louis XVI. 17th century English designers were also interested in vases, though above all in their architectural application (*see also* urns), calling them 'potts'. They were used as *cresting ornament, against the skyline, on parapets and as garden ornament along balustrades. J.-F.*Blondel thought they should be made of different materials, determined by the importance of the site: marble for the best site in the park, precious stone (porphyry, alabaster or agate) for interiors, bronze for less important places such as terraces, and lead for fountains. Iron or faïence were also used with stone matching the façade in question. Vases, sometimes with flowers, appear in ironwork as *finials.

M.*Darly, in *The Ornamental Architect* (1770), drew attention to the differences between vases used on the exterior and interior of buildings: 'Those intended for the inside of Rooms, Halls etc. may be more neatly finished and ornamented than those for external use, which should have pleasing forms and large parts and never to be loaded with trifling ornaments.'

By this period, vases were ubiquitous, appearing, for example as pulpits and fonts, as finials on cabinets, clocks and bureaux, on stretchers of tables and on chimneypieces. This obsession with the form, dubbed 'vase mania', gathered momentum with *Neo-classicism, not least as a result of a series of important publications of archaeological finds. Chief among these was the Hamilton Collection, gathered by Sir William Hamilton (1730-1803), diplomat and antiquarian. His acquisitions were described in *Antiquités Etrusques, Grecques et Romaines* (4 vols, Naples, 1766-67) engraved by F.A. David and annotated by d'Hancarville (the pseudonym of F.G. Hugues). The preface set out the objectives of the publication: 'We think also that we make an agreeable present to our manufacturers of earthen-ware and china and to those who make vases in silver, copper, glass, marble etc. Having employed much more time in working than in reflection, and being besides in great want of models, they will be very glad to find here more than 200 forms, the greatest part of which are absolutely new to them.' These volumes were reprinted, 1785-88 and 1801-18. The fortunate could see the original vases as they arrived at the British Museum, from 1772, but with further publications the Hamilton Collection became increasingly accessible to an ever wider audience. The *Collection of Engravings from Ancient Vases* published by W. Tischbein (Naples, 1791-93) illustrated later finds and was less expensively produced, ' . . . young artists are not often in a situation of making such a purchase'. It also differed in presentation, being, as Hamilton observed, 'confined . . . to the simple outline of the figures on the vases, which is the essential, and no unnecessary Ornaments, or colouring have been introduced'. This encouraged accuracy, where, in the past ' . . . Antiquarians and Artists have been misled cruelly'. Josiah Wedgwood was to use the Hamilton Collection extensively and certain individual items had enormous influence. The Portland Vase (found in 1582 and

originally known as the Barberini Vase) was sold by Hamilton to Margaret, Duchess of Portland in 1784, and since 1810 it has been on loan to the British Museum. Another of Hamilton's vases, the Warwick Vase, was published in G.B.*Piranesi's important work of 1778, four years after its discovery at Hadrian's Villa, Tivoli. Piranesi's engravings of vases were heavy, similar in style to the work of Mannerists such as Polidoro da Caravaggio, but they were also of considerable academic importance.

In the early 19th century *Greek Revival, the vase (often a long-necked version with a single handle called a *lekythi*) was widely used. In 1814, H.*Moses published 170 objects from British collections, which included both vases and *urns. The Warwick Vase was depicted in a spare, linear style far removed from Piranesi's lavish rendering. In 1819 Moses published illustrations of vases from the collection of Sir Henry Englefield. Throughout the 19th century and into the 20th, the vase, whether abundantly ornamented or treated with extreme simplicity, remained a standard ornamental motif.

vaulting. Both in *Islamic architecture and in *Gothic architecture, elaborate systems of vaulting were developed, originally for structural reasons. But the enrichment of rib-ridges and the creation of intricate patterns as a result of ever more complex networks of ribs and intermediaries led to the importance of vaulting as a decorative as well as a functional feature. The meeting of ribs in vaulting systems is often elaborated with *bosses or *pendants that form ornamented terminals to disguise the join.

The best known Islamic variant is honeycomb vaulting or *stalactite work, which was revived in the 18th and 19th century European fashion for oriental styles. Specifically decorative types of Gothic vaulting include the diamond vault, *fan vault, *net vault and *star vault. Gothic architecture used stylised vaulting in the heads of *niches in the way that classical architecture used a *scallop shell. In late Gothic work, especially northern European *Flamboyant interiors, the allusion was made to *tree branches and the structural function of vaulting became somewhat elusive, with ribs sometimes arbitrarily cut off or knotted.

Vaux, Calvert (1824-95). English landscape architect, who moved to America and worked with A.J.*Downing. He was an influential figure in the introduction of the *Picturesque in America. His *Villas and Cottages* (New York, 1857; five further editions 1863-1874) was dedicated to Downing and closely followed the English Picturesque *pattern books of the early 19th century. Vaux's advice was to 'Make the ornament secondary to the construction and not the construction secondary to the ornament . . . it is always as easy to spoil a house by overdoing it as by underdoing it.' His designs, like his own buildings, were either *Gothic Revival or Italian *Renaissance style.

vegetables. The enthusiasm for *naturalistic ornament in the 14th and 15th centuries led to the use of vegetables as decorative subjects, though to a lesser extent than the more obviously attractive flowers,

vegetable. Cauliflower *finial on English silver tureen, made by Thomas Heming, 1763-64.

trees and animals. Louis of Anjou is recorded to have had plates decorated with pumpkins, parsley and leeks in 1380. Vegetables are a strictly northern European addition to the *Renaissance form of the *festoon, and appear in engraved ornament designed by artists of the *Netherlands Grotesque school, such as C. *Floris. A.*Quellin decorated the Town Hall in Amsterdam (1648-55) with festoons which included peas, beans, carrots and turnips. Grinling Gibbons and his followers (*see* Gibbonwork) were influenced by this work and included vegetables in their carvings, alongside *fruit and shells.

In the 18th century, vegetable decoration appeared most commonly on silver and ceramic soup tureens and sauceboats, e.g. *finials in the form of artichokes or cauliflower florets. Both G.-M.*Oppenord and J.-A. *Meissonier published *Livre de légumes*, elegantly composed collections of vegetable engravings. C.-N.*Cochin the Younger commented on the fashion for vegetable ornament in 1754: 'The goldsmiths are begged when they make an artichoke or a celery stem of natural size on the lid of a sauceboat to be so kind as not to set beside it a hare as big as a finger . . . ' During the same period there was a fashion, for the (usually ceramic) piece itself to take the form of a vegetable – tureens were made in the form of a lettuce or a bunch of asparagus, for example.

Carved or painted *trophies representing gardening or *husbandry often included a few decorative vegetables among the implements and a suitably rustic straw hat.

This realistic style of vegetable decoration was not compatible with *Neo-classicism, and it was not until the mid 19th century, when naturalistic plant forms once more dominated ornamentation, that vegetables reappeared, encouraged by the prevailing concept that ornament could be derived from all aspects of the plant: the root and the seed as well as the flower and leaf. Anton Seder's pattern book *Die Pflanze in Kunst und Gewerbe* (Vienna, 1886) includes *grotesques and festoons with turnips, beet, radish, maize and gourds.

Venetian Gothic Revival. The single-handed creation of John Ruskin (1819-1900) who, in publishing *Examples of the Architecture of Venice* (1851) and, more importantly, *Stones of Venice* (1851-53), brought to the attention of architects and builders the existence of the Venetian Gothic. The revival encouraged a version

Venetian Gothic Revival. Templeton's Carpet Factory, Glasgow, Scotland, architect William Leiper, 1889.

of the *Gothic which gave considerable decorative licence, particularly in polychromatic materials. One feature was the use of banded stone and brick, especially where the emphasis to the window or door frames was required. Ruskin commented, with some justification, 'I have had an indirect influence on nearly every cheap villa builder between this and Bromley: and there is scarcely a public house near the Crystal Palace but sells its gin and bitters under pseudo-Venetian capitals copied from the church of the Madonna of Health or of Miracles.' Many architects and designers borrowed details direct from the *Stones*, especially examples of *tracery. The style was also popular in America: the Academy of Design in New York (1865) by P.B. Wight and the Isabella Stewart Gardner Museum, Boston (1902), which incorporated genuine Venetian fragments, were two important examples. Leading British architects such as J.P. Seddon (1827-1906), Benjamin Woodward (1815-61) and the Dublin-based firm of Sir Thomas Deane (1828-99) owed much to Ruskin, and many of the commercial buildings that rose in the City of London during the 1860s were reworkings of the Ca' d'Oro, Venice (c.1425-c.1440) and other Byzantine/Gothic masterpieces.

Venetian Saracenic. *See* arabesque; damascening.

Venetian window. *See* Palladian motif.

Veneziano, Agostino. Engraver and publisher who worked in Rome and Florence, c.1516-36. His work was an important source for J.A.*Ducerceau. He issued 57 plates of ornament, some copies of the antique, some interpretations of the work of S.*Serlio, Raphael and Giovanni da Udine, the best known of which was a series of *grotesque panels.

Venus. Goddess of *love and fertility, the Roman equivalent of the Greek Aphrodite. Born out of the sea, she floated to land on a scallop shell: one of her attributes is a *dolphin and she occasionally appears in *marine decoration.

In more conventional usage Venus is often accompanied by the Three *Graces or by her son *Cupid. Her attributes include *doves, *swans, a flaming *torch and a *heart. Plants sacred to her are the red *rose and the *myrtle. Decorative schemes based on Venus usually appear in women's bedrooms or boudoirs, particularly on objects alluding to beauty, e.g. looking glasses, dressing tables, even bed warmers. The two themes most often depicted are the Triumph of Venus, in which she is pulled on a shell-carriage by swans or doves, and the Toilet of Venus, in which Cupid holds up a mirror for her. Venus sometimes appears with *Mars, whom she loved, and together they stand for Beauty and Valour or the Conquest of Strife by Love. Venus's helpless love for Adonis and his subsequent death while hunting was a theme used by the English silversmith Matthew Boulton (1728-1809) on a clock-case c.1770: Venus weeps at the tomb of Adonis, whom *Time will never restore to her.

vermiculation. A pattern of short, irregular wriggling channels imitating worm tracks, used as a surface decoration on stone. Mass-produced from the late 18th century, it became the most widely used type of *rustication for domestic architecture, picking up details such as *keystones, door or window surrounds.

In ceramics, *vermiculé* decoration is a ground pattern of irregular blobs of colour surrounded by gold which was developed by the Sèvres factory in the 1750s and subsequently copied by other porcelain manufacturers. Wedgwood introduced a similar pattern, c.1810, called *Vermicelli*. A comparable vermicular design appears as the ground pattern on late 18th and early 19th century printed cottons.

vertebrate band. A strip of ornament with a central line to which the rest of the decoration is attached, e.g. a continuous pattern of flower, fruit and foliage designs with a main stem running down its centre. A more literal example can be found on the exterior of the Natural History Museum, London (planned by Alfred Waterhouse, built 1871-81), where a *moulding enrichment based on animals' vertebrae is used as a support for climbing beasts.

vesica piscis (Latin, bladder of a fish) or **mandorla** (Italian, almond). An elliptical form with pointed ends often used in *Christian ornament for the aureole or glory surrounding the Persons of the Holy Trinity and the Virgin Mary in medieval paintings and sculptures. The form is occasionally found in ecclesiastical architecture, usually *Gothic, where it is applied to various features including windows, decorative spaces, panels and *medallions. The form was readopted in the 19th century *Gothic Revival, as in J.K.*Colling's *Art Foliage*.

Vices. *See* Virtues.

Vico, Enea (1523-67). Italian ornamental engraver and medallist, whose work was an influential source in the spread of *Renaissance ornamentation, in particular his suite of *grotesque designs closely based

vermiculation. 1) Gate pier at Chiswick House, London, built 1725-29.
*2) *Keystone, late 19th century house, Ventnor, Isle of Wight.*
*vertebrate band. 3) 13th century doorway, Rouen Cathedral (Seine-Maritime), France. 4) Border from M.A.*Pergolesi's* Designs for Various Ornaments, *late 18th century.*
*vesica piscis. 5) Design composed of 'natural type ground ivy' from J.K.*Collings's* Art Foliage for Sculpture and Decoration, *1865.*

on Roman originals: *Picturae quas grottesches vulgo vocant* (Rome, 1541). These were widely known in Europe, notably to J.A.*Ducerceau who copied them in 1550. Vico's suite of military *trophies (1553) incorporated a wide range of classical Roman arms and armour. He engraved existing archaeological works such as the Tabula Bembi (*see* Egyptian style) and *portrait heads of Roman emperors and later their wives as depicted on coins: *Imagini . . . degli Imperatori* (1554) and *Imagini delle Donne Auguste* (1562) were both sources for this popular ornament. Vico also published some extremely elaborate designs for *vases and ewers in the *Mannerist style.

Victory was personified by the Greeks and Romans as a winged female figure, carrying a *laurel wreath (with which to crown a victor) and sometimes a *palm (symbol of military victory). The figure was revived, particularly for the decoration of arms and armour, during the *Renaissance. Roman prototypes found on the *spandrels of *triumphal arches were copied and adapted for use over arched doorways, e.g. the figure over the principal entrance at Blickling Hall, Norfolk (1616-27); this position had also been used for Early Christian *angels, which were often based on the classical Victory figure. Victory was a common *Empire style motif, frequently shown standing atop the world's globe and accompanied by *Fame, sometimes with vanquished enemies or captured weapons heaped at her feet.

The victory column, usually a decorated shaft surmounted by Victory, was in *Neo-classical styles adapted to monarchical purposes, as well as being used for the recognition of military or civic glory or achievements, e.g. Nelson's Column, London (1839-42).

Vienna Secession. A society founded in Vienna in 1897 by a group of painters, architects and designers to counteract the prevailing tide of indiscriminate *Historicism. The group, which formed a kind of bridgehead between the *Jugendstil and *Art Nouveau styles and the later Modern Movement (*see* Modernist decoration), had some parallels with the *Arts and Crafts

Vienna Secession. Karlsplatz underground railway station, Vienna, by Otto Wagner, 1898.

*Victory. *Spandrel on Arc de Triomphe, Paris, 1806-36.*

movement. Early ornamental work, such as that by Otto Wagner (1841-1918), who was loosely associated with the Secession, was based on formal floral patterns, as on the tiling on his Majolika Haus in Vienna (1898). The so-called 'golden cabbage' dome of the Secession headquarters (1897) by Josef Olbrich (1867-1908) was in the same vein. However these were the last echoes of the Jugendstil and soon the ornament of simple inlay, contrasting materials, metal studs or semi-precious stones, often geometric, chequered and pierced, especially in the work of Josef Hoffmann (1870-1956), was applied to glass, metalwork or woodwork at whatever scale was required. Thus furnishings, artefacts and the architecture were designed in a homogenous scheme. Exhibitions were held to promote the aims of the Secession, with, later, invited guests from abroad, such as the *Glasgow School designers. The magazine *Ver Sacrum* (1898-1904) expressed the designs and beliefs of the group, and the Wiener Werkstätte, founded by Josef Hoffmann and Koloman Moser (1868-1918) in 1903, was a craft workshop-cum-studio set up to translate the aims of the movement into contemporary design. The ceramic workshop Wiener Keramik was founded in 1905 by Michael Powolny (1871-1954) and Berthold Löffler (1874-1960) and traded in association with the Wiener Werkstätte. It produced black and white earthenware pieces decorated with geometric patterns and portrait figures and animal models painted in bright colours. The Wiener Werkstätte opened a sales office in New York in 1919, and continued in operation until 1932. All three organisations shared the principles of the alliance of art with utility: in the words of Hoffman and Moser, 'our guiding principle is function, utility our first condition, and our strength must lie in good proportions and the proper treatment of material. This belief in only vestigial ornamentation led soon to the conviction that function alone should govern the form, and the Bauhaus and Modern Movement came into being, with the energetic Adolph Loos (1870-1933) as the prophet of an age when ornament was to be viewed as redundant.

vignette. Originally, a small, compact, decorative book illustration. Later it described any small decorative scene of similar appearance that was used in painted decoration, e.g. on porcelain, particularly in the 18th century. Photographic printing techniques made the production of the characteristically softened edge of a vignette a simple process and it became a popular decoration on 20th century ceramics and other small artefacts.

vignette. Term occasionally used to describe carved ornament, usually medieval, with a continuous design based on *grapevine leaves and *tendrils.

Vignola, Giacomo Barozzi da (1507-73). Italian architect working in Rome whose treatise *Regola delli Cinque Ordini d'Architettura* (1562) assumed an importance in France comparable to that of A.*Palladio's treatise in England. The engravings were of high quality and more scholarly than those of S.*Serlio, his near-contemporary. Both architects worked for Francois I at *Fontainebleau for a period. Vignola's treatise was based on *Vitruvius, with Roman examples for the *Orders amplified by Vignola's own designs. The French edition was issued in 1629; the Amsterdam edition of 1642 had parallel texts in five languages, including English; the first full English edition appeared in 1694, translated by Joseph Moxon, and it was in its fifth edition by 1782. In 1691, A.C.*d'Aviler published his *Cours d'architecture, qui comprend les ordres de Vignole*, which was constantly revised and reissued with designs by contemporary *ornemanistes*: the 1710 edition, for example, included work by J.*Berain. During the 18th century, Vignola's work continued to be the main source for authors of French architectural treatises: both C.-N.*Cochin the Younger (1757) and J.F.*Blondel (1767) based their treatment of the Orders upon Vignola's account.

In his own architectural work Vignola used the Orders both in a strictly *classical way and, where appropriate, in a more *Mannerist fashion. He was the founding father of *Baroque ecclesiastical architecture, with the highly influential Gesù in Rome (begun 1568).

Viking or **Norse** ornament was based upon *zoomorphic motifs and linear forms. As in early *Celtic ornament there was little *naturalism, and where plants were used they were highly stylised. Historians have identified in Viking art a number of roughly chronological categories: in the latter half of the 10th century the Jellinge style consisted of *interlacing ornament and linked animal forms in a writhing, unbroken pattern; this was followed by the Ringerike style of the 11th century, consisting of frenzied foliate patterns, the plant bearing some resemblance to the *acanthus; the Urnes style of the later 11th century also consisted of flowing ribbon patterns and *lacertine animals. Other distinct regional types have also been identified, but the differences are often extremely subtle. Viking art was to reach Britain fairly late: the early raids did not have any influence and it was not until the later 10th century that it combined with the Celtic (Hiberno-Saxon) style then prevalent and appeared in the north and east of the country. It was soon eclipsed by the *Romanesque style.

In the 19th century a romantic nationalistic revival in Norway found expression in the *Dragon style. At the same time, in keeping with the fashion for jewellery

Viking style. American reproduction of Viking Punch Bowl, by Tiffany & Co., c.1893
Federico di Vinciolo. Peacock design from Les Singuliers et Nouveaux Pourtraicts pour toutes sortes d'ouvrages de lingerie, *1587.*

in the *Archaeological style in Europe, the Copenhagen jewellers Borgen and Christensen copied Viking ornaments. In addition, Viking forms mingled with Celtic ones in the more stylised ornamental vogues of the late 19th century, especially *Art Nouveau and the *Jugendstil. The Fornordisk style (also called Old Norse in Britain), which appeared in Scandinavia in the 1890s, combined traditional vernacular forms taken from folk art with ancient Nordic motifs, and was used in furniture design and architectural decoration.

Vinciolo, Federico di (fl 1587-1599). A Venetian, probably employed by Catherine de Medici, who produced one of the most widely published *pattern books of designs for cutwork and the first for *reticello* lace. It first appeared in Paris as *Les Singuliers et Nouveaux Pourtraicts pour toutes sortes d'ouvrages de lingerie* (1587); by 1612 it had run to 13 editions and was copied in Turin and Lyons. The designs were pirated by Adrian Poyntz who published them as *New and singular patternes and workes of linnen. Serving for patternes to make all sorts of lace, edgings and cut-workes. Newly invented for the profit and contentment of ladies gentilwomen and others, that are desirous of this arte* (London, 1591); subsequent editions appeared in Paris (1595), Strasbourg (1596) and Basle (1599), and across Europe throughout the 17th century. The book included fashionable *Renaissance motifs, such as *grotesques, *scrolling foliage, classical gods and goddesses, as well as motifs derived from Eastern silks such as *peacocks and a *lion with a saddle cloth. One section was obviously intended for ecclesiastical vestments and furnishings, including designs such as the *pelican-in-her-piety and flaming *hearts.

Vinciolo's second collection, *Les Secondes Oeuvres, et subtiles inventions de lingerie* (Paris, 1594), was principally ecclesiastical, with the Deposition, Crucifixion and Annunciation all schematised for cutwork panels.

vine; vinescroll. *See* grapevine.

Viollet-le-Duc, Eugène-Emanuel (1814-79). French architect whose scholarly interest in the *Gothic style made him the foremost exponent of its revival in France (comparable to A.W.N.*Pugin in England), as well as the leading restorer of the great medieval monuments of France. His *Dictionnaire Raisonnée de l'architecture française* was published 1858-68, and dealt with the structure and decoration of Gothic buildings. It was followed by the *Dictionnaire Raisonnée du mobilier français de l'époque Carlovingienne à la Renaissance*, first published in 1858 and then expanded into six volumes 1872-75, which was an extensive survey of medieval furnishings, costume and armour from the Carolingian period to the Renaissance. His *Entretiens sur l'architecture*, published in two volumes in 1863 and 1872, contained illustrations of ironwork which were surprisingly free, more *Art Nouveau than Gothic Revival in form. The first volume of *Entretiens* was translated by Henry van Bunt in 1875 and published in England as *Discourses on architecture* – it dealt with both interior and exterior ornament and noted *Egyptian, Moslem, Roman and *Byzantine motifs. Viollet-le-Duc's works were influential in England, with admirers such as J.K.*Colling and the architect William Burges (1827-81). Viollet-le-Duc regarded the Gothic as a style without limitation: he decorated the railway carriages on Napoleon III's Imperial train in modified 15th century style, embellished with earlier details. Many of his illustrations for furniture were used as patterns by designers and manufacturers. *See also* Worthies.

Virtues and Vices. The idea of *personifications of the Virtues opposing the Vices came from the *Psychomachia* of Prudentius, a 4th century classical poet. It was a popular theme in medieval literature and appeared frequently in ornament, particularly in *Romanesque ecclesiastical decoration. The accepted Christian Virtues of this period were Faith, Hope and Charity together with the four pre-Christian cardinal Virtues: *Justice, Fortitude, Prudence and Temperance, although Prudentius had included more, such as Patience, Humility and Chastity. At least twelve were in frequent use. Ethical allegory was a popular medieval concept and the increasing complexity and obscurity of references appealed to the intellectual preoccupations of *Renaissance Italy. The Vices rarely appear unless in opposition to a Virtue, either in combat: e.g. a beautiful maiden (Virtue) and a bearded man or monster (Vice), or juxtaposed: Pride and Humility, Lust and Chastity, Sloth and Industry, etc. Virtue is always an idealised figure (often based on the image used in classical antiquity, but sometimes a child or *putto*); Vice is

Eugène-Emanuel Viollet-le-Duc. Imaginary reconstruction of the Baths of Caracalla from his Entretiens, *1863-72.*

represented by a grotesque or fearsome creature. The Vices most frequently depicted as the enemies of the Christian Virtues are the seven cardinal sins: Pride, Covetousness, Lust, Anger, Gluttony, Envy, Sloth. Others included Calumny, Ignorance and Ingratitude. The Virtues are sometimes represented with the Heroes of antiquity or the *Liberal Arts or Sciences. Sometimes the personification is combined with its antitype, usually from mythology or history, for example late 16th century embroidered hangings at Hardwick Hall, Derbyshire, show Faith with Mohamet, Temperance with Sardanapalus and a third, now lost, Hope with Judas. A careful selection of appropriate characteristics was made according to the intended application of the ornament, public virtues for civic buildings or tombs of leaders, heroic virtues for the tomb or house of a military hero, religious virtues for a pope or cardinal's tomb, conjugal virtues for a marriage chest or domestic interior, etc.

Many of the 16th and 17th century German, French and Netherlandish engravers provided patterns for the creation of these Virtues; C.*Ripa was probably the most popular source. Later, C.-N.*Cochin the Younger revived the theme of Virtues and opposing Vices in his *Almanach Iconologique*, and engraved about fifty of each over the four years. At this period personifications were also proving a popular subject for ceramic figures, and Meissen produced a series of Virtues during the 1760s. Edward Wyatt's decorative schemes for Carlton House, London (1804) combined *Neoclassical panels of the *Elements, the *Seasons and the Virtues. The subject was fashionable in mid 19th century *Historicist architectural ornament, in which personifications were widely used.

Vitruvian scroll. *See* wavescroll.

Vitruvius Pollio, Marcus (fl 46-30 BC). Author of the only written account of architectural theory to survive from classical antiquity, *De Architectura*. Numerous copies circulated across Europe in the Middle Ages. A manuscript copy was discovered at the monastery of St Gall, Switzerland in 1414, and the first printed version was published in Latin in Rome c.1486. Fra Giocondo's edition (Venice, 1511) was the first to be illustrated, with charming but unscholarly woodcuts. Further editions appeared including the first in Italian in Como (1521) and the German *Vitruvius Teutsch* by Walter Rivius, also known as Walter Ryff, in Nuremberg (1528). But it was the 1556 edition published and engraved by Daniele Barbaro in Venice, which, for the first time, illustrated the rather imprecise and obscure homilies of the text with careful, high-quality engravings from illustrations by A.*Palladio. By the end of the 16th century Vitruvius's treatise was available in most European languages, though an abridged English version did not appear until 1692. Various important architectural theorists were responsible for editions of Vitruvius including Claude Perrault (1613-88) who published the officially commissioned French translation, *Les Dix Livres d'architecture de Vitruve, corrigés et traduits nouvellement en français* (1673, 1684) and *L'Abrège des dix livres de Vitruve* (1674).

Vitruvius established three *Orders, Doric, Ionic and Corinthian. He also referred to a Tuscan Order.

The Orders were designed to match the purpose of the building, thus the temples of *Minerva, *Mars and *Hercules should be Doric, since the 'virile strength of these gods makes daintiness entirely inappropriate to the houses'. By contrast, *Venus, Flora, Proserpine, Spring-Water and the Nymphs are suited by the Corinthian Order, 'because these are delicate divinities and so its rather slender outlines, its flowers, leaves and ornamental volutes will lend propriety where it is due.' Thus Vitruvius introduced the theory of an appropriate degree of ornament which was to underly *classicism in all its manifestations from the *Renaissance. Vitruvius is expansive on the historic background of *caryatids and *persians, and the 1511 edition illustrated these. *De Architectura* was the springboard for the great architectural theorists of the Renaissance, among them L.B.*Alberti, S.*Serlio, A.*Palladio and G.B. da *Vignola.

volute. Merchants' Exchange, Philadelphia, Pennsylvania, architect William Strickland, 1832-33.

volute. Spiral, scrolling form which is the basis of the *capital of the Ionic *Order. According to one theory of the origin of the Ionic Order, the volutes derived originally from ram's horns (*see* aegricanes). In reduced form, volutes also appear on Corinthian and Composite capitals (*see* helix). *Consoles (or *brackets) often take the form of a volute. From the *Renaissance volutes were taken up in ornament and used to link storeys. In the *Baroque the device was elaborated to form a kind of decorative screen and buttress for a cupola. In *Louis XIV decoration the form is squared, adapted to match *reeding and *fluting. In furniture, it is a standard form for extremities, arm rests, feet, etc., and is also used in silver and ceramics. In the 19th century, one of many technical aids to pattern making was the 'voluter', a machine to draw the scrolling shape on wood, stone, or even paper. *See also* Onslow pattern; *os de mouton*.

Vredeman de Vries, Hans or Jan (1526-1604). Painter, ornamentist and designer of the paraphernalia of royal festivities, principally in the form of temporary *triumphal arches, which were a particular feature of celebrations in the 16th century. He trained under C.*Floris and worked in Antwerp, Germany and Amsterdam. His *pattern books, which cover the full range of ornament popular in northern Europe during the latter half of the 16th century, were widely influential in the Low Countries, Britain and Scandinavia, where his importance was comparable to that of J.A.*Ducerceau in France.

In 1555 and 1557 he published suites of designs for *strapwork *cartouches entitled *Multarum variumque protactionum libellus*. Further collections published in the early 1560s clearly show the combination of strapwork with *grotesque details that was the essence of the *Netherlands Grotesque style. Vredeman de Vries was heavily influenced by the work of S.*Serlio and a large proportion of his engraving was concerned with demonstrating the ornamental possibilities of the *Orders, notably in his *Caryatidum* of the early 1560s and his *Architectura*, which was first published in Antwerp in 1563 and quickly went into further editions. He continued the theme of the Orders in *Theatrum vitae humanae* (1577) with a typically *Mannerist scheme that matched them to the *Ages of Man. His final work was *Architectura oder Bauung der Antiquen* (1581).

Vredeman de Vries also produced suites of patterns: in 1566 he published a suite of *portrait heads of Julius Caesar, and in 1572 *Panoplia*, panels of military *trophies with a fearsome collection of antique and contemporary weapons. His designs of fantastic architecture and elaborate architectural *perspective were frequently used for *intarsia* panels (inlays of bone, ivory and pale woods on ebony or other dark woods) in furniture and wall panelling. Vredeman de Vries published two series of engravings c.1560, later reprinted as *Variae Architecturae Formae* (1601) and, in the year of his death, *Perspectiva, Id Est, Celeberrima Ars* (1604). An early work gave patterns for tomb designs, *Pictores statuarii, architecti, la tomi, et quicunque principum magnificorum* (1563), which included supporting figures carefully graded in grandeur: lions for royalty, armoured *monopodia for soldiers and knights and faithful dogs for the less exalted. *Différents Pourtraicts de la menuiserie* (1565, 1588) was one of the earliest pattern books for furniture. It was much copied and included designs (some relatively simple) for buffets, tables, chairs and beds.

His son, Paul Vredeman de Vries (1567-post 1630) collaborated with his father, and in 1630 published two volumes of his own furniture designs, *Verscheyden Schreinwerck* (Amsterdam, 1630, 1658), which were richly decorated with strapwork, *masks and *caryatids. These designs, which were similar to his father's work, but even more elaborate, greatly influenced furniture design in the Low Countries.

*Hans Vredeman de Vries. Engraved designs for *herms.*

waggon chamfer. Type of *chamfering in which a succession of small scoops are taken out of a rectangular wooden section. Traditionally this ornamentation was used in waggon building, but, like *chip carving, it was also widely used on country-made furniture. Adopted as a decorative device by the English *Arts and Crafts firm of Kenton & Co., it later became the hallmark of Cotswold-based craftsmen Ernest Gimson (1864-1919) and the brothers Sydney (1865-1926) and Ernest Barnsley (1863-1926). Charles Rennie Mackintosh (see Glasgow School) used waggon chamfering on wooden beams in the Glasgow School of Art Library (1898-99). Heal & Son of London applied the technique to a range of furniture designed for country cottages from c.1910, mostly on panels and chair-backs.

war. See military decoration.

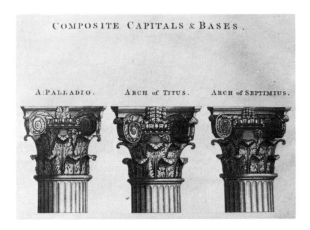

*Isaac Ware. Composite *capitals from* A Complete Body of Architecture, 1756.

Ware, Isaac (d 1766). English architect whose *A Complete Body of Architecture* (2 vols, 1756; many subsequent editions) was an important milestone between *Palladianism and *Neo-classicism, and became an influential standard source book. In it Ware instructed the architect to study the 'great and glorious remains we have of the antique, and to guide himself by no rules but those which can be either drawn from such examples or authorised and illustrated by them.' There was some *Rococo stucco work in the book but 'French crooked figures . . . unmeaning ornament barely and nakedly scattered over the surface' attracted his disapproval. Such ornament could be made 'more decent' if it was properly blended. His own French-style decoration, as at Chesterfield House, London (1749, demolished), was more squat and strictly to English proportions. Ware's first publication had been *Designs of Inigo Jones and Others* (1735, 1743, 1756) and he also translated A.*Palladio's *Four Books of Architecture* (1738, 1755), which he regarded as a book of rules; he was impressed that Palladio was the 'only architect after whom an architectural idiom is named.' Most of Ware's publications were known in America – his translation of Palladio was certainly known by 1754, and *A Complete*

Body of Architecture was an important source for the more sophisticated architecture developing in American East Coast areas.

water. *Classical decoration depicts water being poured from an *urn, symbolising the source of a river. Christian iconography uses formalised water motifs (wavy parallel lines) to represent the four Rivers of Paradise. An obvious symbol of cleansing and purification, it may signify baptism. Water appears in schemes of the four *Elements, both represented by *waves and as the sea personified in the figure of *Neptune. Other ways of representing water in decoration are waves and waved *fluting, also *icicles or congelated drips (see rustication), which are a popular element in *grotto ornament and fountain decoration and, combined with *rocaille, were applied to both exteriors and interiors in the *Rococo period. See also marine; riparine.

*waterleaf. 1) On *capital from P.*Columbani's Capitals, Friezes and Corniches, 1776. 2) Gothic Revival capital in church at Grosmont, Gwent, renovations by J.P. Seddon, 1869.*

waterleaf, hart's-tongue or **lily leaf.** Early *Gothic ornament developed for *capitals and consisting of a broad, blade-shaped leaf with a slightly crimped edge, usually with its tip curling over as it reaches the *abacus; it may have developed from the waterlily leaf. Used particularly in the late 12th century in England and northern France, it reappeared in 19th century *Gothic Revival work.

Waterleaf may also refer to a long strap-like, feather-shaped leaf, as used by A.*Palladio as an enrichment for the *mouldings of the Ionic, Corinthian and Composite *Orders. This form is also known as stiff leaf, particularly when it appears on ceramics. In *Neoclassical ornament it often replaced the *acanthus leaves on *capitals. *Adam style decoration in the 18th and 19th centuries used it as a repeating motif on *friezes, borders and at the top of columns. It appeared in 18th century ironwork dog bars and *cresting, and the term is used in *pattern books of the period to describe any unserrated leaf, in particular that used in egg and leaf mouldings. Like the acanthus, it appears on silver and ceramics (especially in Neo-classical designs) often forming a border around the base of the vessel.

waterlily. See lily; lily pad; lotus.

Watteau, Jean-Antoine (1684-1721). French painter whose work was influential in early French *Rococo decoration (also known as *Régence). Engravings after his paintings and drawings, many executed after his death, notably *Oeuvre Gravé* (published by Jean de

Julienne, 1727-35), formed the basis for ornament in the *pastoral manner and for *fêtes galantes. Watteau also produced purely ornamental designs, some of which were published posthumously, notably his *trophies and Grandes et moyennes arabesques (early 18th century), which presented a new light and airy treatment of *grotesques incorporating *chinoiserie figures, *commedia dell'arte characters and *espagnolettes. Watteau's decoration appeared on tapestries and French, English and German porcelain as well as influencing the composition of the ormolu mounts on Rococo furniture by the leading French ébeniste, Charles Cressent (1685-1758). The Rococo Revival in the 19th century made use once again of Watteau's designs.

waves. Motif used to represent *water or, sometimes, motion. The sea and rivers are usually represented by rippling, wavy forms. In ancient classical ornament an undulate form, sometimes called *strigillation, was used on sarcophagi to symbolise the passing of the soul into the after life. More recently, sound waves have occasionally been depicted as a kind of flattened *wavescroll.

wavescroll, Vitruvian scroll, running dog, Greek scroll or **running scroll.** An undulate scroll pattern based on the *C-scrolls found in classical Greek and other ancient cultures. In late Roman decoration, the form was sometimes elaborated into *scrolling foliage. Readopted in its plainer form in the early *Renaissance,

the *wavescroll remained important as a *frieze and *banding ornament thereafter, and is one of the motifs that invariably reappear whenever there are *classical revivals. It was a common border ornament on 18th century silver and in architecture, and was one of the few motifs considered acceptable in the pared down classicism of the 1930s, when it was used, for example, by Val Myers and Watson-Hart on Broadcasting House, London (1931). See also nebule.

weapons. See military decoration.

weeping willow. Symbol of sadness and mourning that has been widely used in funerary ornament (see death and mourning). In the late 18th and early 19th centuries it was often shown with an *urn placed beneath its boughs. Like *ivy, its graceful hanging forms make it highly appropriate for decorative use.

whales' tails. A type of *scrolled pediment *cresting used on late 18th century American long-case clocks, typical of Connecticut makers.

wheat. In many cultures and since ancient times, both the wheat ear and the wheat sheaf have been important symbols of fecundity and fertility, appearing wherever *husbandry or abundance is commemorated. Wheat is an attribute of the Roman goddess of agriculture, Ceres, and her Greek counterpart, Demeter. In ornamental schemes based on the *Seasons, Summer is

*wavescroll. 1) Mid 18th century English giltwood side table. 2) The Register House, Edinburgh, by R.*Adam, 1774-92. 3,4) Representations of radio waves on Broadcasting House, Langham Place, London, architects Val Myers and Watson-Hart, 1931.*

*wheat. 1) English silver plate toast rack exhibited by Roberts and Hall at the Great Exhibition, London, 1851. 2) *Keystone on façade of Tewkesbury Town Hall, Gloucestershire, 1891. 3) Russian fabric print by V. Maslov, late 1920s or early 1930s.*

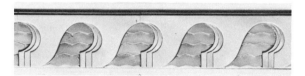

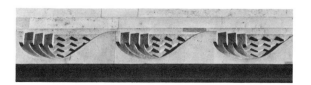

often represented carrying a wheat sheaf. In *Christian decoration, it usually appears with grapes or a *grapevine representing the Eucharist (the wheat signifying the body, the wine signifying the blood of Christ). As a *heraldic device the wheatsheaf is known as a garb.

Wheat ears were a popular motif in the 17th and 18th centuries, often used without any symbolic intent; they appear, for example, in wrought iron work, either in scrolling form, as in the stair railings at Claydon House, Buckinghamshire (late 18th century), or, more stiffly arranged, in a vase, on chair-backs and as a *cresting motif on late 18th and early 19th century overmantel mirrors. In the 19th century, the tendency to select appropriate decoration made the wheat ear and sheaf popular ornaments on bread platters and bread knives – a convention still followed today. *See also* husk.

wheel. 1) Window, Notre Dame, Paris, last phase of works, 1250.
2) Iron supports to canopy, Thetford railway station, Norfolk, 1889.

wheel. Symbol of *time, transience, fortune, the *sun (when the spokes suggest rays) and an attribute of St Catherine in *Christian ornament (she was executed on a wheel).

The Wheel of Fortune was a favourite medieval motif, and was used in the architecture, sculpture and painting of Christian churches. It appeared as a *moulding enrichment on French *Romanesque church arches, and, more dramatically, forming the mullions and surround of a circular window, sometimes accompanied by the inscription *Regnabo, regno, regnavi, sum sine regno* [I shall reign, I reign, I have reigned, I am without sovereignty]. In the more elaborate *Gothic wheel window, figures are seen rising and falling on the perimeter of the Wheel of Fortune, e.g. at Amiens Cathedral in France. Wheel forms are also sometimes pierced in buttressing on Gothic cathedrals.

Wheel-backed chairs are an application of the form in furniture, with numerous local variations according to place of manufacture, both in England and America; but the two main types are: a shield shape pierced in the central flat support of a chair-back, or the whole chair-back, either circular or oval, composed of radiating spindles resembling the spokes of a wheel.

19th century and early 20th century railway stations were often decorated with wheel motifs, e.g. ironwork *brackets, sometimes *winged to suggest speed.

wheel-head cross. Thought originally to have been a primitive sun sign, the wheel-head cross is best known

in the form of the *Celtic cross, widely used as a graveside cross in the *Celtic Revival.

whiplash curve. Whip-like shape, an important form in *Art Nouveau ornament where its use is as ubiquitous as that of *C and S-scrolls in *Rococo decoration. It also appears in work clearly influenced by Art Nouveau design, such as that of the British artists Walter Crane (1845-1915), Selwyn Image (1849-1930) and A.H. Mackmurdo (1851-1942), and was subsequently picked up and elaborated by practitioners of the style in Europe. It remained an important Art Nouveau motif up to and including the debased commercial productions of the early 20th century.

whiplash curve. 1) Stamped leather design by Lucien Gaillard on French mahogany chair, c.1900.
wild man. 2) Misericord with lion attacking wild man, Church of St Andrew, Norton, Suffolk.

wild man or **woodwose.** Human figure covered in shaggy hair, usually wielding a wooden club, and resembling Hercules (*see* Herculean decoration). The figure appeared on 13th century illuminated manuscripts, and later in stone and wood carving, tapestry, etc., as a symbol of lust and aggression. There are rare 15th century examples of the form used as a spoon terminal. In *heraldic decoration, the motif appears as a supporter, and is sometimes termed a woodhouse or wodehouse.

William and Mary style. The reign in England of William and Mary from 1688 to 1702 acted, in stylistic terms, as a link between the heavy, elaborate *Restoration style and the lighter treatment of the *Queen Anne period. The prevailing influences were naturally Dutch (William of Orange was Stadholder of the Dutch republic) and also French. In 1685 the Revocation of the Edict of Nantes forced Protestant Huguenots, many of whom were craftsmen, notably silversmiths and weavers, to leave France, and many settled in England. This resulted in a wider awareness of the work of French designers such as P.A.*Ducerceau, J.*Berain and J.*Le Pautre, which the Huguenots rendered in a restrained manner, favouring animals and figures for handles and *knops, *cut card decoration, *gadrooning and *fluting. D.*Marot, a Huguenot, worked for William in both Holland and England, and his published designs are typical of this amalgam of Dutch and French styles. Tall, thin proportions were favoured for chairs, looking-glasses, beds, etc., and height was accentuated with the application of *crestings, *pediments and *finials. *Chinoiserie became a fashionable decorative element, evident in the designs of J.*Stalker and G. Parker, and indicated by the immense popularity of blue-and-white tin-glazed earthenware.

The Dutch influence also touched architecture with such obvious motifs as the *Dutch gable, and in a continued rapprochement with *classicism, as in the Restoration period. The great architects of that period were carrying out many of their mature works under William and Mary.

willow pattern. A genre of *chinoiserie design used principally on ceramics, but occasionally appearing on silver and textiles. The standard *Picturesque view, painted in blue on a white ground, incorporates a river or lake, a bridge, boat, island, pagoda, willow trees, Chinese figures or fishermen, and birds flying in the sky, with the whole scene surrounded by a *fret design. Willow pattern was reputedly invented by Thomas Minton in about 1780. It was used extensively from c.1800 by English manufacturers, and was copied and adapted in France and Germany.

willow pattern. English electroplated coffee machine made by Padley, Parkin & Staniforth, c.1885.

So popular was the pattern that at the end of the 19th century fanciful stories were invented to fit the scenes depicted. For example, that a mandarin's only daughter fell in love with an unsuitable young man who lived on an island at the top of the pattern. The father forbade the match and the couple eloped in a boat to the island after hiding together in the gardener's cottage. The furious mandarin chased them with a whip intending to beat them to death, but the gods intervened, transforming them into turtle doves. Use of the pattern by many factories and in many variations has continued to the present.

The pattern was sometimes used on teapots, even in silver or electroplate, due no doubt to the association between China and tea.

Winckelmann, Abbé Johann Joachim (1717-68). Archaeologist and sometime librarian to the Roman antiquarian Cardinal Albani. He was one of the few 18th century scholars to have access to the sites of *Pompeii and *Herculaneum and became the superintendent of antiquities in Rome. His *Monumenti antichi inediti* (2 vols, Rome, 1767) was dedicated to Albani, whose great collection contained many of the most important Roman antiquities. The *Monumenti* was illustrated with spare line drawings and, like his other works of scholarship, was more important for its commentary than for its ornamental content. Winckelmann considered that true *classical ornament was extremely simple and it was in this volume that he claimed that the fine red and black figure vases hitherto thought to be *Etruscan were in fact Greek. *Geschichte der Kunst des Altertums* (Dresden, 1764; English edition, 1766; French editions, 1766, 1781), his most important work, introduced a theory of antiquity that was illustrated with more than 200 engravings of little known artefacts; it was widely known throughout Europe and marked a definitive turning away from the *Rococo.

windows. *See* Diocletian windows; fanlight; lancet; lunette; oculus; *oeil de boeuf*; Palladian motif; rose window; wheel.

wind. In classical Greek usage the Winds were personified as gods, most famously on the octagonal Tower of the Winds in Athens, which has a winged figure on each façade: Boreas (north), Notus (south), Eurus (east) and Zephyrus (west), as well as personifications for north-west, north-east, south-east and south-west winds. Their attributes relate to the characteristics of each wind in Greece, the root of much confusion when the theme was applied in northern Europe: Boreas blows a *triton's horn to signify power to raise a storm at sea; Eurus has fruit and flowers in the folds of his robes; Notus pours rain from a vessel and Zephyr carries Spring flowers. The rest hold clouds, a vase of hailstones, a ship's stern (to indicate a good sailing wind) and a vessel full of hot charcoal. Horses were also occasionally used to represent the wind in ancient classical decoration.

In medieval iconography the winds are often subdivided into 8, 12 or even 16, appearing with the year and the *zodiac signs, but *classical revivals reinstated the more usual four, as in J.*Stuart's *Neo-classical copy of the Tower of the Winds at Shugborough Hall,

Staffordshire (begun 1764) and K.F.*Schinkel's Schloss Tegel (1822-24) in Berlin.

Wind motifs decorate maps, globes, sailing ships and, less obviously, organ cases. The precise *personifications and attributes are rarely used, but such literal symbols as bellows or *cherubs and *putto* heads with puffed-out cheeks are common.

winged disc or **winged globe.** Ancient Egyptian motif associated with the deities Horus or Edfu; a symbol of protection both in earthly and eternal life, it appeared on temple entrances and on the ceilings of tombs. Europeans would have seen it from the early 19th century at Philae and in the Valley of the Kings, and it was used in *Egyptian style decorative schemes. C.*Dresser states, erroneously, in his *Principles* that winged discs appeared on all Egyptian buildings as a symbol of protection and advocated their use in this manner.

winged horse. *See* horse.

wings in ornament may signify travel of some kind (e.g. winged *wheels in *railway architecture) or immortality, as on *Renaissance sarcophagi. A winged cap or helmet and sandals allude to *Mercury. In classical mythology guardian spirits were often depicted as winged figures, the origin of the Christian *angel. Wings may also indicate a saintly status, as in the case of the four *Evangelists, represented by the winged *lion, *eagle, ox and man, the convention even extending to revered clerics in Victorian ornament. The position of wings is sometimes significant: outspread they may denote protection, crossed, trust.

In *Assyrian ornament, *sphinxes and winged *lions acted as guardians. Many of the fantastic beasts of classical *grotesque ornament were winged, such as the *wyvern, *griffin and *harpy. Hypnos (*see* night) fanned sleepers with dark wings; wings also appear as an attribute of the *Winds, of *Victory, *Fame and, sometimes, the *Virtues.

In Christian ornament, the Holy Spirit is symbolised by wings, usually in the form of the *dove, but sometimes diversified in medieval Books of Hours into species as various as cocks, cranes, storks, swans, sparrow hawks, flies, ladybirds, butterflies or dragonflies. The Renaissance *cherub is one of the most widely used winged figures. In the 17th century, bats' wings often appeared with the *skull on funerary monuments as a dramatic contrast to the lively child's head surrounded by fluffy wings, which was also used as a classic architectural detail at the same period.

In monuments to heroes, the classically derived winged *horse (Pegasus) was often used. In *Neoclassical ornament, especially that of the *Adam style, winged figures and creatures appear widely, and in *Empire decoration a winged creature based loosely on the sphinx supports tables, armrests or *torchères*. In later architectural ornament, wings act as *brackets supporting balconies, etc. Although wings are usually feathered or webbed (like those of the bat or *dragon), there are also diaphanous insect-like wings (used in the *Netherlands Grotesque style) of the type that were later to be found on Victorian images of fairies and sprites.

*wind. 1) East Wind and West Wind, plate first published 1776, from G.*Richardson's* Iconology, *1779-80. 2) West Wind, Schloss Tegel, Berlin, by K.F.*Schinkel, 1822-24.*
winged disc. 3) Over front entrance of early 20th century office building, London. 4) English redware dish with border of Egyptian subjects, made by Wedgwood, c.1800.

wisdom. *See* learning.

wodehouse, woodhouse or **woodwose.** *See* wild man.

Wood, Robert (1716-71) and **Dawkins,** James (1722-57). Two amateur antiquaries who travelled to Syria to record the ruins of the Roman cities of Palmyra and Baalbec. Their three-year visit helped to lead to the publication of *Ruins of Palmyra* (1753) and *Ruins of Baalbec* (1757). These lavishly illustrated volumes led architects and ornamentists back to the 'true style of the ancients'. The archaeological approach of Wood and Dawkins to their subject was comparable to that of J.*Stuart and N. Revett towards Greek architecture and the two teams spear-headed the *Neo-classical movement in England, and elsewhere in Europe. Robert Adam (*see* Adam style) used more details from the work of Wood and Dawkins than from his own observations on Diocletian's Palace, and a large number of interiors of the 1770s were directly based on motifs from their publications. Wood and Dawkins were strong supporters of the classical antique in the face of other styles. They wished to 'improve the taste of our countrymen and expel the littleness and ugliness of the Chinese and the barbarity of the Goths, that we may see no more useless and expensive trifles.' An example of the speed with which their influence spread is the fine model of the Ruins of Palmyra made by the housekeeper at Erddig, Denbighshire (now Clwyd) in 1773. *Ruins of Palmyra* was republished in Paris in 1819. In the early 19th century, scenery showing the Ruins was painted at Vauxhall Gardens, 'to deceive the eye and appear buildings'. Motifs such as *pulvinated friezes of heavy *oak leaves, *niches, *coffering, *bucrania, elaborate Composite *capitals, *broken pediments, *eagles and the famous *rosette motif taken from the Temple of the Sun were all the stock-in-trade of late Roman architecture as it could no longer be found in Italy. These features were soon to be found liberally applied to the public buildings and great houses of Europe.

Worthies, The Nine. Group of nine heroes, three Old Testament, three pagan and three Christian. Although the membership of the group varies, it is usually Joshua, David and Judas Maccabaeus; Hector of Troy, Alexander the Great and Julius Caesar; King Arthur, Charlemagne and Godfrey de Bouillon. The theme emerged in the late medieval period, rarely appearing in decoration before the 15th century. It is mostly used in plasterwork, on carved furniture panels, as terminal figures on spoons and as *cresting figures on parapets. The theme may have originated in the *Voeux de Paon* composed by Jacques de Longuyon, c.1312. A set of engravings depicting them was produced by the Flemish engraver, Nicholas de Bruyn (c.1570-c.1635). E.-E.*Viollet-le-Duc revived the Nine Worthies (Les Neuf Preuses) as a theme in his *Gothic Revival restoration of the Château de Pierrefonds (Oise), c.1865.

wreath. Crown or garland of leaves, usually *laurel (or bay), *oak or *olive, used in ancient Greece and Rome to honour emperors, heroes, athletes, poets,

*Robert Wood and Richard Dawkins. *Modillion and other details on 'East side of Arch to Temple of the Sun' from his* Ruins of Palmyra, *1753.*

etc. Fruits, nuts and berries are often scattered among the leaves and the wreath may be bound and tied with ribbon. It is used as a symbol of sovereignty, honour and glory and victory, appearing with figures of *Fame and *Victory. It was a popular motif in the early *Renaissance, used alone or to encircle a *portrait head. It was revived in the *Empire style, particularly suiting the range of motifs introduced to recall the glories of the Roman emperors. Napoleon chose a golden wreath of laurel for his coronation. As a symbol of victory over death, the wreath appears in funerary ornament. Because of its classical use as a mark of poetic achievement, the laurel wreath appears in the ornament of academic institutions.

wreathed column. 18th century term for a *spiral column entwined with vegetation.

'Wrenaissance'. A style which began to gather strength in the 1880s following the *Queen Anne Revival, and an important strand in Edwardian architecture. In common with other English classicists, Sir Christopher Wren (1632-1723) had been eclipsed in the mid 19th century wave of *Historicism. However, interest in his work began to be expressed from 1883, mostly by architects, through a number of scholarly publications, and in the adoption of his domestic styles (complete with its range of restrained ornament). His more florid and monumental *Baroque style, as seen in St Paul's Cathedral, was revived to lend weight to commercial and municipal buildings, in particular. Norman Shaw, Mervyn Macartney and John Belcher, joint authors of *Later Renaissance Architecture in England* (1898-1901),

*wreath. 1) Apollo head from G.-P.*Cauvet's* Recueil d'ornemans à l'usage des jeunes artistes, *1777. 2) 19th century tombstone, Abney Park Cemetery, Stoke Newington, London.*

and Ernest George and Alfred Yeates were among the practitioners of this style. The British Stand for the St Louis International Exposition in 1904, constructed by George and Yeates, was a replica of the Orangery at Kensington Palace, 'in memory' of Wren. The Wren Revival, which became a vague domestic *Neo-Georgian style and commercial *Baroque Revival style, was also adopted in America.

wrigglework. Pattern achieved on silver and pewter by rocking a gouge from side to side, thus creating a zig-zag effect. Mainly popular in the 17th century, often confined within a band.

wrythen. Spiral *fluting or *reeding applied to the oval *knop of 15th or 16th century spoons. Also cast spiral moulding on metalwork or swirls of glass coiled diagonally around glassware – wrythening was a popular decoration on 18th century English drinking glasses.

wyvern or **wivern.** Mythical beast illustrated in medieval *bestiaries: a winged dragon with two eagle legs and a serpent-like, barbed tail. Principally used in heraldry and and best known as the symbol of Wales. It is also an emblem of war and pestilence.

zigzag. *See* chevron.

zodiac signs. The zodiac is an imaginary belt or zone in the heavens which is divided into twelve equal parts proceeding from East to West. Each section has a sign determined by ancient astronomers from the positions of the stars in that part of the sky; they are: Aries, the ram, Taurus, the bull, Gemini, the twins, Cancer, the crab, Leo, the lion, Virgo, the virgin, Libra, the scales, Scorpio, the scorpion, Sagittarius, the archer, Capricorn, the goat, Aquarius, the water bearer, and Pisces, the two fish. The zodiac signs survived from *classical decoration and were a popular ornament in northern European *Romanesque and *Gothic churches, possibly because they could be equated with the Twelve *Apostles. The Labours of the *Months were frequently indicated by zodiac signs, the sign relating to the month in which the sun enters it. Thus January is represented by Aquarius, February by Pisces, March by Aries, April by Taurus, May by Gemini, June by Cancer, July by Leo, August by Virgo, September by Libra, October by Scorpio, November by Sagittarius and December by Capricorn. This theme appeared in architectural ornament, and in the illumination of psalters and books of hours, remaining popular until the end of the Middle Ages. It was revived in a light-hearted spirit in *Rococo ornament. Later uses for signs of the zodiac include decoration of ceilings, timepieces, maps and astrological instruments.

zoomorphic forms. Ornamental, usually highly distorted or stylised forms based on animals. The use of animal motifs in ornament was central to the arts of the nomadic cultures of Central Asia, with both a symbolic and formal intention. Nordic animal motifs and ancient *Celtic, *Viking and other Scandinavian variations, inherited this liking for contorted and highly linear decoration. Zoomorphic forms were a favourite choice for the surrounds or frameworks of initials in French and English *Romanesque illuminated manuscripts. They were also frequent in ironwork and stonecarving, where the 'animal' is often scarcely distinguishable from stylised foliage and other scrolling and spiral forms. *Lacertine and *dracontine ornament are two of the most common expressions of zoomorphic forms. In the 19th century Celtic and Viking Revivals and in *Art Nouveau at the turn of the century, zoomorphic ornament reappeared, often even more stylised than in its original form. *See also* beakhead.

Zopfstil (German, ponytail). A style of ornamentation popular in late 18th century Germany that was used principally in ceramics, glass and painted furniture decoration. It consisted of sentimental scenes with figures – often children and animals – wearing contemporary costume and presented in silhouette. Prints after painters such as Daniel Chodowiecki (1726-1801), Angelica Kauffman (1741-1807) and J.B. Greuze (1725-1806) were often used as sources.

Zoppino, Nicolo. Compiler of one of the earliest *pattern books for weaving and embroidery in Italy, *Esemplario di Lavori* (Venice, 1529; six editions before 1539). It included patterns from earlier collections published in 1527: G.A.*Tagliente's *Essempio di Recammi* (Venice) and Peter Quentel's *Eyn New Kunstlich Booch* (Cologne). The designs consist of elaborate *interlacing ornament and *arabesques.

Nicolo Zoppino. Design for embroidery from his Esemplario di Lavori, *1529.*

Zwiebelmuster (German, onion pattern). Blue and white *chinoiserie design used on Meissen porcelain from c.1739. The pattern is an imitation of a Chinese design composed of formalised peaches, mistakenly thought to be onions, that surround the central design of asters, peonies and foliage. The design was copied by other European porcelain manufactories, notably Tournai.

PICTURE CREDITS

The majority of the pictures in this book were specially taken by Philippa Lewis, Gillian Darley, Ian Cameron and Jill Hollis, and processed and printed by Donna Thynne. In the following list of credits for the remaining illustrations, the positions of pictures are denoted by a letter after the page number; the letters read left to right down each of the two text columns on a page.

Arkwright Arts Trust 112a, 112b, 112c

Arts Council of Great Britain 170a, 263d, 298d

American Museum, Bath 272c

Berlin, Kunstgewerbemuseum 172d

Bord Failte, Dublin 23a, 75a, 124c, 163d, 203a, 212a, 249d, 261a

British Museum 34g, 37a, 41d, 57f, 73b, 98d, 125b, 145e, 168c, 200a, 269c, 271b

Campbell Collection 85c, 178a, 307a

The Art Institute of Chicago 118f

Christie, Manson & Woods Ltd 20e, 34f, 37f, 38b, 44c, 45b, 45e, 51b, 57b, 57c, 66c, 77b, 78a, 88b, 92e, 96b, 114e, 119a, 122c, 126a, 129a, 138b, 148g, 150b, 152c, 153c, 177e, 181b, 191c, 191f, 192b, 194a, 203e, 206a, 230e, 235f, 236a, 239a, 241d, 274b, 284f, 314a

Cooper-Hewitt Museum, Smithsonian Institution 45g, 77c, 115b, 137a, 237b, 262d, 293b

The Corning Museum of Glass 92b, 114f

Dan Cruikshank 254d

Raymond Fortt 49a, 254a

Alain Gaucher 35c, 45j, 71d, 84b, 109a, 151a, 210a, 217c, 260a, 309a

The Worshipful Company of Goldsmiths 78d, 100b, 100d, 138a, 200c

Guldbrandsen of Copenhagen 238b

Georg Jensen 169c

J. Jesse and I. Lasky 168b

The Metropolitan Museum of Art, New York 20f, 27d, 109e, 127a, 154b, 204a, 270e

Musée des Arts Décoratifs, Paris 39d, 39e, 39f, 171a, 199b

Norwich Museums 290a

A. Sanderson & Sons 111c, 206b, 299d

S.J. Shrubsole, London 31d, 51c, 52d, 129b, 172b, 179c, 179d, 185d, 251c, 253d

Sotheby & Co. 20c, 24d, 40b, 43c, 44b, 45c, 46e, 52a, 56a, 59c, 74b, 76i, 81a, 115a, 120a, 124b, 145b, 145c, 148d, 169d, 170d, 174a, 174b, 174c, 177d, 194c, 226d, 230b, 278e, 316a

Sotheby's Belgravia 41b, 60c, 78f, 179a, 201c, 256d

Stoke on Trent City Museum and Art Gallery 201a, 256a

Victoria & Albert Museum 23c, 30d, 38a, 68b, 80b, 94a, 95b, 96c, 103a, 121d, 123a, 125a, 132b, 156c, 168a, 169a, 195, 208a, 223c, 238c, 241a

Wadsworth Atheneum, Hartford 29b, 92f

The Wedgwood Group 33d, 33e, 45i, 68c, 69b, 122d, 149c, 161a, 182d, 185b, 212c, 229a, 239d, 239e, 258b, 276b, 284c, 296a

Whitworth Art Gallery, Manchester 78g